③

40
20

an examination on
Revelation.

THE STRATEGY

THE STRATEGY

by

DAVID MILLS

SAXON HOUSE CANADA
TORONTO
2005

Copyright © 2005 by David Mills

All rights reserved

ISBN 0-9693934-7-4

Published by Saxon House Canada
Box 6947 Station "A", Toronto Ontario M5W 1X6
CANADA

Canadian Cataloguing in Publication Data

MILLS, David,
    The Strategy

History. An analysis of the Book of Revelation
    Includes Bibliography

ISBN 0-9693934-7-4

I. Title.

BS2825.52M45 2005   228.06   C2005.901547-0

PREFACE

Since the beginning of civilization in the year 3500 BC and earlier, to the time of Jesus Christ, human life was seen as part of a network which joined all people to communities, to nature and to the powers that rule nature. To the people of Judea, who lived in the last days of ancient Near Eastern culture, that outlook still survived. Although it may seem strange to some, there actually was a man called Jesus of Galilee who lived during this period, at the first part of the first century of the Common Era. He was not a myth nor a figment of anyone's imagination, but an historic figure of considerable ability and remarkable leadership.

It was said of him that he opened the Hebrew Scriptures to the understanding of his followers. This would appear to indicate that the meanings of the scriptures were sealed to most readers. Why their meanings were sealed is a complex question. Yet resolving their meanings was akin to interpreting dreams. Dreams were universally regarded as communications from the deities (or spirits) governing the world. These communications, they believed, could be understood only if someone of great wisdom would interpret them. You will remember, for instance, that Joseph, by interpreting the dreams of Thutmose IV, revealed himself to be a man of great wisdom. This marked him as a man well qualified to govern well.

Interpreting dreams and solving riddles were mentioned frequently in chronicles of different kings as being a sign of their great wisdom. King Assurbanipal of Assyria tells of how he had been trained for solving them. King Solomon was celebrated for his own ability in resolving "riddles and dark sayings". It was a quality which ancient people looked to find in leadership. Because Daniel could interpret dreams and riddles, Nebuchadnezzar II made him the Prime Minister of Babylon. It is apparent therefore that when Jesus trained his own disciples for roles of leadership, he spent much time teaching them in parables and showing them how they must interpret them.

Even the final communication Jesus sent to one of his early disciples (a man called John the revealer) was written in symbols, to disguise its meanings from those not trained in understanding them. This served to hide its meanings from those who were self-satisfied and did not have the patience to resolve a problem properly. It also served to hide their plans from any enemy. Yet this letter (sent to every church in Christendom) revealed a well-constructed plan to save the world from the murderous cycle of false leaders, violent wars, economic depressions and death from war, famine, social upheavals and persecution.

In the plan (now known as the Apocalypse) Jesus clearly understood that mankind was not only destroying himself; he was destroying nature and the very source of life itself. In a well-considered strategy therefore, he showed all those who took world conditions seriously, what they had to know if they would establish a new world system which honoured God and Nature and Mankind.

Jean Lesage

TABLE OF CONTENTS

TABLE OF CONTENTS
(Continued)

Page

"Do not interpretations belong to God"

(Genesis 40: 8)

PROLOGUE

The Dream of God

In 1965 a great American, whose biography and speeches now arc found in all important libraries throughout the world, stood in Washington D.C. before a large crowd of humble men and women, and in words that rang with passion and conviction, he gave a voice to their most fervent hope. These in part were the words he spoke:

"I say to you, my friends, that even though we must face the difficulties of today and tomorrow, I still have a dream...I have a dream that one day on the red hills of Georgia, sons of former slaves and sons of former slave-owners will be able to sit down together at the table of brotherhood. I have a dream that one day, even the state of Mississippi, a state sweltering with the heat of injustice, sweltering with the heat of oppression, will be transformed into an oasis of freedom and justice. I have a dream my four little children will one day live in a nation where they will not be judged by the colour of their skin but by the content of their character. I have a dream today..."

The speaker was Martin Luther King Jr. and the full text of his words are now available in schools and libraries everywhere. It was a dream that could not be suppressed, for it kindled the imagination of people and spread like fire throughout the world. For it wasn't just a dream. It was a vision. And it wasn't just a vision. It was a prophecy. Allusions to the words of the ancient Jewish prophet, Isaiah, in this speech, is worth examining. For Isaiah also had a dream that echoed through the centuries:

"Of this you can be sure, that I will one day make new heavens (governmental systems) and a new earth (social practices): for all those (corrupt governments and degenerate social practices) of the past I will sweep away. They shall be forgotten and nevermore return. Be confident therefore and be glad, and celebrate the customs and the government I am creating, for I shall fill Jerusalem with joy and give her people happiness. The sound of sorrow and weeping shall not be heard in her again. No longer shall the life of any infant be cut short. No aged person living there shall die before he has lived out his days. In that new world which I am building, anyone who dies at a hundred years of age will be looked on as a child, and for anyone to not live to be a hundred would be regarded as an undisputed travesty.

"In that day my people shall inhabit the houses that they build, and shall enjoy the fruit from the vineyards that they plant. No longer shall they build (their houses) for someone else to occupy, nor plant their food for someone else to eat. For their lifespan shall be in its duration like the lifespan of a tree, and they shall long enjoy the labour of their hands. Never shall they work in vain, nor shall the children that they bear ever have to face the terrors of calamity (and war), for they will be the children of those Jehovah has blessed – they and their children after them. And it will surely be, before they call upon my name, that I will answer them. Even as they speak to me in prayer, I will respond to all their needs. The wolf and the lamb will feed together peacefully, and the lion shall eat straw like an ox, while dust shall be the serpent's food. In all my kingdom, no creature shall injure or destroy another one, Jehovah says."   (Isaiah 65: 17-25)

Now Isaiah lived almost three millennia before the time of Martin Luther King Jr., and he spoke a language common at that time. The idioms he used were far different from the idioms we use today, but his dream (like that of Martin Luther King Jr.) continues to survive in many hearts—like the seed of a great tree waiting for the rain. In its time that dream gave the Jewish people courage to rebuild the ruined cities in the land of Israel after their return from a long captivity in Babylon.

That is the gift of prophecy. It makes it possible for people to find courage in the face of overwhelming odds, and it gives them goals to work toward. These possibilities that prophecies express, inspire great faith. And faith, a vision and a plan, is all it takes to build a better world.

Now the capstone of all Bible prophecies is the *Book of Revelation* written in the year 98 AD by a venerable old man called John the Revealer. Tradition tells us he was a disciple and close personal friend of the man whom Christians call the Christ, Jesus of Nazareth.

What makes John's *Book of Revela*tion such a powerful and compelling work is that it sums up the teachings of all Bible scriptures from *Genesis* to the Christian gospels, and it lays out a strategy for reaching a goal that ancient Jews and early Christians once believed was possible to reach, and later Christians would forget had ever been laid out for them at all. For later centuries would make the *Book of Revelation* the most abused book in the entire canon of scriptures.

Because it has been so thoroughly misused and its meanings far from universally agreed upon, many intellectuals today conjecture periodically as to whether the *Book of Revelation* is not actually a volume of apochryphal literature rather than a true prophetic work. In such a manner then they successfully imply that The *Book of Revelation* is no more than a mere part of a larger body of obscure Jewish literature that almost no one understands, but which scholars can endlessly debate upon without feeling anything of worth has actually been lost in not resolving any of their arguments. So let's settle the matter now conclusively. The book refers to itself as prophecy. That should answer us effectively enough.

The real confusion rises not from the book itself, but from ourselves. It rises from the expectations in our understanding and our misuse of the word "prophecy". Some will tell you, for instance, that two-thirds of all Bible literature is prophecy. So let us correct that statement too. The Bible doesn't contain prophecy. The Bible is prophecy.

Every text contained in the Bible (from "In the beginning God created the heavens and the earth" in *Genesis* to the words "The grace of our Lord Jesus Christ be with you all. Amen." found in *Revelation*) is prophecy. For prophecy is not fortune telling. It is revelation – the revelation of God's will, purpose, work and plan, as well as all the promises of the kingdom that God desired to build on earth. Being told what God is like, is prophecy.

The Book of Revelation is beyond all doubt a great prophetic work. Yet having read the stream of utter balderdash in books like *The Last Great Planet Earth* and other writings of its kind, I have been shocked to find the great extent of confusion that exists in many Christian minds when it comes to reading it intelligently. Whatever we might think of people in the past, ancient men and women were not idiots. They lived in a different social atmosphere from what we know today, and they frequently expressed themselves in different idioms of speech. But to read more into their words than what they meant to convey is very dangerous.

There are, of course, those who deliberately deceive, and Paul, the first Christian evangelist to the Gentiles,

has warned us about them in this description to the
Colossians: "Don't let yourself be tricked out of your
reward by anyone pretending to be pious or claiming to
have spoken with angels. Such a person will tell you in
great detail about the things that he has seen, and his
unscriptural mind will be full of worthless notions."

(Colossians 2: 18-19)

We should avoid as well, the pragmatic attitude of
being far too literal. For ancient writers did use figures
of speech like similes, metaphors and hyperbole to put
their ideas across. Being adamantly literal in one's
interpretation of some Bible texts is closely related to
idolatry. Does anyone actually believe the inhabitants of
Canaan were driven out of their land by swarms of
hornets (as the Bible says) and that Israel was carried
across the Sinai desert from Egypt on the wings of the
eagle or that a man should cut off his hand if it offends
him, or that Pharisees being careful not to swallow gnats
actually swallowed camels. We must take time to look at
Bible symbols with some measure of intelligence.

The Bible is not an easy book to read. I have known
some Christians who haven't even read it once. One man
told me he could never get past all the begats. I knew
what he meant, but I was certain that more than the
begats stopped him reading it. One can easily leap over
genealogical lists. It's the imagery, the numerology, and
the devastatingly boring parts of long descriptive
passages on priestly ceremonies that get in many people's
way. In this study on the *Book of Revelation* I shall try
to compensate for some of that, by making the text
itself more readable and comprehensible.

Still, the images themselves require interpreting.
Therefore I interpret all of them as we encounter them,

then later on, I try to show you where the Bible parallels have made them plain. For I realise that all the super-stitious prattle we have heard about tatooed arms and foreheads, or people floating up to heaven in a secret "rapture" while motor cars cascade from highways and the planet earth goes up in flames can be discouraging. I will admit John's prophecy can prove sometimes difficult to read, but understanding it is not impossible.

John's *Book of Revelation* was an open letter to encourage Christians and to give them hope, like the speeches that I quoted earlier. It wasn't meant to frighten them to death. Although it mentioned troubles that still lay ahead of them, the *Book of Revelation* was meant to show the early Christians that their faith could overcome these troubles, no matter how formidable they seemed. As Martin Luther King Jr. said in his now famous speech: "Though we must face the difficulties of today and tomorrow, I still have a dream." Likewise John did not minimize the difficulties that his people faced.

The Bible uses many symbols to express its words. To mention roughly just a few of them: "The finger of God" was symbolic of the Holy Spirit, "The right hand of God" was the throne of Israel's earthly king—the focal point of God's authority on earth. A "mountain" was symbolic of a powerful kingdom which dominated smaller ones, and the "sea" represented turbulent, restless and rebellious mankind. Precious jewels reflected all those glowing qualities of character as they were found in God himself or in mankind: Emeralds—mercy, Jasper —holiness, diamonds—stability, and precious metals such as gold stood for wisdom, integrity and trustworthiness. Even so it is the scriptural context that we must consult to ultimately define all symbols.

Then there is the language of numbers. I don't like the word numerology really. It sounds too superstitious. The language of numbers, like the language of glyphs, conveys ideas. There is no magic charm in them. Those who read them literally often close the door to their real meaning, for the numbers may not always indicate the actual number of objects to which they refer. Such numbers rather are a language to be read, and serve as symbols that convey a meaning that must be interpreted: Seven means perfection or completion in the eyes of God. The world, for instance, wasn't necessarily made in seven days, as I will later show. It was brought into perfection by the power of God. Ten marks completion in the Gentile world. The number two affirms that something is made certain and is attested to. Three is affirmation in the strongest possible terms. Four refers to all directions in the world or in the universe. Six is a tragic number of human imperfection and it calls attention to the power of human wisdom without God. Opposed to the way of life, it is the way of death. And it inhibits, curses and destroys all life in the world. There are other numbers too, but I shall read them in the context of John's words.

Ancient people were quite accustomed to reading symbols as many ancient languages were made from pictures or glyphs, and many people still retained and were accustomed to interpreting them with ease. It is the modern man in his prosaic sterility who has lost touch with the concrete speech of poetry and the powerful meanings it conveys. So before we shrug off scriptures as the superstitious nonsense many people make of them, I think we should at least take time to thoughtfully examine what those ancient writers had to say and to credit them with some degree of sanity. For they were men who had a dream and lived in hope of seeing it made real.

Some scripture is, of course, deliberately obscure and puzzling. Samson, for instance, spoke in riddles so that his enemies wouldn't understand his words, and he considered it a betrayal when his (betrothed) wife told his enemies the meaning of his secret words. When Jesus's own disciples came privately to him to find out what his words meant, he said: "You have been selected to know about the secrets of the Kingdom of God; but others will only hear about them in parables (or symbols) so that even as they watch they will not see, and even as they hear it spoken of, they will not understand what they have heard." Jesus didn't teach the careless listener.

Nor did John. He didn't want the Kingdom's enemies to know his plans. He had just returned from prison for having taught about his new heaven and new earth (i.e. a new governmental system and a new society), and it wasn't likely he would want to find himself in prison once again. Nor did he want the ridiculing and trivializing world to interfere with what he had to say or counter what he planned. So John wrote his letter in "the language of angels" so that it would require an interpreter to read. Therefore, very appropriately, he addressed his words to the angels (those interpreting spirits in the various churches which were – by their very character – close to the throne of God) rather than directly to the ultimate recipient – the faithful individual who must hear and understand his words.

These angels were not individuals. They were spirits binding the communities together. John's words, therefore, might easily have read: "To the interpreting spirit in the body of believers at Ephesus," or "To the power of interpreting tongues in the body of Christ at Smyrna." for John fully intended his words to be read and understood, as they contained instructions and commands that he wished acted upon. Without them having been obeyed, establishing the Kingdom of God (on earth) would prove impossible.

Ironically, today, a modern Jew is far better equipped than most Christians for reading The *Book of Revelation* and understanding it. For the basic plan on which John has built his work is the so-called "Jewish" holy days. And any Jew can tell you, the seven sets of holy Festivals were far more than memorials of the past. They were the systematic path to salvation. Moses used them as the strategy for coming out of Egypt and preparing the children of Israel for entering the Holy Land. Now, in his instructions to the churches, John uses these same holy days of God in the same way Moses did, as steps for entering the Kingdom of God.

Yet many Christians seem determined not to think of these holy days at all, imagining that somehow "they were done away," even though our history books prove otherwise. John and all of the apostles celebrated them, and Paul himself referred to them as "shadows of the things to come". I suggest that we should look again at Paul's now famous words, where he said: "Don't let anyone outside the body of Christ (i.e. the Church) judge you in matters concerning what you eat or drink, or in relation to religious festivals, a New Moon celebration or a Sabbath Day. For these are shadows of the things to come." (Colossians 2: 16-17)

In other words, they are the ground plan to be followed toward the reality of God, until Jehovah's kingdom is established on the earth, and rules the world. They are the strategy of salvation. Paul kept them faithfully and urged the churches to do the same, as is apparent from these words and from his words to the Corinthians, when he said: "Christ our Passover is sacrificed for us. Therefore let us keep the Feast (of Unleavened Bread), not with the old leaven of malice and wickedness, but with the unleavened bread of sincerity and truth."   (1 Corinthians 5: 7-8)

It is unfortunate that many versions of our modern Bibles do contain a number of misleading texts because of awkward mistranslations from the Hebrew or the Greek. What causes this is mostly due to forcing texts to stay in keeping with accepted doctrines and traditions of the modern Church. So if I had a choice I would either sidestep or ignore this matter and proceed with simply showing what John said. Unfortunately John's words won't permit my doing this. Ignoring mistranslations of essential verses in this case would only mean corrupting and destroying words essential to the message John communicates, and he has told us it is essential to our lives. One such example is that one I have named, found in Colossians 2: 16-17.

How else can we explain how one small phrase "the body of Christ" which means "the church" came to be translated as "the body is of Christ", then gradually became "the reality is of Christ" and finally "But what is true and real has come to be found in Christ." I understand the need to make the scriptures readable, but such warping of the words as we find here doesn't constitute translation. This is warping just to suit our personal convictions, or to make the scriptures say what we believe should have been said.

"What difference does it make?" you're bound to ask. The difference is that Paul was defending Christian holy days, which differed from those celebrated in the pagan city of Colossae, and was telling "the body of Christ" there, not to be intimidated by the pagan world, because the holy days of Jehovah were a plan of things that were to come. The implication, in the warped translation of this verse, is that Christ had done away with all things "Jewish", including holy days. This warping of the scripture here was done (no doubt unconsciously) to make it fit a doctrine Christianity in later centuries evolved, namely: "Christ did everything that needed to be done, and there was nothing else for anyone to do, but wait in expectation of that time when Jesus Christ would come and snatch all true believers up into the sky."

But open up your interlinear translations from the Greek. The Greek clearly says "body", not "reality", and the verb "is" just can't be found anywhere at all. We have to put it in where it does not belong. Then after some embroidering we get the words which satisfy our modern prejudice. That is not translation. What the Bible says is "Let no one but the body of Christ judge you in the holy days you keep, because they are a shadow of the things to come." That was the message of those words. Now John gives concrete substance to Paul's instructions, by showing us the way that they apply to things to come. So my whole point here is not to cause unnecessary controversy, but rather to clarify the meaning of the texts we will be examining. And this verse is an important key to understanding what John said.

The feasts of Jehovah, as the Bible calls these days, are important festivals since they memorialize the victory over Pharaoh and the entrance into the promised land, and they set a standard plan for warfare against Satan and the pagan world. So I shall make a short review of them:

Passover: marked the final stroke in overturning Pharaoh's power.

The Feast of Unleavened Bread: brought Israel out of slavery.

Pentecost: gave Israel the law of God from Sinai.

The Feast of Trumpets: was a prelude to the final judgment on the idolatrous world, and a time for strengthening the sons of Israel.

The Day of Atonement: was a day for confessions of all wrong doings and for generous forgiveness of our brethren so that sin could be put out of the community of God.

The Feast of Tabernacles: was a time to rejoice and learn the way of God and good government.

The Last Great Day: was a time to enter the new world and deliver judgment on God's enemies.

In short, the holy days were the creative gospel of salvation. And it is no accident that they supply the format for all four gospels in the Christian scriptures. In the gospel of Matthew, for instance, Jesus (the Lamb of God) entered God's covenant when he was baptized at Passover; and overcame the temptations of Satan in the wilderness during the Feast of Unleavened Bread; and then went up into the mountain at Pentecost to deliver the Sermon on the Mount, to reveal the way of God to his followers. During the Feast of Trumpets, he gave warning of impending judgments to those who had not repented. On the Day of Atonement, before three of his disciples, Jesus revealed the meaning of true unity with God by projecting his return in glory in his transfiguration. During the Feast of Tabernacles he taught his disciples the secrets of the kingdom of God, and rode into Jerusalem for the Last Great Day of triumph over Satan and his rebellious world.

For that is the strategy of God's plan. We find it in the gospel messages, and in *The Book of Revelation* we find it used as the basic plan for entering God's new world. As Jesus, with his life, prophesied the things to come, so John now shows us the reality of what he prophesied. Jesus, with his life, revealed the way. Now we are called upon to follow it. That is the strategy.

Keeping the holy days of Jehovah, is not simply a celebration of them in form, as merely days upon the calendar. That would be a mere mechanical formality. What Christians were to do was keep them in the very manner Jesus did, as real reminders of the plan that God would one day ask them to fulfill. The festivals themselves (which should not be ignored) attempt to show the Christian exactly what it is that is required from him. Moses used these festivals as the first means for teaching Israel. For in those very early days, there was no way of placing scriptural material in every person's hands, so other teaching methods had to be employed. The holy days of Jehovah were but one important means they used.

In interpreting John's letter, I have tried to make the text as comprehensible as possible, and so I've made insertions all along the way. I have not done this irresponsibly, as all of my insertions are derived from other Bible texts. However, I do not ask my reader to submissively agree with everything I say. The benefit of any commentary is that it presents the scriptural evidence to the unencumbered mind. It is the individual who is ultimately responsible for weighing it and reaching conclusions without pressure or intimidation.

In the process, though, of interpreting John's imagery, I've found myself sometimes at odds with what different churches teach. And for a time that bothered me, as I had no wish to be at odds with them. I simply hoped, when I began this work, to do nothing other than interpret the message hidden in John's words. And I believe I've done that honestly. I did not try to bolster or tear down what any churches preach. However, when I found that certain Christian doctrines did get in the way, I felt obliged to speak about them openly then let them stand or fall according to the individuals or churches which would have to deal with them. The onus of accepting or rejecting what John says must rest entirely with anyone who fosters doctrines other than those found in this Bible document. It is they who must decide on whether they will follow those traditions they have grown to love or take the course which John has recommended that we take.

John doesn't call on any one to fantasize or to imagine the impossible. His imagery is drawn entirely from selected Bible texts, and the picture that he draws for us (when properly interpreted) and the new world he describes is one completely possible and credible. So let's put all our superstitions to one side and read the letter to the churches sensibly for what it is primarily: a letter of encouragement and hope, and a revelation of the plan the churches have been called on to obey in order to translate the dream into reality.

THE BOOK
of
THE REVELATION
of
JESUS CHRIST

(containing his plan for establishing
God's Kingdom upon earth)

Chapter One

The Perfect Man Revealed

The plan (of salvation) disclosed in this document was given to Jesus, the anointed leader of Israel, by Jehovah so that he could show his trusted workmen what needed to be done at once with care and thoroughness. So it was that Jesus sent his messenger directly to his loyal servant John who, in this book, describes in detail everything that he was shown, and who gives his personal assurance that everything he says is nothing other than the very word of God, as Jesus (the anointed leader of Israel) revealed it to him. Anyone who therefore reads these words or hears and understands them, and does those things which are required, will receive the promised benefits. For the time is very near at hand (for establishing the Kingdom of God on earth).

(At this point, John begins an open letter to every church in Christendom — a letter which ends only with the last words written in this book.)

John:
To the seven churches in Asia (now called Turkey): Greetings and best wishes for your prosperity and well-being,

from Jehovah,   who is and was and is to come;

from the seven creative spirits,
             which stand (as lamps) beside his throne;

and from Jesus (God's anointed priest and king)
             the faithful witness, the first revived from
             death, and greater (in authority) than
             every king who rules on earth.

Our service and our loyalty belong alone to him who
loves us, and who freed us from the power of sin (and
death) so that we might be a kingdom of priests who
serve his God and Father (Jehovah) forever. Yes! Let
these things be. For look! Already he is coming on the
clouds (of heaven) and everyone will shortly see him
come, even those who impaled him. And people out of
every nationality on earth will mourn because of him.
Yes, Let these things be.

"I am the A and the Z, the beginning and the end,
(the only God—before me there were no Gods and after
me there shall be no other Gods)" says Jehovah of hosts,
"which is and was and is to come, the Mighty One of
Israel."

I, your brother John, have shared in your afflictions
and sufferings with patient endurance for (the sake of)
God's kingdom and Jesus (his anointed representative).
Now I am writing you this letter following my imprison-
ment(upon the isle called Patmos) because of my devotion
to the word of God and my acknowledgement of Jesus
Christ (as the ruling power on earth above all kings).

Now in spirit I was present on the day of Jehovah,
and I heard a great voice behind me like a trumpet
(sounding to alert the troops to action), saying, "I am

the A and the Z, the first and the last" (which is to say "the author and the finisher of our faith" — the Bible's way of saying that Jesus initiated the plan of Salvation and would bring it to a successful conclusion). Therefore, write down everything you see in a book, and send it to the seven churches in Asia: to Ephesus, to Smyrna, to Pergamos, to Thyatira, to Sardis, to Philadelphia and to Laodicea.

Then when I had turned to see who it was that spoke to me, I saw seven golden lampstands (signifying John was in the spiritual temple of Jehovah), and I observed among them what appeared to be (the mysterious figure of) a man wearing a long robe (of righteousness) that reached down to his feet, having a golden sash (of trustworthiness) across his chest. His hair which resembled white wool (indicating wisdom) was as white as snow (the pure wisdom of God's unpolluted word), and his eyes were like flames of fire (showing that he will not judge superficially from circumstantial evidence).

His feet shone like polished bronze (like that of the sustaining angel who had walked with Shadrack, Meshak and Abednigo upon the flames in the trying furnaces of Babylon. For such is the manner that this judge too is ready to strengthen and sustain everyone walking in the counsels of Almighty God, during their adversities). For his feet had been tried in the furnace (of painful experience), and his voice was like the sound of running water (having the authority of God's word). In his right hand he held seven stars (the seven interpreting spirits who could clarify the message of John's letter), and from his mouth there came a sharp double-edged sword (for his words were the keen unerring words of God, able to bring judgment to the earth). Also his face was as brilliant as the sun shining at its brightest: (Since nothing in his countenance, his deeds and words were clouded by indecision or uncertainty, they revealed the perfect will of God).

The very moment that I saw him, I fell at his feet as if I were dead, whereupon he placed his right hand upon me and he said: "Don't be afraid! I am the First and the Last (the one who began and will finish the plan of salvation). I am the Living One who died, but is now alive for ever and ever. For look! (There is nothing to fear.) I have the keys to death and the grave. ('And the gates of the grave shall not prevail against my chosen ones.'" Jesus would not need the keys to death and the grave if the righteous dead were already alive in heaven. But the Bible says they sleep and will be raised up at the last day. — 1 Thessalonians 4: 13-14; John 6: 39)

"Therefore write down everything I show you, of what is now and what shall later be. There are many secret meanings in my words, as in the seven stars I hold in my right hand and of the seven golden lampstands: The seven stars are the interpreting spirits present in the seven churches, and the seven lamp stands are the seven churches."

(So right from the start, John tells us that the imagery he uses is symbolic. To read it literally is dangerous. His imagery, however, can be readily interpreted because it is drawn entirely from parallel passages in other Bible books.)

*

John clearly states that his letter is a commission from God bestowed on all those who understand his words and are ready to obey them, being loyal only to God and his messiah — Jesus, the anointed leader of Israel.

Those addressed are told that they should avoid confusing entanglements of loyalties, customs and practices which hinder an immediate and unreserved obedience to "him who loves us"—namely Jesus Christ— as they are to be "a kingdom of priests that forever serve his God and Father (Jehovah)." John here, and throughout his letter, makes a clear distinction between God and his messiah Jesus Christ. For that reason only I also will take care to preserve the same distinction.

"Through a vision I was present on the day of the Lord." This verse sets the tone for the whole letter. Words similar to this are to be found in various parts of what Christians seem determined to call the Old Testament, but which Jesus called the "word of God" or the "Holy Scriptures". For example, when the prophet Ezekiel was carried in a vision to the Valley of the Bones, he spoke of being in the spirit and being brought there. And even John, in the course of this very letter, speaks of being present in heaven after saying, "And instantly I was in the spirit." This tells us that the vision we are shown is spiritual and not a carnal experience.

This day of Jehovah that is mentioned here is not a single day but, as we read the letter, proves to be a great period of change encompassing seven great creative acts (or holy festivals) which will establish God's new world. So logically our story (which covers the whole year of Jehovah) begins with the ultimate and great spiritual Passover of God. Upon hearing a clear commanding voice behind him, John turns and brings his readers face to face with a very powerful depiction of Israel's messiah, who stands (like the High Priest) in the Temple sanctuary of Jehovah's city of Peace (spiritual Jerusalem). Snow white hair, tempered feet of brass, eyes of fire, a voice like rushing waters, a sharp sword flashing from his mouth is an awesome spectacle no reader can easily

forget. To read it, or to hear it, is to see it as a real experience. We share directly in the vision John has seen.

In such a manner then, John captures easily the
imagination of all those following his words. Whoever
was the author of this letter obviously knew that people
are more readily moved and governed by their
imaginations than by any written rule or law or tedious
instruction. Even Albert Einstein, the most celebrated
physicist of the twentieth century, said, "Imagination is
greater than knowledge." Yet powerful as this visual
depiction of God's messiah is, this is not a physical
description of the Christ, but a symbolic one. What John
alludes to in such powerful terms is Isaiah's prophecy.
John has taken it and made it visual by expressing it in
concrete images:

"Eventually a shoot will spring from the tree stump
of Jesse('s cut-down kingly line) and a fruitful branch
(that is to say an heir to the throne of Israel) will grow
from its roots. And the spirit of Jehovah will rest on
him, and endow him with wisdom, perception, good
judgment, strength, knowledge (of Jehovah's will), respect
for God and his creation, and the joy of obedience to
God. When he judges, he will not be deceived by
circumstantial appearances or by hearsay; but he will
be fair when he judges the poor, and he will be just when
he decides the cases of the non-illustrious. He will speak
with authority when rendering judgment in the land, and
by the power of his words he will commit the wicked to
death. He shall be clothed with the righteousness of
God, and girded about the waist with trustworthiness.
(He shall be fair and impartial.)

"(Even creation will be at peace when he appears.)
The wolf and the lamb will live together in harmony; the
leopard, the goat, the calf, the lion and the fatted

yearling will all lie down together; and they will be
placed in the care of a small child. Even the cow and
the bear will feed together, and their young ones will
mingle peacefully. Lions, like oxen, will eat straw. An
infant will play near the hole of the cobra, and a young
child will put his hand into a viper's nest (and not be
harmed). No creature in all of my holy mountain will
harm or injure another; for the whole earth will be filled
with the knowledge of Jehovah, in much the same way
that the sea is filled with water."   (Isaiah 11: 1-9)

John's picture of the messiah then is deeply rooted
in the Hebrew Scriptures and in the expectations of
Israel: a leader clothed in the righteousness of God; girt
about his body with trustworthiness, whose wisdom is
the pure wisdom of God, whose eyes do not judge things
superficially, whose spoken word (because it is God's
word and not his own) is like a two-edged sword "able to
divide both soul and spirit" and because he has suffered
in the fire of life's adversities, he can strengthen all who
walk with him.

The very nature of this vision (expressed in
concrete terms) of a man whose voice is like a trumpet
call to action, carries with it an indirect command. You
may well ask: "What must we do?" Paul—the man from
Tarsus—answers that for us: "Put on the new being,
made with true righteousness and holiness, in the very
image of God." (Ephesians 4: 24). John has clearly shown
us here—in concrete imagery that makes him visible—
the spiritual man we must put on. Present in the midst
of all the churches, this spiritual man is ready to
perform a miracle and give unity to them. And Paul has
readily defined the kind of influence that such a vision
has: "All of us, looking with uncovered faces upon the
character of God, reflect—as if we were a mirror—the
very glory that we gaze upon. For we are all

transfigured by the vision that we see and become by gradual degrees more and more like him that we behold."
(2 Corinthians 3: 18)

In truth all of us are influenced and invisibly governed throughout our lives by all the things we see and hear and imagine. Everything effects some kind of change in us. So John takes time to clearly show us the character of Christ—the spiritual man designed by God. And we are changed by it. We grow, and are fashioned by a power beyond ourselves. Jesus said, "Behold the lilies of the field, how they grow." The hidden seed reaches toward the light. The blossom bursts forth into full bloom. Our fruits grow and ripen according to whatever vision we are shown. We only need to briefly think upon the power of popular celebrities to see that point. All life is a religious experience, and we grow continually to be like those we most admire. John has therefore lifted up for us, the concrete vision of a man made in the image of God, and shows us that the character of God is not a thing beyond our comprehension, but something that we can imagine and reflect. This is not superstition. It is real.

The character of God made flesh is in our midst. This is the judge, who comes to put his house in order, before he tries to lead the world toward that harmony with nature which Isaiah has foretold.

You will have noticed by this time that in all my comments I refer to God by the anglicized version of his name, Jehovah, instead of the traditional The LORD, and you might wonder why. The Greek text, after all, does not use the Hebrew Tetragrammaton יהוה . The reason I do so is to avoid confusion. John's letter calls for an interpreter, and an interpreter must remove confusion from the text. Since John's allusions are to Hebrew Scriptures where the Tetragrammaton is used, I have incorporated it into the translation of John's text, and to be consistent, I have maintained the name throughout.

Also John does make a difference between Jesus and God, and so it seemed appropriate for me to use the name of God wherever it had been implied. The custom of refraining from its use, began with the Pharisees. So as not to dishonour it or use it blasphemously, they stopped using it at all, and wouldn't utter it even in the reading of scriptures in the synagogue. But since the name of God can only be dishonoured by an unhealthy attitude toward Jehovah's word, or by the careless way we treat our fellow man or any other part of his creation, I see no folly in the use of the symbolic word that stands for the reality of what he is. Martin Luther (the sixteenth century German leader of the Protestant Reformation) reflecting on this matter, said: "If (the name of God) can be written with pen and ink, why should it not be spoken, which is much better than being written with pen and ink? Why is it not also called unwritable, unreadable or unthinkable? All things considered there is something foul?"

Now when John presents us with Isaiah's Messianic priest, standing in the temple of God, he says that he was walking in the midst of seven lampstands. That may seem confusing just at first, for the Temple in Jerusalem had but one lampstand with seven branches. These seven branches respresented the seven days of creation, and the power of God's word to give light to the world. How is it then that in the Temple John describes for us, we find seven lampstands which would have seven branches each?

The answer is of course that the High Priest's words are directed to the seven churches — and the spirit of

Christ exists in all of them. Remember Jesus's words to the woman by the well in Samaria: "Believe me, woman, a time is coming when you will worship the Father not only in this mountain (of Gerazim at Samaria) nor in Jerusalem (but anywhere on earth)... The time is coming, and has indeed now come, when true worshippers will worship the Father in spirit and in truth (wherever they may be). For they are the kind of worshipper the Father seeks."   (John 4: 21, 23)

To the one who wrote this letter, it was that entire body of (believers in) Christ known as the church (existing individually in each city of the world community) which was a living temple sanctuary (or Mishkan) for God. For it was written not that "God dwelt in it," but that "God dwelt among them." Just as Isaiah referred to Jerusalem and her citizens as citizens of Sodom and citizens of Gommorah, so this letter to the churches makes it clear that the Mishkan of God's Temple is anywhere on earth where people worship God in the right attitude of spirit. There was no longer any need for a sacred pilgrimage to a "Holy City" anywhere on earth. For God's Divine Presence (or Shechinah) was available to God's people everywhere, just as the prophet Ezekiel in his vision once had shown. Perhaps it should be noted too that there is no reference made at all to any Pope or Mother Church. There is but One High Priest: the anointed, resurrected Jesus Christ—who lives. See Matthew 17: 20. Each church, therefore was autonomous and individually responsible to no other than to the High Priest in the Temple (Jesus Christ "who loves us").

John was not initiating any new idea, for many Jews by this time also believed that the Temple of God was present anywhere on earth where people served and worshipped God according to the spirit of his word. Even at the time when Jesus did his missionary work in Israel, the Pharisees maintained that God was present in their synagogues throughout the world. Many Jews as well began to feel that the sacrifices made on their behalf, in old Jerusalem, were not entirely to their taste.

The smelly temple offerings left much to be desired. There was an awful stench to them, and no matter how thorough the priesthood was in cleaning up around the altar of the temple afterwards, flies still clustered on the paving stones and on the altar's sides. Yet abandoning such sacrifices was unthinkable for no one possibly could sanctify himself merely by saying, "I will never sin again." The purpose of the sacrifice was to impress upon the sinner the gravity of his sin. The lives of others suffered from his deeds, and a sacrifice impressed this fact upon his mind. So it came to be that many Jews looked forward to a time when "a clean sacrifice" could be made. Christianity apparently believed that they had found the means for doing this, for the perfect sacrifice, they said, was found in Jesus Christ, whose life personified (the lamb of God) the man of heaven which Isaiah had earlier described and whose death could be recounted every year, and celebrated in a yearly sacrament on the fourteenth day of Nisan.

In a little-understood vision of the prophet Ezekiel, Jehovah made it evident to his people that God's throne was present anywhere, and at any time, when there was need for him: "Wherever the living creatures moved, the wheels (of God's chariot) moved, and when the living creatures rose from the ground, the wheels (of God's chariot) also rose. Wherever the spirit would go, they would go, and the wheels would rise along with them, because the spirit of the living creatures was in the wheels."   (Ezekiel 1: 19-20)

God's chariot is made up of his living creatures, and the living spirit of creation drives the chariot of God. His chariot also moves with the speed of light to anywhere in the universe. That is the message in these words.

Now it should be noticed from the start, that this long awaited letter of instruction from the Christ to the seven churches in Asia is not a letter to unconverted men and women. It is a letter to faithful Christians and alerts them to a necessary line of action, and serves as a powerful reminder of what manner of spirit they are: "The spirit of Jehovah is upon me because he has anointed me to preach the gospel to the poor. He has sent me to proclaim freedom for those held captive, and recovery of sight to the blind, to set free those who are oppressed, and to proclaim the year of Jehovah's salvation." (Luke 4: 18-19) This vision then of Christ is one that assures renewal and encouragement from him who has authority to direct their ways.

The seven special messages inserted in the letter particularize the commendations and critical complaints of shortcomings that must be tended to, before the great proposal of God's plan can be made workable. Without all steps being carefully carried out, all that follows each of them is doomed, as John's own words will later verify. The letter John has written takes the form of a divine mandate from God and commissions individually the church of each community to play its part. The cleansing of that church is the prelude to the plan which the great creator of the world has asked it to initiate. So putting on the nature of the one whom he has seen and should reflect, each Christian has been urged to promptly carry out with thoroughness the first step in God's strategy.

CHAPTER TWO

Grooming the Bride to Meet Her Lord

Write these words to the guiding spirit in the body of believers at Ephesus: "The one who has authority over all who act as his interpreters (which John depicts as seven stars held in the saviour's hand), and who walks among the gatherings of those who bear his name, has this to say to you: 'I know how hard you've worked on my behalf and all you have achieved. Even in the face of overwhelming difficulties you have patiently endured, and no evil person ever was allowed within your midst. So thorough were you in examining all those who tried to find a place amongst you that you laid bare the lies of even those who claimed that they were sent by me. In every case you showed yourselves to be extremely capable, for you were thorough, diligent and patient in everything you did on my behalf, and you never let yourselves despair.

"'Nevertheless you are not perfect in my sight. For I have this against you: That you have turned away from your first love (the genuine pure doctrine you were taught at first). Take time to notice therefore, and confess the height from which you've fallen and return to the teachings and the practices that first were given you. For if you don't repent, I will take away your lampstand from its place (which is to say, "I will take away the light of my presence from your midst"). Still I must credit you with this, that you hate the practices of the Nicolaitans, which I also hate.

"'If anyone has ears (to comprehend my words), let him do those things the guiding spirit of interpretation directs all bodies of the faith to do; for anyone who overcomes (the snare of all false teachings and false practices, and all corrupting influence) will be given fruit to eat from the tree of life which grows in the garden of

God. (Fruit growing from the seeds of love, joy, peace, longsuffering, gentleness, faith, meekness, and self-control which you have sown. "For what you sow, that shall you also reap.")"

Next write these words to the guiding spirit which interprets tongues in the community of saints at Smyrna: "The First and the Last (the author and the finisher of our faith), who was dead and is alive, says this to you: 'I know the great extent of all your suffering and poverty, although (in spirit) you are very rich indeed. But I know about the slanders of those maligning you, who falsely claim that they are Jews, when actually they are nothing of the kind but members rather of a Satanic group.

"'Don't allow yourselves to be intimidated by them or by any of the things that you will shortly have to suffer for my sake. For the devil certainly will test your faith – severely trying you – by throwing some of you into prison, where you will suffer to the limit (literally "ten days", which indicates the ultimate of suffering) and the very worst that can be done, will certainly be done to you. Be steadfast therefore, even in the face of death, and I will give you the (victor's) crown of life (which is immortality) for having run the course of life so well.

"'Let whoever understands these words therefore do everything the spirit (of wisdom) says to all the churches. For whoever triumphs (over all such obstacles) cannot be injured by the second death.'"

Next write these words to the spirit of interpretation in the church at Pergamos: "The one wielding the sharp double-edged sword says this: 'I realise that even though you are living in the very place where Satan has his throne you've held fast to your faith and haven't once denied my name. You stood firm even at the time when

Antipas, my faithful witness, lived there in your midst and was cruelly put to death in that very place where Satan has his home.

"'However, I do have several things against you: you have allowed into my flock those who follow the practices of Balaam who taught Balac how to lead the children of Israel into sin. These persuaded them to eat unlawful food which was sacrificed to idols, and lured them into sexual immorality. In this same spirit you have brought into your midst those who follow the teachings and the practices of the Nicolaitans.

"'Repent, therefore, (and get rid of all the practices and doctrines that are not of God, so that you will be ready for the work I have in mind for you). Otherwise, I will personally come against you with the sharp sword of my mouth and fight against all those (who bear the guilt of condoning such unrighteousness).

"'Let anyone who understands these words do what the guiding Spirit of interpretation tells the churches they must do. To anyone who overcomes (the power of all the evil influences I have named) I will give the hidden manna (of God's wisdom) to eat, and a white stone (of acceptance) with a new name engraved on it (indicating a new character), known only to the one receiving it.'"

Next write this message to the spirit of interpretation in the congregation of believers at Thyatira: "These are the words of the Son of God, whose eyes burn like fire and whose feet are like polished bronze: 'I have observed your deeds, and I know of your love, your faith, your service, and your patient endurance, and I realise that you are doing even more now than you did at first.

"'Nevertheless, I do have this against you, that you tolerate that woman Jezebel, who calls herself a prophetess, to teach and lead my servants astray, justifying fornication and the eating of food that is offered to idols. Though I have given her the time (and the counselling she needs) to repent of her immorality (that is to say of her "idolatry") she stubbornly and wilfully persists in it.

"'For this reason I will bring her down into a bed (of sickness and suffering), and all her paramours (kings and rulers who have used her for their purposes and licentiously have lain with her) will be afflicted with severe distress, unless they turn away from her, and repent of their depravity. All the children (men and women who spiritually came out of her womb and are fed as members of her congregation) will be struck dead with a pestilence so great that churches everywhere on earth will know that I am he (the judge of Israel) who searches and who knows (the thoughts and wishes of) the heart and mind; and (justly) judges all according to their deeds.

"'However, to all the rest of you in Thyatira, who have rejected such teachings, and have not experienced "the deep mysteries of Satan" — as they are called — I will not further burden you with anything, except to caution you, to hold fast to what you have until I come. For anyone who overcomes (the influence of those seducing and alluring trends — or spirits), and who does my works until the very end, I will give the same authority over the nations that I have received from my father (Jehovah) to rule over them with an iron sceptre and break them into pieces like pottery.

"'I will also give that person the morning star (which is to say "I will be his close companion and will dwell with him and counsel him." Rev 22: 16 and "I will come in to him and will sup with him and he with me.")'"

Everyone with the ability to understand these words should do what the guiding spirit of interpretation says here to the children of God.

(It is clear from this last statement, and others like it, that these messages to individual congregations apply to the people of God everywhere. Notice as well that the accent is always placed upon the actions and decisions of the individual — not solely on the group itself. There is no room for saying "It's all your fault for not guiding me," or "my minister says...." The scriptures counsel every individual. And as it says in the song: "The things that your preacher is liable to teach yer, it ain't necessarily so." The onus is on you.)

*

There is a need to clear the air of some of those deceiving superstitions many people have, before continuing. Today we frequently use terms like "spirit of the times," "spirit of learning," "spirit of the community" or "spirit of the crowd" and have little difficulty understanding what is meant by it. But let the Bible say that there are many spirits present in the world (many of them malignant ones), or even say that we should test the different spirits that we find, then instantly superstitions of all kinds abound to cloud the minds of even those who otherwise would seem most sensible.

This also is the case whenever angels are referred to there, or if demons are the subject of the text. In such a superstitious frame of mind even Satan (or the devil) is crudely and outrageously depicted and personified (some think realistically) as a malevolent freak of nature residing deep within the hidden caverns of the earth.

The angels of the church which Jesus mentions in this letter that he sent to them, refers directly to the spirit of community existing in each body of believers joined in a fellowship. For it was in that single body of believers that special gifts which God had given them were shared among the membership. This letter was not sent to any individual within the church community, say like a bishop or a clergyman. Nor was it written to a creature out of heaven which enjoyed existence independently outside of natural phenomena. It was addressed to the spirit which united the community of saints making up the church. That is to say that it was written to the body of ordinary members who relied upon the spirit of shared gifts for interpreting the message John relayed.

As the scriptures clearly say: "To one the spirit gives the word of wisdom, to another one the word of knowledge, and by the same spirit another has ability to do great works (literally miracles). Another by the spirit has the gift of prophecy, while yet another one possesses insight and ability to challenge any spirit (differing from the doctrines Jesus Christ and the apostles taught). Still yet another has great fluency in languages, while the spirit gives another one the necessary ease in their interpreting."   (1 Corinthians 12: 10)

Such a congregation did not have a hierarchy of priests. For Jesus had forewarned them in these words: "You all have noticed how the rulers of the nations exert great power in making others subject to their will, and how their high officials flagrantly display authority. That is not the way that it must be with you. Instead, if anyone among you would be great, he must do the duties of a servant. And whoever would be greatest in your midst must do the duties of a slave." (Matthew 20: 25-27) So it was that Jesus called upon the members of the church to serve each other with their special knowledge and their gifts, giving strength to others and receiving strength from them in any area where they were weak, so that as a body this shared fellowship would make them strong.

The members of the church enjoyed a fellowship which Luke describes like this: "All that believed were together and had all things common; and sold their possessions and goods, and parted them to all men, as every man had need." (Acts 2: 44-45) He further said: "For the multitude of them that believed were of one heart and of one soul: neither said any of them that any of the things which he possessed was his own; and they had all things common." (Acts 4: 32)   In other words, they were all mutually responsible for the welfare of each other. It was this fellowship that Jesus in his letter calls "the angel of the church."

In contrast to that "angel" of the church community, another angel of community stood ruthlessly opposed to it.   That angel bore the name of Satan – since it was opposed to the spirit of God. Leaving for a moment all the superstitions and symbolic images our minds have drawn of it, this angel is identified in scriptures as "the prince governing the power of the air." Ancient people knew (like many people now) the power of a community spirit to mold the human mind. We only need to think about the national spirit prevalent in Nazi Germany or in the whole of North America during the Cold War years to realise just what that spirit is, and what it does to human consciences and character.

In Bible literature Satan is shown to be that power which governs and controls the public atmosphere, an atmosphere which like strong wine deceives the human mind. It rules the world and lures humanity away from God with envy, greed, suspicion, lust, hatred, war and violence. Satan didn't fall from any heaven which God made, as many people (even the English poet John Milton) have believed. It was the character of man which fell. Satan was a spirit born on earth within the rebel heart of man. For as the Jewish prophet Jeremiah said: "The human heart is desperately sick and deceitful above all things. Who possibly can understand it?" (Jeremiah 17: 9) Jesus also called attention to the human heart as being the prime cause of evil in the world, clearly saying: "Out of the heart comes evil thoughts, murder, adultery, sexual immorality, theft, false testimony, slander. And these are the things which make a man unclean."

(Matthew 15: 19)

It was the spirit governing the world community which first drew people from the way of following their God. It was the spirit governing this world community which the early Christians were suspicious of. And at the heart of this community was Satan's throne. That throne set the pattern for all customs, attitudes and practices degrading to the character of man, or should I say the character of God in man. For this reason, John reveals his vision of the Son of Man — a person in the character of God — having all the attributes that God originally designed for man (male and female). Such a vision tends to slay the old man of the world which lives in us, and raise up in its place a new man of the spirit. "As it is written: 'Whereas the first man Adam was a living creature, the final Adam was a life-giving spirit.'" (1 Corinthians 15: 45) The messianic vision we are shown gives birth to that new man in us.

Still before continuing, there is another matter yet
to be resolved. We must settle finally upon a definition
for the "church", and find out what "religion" really means.
We cannot just presume to know from what the world
around us says. Too many people are preoccupied with
furthering the attitude of "I'm a Christian; you're a Jew,"
or with calling different segments of the Christian church
"someone else's religion." I realise (as many Christians do)
that there are more than 25,000 different sects, denominations and cults today dividing Christianity. More than
just a few of these declare themselves to be exclusively
"the true and only church of God." These confidently
laud themselves, and praise the purity of their own
doctrines before the world. Then not content with that,
they vehemently speak against all other Christian groups
whom they identify, and collectively condemn, as being
part of "Babylon the Great", that horrendous monster we
will very shortly meet in later chapters of this book.

It is not my purpose here to either ridicule or praise
such claims as any of these churches make. I simply say
we must not let such claims interfere with a dispassion-
ate appraisal of God's word or with reading scriptures
without prejudice. I make no pretense of judging anyone.
I only wish to point out here that Jesus's intent in
sending out this letter to the churches of the world was
to call them to repentance and to unity, by being humble
before God and honestly admitting where they'd erred.

Some of course may say: "These admonishments
were not meant for us. We are the people God has
chosen for himself — the Church of Philadelphia. We
have never sinned as other churches have, for we have
God's pure light in us. We are not the children of
fornication as other churches are. So thank God we are
not like them." But John, in yet another letter that he
wrote, told the church: "If we acknowledge our sins,

(before God), he is faithful and just to forgive us our sins, and to cleanse us from all unrighteousness. Yet if we stubbornly maintain we have not sinned, we make him a liar, and his word is not in us." (1 John 9-10) Self-righteousness has no place in Christianity.

Consequently Jesus only recognized one church in each of all the cities that he named, in spite of any differences in doctrine which divided different segments of that church. In his eyes they remained one church. Yet he exhibited no qualms in severely criticizing them, regardless of the tender sentiments and feelings any of their members may have had. Of course he had that right, we're bound to say, for he established them. That being so, we certainly must turn to him to properly define the church for us. And he does so very beautifully when he compares it to the fish in a fisherman's net being drawn to shore. The net (which is God's word) is thrown upon the open sea of mankind and gathers in it many different kinds of fish – both good and bad (the church).

Regarding this, Jesus told his followers: "the kingdom of heaven is like a net which is thrown into the sea to gather every kind of fish in it. When it is filled, the fishermen pull it to the shore, where they sit down to sort the fish, crating all the good ones and throwing all the worthless ones away. This separating of the fish will take place at the end of the age, when the angels of God will separate the wicked from the just." (Matthew 13: 47-49) Those "angels of God" Jesus speaks of in this parable are the very angels John so carefully describes for us in the fourteenth chapter of this book. They symbolize those powerful social forces which compel us all to choose the kingdom and the government we serve when times are critical.

The imagery which Jesus uses in this parable is simple, easily imagined and serves to illustrate the point he wished to make. The Kingdom of God was comprised of all those righteous Jews who lived according to the word of God, and from whose midst Jesus drew the emissaries he commissioned for the preaching of that word. The net they threw into the water was the word of God. The water was mankind, and the fish which they drew in were the people who had come to hear them speak. This story clearly illustrates the varied and differing collection of people who were pulled up from the waters of the world — as willing listeners, but not all willing to be changed. Only at the end of a period of time which God alone would designate as suitable, would they be divided into what was good or bad. That period is referred to in the Bible text as "the end of the age" which, for a time, we erroneously called "the end of the world".

We hear in Jesus's description of the church, an echo of the psalmist's words, which said: "Therefore the ungodly shall not stand in the judgment, nor sinners in the congregation of the righteous. For Jehovah knows the way of the righteous; but the way of the ungodly shall perish." (Psalm 1: 5-6) Those chosen by the angels at the end of this present system of the world, will truly deserve the title of ecclesia (which means the chosen, or the church). For having endured the many trials of tribulation in the furnace of the world's adversities, they will be deemed worthy to come forward from their graves on the first day of resurrection from the dead.

Jesus was quite definite, however, in his assessment of the present churches of the world as bodies having in them good and evil, for earlier he had compared them to a field of grain, saying: "The servants came to the owner of the field (God) and said to him, 'Sir, didn't you plant good seed in this field? How is it then that worthless plants are growing there as well?' When he replied, 'An enemy has done this thing,' his servants instantly responded saying, 'Shall we go then now into the fields and root them out?' 'No,' the owner wisely cautioned them, 'because in pulling out the weeds you will certainly uproot the good wheat too.'"   (Matthew 13: 27-29)

To imagine then the church as ever having been infallible does not correspond to Jesus's description of it as a body having in it good and bad. The one essential element in any church is that it has the word of God "to draw the people in" so that they are free to glean whatever benefits they can derive from it. No history book can ever show you any church that was not flawed. Not even if we go back to the church of Jesus's own day. Read the letters in the Christian chronicles of scripture and they will show you that the early Christian church was not a flawless paragon.

* *

If we would better understand the church, we would be wise to trace its pattern of development and take the necessary time to learn what true "religion" is. To do that we must do what Jesus did whenever he was faced with answering a question others had believed to be impossible to solve. In such a case, it always was his custom to go back to the origins of faith, even overstepping Moses, to reach the primal cause. There he found the principles on which the written law of Israel was framed.

By going back to *Genesis*, we find the first scriptural account of formalized religious practices in the different sacrifices Cain and Abel offered God. Moved by jealous rage because his brother prospered in religious practices which differed from his own, Cain rose up and slew his brother in the field. By reference to an elementary case involving fratricide, the Bible text of *Genesis* reveals that the world's first murder was unmistakably religious in its origin. The lesson in religion that we learn from it, is that we cannot worship God with envy, anger, sullenness or violence, and that all mankind — related as they are through Adam — are answerable to God for any human blood they shed. These principles are just a few of those on which Biblical religion first was framed.

So if we truly would appraise the sacrifice of Cain we must do so purely from the Bible text in *Genesis* rather than relying on some Bible commentaries we might read. God reprimanded Cain only with these words: "If you do what is right will you not be accepted? But if you do not do what is right, sin is crouching (like a wild beast) at the door; it desires to have you, but you must master it." This should surely tell us that the sacrificial ritual was purely a symbolic one.

Cain's nature was the real sacrifice he offered before God, and it did not display the healthy fruits of the spirit God desired from him. Spiritual fruits like tolerance, caring love for others and patience were completely missing in his character. His belligerent disregard for others is aptly summed up in that defiant question that he asked of God: "Am I my brother's keeper?" It wasn't actually a question. For he did not really seek an answer. It was a bold outrageous statement of total disregard.

Religious ceremonies are not worship in themselves. They are only meaningful if they have a positive effect on human lives. "The multitude of your sacrifices," God said, "what are they to me? ...I take no pleasure in the blood of bulls and lambs and goats." If sacrifices people make do not instruct them in the way of God, they are no use at all. "What I really want from you," said God, "is surrendered loving care for others rather than sacrifice; and loving loyalty to God rather than burnt offerings." (Isaiah 1: 11, Hosea 6: 6) Religious rituals and ceremonies of any kind are no more than devices for instructing men and women in the way of God and leading them again to paradise on earth — that garden in which all mankind and nature are at peace.

Humane regard for others was the true religion from the start, and later scriptures would affirm that early theme: In later chronicles Isaiah said: "'Put all evil from your midst and stop doing what is wrong. Practice doing right by ensuring justice in the land and helping those who are oppressed. Give help to the fatherless and speak out on behalf of widows (disadvantaged women) in your midst. For it is through such things as this that you will make all matters right between us,' Jehovah says."
(Isaiah Chapter 1: 16-18)

Later on he said: "Is not this the fast that I require from you? that you will free the land from wickedness by lightening the burden of labour, letting the oppressed go free and breaking the chains of slavery? Are you not called upon to share your food with the hungry? to bring the homeless who are thrown into the streets into your homes? when you see the naked to clothe him? and not neglect the needs of your own flesh and blood?"
(Isaiah 58: 6-7)

As James (Jesus's own brother of the flesh) observed: "True religious worship in the sight of God is this: to visit and help orphans and widows who are in need, while keeping oneself unpolluted by the spirit of the world."
(James 1: 27)

One striking error often found in text books written on comparative religions is the blind but confident assertion that so many of them make: that the Jewish religion was founded by Moses, and that Jesus was the founder of Christianity. Such statements tend to cloud the mind and poison it with prejudice. The truth is Moses would have been surprised if anyone had told him that in the process of building up a nation known as Israel, he was the father of a new religion too.

Jesus would have been surprised as well by any notion which suggested that his mission in the world was to build a new religion that opposed the teachings of the Jews. Jesus lived his whole life as a Jew. He kept all Jewish holy days. He called the faithful Jewish people "the light of the world," and the Jewish temple in Jerusalem "my Father's house." He worshipped every sabbath day in Jewish synagogues, and he told a woman in Samaria, "Salvation is of the Jews."

Jesus worshipped the same God as Moses and as Abraham, and as the Bible clearly shows there were other worshippers before the time of Abraham who worshipped that same God as well. Moses had enjoyed a close relationship and fellowship with a priest from On, and Abraham willingly paid tithes to King Melchizedek, a man who ruled a city state whose citizens were also worshippers of him who made the earth and skies. Job from Uz, along with all his friends, reverenced the creator in the company of those known as the B'nai Elohim (or literally translated "the sons of God").

Long before the flood, this same congregation to which Noah had belonged could trace its origins to Seth and earlier. Moses did not make a new religion for the world. That I do not distort in any way the meaning of the Hebrew words, B'nai Elohim can be verified in the ancient Books of Eden, which refer to all of Seth's disciples by that name. I realise that there are many now who have a different view of them. Some sincerely hold to the belief that the B'nai Elohim were "angels in heaven", but nowhere in the Hebrew text can such a rendering be justified. Much as I respect all those who hold this view of them, it seems to me presumptuous that some translators take it now upon themselves to write this mere presumption into translations of the Bible text.

Also if we remove one of the unnatural Bible barriers to reading, set up in more recent centuries (I speak here of dividing the Hebrew text into chapters which causes us to halt between connected thoughts) we will notice instantly that the natural flow of Hebrew words between Chapter Five and Chapter Six of *Genesis* carries the reader from the genealogy of Seth directly into the mention of "the sons of God." The allusion then to the genealogy just named becomes apparent. "The sons of God" is (as it is in all grammatical constructions of thought) a direct reference to the line of Seth directly mentioned just before. The implication then is that, like Abel, the sons of Seth had found favour in the eyes of God, and therefore were regarded as his sons.

There is no good reason to assume that the assemblies of "the sons of God", mentioned in the books of *Genesis* and *Job*, congregated anywhere besides on earth. They met as a community before the throne of God, as modern worshippers still do. Consequently, Satan too was also in their midst, just as he appears in congregations now throughout the world. If heaven were a place for backbiting and rebelling angels who ogled women lustfully, railed against God and those who worshipped him, we couldn't with an open conscience pray, "Thy will be done on earth as it is in heaven." In such a circumstance there wouldn't be a model for true worshippers on earth to emulate. Men on earth alone rebelled against the living God. There would be no point in asking God to make earth like heaven if all earth's problems had originated there.

After all, isn't it the purpose of these early Bible texts to communicate to readers through their real experience how the two religious congregations in the world were divided into those who served their God (the sons of God) and those who were opposed to him (the sons of willful Adam who had disobeyed). These groups upon occasions were so closely interwound, we can only with great care discover them. If we take time to briefly look at them, we might divide them in this way:

The Two Congregations

The Sons of God	The Children of Iniquity
Congregation of the Righteous (The Seed of Woman)	Congregation of the Wicked (Generation of Vipers)
The Tree of Life	The Tree of Knowledge of Good and Evil
(following the wisdom of God)	(Doing anything that seems right in their own eyes)
Social Empathy, Compassion Co-operation	Self-sufficiency, Envy Competition
Emotional stability and self-control	Dominated by anger, resentment, envy, self-pity, possessiveness and sexual desire
Meekness (easy to approach), Humility, Respect for others	Haughtiness, Pride, Arrogance

| Mercy, Seekers of Truth Patience | Cruelty, Superstition, Impatience |
| Willing to yield, listen graciously | Stubborn, Unwilling to listen, Insulting |

THE HARVEST

| Fruit of Spirituality eternal life | Fruit of instant gratification eternal death |

One basic principle of real religion that existed from the very first, long before the time of Moses or of Abraham, was accountability for life on earth. Man had been made responsible for every living thing. In the first chapter of *Genesis* God said: "Let man have jurisdiction over all life upon earth, over the fish of the sea and the birds of the air, over all domestic animals and over all wild beasts of the field, and over everything that moves upon the earth."

Moses took such ancient principles as this. How much was orally passed on to him and what was written down, we do not know. The Bible only shows us that he felt the grave necessity to make a written law for Israel. Having led the twelve tribes of Israel out of slavery, he became responsible for them and knew he could not walk with them forever in the wilderness. So he had no choice but to organize them, settle their disputes and make a nation out of them, then find a land for them to settle in.

There was no other man on earth so well equipped for doing this. In early boyhood Moses had been schooled and tutored in the lore and learning of his mother's Hebrew faith. From her he learned to dream the dream that Abraham had dreamed: Of building upon earth a nation that could bring mankind and nature into harmony again, and thereby bless all people upon earth.

Through a strong and well-considered code of national laws, Moses laid the groundwork for a solid, stable state. More advanced in almost every way from any other law codes existing at that time, the law of Moses gave Israel the basis of a system which could have made that nation the envy of the ancient world.

Today that law code still remains a wonder and serves as a solid basis from which three religious faiths have grown. Quite naturally there are those who are disparaging of it and say that Moses copied freely from the Hammurabi code of Babylon. That may be so. Perhaps he did. For Moses was not proud and arrogant and very often learned from what others said and did. But utter honesty compels us to admit his law depended more upon the faith he had in the creator — the God of Abraham and all the ancient men who lived by faith throughout the past — whom he relied on most. Also, what was unique about the law of Moses was that it was not built on retribution but on the principle of love. Love of God and love of one's neighbour were the principles he emphasized. Therefore, mercy was a recommended feature of the law.

* * *

Very often we forget as well that Moses had been educated as a royal prince in Egypt and (so the Bible says) knew all the arts and sciences of that land. Since this is so, Moses must have studied in such higher seats of learning as the colleges of Karnak and Memphis as well as under palace tutoring. This made him undeniably a man well schooled in foreign and domestic governments. In addition he was a man of very broad and practical experience. He knew everything from shepherding to the governing of states, and what a fugitive must do in order to survive out in the wilderness. Even so, a careful study of the Hammurabi code of law should show us instantly the striking differences that separate it from the law which Moses gave to Israel.

It was only after he consulted with Jethro, a bronze age priest from On, that Moses made the great law code of Israel (according to the word of God) and so as not to wear himself away, he delegated many of the powers he once exclusively had exercised. After he considered it, Moses took the priest's advice and appointed judges, tribal princes and a priesthood which would serve the nation in the settling of disputes, and act as educators and a board of health. For Moses had determined that the ordinary citizen of Israel should not remain illiterate or suffer from diseases that were prevalent in other lands. So in the writing of the Torah, Moses gave the world its most lasting and effective document of law, religion, education, government, health, hygene, and dietary rules. To neglect such necessary things as these was sin, and led to sickness and criminality. He also worked out ways for periodically redistributing the wealth of Israel so as it would not fall exclusively into the hands of just a few.

As a base for all of this, he gave the ordinary citizen a moral code of ten commandments that no judge besides the individual could oversee. Perhaps it is significant that there were exactly ten of them, for whether by intention or by accident, the number in symbolic terms suggests that they were meant to be a solid moral base for all the nations in the world.

That they were "written by the finger of God" also is significant, since such a phrase suggests that Moses had received these basic laws directly "by the power of God's own Holy Spirit." Jesus later on would use this phrase to show the legalized religious leaders of his day the power by which he did his miracles and their significance. For he addressed them with these very words: "If I drive out demons by the finger of God, then the kingdom of God has come unto you." (Matthew 11: 20) So this phrase underlines for any reader that the ten commandments would endure forever and never pass away.

You will remember too, that the religious advisers of Pharaoh in Egypt in speaking of the miracles of Moses indicated this same origin: "This is the finger of God," they said. (Exodus 8: 19) But Pharaoh's heart was hard, and he would not listen to such words. We must conclude, therefore from this, that Moses in founding Israel and giving them the ten commandments, was by his work laying the foundation of the world. His religion therefore was a constantly progressive one.

I know that there are Christians now who say the ten commandments (like the holy days and all the other laws of Israel) were done away. Yet Jesus Christ emphatically declared: "Don't imagine for one moment that my purpose is to do away with anything the law and prophets said...For if anyone deliberately should break the very least of these commandments, and teach others that they may do the same, that person shall be called the least in the kingdom of heaven (being built on earth). Likewise anyone who keeps and teaches these commandments, shall be called great in the kingdom of heaven." (Matthew 5: 7-19) There is no question that these laws were meant for everyone who wished to be "a son of God" and a citizen of that kingdom being built by God on earth, through men like Moses and like Jesus Christ.

Moses gave the tribes of Israel a stable law and stable state. Yet he never meant the state of Israel to be a rigid static one which never could advance beyond the teachings Moses had laid out for them. For Moses was a forward-looking man and made adjustments in the law to suit those situations where the people's needs required such change. One such case occurred when the daughters of Zelophehad came before Moses to complain about the

way the law code, as it stood, had disinherited their
father's line, and they argued for a right to be included in
the lineage of inheritance, which was strongly biased
toward male heirs. Moses listened to them, and the law
was changed. But the basic principle on which it had
been built remained.   (Numbers 27: 1-11)

Some republican idealists today I know will
vigorously complain at what will seem to them a totally
unjust imbalance in the law. However, you cannot
ignorantly impose upon the people of any nation laws
completely foreign to their temperament. The community
of Israel in ages past was looked on as a unit. No man or
woman stood alone in it. Women benefited from all
concessions made to men in general, and men were made
responsible for seeing women were not deprived or
destitute. Moses simply honoured customs which the
world developed on its own, and made a law accommo-
dating some of them, a law which to some degree was
flexible, and like a suit of clothes could be comfortably
worn – as Moses own example showed. The principle
established by the case involving the daughters of
Zelophehad was that if a woman – at any time – could
show just cause of complaint, the law (although retained
in spirit) must be eased to fit the circumstance. For the
law was made for mankind, not mankind for the law.

In such a spirit Moses could foresee a time when
there would be another prophet coming after him, who
would rise out of the brotherhood of Israel. The
scriptures introduce him in this way: "Jehovah said to
me...'I will raise among his brothers another prophet very
much like you. I will put my words into his mouth, and
he will tell them everything that I instruct him to. If
anyone refuses to accept the words that prophet speaks
on my behalf, I will call that person to account.'"
                                   (Deuteronomy 18: 17-18)

But Moses did not leave the people of God with no way of testing such a man. For earlier he had said: "Imagine that a prophet or interpreter of dreams is found among you, and tells you of some miraculous sign or wonder that he claims will soon take place. Even though that sign or wonder which he speaks of does occur, you must not follow him if he tells you, 'Let us follow other gods (gods you have not known) and let us worship them.' Such a prophet or a dreamer does not speak by me. Take no regard of anything he says. For this is but a way Jehovah, your God, has of testing you."

(Deuteronomy 13:1-3)

Such counsel was very wisely given, for many dreamers and false prophets have appeared throughout the centuries. Many of them significantly relying on "guidance by the spirit," in order to negate the word of God. "Let your own heart speak to you," some say. Others claim, "I have had a vision," and yet another one will tell you, "The word of God has now been done away." So even John, Jesus's apostle, in later centuries, felt it necessary to remind the Christian brethren of this necessity to: "Test the spirits to see whether they are actually of God; because many false prophets now are going to and fro throughout the world." (1 John 4:1)

If the word of God does not "endure forever", as Jesus and the prophets once assured us that it would, we have lost all means of testing any spirit by measures which are clearly recognized and understood. Throughout its history, the core of true believers in the heart of Israel were led not so much by any human leader, as by principles embodied in the Torah Moses left to them as "a lamp to light their paths." Good human leaders did from time to time arise among the populace. But they were those who kept the vision alive which Moses gave to them. So it was that prophets, who appeared among the people, have been rightfully considered to be of far more importance as leaders of God's nation (at the heart of Israel) than any priest or king who governed them.

The Torah, as Jesus might have said, was like a net that held all sorts of men in it. For Israel survived, not because of any virtue in the vast majority of citizens nor in the goodness of the leaders after Solomon. It was the inner nucleus of those who had endured the furnace of the world who were the citizens of that kingdom God was building upon earth. These were they who through the centuries preserved the word of God, and kept before the populace a vision of the perfect man. Whereas other nations boldly used the symbols of dramatic beasts of prey — the lion, the leopard, or the bear — to show the sort of spirit that they were, Israel expressed its character in the depiction of the common man ennobled by the wisdom God had (like a crown) placed on his head. This vision was referred to by the prophets as "one like the son of man". There was a subtle difference though in him. That difference was his character. So it was, "the son of man" became synonymous with Israel's messiah.

In addition to this spiritual celebrity held up for them to emulate and strive to be, there was the oft-repeated vision of the world to be. This became the essence of all prophecy: Visions of (1) the God of Israel, (2) the ideal man, (3) the world to be, (4) and finally the plan which lay behind the "Jewish" holy days. Together they revealed the strategy of God, and held out hope to them that a truly noble kingdom could be built on earth.

I realise that there are many now who actually malign the Jews for having failed at this. I marvel that they even tried, or that they proved successful, even in small groups, to walk as citizens of God on earth. Yet even more I marvel that they were successful in the preservation of God's word. I doubt that any other nation upon earth could have done as well as this. This of itself is no small miracle. And if the God of Israel is true to his own word, he has not deserted them.

* * * *

You cannot possibly imagine how refreshing it must have been for many people in Judea to hear a man like Ya'shua bar Ya'seph speak. This courageous Jew spoke of God in terms so intimate and personal, it seemed to many that the door for entering God's kingdom upon earth was already in their midst and had suddenly been opened and they could enter by it, if they wished. The mission of this Jew (whom we call Jesus Christ) was to revitalize God's nation in the world according to the word of Moses and the prophets, by making a new covenant with all courageous Jewish men of faith. However, he did warn them, that if they didn't hear his words, Israel would perish in the flames.

To accomplish what he hoped to do, he preached God's word to all who were disposed to hear him speak, and he lived his life to make "the son of man" crowned with the character of God (and with the wisdom of his word) a visible experience for them. In doing this, he did not try to build a new religion or a "new church." The ecclesia of God (those people God in time would choose) remained for him the only church. And because the words he spoke were only those of God, he called that congregation "my ecclesia." That is to say "my church." That church was founded, so he said, upon the word of God. For he told his listeners: "Whoever hears these words of mine and does them, I shall compare to a wise man who built his house upon a rock." (Matthew 7: 24)

Yet Jesus said of his own words: "These words I speak to you are not my own, but are those of (God) who sent me." (John 14: 24). So that the rock he spoke of was the rock of God — the strong, unchanging rock which is able to withstand the storms and tempests of the world, like warfare, famine and social turbulence. Relying on this rock, Jesus did not surrender God's authority to any man, but was faithful to the scriptures which had said: "Do not put your trust in any prince whose life is only in his breath." "Surely all flesh is like grass," Isaiah had affirmed. "The grass withers and the flower fades, but the word of God endures forever." So Jesus easily had passed the test which Moses gave. Instead of saying, "Let us follow other gods," he reaffirmed the psalmist's words, which said: "Jehovah is my rock and my strength. In him I put my confidence."

Those Jews who listened to his words and did them, he referred to as "my brothers and my sisters and my mother." And he told the Jewish hierarchy "the kingdom of God is in your midst," by which he meant all Jewish men and women who by faith obeyed the voice of God and sat each sabbath day in Jewish synagogues. Those who listened to and obeyed those words were the very heart of God within the midst of Israel.

Jesus did not go about the nation telling them that he was Israel's messiah, who had come to rescue them. Instead he let his own disciples (through their knowledge of God's word) identify him as the seed of Israel (who came forth from the virgin bride of God — the faithful Jewish populace). In this way he fulfilled the prophetic words of Moses which had said a prophet was to rise among his brothers to lead his nation Israel. From this we find the meaning of Jesus's own words when he called the faithful Jewish people "my mother". So it was that he told his followers, "my church" is founded solidly upon God's word, and not upon the shifting sands of human attitudes. He did not found it on the rock of any clergy

— professional or otherwise — but on the foundation stone of God's word, on which "anyone who hears these words of mine and does them," builds his life.

When Peter therefore made his great confession of Jesus as the Christ, he in no way introduced any new idea amongst the others. He merely said what all the rest of them already knew, but he himself had very slowly learned.

It had been Peter's own brother Andrew who three years earlier had gone to Peter (who was known as Simon then) and confessed his own belief to him. Excited by the knowledge that he had, Andrew told his brother eagerly: "We have found the Messiah." In doing this Andrew didn't need a special vision from the skies to help him make that claim. He discovered it in just the same way Philip did. Philip's words to Nathaniel identified the source from which he gained the strength of his conviction, for he said: "We have found him of whom Moses in the Torah and the prophets did write, Jesus of Nazareth, the son of Joseph." So three years later, when Simon eventually confessed that Jesus was "the Christ", he too had found his confirmation in the scriptures just as all the others had.

Yet at first, when Andrew had brought Simon (Peter) as a novice to Jesus, Jesus said to him: "You are known as Simon now, the son of Jonah, but you shall be called Peter." Jesus was promising him a new character. Peter had to grow in faith, and only gradually did he eventually become strong enough in spirit to be called "Cephas" or "Peter" — or "Rocky" we might say today. For Simon was unstable as water, but Simon would become Peter — a rock. So as they neared the final testing place where the fire of social tensions would try all of them, this incident took place:

"When Jesus came to the region of Caesarea Philippi, he asked his disciples: 'Who do people say the Son of Man is?'

"They replied, 'Some say John the Baptist; others say Elijah; and still others, Jeremiah or one of the prophets.'

"But what about you?' he asked. 'Who do you say I am?'

"Simon Peter answered, 'You are the Christ, the Son of the Living God (which is to say 'You are born of his word').

"Jesus replied, 'Good for you. You have answered very well, Simon bar Jonah, for this was not revealed to you by what any person said, but you learned it from my Father in heaven (through knowing the word of God). And I tell you that you have now become Peter (a new name signifying a new character) and on this rock (the power of God's unchanging word to change the human character) do I build my church.'"

In a manner similar to this, Moses (as he stood beside the burning bush) was shown the power of God's word to change the very nature of a man. "'Put your hand into your bosom,' Jehovah said to him. So Moses put his hand into his bosom just as God instructed him. Then when he took it out again, it was leprous white — like snow. 'Now put your hand into your bosom once again,' Jehovah said. This time when he took it out, he found it was made whole again, like the rest of all his flesh." (Exodus 4: 6-7). So, in this way, Jehovah was able to show Moses the power of his word to change the very heart in him. God, then, was the seat of all authority.

Upon this very matter of authority, Peter said, "Each one of us (all Christians educated in God's word) should use whatever special gift he has to serve others, faithfully revealing God's good will in various forms. If anyone speaks he should do so (as Jesus did) as someone speaking the very words of God. If anyone serves, he should do it with all the strength that God provides, so that in everything God may be praised through Jesus Christ." (1 Peter 4: 10-11). Then he went on to say, "To those who work as elders in your midst...Feed the flock of God that is among you (with understanding of God's word), tending to their needs, not because you must, but because you are eager to serve; not lording it over God's people, but as examples to the flock." (1 Peter 5: 1-3)

* * * * *

Paul, a Pharisee disciple of Jesus, was the inventor and establisher of churches in the Gentile world. Sent by James (the brother of Jesus) to speak to Jews in foreign lands, Paul went at first to all the synagogues. But many Jews had settled down into the world and wanted peace with those who didn't share a common faith with them. Some Jews even came to feel that they were more a part of those communities which they had grown up in than they were with any warring faction of their people in Jerusalem. Troubles in Jerusalem brought many unwanted difficulties into their lives. Jews of the Dispersion were constantly assailed by those who tried involving them in insurrections of some kind. And Paul, who spoke to them about the uprising of Jesus (by which he meant the resurrection, not insurrection) didn't get much sympathy from his fellow Jews. So Paul turned his attention to the Gentile world.

In creating the synagogue, the Jews created the structure that was to influence Christians and other religions' congregations after them. Being a scattered people without ready access to their temple in Jerusalem, the Jews of the Dispersion poured out their hearts in worship in places set apart in individual communities throughout the world. Here they could pray, sing praises to the creator of the world, hear the law of God, be instructed in the principles of living, enjoy the fellowship of like-minded people, and refurnish their own minds with God's exciting vision of the world.

So it was only natural that Paul should copy the synagogue in establishing the churches throughout the world. Putting his knowledge as a Pharisee to work for him, Paul made the church a Christian synagogue, fashioned in the pattern of the Jews, for it seemed to him the ideal form. For this new task of turning Gentiles into spiritual Jews, Paul was the ideal man. He was a Jewish Pharisee of great learning in all the culture, lore and learning of his people—their Scriptures, customs and traditions including the oral teachings of the fathers of his faith.

At this point I should remind you that Paul had been taught the precepts of the Jewish faith by none other than the revered Gamaliel the Elder, who in Sotah 9: 15 of the *Mishnah* is described in these terms: "When Rabban Gamaliel the Elder died, the glory of the Law ceased and purity and abstinence died."   (Translated by H. Danby)

Yet having read the literature of the Greek and Roman world as well, and being thoroughly acquainted with their customs and their learning too, Paul was adequately armed to meet the challenge facing him. No one knew the plays of Euripides better than Paul himself. Any scholar of the classics who has read Paul's letters knows just how much Paul's own style of writing was indebted to this Gentile writer's works. Often he would paraphrase lines from some of them, to gain the confidence of Gentile listeners.

The mature Christian might wish to read Euripides' play *Ion* for instance. The entire speech of Hermes, at the opening of the play, is reminiscent of the opening of Paul's epistle to the Hebrews. Paul's description of Melchizedek as being "without father or mother" coincides exactly with what Ion (the son of Apollo, born of a virgin mother) says about himself. "Yes, I know neither my father nor my mother." And one of Paul's chief arguments against pagan beliefs is found in many of Ion's own speeches: "How is it right," Ion asks, "for you (the gods of Greece) to make laws for men, and appear as lawbreakers yourselves?...You put pleasure first and wisdom after – and it is sin! It is unjust to call men bad for copying what the gods find good: the sin lies with our examples!"

Paul was later to turn this same argument upon those Jews who looked upon themselves as righteous – breaking the laws of God while condemning those that they looked on as outside the law. He said: "Now you call yourself a Jew; if you rely on the law and brag about your relationship to God; if you know his will and approve of what is superior because you are instructed by the law; if you are convinced that you are a guide for the blind, a light for those who are in the dark, and instructor of the foolish, a teacher of infants, because you have in the law the embodiment of knowledge and truth – you then, who teach others, do you not teach yourself? You who preach against stealing, do you steal? You who say that people should not commit adultery, do you commit adultery? You who abhor idols, do you rob temples? You who brag about the law, do you dishonour God by breaking the law? As it is written: "God's name is blasphemed among the Gentiles because of you."

(Romans 2: 17-24)

Even in a tight situation Paul knew exactly the right words to use to win the confidence of anyone who was not a Jew. "I am a Jew, from Tarsus in Cilicia, a citizen of no ordinary city," is an almost exact paraphrase of Euripides. Through these words he won enough of the confidence of the Roman officer who had arrested him to be granted permission to speak to the crowd which had gathered against him. Then when Paul was prepared for flogging, he sent for the officer again. When Paul told him he was a Roman citizen, the officer responded with the words: "I paid a great price to attain this freedom." And Paul always ready with apt words responded with another line from *Ion*, "But I was freeborn."

These answers were not accidents. When Paul told the Corinthian congregation, "I speak in tongues more than all of you," he was not making an idle boast. He spoke more than in just translation of the words. He knew the way to level in upon the sentiments of those whom he addressed. You might for instance like to hear his own defence before the Areopagus in Athens. This ancient civic court, comprised of those from noble families, was empowered to try any serious offense against the well-being of the community, or any individual who degraded moral standards set by them.

Paul was brought before this court for questioning, as he had been accused of advancing teachings of a foreign god. But Paul was masterful in answering the charge: "Paul stood up in the meeting of the Areopagus and said: 'Men of Athens! I see that in every way you are very religious. For as I walked around and observed your many monuments of worship, I noticed that you even had an altar bearing an inscription: TO THE UNKNOWN GOD. You therefore have been worshipping in ignorance the very God whom I shall teach you of."

(Acts: 17: 22-23)

The whole sermon he was able to deliver was a masterpiece of tact and eloquence. This is what he meant by "speaking in tongues." He could communicate on every level and find appropriate words to respond to whatever the occasion required of him. For his day Paul was a very learned man. No one anywhere on earth could possibly compete with him. Few speakers among the Jews or in the heathen world could match his skill in oratory and many often had to resort to shouting or frenzied rioting to prevent his being heard. Even Festus, the Roman procurator of Judea, was aware of Paul's vast knowledge and ability even though he spoke to him in a derogatory way, saying, "Much learning has made you mad." (Acts 26: 24)

Yet anyone who thinks Paul Hellenized the teachings of Jesus have not read Paul's words carefully enough, and have read meanings into them that are not there. It should be stated clearly then, that nowhere in Paul's letters to the different churches is there anything written that would directly teach or suggest that he revised or did away with anything essential to the word of God. Paul's teachings in essence were really quite simple, and in no way contrary to "Old Testament" principles. What he taught was this: The death of Jesus, the Messiah, had broken down the wall between the Jews and Gentiles and had made the promises given to Abraham available to Jews and Gentiles alike, if they would simply live by faith as Abraham had done.

Hasty readings never should obscure the fact that Faith entailed far more than simply believing that there was a God and that Jesus was the promised messiah and then waiting to be taken up to heaven after death. Faith meant taking time to hear or read what Moses, the Prophets, Jesus and the Apostles taught, and then make those teachings the foundation stone of life. The purpose of the Law, so Paul affirmed, was to identify sin and make it recognizable, so as to deal with it, in a meaningful and constructive way.

Overcoming sin was the work of faith, battling with sin with the help of God's holy spirit. Paul, however, taught that the Law of God did not condemn a person who was engaged in overcoming his habitual sinful traits. Since overcoming sin required God's help, and time, the sacrifice of Christ removed the condemnation (or curse) of the law. The idea that the "law" was done away, or that "grace", in some strange and mystic way, had replaced the "law" of God, was something never mentioned in Paul's words.

Paul simply said that there are two ways in which a man can live — the way of the flesh or the way of the spirit. What Paul accomplished in the Gentile world was miraculous. The churches he established were but schools which trained the people to walk as citizens in a new kingdom being built on earth. It was a Kingdom of which they hoped to be a part, and they wished to play a part in building it.

When we think of preaching to the Gentiles, we usually think of Peter and of Paul. However, the first missionary to the Gentiles actually was centuries ahead of them. His name was Jonah. Jonah also was a Jew. He went to Nineveh — reluctantly of course — and his preaching saved them from destruction by the sword. The lesson to be learned from this is that he did not preach to make them Jews. He preached to teach them the principles of salvation. That's what Paul and Peter both did too.

Neither Paul nor any other apostle ever tried to pose as a mediator between God and the church's "laity". There was no "laity" in Christianity. There was only one High Priest as Paul once wrote to Timothy: "There is but one God and but one mediator between God and men, the man Jesus Christ." (1 Timothy 2: 5)

Jehovah was the first and last—the only God, and Jesus was the first and last—the only mediator. Therefore Paul could say to every Christian: "Let us come therefore before the throne of grace with confidence for help in time of need." (Hebrews 4: 16). Like "the sons of God" in ages past, the Christian worshipper could boldly come before the throne of God. The believers themselves were appointed to be a priesthood of equal brethren not being dominant one over another.

To reach this point, however, the churches had to "grow in grace and the knowledge of Jesus Christ." At first they leaned heavily upon the spoken words of Paul and those who had intimately known the Christ. Such human contact made the son of man appear to them no more than just a touch away from them. But it was physically impossible for Paul to be constantly in every place. So Paul sent letters out continually to all of them.

Right from the first the churches all had access to copies of the *Septuagint* (the "Old Testament" scriptures translated into Greek). Paul's letters were a boon to them as well, for he supplied a living contact with the past and present as it was, and with the resurrected Jesus Christ whom they had never seen. The letters that he wrote were copied eagerly and circulated so as to share the wisdom of his words. Because his words were so revered, the churches elevated them at once to the level of all scriptures that they had, reading just as frequently from them as they did from the ancient books of scripture that they had.

Soon letters came from all of those whom Jesus had entrusted with his word: James, Peter, Jude and John. It made the scriptures seem alive to them, and Paul himself was moved by this, as is apparent from his words when he said of those who learned from him: "You yourselves are our letter, written on our hearts, known and read by everybody. You show that you are a letter from Christ, the result of our ministry, written not with ink but with the spirit of the living God, not on tablets of stone, but on tablets of human hearts."   (2 Corinthians 3: 2-3)

The church in each community was growing in maturity and soon would be capable to stand completely on its own. But those men who had known "the son of man" most intimately realised the warping power of time and the evilness of those who could and would manipulate the spoken word, misquoting it if they should choose. They realised as well that everyone who had known the Christ would die, and if the kingdom had not come, there would be no one in the world to pass their message on. The gospel needed to be written down.

Even before 70 AD all four gospels that we have today were in the hands of churches of the world. These soon, along with all the other documents, were looked upon as equal to the ancient texts within the Septuagint. Peter in one letter showed how he regarded all the writings of his peers as scriptural. For in this letter he said: "So, dear friends, since you are making every effort to become spotless, blameless and at peace with him, bear this in mind, that our Lord's Patience means salvation, just as our dear brother Paul also wrote you with the wisdom God gave him. He writes the same way in all his letters, speaking in them of these matters. His letters contain some things that are difficult to understand, which ingnorant and unstable people distort, as they do other scriptures to their own destruction."   (2 Peter 3: 14-16)

Yet it was Paul who pointed out that everything essential to salvation was now in Christian hands, and he also stressed the method of the Christian fellowship in getting at the truth. He said: "You should realise from having heard my teaching and observed my way of life...(that) everyone who tries to live a godly life in Christ Jesus will be persecuted, while evil men and impostors (hypocrites) will increasingly grow worse in deceiving and being deceived themselves. But as for you, you will go on learning because you were convinced by those who taught you, and you trusted them, so that from infancy you learned to know the holy scriptures which are able in themselves to make you wise in the way of salvation through faith in Jesus Christ. All Scripture has come as breath from God's own mouth, and is sufficient for teaching, rebuking, correcting and training in righteousness so that the man of God may be thoroughly equipped for all good works." (2 Timothy 3: 10-16)

I know there have been those throughout the centuries who've felt the need to write "missing doctrines" into Christianity. There have been more than just a few who have elaborated on the texts to create doctrines of their own. So Paul whose own words have been twisted many times said this: "Brethren, I speak in terms of human relationships when I tell you that even in a man's covenant, once it has been ratified, no one sets those words aside, and adds conditions different from those given at the first" (Galatians 3: 15)

What could be clearer than that. There is nothing to be written in. Jesus predicted two things: the fall of Jerusalem, and his return to the world to establish God's Kingdom upon earth. Then in 70 AD Titus conquered Jerusalem. The city was laid waste and 600,000 Jews were slaughtered. Those who survived were sold into slavery. The Nazorean Jews (who accepted Jesus as the Messiah) were able to escape the massacre because they heeded a warning Jesus gave for them to leave the city as soon as the Roman armies withdrew for a time.

The first prophecy then had been fulfilled. Jerusalem did fall as Jesus said it would. The city he had wept for perished, and "not one stone (of the temple) was left upon another. Every one had been thrown down." The fulfillment of this prophecy meant that Jesus had passed both the tests that Moses specified. Yet from Jerusalem there emerged (like twin brothers from the same womb) two witnesses, whom God in his good time would use— the Christian churches and the Jewish synagogues. Christians now awaited further word from Jesus Christ himself, to establish his new kingdom upon earth. At the last trumpet of a well-laid plan, Jesus would return.

Then in 98 AD, the last of all of Jesus's apostles sent an open letter to the churches of the world, which purportedly revealed a strategy for establishing the Kingdom of Heaven upon earth. The plan required complete obedience from churches everywhere. These churches were asked to follow the plan in its entirety in preparation for the coming of their Lord. The letter stressed the fact that it was Jesus Christ himself who had revealed this plan to John.

* * * * * *

John forwarded the letter he received from Jesus to the angel in each of the seven churches in Asia (now called Turkey). Being written as it is in symbols, it required the power of an interpreting spirit in the Christian congregation to unravel it. The whole plan of the letter that we call the *Book of Revelation* or *The Apocalypse* is firmly grounded in the pattern of the Jewish holy days: the same festivals that Moses had used as a battle strategy for Israel 1500 years before. Understanding this makes it possible for anyone with a fundamental knowledge of Israel's past history, to easily unveil the meanings hidden in this code of images, images so apt that it is startling just how clear the message is once we have the key to open it.

Jehovah's holy days (as they are called in scriptures) concern themselves with triumph over Pharaoh (the dominating and enslaving spirit of the world), the coming out of slavery while putting leaven (the world's corrupting influence – or sin) out of the midst of Israel, receiving God's instruction in the wilderness, and then entering the promised world after forty years of wandering (which is to say, however long it took to gain the necessary discipline, and to understand what God required from them).

In Chapter One of *Revelation*, we were shown a powerful vision of the God-begotten son of man, who has the power to slay the first-born man of sin, and the power to raise him up from death as a newborn man of spirit, ready to give obedience to God. This is the Passover. It is a time for congregations everywhere to renew their covenant with Jehovah, and for each individual to imbibe the spirit of Jehovah's man of heaven, and by obedient deeds ingest his character.

Swift upon the heels of this inspiring vision, the festival of unleavened bread begins. All churches everywhere throughout the world are called on to repent and put off their captivity to sin. They must repent. No church is made exempt from this. All churches are obliged to re-examine themselves, their doctrines and all their practices in accordance with the spiritual measuring stick of God's unchanging word. To show the Christian church that this phase of the plan has seven steps to it,

Jesus very purposely has chosen seven churches in the heart of seven cities of Asia (known today as Turkey) which directly follow one another on the mail route linking them. Their very number indicates that the lessons learned from them must be applied to every church throughout the world, and their order shows that the lessons learned from each of them must be dealt with in their turn, like separate segments of the feast that Moses used to overthrow the power of Pharaoh and deliver Israel from the armies that would follow them.

Jesus Christ reveals the only way that any group of individuals can re-instate themselves with God. There is no church on earth at all with any right to claim infallibility. The only formula for being in God's church is obedience to the written word of God. Not one can claim that they alone possess the truth and have the right to act exclusively on his behalf. "If any man hears my voice and opens the door, I will come into him," Jesus said. Whoever hears the words of God and does them, that is all that God requires. The Church itself is in God's hands — for those whom he will choose will be from those who are obedient to him. But if they heed a voice that is not God's, then they are Satan's lot.

The fact that Jesus calls on every church and individual to re-examine what they do and teach, indicates the only method for staying in his church. All his followers are called on to repent where they have erred. Nor is anyone allowed to add new teachings to his word. As Paul so aptly said, no covenant once it has been ratified can possibly be changed by adding other words or church decrees to it.

It is significant that Jesus calls upon all churches to repent, and that there is but one church only in each city that he names. The angel spirit of each community, regardless of the sins which the word of God identifies and the number of divisions in each church that's named, is made responsible to Jesus Christ, God's sole High Priest. For there is only one lampstand in the temple there. This gives the body of believers unity, and makes them members of one flock. Those who are his sheep will hear his voice. The angel, like the voice of wisdom "cries at the city gates" and speaks with Jesus's authority the words of this last message that he gave to them. So what the angel spirit says "to all the churches" is important for our day.

Written in symbols "the tongues of angels", this message requires an interpreter, the spirit of true church fellowship. It could be very dangerous, considering the persecution in the early church for a message of this kind to be written in any other way, since it tells of the "end of the world", which is to say "the end of the oppressive governments of this world" — or as almost any clergyman can tell you "the end of the age," not, as you will hear from those who masquerade as angels of light, the end of "the late great planet earth." "For God made the earth," so the psalmist says, "to be established forever." (Psalm 78: 69) Or as Solomon maintained: "The earth remains forever." (Ecclesiastes 1: 4) "For God did not create the earth to make of it a ruined waste. He made it to be inhabited."   (Isaiah 45: 18)

The Greek word "angelos" literally means "angel" or "messenger of Jehovah". However, many interpretations of this word abound in Bible commentaries: the heavenly spirit that directs the church, the officiating church officer or secretary, the church bishop, the reader who communicates messages to the congregation etc. Since angels were regarded as guiding spirits of God's people generally, and faith was the essential element of belief, whether you decide the angel was natural or supernatural, the important thing to realise, is that it was the angel's duty to translate this message into words both clear and unequivocal.

I earlier have shown with scriptural reference how the scriptures would interpret it, as being that spirit of fellowship where gifts were shared within the church. However, when this very minor barrier is breached, it is the faithful individual to whom John wished to speak — those guided in their faith to obediently act upon his words as sons and daughters of Israel and who without hesitation serve their God the moment that they recognize his voice.

Two things here are worthy of our notice. In these addresses to the different churches: (1) No church is infallible. All are capable of straying from doctrine and from practices that rob them of their place in God's scheme and take away the light of God from their midst. (2) The church as a whole is called on to repent — examine its doctrines and its practices and put them right. Repentance is not just an individual matter; it is a matter for whole communities of Christians. It is also worth remarking on, that not one of these seven churches is spoken of as the "Mother Church". Their sole source of Guidance is God's word and the Living Christ.

Throughout this letter, the final emphasis is always placed upon the individual rather than the group. It is to the individual who "overcomes" that great rewards are given. Jesus speaks in this same way in his parables, saying: "Anyone with ears to hear, let him hear." Yet there are also bad fish in the net, and these eventually will be thrown away. It is the individual who hears and does his words who is in the Kingdom of God on earth. Such a person looks to God alone for any plan of action that he takes — not to those who say they are prophets and apostles sent by him, then tell you that they have a fuller gospel in their hands.

There is no shortcut to the plan which Jesus Christ himself has set out for the church. So it is apt that he calls upon the churches first to show humility. "I tell you the truth," Jesus said, "the man who does not enter the sheep pen by the gate is a thief and a robber." (John 10: 1) When Jesus has set out the plan there is no other way.

There is no safety in numbers, and there is no room for the attitude which says: "You're just a layman; he's a minister. He knows the Bible better than you; you must do what he says." The individual is responsible. There is no such thing as professional and non professional in Christendom, in Judaism or in the Islamic faith. A minister, at best, is no more than a man selected from the midst of those mature enough in faith and learning of the scriptures to choose a representative to speak for them. Hopefully he is a person with a special gift, perhaps of speaking well. For that gift alone they have placed their hands on him.

This symbolic act of laying on of hands goes back to very early times. Moses, when he delegated powers to other members of the sons of Israel, did it publicly to show that those areas of government which he had once controlled were now assigned to others upon whom his hands were laid. This act of public recognition transferred the jurisdiction of authority in certain offices of government. It was an ancient means used by communities for showing publicly that authority had been transferred, or that someone had been sent to act as an ambassador for them.

Yet there was more involved in this transference of power than just that simple public act. Moses had to train all those on whom such offices were laid. That training did not flow out of his fingertips. He had to instruct these officers in the duties of their offices. But by the laying on of hands, he indicated publicly that the spirit of governing those offices now had been been transferred to them on whom he laid his hands. These new officers were seen henceforth as having been approved, so that the people turned their faith and confidence to them.

Jewish rabbis in the time of Jesus Christ also laid their hands upon disciples to publicly affirm that they were masters of the spoken word. The church of early times took up this practice too so as to show the congregation publicly that those whom they approved of had reached that necessary stature of maturity of learning and discretion to speak the word of God effectively. They also used it to confer on them responsibilities of mission or of leadership. God bestowed the gifts. The laying on of hands was but the elders' way of indicating that they recognized the talents God had given them. It was the duty of elders in the faith to help the younger ones to grow. The laying on of hands provided them with confidence.

The closest that we come to any Mother Church, in all of this epistle, is "the woman Jezebel" in the church of Thyatira. For it says of her "And all her children (those members whom she nourishes with teachings contrary to God's word) will be struck dead with pestilence so that churches everywhere will know that I alone am he (the judge of Israel) who searches and who knows (the thoughts and wishes of) the mind and heart; and (justly) judges all according to their deeds." We cannot doubt these very words rule out any possibility of any Mother Church appointed as a guide with special powers, to act as other churches' consciences or to interfere with or dictate policies followed in another city's church community. The text affirms that God alone is judge of each "according to their deeds." Those churches that John wrote to in this letter were individually responsible for handling their own affairs and correcting any problems locally.

In the letter John sends to "the angel of each of the seven churches in Asia," city by city is asked to overcome the power of Satan in its midst. By this John means the power of national, worldly practices and philosophies contrary to the way of God and his creation. John's letter was designed to be freely circulated among all church communities so as to offer them a comprehensive plan for achieving unity with one another through unity with God — the spirit of creation. His instructions therefore show the need and the method for cleansing the churches from all unrighteousness, by focusing their attention upon the goals to be achieved.

* * * * * * *

John, begins instructing the church at Ephesus, by telling them that the one addressing them is "He who walks among the lampstands of the world and holds the seven stars in his right hand." The imagery is apt, for each church (having a lampstand of its own) is shown to be autonomous, and Christ (who holds the seven stars in his right hand) is shown to be the only one to whom each church is individually responsible. As Paul once said: "by their own master they stand or fall." Even congregations in a city are united by one angel — one perfect vision of what the church must be.

Yet spiritually all cities are united in the capital of God, by a single priest — the son of man from heaven — Jesus Christ. There is no need therefore to make a pilgrimage to any other place on earth, or turn to head offices in New York, Los Angeles, Pasadena, Salt Lake City, London or Rome for guidance, assistance and authoritative edicts and declarations from any earthly man or throne. The whole test is whether we put our confidence in God or men.

Flesh and blood cannot reveal God's will to you. As Jesus told his followers "only the word of God is able to." And "Look! Even now he is coming on the clouds of heaven," so John has said. And how appropriate it is that this man from heaven (who alone has the authority to govern them) should accuse the church in Ephesus of turning from its "first love". That is to say that they had turned away from Jesus Christ himself to a Jesus Christ which they had shaped in their own minds to fit the inclinations of their own ideas and biases: a Jesus Christ quite different from the one that the apostles taught and directed them to love.

I have heard many powerful sermons preached upon this theme of "first love" by ministers who imagined that it meant the initial glow of enthusiasm accompanying the early days of conversion to the Christian faith. This is not the case. We cannot merely read our own emotions into biblical passages. We must look into what the scriptures say of them. Paul explained its meaning in these words: "I made a personal promise that I would betroth you to only one husband, so that I might present you to Christ as a pure virgin bride. But I am afraid of your being turned aside from the simplicity of true devotion in your love for Christ, just as Eve (through the serpent's artful deception) was turned aside. For you are far too pliable when others preach about another Christ, who differs from the one we preach, and you willingly accept another spirit and a very different gospel from the one that you received from us." (2 Corinthians 11: 2-3)

So when he who holds the seven stars in his right hand (which denotes his sole authority over every church) says that all the churches have turned to another Jesus Christ, we need to seriously pause and examine this. Has the Christian church (in the city where we live) turned away completely from the one that Christians first were taught to love and prepare to meet. If such is the case it would explain the many great divisions in the church. Are the doctrines that we preach the same as those that Jesus and his apostles taught?

The first step then in this festival of self-critical examination, needs discussion by the church's member-ship — everyone within each city's church. For if the church of God's community in every city upon earth does not take these words to heart, the lampstand giving them autonomy and guiding them and those they lead will be taken from their midst. Those communities and individuals which overcome and learn to know the true character of Christ, will be given fruit to eat from the tree of life.

Now the tree in the midst of the Garden of God is that special wisdom that permits us to live truly successful lives. For we read in the *Book of Proverbs*, "Blessed is the man who finds wisdom, the man who gains understanding, for she (Wisdom) is more profitable than silver and yields better returns than gold. (Wisdom) is more precious than rubies; nothing you desire can compare with her. Long life is in her right hand; in her left hand are riches and honour. Her ways are pleasant ways, and all her paths are peace. She is a tree of life to those who embrace her; those who lay hold of her will be blessed." (Proverbs 3: 13-18) Such then is the tree of life, and its fruits are great. Solomon further says: "The fruit of righteousness is a tree of life, and he who wins souls is wise." (Proverbs 11: 30) The scriptures say even a great

deal more of this wonderful wisdom of God, "whose fruit
is healing and the uplifting of the spirit, and those who
seek it earnestly will surely find it."

I cannot overstress just how important this step is to
Jesus's whole plan. If the whole church fellowship in the
community where we live has not done its part and, as
one body standing bravely before the world, declared one
Jesus Christ, how can we expect to recognize him when
he comes or for the world to see him as he is.

Jesus himself has shown the church that he alone
has sole authority over all the churches in the world, and
that their loyalty belongs alone to him — not to any
founder of a secular denominational branch. As Paul said
to the Corinthians: "What after all is Apollos? And what
is Paul? No more than servants through whom you came
to believe....Neither he who plants nor he who waters is
anything, but only God who makes things grow. We are
no more than God's workers. You are God's field. It is
God alone who builds you up."   (1 Corinthians 3: 5-9)

We must remain solely in him or be cast off. And he
has called his followers (in each community) to assemble
periodically in one place, and settle for themselves in
that autonomous community upon such basic questions
as: Who is Jesus Christ? and what exactly did he preach?
Nor should any Christian ever feel that he must turn to
London, Moscow, or New York or Rome. Let the angel
speak in the community of East End Saskatchewan or in
Pickering Ontario and in each community upon earth.
Let all branches of the faith come together of one accord
in one place, and look to find a miracle.

Let them gather with humility and settle finally this
question for themselves: Who is the bridegroom they

expect to see? Whom do they teach the bride to love? So
when he comes, the son of man will have a virgin bride
who knows his voice. Until they have fulfilled that task,
the Church of their community remains in Ephesus. They
have not equipped themselves as yet for moving on from
this, to the next step in the plan that Jesus left for them.

In the second step of Jehovah's Festival of
Unleavened Bread, Smyrna is addressed by "the first and
the last, who was dead and is alive." This very title
assures the flock that the shepherd (who is first and last)
will not leave his sheep in any other hands. He will not
turn them over to any shepherd other than himself. For
he was raised from death and has the power to raise
them all from death as well. Such a reassurance calls to
mind the words that Jesus spoke to Peter and the rest of
the apostles at Caesarea Philippi: "Upon this rock (of
God's unchanging word) I establish my chosen ones, and
the gates (to the city) of Death shall not close on them
forever. (For they shall rise from death and live again.)"
(Matthew 16: 18)

Having obeyed the first command of Christ, the
Church at Smyrna has its priorities set right. They do
not look to any other person than to Jesus Christ
himself to lead them out of slavery to the world. The
first and last addresses them, the only Jesus Christ who
is to come, the only bridegroom sent to unite them as
one people in the character of God. "The wind blows
where it will and you hear the sound thereof, but you
cannot tell from where it comes or where it goes. So it is
with everyone who is born of God's spirit." (John 3: 8)

Having a true vision of their "first love" and a
proper understanding of his word, they are every bit as
rich as Jesus says they are. For rubies cannot compare in

value with the understanding that they have. The *Book of Job* speaks at great length upon the value that true wisdom has. Here is just a fragment of those words: "Neither gold nor crystal can compare with it, nor can it be had for jewels of gold. Coral and jasper are not worthy of mention; the price of wisdom is beyond rubies. The topaz of Cush cannot compare with it; it cannot be bought even with pure gold."   (Job: 28: 17-19)

Then King David calls attention to the value of the Law, saying: "The law of Jehovah is perfect, reviving the soul. The statutes of Jehovah are trustworthy, making wise the simple. The precepts of Jehovah are right, giving joy to the heart. The commands of Jehovah are radiant, giving light to the eyes. The fear of Jehovah is pure, enduring forever. The ordinances of Jehovah are sure and righteous altogether. They are more precious than gold, than much pure gold; they are sweeter than honey, than honey from the comb. By them is your servant warned; and in keeping them there is great reward."   (Psalm 19: 7-11)

It is no wonder then that the Christians of Smyrna are told that even though they are poor in the riches of this world, they are actually very rich. Yet they are slandered by the world community — namely by a group they wouldn't think would slander them. For by appearances they both are brothers from the same womb, the virgin bride of God — namely Israel. They are a group who say that they are Jews. John, however, makes it clear they are not Jews at all, but members rather of "the synagogue of Satan." Satan, to the Christian mind, was the spirit governing the pagan world, of which the Jews were not a part.

So who was this group John spoke of here? If we really wish to know we must look at very ancient history. We must go back to that time when the children of Israel came out of Egypt (during the festival of unleavened bread). Pharaoh had determined that the Israelites should not leave his land, and sent his minions after them to bring them back by force. Satan's world just can't bear to lose so many of its slaves. They want all those who serve them to continue serving them throughout their lives. So Satan's armies are sent out hastily either to bring their former captives back or slaughter all of them. They know no other way. Satan cannot bear to have a people—any people—live in any way that differs from the world he dominates and rules.

So the synagogue of Satan could be any group at all closely allied to the ruling power within the pagan world, who act as Pharaoh's armies and hinder or venomously assail those dedicated to God's will. We will later speak of such alliances in the third step of this Festival of Unleavened Bread, which Christians have been asked to celebrate. Yet I realise this passage has been used at times by certain groups to fan the current fires of prejudice. In doing so the two-edged sword of God's sharp word also has included them in that same synagogue. The label worn by any man does not entitle him to any special exemption from the principle these words involve. A Christian who persecutes or harasses people of another faith is not a Christian. Nor is a Jew a Jew when his words do not reflect the wisdom of his God.

When he who was dead but is alive tells the church of Smyrna that they will have to suffer to the limit, we realise that some of them will be put to death. We picture then the armies of ancient Egypt once again, when they hemmed in all the people Moses led. Escape appeared impossible until the Red Sea opened, and God's people walked safely through it and came out on the other side unharmed. Yet Pharaoh's armies lost their lives as the waters of the Red Sea covered them.

If we treat this story as a parable, then the Red Sea is the grave or death. Those obedient to God will pass safely through and be delivered from the grave, and triumphant will commence living a new life. But those who serve the Pharaohs of this world will not be raised again, for the grave will be triumphant over them.

No one who has lived through the twentieth century can overlook the evolution of that strange word "Pharaoh", which at first meant "royal house". Later it referred to the ruler in that house. The Assyrians changed its sound and used the word "Pharor" to refer to the man who sat on Egypt's throne, a word not far removed from Führer in the modern German tongue. So a great deal of this ancient tale makes me think of Jewish suffering, as does the prophecy in John's *Book of Revelation.* "The devil will throw some of you into prisons and you will suffer the most terrible of persecutions (literally ten days which signifies suffering to the ultimate degree). If you prove faithful to the point of death, I will raise you up again and crown you with eternal life." (For "I will take you through the flood" or even "I will take you through the waters of the Red Sea.")

There is of course a command implied in this message to the Church in Smyrna, which we find in this allusion to the words of Jesus Christ as Matthew has recorded them: "Blessed are those who are persecuted because of righteousness, for theirs is the Kingdom of heaven. You shall be blessed if people insult you, and persecute you, and falsely say all manner of evil things against you for my sake (that is to say 'for the sake of righteousness and all the qualities of godly character'),

for great reward is kept in store for you in heaven, for all
the prophets were persecuted in this same way you have
been."   (Matthew 5: 10-11)

In case you missed the full implication of these last
words, they imply that anyone who lives a godly life is
making a prophetic statement to the world. God includes
that person with the prophets because his life not only
reveals the way of God, but it also predicts the coming of
God's kingdom into the world. We are reminded briefly
of Paul's letter which I quoted earlier, that says: "You
show that you are a letter from Christ...written not with
ink but with the spirit of the living God." Should he also
have said: "with the finger of God"?

The prophecy which offers the children of God in
Smyrna eternal life, offers it as a gift to those who keep
God's word. That fact clearly underlines for us that
immortality is not a quality we have inherently in us.
This letter interprets it as the winner's prize awarded to
all who run the course of life so well and overcome all
obstacles that they encounter in the world. Immortality
is the gift of God.

To achieve it we should follow Paul's advice: "Let
this attitude of mind be found in every one of you which
was found in Jesus Christ: Who being in the image of
God, did not consider robbing God of his authority by
claiming to have equality with him. Instead, he humbled
himself, and assumed the duties of a servant, and became
obedient until death, even (a shameful) death upon a
(criminal's) cross."   (Philippians 2: 5-8)

So the command from God is this: "Learn to be like
your 'first love' Jesus Christ, and walk according to that
way of righteousness you learned from him through
knowing who he is. Pursue that path regardless of the

consequence, and regardless of the enmity that others heap on you."

The next step in this Festival (to purify the bride of Christ) is illustrated by what is said to the unifying angel of the church in Pergamos. What shows this step to be consecutive in the festival of God to the steps which have preceded it, is that Satan has his throne in Pergamos, and Antipas, a model servant of Jehovah who has suffered to the limit, is put to death in the very place where Satan lives. In the first step of this plan, the church is called upon to learn to recognize the messiah as he is. Secondly it is instructed to grow to be like him in order to live as he had lived and be able to withstand all persecution if and when it comes regardless of how fierce it grows to be. Now in the third step of God's festival, the church in Pergamos is shown the source of all its ills: the very throne of Satan in the city where they live.

The city of Pergamos is very aptly chosen as a concrete illustration of "Satan's throne". The city typified in every way the perfect image of those words. Any modern tourist who visits Pergamos today will no doubt be taken to the top of the hill there and be shown the remains of Jupiter's Temple and be told by a knowledge-able guide that that was what was meant by Satan's throne. But Jupiter's Temple didn't even represent the half of it. Pergamos was a city which fiercely advocated the worship of a political ruler, the Roman emperor, and this combined with the worship of all pagan gods constituted an actual example of that throne on earth which rules the world and controls the social atmosphere.

Every facet of life in that city was affected by that atmosphere. You couldn't get away from it. Entertainment, theatre, national and civic holidays, sportive holiday parades, social customs, business practices, music, formal worship, everything that constantly assailed the ears and eyes and soul. The worship of carnal love especially was prominent. Venus (the love goddess) called for full surrender and commitment to the carnal appetite —which to the Christian and the Jewish mind was responsible for many enfeebling diseases, and therefore regarded as unclean by them. Ironically Pergamos was the centre of healing in the pagan world as well, a practice which pretended to heal, by the power of those pagan gods, the very sicknesses and plagues the worship of them had brought down upon the world.

Jesus, though, does not depend upon this reference alone to clarify his meaning of the term "Satan's throne". He calls attention to a well known part of Jewish history by deliberately alluding to the two men who stand out in it: Balaam and Balac, who tempted and corrupted Israel. By such a reference he shows all Christians educated in the word of God exactly what he means by "Satan's throne". All Christians who have done their homework well, as he presumes they should, will instantly recall the situation he is speaking of, when he says: "You have allowed into my flock those who follow the practices of Balaam who taught Balac how to lead the children of Israel into sin." Balac was the Edomite king who used the powers of a supposed "holy man" to assist him in a plan to corrupt and ruin Israel.

Balaam was certainly well gifted and educated in Jehovah and his ways, but he sold his knowledge for a price to anyone who wished to pay him liberally for it. His knowledge was so vast concerning God, he knew every trick and lure by which a holy nation could be wrecked. He was what the Bible calls "a wandering star" or a fallen "son of God," or in the text that we are reading now "an angel fallen from the sky."

He is that false prophet that the Bible warns us of, who toadies to whatever government or group of entrepreneurs can pay him well with money, favours or with influence. Elsewhere such a combination is explained like this: "The elder statesmen and the honourable men are the head, and the prophets who teach lies are the tail." (Isaiah 9: 15) This is where the "synagogue of Satan" now comes in. It is that fatal combination of celebrity — a seeming holy man or group of holy men — who are publicly esteemed, yet lend or sell their services to powerfully ambitious men who set themselves against the will of God and pervert the social atmosphere.

Balaam having failed three times in his attempts to curse the church of God in Israel through any weaknesses he could find in that protecting spirit guiding them, he apparently showed Balac that the best and only means of weakening Israel was to sap its strength through infiltration into their camps. Appealing to the natural appetites of Hebrew men, they could lure them subtly into practices which would totally corrupt them spiritually. Moses tells us how this spiritual invasion of the camp of God's kingdom took place. Moses speaks of it like this: "While Israel was staying in Shittim, the men began to indulge in sexual immorality with Moabite women, who invited them to the sacrifices offered to their gods. The people ate (of sacrificial meat) and bowed down (worshipfully) before those gods. So Israel joined in worshipping the Baal of Peor. And Jehovah's anger burned against them." (Numbers 25: 1-3)

Loose sexual practices with pagan women, in the time of Noah and earlier, had caused "the sons of God" to fall down from their first estate. In the *Genesis* account we were told that there were Nephalim ("those who cause others to fall down") in the land, who were responsible for enticing the "sons of God" to go in to pagan women and desert the way of God. This same scenario was repeated now in Israel when temple prostitutes were brought in to their camp — no doubt by Nephalim ("those who cause others to fall down") — seducing them and turning them from God and leading them to worship idols of the Edomites.

How devious and subtle all this was we have witnessed in our time. We've seen whole nations led astray by rhetoric of statesmen, by the media which supported them, and by the luring power of political ideologies. We have seen children turn away from values taught to them at home by those who gained power over their young minds. For Satan's throne is not a part of some strange world below the earth. It is in the midst of every city in the world, and Christians have to learn to recognize it if they are to battle with it in the later stages of this plan.

Satan's throne is established in all communities where any venerated individual or government has at its command a prophet or a department of propaganda of some kind that assures him of great power to influence human minds and rule the masses with an agenda which leads the people of the land he rules, away from the Creator and his ways. That individual can be allied, as Balac was, with someone who to all appearances is a "holy man of God" or even by a whole church or churches, as was the case in Pergamos, where the Emperor of Rome, was allied with values of a pagan world, typified by national gods inflaming human appetites. In the case of Nazi Germany, it was Adolph Hitler supported by the creed of nationality, his ministry of propaganda and gestapo police. Do I dare go on? or shall I leave it to the church in each community to discover for themselves the throne of Satan governing the temperament of their own community? It is a very tricky thing to do when churches of the world allow themselves to fall beneath the spell of those infected moods which govern those societies.

In any case it is that core of men who for money, power and for the adoration of the crowd exert an influence on social behaviour and act as models for society to emulate, while leading them into a way of life contrary to the standards of behaviour set by God. The test of course is in the fruits such rulers yield (for elsewhere they are spoken of as trees). This throne of Satan (the god who pulls the world toward war and strife) with which I shall deal more fully at a later time, has been identified for Christians during the festival when they renew themselves and groom the bride of Christ for the Atonement Feast — or Marriage Feast — with him. Christ already who is one with God is able (as Christianity's High Priest) to make all men one with him. "Behold, Jehovah whom you search for shall come suddenly to his temple through the messenger of the covenant (Jesus Christ) whom you delight in. Behold, he shall come says Jehovah who commands all powers." (Malachi 3: 1)

Christians therefore are alerted by this vision and are shown by what means they might recognize Satan's earthly throne. They are told to be aware of those ways he employs to bring them down and hinder them. They are also asked to recognize the wiles he uses for seducing them and turning men and women from the path of God. The letter Jesus sent through John to Pergamos lays great stress upon the eating of food sacrificed to idols, sexual immorality and the following of practices introduced into the Christian body by the Nicolaitans (who like the ancient Nephalims apparently caused others to fall down).

The eating of food sacrificed to idols was looked on by the children of God, since very early times, as something that was especially abhorrent. It was so revolting to the children of Israel that the Canaanite practice of boiling a kid in its mother's milk was written emphatically into the Mosaic law in a double reference.

(Exodus 23: 19; 34: 26)

An ancient Ugaritic text (found in the twentieth century) describes the rite itself in almost the same words that the Bible does. In part this ancient cuneiform tablet from Ugarit says:

"They cook a kid in milk
A goat in butter."

Apparently the Canaanites hoped to gain eternal youth and immortality by such rites and practices as they employed, such as eating sacrificial meat shared by gods and godesses of fertility. Many of such ceremonies also incorporated sexual enactments of fertility and other rites that early Israelites considered gross, obscene and blasphemous, for they demeaned the character of man, who was called upon to walk according to the way of God.

However, by John's time, sacrificial meat was a marketable commodity — and though buying it did not of itself constitute any obligation to indulge in the rites of any cult, it was still seen as an entrapment to others who formerly had worshipped such gods and were suggestible to any act that once had been associated with worship such as that they had once participated in. Paul, because of this, advised the Christians: "Do not those who eat the sacrifices participate in the altar?...The sacrifices of pagans are offered to demons, not to God, and I do not want you to be participants with demons," (1 Corinthians 10: 20). Demons are those varied detrimental spirits of the age which find their way into the human character and mold it into ways perverse to God. These life- and mind-destroying ways are legion and inimical to nature, God and man.

On a par with this, Paul also mentions eating things so as to offend others: "If your brother is distressed because of what you eat, you are no longer acting in love. Do not, therefore, by your eating destroy your brother for whom Christ died." (Romans 14: 15)

Yet there are some, in today's world, who do eat to give offence. I remember once being told of a group of so-called "liberated Jews" who stood in front of a Jewish synagogue and, in an exhibitionist manner, ate pork chops and pork sandwiches. There is nothing liberated, humorous or commendable in actions of this kind, regardless of what may have prompted them. Even so, their action called to my mind a piece of Christian history that is none too flattering.

While anti-Semitism may be the farthest thing from most Christian minds today, when they enjoy the "traditional" Easter ham at dinner time, it wasn't the most inconsequential matter prompting those in early times who introduced that practice into Christianity. Although most Christians are today completely unaware of it, in early England, anti-Semitism played a major part in Easter celebrations. Because Easter fell so close to the Passover season when lambs were slain by Jews to celebrate their deliverance from the angel of death, Christians began slaying pigs instead, and ate pork in order to offend the Jewish people (See the *Encyclopaedia Britannica's* article on Easter). This was in direct opposition to Paul's own words that we should never eat to give offence.

Often it has seemed to me something of an irony that this tradition to commemorate the sacrifice of the

Lamb of God (Jesus Christ) is celebrated by the slaying
of pigs and the eating of their flesh. Isaiah's words in
such a context seem like a rebuke to us: "These people
spend their nights keeping secret vigil; and eat the flesh
of pigs." (Isaiah 65: 3-4) I think too of Antiochus of
Epiphanes who, to insult the Jews, killed a pig and offered
it as a sacrifice upon the altar in Jehovah's Temple in
Jerusalem. Such insults are insults to God himself, as
Paul, Isaiah and John here clearly show, and such
exhibitionism is idolatry.

In spite of some very elaborate descriptions of them,
all that we really know about the Nicolaitans is what we
read about them in the *Book of Revelation.* The one
advantage of the passage here describing them is that it
underlines the fact that Christianity, even in its early
days, was divided into varied groups which were a mutual
influence on one another. There were the Nicolaitans,
the Gnostics, and the congregation of Jezebel, among
others. From the very start, Christianity wasn't unified
in all its teachings and its practices. What gave unity to
Christians in each city was the spirit or angel of the
church, which kept alive the vision of Jesus Christ and
the work which he set out for them to do: remembering
the nature of his character, the goals to be achieved, and
the definite commands to be obeyed.

It is mere speculation that ties this group of the
Nicolaitans to Nicolas of Antioch, who had become a
proselyte from the Jewish faith. There is absolutely no
grounds for such a claim, and all Christians would be
well advised to abandon it. As for the practices of the
Nicolaitans, which is the real issue here, we have, from
scripture, only that they were related to the teachings of
Balaam who corrupted Israel with licentious practices,
while antiquity suggests they mixed idolatrous practices
with their worship. Whatever they were, the important

thing for us to realise is that we ourselves must put our own lives in order, and not be intimidated by the many sects around us, nor by the practices of that particular denomination with which we have aligned ourselves. We are called on to examine ourselves individually and as a civic community of equal brothers and sisters, in the light of scriptures:

"Blessed is the individual (man or woman) who does not walk in the counsel of the ungodly (of even his own church ministers), and does not stand in the way of sinners (the teachings of our modern Nicolaitans), and does not sit in the seat of the scornful (believing smugly that he knows it all), but his delight is in the instruction of Jehovah (the enlightenment of God's written word), and in this law he meditates both day and night. And he shall be like a tree (of life) planted by the rivers of living waters that brings its fruit forth in season. (The same reward promised, in a slightly different way, to the overcomer in the church of Ephesus.)

"Neither shall his leaf wither, for everything he does will prosper. That is not the case with the ungodly, for they are like the chaff that the wind drives away. Therefore the ungodly shall not stand in the judgment, nor sinners in the congregation of the righteous. For Jehovah knows the way of the righteous, but the way of the ungodly shall perish."

Here we have the whole responsibility of the individual clearly defined – for Jews, for Christians or for Muslims. "Put your doctrines and your practices in order, regardless of pressures put on you by other individuals, faiths, sects and congregations – outside or in your own faith." It is the individual who must answer, for whatever stand he takes.

Had Christians more fully understood the benefit of the "Jewish" holy days (especially the feast of unleavened bread), they could have regularly reviewed their doctrines and their practices and put sin out of their midst. For Christianity was not a highly stratified hierarchical society in early times. Members looked on one another as equals who could admonish brothers and sisters in the faith from the written word of God. As Paul said: "All scripture is the very breath of God, and is useful for teaching, rebuking, correcting, and training in righteousness, so that the man of God may be thoroughly equipped for every good work."   (2 Timothy 3: 16)

So, fittingly, the spirit (or angel) of the Church in Pergamos is strongly admonished by God's word, which is to say by "the one wielding the sharp double-edged sword". As the scriptures say, "The word of God is sharper than a two-edged sword and able to divide both soul and spirit." Soul and spirit are not synonymous, as many seem to think. Soul relates to beings living in the physical realm, not the spiritual. Quite clearly then, the church of Pergamos is visually instructed to use the word of God to help them distinguish the difference between the things which are of God from those which are of Satan's world. The symbolism is keen and visual, and stresses the importance of not merely doing what is right in our own eyes, but making clear distinctions between right and wrong.

Although Pergamos held firm to its faith in Christ's name, they had been lax about doctrines and had been lenient toward immoral practices. Overcoming such practices is not an easy thing, yet those who overcome them are promised the reward of manna from the Ark of God as well as a white stone with a new name written on it. These symbolic rewards are charged with meaning.

The manna from the Ark of God (which was like coriander seed and sweet as honey — nourishing and delightful to the taste) is the pure unadulterated wisdom of God, received directly from God's own lips, to strengthen and encourage his people. Such a promise would be quite meaningless if the Law of God were done away. Yet like the children of Israel in the wilderness, overcomers are told that Jehovah will feed them with the manna of his wisdom, hidden in the Ark of God. This is said so as to remind the church in Pergamos that "Man does not live by bread alone but by every word of God."

The white stone with a secret name written on it which is promised to the overcomers, indicates that like Moses and the twelve apostles, they will have won God's confidence and be admitted to his most intimate councils. "Things hidden from the foundation of the world." "Henceforth you will be called no more Jacob, but Israel." Names had great significance. Abram became Abraham. Saul became Paul. Simon became Peter. Shadrak, Meshak and Abednigo were but the worldly names for Hananiah, Mishael, and Azariah. The change of a name meant the blessing of a new standing with God. Of course the white stone or voting pebble ("Psephon" in Greek) indicated they were declared innocent of any crime. White pebbles meant innocence or acquital; black pebbles meant guilt and condemnation.

Another image has been very aptly chosen next, for the angel of Thyatira is addressed "by the Son of God, whose eyes burn like fire and whose feet are like polished bronze". The image very sharply reminds all Christians whom it is they serve. He does not tolerate any form of wickedness in those whom he will choose. Yet he stands ready to uphold and strengthen any individual who turns to him when even his own church has failed. These will

shine like stars in heaven as companions of the morning
star.

This church at Thyatira is far too tolerant and has
admitted to its midst "the woman Jezebel". This whole
letter is a symbolic book of well-selected images. Yet
there are those who in spite of Jesus's own words remain
too literal. This often is the case in reading of "the
woman Jezebel" who is called a prophetess. Since there
are some lessons to be learned from doing this, we will
for a moment yield upon this point. However, it is foolish
to speculate on who Jezebel was in such a case, but we
should warn ourselves against presuming (as some have
done) that because she was a woman, she had usurped
the man's place and idolatry was the consequence.

Neither history nor the Bible supports this claim.
For both these sources confirm that women played
important roles in the early Christian church. As Paul
himself said: "In Christ there is neither Jew nor Greek,
male nor female. For all are as one in Jesus Christ." Nor
should we be deceived by that apparently contradictory
text in Paul's letter to the Corinthians, saying women
should keep silent in the church. For Acts 2: 17 confirms:
"I will pour out my spirit upon all flesh." That meant
male and female equally. Luke was quite explicit here, for
he went on to say, "and your sons and your daughters will
prophecy." There was absolutely no discrimination then.
Even the prophet Joel had left no doubt that this
equality was to be an essential term of the new covenant
with God.   (See Joel 2: 28)

But there can be no better example than that of
Jesus himself, who taught women and used them as
ambassadors. He not only instructed Jewish women, he
taught foreign women too. Greek scriptures also give a
lengthy list of women who played important roles in the

spreading of the gospels. Then quite apart from all the women that are named in the "New Testament", the early history of the church, as well, tells us of early Christian women such as Balinda, the slave, who in 177 AD at Lyons vocally testified along with her mistress and other Greeks and Romans. In 283, Perpetua of Carthage became the first woman in all of history to create a lasting written document.

There are many other notable examples as well, but my purpose here is not to make a long discussion of this point. For I realise that there can be endless arguments of this. I merely wish to show, that the sex of Jezebel played no part in the condemnation of her given here. As Paul has told us, there is no distinction made between male and female. "They are as one," in the community of saints making up the body of Christ. If taken literally, Jezebel's teachings were condemned for exactly the same reasons that those of the Nicolaitans were condemned. Had her sex been, in any way, a barrier the writer would have made that clear, and been unequivocal. Jezebel was not condemned for preaching in the church, she was condemned for preaching the wrong doctrines.

The *Book of Revelation* is more concerned, however, with the symbolic meaning of these words. "Meat" itself is symbolic. For Jesus said, "My meat is to do the will of him that sent me." (John 4: 34) So to eat meat from pagan altars was to do the will of those (like Hitler, Balac or Pharaoh) whose ways corrupt the world. Mixing idolatry with worship of Jehovah is spoken of many times in the Hebrew and Greek scriptures as fornication or idolatry. We find many good examples of this in the days of early Israel.

In Chapter 17 of the book of *Judges* for instance, we read of a man called Micah, who lived in the hill country of Ephraim during the 12th century BC. Micah was not a very admirable person. He was a thief and an idolator, and was extremely superstitious. We are told that he built "a house for God (Elohim)" and that he hired a young Levite (a member of Israel's priestly family) to act as his own personal priest. He even clothed him in rich priestly garments.

Then having done this, he said: "Now since I have a Levite for my priest, I know that Jehovah will bless me."

Yet even though the house he built for God was filled with many graven images (representing different powers in the hierarchy of God) Micah imagined that he was still a worshipper of Jehovah.

Such concrete scriptural illustrations help to teach us what false worship is and to remind us what is meant by Satan's throne. That John now, in writing to the church fellowship of Thyatira makes a strong clear reference to Jezebel (the prophetess queen of Israel) who brought idolatry into Israel, serves to indicate that such idolatry had come into the Christian church as well. For it was this queen and the congregation of Baal worshippers and idolators which she brought into Israel who were the synagogue of Satan in that case. It was a term we should not use carelessly. The adoption of doctrines from pagan teachings was itself viewed, throughout the Hebrew Scriptures, as fornication, as was eating food from pagan altars.

In hearkening to men rather than to God, the food of corruption is eaten. The unleavened bread of Christ's body, was symbolic of the unadulterated word of God. So in this feast of unleavened bread, we see that true worshippers must put the leaven of this world's practices out of their lives or be in danger themselves of becoming "the synagogue of Satan". They are therefore warned that they must live completely on the bread of truth and deeds which Christ approved and taught and showed his followers in the way he lived his life. "I am the way," he told them openly.

Paul himself, to some extent, may have been responsible for this, for he laid the ground plan when he said: "I am fully convinced that no food is unclean of itself." Now the consequence of his words was being realised within the Christian church. But to be fair Paul did warn those practicing the eating of meat offered to idols, that their practice would lead to some undesirable side effects. For though not physically harmful, it would lead to misunderstanding and cause others to err in their worship. In speaking plainly as he did, Paul neglected to lay much emphasis upon the symbolic meaning of those acts.

The reference to Jezebel of course is not to any person, but to a group. A group being receptive to spiritual conception was throughout the Bible personified as a woman, a harlot or a virgin. We know for instance that God is not a man, but a powerful, spirit of intelligence which created the heavens and the earth through the power of "his word". He is called Father — not because he is a man — but because he plants the seed of life in his created things. Mankind in relation to God plays a female role. She may, if she desires, receive the seed of God's word. God, however, does not rape a people. They must yield to him of their own free will and because of their sincere desire to be with him.

Jezebel is that group of people who mingle Jehovah's teachings with those of "another god". Here, seemingly part of the Christian fellowship, the sect of Jezebel are actually worshippers of other gods and of "another Jesus

Christ". Their teachings are adulterated teachings since
they have been mixed with teachings from the pagan
world. They even claim to have another word besides the
word that Jesus and the ancient prophets gave to them.

The sect of Jezebel are they who believe themselves
to be in possession of "a deeper, fuller and more revealing
word of God"—or as John fittingly worded it "the deep
secrets of Satan". It is unlikely though that they
themselves would refer to these secrets as that. But what
they consequently teach is not the word of God at all.
This group which mingles the word of Satan with the
teachings of God causes spiritual sickness that will lead
eventually to death. Therefore the many paramours of
Jezebel (those with whom she has allied herself
politically) will fall into the same sick bed as she and her
children (those individuals within her midst who draw
their spiritual sustenance from her).

All of them will die because of the false doctrines
that they feed upon. This is the same warning that was
given to Adam at the beginning of the world when God
said to him, "You must not eat from the tree of the
knowledge of good and evil, for when you eat of it you
will surely die." (Genesis 2: 17) You will remember that
the one great hope for those living Christian lives, and
who die in Christ, is resurrection from the dead followed
by eternal life. So John here makes it clear that there is
no salvation in false teachings, even if they wear a
Christian face. Idolatry must be put out of the Christian
church, for the consequence of all idolatry is eternal death.
Idolators will never share in God's gift of eternal life.

Those who overcome will be given the morning star,
which means that Jesus himself will be their close
companion. For it is written: "I am ...the bright morning
star." (Revelation 22: 16) He will be their close companion

and will walk with them through the furnace of affliction and adversity. For he has feet of brass that have been tried in that furnace. In this context, these words from the psalmist also are appropriate: "Yea though I walk through the valley of the shadow of death, I will fear no evil, for thou art with me." Then Jesus promises to give them his authority over all the nations as a suitable reward, since he told them earlier, "Blessed are the meek (those who are approachable and willingly yield themselves to God) for they shall inherit the earth."

CHAPTER THREE

Recognizing the Brotherhood

These are the words that you must write and send to the interpreting spirit, in the body of believers at Sardis: "The one who has the seven spirits of God (and therefore is informed of all events occurring in the world, Rev 5: 6), and who has the seven stars (as spirits guarding his community and knows the full condition of his flocks, Prov 27: 23), has this to say to you:

"I have very carefully observed your works, and although I realise that everyone who speaks about you says you are a very lively church, the truth is you are perishing. So wake up now and arouse yourselves and try to stay alert. Otherwise you'll lose everything you have. You and everything that you now have will vanish, since nothing that you do is of the standard God requires. So take the necessary time to carefully consider everything that you were taught at first (in the scriptures) and then obey (what you have learned from them). Turn away from your gross negligence. For if you go on slumbering, then you will find that I will come upon you like a thief, and you won't even know the time I came. (For it is written: 'Jehovah of Hosts has said: "I will send my messenger, who will prepare the way for me. Jehovah whom you are seeking, will come suddenly to his temple, with the messenger of the covenant — Jesus Christ — whom you desire to see." ')

"Even so there still are individuals in Sardis whose garments are not tarnished (with worldly practices). Therefore, they shall walk with me in white (linen, which indicates the good things they have done. Rev 19: 8) for they are worthy. Everyone who overcomes (those difficulties keeping him from that obedience that I require of him) will be clothed in white, and his name will not be erased from the *Book of Life*, but I will acknowledge him as mine in the presence of my Father and his hosts." Let the one with understanding hear (and obey) what the spirit says to the bodies of believers (throughout the world).

This is the message that you must send to the interpreting spirit in the community of saints at Philadelphia: "These words are from the One who is holy and true (that is to say the Christ: 'my beloved son in whom I am well pleased,'—the true light...the true bread...and the true vine) who has the key of David and has the authority to open so that none can close, and the authority to close so that none can open.

(These words are a reference to the king's closest adviser, as we see in *Isaiah* 22: 22-23, and emphasizes his full authority to act on the king's behalf and to make decisions that are binding. It is the same authority that Jesus bestowed on his followers when he gave them the keys to the kingdom of heaven, saying: 'Whatsoever you shall bind on earth shall be according to what is bound in heaven, and whatsoever you shall loose on earth shall be according to what is loosed in heaven.' This was not a license to act irresponsibly. It was a trust of power. Such a one was to act in the name of the king. In this case God. He was to do God's will—not his own. Such a verse then implies that Jesus had a king over him— namely God, who sat upon the throne.)

"I have observed your deeds. So look! (to show my approval of you) I am placing an open door before you (that all the world may see how close I am to you). It is a door that no one possibly can shut. (I give you access to my presence through it because) even though you barely had the strength, you always obeyed me and never have denied my name. Now watch, for I will make all those belonging to the synagogue of Satan (those liars claiming to be Jews, but who serve the pagan world and so really are not Jews at all) fall at your feet, acknowledging that you possess the blessings of my love, because you have obeyed my word and patiently endured and kept the faith. For this reason I will preserve you in the time of trouble when it comes upon the world. Since I am coming soon, hold closely to everything you have (continuing to walk in my ways) so that no one takes away your (winner's laurel) crown (of immortality).

"I will make of anyone who overcomes (the power of this world's subtly persuasive spirit) a pillar in the temple of my God that shall never be put out of it. (Since these words were not merely spoken by Jesus, but by the resurrected Jesus, we should observe that Jesus has a God — his Father — Jehovah, who sits upon the throne of heaven, as the next chapter itself will show.) On such a person will I write the name of my God, and the name of the city of my God, the New Jerusalem which descends from heaven. (The New Jerusalem is a spiritual presence that can exist anywhere throughout the world in any city: Paris, London, Ottawa, New York, Moscow, or Medicine Hat and Moose Jaw, Saskatchewan. It is the character of life in a city then that makes it spiritual Jerusalem, not its geographical location. Just as the throne of God is wherever people call on him, so the Holy City is wherever city life reflects the love and compassion of God — and the atmosphere of God's Spirit is on all its citizens.")

Let whoever understands these words, obey what the spirit says.

Here is what you must write next to the (interpreting) spirit in the Laodicean community of saints: These are the words of God's assurance (literally "the Amen"), the faithful and true witness (the righteous judge of Israel, Isaiah 11: 1-5; whose power can do amazing things, Psalm 45: 4):

"I have observed your deeds and know that you are neither cold nor hot, although I would prefer that you were one thing or the other. But because you are luke-warm — and neither hot nor cold — I will spew you from my mouth. For you have said to yourself, 'I am rich and well supplied with goods, and I have everything I need,' but you cannot see how wretched, miserable and poor you really are, and how blind and naked you've become. (For it is truly said that it is difficult for a rich man to enter into the Kingdom of God. 'For all his profits will not expiate the guilt he has incurred.' Hosea 18: 8)

"My advice to you, then, is to purchase gold (wisdom) from me — pure gold (unpolluted wisdom) refined by fire (tested in the adversities of life) — that you may have true riches (that is to say wisdom and the sterling qualities of character that are developed by experience...for it is better than silver or fine gold) and to buy white clothes from me (by 'being rich in good works — always generous and ready to share') to cover up your shameful nakedness. Also anoint your eyes with ointment (God's word which gives sight to the blind, and is a lamp unto your feet) that you may see.

"(Nor should you take offence by what I say, for) I always rebuke and chasten everyone I love. And so I earnestly entreat you to repent. For Look! I am standing at the door and knocking. If anyone acknowledges my voice and opens the door (that is understands my words and does them) I will enter his house and will eat with him, and he with me. ('My meat is to do the will of God who sent me'. To eat with Christ is to do the same work he would do).

"To anyone who overcomes, I will give the right to sit beside me (at my right hand, when I am seated) on my throne (the throne of David — God's right hand upon earth), just as when I overcame (I received the right) to sit beside my Father (at his right hand, as he was seated) on his throne."

Anyone who has the understanding, listen to and obey what the spirit says to the community of saints.

*

There is something very much wrong with Christianity. Everybody knows there is. Christians themselves are well aware of it. That is why Jesus recommends we keep the Feast of Unleavened Bread each year so that we may periodically review ourselves. In Chapter One of this book we presently are examining, we meet the judge of Israel — a judge who doesn't judge things superficially or deal with hearsay evidence, who like a shepherd holds the fate of all the flocks in his hand and walks in all the sanctuaries of the world; but whose speech like a two-edged sword — "dividing soul and spirit" — is the word of God, with power to curse or bless the world, according to the path that people choose to take.

If we make a covenant with him, he will be our close companion and will walk with us through all the fire and tribulations that the world can force upon us during the experiences of life. That covenant, which was made at Calvary with all assemblies of God, symbolized all the blood of innocence that was ever shed so that we might see and understand the havoc that our sins have brought upon the world. The guilt of all of it is on our hands if we adopt the careless practices made available by those societies which murder Christ in all their God-denying ways. For after all an atheist or a God-denying person is not merely someone who honestly believes there is no

God. An atheist is someone who, although he may believe there is a God, deliberately denounces him in the way he lives and in the way he treats the world the great creator made.

But Jesus says that if we make a convenant with him and with his God, that he will take upon himself the guilt of those past sins separating us from God, regardless of how red with blood they are. Then he will lead us to a new and better world. For this reason Jesus, in this one decisive act, revealed all the enormity of that bloodguilt which all the nations share and which they have incurred through all the centuries through the maintenance of their traditions, cultures and aggressive governments with armies for preserving them.

Yet *Passover* – which has its pain – is a time for giving birth. When we recognize and acknowledge all our sins, (offences against God, against others, and against creation) we start off on the journey of personal transformation toward a new and better world with new and better citizens. Therefore we must keep the *Feast of Unleavened Bread.* As we examine each of the churches in Chapters Two and Three, we see that they can be interpreted as symbolic steps meant to be followed by every congregation, in examining themselves, during the Festival's symbolic days. I do not doubt that these churches, which John mentions in his letter, did exist in the very state in which he pictures them. That is what has made them such meaningful and powerful examples as we study them. Yet they are now much more than just history. Like the Menorah lamp inside the temple of Jehovah in Jerusalem, they represent the seven days of the creation of the world.

On the first day, God said: "Let there be Light." Therefore let the light of God's unpolluted word be established in the church. In his command to Ephesus, he commanded them, "Return to your first love," the meaning of which Paul revealed to us as being "Return to the first pure doctrines you were taught." I cannot stress too much the importance of these commandments that we find in these two chapters at the first. For if they are not carried out, when the bridegroom comes none will be prepared for him. Only darkness will be in your world. As Jesus says: "If you do not repent (of turning from the teachings in the word of God) I shall come and take your lampstand from its place."

On the second day of Creation, God said: "Let there be a space dividing the waters above from the waters below." So the church as well must make a clear distinction between the waters of God's word and the waters of philosophies in the scholastic and the entertainment worlds. So "he who was dead and is alive", told the church at Smyrna they were rich for having put away the power of Satan from their midst, even though it brought them suffering. Putting a space between the waters of heaven and the waters of the world did not prove to be an easy thing. Yet this would prove to be the vital step toward immortality.

On the third day of Creation, God said: "Let the waters under heaven be gathered together to one place, and let the dry land appear...and the earth bring forth life." Then to the church at Pergamos, the one who had the power to curse and the power to bless because his word could separate the spiritual things from the things of the flesh, said: "Get rid of all the fleshly practices that tie you to the corruption of the world, such as Balaam's sin of pagan enticements toward immorality." In other words become a stable church. Rise from the waters of baptism and leave behind all the former things and lead a different sort of life—a life that is more stable and founded on the solid ground of God's enduring word (so that new life will abound).

On the fourth day, God placed lights in the firmament of heaven, which divided the day from the night and served as guides to warn the world and Christians of the changing times and seasons. That is why the son of God, whose eyes can see through superficial evidence, and who stands ready to walk with us through all adversities, gives this next command to rise above the pagan teachings of the church and stand like stars to guide the flock. For the immoral practices of the woman Jezebel may be a part of Christianity in the community where you serve, seducing you with all her pagan practices and the idolatry that she has brought into the congregation from the city where we hope to found our spiritual Jerusalem.

I cannot overstress the great importance of these holy days, for what God shows us in this very plan he has revealed, is the actual scheme itself by which he made the world. To say these days were done away, as well as all the great commandments that he gave, is to say that God himself is obsolete and that Creation has been nulled. For what we're witnessing, in this important festival, is a new creation of the world, and the seven days of self-examination are the first important steps in making it a visual reality. Are we merely standing by and looking at the clouds to see if or when the Christ will come? or are we sensibly, in faith, making preparations for the tasks he has in mind for us?

Now the church at Sardis was a very lively place. Lots of things were going on. It was the kind of church that filled the heart with wild exhilaration. But nothing very much — if anything —was being done to give real glory to the name of God. It was a church that didn't have a plan. It wasn't going anywhere. Yet God had said, "Let there be life." and every kind of life abounded in the waters of the world and in the firmament and upon the earth itself. It teemed with life. Had you been there, you would have been impressed by it. But there was no direction yet for any of this life. ("There was not a man to till the ground"). So to the church at Sardis Jesus said, "Arouse yourselves lest you lose whatever truth you have." Liveliness was not enough. There had to be a plan.

Then on the sixth day, God made man (male and female) in his own image — "a man after his own heart" — so that he could be the one who ruled the world. For this reason, God put all things under him, making him the responsible protector and the overseer of all life on earth. That is why Jesus, who had the keys of royal authority, placed them in the hands of these loyal followers in Philadelphia and made them equals of himself. For it is written: "No servant can be greater than his lord or stand above the one who tutored him. It should be enough for any disciple to be like his teacher, and the servant to be like his lord." (Matthew 10: 24-25)

This is the message that we have from Philadelphia. This is the ideal toward which all Christians strive. To such a congregation, God gives access to his personal counsels, for he has opened heaven's door and speaks with those disciples face to face — as he once did with Moses in the wilderness.

This community, then, is Adam (or mankind) — the New Adam — who will (if they are faithful) rule the world as equals with their lord. Being equal to Jesus doesn't mean standing in the temple of God and saying "I thank you Lord God that I am not like other men." It means humbling yourself to look after the needs of others, as Jesus did when he clad himself in a towel, like a slave, and washed the feet of his disciples — the most menial task that he could do.

Paul's advice to the Philippians reflects this attitude, for he said: "Let this attitude of mind be found in every one of you which was found in Jesus Christ: Who being in the image of God, did not consider robbing God of his authority by claiming to have equality with him. Instead, he humbled himself, and assumed the duties of a servant, and became obedient until death, even (a shameful) death upon a (criminal's) cross." (Philippians 2: 5-8) This is the picture of the perfect man. In what manner would you speak to such a one?

There are those who cannot enter the Kingdom of God. Their very nature has excluded them. They are those who constantly find fault in others. They cannot overlook the slightest defect in another individual. They are impatient and intolerant with everyone who errs, and they do not let their own strengths compensate for someone else's weaknesses. They are impatient, judgemental and snappish. Such is not the way of God. The man of God does not hold others up for ridicule, or only deal exclusively with righteous men. He makes all men righteous by the way he deals with them, and he controls his tongue in the way he speaks to others or addresses them. Being righteous is an art requiring grace and a kindly attitude. Lord deliver us from the acid tongues and fierce defenders of the faith whose every word is withering and cruel and totally unrighteous in their zealousness. One does not gather grapes from thorns.

Walking in God's Kingdom is not something that we do after death has carried off our soul into the prison house. It is something we are called upon to do each day. It is the manner that we walk and speak to others and treat them now which determines whether we are walking in the Kingdom of God today. If we only treat another human being "as he deserves," then we have made ourselves a judge. And if others treat us too in that same way, the lot of this world will not be an easy one.

Finally there came the last day of Creation, and God's rest. For there were seven days in which God made the world. It wasn't made in six. Yet for each day, as it is named, we are told of all the things that he created in the world. So the question must be asked, "What did God make on the seventh day?" Why, sir, or madam, don't you know? On the seventh day he created what we call the sabbath day – to be a day of rest. Jesus said of it: "The sabbath day *was created* for man" and then referring to himself he said, "The son of man is lord of the sabbath day." These same words could now be said of any man who was obedient to God.

The sabbath took place always on the seventh day of the week rather than the first, because it required preparation. All seven days were holy days, for God gave commands concerning all of them – the general commandment being six days you must labour and do all your work. Then on the seventh day, the man of God was called upon to do those things the other six days of preparation had made possible. God's servants always must prepare themselves for doing any work that God requires of them.

Yet Israel and Judah too, or so the Bible says, went into captivity for abusing all the sabbath festivals. It said they didn't keep the sabbaths, even though formally they probably observed them faithfully. What they didn't keep was the commands implied in them. They didn't rid themselves of all the pagan teachings, or their carnal practices. Their daily lives were marred by them. Just as those of modern Christians are who have junked the formal festivals as well, so as to celebrate those holidays which are more fun to them—watching for the yule tide fire god wearing his red suit in the chimney place, or hunting for the Easter bunnies and for Easter eggs before they eat the Easter ham on Ishtar's holy day. Such practices may indeed be harmless as the modern Churches say, but none of them will free the world from its captivity.

That is why, when speaking to the congregation in Laodicea, Jesus (whose power can do amazing things) had this to say to them: "You cannot seem to fathom just how wretched, miserable and poor you really are, and how blind and naked you've become." He said this to a smug, self-satisfied and easy-going church that wasn't doing anything it should, because they thought they were rich and well supplied with everything they needed in the world. "Jesus did it all," they may have said. "Oh, you should hear our minister. He's really good. He's such a friendly man and full of fun. And his sermons are so marvellous, we just keep going back to hear him all the time."

The church in Laodicea was a church that had settled down to take their ease. Having filled their barns with all good things, they said: "I will tear them down and build bigger ones." This church just hadn't learned that "to whomever much is given much shall be required," and so they left almost everything to the professionals. "I'm just a layman after all. I don't pretend to understand the Bible or theology. We pay a minister for looking after that."

Jesus taught his followers that the sabbath day was to be used to glorify God—not themselves—with every kind of good work they could do. Then he taught them—through his miracles—to heal the sick, console the sorrowful, feed the hungry, and visit those who suffered ills. He taught them they should teach (through word and deed) the glory of the God they served, until the world was filled with light. "My Father laboured until now, and I also work," were Jesus's own words.

So each church, in this review of admonishment and praise, is used by the risen Jesus Christ to teach his followers the way. Each church, symbolic of a separate day in the *Festival of Unleavened Bread*, serves like an imperative command to search ourselves for follies that are similar and cleanse ourselves of them. Only by this means can we be ready for the work that he will afterwards reveal. Briefly then, he asks us all:

(1) To give the light of his pure doctrine to the world.

(2) To understand the difference between the philosophies of men and the untainted word of God.

(3) To come out of the waters of baptism (that great flood that inundates all the world) and begin to live a new life by putting away all the things that had corrupted us.

(4) To grow in knowledge so we can be a light in the firmament of God and act as guides to lead the world.

(5) To take the necessary time to critically examine the nature of our activities and to make certain we are serving God with them.

(6) To strive against all obstacles till Christ is born in us, and never to give in, serving in humility and not in arrogance of heart.

(7)   Do not confuse the ease that material wealth affords with the rest that God offers us through serving him.

These commands were meant to be obeyed. The church — every church — was called upon to perfect itself, and the Church of God in each community was to be responsible directly to their "lord" and not to any other overseeing church, which presumed to have authority. Also each city was declared by Jesus Christ to be autonomous, and he called on them to deal locally with problems in their midst.

This brings us to another point. John, himself, could never have anticipated the exact developments of history. He didn't speak of any mother church, but that doesn't mean a mother church did not develop in the Christian world. Protestants, however, have often shown themselves ready to incriminate the Roman Catholic Church, accusing her of many crimes, while refusing to see anything that links themselves to her. Some will even argue quite vehemently they never were a part of such a church. Yet history says otherwise.

Most of the Christian churches in the world are daughters of the church of Rome, which separated from her in the sixteenth century. Even those who claim that they are not Protestants at all, since they don't consciously believe they protest anything, still bear the characteristic markings of their mother church in all their practices. Though some of them affirm they are the re-established church of Jesus Christ, history belies their words. Their mother's blood is in their veins. Sunday worship was initiated by the Roman Catholic Church, as any Roman Catholic bishop or priest will be ready to confirm. In the early days it was the celebrated day of Sol Invictus prior to the Christians celebrating it.

Christmas, too, was an adopted custom of the Roman Catholic Church. When the Christian church came into power, the world was full of pagan practices. Rather than lose many new Christians to pagan gods, the Roman church found ways to deal with them. Since most of their parishioners enjoyed a pagan festival which celebrated the birthday of the Sun – Sol Invictus – the Christian church was forced to deal with it. It was a delightful time, filled with fun and sportiveness. Unable to prohibit the people from joining in this feast, the Pope, in wisdom, tried to overcome its harmful practices by introducing Christian ones replacing them. By celebrating in its place the Birth of Jesus Christ – the Light of all the World – he gave the feast a Christian face. Was he wrong? That is not for me to say. You, with the wisdom of God's word, must be the judge of it. But Protestants still bear the birthmark that their mother left with them.

Other practices, as well, were instituted by decree: Easter celebrations, Church processionals, a priesthood and a laity, the teaching of a Godhead trinity which was formalized around 400 AD, long after every Bible book was written. There are many other little things as well that aren't the least bit biblical. I call these things to mind, not to point the finger anywhere accusingly, but merely to show there is no denying the relationship that other churches have to the Roman Catholic mother who gave birth to them. Even among those who claim to be the re-established church of Jesus Christ, we find the birthmarks that are unmistakable.

It doesn't take another special vision from the sky to re-establish "the true and only church of Jesus Christ". Any community of believers upon earth can do it on their own, at any time, by simply following all of the instructions which Jesus Christ himself sent by

messenger "to his loyal workman John." The purpose of
the now forgotten *Festival of Unleavened Bread* is to
reinstate the church of God in each of all the world
communities. Every congregational community is merely
called on to repent and openly examine all the things
they teach in the light of God's unadulterated word.

For God's word — not tradition — bestows authority
upon a church or takes away the light of God from it. No
less a personage than Jesus Christ himself affirmed the
truth of that when he admonished those who thought
they had authority: "By your own traditions you have
made the word of God of no effect." And Christianity
itself has substituted other doctrines, practices and plans
for those which God revealed. Upon whose word did
Jesus build his church? Upon the shifting sand of human
understanding? or on the solid rock of God? surely not
upon a man — not on flesh and blood.

Some will keep on asking though, "What church
must I go out and join?" to find the Church of God. No
church at all. Don't go running here and there saying,
"Here is Christ!" or "There." If you simply follow God's
plan, and obey all of the commands that are given in
this strategy, God will put you in his Church right now.
No one else can ever put you there. Its only roll of
membership is in the *Book of Life.* And God alone
reserves the right for putting any name in it. That's the
Bible meaning of the Church of God. "Where two or
three are gathered in my name," I tell you now, "I am in
the midst of them!"

The visible churches of this world are but a net for
gathering the fish. But God's church, which is invisible, is
simply what Paul said: "Neither he who plants nor he
who waters is anything at all. It is God who makes things
grow.... You are God's field. It is God alone who builds

you up." (1 Corinthians 3: 7-9) "The wind blows anywhere it will, and you hear the sound of it. But you cannot tell from where it comes or where it goes. That's the way it is with everyone who is born (of the spirit) of God." (John 3: 8)

So even if you only meet each week with friends in your own home, to read the Bible and to study God's intent, singing songs of praise and addressing God in reverence, and finding out what is required of you, you will find your way into the presence of your God. If you have access to the ear of God, and enjoy his counselling, you cannot ask for more. And no one anywhere can keep the promises of God from you. Beware of charlatans, of course, whose only purpose is to gain power over you. No one besides God has any power to excommunicate or disinherit you. The holy spirit is your guide and will govern you. However, you may be admonished and corrected if you vary from the written word of God. And you will humbly listen to admonishment from God's words whether it be from another Christian or a brother Jew. For that, and that alone, is God's foundation stone.

John tells all Christians, in these chapters, they must examine all their doctrines carefully and measure them according to the word of God. Not all congregational doctrines are the same. They ought to be, of course. That is living proof of why each church must re-examine what they preach. Each individual, as well. is called upon to periodically re-examine his beliefs. That was why the early Christians used the annual Festival of Unleavened Bread to critically re-examine their beliefs in the light of God's word. For we must never be dependent on what others say. The Christian has to know the scriptures for himself, lest he become the slave of charismatic men or stand in awe of those who hold high offices.

"How can you believe, you that receive honour one from another, but seek not the honour that comes from God only."

CHAPTER FOUR

The Pattern of God's Government

Afterwards I looked and saw in front of me a door opening in heaven: and the voice that I had heard at first, which sounded like a trumpet, spoke to me again, saying: "Come forward, and I will show you things that must shortly come to be." (What John is shown then in this vision is the basic spiritual ground plan for the new theocratic government which God calls upon his workmen to establish upon earth, so that it may replace the earthly governments of mankind's super powers, which are opposed to him and sustain themselves with military might. Because this governmental system that John describes for us is not as yet established amongst mankind, it is spoken of as "things that must shortly come to be.") Then instantly I was there in spirit.

What I saw in front of me was a throne (the symbol of governmental power) and someone sitting on it (revealing him to be the ruler of creation). The one who sat there had the appearance of jasper (holiness) and carnelian (divine justice), and there was a rainbow (symbolic of divine mercy, or grace) resembling an emerald (whose very costliness and beauty illustrate how precious and desirable the quality of mercy is) encircling the throne. (This vision then reveals that both the law and grace exist together in the character of God. The carnelian represents the administration of the law. For without the law there is no justice. Yet the rainbow, representing grace – or divine mercy – is there as well, indicating God is always merciful and ready to forgive all those who learn his ways and live by them.)

Around the throne were twenty-four other thrones: and seated on them were twenty-four elders (world rulers) dressed all in white (symbolic of Jehovah's righteousness), with golden victors' crowns (Greek: stephanoi) upon their heads. (These righteous individuals, who had been tried in fires of life's adversities, like Job, had proved themselves to be triumphant over them. They were those before whom heaven had seen fit to place an open door. Like the sons of God in ancient times, they took their places in the court of God as members of his government.) Then from the throne came lightning (symbolic of divine wisdom) and sounds of thunder (representative of God's great power to shake the nations of the world).

Seven lighted lamps, which are the seven spirits of God, burned before his throne. (These are the angels of the seven churches which burn as lamps in God's obedient communities, throughout the world). In front of the throne there was a sea of glass which was as clear as crystal (representing God's promise to remove deception and dishonesty from the turbulent world system and install a new world government to calm the troubled waters of the world.) Placed around the throne, four living creatures (the seraphim) were covered in front and behind with eyes. The first living creature was like a lion, the second like an ox, the third had a face like a man, and the fourth was like a flying eagle. (These four living creatures are definitive of those areas of creation whose jurisdiction God had placed in human hands when he commanded man to keep a constant watch on them.)

Each of these four creatures had six wings (six indicating that it was the duty of mankind to oversee these areas of life and act speedily in ministering to all their needs). These (seraphim or) living creatures were covered all over with eyes, even under their wings. Day and night they never stop saying, "Holy, Holy, Holy is Jehovah the Almighty God who was, and is, and is to come." (Creation being the glory of God is an open testament of him and, by its very being, praises him continually.) Whenever the living creatures glorify, honour and give thanks to him who sits upon the throne and who lives for ever and ever, the twenty-four elders (the rulers of the world) fall down in front of him and cast their crowns before the throne of God, saying: "You, Jehovah, are deserving of glory, honour, and obedience: for you created all things, and by your will they were given existence and life." (Not only is it characteristic of the seraphim then to offer praise to God, it is a necessary feature of every ruler serving in the new world government.)

(Creation by its very nature is the master teacher of mankind and therefore teaches everyone who carefully observes its ways. God's authority is affirmed on the basis that he is the creator and sustainer of all things. Therefore all power, honour and glory belong to God alone. From this standpoint, mankind is called upon to witness the judgment of God which follows — ending like the promise of Isaiah — in a vision of the ideal kingdom to be built on earth. Notice as we study this whole plan that there is no "rapture". Even at the very end no one actually "goes to heaven" for protection from the world. The riches of heaven are to be established upon earth when the dead have been raised and all creation rejoices in a world that is at peace. It is not the luxury of God's servants to be taken from the world or to flee from any of its ills. They are called on rather to overcome those ills and free the world from them.)

*

I can think of no better illustration of a theocratic world government than that which is described in Chapters Four and Five of the *Book of Revelation*. Here we are shown a throne surrounded by four living creatures, symbolic of the different areas of created life: a lion (representing all wild life on earth), an ox (representing

all living plants and creatures in domestic environments),
a man (representing the entire realm of human affairs),
and an eagle (representing all created things existing in
the sky above). Since God is the one great vital force
enlivening all of these, God reveals himself in them.

It becomes significant then that the great creator of
the universe is seated behind these living creatures which
speak on his behalf, and the only living being directly to
approach and look upon the throne of the living governor of heaven and earth is the faithful servant (the lamb),
who will be introduced in Chapter Five. This whole scene
then is strongly reminiscent of the sage Priest-Kings we
read about in histories of very early times.

Certainly in the *Genesis* account of Abraham, we
find that famous patriarch paying tribute to the great
Priest-King of Canaan, known as Malki Sadeg* (or
Melchizedek), whose long effective rule was centred in
the impregnable walled fortress of Ur Salem (called
Urishlim* in Canaanite poetry). The very fact that
Abraham paid tribute to this king would indicate that
Abraham (as a royal prince) acknowledged his
dependency on him as the only legal unifying power
amongst the princes of the regional communities. The
God who authorized Melchizedek to rule was known as
El il or El Elyon (the same God who was later known as
Allah by the Arab peoples of the world). This had been
the God of Job and Abraham. El il or El Elyon in times
much earlier had been the God who unified the ancient
land of Sumer. It was he who had secured such kings
upon their thrones as the legendary shepherd king
Dumuzi, whose name meant "faithful servant", a title later
given to all those kings who followed him.

It was the duty of all such Priest-Kings (known in
Sumer as Sanga-Lugals), on whom the spirit of heaven

had come down, to approach the one Elohim who could unify the city states, receive instructions from his hand and make them known to all the kings (or ensis) serving under him. We would refer now to such revelations as these Priest-Kings made, as the throne speech of the government. This ceremony was performed each New Year's Day even in the ancient city state of Babylon, where the Great God El il had been deposed and made subordinate to the mighty warrior God called Marduk (or Merodach). Still the kings of ancient Babylon continued every year to read the will of heaven (in the same time-honoured custom of the past) from what was known as "The Tables of Destiny" (ancient stones with strange markings carved on them dating from a time before the great sage King Adapa reigned).

All ancient kings of the Near East (so we are told) without exception claimed they were descendants from that legendary sage. Adapa was supposedly the first Priest-King of all the world who ruled in Sumer during the early Bronze Age years. It was he who civilized mankind and established theocratic governments on earth. Some Jewish scholars even say that King Adapa may have been the person whom the Hebrew Scriptures renamed Adam because (as King) he represented all Mankind. No one ever doubted that it was the plan of heaven for one Priest-King to be the central governor of all the lands. They only had to look into the sky and see it written in the stars. All constellations had a shepherd star which guided them, and these in turn all moved about a single star which was referred to by Sumerians as "the good shepherd of the sky". "Thy will be done on earth even as it is in heaven," was the early creed of every man. Kingship came from heaven, for that is where all governments began.

The one man who first associated Jesus Christ with all these early Priest-Kings of the past which date back to the time of King Adapa, is none other than Christianity's most powerful missionary, Paul of Tarsus. In his letter to the Hebrews, Saint Paul writes: "Melchizedek was King of Salem and Priest of the Most High God (i.e. El il who unified the tribes and early city states of Canaan). He met Abraham who was returning after he had battled and defeated hostile kings. Then after greeting him, Melchizedek blessed Abraham, and Abraham responding, paid tribute to Melchizedek by giving him a tenth of everything he'd gained."

(Hebrews: 7: 1-2)

Now John in *Revelation* unmistakably confirms what Paul had said: that Jesus was indeed a part of that same ancient line of kings. He shows us clearly that "the lamb" approached God's throne, and took a sealed scroll from his hand. Then afterwards he interpreted the hidden meanings written on the scroll, by opening the seals in front of all the Kings assembled in his presence. Such sacred rites as this could only have been carried out by someone who as Priest King was regarded as the King of Kings and undisputed leader of the world. For no one other than a High Priest had been ordained to come before the throne of the Most High God which governed all the tribes of men. Nor would someone other than the King of Kings presume to read the resolutions of the government he led or even speak for that one God to whom all other Gods paid tribute through the Kings who represented them.

Many ancient documents confirm that "Kings were chosen in the womb". That is to say that they were chosen in "the temple school" where Kings were trained and educated by the priests. And these same temple priests it seems would always choose whatever candidate was favoured in their eyes. Yet only after such a candidate was brought before the King of all the Lands, and he acknowledged and accepted him could such a candidate for Kingship actually become the ruler's legal son and heir. That is why all Kings were looked upon as sons of Gods if not actually the Gods themselves. It therefore was acknowledged as a universal truth, that all Kings (having been ordained by the nominating God presenting them) had been conceived and chosen in the womb (the temple school) – which is to say within the virgin bride of God.

In this vision John has seen, the rulers of all sovereign states throughout the world are spoken of as elders. These are prominently seated right before God's throne, and God who is surrounded by the living creatures glorifying him, instructs the elders in his government through them. These theocratic elders all wear golden stephanoi (or victors' crowns) to show us that their authority had been bestowed on them for having triumphed, after being tested in fires of life's adversities. That they are twenty-four in number simply shows us they are living men and women gathered from all quarters of the earth (not supernatural beings), whose duty is to serve their God both night and day as faithful guardians and watchmen over that created world which God had made. The number of these elders then is not a literal one by any means.

Yet for the sake of those who do not understand the Bible's use of numbers in prophetic texts, I shall take a little time to show you what they are and how they're used. There are three decisive numbers of perfection in the Bible: seven (7), ten (10), and twelve (12). All of them were perfect numbers, and all peoples in the Near East used them for resolving complicated problems which were difficult to solve. Any task related to the question of creativity and death always was completed in seven steps. There were seven moving bodies in the sky which were visible to the naked eye. These were the sun, the moon and five planets, whose movements (everyone believed) affected life on earth.

There were seven gates of death which stripped the soul of life. The great dark beast of waste and ruin (called Leviathan) had seven heads, and every battle fought with it took seven days, or seven weeks or seven months, or seven years. You may remember there were seven years of famine (when Joseph could be said to have struggled with the beast of waste and ruin so he could feed the peoples of the world). Therefore there were seven days of creation, seven days of the week, and seven holy festivals, and the lifespan of a man was divisible into seven units multiplied by ten (each ten years standing for a day in each man's life).

Ten was the number which defined completion in the Gentile world. There were ten fingers on human hands and ten toes on the feet. Gentiles consequently counted in tens. So in Bible prophecy ten was used to indicate completion in the Gentile world. Ten nations simply meant all Gentile nations, regardless of how many nations there actually might be. To suffer ten days implied the full extent of human suffering that Gentile nations could inflict. Ten therefore, in addition, represented trial and suffering. When multiplied by four it represented widespread suffering and emphasized how severe that suffering must have been. Multiply that number by another ten and you find the kind of suffering that Israel underwent in Egypt. It didn't mean that Israel spent four hundred years in Egypt. Yet because the number ten lacked the full perfection of God expressed in the number twelve, two became God's perfect witness to the world.

Twelve was the perfect number that revealed the character of God. The psalmist said, "The heavens declare the glory of God." And there were twelve signs in the zodiac, by which the seasons of the year were measured and there were twelve new moons in every year. Consequently there were twelve months on the calendar, twelve hours in the day and twelve hours in the night. As all creation was regarded as the glory of God, there were twelve stones in the breastplate of Israel to represent the twelve chief virtues in his character. Those twelve virtues were supposedly revealed in all twelve tribes of Israel. That is why their names were etched upon the stones the High Priest wore. Because a man's foot could be measured by twelve thumb widths, man was the glory of God's creation and was expected to walk in a manner that would not desecrate his name. A man was called upon to walk with God. This meant that he must walk according to the torah (the instruction) of God's way.

When multiplied by two, the number twelve (which measured night and day) became a symbol of the perfect watchfulness of God, and found expression in the number twenty-four. This number therefore indicates that the "watchers" in God's government revealed by John performed their tasks as perfect witnesses (for him who neither slumbers nor sleeps). Since twenty-four was universally regarded as the number of perfect watchfulness, it was taken as a sign of true perfection and a circle soon became the symbol of that truth. That is why all ancient people thought the world itself was round and surrounded by a great bubble of air which floated in the waters of the universe, where the great God An ("the Ancient of Days" and "the Father of all Lights") was said to rule.

As a second witness of this truth, the twelve constellations in the night sky over them took approximately three hundred and sixty-five days to move around "the one true shepherd star". But because that number couldn't be divided evenly by twelve, these wise people living in the past believed the world was somehow out of harmony with God, and so they made the measurement of every circle 360 degrees: a scheme of measurement which we still use today. There were three imperfect numbers though: three and a half, five, and six. These were half of seven, half of ten and half of twelve. Yet when the number seven frequently was separated into four and three, four was used to stress the universal application of the prophecy while three affirmed its certainty. There is of course much more that I could say regarding this important field of symbolism used in many Bible texts, but to do so would require much space and would only lead us far afield from what we are examining.

It is the number 24 (which is 6 x 4) which tells us that the men and women in God's council are representatives of all mankind (as the number "6", which is Man's number, clearly shows), and the number four "4" (which stands for all directions of the compass) quietly affirms they come from every place on earth. That's the reason why the cross became the symbol of all Priest-Kings who acted as the head of super states. The four extended arms upon the cross affirmed the right of each anointed King of Kings to govern all the earth. Branching outward from a common centre visually affirmed the ruler's right to rule the circle of the world in heaven's name. His royal influence stretched out (like rays of sunlight) into every portion of the world. Even French Kings of a later time, who took upon themselves the name of "Roi" (or "Re" which meant the "Sun"), built their royal city like a cross to indicate their right to rule the world.

This number "twenty-four", which also can be broken into 12 + 12, tells us that these individuals are the watchmen or "the watchers" who keep a perfect vigil over all creation night and day. And then, because the sea in front of them is calm and crystal clear, the role that these kings play as "watchers" is carefully defined for us. It is the calling of these elders (kings and queens) to keep the sea of mankind's formerly destructive and turbulent world system free from violence, and clear from all deception and dishonesty. They are those entrusted with the elements of life (water, land and air) and protect these from pollution and abuse.

In Chapter Seventeen of Matthew's Gospel we read that Jesus took three of his disciples (Peter, James and John) into a high mountain. This was equivalent of inviting them to join him in the government of heaven. Like John, he opened heaven's door to them and made them witnesses to what is commonly referred to as "the transfiguration". Matthew tells us that the face of Jesus "shone like the sun, and his clothes became white as light." Most Christians are familiar with this passage and generally agree it was a foreview of Jesus's return in glory. However I suspect that it was even something more than that. It represented Jesus's induction by "angels" into the role of Priest-King in God's government.

Like that transfiguration though, the twenty-four elders depicted in John's vision also are inducted into governmental roles, and at the same time they are a strong projected image of the future Parliament of God to be established upon earth. This is the government that shall one day rule the world when the plan which Jesus gave his workmen is achieved. These rulers being shown to us in heaven represent a strong command from God, which communicates the will of God to all of those who understand the scene. The "stephanoi" they wear, like the headplate worn by Israel's High Priest, marked a human mind anointed and conversant with the mind of God. In other words these elders had been sealed like living letters after God had placed his signature on them.

What is most notable about this government (which John calls heaven) is the manner in which it rules the world, and combines the powers of deity with the powers of human rulership. The seat of ultimate authority is God, who is unseen, but is perceived and speaks to all mankind through the powerful voices of creation. The men and women who sit in his royal court are those tried and tested workmen serving God. For this is the court which no one possibly can enter unless he understands the principles by which he is to rule. Psalm Twenty-four addresses this important question when it says: "Who may ascend to the hill (that is the government) of Jehovah?" and the writer answers this by saying: "He who has clean hands (unstained by innocent blood) and a pure heart; and does not take my name in vain or swear deceitfully."

It is Job though (in a book named after him) who admirably describes the duties of a theocratic government official when he says: "When I went to the gate of the city and took my seat in the public square, the young men saw me and stepped aside and the old men rose to their feet; the chief men refrained from speaking and covered their mouths with their hands; the voices of the nobles were hushed, and their tongues stuck to the roof of their mouths...because I rescued the poor who cried for help, and the fatherless who had no one to assist him. The man who was dying blessed me; I made the hearts of widows sing. I put on righteousness as my clothing; justice was my robe and turban. I was eyes to the blind and feet to the lame. I was a father to the needy; I took up the case of the alien. I broke the fangs of the wicked and snatched the victims from their teeth." (Job 29: 7-17)

God has called such men "Elohim" because they are a most essential part of government, and sit on thrones before his throne. That is why it is written in the Psalms: "God stands (to open the proceedings) in the assembly of the Elohim and in the midst of other judges, pronounces judgments." (Psalm 82: 1) And he also says directly to everyone whom he has sanctified to sit with him upon his holy hill as members of his government: "I have told you, you are Elohim, and the sons of the most high."
(Psalm 82: 6)

Elsewhere in the Psalms we read: "What is man that you should be concerned with him or the son of man (i.e. 'the common man') that you should even care for him?" Then he defines the place of all men and women in the world as being "just a little lower than 'the Elohim' (all those in the government of God)". This word "Elohim", which refers to this council of divinely chosen rulers is variously rendered as "God", "gods", or "angels" by translators of the scriptures, even when the word is used in reference to those human councilors who sit in council with Jehovah upon his "holy hill" (that is to say as part of the government of heaven ruling in God's name).

This brings us to the question then, "What are angels?" It is a question which needs to be asked for it is apparent that men and women in very early times did not think of angels in the same way that we do today. There was frequent reference to and communication with these beings throughout scriptural accounts. The cherubim (or keruvim) guarded the gates (or doorways) of spiritual access to God, and they guarded the way to the tree of life with flaming swords (God's chosen vessel then required a body guard). Yet they also carried the throne of God (at the speed of light) to every place on earth in much the same way that certain of the Levite priests had done in Moses's own time when they had carried God's tabernacle through the wilderness.

The seraphim on the other hand gave continual praise to the creator of the world, and revealed Jehovah's will to everyone who understood the way of life. Angels, therefore, were beings men and women were familiar with. Who were they then? or what were they? Jacob, in a dream, envisioned angels as having access both to God and to mankind (as they ascended and descended the great stairway of the ziggurat, which he imagined in a dream at Bethel).

The practices of the ancient Essenes, as they are described by Flavius Josephus in Book II Chapter 8 of *The Wars of Jehovah*, bear a striking resemblance to the School of Prophets founded by Samuel, the last great judge of Israel, and I suspect that the Essenes may have looked upon themselves as a continuing community of them. Josephus says that they kept alive the names of angels. It is a fleeting comment, but a very revealing one, for it can only mean one thing: that all who belonged to this group were named after angels and carried with them the spirit of the names they bore. That is to say that they perpetuated names like Michael and Gabriel and no doubt well known patriarchs as well, like Abraham, Isaac, Jacob, Joseph and Moses, or names of Hebrew prophets like Elijah, or priests like Zadoc.

These men then looked upon themselves as angels of God, but they did not think of angels in the same way that you think of angels now. They simply saw themselves as being set apart, reserved to do and speak the will of God. They therefore saw it as their duty to descend the holy hill of God whenever there was any special message to convey from God regarding situations in the world. I do not think that I exaggerate at all or overstress the point because the practice that Josephus named is clear. This so-called "sect" (of the Essenes) knew that they were angels because they read it in the Psalms, and they knew that they were following the practices the prophets of the past had followed ever since the time that Samuel established them. They therefore saw it as their duty (as a part of God's elected angel government) to warn and caution the people of God and bring messages to them from God which heartened and encouraged them.

After all that word "angel" simply means "messenger of God". Therefore "angels" were no more than "ambassadors" of God who directly spoke the word of God (not changing it in any way). We are told in scriptures that three men came to Abraham as he was sitting near his tent. Elsewhere we are told that they were angels. Angels therefore (in certain instances) were men. The two angels whom Lot brought into his house were also spoken of as men. Yet Moses came into contact with the "angel of Jehovah" who spoke to him from the curious phenomenon of a burning gas plant which was not consumed by the flames engulfing it. An angel then can also be a strong communicating spirit speaking from any natural phenomenon which reveals a meaning that is deemed to be significant. The stars of heaven therefore were angels and so was every strong traumatic moment experienced by anyone.

God then speaks directly to mankind either through the natural forces of creation (See Psalm 8 or Romans 1: 20) or through those men and women he has sanctified (John 10: 35-36). The scriptures therefore show us that angels are not disembodied souls. Rather they are spirits which we find revealed (1) in men and women God

selects to speak his word. (2) in those communities which
carry out a special plan which God through scriptures
has revealed to them, (3) in thoughtful visions which
some might picture emanating from all natural
phenomena and (4) in dreams God's word inspires in
those who keep its treasures stored up in their hearts.

Prophets were angels and so were all the members of
Israel's high parliament. Those apostles Jesus trained and
sent into the world after he commissioned them were
angels of his government. As Jesus told Nathaniel,
"Hereafter you shall see heaven opened, and the angels
of God coming and going to and from the Son of man."
(John 1: 50) So when Jesus's apostle John tells us in a
letter that we must test all spirits that we meet, he is
not speaking any pious platitude or superstitious
bugaboo. (I John 4: 1) He is telling us directly that we
must never let ourselves be fooled by pious charlatans or
any superstitious notions we might entertain. And even
Paul, the most mundane and blunt of all the scriptural
writers flatly warns his readers, saying: "Don't let
yourself be tricked out of your reward by anyone
pretending to be pious or claiming to have spoken with
angels. Such a person will tell you in great detail about
the things that he has seen, and his unscriptural mind
will be full of worthless notions." (Colossians 2: 18-19)

It is the nature of the task itself which the angel asks
us to perform, and the spirit in which it is to be
performed which identifies the origin of the messenger
and the message he conveys. Piety and lofty words are
not enough. The scriptures never ask God's people to
rely on supernatural phenomena as crutches for the lame
to lean upon. It is the task itself (which lies behind the
symbols) we must examine carefully to see if it has been
endorsed by God and bears his seal. Yet when I hear the
fiery rhetoric of war inflaming all the populace with

"Outrage" and "Righteous Indignation", I have to ask myself what manner of spirit they promote. Are the men and women leading us to war (who call all those that we are asked to hate "mad dogs", "rats caught in a hole", "monkeys without tails" or any other such demeaning epithet) angels of God or Demons.

In Chapter Nine of the gospel of Luke we read that Jesus's own disciples were angrily indignant after being refused entry into a Samaritan village. James and John (who were called "the sons of thunder") wanted Jesus to "call down fire from heaven ('holy war') and consume them, even as Elias did." Then, according to the King James text, Jesus "turned and rebuked them, and said, Ye know not what manner of spirit ye are of." God's people had been called on to assuage the wrath of mankind, not incite it.

The scriptures offer us many examples of how we are to speak to keep the waters calm. The book of *Proverbs* gives us this advice: "A soft answer turneth away wrath: but grievous words stir up anger" (Proverbs 15: 1). Yet how many world statesmen do you know who follow that advice. The book called *Judges* gives us two contrasting instances which illustrate those words for us. In Chapter Eight of that book we read: "And the men of Ephraim said unto (Gideon), why hast thou served us thus, that thou calledst us not, when thou wentest to fight with the Midianites? And they did chide with him sharply. And he said unto them, What have I done in comparison to you? Is not the gleaning of the grapes of Ephraim better than the vintage of Abiezer? God hath delivered into your hands the princes of Midian, Oreb and Zeeb: and what was I able to do in comparison to you? Then their anger was abated toward him, when he said that."

(Judges 8: 1-3)

A similar scene to this is found in Chapter Twelve of that same book, but the outcome is quite different. It is no accident that both these incidents have been presented to the reader as they have. So we read: "And the men of Ephraim gathered themselves together, and went northward, and said unto Jephthah, Wherefore passedst thou over to fight against the children of Ammon, and didst not call us to go with thee? We will burn thine house and thee with fire.

"And Jephthah said, I and my people were at great strife with the children of Ammon; and when I called you, ye delivered me not out of their hands. And when I saw that ye delivered me not, I put my life in my hands, and passed over against the children of Ammon, and the Lord delivered them into my hand: wherefore then are ye come up unto me this day, to fight against me? Then Jephthah gathered together all the men of Gilead, and fought with Ephraim: and the men of Gilead smote Ephraim, because they said, Ye Gileadites are fugitives of Ephraim among the Ephraimites. ...and there fell at that time of the Ephraimites forty and two thousand."

                                        (Judges 12: 1- 6)

Clearly then it was a different sort of angel in each of these two cases which addressed the Ephraimites. In the first case it was God who answered them, and in the second case it was simply peevish human pride.

Some may wonder, though, why I have called these creatures standing close beside the throne of God the "seraphim", for physically they do resemble those Ezekiel in another vision had called the "cherubim". Jewish tradition frequently depicts these "supernatural creatures" in a variety of ways. We read, for instance, that the Cherubim (or Keruvim) which were upon the Ark of God were "manlike from the head to the shoulders, and from the shoulders downward...shaped like birds." (Rabbi Avraham ben Ha Ramadam). Elsewhere in the Talmud we are told that one of the Keruvim had the features of a male, while the other had the features of a female.

(Yoma 54a)

Even so, it is not the physical depictions of these angels, nor where they stand which tells us what they are. It is the function that they serve. A man might be a trumpeter or a taxi driver. He might be even both. But he does one job at a time. The Bible clearly has defined the functions of the cherubim as "creatures" who transport the throne of God at lightning speed to any place on earth. It isn't difficult to find scriptures which define the services that they perform. Two examples of these are 2 Samuel 22: 11; and Psalm 18: 10. The cherubim are also called upon to guard the throne of God and keep it free from man's defiling willfulness. That is why we find the cherubim in the Garden of Eden guarding the way to the tree of life (Genesis 3: 24).

The occupation of the seraphim, however, is to celebrate and praise Jehovah's holiness and power. They also give a voice to God. For it is through these creatures that God communicates with man (Isaiah 6: 2). They also are engaged in commissioning God's servants for any special task (Isaiah 6: 6-7). This is what "the living creatures" in John's vision do. The passage in John's text which describes these four living creatures with six wings who never stop saying Holy, holy, holy, would be quite ludicrous if we were to take it literally. What could be more tedious than lip service of this kind. But symbolically, the scene which John describes carries in it the potential of a powerful meaning. For all creation by its very being glorifies the great creator of the heavens and the earth. As I said earlier, Nature can and does communicate with man.

One poet even wrote:

> "And this our life, exempt from public haunt,
> Finds tongues in trees, books in running brooks,
> Sermons in stones, and good in everything.
> (Shakespeare: *As You Like It*. Act II. Scene 1)

That is not pantheism. John is not telling anyone to worship such things. Rather he is showing his readers that all living creatures constantly praise God. The Scriptures even tell us that God reveals himself through everything that he has made. And the four areas of creation through which he speaks are seraphim giving constant praise to him. Those spirits guarding God's creation (with the flaming word of God) are known as Keruvim. It is they who guard the throne of God, and carry in their persons (everywhere they go) the Shekinah or Presence of God. As Jesus (whom all Christians have been asked to emulate) once said, "I am in the Father and the Father is in me." So like angels in God's garden, which guard the tree of life, those who walk with God are guardians of the Shekinah and keep it safe from all defiling hands. Yet like the tree of life itself they bear good fruit for all who honour God and wish to eat.

Now there are three great visions of God given in the scriptures. We find the first one in the sixth chapter of *Isaiah*, when the Jewish prophet, while standing in the Temple of God, saw Jehovah sitting on his throne, high and lifted up as the train of his robe filled the Temple. The second vision is found in the words of the Jewish prophet, Ezekiel, in Chapters One and Ten of the book which bears his name. In the pages of that book the prophet shows us that Ezekiel (while standing by the canals of Babylon) saw Jehovah's royal chariot propelled by wheels that moved it at the speed of light to any place on earth or in the universe. The third great vision though is that one we are reading now in the *Book of Revelation*, which depicts Jehovah seated on the throne of heaven, with the whole ingenious scheme of heaven's government surrounding him.

Now none of these three visions was revealed just to dazzle and amaze an awe-struck audience. All three of them were written solely for the purpose of visually defining what each prophet had to say. For every vision underlines a special truth and makes each prophet's message memorable and clear "to everyone who has the eyes to see and ears to hear." It serves no purpose just to stand in awe of what we read, and worshipfully adore the sacred images which we discover in the Scriptures. For God is not an image anyone can see. The only thing we are concerned with here, is what the message of Jehovah really was and how that image in the vision helped communicate and clarify the prophet's words. What great commandment did the vision serve to underline? and how did it encourage everyone to whom the message was revealed?

The first of these three visions was written at a time when the glory that had once been Israel had waned. Israel was divided into broken and conflicting lands: Israel and Judah. The golden age for both of them was gone, and as far as anyone could see, there was no future left at all for either one of them. Judah's day was done, for Judea, like any other nation in the world, was about to fall and there simply was no vigour left in her.

And yet Isaiah, while praying in God's Temple at Jerusalem, envisioned clearly what he knew undoubtedly would strengthen and encourage everyone who still was faithful to the God of Abraham. So he described God's throne as he envisioned it in all its splendour, and the overwhelming picture of the spirit governing creation seated firmly in their midst. God was with his people, he maintained. And even at this crucial moment in their history, the righteous God of justice still could rescue them from any peril which endangered them. That is to say that God (who was the fount of life itself) could "save his people" if they only would rely on him and call upon his name. God was in their midst. And the vision that the prophet had perceived, revealed the meaning of that truth and underlined its full significance.

Isaiah therefore went to see that very foolish king called Ahaz (736-716 BC), and the message that he gave him was, "You have nothing to fear from any of your enemies, if you rely upon Jehovah — God is with us." Then as a sign he said: "A virgin shall conceive and bear a son, and shall call his name Immanuel — God with us." God's presence in the land of Judah would be verified to Ahaz through someone that the temple priests would bring to him.

Ahaz couldn't fail to understand the meaning of those words, for the virgin that Isaiah spoke of must have been apparent to all Kings living in a world of Kings, most of whom claimed virgin birth in Ishtar's temple womb. To Ahaz though, it should have meant that, in a short while, he would be asked to choose an heir to follow him upon the throne. The Temple Priests who tutored Kings would bring a worthy candidate to him who would ensure his throne's continuance in years to come. This was certainly a sign the King could understand. And yet the virgin bride of God was Israel itself, as other scriptures have maintained, and so Isaiah's words did hold a deeper spiritual meaning in them that later prophets would enlarge upon. For the True and Faithful spiritual core (which was in the midst of Judah) would eventually give birth to one whose hand could bring deliverance and reunite the now divided lands of Israel.

And yet whatever merits or demerits you might attribute to this argument, my whole point here is just to say, that the vision which Isaiah saw was given simply to affirm that God had never left his people in the past or at any time. God was always in their midst. He was with them then, and would remain with them as long as they remained with him and humbly called upon his name. The vision that Isaiah saw was powerful: "God was with his people (the righteous Jews of former Israel) and would fight for them." Even though the Ark of God apparently was gone, God was still a strong and stable presence in their midst.

Centuries later though, both John the Baptist and Jesus of Nazareth continued to proclaim that same prophetic truth: "The Kingdom of God is at hand," (another way of saying, "God is with us," or "The Kingdom of God is in your midst," or "the Kingdom of God is within you".) Even the gospel writer Matthew (from the tribe of Eli) recognized the powerful meaning that Isaiah's words possessed. First spoken at a time when Judah's social atmosphere was darkened by the arrogant intimidation of her enemies, Isaiah's words encouraged Judah, and her people had survived. And the promise of that ancient prophecy was just as true as when Isaiah first had uttered it: "God is with us," and he has given us a sign to verify his words. That promise in the past had made them strong, and it could strengthen them again because a heaven tutored King had risen in their midst who was to lead and govern them and overcome the armies of their enemies. That is to say the King whom God had sent would save them.

According to the ancient prophet's words, repeated now by Matthew, God would once again supply an heir to take the throne of Judah's theocratic government and bring salvation to his people in the midst of all her enemies. He would offer them a king to which all nations in the world would turn and ask for guidance. That was the purpose Matthew had in mind when he restated what the Jewish prophet said: "Behold a virgin shall conceive and bear a son, and she shall call his name Emmanuel — 'God is with us.'" "God is with us" was Isaiah's theme. By saying this he was telling Judah that the Israel of God would be restored, if there was still a virgin remnant of the people who believed the unpolluted word of God. As it is written in Isaiah's words: "Do you believe that I would bring (my people) to the point of birth, then not allow her to bring forth?...Shall I who am the cause of birth seal up the womb of Israel?"   (Isaiah 66: 9)

Like the tree of life in the garden of the world, Israel was called upon to bear good fruit from which all nations of the world could eat and find abundant blessing and enlightenment. That hope is wonderfully expressed in the blessing Jacob gave the son he chose to be his heir, namely Joseph. His fruitful branch would reach beyond the vineyard's wall where Judah had so carefully confined his animals so that they would not stray from it.

The second vision, too, is worth examining for it extends the meaning of the vision which Isaiah saw. Isaiah showed the throne of God securely anchored in the Temple at Jerusalem, while Ezekiel radically depicts it on a mighty chariot moving at the speed of light to any place on earth or in the universe. He tells us that it is propelled by wheels of living creatures with the spirit of their God in them. These wheels are full of eyes, and move the throne of God with their intelligence. That is not a fantasy; it is a blueprint man is called upon to recognize as the Tabernacle that God's people carry with them in their hearts. For God's Tabernacle is the heart of man after it is filled with the wisdom of God's enduring word. That is why even the Jewish writer John (a disciple of Jesus of Nazareth) began his gospel with the words: "In the beginning was the word, and the word was with God, and the word was God."

What Ezekiel saw was a ground plan for constructing an impressive chariot for God to ride upon. It was a plan especially designed for uniting all the scattered tribes of Israel. All Jews of the Dispersion had the makings of a powerful craft within themselves. They only had to recognize the power that God had put into their hands. This vision told them God was with his people anywhere on earth that they might be. Ezekiel (by this vision) called upon God's people to renew themselves in God's unchanging word and call upon his name. For God was with his people anywhere and everywhere that they might be. "If I say to this sycamore tree (the Temple where God lives) be uprooted and planted in the midst of the sea (the turbulent world system of mankind) it would be done even though your faith should be no larger than a grain of mustard seed."   (Luke 17: 6)

God's mighty chariot was Israel itself and in this vision, Ezekiel has shown the Jews that they can move God's throne to any place (on earth or in the universe) that they might choose to be. Upon the power of prayer alone, God's chariot would move. Men and women only had to recognize God's presence in their midst and he would strengthen them. Though Jews were spread out now throughout the world, the word of God united them. "Hear oh Israel, the Lord your God is one." However scattered upon earth they had become, God's people still possessed within themselves the power to influence mankind, point them to the way of peace, or shake the pillars of the world and bring the social order down. "God is with us," Isaiah once had said. Ezekiel simply added "wherever we might be." And yet what powerful meanings were contained in those few words.

Now Jesus's apostle John, in the vision he describes, substantially extends those first two visions we were shown. He uses jewels so that we can see the nature of the God he calls on us to serve, and that description provides this government with a working constitution everyone can understand. By drawing our attention to specific qualities in God, John defines the fundamental principles on which God's government is built. All their actions must be righteous, just and merciful. Even so, this third trait I've called "Mercy" means much more than that. It stands for "Grace" for it is represented by a "rainbow" (like an emerald). As many scholars note, the stones upon the breastplate of Israel's High Priest when taken together, made up the colours of the rainbow. So by showing us a rainbow, John blends many traits of Godly character into an aura of infinite mercy surrounding every act of God.

Taken individually, however, each of the twelve precious stones making up the rainbow represents a special quality of character. These stones were the ruby, the topaz, the beryl, the turquoise, the sapphire, the emerald, the jacinth, the agate, the amethyst, the chrysolite, the onyx and the jasper. Throughout the scriptures, we are told in many different ways what God is like: God is holy, God is just, God is merciful, God is patient, God is wise, God is provident. He is watchful and upholds the weak, God is incorruptible, God is far-seeing, God is loving. He is fair and righteous in all his dealings. Search the scriptures and you will find them all. There are many more such traits I have not named, but like the colours of the spectrum they blend in colouring.

The reason we are told of them is not to flatter any being's vanity. They are there to show us who it is we represent so that we may proudly share that character, and reflect the qualities that we are shown. Without godly character no one possibly can carry out the work which God assigns. Those serving in his government are called on to be wise, just and merciful. John's simple illustration shows what God requires from all those serving him.

These jewels from the breastplate of Israel's High Priest help us to appreciate how beautiful and valuable those virtues are. In very early times of Israel's history, the High Priest was the one essential link between God (who sat upon the throne) and all the sons of Israel. From that High Priest, adorned with godly traits, Israel visually perceived God's character and imbibed the traits revealed to them. For this reason Christians look to Jesus Christ who (as their High Priest) links them to the character of God "from whose fullness we all receive our various gifts and blessings one after another."   (John 1: 16)

These were traits God's people were to carry with them everywhere they went, and the voices of creation (by glorifying God) serve to make his will and purpose known. The chosen rulers of the world, who sit before God's throne (wearing golden victors' crowns) reveal themselves as being wise. Having triumphed over life's adversities, they are able to perform their role as "watchers" of creation, and remove dishonesty, deceit, and malice from the turbulent world system and calm the troubled waters of mankind.

A difficult objective really! Especially for well-meaning souls who lack experience in life's adversities. Yet future chapters will reveal the recommended plan that Jesus gives to those who wish to follow him. But this is only given to those members seated in his government and to the seven strong united churches of the world. This government of God (though real) is only plainly seen by those who are a part of it. As Jesus said, "Except a man be born from above he cannot see the Kingdom of Heaven." Yet John has opened many eyes of those to whom it was invisible. In doing this he also shows it as a plan for building and measuring any government of man. It is therefore something like the blueprint of a house that we are asked to build. We see the plan, and step by step begin to build what we have seen until it can be seen by everyone.

In some measure Paul's words seem appropriate to mention in regard to this, for he realised his own inadequacy in undertaking a work of such great magnitude. He said: "Even though I am the least of all God's people, God gave me the privilege of bringing Jesus Christ's good news to the Gentile world, so that I could clearly show them how the secret plan of God was to be put into effect. For God who created all things chose to keep this plan hidden from the world until the time was ripe for it. Now that the time has come, by means of the church he will make known (to all authorities and rulers who govern spiritually) the great wisdom of the heavenly realm. For Jesus Christ our lord has made it possible through faith in him to come before the throne of God with freedom and with confidence." (Ephesians 3: 8-12)

That is precisely what John has done, and through his eyes we see the vision he has seen. By showing us the end to be achieved at this point, rather than the beginning, the aims have been defined for us. To do this makes good sense. For as it is written in *Isaiah*: "I am God and there in none like me (amongst gods or men). I make known the end from the beginning, from ancient times, what is still to come. I say: 'My purpose will stand, and I shall accomplish all that I set out to do.'"   (Isaiah 46: 10)

A project that does not clearly define its aims for all to understand is one that usually degenerates into fruitless arguments and anarchy. George Bernard Shaw, the waggish Irish playwright, once defined a fanatic as "someone who has lost sight of his aims and doubles his efforts." Christianity has an aim. It still has not accomplished it. Could it be they have forgotten what it was? To remind all Christians of the reason they were called, God proclaims the end for us at the beginning so that we will not lose sight of it and waste our energies in petty quarrels and arguments.

Jesus himself addresses the matter in these words: "Suppose a man should choose to build a tower. Does he not sit down at first to estimate the cost to see if he has the money for completing it? For after the foundation is put down, if he should lack the means of finishing his work, others looking on will ridicule him cruelly, saying, 'This man started out to build a tower but could not finish it.'

"Or imagine that a King should choose to go to war against another King. Will he not take the time first to consider if he has the means with ten thousand men to overthrow the one whose army has twenty thousand men in it? If he is not able to do that, he would be shamefully obliged to send a delegation out while the other one is yet a long way off from him and negotiate for peace. (But I will not make peace with Satan and his world.) So if any one of you wish to follow me, he must be prepared to lose everything he has."   (Luke 14: 28-33)

In yet another place he told his disciples: "If any man wishes to follow me, he must deny himself and take up

his cross and follow me." (Matthew 16: 24) He must be
willing to lose everything he has including his own life. It
wasn't just the rich young ruler that he told, "you must
give up everything you have." This is a very serious
situation. Do Christians realise what they have gotten
themselves into? Jesus expects something of them,
especially for the final push of this great task he has
assigned to all who wish to follow him. Like Gideon, he
is deliberately thinning out his army. So Jesus in effect is
telling us through the vision he has shown to John, "Here
is the task. This is the goal that we must strive to reach.
Now listen to the method I put forward for achieving it."

CHAPTER FIVE

The Great Designer and the Builder

All at once I noticed a scroll in the right hand of him who sat upon the throne. It had writing inside it, but it was sealed on the back with seven seals. Then a powerful angel crying out with a loud voice, asked: "Who is able to break the seals and open the scroll?" But there was no one to be found anywhere in heaven or on earth or even under the earth (i.e. not among the living or the dead) who was able to open the scroll or look inside it. So I wept bitterly because no one anywhere was capable of opening or reading the scroll nor even of looking at it. But one of the elders assured me, saying, "Don't worry! For notice that the Lion of the tribe of Judah (that is to say the strength of Judah's Kings), the Root of David, has prevailed. He has the power to break the seven seals and open the scroll."

Then, I noticed that before the throne which was encircled by the four living creatures and surrounded by the twenty-four elders, there stood a lamb directly in front of it. The lamb looked as if it had been slain. and it had seven horns and seven eyes upon it, which are the seven spirits of God. These (correspond to the spirits of community governing the seven perfected congregations in the world for they) represent him throughout the earth.

Stepping forward, the lamb took the scroll from the right hand of him that sat upon the throne. But when he took the scroll, the four creatures and the twenty-four elders immediately bowed down before the lamb in reverence, each one holding a harp in his hand (indicating he was free and under obligation to no one other than God) and a vessel made of gold (a wise heart) full of incense — which are the prayers of God's people. (For the lamb was responding to the prayers of everyone who respected the creation God had made).

Then they all began singing a new song: "You have the right to take the scroll and open its seals, because you were slain, and with your blood you purchased men and women out of every nation, language and race and you have established them as a kingdom of priests to rule in God's name on the earth. Then, even as I watched and listened, many angels gathered around the throne along with the living creatures and elders. Together, they numbered myriads upon myriads and thousands upon thousands (of myriads), and they sang with a lusty voice: "The lamb that was slain is worthy of power and riches, wisdom, strength, honour, glory and praise."

After that, I heard every creature in heaven (the government) and on earth (the governed masses) and under the earth (the dead) and on the sea (men of commerce and trade), singing together: "All praise, honour, glory and power belong to him that sits upon the throne (Jehovah) and to the lamb (the anointed Priest-King) for ever and ever." At these words, the four living creatures shouted their enthusiastic assent and the elders all bowed down worshipping.

*

In Chapters Two and Three of *Revelation*, we were shown the means by which all members in the different church communities throughout the world were trained for entering the heaven John describes. He showed us this same doorway that we enter now with John, existing in the Church at Philadelphia (a city church completely unified). The members of all churches therefore (if they are obedient to all of those commands which are implied) have now been fully trained for entering God's government with Christ.

This entrance into heaven is based upon the festival of *Pentecost*, when Moses brought God's law down from the mountain in the Sinai wilderness (that womb where Israel was born). In John's vision, the mountain is revealed to be the place of God's government, and it is here that John is made a witness to the revelation of Jesus's strategic plan to liberate mankind from war and violence so that the sea of world affairs will be calm and clear. The first celebration of this day (which Moses later formalized for Israel) was indicated when Adam and his wife were brought into the Garden of Eden, where two trees grew. By choosing the way of the forbidden fruit, Adam and his wife brought God's curse upon the world. It should be stated, though, there was a law of God built into his creation—a law which could both bless or curse mankind according to whatever path they chose. Cause and effect is what we call this process now.

The power of God's law was revealed to the world through Adam. Although it brought adversity, Adam was forewarned of it. But still he chose (on behalf of all the people that he governed) to pursue a way of life not in harmony with God. Moses on the day of *Pentecost*—having climbed Mount Sinai—brought the ten commandments down, engraved on stone. In such a fashion, Jesus also climbed a mountain in the land of Israel where he taught his followers, in "the sermon on the mount", those principles to live by in order to find harmony with God. Now John, in this same fashion, by the spirit of inspiration, is present in heaven and is able to describe the goal of heaven before he starts unveiling the plan for reaching it. That plan lies hidden in the scroll that God holds in his hand, and no one but the lamb of God can take it from his hand. And no one but the lamb of God can open it.

Pentecost therefore is shown to be a time of revelation. It does not come before God's servants have been properly instructed and prepared for governing. Eden revealed the curse of God upon the world because Adam showed himself to be unfit for governing the creation God had placed into his hands. Moses, by giving Israel the law, revealed the power of God to either bless or curse the people according to whatever path they chose. If they obeyed God's law, then they were blessed; if they dishonoured it, then they were cursed. So it was, that throughout Hebrew history, Israel sometimes thrived and sometimes failed. Still, Jehovah's virgin bride, was always present in their midst, and she was destined to give birth to someone who in God's name would establish a better covenant between them and their creator.

Now in the vision John has given us, we are led by John into heaven on the day of *Pentecost*. There the lamb of God reveals a plan which can restore the world of God to one of peace and harmony with all the innate laws which govern it.

I am certain that I am not the only person in the world to have noticed the strong visual similarity which exists between the passage in the *Book of Revelation* which reads, "I saw the lamb...standing before the throne of God encircled by the four living creatures and the elders", and the one in the book called *Job* which says, "One day the sons of Elohim came before the throne of Jehovah, and Satan was among them." There is a great difference though in the text which follows each of these two passages. In one "the lamb" takes a scroll from the hand of him who sits upon the throne in order to reveal the instructions of God to all mankind. In the other Satan shows himself to be arrogantly contemptuous of God's judgments and accuses those who appear righteous before God, of cupidity. Maybe you have wondered, just as I have done, what the reason for this similarity and difference is.

This similarity which we encounter here can only be attributed to the fact that Jesus was the sole Priest-King in God's new government. As such he had access to the throne of God just as Satan did when he had been Priest-King of all the city states on earth. Since very ancient times, no one ever doubted that it was the King with the greatest military strength who automatically assumed the right to rule as King of Kings (the chief executive who set the tone and policies pursued) by all world governments. All Kings who ruled on earth were governed by his word, and paid him tribute, bowing down before his feet and kissing them. There is a picture to be found in many history books today which shows the King of Israel doing this. It shows him bowing low (a humbled man) before the great King of Assyria. Does that not make you think of Job who suffered under Satan for a while?

So the great Priest-King of every super power which ever ruled the world, was looked upon as having access to God's throne, and all the other major powers on earth depended upon him to reveal their future from "The Tables of Destiny" and set the international policy that they were called upon to follow. The words he read to them were said to be the words which the Elohim had given him to read. Satan then defines himself as the spirit of fallen man, which finds expression in the person of whatever King (or leader) governs all the nations in the world through social influence, economic strength and military power. For if lesser nations did not do obeisance to him, he would invade and humble them. All Kings therefore feared the King of Kings and feared his God.

That view is abundantly confirmed in many Bible passages such as the one Isaiah wrote as a rebuke to taunt the King of Babylon after his traumatic fall "from heaven" (an expression parallel to being expelled from the "Garden of God"): "Jehovah has broken the rod of the wicked, the septre of rulers which in anger struck down peoples with unceasing blows, and in fury subdued nations with military power and might.... Now you have fallen from heaven, O morning star (standing closest to the throne of God) son of the dawn!"

(Isaiah 14: 5 and 12)

Satan then is the anointing spirit of all Priest-Kings who rule as King of Kings and encourage international and domestic policies not in keeping with the way of the Elohim or his creation. While they may serve Elohim, these Kings (or leaders of super powers) use their cultural influence, economic strength and military might to humble weaker nations, and exploit them only to increase the glory of their own great super state. No one dared resist such Kings because they had it in their power to call down "fire from heaven" in the sight of all the people, to frighten and to humble them. That is to say that if it challenged other states in war, the Gods would aid the ruler of the super state.

The lamb, however, (who as the chief executive in God's new government and the representative of all mankind) had taken on himself the full responsibility for every crime committed in the world. His death and resurrection show that he has paid the price of every crime, and now is ready to initiate a plan to remedy the wrongs which Satan's world had caused. As representative of Man before the throne of God, and representative of God before the world, he seeks to heal the painful rift dividing God from Man.

No interpretation of any other image in the *Book of Revelation* has been so universally agreed upon by all denominations making up the Christian church than that which says the lamb which we encounter here in Chapter Five is none other than the resurrected Jesus Christ. Nor have I any wish to set myself against such a strong and confident assertion of Christian unanimity. Yet I would be remiss if I should fail to point out to my readers that if we were to interpret this same symbolic image of "the lamb with seven horns" in exactly the same spirit that we interpret other biblical descriptions of such animals with horns, we would be forced to say there is a deeper meaning hidden in these words.

All other beasts which we encounter in the scriptures are representative of united masses of people being led by leaders (who are depicted as the horns upon the beasts they govern). Would it be wrong then to assume that the lamb in this case is none other than the united "body of Christ" (the Christian Church)? and that the horns that lead it are the spirits of the seven churches which have unified the congregation of the church in each community? For Jesus Christ commissioned them to continue in his name, the work which he began. And he taught his followers, saying: "I tell you the truth, unless a kernel of wheat falls into the ground and dies, it remains only a single seed. But if it dies, it produces many seeds."
(John 14: 24)

Perhaps it should be pointed out as well that the seven horns upon the lamb give equal rule to each united body of the Christian church who are situated in cities everywhere throughout the world. Not one horn (or leader) on the lamb enjoys superiority over any of the other six, as they are all dependent only on the one High Priest (Jesus Christ) who we saw (in Chapter One) was present in the midst of all of them.

These seven congregations all have been commissioned individually by Jesus Christ himself. It was he who (in this very letter) promised he would give them full authority to speak and act on his behalf, the very moment they returned to "their first love", and overcame the differences dividing them. Only after they repented of their deviations from the truth, could heaven's door be opened in their midst and give them access to the throne of God. The fact they now are shown to be the horns upon the lamb, tells us they've accomplished this. "Be ye one even as I and the Father are one," was the basic need that Jesus stressed to those who followed him. So having now repented of those deviations from the truth which formerly had hampered them and made them the accomplices of Satan's world, the churches all are given access to the Ark of God in heaven as members of one body.

Yet the seven horns upon the lamb show us even more than this. What they indicate is the very nature of the enemy the lamb is called upon to fight: the seven-headed dragon from the pit of death, which the Canaanites once called Leviathan. This dreaded monster which brought waste and ruin to the world, often showed himself in many forms: drought and famine, darkness and death, warfare and destruction, and every other kind of world calamity. The Canaanites therefore often called upon their hero God, the mighty storm God Baal, to come and rescue them. But frequently their God went on a journey or fell asleep somewhere, and so they sent another God in search of him. The seven horns upon the lamb, however, represent the rods of royal authority the seven churches have received from Christ. It is they then who shall give the seven great commands which shall destroy the enemy of nature and mankind, and overcome the power of death itself.

We should remember though that seven is not a literal number. It is a symbolic one which stands for every Christian body in the world, who earnestly have cleansed themselves according to the pattern Jesus Christ has given them. Renewed, these churches (whose members have become the body of Christ) can speak now with his full authority because he has commissioned them to be his representatives on earth and has endowed them with his power (providing they have followed his commands and not altered or diluted them). Having eyes to see what has been done in heaven, they are asked to search the earth for opportunities to do the many things that he will now reveal. Any revelation coming after this (which presumes to take another course from that which John has given) has by the words of Jesus Christ himself been rendered void. For there is but one plan to follow, not two, or three or four or five. Not even 25,000.

In this chapter we are told that a "new" song was sung. This is just another way of saying that because the scroll could now be opened, that there was a new and greater reason to praise God. As every Jew and Christian knows, Psalms are songs of praise. In Psalm 96, for instance, we read: "Sing to Jehovah a new song;...sing praises to his name; proclaim his salvation day by day. Declare his glory among the nations because of the marvelous things that he has done for his people." The "old" song is that same song that the nations of the world have been singing ever since the day that Adam (by his disobedience to God) first taught them all to sing. So there is a greater reason now for praising God. Underneath the seven seals there is a plan which is designed to rescue and preserve all life on earth from the abusive hand of those who are corrupting and destroying it.

There always is a reason why the prophets show us what they do. We are shown this government of God because it is a gauge by which to measure other governments we are acquainted with. Such a standard helps us understand their strengths and weaknesses.

Therefore I shall take a moment to compare the government of God with other governments we know, so that you might thoughfully consider how they resemble and yet differ from the standard John has given us. Sir Winston Churchill, the foremost British statesman of the twentieth century, once said that the farther we look back in time is how far that we can see into the future. So maybe we should take his word for this and begin our study by examining the Constitution of the Anunnaki Council which governed ancient Sumer, the world's first civilized society.

The Anunnaki councillors were representatives from every area of life ruled by the Gods. The great God An (or Anu), as far as we can tell, first chaired the meetings of this government. Later though, El il became the Most High God and sometimes was advised by An (who was regarded as the Ancient of Days and the Father of all Lights). One of the primary functions of this Anunnaki Council was to appoint Kings to rule all the different city states and maintain peace amongst them. Another was to act as a court of justice for the world. Questions of concern were openly debated in their midst and voted on. If unanimous agreement was reached the councillors would all cry out "Haem" (So be it). Yet if agreement wasn't found, the voice of Sumer's Most High God would intervene as the deciding voice to be obeyed. Yet El il's voice was that of Nippur's Sanga Lugal (whose spirit was passed on from age to age). The well known cry, "The King is dead, long live the King" no doubt originated here.

This Anunnaki government concerned itself with nature and its ways. Yet even though Sumerians acknowledged many Gods, they did not really "worship" them at all. Not in any modern sense at least. What the people and their leaders tried to do was simply understand and know their will, because (according to the consensus of opinion in that time) mankind had been created by these hidden powers of life so that they could be the servants of these deities and the elements sustaining them. The Gods of the Sumerians (which they called "Els" or "Ens" or "Nins" meaning "Powers" or "Lords" or "Governors") were actually real entities. When measured by whatever standard you might choose, these "Powerful Forces" represented all life-giving properties existing in such basic things as water, air, land and sunlight (which caused all things to be).

For reasons which we do not fully understand, ancient people living in Near Eastern lands frequently depicted wisdom as a serpent. Yet serpents (to their minds) were as varied in their character as the special wisdom that the different deities conveyed. Kings became wise (and therefore strong) through the special serpent learning they received in the temple school, which was regarded as the womb of the Mother Goddess Nin Khursag. (The virgin Goddess Of Love, Inanna, would later take her place).

Though spoken at a time much later than the reign of King Adapa, the words of the Assyrian King, Ashurbanipal, help in part to define the kind of learning that a King received. Almost face to face with us, he says: "The God of the scribes has bestowed on me the gift of knowledge of his art....From the art of the Master Adapa [Sumer's first human Priest-King] I acquired: the hidden treasure of all scribal knowledge, the signs of heaven and earth...and I have studied the heavens with the learned masters of oil divination; I have solved the laborious problems of division and multiplication, which were not clear; I have read the artistic script of Sumer and the obscure Akkadian, which is hard to master, taking pleasure in the reading of stones from before the flood [i.e. 'the Tablets of Destiny']....

"This is what was done of all my days: I mounted my steed, I rode joyfully, I went up to the hunting lodge. I held the bow, I let fly the arrow, the sign of my valour. I hurled heavy lances like a javelin. Holding the reins like a driver, I made the wheels go round. I learned to handle the aritu and the kababu shields like a heavy-armed bowman...At the same time I was learning royal decorum, walking in the kingly ways. I stood before the King, my begetter, giving commands to the nobles. Without my consent, no governor was appointed; no prefect was installed in my absence."

Such wisdom (and the strength derived from it) was symbolically depicted in the rod of authority a royal prince received the moment he became the King. The Sumerians tell us:

"Before Kingship descended from heaven
Septre, crown, headband and staff remained with
Anu in heaven....[During that time]
There was no counseling of the people;
then Kingship descended from heaven."

Nothing better illustrates the value that a King placed on this special kind of wisdom, than does the building of the vast library that Ashurbanipal established at Nineveh to house all the lore, knowledge and literature that mankind had committed to writing since "the beginning of the world." It was such writing which had made Adapa strong, and the Sumerians had this to say of it:

"[Adapa's] command was like the command of Anu.
With wide understanding En Ki [the earth God]
                                        had perfected
him to expound the decrees of the land.
Yet even though he gave him wisdom
he had not given him eternal life.

...Yet of this wise King, no one treated his command
lightly."

It certainly must be significant that Moses (at a later
time) held a rod which (as a serpent) swallowed up the
rods in Pharaoh's court. For the rod of Pharaoh's royal
authority did (on occasion) swallow up the strength and
wisdom of all weaker Kings. Few would dare to
challenge any King whose power was greater than his
own. Yet Moses did not hesitate to challenge Pharaoh
with the strength and (serpent) wisdom of his God.
Later on he used the rod (of that same learning) when he
fought against the Edomites.

We could easily interpret modern history in such
terms too. To speak symbolically, the rod of Joseph
Stalin swallowed up the powers of everyone inside the
Communist Government. Adolf Hitler standing in the
legislature of the Weimar Assembly swallowed up the
powers of all the members there. Any powers usurped
from other ministers in governments or from other
governmental bodies are not looked upon today as
serpents or as Gods, because we speak in different idioms.
But readers all the same should still appreciate the truth
revealed in ancient texts.

The constitution of the Sumerian state has been
described by Henri Frankfort (in his book called *Kingship
and the Gods*) as being "religious, democratic and
communist". I do not fully share his views because the
common man did not choose his government, although
he did choose to be obedient to it. Also judging from
the literature we read of them, these early leaders
apparently did care about the people that they ruled.
They debated many questions openly and tried to reach a
unanimity of views, and (as far as we can tell) they ruled
the people by persuasion rather than by force. How far

the Council's dictums were obeyed, depended on the different city states and the power of their King (or Ensi) to persuade the people serving under him.

We cannot overlook the fact that the Anunnaki system of government was unquestionably a polytheistic one. Yet it is difficult today to explain (to most of those who are emersed in monotheistic teachings and beliefs) the advantages and disadvantages of such a government. Polytheism acknowledged and respected the uniqueness of the qualities existing in all individual living plants and animals and the individuality of every living person in the world. Every person had a God communicating with all other Gods outside himself. In other words, the Sumerians were scientists, but unlike modern scientists they did not look on anything at all with what we today would call scientific detachment or with cool unfeeling eyes. They empathized with everything. The things that they examined spoke to them. So they respected all the Gods (or powers) which dwelt in them. And all of these were represented in the Anunnaki Council of the Gods through priests or priestesses who spoke on their behalf.

What unified this Council, though, was the centralizing God presiding over it. Its whole structure (of many Gods united by a single God) laid the basis for responsible government. Yet the purpose of the Council was not to serve the needs of man; its prime purpose was to serve and feed the Gods themselves. Sumerians therefore saw it as their calling to be responsible towards the "Lords of Life" which governed them. The revelations from the living world of which they were a part, defined the duties which the "Lords of Life" assigned to them. So taking care to see that they fulfilled their duties to the different Gods and Goddesses became the issues that the Council chose to speak of and debate upon.

The great Priest-King interpreting the voice of El-il
in the Anunnaki Council hall was apparently regarded as
being half-human and half-divine. Although divine, he
died each year in public ritual, and then was raised from
death by the semi-divine Inanna (the virgin sister of the
great King Gilgamesh) who secretly had stolen all the
powers of life and death from En Ki and Erishkigal (two
deities who ruled the upper and the lower regions of the
world). She therefore could defeat the grave and confer
continuing life upon her husband-son, "the faithful
servant" of the Gods, Dumuzi. Even when the reigning
King did die, Inanna through this same festival (of
mourning and rejoicing for the dead and resurrected
King) reestablished yet another King upon the throne in
one unbroken cycle. Doing this set the tone of long and
stable government. "The King is dead," the people
shouted lustily, "Long live the King."

The greatest disadvantage of this system though was
that the domicile of its chief God was always localized.
His home (located in a certain city state) became the
envy of other Kings, who no doubt felt their own
abilities were just as great, if not greater, than the man
who was the voice of Sumer's leading God. This made
the Sumerians prone to petty wars amongst themselves.
The entire uncivilized world as well, looking in on them
from outside areas, greatly envied Sumer for its stores of
grain and wealth, and this made standing armies a
necessity. The first great upset of Sumer's royal throne
occurred when Sargon, the royal cupbearer (and steward
of the vine) led a palace revolt in Kish and murdered its
shepherd King. Then he established a new state to the
north called Akkad, and eventually he humbled all of
Sumer and made it subservient to him.

Even though El il still remained supreme, and in time
Sumer once again was able to assert her own authority

through making Ur its capital, times had changed. A great flood of invaders in the land, gave Elam the opportunity to assert its own advantage and lay siege to Ur reducing it to ashes. The Amorites (who showed themselves to be the rising New-World power) eventually incorporated all the city states of Sumer into their empire. When one thinks about it, this was a most unusual phenomenon. What was taking place was the birth of world civilization itself. When Sumer's royal house fled to Haran, the Amorites (or Hammurites), made Babylon the new world capital governed by a mighty warrior God called Marduk. The whole land had become a place of great confusion, new peoples and new tongues as new Gods vied to be supreme. As the Bible in so few words says, Nimrod (a mighty warrior opposed to God) challenged El il for supremacy. Yet El il still was served from that time forward as the principal and reigning God governing the Jebusite community of Ur Salem.

Ancient Egypt (the most stable of all nations in the world) like Sumer also was a polytheistic society. But in Egypt the Government and the Law were centred in the King. The King defined the Constitution of the land. Apart from him there was no legal written document. It was the person of the King who defined Government and Law and was the object of all worship. It was the person of the King (whom we call Pharaoh) who made the nation strong. Regarded as a God in human form, he was far more than just a man. He was the fount of all power in the land, natural and political. In fact he owned the land. As the one supreme judge he appointed all officials serving under him, and he ruled through a network of appointed subordinates, ministers, and feudal chiefs. Yet all power (because it had devolved from him) made it possible for everyone to say that everything accomplished by his will had actually been done by him.

He was the one who (as head of religion) spoke for all the Gods whose spirits all had been conferred on him. In order to legitimize his right to rule as God of all the world, Pharaoh had to journey through and let himself be crowned in every area where different Gods prevailed. Only after that could he proceed toward the nation's capital, and receive the double crown while sitting on his virgin mother's lap, (which is to say the throne of Isis) which identified him as the great God Horus, her newborn son. It is from this image of Isis holding the Egyptian King (Horus) that we find in art the first image of the Madonna and her Child. It is an image signifying Kingship and the right to rule the world.

In the eyes of all Egyptians the Pharaoh never died. At least he never died a natural death. Whenever death eventually did come to him, he supposedly was slain by his envious brother Seth—the God who ruled the wilderness, but Horus always was reborn because his sister, wife and mother (all of whom were Isis) raised him from the grave so that (as a newborn child) he might sit upon her lap again. Because he had to move from place to place in order to establish his authority with all the Gods, all the Gods of Egypt became resident in him. The requirement of Pharaoh was that he be well educated and well informed. Even after he was crowned, though he had many counselors, military, foreign and domestic ones, it always was the King himself who rendered judgments and made decisions. Yet the chief of all of his advisors was his vizier. But what finally weakened Egypt was the presence and the influence of foreign elements.

King Thutmose IV (1419 - 1386) adopted a great vizier known to history as Yuya (which was actually the name of his God). Yuya (pronounced Iouiya) was the interpreter of Pharaoh's dreams, and King Thutmose IV who adopted him as friend and counselor became known to history as the dreaming monarch. Yuya became so great in Egypt that he was equal to the Pharaoh in his power, and the many titles that the Pharaoh bestowed on him is ample testimony to that. He was the only vizier to be mummified and given royal burial amongst Egyptian Kings. Yet Yuya was a foreigner, and many speculate that he originally had come from Canaan or the land of Syria. The Pharaoh even looked on Yuya as having royal blood of sorts in him, relating him in some way to Egyptian royalty. So greatly did the King of Egypt value him, that he gave his son Amenhotep III (1386 - 1349) in marriage to his vizier's only daughter, Tiy.

Although there is no doubt that Yuya's name was great throughout the land, and that the people loved him for reasons that we do not know, not everyone was pleased to see his daughter taken as the Pharaoh's wife. Those in powerful places did not like to see a Semite marrying the King who eventually might give birth to someone who would become the heir and ruler of the land. The Hyksos rule, which had recently humiliated the Egyptians was still fresh in their minds. And we cannot honestly say that the fears these nobles entertained were totally unjustified because Yuya's daughter Tiy did give birth to a royal son who was called Amenhotp IV (1350 - 1334). And it was he who changed his own name so emphatically to Aknaton and in defiance of all ancient practices introduced the worship of only one God into the lands he ruled.

The one God that he introduced and forced upon Egyptian life was that obscure Semitic God called Adon (or Aton). This proved to be a blow to Egypt for it sapped her strength completely and proved to be her ruin, showing that you cannot simply legislate a God upon a people in defiance of their customs and traditions. If we take an external look at what Aknaton taught and tried to do, it might appear quite beautiful, but it spelled the finish of a strong and mighty land. What Aknaton was attempting to accomplish was the complete rebirth of Egypt and the spiritual union of the lands he ruled, for Egypt had become an empire, and it held all other lands outside its own by military force of arms. That would not be necessary, Aknaton thought, if Egypt and the other lands he ruled were governed by a single God (whose power could heal their differences) and a King who was thoroughly human and showed himself to be understanding of the common weal.

This outlook is apparent both from his writings and the new art forms he introduced into Egyptian culture. Although he hoped to change the social atmosphere through these, he failed to realise that it is quite impossible to force new values on a people whose tastes, customs and habits are completely at variance with them. Aknaton failed not because he was a madman or a lunatic, but because he did not show respect for any of his people's ingrained thoughts and feelings. Nor did he take into consideration the natural brutality and indifference he would meet from those who wanted nothing other than to satisfy their own increasingly ambitious powers to conquer and control those lands on earth which promised them new wealth. Fortunately for Egypt though it was a strong and patriotic military general known as Horemheb who rescued Egypt from Aknaton and the weak Amarna Kings who seemed to be destroying it.

That may have been the reason why the Israelites, when they approached "the promised land" relied on military force to conquer it. For until Aknaton weakened Egypt's hold on Canaan, it had been a corporate part of the powerful Egyptian Empire, ruled by military force of arms. I expect the former Hyksos rulers too may have settled there. All the same, there was something very wrong with the policy of war which Joshua pursued in taking the land so brutally from its inhabitants. The Bible even says there was. Though space will not allow me to deal more fully with this question here, the scriptures do give ample arguments against this "holy war" and others of its kind. The entire book of Jonah alone will serve to illustrate that point. One New Testament citation though is worth a thousand words. In his letter to the Hebrews, St. Paul writes: "If Joshua had actually (by these battles) given Israel real peace and security God never would have spoken about another day." (Romans 4: 8)

The truth of Paul's words is underlined by the fact that the whole history of Israel (right from the time they entered Canaan in the year 1215 BC until their expulsion from it in the year 70 AD) was one long series of wars and battles against "the evil empire" and "the axis of evil". These battles (which were all fought supposedly to bring peace and security into a troubled world) actually set loose a whole chain of destructive wars which have continued right up to the present day. Ironically they are always painted even yet as wars of "good against evil", even though the wars themselves are evil things. They who tell us that the aim does not justify the means still revert to "holy wars" which nations still continue fighting "in the Valley of Decision."

According to Jesus of Galilee, violence was not the answer. "Put up your sword into the sheath," he admonished his disciples, "for anyone who relies upon the sword will perish by the sword" (Matthew 26: 52). Jesus spoke and the troubled waters were made calm. (Matthew 8: 26). He taught his followers that if a holy war is fought, it must be fought only with carefully chosen words, like metal tempered in the fire of God's wisdom. In this very vision, Jesus reveals that conventional warfare is inspired by demons (Revelation 16: 13), and that worshipping a piece of land (supposedly thought holy) is idolatry. And to destroy human life for it is equivalent to sacrificing your children in the fires of Molech (Jeremiah 32: 35). As the scriptures say "The whole earth is Jehovah's and everything that's in it." (1 Corinthians 10: 26). This is why Jesus tells us that God carefully laid out a plan to save the world from mankind's egotistically destructive ways.

If we leap ahead now six millennia from the time of King Adapa and the Anunnaki Council which appointed him, we come rather close to the kind of government that John describes for us, in the United Nations Organization, which was established after World War II. This Organization is by far the largest representative body of world peoples ever assembled in one place since "the beginning of the world". It is certainly much larger than that council in which "all the sons of God shouted for joy" to celebrate the beginning of the civilized world "when kingship descended from heaven".

Its purpose (as defined within the first article of its Charter) is to maintain peace and security, and to develop friendly relations among nations. Based on the principle of equal rights and self-determination of peoples, it lists as its aim the achievement of international co-operation in solving international problems which are economic, social, cultural or humanitarian in character, and to serve as a centre for harmonizing the actions of nations in the attainment of these common ends.

It is the United Nations' Charter then which actually defines the spirit which is sitting on the throne of this world Council (a council representing all the different areas on earth). And the spirit it defines can logically be called its God. The United Nations' Charter therefore (by defining the nature of its purposes) defines as well the character that those nations making up the Council are called on to adopt. Like the jewels which we saw on "him who (in John's vision) sat upon the throne", it is the spirit of the United Nations' Charter which sets forth the expectations and requirements for becoming members of this government. Like John's Council too, the nations making up this Assembly all were tried in fires of life's adversities. But did they overcome their personal resentments and their lusts?

Article Two of that same Charter goes on to define that spirit when it says: The United Nations is based on the sovereign equality of its members; disputes are to be settled by peaceful means, members undertake not to use force or threat of force in contravention of the purpose of the United Nations; each member must assist the organization in any action it takes under the charter; and any state which is not a member of the United Nations is still required to act in accordance with these principles in so far as may be necessary for the maintenance of international peace and security.

In addition, Article Two goes on to make it clear that the United Nations will not intervene in any matter which is "essentially within the domestic jurisdiction of any state, except to take enforcement measures." The principal UN organs include (1) The General Assembly, (2) the Security Council, (3) the Economic and Social Council, (4) the Trusteeship Council, and (5) The Secretariat.

The General Assembly certainly resembles the Assembly of Elders mentioned by John and their functions are identical: to keep the waters of the whole world system calm, and clear from all deception and hostility. Yet their advisory councils take only into account the affairs of mankind, not the forces of nature:

wild and domestic animals and creatures of the air. Therefore from the standard set by John the council is incomplete, but as far as it goes, it has some of the qualities which John described.

Nationalism however is its bane, for nationalism still remains a potent force frustrating mankind's fondest dreams and hopes for lasting peace. Although the Cold War served its strongest blow, even when the organization was still in embryo, the great powers in the world exhibited a lack of faith in this new child about to be born. Great Britain was obsessed with establishing a western European bloc, the United States with expanding their control in the Americas, the Caribbean and the Pacific, and Russia drew a broad security zone around itself as well. These actions set the tone for mutual distrust and caused other nations to scramble for positions of security from any possible collapse of their new dream. In spite of this, the United Nations still remained a powerful educating force, publicly debating on the great world stage all the major crises existing in the world and proposals that were made regarding them.

So Satan in this body greatly weakened its resolve to maintain peace, and national ambitions frequently took precedence over the organization's own resolve to be the one world arbiter of peace. The quarrels between the United States and the Soviet Union caused many of the Assembly's majority decisions to be ignored. It became especially clear when a coalition of western nations formed the alliance of NATO that world nations had made a firm decision to set their own interests and agendas above those of the international assembly of nations and to choose alternate paths.

There is really only one legitimate and undeniably natural government which is qualified for governing the world. John reveals it most effectively in the vision he has drawn of heaven in Chapters Four and Five of *Revelation*. To resketch that government in more modernly accepted terms than John has used: it consists of (1) A Royal Charter, (2) Four Advisory Councils, (3) A General Assembly, (4) A Security Council, and (5) A Standing Army.

I. The Royal Charter is the power behind creation which we find expressed in jewels and in a rainbow. These serve to list the qualities of character to be venerated and upheld in all the sons of men (not all of whom are Christians, Jews or Muslims). These qualities are:

(1) Righteousness: Fair and honest dealings and reliability in every field of human endeavour.

(2) Justice: Based upon laws upholding righteousness (i.e. fair and honest dealings and reliability), and a court of justice to uphold them.

(3) Grace: All Godly qualities of character and those abilities derived from them. As one Gospel writer summed them up: "All of us have received from this fullness, many gifts and rewards (of character and ability that we enjoy) one after another." (John 1: 16)

We must look then for all these virtues— Righteousness, Justice and and exceeding Graciousness— in all those serving in the government of God.

II. The Advisory Councils: These councils include:

(1) The Department of Wild Life   (the Lion)

(2) The Department of Domestic Creatures (the Ox)

(3) The Department of Human Affairs   (the Man)

(4) The Department of Aviation Creatures (the Eagle)
Birds, bats and everything that moves in the sky.

These departments are all directly concerned with the elements of life supporting them: Air, Water, Land and Sunlight and the availability of food for sustenance.

III. <u>The General Assembly</u>: These are the twenty-four elders representing every area upon earth. It is their duty to keep the whole world system free from violence, deception, and pollution of all kinds. These are the watchers and the guardians of all life on earth.

IV. <u>The Security Council</u>: (the Lamb) A large body of men and women drawn from every area upon earth which do not constitute an armed state serving national interests of any kind. It is their duty to reveal the present dangers and suggest the plan for dealing with them. The plan they recommend must be supported by the Charter – like a scroll taken from the hand of him who rules the elements of life.

V. <u>The Standing Army</u>: These are the myriads upon myriads of conscientious messengers armed only with the sword of the spoken word of truth. The glory and the praise they give to the Creator is their only weaponry. And the enemy of this heaven John describes for us is the seven-headed beast of death and devastation, which the ancient Canaanites once called Leviathan.

This is the only Constitution God has ever written with his own hand, and it is written on the fabric of creation itself. All other Constitutions that we read were written by the hand of Adam and of Cain. The right to kill is an important part of some nations' constitutions which we find framed even in the Constitution of the United States under the words "the right to bear arms." In the Constitution of God it is written, "They shall not injure or destroy in all my holy mountain."

It was the life and death of Jesus and his resurrection afterwards that made it possible for us to understand the sequence of events that lie beneath the seals of the great scroll of reality. For there is a pattern to the following events, that we have often witnessed throughout history. But none of us would recognize the pattern that the lamb of God reveals had Jesus's own life not made it clear to us.

Therefore in response to the prayers of all creation, the lamb alone is able to approach God's throne, and take the scroll from him then open it. No one else, alive or dead — among scholars or among humble men (not in heaven, or on earth or even under the earth) could make known the secrets of the scroll. Many, though, have tried from scholarship and human wisdom, but have failed. Yet Jesus had already opened it, and told his followers the things that were to be.

In Chapter Twenty-Four of Matthew's gospel, all the secrets of the seals were told by none other than the lamb of God himself. For on the Mount of Olives when his disciples came to him privately, they asked: "What will be the sign of your coming? and of the end of the age?" To which he answered them: (1) "Many will come in my name (that is pretending to be saviours of the world). They will make the claim, 'I am (the one who can deliver you, that is to say) the Christ.' And many people will be fooled by them. (2) Then you will hear of wars and rumours of coming wars. See that you are not afraid. For these things are inevitable, but that is not a sign that the end is near, since many wars shall follow one upon another as nations rise against nations and empires against empires.

(3) "Then famines shall follow. (4) and after that will come disease and earthquakes (national upheavals and disruptions). (5) At that time you will be turned over (to the authorities) for trials and punishment and torturing and they shall kill you too. (6) Following this tribulation (Notice that it is the saints who suffer during the Great Tribulation) the sun will be darkened, the moon will not give light, stars will fall from heaven and all the powers of heaven will be shaken. (7) Then a sign of the son of man will appear in heaven, causing every tribe upon the earth to mourn, for they shall see the son of man coming upon the clouds of heaven with great power and splendour. He shall send his angels forth, at the sound of a great trumpet, to gather his people together from (all directions) where the four winds (blow) from one direction under heaven to the other."

Maybe you can recognize the pattern that Jesus was describing here with these prophetic words. It is a pattern that has been repeated throughout history. False messiahs come to lead men to an unforeseen doom with promises of a new and better future for their nation, by giving them a better government, or appealing to their national sentiments. Wars soon follow in the wake of them, then famine comes upon its heels, and after it comes epidemics of dread diseases. Then the earth is shaken by great changes in the world. Persecutions start against the Jews and radicals and Christian heretics, as blame is laid on them for everything that has gone wrong.

Then the government of the false messiah starts to fall, the national religion gives no light, and all the great men lose their place in government. In the vacuum that is left, there is the opportunity for real deliverance. The question always is: "Who will fill it when the time is ripe for it?" The traditional belief of Christians is that Jesus, when he comes, will show the way.

I'll say no more of this right here, for John himself will show the churches in much greater detail than what we find described by Jesus in his *Matthew* narrative. The only point I wish to make is that Jesus — the lamb of God — has already told his faithful followers the pattern they will find disclosed beneath the seven seals: (1) A false prophet, (2) Warfare, (3) Famine, (4) Epidemic plagues and revolutions (literally earthquakes), (5) Great tribulation for the innocent, (6) The fall of leaders from the firmament, (7) Trumpeting angels (the spirit of the churches) and the appearance of "the son of man", when the members of the tribes of Israel (which are the clouds of heaven) reveal him in their midst.

This is quite a different picture from the one you might expect after having read and heard the great body of superstitious nonsense many writers give us when they put pulp fiction in the place of prophecy. Keep this in mind: The pictures that John paints are real. They only need interpreting, and the Bible itself does a good job of that.

CHAPTER SIX

The Tragic Pattern of Man's World

1.

I watched as the lamb opened the first of all the seals, and I heard what seemed to be the sound of thunder. It was the voice of one of the four creatures saying: "Come!" Then immediately in front of me I saw a white horse (which meant a national liberator would arise). Seated on it was a man with a bow (like Nimrod the hunter, indicating that he was a false messiah) and a crown was given him (to rule, like leadership bestowed on Hitler, who was elected as the people's choice), and he went forth conquering and to conquer.

When the second seal was opened by the lamb, I heard the second living creature say, "Come!" And instantly a red horse (symbolizing war) came out, and the one who sat on it was given power to take peace from the earth. (This condition is the direct result of the first — the false prophet. All of us have seen it happen throughout history, when men like Adolf Hitler — by popular choice — come to power as those who can restore national pride and strengthen cultural ties and values while catering to human biases. War inevitably follows them.)

Then after the lamb broke open the third seal, I heard the third creature say, "Come!" and a black horse (which represented famine) appeared in front of me; and he that sat on it had a pair of balances in his hand. From the midst of the four creatures, a voice said, "A quart of wheat for (a day's pay) a denarius, and three quarts of barley for (a day's pay) a denarius. But there is very little oil and wine. Be careful not to dilute or pollute them."

*

In ancient times oil and wine were universally regarded as essential needs. The scarcity of them was more than just a dietary loss; more importantly losing them would mean losing those commodities essential to a nation's health. Wine and oil were medicines and used to bind up wounds. Diluted, wine might be unappetizing as a drink, but as a disinfectant it would be no use at all. Yet food and medicine during any famine are in short supply, and shortages of wine and oil as food can also have disastrous results. During Prohibition years in North America, people drank perfumes, food flavouring, and wood alcohol. Shortly following the Second World War black market merchants in some countries, prompted by their greed, sold motor oil as cooking fat. The result on human lives was devastating. Usually upon the heels of any war, food and medicine are frequently in short supply.

2.

When the lamb had opened the fourth seal, I heard the voice of the fourth living creature say "Come!" Then all at once in front of me, there appeared a pale horse (of the plagues and earthquakes Jesus named. Yet in Bible language, even earthquakes are symbolic, and represent social turmoil and upheaval following catastrophes). The name of the one who sat upon the horse was Death, and the grave (or opened earth) followed him. Throughout more than a quarter of the earth, a great slaughter prevailed because of war, hunger, disease and marauding beasts (those groups and rabid mobs which bring about social upheavals). (The cause and effect principle in all of these occurrences is unmistakable. False prophets lead to war, war to famine and disease, and famine and disease to death. These are the curses Satan's world incurs. Christians have been warned of the phenomena and must learn how they should deal with them.)

But when the fifth seal was broken open, I saw —
under the altar — the lives of all those who had been
slaughtered in the course of doing God's will and for
affirming the spirit of his teachings to the world.

*

Remember the Jews of World War II. They were
made the target, and blamed for everything that went
wrong in Nazi Germany, so that following the war we
had the Nuremberg trials. Some will argue, I am sure,
that many Jews do not even believe in God. That may be
true, but — whether from choice or not — they bear God's
name, for they are associated in many people's minds
with God. It is a fact from which they can't escape. And
all humanity because of their great suffering stands now
before the judgment seat.

John, in this brief passage, deliberately reminds
the readers of everyone who throughout history was
slaughtered for his dedication to the way of God. There
was a crime of long long standing waiting to be judged,
and John saw all the nations' governments, their national
religions and the people serving them, as being collectively blood guilty of deaths of all the righteous and the
innocents. Religion in John's eyes, was not a superficial
ornament tacked on to people's lives. It was the way that
nations and their people lived, and the institutions of
society were, in one way or another, all a part of it. To
preach or teach a different course from the way the world
had gone, was ruthlessly assailed by those who held the
reins of power. Cain had slain his brother Abel for
worshipping in a manner much different from his own.
Now in John's time, the living messengers of God daily
faced the threat of death, imprisonment, torture and
humiliation, for the sake of making God's will known.

3.

I watched as the sixth seal was opened and a great earthquake took place. (This symbolized social upheaval.) Upon that, the sun instantly grew black as sack cloth made with goats hair, the moon turned red as blood, and the stars in the sky all fell to the earth in the same way that a fig tree will drop her figs late in the season when they are shaken by a strong wind. The sky disappeared like a scroll when it is rolled up; and every mountain and island was moved from its place.

*

Such a phenomenon as John describes in these last words is not entirely an uncommon event. What is described here as the heavens being rolled up like a scroll is the disappearance of those institutions governing the Gentile nations of the world. The occurrence was seen during the French Revolution, the Soviet revolution, and again at the fall of Nazi Germany. For it symbolically describes the fall of governments, and the eventual disappearance of nations themselves. The sun is the governmental ruler. The moon is the national religion (in Hitler's case the Nazi party). The stars are all the great important office holders in the governmental hierarchy, like Goebels, Himmler, Goering and the rest, who were illustrious luminaries in that nation's firmament.

The same situation is described in other Bible passages, which leaves no doubt that it is the governmental powers which fall. Psalm 89: 36-37 gives us a strong lead in understanding this for it says: "(David's) line will continue forever and his throne will endure before me like the sun; it will be established forever even as the moon (the Jewish faith) upholding it, that faithful witness in heaven." Then Isaiah using these poetic images asserts: "Jehovah is angry with all nations; his wrath is upon all their armies. He will totally destroy them, and will give them over to slaughter. Their slain will be thrown out, their dead bodies will send up a stench. The mountains will be soaked with their blood. All the stars of the heavens will be dissolved and the sky rolled up like a scroll: all the starry host will fall like withered leaves from the vines, like shrivelled figs from the fig tree." (Isaiah 34: 2-4). Can anyone doubt that these last words are in reference to the governments of nations themselves.

We surely cannot miss the meaning underlined in Jeremiah's words which say: "(Backsliding Israel's) sun will set while it is still day; she will be disgraced and humbled. I will put the survivors to the sword before her enemies." (Jeremiah 15: 9) For what is spoken of is spiritual light from a throne (or government) no longer able to guide its people. Like the sun, its light has gone out. Jacob and his other sons had no difficulty in interpreting the meaning of the dream which Joseph tactlessly revealed to them when he said: "In another dream, I saw the sun and moon and eleven stars bowing down to me." For his father, rebuking him, replied: "What kind of dream is that? Do you imagine for one moment that your mother and I and all your brothers will actually bow down to the ground in front of you?"   (Genesis 37: 9-10)

Jacob didn't take his own son's words literally, so why should we force literal meanings upon scriptures which elsewhere have been interpreted for us. None of the things that John describes in images is unusual. We have seen such things again and again throughout history. *The Book of Revelation*, merely tells the various churches to expect all of these occurrences. Jesus himself would say of them: "Don't be alarmed when you see any of these

things take place, for things like this are sure to come
about." Significantly, however, John, in the *Book of
Revelation*, reserves the opening of the seventh seal for a
later time. Yet as we've seen already, Jesus, in his talk to
his disciples, when they sat upon the hillside overlooking
Jerusalem, told them everything they could expect to see.
And he clearly said what lay behind the seventh seal. For
your convenience I will restate his words for you:

"And then shall appear the sign of the Son of Man
in the sky, and all the nations of the world shall beat
their breasts in lamentation when they see the Son of
man coming on the clouds of heaven in power and glory."
We might be inclined to ask ourselves if these words
refer to Jesus's appearance in the centre of prominent
public events, say in a march like that of Dr. Martin
Luther King Jr. etc. who in the name of Christ led his
people out of oppression. I leave that solely to the
discretion of the reader. Yet, as every Christian knows,
care must be observed in this. For false messiahs have
also plagued the world throughout history. I do not need
to name them all. For a church that has fulfilled the
necessary first step in the Kingdom strategy, recognizing
Christ should not be difficult. For Jesus said: "My sheep
shall know my voice." Those words caution us of the
need to know the scriptures well because he can be
misidentified.

Jesus's disciples will not follow any man who charms
them with the spell of his charismatic personality, or
tries to rouse them with inflaming oratory. They will
recognize him by his words and deeds. As Jesus said
again: "By their fruits you shall know them." No one's
intuition or mystic feeling will be called upon. The Word
Of God will be clearly recognizable through what is said
and done, for what is said and done will be what you have
learned from having supped with Christ.

These then are the seven seals. John, in the *Book of Revelation*, however, is much more elaborate in the description of what lies underneath the seventh seal. He begins unfolding its mystery at Chapter Eight verse 1, and doesn't end it until the book's last word. Yet, in this present chapter, John has not yet finished showing us what lies beneath the sixth seal. The text of the chapter continues in this way:

4.

All of the earth's rulers, its leaders, its wealthy citizens, its high-ranking military officers, its influential business men, its freemen and its slaves (every level of society) tried to hide themselves in caves and among the rocks of the mountains. Then calling to the mountains and the rocks, they cried: "Fall on us and hide us from the face of Jehovah who sits upon the throne and from the anger of the lamb!" For the great day of their anger has come and who can possibly survive?

*

I have deliberately separated this portion of the sixth seal from the earlier part, as the first portion of Chapter Seven actually lies between this and what was earlier described for us as lying underneath the sixth seal. Chapter six, however, appropriately ends with the question *"Who can possibly survive this dreadful time?"* Chapter Seven, logically, sets out to answer that question for us. By showing us the tribes of Israel, John, by allusion, instructs the children of God on how they must prepare themselves for meeting the disasters that he describes as being under the latter part of the sixth seal.

CHAPTER SEVEN

The Solid Base on which to Build

Immediately following this (important question of who can possibly survive these trying times?') I saw four messengers of God stationed in all four regions of the world (four denoting everywhere throughout the earth, in all directions of the compass). These restrained the winds (of social maladies which we earlier identified in the four horsemen) from blowing on the land, the sea or on any tree. (Winds generally are used in many Bible texts to represent prevailing spirits in the world which influence public attitudes and human thought. We read, for instance, about being blown about by every wind of fashion. Land, sea and trees taken together represent the people, the turbulent world system and the illustrious leaders of the world. Having had a foreview of what lies in store for this world and its turbulent way of life — war, famine, disease, pestilence, social upheaval, persecution and death — God's people must prepare themselves. But how?)

That was when I saw another of God's messengers coming (like the rising sun) up from the east (offering the world hope of a new day about to dawn). This angel spirit from God had the seal of the living God with him (indicating that he was a scribe who had written letters for his master and now was authorized to add his master's seal to them). He cried out in a loud voice to the four powerful spirits who had been given power to harm the nations (the four horsemen that were mentioned earlier — for God is always in control and the four devastating calamities of false ideals, war, famine and pestilence are direct results of saying that we have no God besides Caesar). "Do not harm the nations, the people or their leaders," he cried out, "until we put a mark on the foreheads of all God's servants." (That is to say that God will seal them with his name because they know his word and live by it.)

Then I learned the number of those who had been marked on their foreheads (signifying that the torah, or instructions, of God had been written on their hearts and minds. This reminds us of a certain promise which God made: "I will put my law, or torah, on their inward parts and I shall be their God, and they shall be my people.") The number was 144,000 from all the tribes of Israel. ("For God has not forsaken those whom he first called.")

From all the tribes of Israel, there were marked
twelve thousand from the tribe of Judah,
twelve thousand from the tribe of Reuben,
twelve thousand from the tribe of Gad,
twelve thousand from the tribe of Asher,
twelve thousand from the tribe of Naphtali,
twelve thousand from the tribe of Manasseh
                                        (replacing Dan)
twelve thousand from the tribe of Simeon,
twelve thousand from the tribe of Levi,
twelve thousand from the tribe of Issachar,
twelve thousand from the tribe of Zebulun,
twelve thousand from the tribe of Joseph, and
twelve thousand from the tribe of Benjamin.

(Such scriptures tend to make us think about Paul's words to the Corinthians "You yourselves are the letters that we send, written on the heart, and understood and read by everyone."— 2 Corinthians 3: 2. The God-sent angel rising from the east and establishing all the tribes of Israel, as representatives of God on earth, indicates that Israel — which bears God's name and character — will be the sun in that new heaven of celebrities being established upon earth to influence and to govern in God's name. We cannot help but think about the words which Jesus spoke: "Then shall the righteous shine as the sun in their heavenly Father's realm."   — Matthew 13: 43)

After this took place, I looked again and saw an enormous crowd of people who were so great in number that it was impossible to count them. (This crowd was representative of the new earth which God was promising to build). They came from every nation, tribe, people and language upon earth to stand before the throne (of God) and before the lamb. (Led by the sunshine brightness of Israel, this great crowd would come like other worshippers before the throne of God and, being ruled by him, live according to his ways. The great crowd (who came before the throne of God) were wearing white robes and holding palm branches in their hands. (John deliberately creates a scene which is reminiscent of the text which reads: "A great crowd...when they heard that Jesus was on his way to Jerusalem, took palm branches and went out to meet him, shouting, 'Hail to the saviour that Jehovah sends to us! Long live the king of Israel!" – John 12: 12-13) (So likewise) this crowd cries out in a loud voice: "Salvation comes from God who sits upon the throne and from the lamb (the meek submissive servant, obedient to God – of whom it has been said, 'he was led as a lamb to its slaughter'.)"

Then all the holy angels (who like morning stars herald the coming of God's full majesty into the world) stood about the throne of God, and about (the other sons of God) the elders and the four living creatures. Together they bowed their faces before the throne (in recognition of God's supreme authority). Then they worshipped God (by shouting for joy) and saying: "Certainly blessing and glory and wisdom and thanksgiving and honour and power and might belong only to God for ever and ever. There can be no doubt of this. (literally 'Amen')."

Then one of the elders asked me: "Tell me, who are all these people that are dressed in white robes. And where did they come from?" (But desirous of his answer) I replied: "Sir, you know who they are. Tell me." So the elder then (responsive to my own desire to learn from him) instructed me, "These are those people who have come out of great suffering and who have washed their robes and made them white in the blood of the lamb. Therefore they are able now to come before the throne of God, where they worship him day and night in his temple."

(These words do not imply that this great crowd — which was past numbering — were assembled in some building made with human hands or "up in heaven" as some ministers have said, imagining them to have died a noble death. They were in God's temple because their deeds had put them there. For it is written: "Pure religion and undefiled before God our Father is this: To visit the fatherless and widows in their affliction, and to keep oneself unspotted from the world." (James 1: 27) So what these people actually were doing was behaving in a way that Jesus would have done — not in lip service — but in deeds of compassion toward those who were fellow sufferers with them. They were, therefore, spiritually in God's house in much the same way John was now in heaven. For God is praised, not by pretentious ceremonies, but by righteous deeds, administered with love to those requiring strength and comforting.)

"They shall hunger no more or thirst any more (They shall not be denied food or drink for the spirit, body or the mind), neither shall the sun beat down on them nor any heat of oppression (no ruler, officers of human government or zealous 'fundamentalists' of any kind shall oppress them), for the lamb (the meek anointed king who serves as God's right hand on earth) shall rule the earth and be their shepherd, and he shall guide them to the springs of the water of life (the word of God); and God shall wipe every tear from their eyes." (God defines his aim: to comfort and relieve the suffering.)

* * *

The purpose of Chapter Seven in the body of Jesus's great plan, primarily, is to answer that one question which was posed in the chapter just preceding it: "Who can possibly survive these trying times?" To help us find the answer for ourselves, John shows us how the winds that blow calamity upon the world shall be restrained and held off while God's secretarial scribes and ministers (who wrote the scriptures or who speak according to the word of God) have written God's word (torah) indelibly upon the hearts and minds of all whom God will choose (as living letters to send out in his name) and place his royal seal on them.   These people are identified as Israel. For God is building upon earth a heaven that shall rule the hearts of men.

We read for instance, in the *Book of Zechariah*, about those spirits who hold back the winds of those destructive horsemen which assail the earth, restraining them. For Zechariah says: "I looked...and before me were four chariots (of destruction) coming from between two mountains....I asked the angel who was speaking to me, What are these, sir?' The angel answered, 'These are four spirits going from the presence of Jehovah into the whole world. The chariot with black horses is going toward the north country, the chariot with white horses is going toward the west, and the dappled horses are going to the country in the south. And the chariot with (red horses) has gone forth to patrol the earth."   (Zecharaiah 6: 1- 8)

That the winds the angels have restrained is representative of those destructive horsemen we encountered earlier is confirmed for us in words like this: "See, the anger of Jehovah will burst out furiously, like a driving wind that swirls down on the heads of the wicked. His fierce displeasure will not turn back until he has accomplished everything that is in his heart."   (Jeremaiah 30: 23-24)

There are many superstitious notions now about heaven which have been garnered from the pagan world and read into the scriptures. These sometimes make it difficult to recognize God's meaning in the Bible text at all. In the heaven God was building upon earth, Israel was to be the sun, shining in its firmament to give light to the world, so that the people of the world no longer would be forced to walk in darkness — according to the passions of their hearts, or (to the detriment of others) doing only what was right in their own eyes.

So God will keep his promises to Israel because he has a plan for them that will benefit mankind. The moment they are ready and observe their covenant with him and willingly put on his character, he will make them like the sun to shine upon the earth. For "in the beginning was the word and the word was with God and his word did not vary from what God was." His character would be written upon human lives. As Jeremiah said: "I will put my law on their inward parts and will be their God and they shall be my people." God's word was not something that was merely set apart on scrolls and read each sabbath in the synagogue. It was the breath of God breathed into human life, so that "as many as received it (into their character) received with it the power to become the sons of God." For this reason Christians have been told to put on Jesus Christ. And for the same reason Israel was told to "Tie (the words of God) as symbols on your hands and bind them on your foreheads. Write them on the door frames of your houses and on your gates."

Scriptures constantly make reference to markings on the forehead, which leave little doubt about the meaning of these words. In Ezekiel's prophecies we find: "Then Jehovah called to a man clothed with linen (a righteous man) who had a writer's inkhorn at his side (indicating he was a scribe who wrote letters for his lord) and

Jehovah said to him, 'Go through the midst of the city, through the midst of Jerusalem, and set a mark (with the seal of my signet) upon the foreheads of the men who sigh and groan over all abominations that are committed in the midst of it.' (As Jesus—God's messenger to Israel—said, "Blessed are they that mourn, for they shall be comforted") Then Jehovah said to the others in my hearing: Follow (that man with the ink bottle) through the city and smite, let not your eye spare, neither have pity..." (Ezekiel 9: 4-5.)

This seal or mark on the forehead has been explained in various ways by commentators ranging from tattoos on the head, to belonging to the right sect representing Christ in Christendom. But the Bible is quite clear about the meaning when we no longer force the text: "Hear, O Israel: Jehovah our God is one Lord: and you shall love Jehovah your God with all your heart and with all your soul, and with all your might. And these words...shall be in your heart, and you shall teach them to your children...and you shall bind them for a sign on your hand (so that the will of God is evident in all your deeds) and they shall be as frontlets between your eyes... (that is on your forehead, signifying that the word of God is always present in your thoughts)." (Deuteronomy 6: 4-9)

Such language is always figurative, not literal in any modern sense, for a man was known by his thoughts (the mark upon his forehead) and his deeds (the mark upon his hand—not by the phylacteries that he put on for ceremonial show). As Jesus says in reference to this, "I am in the Father and the Father is in me."

That God is not worshipped by ceremonies, but by deeds has been a constant theme throughout the whole Bible: "Stop bringing me your vain offerings; the stench of your incense is odious to me; and your pious gatherings—your New Moons, Sabbaths and Holy convocations — are utterly abhorrent. I hate all your New Moon festivals and appointed feasts. They are tedious and boring, and I am sick to death of them. So when you lift your hands in prayer, I will not even look at you or consider your words; even though you multiply the number of your prayers to me, I will not listen: for your guilty hands are thick with blood. Wash and make yourselves clean, and put away the evil of your ways. Stop practicing evil, and learn to do right. Ensure justice, give help to the oppressed, defend the fatherless and speak on behalf of women who are disadvantaged by the world (literally 'widows')." (Isaiah 1: 13-17)

Israel, throughout the Bible, was frequently compared to a fig-bearing sycamore tree, from which anyone who chose might eat. That is why Jesus, who called righteous Israel "the light of all the world" instructed them to love even their enemies, saying, "If you love only those who love you, what benefit is that? Don't even tax gatherers do that?" (Matthew 5: 46) God's people had been called to benefit all men. "For God's sun is made to shine on the evil and the good, and his rain is allowed to fall on both the righteous and the unrighteous." (Matthew 5: 45)

This speaking out on behalf of disadvantaged women, which Isaiah mentions, goes right back to Moses and the daughters of Zelophehad. It was a principle set forth in the Jewish law. Not to honour it was to break a basic principle in the law of God: The law was made to fit the needs of all.

So who will see to it, that God's will is done? on earth? even as it is in heaven? John tells us it will be the sons of Israel. There would be no point in John having taken time to name the different tribes if he were speaking of a different Israel from what is found in other scriptures that we read. He names them to assure us that God has not deserted them. All tempering and refining of this people in the fires of rigorous adversity, throughout the Bible texts and history, would be quite meaningless if in the end God only were to choose another bride. God chose Israel (as Jesus said) to be the light of all the world. "For salvation," he declared, "is of the Jews." In later chapters we will see how God will gather and assemble Israel. Here he simply takes the time to show us those who will be able to survive the dreadful time which is in store. For "even though (they) must face the difficulties of today and tomorrow, (they) still have a dream."

The tribes of Israel, tempered in the furnaces of rigorous adversity, alone will have the strength and character to withstand the great calamities about to fall upon the world. The Bible clearly teaches that all of these calamities which will assail the nations of the world are the direct result of man's accumulated sin against God, against himself, against creation and against his fellow man. In identifying Israel, John is not concerned with any man's "religion" in the narrow sense. It is character on which he lays the emphasis. Like letters written by "the finger of God," the people of Israel will by righteous, just and merciful deeds display the signature of God on them. The character of their deeds reveals God's name to the world. Therefore they shall shine as sunlight to the suffering, who will turn to them in masses, and in doing so will also turn to the very God directing Israel.

However, I realise that many will waste much time in debating endlessly on whether John's words were actually a reference to physical Israel rather than to spiritual Israel (as though a physical Israel could not have any spiritual side to it). John has told us it is Israel. That's all we have to know. For without a physical Israel there could never be a spiritual one, any more than there could be a spiritual America without a physical America. And this Israel John speaks of is complete as all the symbols in this chapter indicate. I expect, though, that such arguments are raised more as an attempt to cheat the Jews (after all their suffering) out of any claim they have (as elder brothers in the House of Israel) to any portion of the great inheritance which God promised to all Israel, and which John's words affirm that they shall have.

The number 144,000 (as many of you know) is not literal. It is symbolic and it signifies godly completion (or perfection) in the fullest sense. It is derived from the total number of all the tribes assembled as the heavenly letters (of the kingdom) of God to be sealed with God's royal name. Twelve is the number of God's character, indicating all his virtues – compassion, wisdom, justice, righteousness, goodly speech, reliability, and all the other virtues we will later on explore. It also is the number of God's people, Israel. The matching and combining of these numbers indicates that God (who is capable of accomplishing all things, and who can cleanse the human heart) will make all Israel reflect his character. In reflecting it, they will be the light of all the world as Jesus said of them.

Twelve times twelve (12x12 or 12^2) therefore is a number emphasizing, in the strongest possible terms, the perfecting of Israel. "God is with his people" was the message that the Jewish prophet Isaiah brought to King Ahaz centuries ago, as he stood by the Upper Pool on the highway leading to the fuller's field. Here the same message is given to the reader: "God is with his people. There is nothing to fear." God is with all those instructed in his word who choose to reflect the virtues of God in all their ways.

Three is the number which emphasizes any matter in the strongest of terms. It is like the affirmation of

"Amen". Isaiah's "Holy, holy, holy is Jehovah of Hosts," is a well-known example of this. Then Moses tells us (in both *Deuteronomy* 17: 6 and 19: 15) that three constitutes the perfect witness. For this reason ten is multiplied three times (10x10x10 or 10^3) so that there will be no doubt that God will call his people out of every nation in the world. For ten is the number of Gentile completion. This then is the Israel which has been tried and refined in the harsh fires of adversity and which Moses saw depicted in the burning bush. Here then Israel rises like the sun to give its true light to all the world. Yet Israel is numbered in this passage like an army (assembled under captains) to battle with an enemy. That enemy is darkness (or world ignorance of the way of creation).

In combining these two numbers (144 x 1000) John stresses in this vision that the promises of God (the Creator) can be relied upon. God has not deserted those whom he first called. He shall be faithful to all the promises that he has made. For God is his word. There is no other way of reading this numeric message John has given us, for all the scriptures that we have, bear witness to its truth.

Israel was called to be the word of God made flesh. They were to shine as light in this dark world so that the people of the world who lived in darkness could be given light and turn to Israel for knowledge of God's word. Anticipating such a time, this is what Isaiah the son of Amoz saw in store for Judah and Jerusalem: "In the end this is what will happen: The mountain (or kingdom) of Jehovah's house (the people) will become the most prominent Mountain (or esteemed nation) in the world and will tower over all the hills (the prominent nations), and all the (people from those) nations will flow to it. And many people anxious to visit it will say, "Come, and let us go to Jehovah's mountain (Israel) to the house (the people: the spiritual temple) of the God of Jacob; and he (God who speaks through his holy people) will teach us his ways, and we will walk in his paths." For instruction (torah) shall come from Zion and the word of God from Jerusalem.

"He (God through his righteous people) will render judgment for the nations of the world and settle the disputes of many people; and they shall beat their swords into plowshares and their spears into pruning hooks: nation shall not lift up sword against nation, neither shall they learn war any more. O house of Jacob (Israel) come and (with this vision of the future) let us walk (today) in the light of Jehovah's will."   (Isaiah 2: 1-5)

In contemplating such a glorious time, we might turn again to read the blessings which Jacob (known as Israel) bestowed on all his children. When we read these blessings, though, we must retain a certain measure of reserve, as most of us must surely realise that there are those who do attempt to milk them for whatever superstitious meanings they can wrest from them. Often such people will rely upon the King James text for a certain aura of obscurity its now archaic language lends, for it helps them cast a spell of mystic awe. We must agree on this: that there is no magic charm in any of the things that Jacob told his sons. However, there is much that we can learn from calmly reading what was said, in those now ancient blessings, with some degree of rational intelligence.

Without any further comment then, here is what was said (in Genesis 49) by a very aged man to his twelve sons approximately four millennia ago:

Then Jacob sent word to his sons, saying: "Come together so I can tell you of the things that shall happen to you in the days that lie ahead. Come and hear me, sons of Jacob; hear the voice of Israel.

"Reuben, as my eldest child and the evident firstfruits of my manhood, was endowed by birth with family pre-eminence and authority. But since you are undisciplined and as unstable as water, like the wild waves of the sea, you shall no longer be the foremost among your brothers. For in taking possession of your father's bed you dishonoured it.

"Simeon and Levi are kindred spirits, very much alike, and quick to take up arms. I will not let myself be joined with their conspiracies, nor, on my honour, be a part of their assemblies, for in their treachery they murdered helpless people and slaughtered cattle senselessly. I curse their anger, for it was fierce and cruel. Therefore I will separate them in the family of Jacob and scatter them in Israel.

"As for Judah, all your brothers shall praise you. You will subdue your enemies, and your brothers will bow down before you. For Judah is like a young lion: returning from pursuing prey, he will lie down and stretch himself out as lions do, and no one will dare to disturb him. He shall bind his ass to the grape vine, and the colt of his ass to the very finest vine, and wash his clothes in wine, and his laundry in the blood of grapes. His eyes will be glazed with wine and his teeth white with milk.

"Zebulun will live near the sea, where his coastline will be a harbour for ships, and his outer border will extend to Zidon.

"Issachar, however, is an awkward and ungainly ass, who will carelessly lie down between his saddlebags, (that is to say he will neglect his own responsibilities) and even when it is apparent how wonderfully pleasant his resting place is, he will still allow himself to be enslaved by others and shoulder burdens that they force on him.

"Like any tribe in Israel, Dan shall be self-governing and protect his people. But like a poisonous roadside snake with deadly fangs, Dan will lie in wait for (Israel's) enemies, biting the heels of their horses, so that their riders will be thrown off backwards.

"O Jehovah, I rely upon your great deliverance!

"Gad (whose name means a troop comes) will be savagely attacked by marauding bands of robbers, but in the end, he shall skillfully upset their strategies and plunder them.

"The land of Asher will provide abundant food, and produce choice edibles fit for a king.

"Naphtali is a freedom-loving hind, conceiving healthy young. (There is some word play in this blessing as there is in many of Jacob's blessings. Allusion is made to fair speech-implying that the sons of Naphtali shall be vigorous and healthy in their speech and in the arts of communication.)

"Joseph, like a vigorous fruit-bearing vine flourishing beside a flowing spring, will shoot his sturdy branches out beyond the vineyard's separating wall. Men of war, covetous of his prosperity, have repeatedly harassed him and assaulted him in fury. But the mighty God of Jacob, the guiding shepherd and protector of Israel has given him a steady hand and made him strong. For you are sustained by your father's God, the Almighty One who blesses you with blessings from above (rain and sunlight in their season) and blessings from the wells of living water underneath the ground, blessings of children and cattle. The blessings which God bestowed on me and on my fathers are now passed on to you, because you

have succeeded as their heir to all the blessings which
are everlasting like the mountains and the hills. They
will continue now upon the head of Joseph, for God has
set him apart from all his brothers.

"Benjamin will prowl like a voracious wolf: by day
marauding and flaying his victims, and at night
covertly surprising them."

These pronouncements of Jacob, regarding the
fortunes of his sons, have far reaching social implications
that cannot be ignored. What is said of one son must be
applied to all the sons of Israel, for Jacob's words serve as
warnings and promises to that nation God will choose to
bless the world. Nothing better illustrates the disastrous
effects of one man's sins upon the nation as a whole than
do the words that Jehovah spoke when Judah's
descendant, Achan, violated God's commands: "Israel has
sinned," he said. "They have violated my covenant which
I commanded them to keep." (Joshua 7: 11) Notice that
he does not tell us "Achan has sinned." He points to the
spiritual result as affecting all of Israel.

In the *Genesis* account we are now considering,
Jacob calls all his sons together as a unit, to consider the
effect that their virtues and their sins will have on the
entire nation of Israel when it is born in future times.
That time will be when all the nations of the earth will
turn to Israel. Yet while these great prophetic
revelations are forward looking, we lose much of their
meaning if we treat them as little more than fortune
telling oracles. The negative and positive words that
Jacob speaks to each of all his sons serves to instruct
them and the future reader of these words in the kind of
character which God requires from those whom he has
chosen to instruct the world.

From what is said to Reuben, we are shown that anyone who abuses the authority God places in his hands does not deserve a place of leadership in the House of Israel. To re-enforce this same idea, Jacob chooses Joseph as his heir, reminding the reader of the various ways that Joseph used his authority (in Potiphar's house, in Prison, and as chief adviser to the throne) so that all power came into his hands. In all capacities he blessed all who came to him, even those same brothers who had abused him earlier. The perfect will of God was shown in him. Then what Jacob says to Simeon and Levi serves to teach us that murderous revenge has no place in the assemblies of God. God's advice to Cain is especially appropriate in this instance.

Next of all, in praising Judah for his faithful stewardship in the vineyard of God, Jacob tells him that the rulership of Israel will come from him. The words that "the rod of authority shall be his and it shall not be taken from (him or) his descendants, until the nations come to him with tribute and obey him," are especially significant for us; as they refer directly to the very moment John has just described for us when great crowds from all nations turn to all the tribes of Israel with the tribe of Judah leading them.

The fortunes Jacob bestows on Zebulun and Issachar are also twinned so that we might see (through this antithetic parallel) the negative and positive effect of industry. The virtues of Zebulun (expressed in concrete imagery) were to bring prosperity to Israel through the tribe's honest and fair practices in world trade. Moses further underlines that meaning when he says: "(Zebulun) will summon people to the mountain (of

God) and there offer sacrifices of righteousness; they will feast on the abundance of the seas (world trade and commerce) on the treasures hidden in the sand (advantageous harbours for ships)." (Deuteronomy 33: 19) The blessing found in Jacob's words clearly indicates then that Israel will flourish in world trade and have unlimited access to all the world's trade routes.

The attitude of Issachar, however, is just the opposite. In Issachar we are shown a negative approach toward industry. He has a nature that despairs too easily, and he displays an habitually careless disposition toward the maintenance of what he has. Not appreciating his advantages (and lacking both imagination and initiative to use whatever power is in his hands) Issachar lets himself become the drudge of others. Here also it is Joseph who supplies us with the best example of what all Israel must be. For even in prison he was guided by the word of God. He drank thirstily from it, and because of this, he bore every kind of fruit to feed the world. For good reason he received the birthright from his father, and the right to use the name of Israel. To be an heir of Israel, then, one must drink continually and deeply from the water of God's word. And as the first psalm illustrates so perfectly, it is through drinking of the water of this word that the birthright of Israel is passed on.

While there are many things to learn from studying Jacob's words, my main purpose is to show that any prophecy read open-mindedly, with no attempt to force the text, offers us great lessons that can enlighten us and help us understand the will of God. In Jacob's blessings of his sons, we find those qualities to be developed in perfecting Israel, and those that must be changed and overcome. Whatever curses or blessings we discover in these words were written so that the Israel which is of God might intelligently appraise itself and overcome whatever weaknesses it has, while developing those traits which were more commendable. So although Joseph's physical descendants apparently did fail to follow in the footsteps of Joseph, the spiritual qualities he had cannot be denied and will be present in his spiritual descendants, and all who are the heirs of righteous Israel.

Those who by their nature are the sons of Reuben (abusing whatever small authority they have and who take unfair advantage of all those whose lives and welfare are under their control) must change their ways and rise above their natural inclinations. They must become the paragons of family honour and champion the cause of all who have no means to voice the wrongs they suffer in this world.

Since Reuben, in the *Book of Revelation*, is named among the tribes of perfected Israel, as is Issachar, Simeon and Levi too, we may assume, the qualities that Jacob found wanting in these sons were overcome. Spiritually perfected, Reuben would stand for family honour and the rights of the oppressed (especially women). Issachar would stand for loyal service and bear his burdens well. Judah's blessing, though, would be unchanged. But its deeper inner meaning is worth remarking on.

A vineyard is symbolic of the kingdom of God. We are told that Judah's eyes glowed with the wine from it, and that everything he did was in accordance with its hope. Even his animals were not allowed to stray from the vineyard of God, but were tied to the vines of it. His spiritual garments were all washed in God's word. Jacob was astute, and saw in this one son, someone who was stubbornly loyal to God. Judah had tenacity. This was a quality to be admired. And Judah to this day has proven to be the strongest and most tenacious of the tribes of Israel in offering real leadership to his people throughout history, quietly preserving the holy scriptures for posterity and offering a focal point to rally Israel. It was from Judah that Israel received its kingly line: the royal house of David, from whom the great messiah did (or was to) come. This must certainly explain why John placed Judah's name above the rest of all the tribes in Israel.

Surprisingly, Dan's name has been omitted from John's list, and we might wonder why John has not included it. It can only mean one thing. The blessing that Jacob gave to Dan was called into question. Perhaps physically Dan's sons remained in Israel, but he has been replaced upon the list of tribal leaders by Manasseh rather than by Ephraim which might have seemed more logical. But then Dan was a backbiter, and Ephraim's descendants were idolaters. And in God's kingdom there was no place at all for backbiters nor idolaters. So what is emphasized by just this one change is that the sons of Israel must be without guile and without deception.

Naphtali, the vigorous young roe, must guard his speech for the sons of Israel must speak goodly words, in order to give birth to healthy offspring. Much evil comes into the world by way of those who do not control their tongues. Perhaps you see far more now, in the naming of these tribes, than just a simple recitation of the family names of Israel. Like the gems upon the breastplate of

Israel's high priest, these tribes display for us the
essential qualities of character which reflect the very
God they serve. These alone are able to withstand the
hardships of the world. Like living letters from the hand
of God, they bear his signature and have his royal seal on
them. The question that John posed for us at the end of
Chapter Six was: "Who can possibly survive this dreadful
time?" The answer is of course the children of Israel
who have overcome the natural weaknesses their father
saw in them, and have, through faith put on the word of
God in order to become his perfect representatives.

During the time of tribulation, they will be a city on
a hill that all can see as offering the world a real
alternative. They will be the lamp upon the lampstand
that gives light to everyone within the house. This
relatively small nucleus, by the light of their example will
draw men and women out of every nation in the world.
These together will make up "the new earth" God will
build. The great crowd we are shown represents all those
who (in the light that they receive from the sun of that
new heaven that God will build on earth) perfect their
ways and turn to Israel for guidance in the way of God.
These will take no part in nationalistic or partisan
warfare, but (by looking to the mount of God) will
overcome the difficulties facing them and now glorify
the God of life through deeds of true compassion, in
accordance with the way of God. For the sons of
Abraham were called by God, not to serve themselves,
but to serve God and to bless the world.

So John's words waken in our minds the echo of
Isaiah's prophecy which says: "'For as long as the new
heavens and the new earth shall endure before me,'

Jehovah has declared, 'so shall your offspring and your name remain. So people everywhere must come from month to month and week to week and worship before me,' Jehovah has declared." (Isaiah 66: 22-23)

We also are reminded of the prophet Daniel's words which say: "While you watched, a rock was cut out without human hands. It struck the statue on its feet of iron and baked clay and smashed them. Then the iron, the clay, the bronze, the silver and the gold (all representing different kinds of kingdoms in the world) were smashed and broken into pieces and were like chaff upon the summer threshing floor. So they were swept away by the blowing winds (of calamity – the four horsemen which John earlier described) and not a trace was left of them. But the rock which struck the statue grew into a mighty mountain filling the whole earth." (Daniel 2: 34-35)

So this large flow of people toward the Mountain of Jehovah, itself becomes a part of that same Mountain which attracted it, as John's vision later on will show. There is no place in God's Kingdom for second class citizens, as some denominations lead us to believe. In one sense, though, we are looking at world conquest. But it is conquest of a different sort. It is voluntarily surrendering to God. As Isaiah in his prophecy maintained of that New Jerusalem which God would build: "Your gates will be left open all the time, they shall not be closed either by day or night so that men might bring you the wealth of the nations, and their leaders will voluntarily submit themselves to you as captives." (Isaiah 60: 11)

This depiction also makes us think about that time "When the morning stars all sang together, and the sons

of God (B'nai Elohim) shouted for joy." (Job 38: 7) The
morning stars of course are all those who herald the new
day of God about to dawn upon the world, and the sons
of God are those who turn to him and put on his
character. Surely Jesus had this scene in mind when he
declared that "There is more joy in heaven over one
sinner who repents than over the ninety and nine just
persons."   (Matthew 19: 13)

We should remember though that these people
John describes as moving toward the Mountain of
Jehovah, are people upon earth, not "up in heaven" as
some apparently believe. Though John is said to be "in
heaven", much of what he is describing is happening upon
earth. There he sees the growing crowd on earth, and the
sons of Israel who, by the light of knowledge that they
give, attract a growing multitude which grows continually
into a mountain (or a kingdom) of enormous size.

In reality, however, God does not really sit on any
throne. No one ever should become so tied to imagery
that he becomes a worshipper of idols. God, in visions,
sits upon a throne merely to convey to us the idea that
his power exceeds all of those who rule on earth, and his
authority is greater than all those who really sit on
thrones. As creator of the universe, he possesses sole
authority to govern it. No literal multitude will move
toward any hill. We are simply shown that the people of
God will offer the light of wisdom to the world, and
people everywhere on earth will learn the way of God
from them. This will make them part of a great nation
that has no boundaries, but is present everywhere
throughout the world.

Since I have taken you this far, perhaps I should
uncover just a few more of those images which we saw
earlier, in that spiritual heaven which John entered on the

day of Pentecost. Of those things seen by him, the most
prominent of them were the living creatures that
surround God's throne. These seraphim which we read
of in Isaiah surrounding God's throne are those spiritual
powers which speak for God and give him utterance:
"Each one had six wings, with two of these he covered
his face (for no one possibly could look on God) with two
others he covered his private parts (his feet to speak
euphemistically. For God made sex a sacred thing. Men
swore oaths by it, as is evident in the oath that Abraham
required from his slave Eleazer in *Genesis* 24: 2, 9. See
also *Genesis* 47: 29. It was realised that God was present
in the world throughout all generations). With another
two of these, each living creature flew about (for God
was present with all living things throughout the earth)."

God's living creatures, being closest of all things to
him, continually give praise to their creator night and
day. We must remember though that John's vision is
symbolic and we must interpret it as such. In the reality
that we experience, we are called on to consider what
these creatures represent, and by comparing other Bible
passages we see that they refer to those spiritual qualities
which are present in all living creatures of the world. It
is wrong though to suppose that we should worship
these (as certain heathen nations sometimes do). Still
these creatures speak for God – or rather God is able to
reveal his will and purposes through them to anyone
whose mind has been attuned to understanding him. But
how can they reveal his word?

As David said of God's creation: "The heavens
declare the glory of God, and the firmament testifies to
the work which he has done." (Psalm 19: 1) Or as Paul
observed: "What may be known of God is plain to all
men, because God has made his purpose clear to them.
For ever since he made the world, God's invisible nature –

his eternal power and personal qualities — may be clearly
seen, being understood from what he has made, so that
no man anywhere on earth can really say he is excused."
(Romans 1: 20)

It is this creation then which speaks for God, as the
glory of nature is closest of all things to his "throne". Yet
nature cannot look upon the God's face, yet by its very
closeness to God's presence, it is able to reveal his
purposes. Even so the carnal-minded man cannot
recognize the word of God in it. Yet all life can instruct
mankind, not only by the physical sciences alone but,
spiritually through the essence of those qualities that
God has placed in them. He therefore calls on man to
preserve and care for the great creator's work. For God
placed man in the garden that he made "to care for it
and protect it carefully." In the heaven that John sees,
the elders have been called upon to calm the sea of men
by holding back the winds of world calamities until the
sea is calm and the Israel of God might shine as the sun
above it (calling forth a new earth out of all the nations
of the world) and ruling as Adam ruled in Eden long ago.

When Yuri Gagarin, the world's first cosmonaut, was
catapulted into space, he proclaimed triumphantly that
he could see no sign of God out there at all. His words
should not have come as any great surprise to anyone for
his observation was predictable before he even uttered it.
He knew what he would say before he went up into space.
As he had not found God at all on earth or in the social
milieu of the land where he was reared, it wasn't likely he
could find him easily in any other place. The proud man,
whose mind is like a heavy iron gate which has been
closed and barred, cannot look upon the heaven of the
living God ה ו ה י, whose very name reveals his character
and power.

The spelling of God's name begins with the smallest of all letters in the Hebrew alphabet, the ‫י‬ . It is the one letter from which all other letters in the alphabet receive their basic character. No other letter there can possibly exist without employing it. It is the seed from which all the other letters grow. It is called the yot, whose articulated sound of "yuh" is like the drawing in of breath. It is followed by the ‫ה‬ "heh" whose articulated "huh" is like the sound of breathing out again. This is followed by the "‫ו‬", "veh" or "vuh" which by itself means "and". But its sound is like the breathing in of breath again. This is followed instantly by still another "huh" or breathing out of breath. So taken together these letters spell the very nature of God who made all things by his breath. Fittingly it is a verb form, and it means "what is, causing to become". Or as God told Moses once: "I am who I show myself to be."

"Oh Jehovah," the psalmist says, "how great and varied are your works! In wisdom you have made them all. The earth is full of your living creatures. Even the great wide sea is teeming with creatures beyond number, every kind of creature – great and small....When you hide your face from them they are disquieted; you take your breath away they vanish into dust." (Psalm 104: 24-29) The power to give life and to give expression to that life resides with God.

Where is heaven then? It is found in that unseen place where God resides. For God and heaven both are very close to us. Those who walk according to God's will converse with him continually. His door is open to us when we do his will, and we may walk in heaven every day we live. The only question is: Is heaven real to us or just a dream or wish? Jesus says he stands at the door and knocks. John tells us that the church of Philadelphia was given access to the very throne of God through the open door that God placed in their midst. We surely are reminded then of what Jesus told Nathaniel: "Hereafter you shall see heaven open (as a door is opened) and God's messengers descending and ascending to and from the son of man." (John 1: 51)   But the work God's servants do is not in heaven; it is work that they are called upon to do on earth. Heaven helps us find the spirit of that world we are to build, and then supplies the plan for building it. And that plan must be in harmony with the creation God has made.

If we are fully to appreciate what has been said in Chapter Seven, we must review all the necessary steps in the strategic plan which have occurred till now:

(1) The judge of Israel has appeared, revealing his full character, and has shown a willingness to walk with those of us who are willing to walk according to his way.

(2) God has called upon all synagogues and churches to perfect themselves, so that the will of heaven will be known by every member of that congregation, who will then be given open access to the throne of God.

(3) Those features of God's character (essential to the work he calls upon his followers to do) were clearly shown: holiness, justice, mercy.

(4) Elders in the government of God are those who conquer human frailties, understand the word of God, keep a faithful watch both night and day over God's creation, and use God's word to calm the restless sea of mankind.

(5) All creation, over which the sons of God keep faithful watch, proclaim God's righteousness by their humility, their mercy, their wisdom and their far-sightedness. His living creatures too, through their very being, also give him praise.

(6) The lamb of God alone, of all beings (living or dead) in God's government or out of it, has power to open and reveal the plan of God.

(7) The lamb began to open all the seals, and opened six of them.

Underneath the first Six Seals we found:

(1)   False prophets who excite the populace.

(2)   Warfare that destroys the world.

(3)   Famine which results because of this.

(4) Disease, rioting and rebellions occurring upon earth (symbolically spoken of as 'earthquakes').

(5)   Persecution of the Innocent.

(6)   Failure of the heavens. In this case "the heavens" refer to those ruling bodies which man has built to rule and guide his world: governments, celebrities, scholarship, arts and religion. When these fail to give light, the world in which man walks is dark.

There is really nothing which is unusual in what we find beneath these seals. All of us are well aware that identical phenomena to these have constantly been present throughout history, in every age that man has known. We have them with us now. They have been always present in the world. Governments still flounder, and the institutions of the nations give no light. Not the churches, not the educationalists, not the entertainment world and not the arts. All the world is dark, and crime is flourishing.

Great tribulation is about to fall upon the world, because we have mistreated the creation of God and have neglected the responsibilities that God put into our hands. "Who can possibly survive it?" John asks us earnestly. Then he shows us those who can: the members of the tribes of Israel, who stand as living letters written by the hand of God ready to enlighten what mankind's darkened hearts have made into a darkened world. When great tribulation falls upon the world, John says that multitudes will turn to the mount of Israel for enlightenment, because of the great example Israel (when it appears) will give.

If the churches and the synagogues are not prepared, then let them trim their lamps, because the bridegroom comes, and Chapter Seven gives us clear and definite commands: Four messenger spirits of God are ready to unloose the winds of war and tribulation upon the world, but they have been restrained by heaven (i.e. God's government) Such an action indicates that all God's servants must do everything they can to prevent social upheaval, blind rebellion, or war from taking place, so that everyone can be prepared with the word of God inscribed upon his forehead. These are the children of Israel called out by the spirit from the world.

Yet many churches apparently imagine that the church of God is only called upon to watch and wait, or to encourage and abet the conflicts in which the nations of the world become embroiled. Some watch for an unscriptural miracle of some sort, to snatch them from the world. And worst of all, many throughout the centuries have made themselves the puppets of world governments as they stir up patriotic zeal in those whom they send off to perish in the very "fires of hell" which they eschew. The church (as John defines it) is called upon to be the eyes and horns upon the lamb—the wheels which propel God's chariot. We, however, have been given access to his plan, and are called on to obey all of those commands that he has written out for us. All who are God's servants will obey. God's instructions are to be so written on the hearts of all the members of the tribes of Israel, that they may recognize his cause and see what parts they are to play in it.

Chapter Seven briefly pauses in the progress of this plan to help its readers understand the role the sons of Israel must play. The crowds will only turn to Israel when Israel, by its actions, shows them how different God's way is from that which motivates the world. Later Chapters in this book will reveal the gathering of Israel, but in the meantime Christians and Jews alike must earnestly prepare themselves for becoming part of it. For the moment, though, the church in each community is asked to give prophetic warnings to the world.

CHAPTER EIGHT

Early Warnings

Chapter Eight of *Revelation* opens with these words:

When the seventh seal was broken on the scroll, a silence lasting a full half hour fell upon all those in heaven. Then when the silence ended, I saw the seven angels (of the churches) presented before God. These were given seven trumpets (of God's golden wisdom to alert God's people and warn the kingdoms of the world). At that time another spirit messenger from God arrived. This priestly spirit stood beside the altar with a golden censer (or pan for holding incense).

This angel was given much (prayer or) incense to offer on the golden altar before the throne (of God). The smoke (or reverence) from these prayers was mingled in the golden pan (or vessel of true community with God), with the aroma of the prayers from all God's people, and offered on the altar (of the humble human spirit) before God's throne. (Great reverence like) smoke from the incense (that this angel offered) ascended up to God from the (priestly) angel's hand.

After this the angel priest of God immediately took the incense pan and filled it with the fire (of God's word) from the altar and hurled it directly at the (system of Satan's) earth. After that there followed peals of thunder, rumblings and flashes of fire and earthquakes (public disturbances and social upheaval).

Then the seven spirits (of the churches) who had the seven trumpet warnings, prepared themselves for sounding them.

***

Like all the scenes to which we are made witnesses in this dynamic "apocalypse", or dramatic unveiling, (that Jesus shows to John) the one presented here for us, in Chapter Eight, is powerful, definitive and memorable. Yet like the other scenes that we were shown, it is symbolic too – not literal. Its meaning has been sealed to all who worship images. So it is important that we realise that what we see is purely spiritual and has no form at all in substance. These images that John has drawn for us are what teachers would refer to as "concrete illustrations". They define relationships so that the reader may visually appreciate the church's source of unity and the tasks that Jesus the Christ (as heaven's sole High Priest) has commissioned them to do as they memorably engraft upon the mind the nature of the message Jesus sent them to the Gentiles to proclaim.

In this vision we are shown the spirit of community existing in each city's church present "in heaven", through the power of prayer, before God's throne, and unified beside the golden altar by the only High Priest heaven has placed over them: Jesus who is called the Christ. Paul's letter to the Ephesians helps us to appreciate the meaning of the scene that we are witnessing.

In it he says: "Although I am the least of all those vessels God has chosen, he graciously entrusted me with showing to the Gentiles the unlimited riches that Christ has made available to them. For up till now these hidden truths, which God – who created all things – had kept concealed, he has chosen to make known. Now, through the power that he has given to the church (the power of his pure truth), he has asked them to make known the many-sided wisdom of God to (everyone, including) all the ruling powers which spiritually guide and govern the imaginations of men (literally 'in the heavenly realms') and to clarify for them the purpose of the work that

Jesus Christ our lord performed. So now, in union with
Christ through faith, we are able to come before Jehovah
(in prayer) with freedom and confidence."

(Ephesians 3: 8 -12)

Is not this the vision John has shown to us? In John's
vision, each autonomous church community is given its
commission directly by Jesus Christ himself — not by any
intermediate authority made superior to it. For that
reason Paul emphasized his own unworthiness. Therefore
such an illustration serves to underline the fact that the
only place of ultimate authority is heaven (where God
dwells) and the only High Priest ruling over those who
serve him is Jesus the Messiah who stands beside the
golden altar of God.

So I must emphasize the point, that since these
images are not corporal, but depictions rather of
relationships, translating them involves far more than
mere transliteration of the words. There is no throne of
God "up in the sky". We are shown this image so that we
might visually appreciate the fact that God is the head
of government, whose rule takes precedence over all
kings and rulers upon earth. Angels (those spirits in
nature and in people which reveal God's will) are shown
to us so that we might understand that God, who is the
creator of all things, delegates his own authority to all
powers and "spirits" serving him.

What heaven is, then, is an awareness of God's
presence in whatever place we are. King David wrote
one whole psalm (Psalm 139) explaining that. Jacob
became aware of God when he was at Bethel and, awoke
there from a dream. Realising where he was, he declared:
"How awesome it is here! Jehovah most certainly is in
this place, even though I did not realise it. Beyond all
doubt, God's House is here, for this is the gate of heaven."

(Genesis 28: 16-17) Isaiah, while in God's temple at Jerusalem, envisioned God there sitting on a throne high and lifted up. It was that experience of God which inspired him to say: "God is with us."

Then, the children of ancient Israel (when coming out of bondage in Egypt) actually carried a tent for God with them wherever they went, so that he could have a place to rest. This was done so as to impress upon the minds of all the people that God was in their midst. Even Ezekiel, following a vision that he had beside the canals of Babylon, tried to make God's scattered people realise that God's throne remained with them however scattered they might be. All they had to do was call upon his name.

Heaven, therefore, is everywhere where God is, and Moses himself expressed that sentiment in these words: "What other nation is so great as to have their Elohim (gods) near to them in the way that Jehovah our Elohim (God) is near to us whenever we pray?" (Deuteronomy 4: 7) He is always with us for he wears creation like a garment, and Paul expressed that sentiment when he said: "(God, our Father,) rules over all things; he is through all things, and in all things." (Ephesians 4: 6) The psalmist too was conscious of this when he said: "When you take away their breath, (your creatures) die and turn to dust, but when you send your spirit forth, they are created, and you continually renew the face of earth."

(Psalm 104: 27-30)

So when John, in this vision of heaven, shows us Jehovah "sitting on a throne" and the angels of the seven churches present there with the spirit of heaven's High Priest, we should realise that the churches in the various communities have been unified through Christ alone, by approaching God in prayer. Just as one brother was not to lord it over another, neither was any earthly city called upon to be more exalted than the rest.

It is significant, of course, that it is the spirit of the seven churches which appear "in heaven" (with the spirit of Christ) before God. For this signifies that all those from the various churches who "walk in the spirit" with Christ will be present there, and commissioned for the work that they have been called upon to do. As Jesus told his followers "many are called but few are chosen"... "for straight is the gate and narrow is the way that leads to life, and few there be that find it."

In a parable that Jesus once told, he spoke of a householder who gave gold talents to his servants for them to use during his absence, and two of these increased the substance of their lord. John's vision, like that parable of the talents, shows the servants of God entrusted with sounding golden trumpets rather than with spending money. Yet both illustrations depict for us a commissioning of God's communities, and both of them deal with the wisdom God has called on them to declare before the world.

Now the sounding of these trumpets serves two purposes. They are alarms to assemble the children of Israel, and they serve as warnings to a God-forsaking world. Chapter Seven specifically identified the nature of the tribes which were being called, and showed them what their purpose was to be. They were to be the sun of God's new firmament, truthfully revealing the light of God in words and deed ("in spirit and in truth", as scriptures say). Having had that shown to us, the purpose of the trumpeters is clarified for us. They are the priesthood God commissions, through his anointed High Priest, to assemble Israel, and we realise that Israel is being called from its captivity as slaves to spiritual Babylon.

So if you are anything at all like me, you will have
noticed that throughout the chapters we've been
studying, there has been a growing pattern of steadily
increasing unity amongst the people God has called upon
to do his work. This began in Chapter One when the
individual was shown the character of Jesus Christ – the
man from heaven. Jesus was the golden standard by
which to measure human character. All those serving
him · would reflect the qualities of character that were
seen in Christ, not set their standards by those spiritual
idols which the pagan world supplied for them. The
Christian character was the basis of all Christian unity.
As Jesus said: "Be ye one even as I and the Father are
one." For the unity that Christ requires amongst his
followers is that unity with God derived from knowledge
of the character that God has written in his word – a
unity that only heaven can supply.

In Chapters Two and Three, the churches all were
shown the great necessity for re-establishing one
Christian fellowship within the nucleus of each city in
the world. For a divided Christian community cannot
possibly provide a solid base for unifying a divided world.
Jesus made it their responsibility to follow those
instructions he had given them. Like any building
carefully constructed (from the bottom up) a healthy
civic church depended on a firm foundation, carefully
laid. The church therefore was called upon to make
certain that the base they built upon was founded on the
strong, sure rock of God's own word. Shortcomings
which had separated them from God and therefore from
each other needed to be remedied. These shortcomings
were all specifically identified so that there would be no
wild speculation regarding what they were. Then the
churches all were shown the way for dealing with them
and for overcoming them – using as their golden
standard, the unchanging word of God.

John next, in Chapter Four, shows the churches of the world the purpose of the work that they are called on to achieve. John does this by visually depicting for them a memorable and unifying scene which defines the church's aim and nature of all relationships existing amongst those serving him in "the heaven" where he dwells. This visual depiction forcefully inscribes upon their minds the goal his servants are to reach in building upon earth a kingdom like to that which they are shown. This portion of John's vision is the only blueprint that was ever given to the followers of Christ for establishing that Kingdom Jesus had proposed.

Afterwards, they are shown the difficulties they will have to face and overcome in taking on that task: world calamities whose violent and destructive brutishness is threatening to lay waste the world. These are found beneath the seven different seals upon the scroll the Lamb of God alone is able to unseal and take from God's own hand. This rules out the possibility of any other prophet contravening Jesus Christ's commands or altering the method Jesus, "the first and last" has given them.

Having these things graphically and memorably revealed to them, the churches next are shown the nation Israel. This vision is a foreview of what must be achieved — a holy nation on a hill to whom all suffering humanity can turn for solace and for comforting, and which offers them a more rewarding way of life as well. Such a vision often makes one thoughtfully reflect upon that very noble sentiment inscribed upon the American Statue of Liberty, which says:

> "Give me your tired, your poor,
> Your huddled masses yearning to breathe free,
> The wretched refuse of your teeming shore
> Send these, your tempest-tost to me,
> I lift my lamp beside the golden door."

That certainly is the sentiment of God's kingdom, but I must hasten to say that "The United States of America is not the Kingdom of God." Nor is any other nation in the world – Christian or otherwise. If any of them wish of course to be a part of it, they must begin to build it now in the humble way suggested in this document which John has given them. There are no shortcuts for building it. Its citizens must be "above" all petty strife which gnaws the human heart and sets mankind against itself. Being the light of the world, even as God is, they must shed all animosity and "Love your enemies, bless them that curse you, and do good to them that hate you and pray for them who contemptuously abuse you, so that you might be the offspring of your Father in heaven. For God's sun shines upon the evil and the good and lets his rain fall alike upon the righteous and unrighteous. Of what use is it to bless only those from whom you will receive a like reward in return."   (Matthew 5: 43 - 46)

Now in Chapter Eight of *Revelation*, we move on to the next step in this intricately presented plan leading toward world unity. For in this chapter we are shown the seven angels of the churches "in heaven" standing at "the golden altar" before God where they are met by an unpresuming angel that we (as individuals) should be able easily to recognize. The very image of this angel in the sanctuary with seven other angels waiting on his word to act, instantly reminds us of the vision we were shown in Chapter One, when John said: "When I turned I saw seven golden lampstands, and among them what appeared to be a man wearing a long (priestly) robe (of righteousness) that reached down to his feet."

Then to emphasize what we should notice later on, this priest was careful to point out to John: "There are many secret meanings in my words, as in the seven stars I hold in my right hand: The seven stars are the angels in the seven churches, and the seven lampstands are the seven churches." Vessels in God's sanctuary then are his human vessels upon earth. And the seven angels waiting at the priestly angel's right hand to receive commands are the angels of the seven churches. Each angel (in the chapter we are reading now) is given "a golden trumpet" which, like the golden talents that the master gave to every church, is representative of the wisdom of God's word. So the angels are next told they must *prepare themselves* for sounding these. As the talents in the parable that Jesus told his followers was money for purchasing the souls of men from their captivity, so the golden trumpets call God's people out of their enslavement to Babylon, and warn all those who don't respond of the consequences that they face.

The golden trumpets (or the wisdom of God's word) should not be sounded carelessly. Nor should any self-appointed prophet piously presume to add or take away from what Christians have been asked to herald to the world. They are called on to give warnings that are definite and sure and summon all the sons of Israel from every nation in the world. To do this, they cannot deviate from that course of action Christ himself has given them. To alter it would only cause confusion in the ranks. Until these battles have been fought and won, this plan alone remains the only plan. To underline this fact for every Christian church, we were told that no one living or dead — in heaven, upon earth, or under the earth — was able or worthy enough to take the scroll from God's hand or to reveal its many mysteries by loosening the seals. Only the lamb of God himself was able to do this. Can anyone, therefore, presume to improve upon a plan which God himself prepared, and only his messiah could reveal?

It starts off as a plan for building "Christian" unity amongst the congregations scattered through the world.

However, this plan did not really start with John or Jesus Christ. A careful reading of the scriptures readily reveals that Moses laid the firm foundations for it when he used principles identical to those which Jesus uses, for unifying ancient Israel. John's reference here to "the golden altar", the golden censer of the Mishkan where God resides, the angel (acting as High Priest) burning incense and the angels charged with blowing trumpets for assembling the sons of Israel (in this case for battle with God's enemies), calls to mind the Jewish origins of Christianity. Such origins cannot be ignored as all the symbols in this chapter we are reading now allude to them.

"The man from heaven" was not a new invention of the Christian faith. The Hebrew scriptures make constant references to him. And the whole idea of unifying Israel through him began with Moses in the wilderness. Isaiah refers emphatically to him throughout his texts. Yet Moses centuries before, when he built the tabernacle in the wilderness, symbolically depicted him for Israel. This tabernacle immediately became the centre of all public life during Israel's wilderness experience. The whole complex of Israel's camp was built around the tabernacle which was the dwelling place, so we are told, for the Divine Presence (or Shekinah). God was in the midst of Israel.

Early Israel had no human king. God "dwelt among his people", and it was the Shekinah which governed them, and the High Priest and the Levites were his courtly ministers. Through these they became one body united in its parts like the body of one man. The temple complex, therefore, and the assembled tribes of Israel together became the great design for the man of heaven which Isaiah was to speak of at a later time. The various tribes of Israel were the members of that body. And the holy sanctuary (or Mishkan) was representative of the head and heart. By this means then, Israel itself was chosen to become the physical manifestation of God's spiritual presence upon earth.

I remember once in the 1950s talking to a man who had recently returned from visiting the Soviet Union. He was a communist and he spoke glowingly of the great feat the Soviets had achieved in rebuilding Volgograd, which at that time was known as Stalingrad. There was much to be admired in what he said. "The first building they erected," he informed me, "was the theatre" When I asked him why, he told me simply, "That's because it would be the centre and the inspiration of their lives."

His words "carried me in spirit" to another time several millenia before when the Jewish people on returning from a long captivity in Babylon set about rebuilding old Jerusalem. It was a noble task as well. And the first building they began rebuilding was the Temple of Jehovah. For what the theatre was to the Russia of a later time, the Temple of God had been to ancient Israel. It stood for all the values on which their lives were built and it was the centre for awakening the spirit of new life in them — the unseen Shekinah which ruled and guided them.

Like nations of the past, the modern western world, as well, has temples of its own unobtrusively but spiritually instructing all its citizens. Not long ago the motion picture cinema was the focal point of life. For many decades, in almost every nation of the world, motion pictures taught the people all the values of their world. To enter such a cinema was to experience the heaven which the nations of the world provided for the populace. The people actually adored the characters they saw in them, and the way of life of whole communities was governed by the images they saw. The public mind and heart were shaped and ruled by artificial worlds which the media made large and glamorous. Later on radio and television sets were made the family altar of the home to re enforce the doctrines taught to them in cinemas. Their doctrines and the way of life they preached became the models which families, adolescents and young children tried to emulate. Imaginations were shaped, and grew and reached maturity through them.

Temples always were and still remain important to the way of public life. They simply have disguised themselves and go by other names. Emanuel Anati, an Egyptologist, apparently believed he'd found one of the places where Moses and the Israelites had camped during their long wilderness experience. His various findings in 1985 at Har Karkom (a mountain between Beersheba and the gulf) so exactly coincided with the *Exodus* accounts he'd read, he was convinced that it had been the place where Moses met with God. One such finding there had been the ruins of an ancient Bronze Age temple, which even certain Christians now imagine might have been the prototype from which Moses took his pattern for the tabernacle which that prophet built for Israel. The view these Christians hold is based upon the Bible text which says: "See that you make these (vessels for the temple) according to the pattern that I showed you in the mountain." (Exodus 25: 40)

Of course what they suggest is possible, but it is also true that there never was a city built at any time in history that did not have a temple of some kind. What distinguishes the tabernacle which Moses built for the God of Israel is the nature of the God who dwelt in it. All nations worshipped national gods — exalting local gods whose spirits were reflected in the images they made. Israel worshipped the creator of all things, whose spirit (not being defined by images) could be found in every place. God therefore dwelt "among his people" as an invisible presence. The tabernacle built them up as a nation and as individuals into the divine man who would eventually restore the earth to the ways of the creator who had made all things.

The Mishkan (or sanctuary of God) whose inner workings were not seen was like the hidden thoughts and passions of a man. These, so we are told, were to be made holy and not to be corrupted or defiled, so that the mind of Israel (through its wilderness experience) could be made free from every unclean, death-promoting influence and practice they had learned in Egypt. Through living intimately with God, they were to learn to be like him and adopt the virtues of his character. "Be ye holy," they were told, "for Jehovah your God is holy." To emphasize this fact to them the High Priest wore a golden plate across his forehead. It was called the Tzitz. Inscribed upon it were the words: "Holy to God." This made plain to them that they were not to be defiled with evil thoughts and practices, so that their minds eventually could become the living sanctuary where God dwelt.

The Ark of God itself was carefully designed to represent that human heart which God was fashioning for Israel. In this regard its structure is significant. The Ark of God was a box within a box within a box. In the innermost of these three boxes was placed the law of God, manna (or daily bread of life) and Aaron's budding rod.

The wooden box, which is the natural heart of man, was placed inside a golden box of wisdom. Another golden box of wisdom was then placed inside the wooden box. These three boxes were then sealed around the top with gold as well. Such symbolic measures remind us instantly of that experience which Moses had beside the burning gas plant in the wilderness. There the angel of

God (inside the burning fraxinella bush) like the seraphim around God's throne, commissioned Moses to do a mighty work in Israel. The Holy Land, which Moses was commissioned by the angel in the bush to lead them to, was the character of God within themselves. The Wicked Land of Canaan which would become the Holy Land was no more than a carnal depiction of the first step in a long journey toward a better world. What God desired was a holy people who would spread out and one day fill the whole earth so as to care for that creation God had made.

Through being twice asked by God to place his hand into his bosom and then examine it each time, Moses learned that the creator's great intent was to change the wilful human heart in Israel and then eventually in all mankind. So if God cast Israel off as certain Christians continually insist he did, then God did not accomplish what he said he would. And it was God—not Israel—who consequently failed. For Israel was God's example to the world. God had set about to work a miracle in them (and as the Bible unmistakably has said, nothing is too difficult for God). So this miracle was one to which God had set his hand, and one which he had sworn to do. Consequently God was now obliged to bring about that miracle. If God failed to do what he had said he would, then God was not the being that he claimed to be, since he told Moses at the burning bush, "I am who I show myself to be."

In considering the Ark of God, we are reminded of the words which God once used in his address to Job. "Who endowed the heart with wisdom or gave understanding to the mind?" he asked. (Jobn 38: 36) Jeremiah's prophecy, as well, enlarged upon this theme of training of the human heart, and was consistent with the placing of God's law and the shewbread inside the Ark: "I will put my law in their minds and write it on their hearts," he wrote (Jeremiah 31: 33). Such a heart which feeds upon the daily manna of God's wisdom will possess within itself the ever blossoming staff of God's authority. "And he shall be like a tree planted by the rivers of water which brings forth fruit in its season." The Shekinah of God will continually reveal itself "above" such a heart and be guarded by the cherubim (those discerning spirits present in creation which reveal God's presence to all who seek him earnestly, but conceal it from all who aggressively oppose his will).

This tree of living truth abounding with the fruit of life was illustrated for the tribes of Israel through the breastplate which the High Priest wore. The many different jewels on it were illustrations of the precious qualities the sons of Israel were called on to imbibe and bear as fruit to feed the world. Significantly, the tribal names were all inscribed on them so as to illustrate and meaningfully teach that principle. The symbolism and the wording of the scriptures leave no doubt that it had been the calling of this people to be a living tabernacle for the world and, through their living presence in the midst of all humanity, reveal to every nation there, the very character of God as it had been revealed to Israel and inscribed upon their hearts and minds.

The Shekinah, which was to dwell in them, was to govern all their words and deeds so that Israel might feed the world the fruit of life they bore. As the tree of life amongst the nations of the world, they were to bear the fruit of healing words and righteous deeds so as to teach the world the way of God. As Jesus told the Jews before the fall of Old Jerusalem: "Let your light so shine before men (in all nations of the world) that they may see your good works and glorify your Father which is in heaven." That those words were said to any Jew who heard him speak is verified by what Jesus said in that same speech: "*Anyone* who hears these words of mine and does them, I shall liken to a man who built his house upon a rock."

The whole structure of the tabernacle in the wilderness was no more than an illustration of God's real dwelling place. It had been designed to waken in the hearts and minds of Israel a consciousness of God's reality and his presence in themselves. So for that reason we are told by scriptures not that God dwelt "in it" but rather that "God dwelt among them." He "was with his people" That is "in" the people themselves. "I am in the Father, and the Father is in me," is a confession any truly faithful Jew (in whom the word of God had taken root) should have been able to have made.

So as to make this clear to them the sons of Israel were told that they should bind God's word upon their arms and wear it as frontlets between their eyes. God was to be for them a living presence in their lives. He was "in" his people – and the tabernacle which he fashioned was designed to teach them this. Israel was chosen to reveal, to every other nation upon earth, the man of heaven dwelling in themselves (within the inner sanctuary of their hearts and minds). As Jesus's disciple John, much later on, would write: "As many as received him (this man of heaven, revealed and written in God's word) were given the means of becoming the sons of God."   (John 1: 12)

Israel was to be the tree of life from which all people of the world could eat and live. They were to be the sycamore tree bearing good figs in the very midst of the Garden of God. To eat from that tree meant emulating those on whom the seal of God was placed – those who knew God's word and displayed his character in all their deeds and words. As King Solomon once said of the

good figs growing on the tree of Israel: "The fruit of
righteousness is a tree of life."   (Proverbs 11: 30)

So it was that the man from heaven was illustrated
in the tabernacle services of Israel. Yet what the temple
was to ancient Israel, one solitary Jew became for
Christianity. Jesus was to be the focal point uniting all
church fellowships in cities spread throughout the world.
He was the man from heaven made flesh and therefore
was their sole High Priest. No other man on earth was
ever called upon to supercede him in that role — even
temporarily. As the tabernacle was the place where Israel
was united in one body, so Christians (looking to the
character of God as it had been revealed to them in
Christ) were gathered in one body by the spirit of their
resurrected lord who stood beside "the golden altar" of
heaven where he commissioned them for spiritual battle
with the world.

The golden altar too must be observed, for it was the
altar in the sanctuary of God. This of itself stresses the
great need for unity in the tasks to be performed. This
altar had three names: "the golden altar", "the incense
altar", and "the inner altar". It was the altar to atone for
the sins of Israel and to unify them in the name of God.

Although this altar was inside the Mishkan (or
sanctuary of God) it wasn't listed when the instructions
for building the other sanctuary vessels were given — the
table of shewbread and the menorah. It is significant
that the instructions for building it were given separately
as that served to underline the altar's great importance in
the holy place. Because the incense offering was as
important as it was, the incense sacrifices offered on it
were the first and the last sacrifices of each day. Some I
know will wish to argue that no sacrifice was ever
offered there at all since no animal was ever burned on it.

Yet because it was the altar on which the blood of innocence was laid, all prayers (or incense) rendered there were sacrifices, as it was the blood of innocence which ensured their being heard.

To help us better understand that unity of spirit which God desires from all those serving him, we should take time to consider earnestly how significant it is that the Hebrew word "Elohim" which we translate as "God," is given several meanings when translated from the Hebrew text. It can singularly refer to Jehovah (the creator of the world) or be collectively applied to all the different Gods the Gentile nations served. In other places too, translators (at their own discretion) have rendered that same word as "angels" in their translations of the text. However, what "Elohim" really means is "great powers" and "Elohim" possibly should be translated just as that.

The first chapter of *Genesis* therefore was meant to be a text which could speak to everyone and not arouse dispute. The words of Moses here were looked on as self-evident for Moses took a very simple "look and see" approach. In ancient times, therefore, the *Genesis* account most probably would have been read like this: "In the beginning great powers made the heavens and the earth. But the earth was shapeless and without life, and darkness covered the face of the universe." No heathen rebel against God anywhere on earth (or in any heaven governing the earth) could possibly have found much quarrel or argument with that.

Even the seven days of creation were never meant to be contentious grounds for argument, for "day" was variously used in scriptures to mean any length of time at all in which a certain thing had been achieved, and "night" was frequently regarded as a period of unconsciousness (regardless of how long it was) which preceded an awakening. The coming out of darkness into light was used in *Genesis* to refer to the first awakening of many different things from unconscious non-being into the light of being. What unifies the great powers (or the Elohim) for Israel's descendants, however, is found later in the Bible texts which say, "Jehovah, your Elohim, made the heavens and the earth." It is God's name which gives God's people unity while not negating their diversity. It is God's name that unites all spirits into one.

In the meadows there are many kinds of flowers. All bloom at different times, in different ways and have many different forms and shades and colours. There are many different kinds of fruits and trees, as well as many different kinds of animals. People too are made in different ways. It is the character of God – his name – which makes them one with him so that they do not war against their fellow man or mistreat that world of nature which God put "under" their control. Mankind (male and female) as God established them in unity with himself, were to be a living part of that heaven which he made to rule the world. Jesus, understanding this, commanded his disciples: "Be ye one even as I and my Father are one." They were made to be a part of those "great powers" by which Jehovah ruled. As the psalmist said of the people whom Jehovah sanctified: "You are Elohim, and all of you are sons of the Most High." (Psalm 82: 6)

The emphasis then that John makes in so few words on unity has many ancient references in it. But the imagery he uses makes it clear that the only source of unity for the churches of the world is not dependent upon kings, princes or exalted individuals of any kind. "Do not put your trust in princes," the psalmist said, "in mortal men, who cannot save." (Psalm 146: 3) The unity Christ offers them is "up in heaven" with God and with

the risen son of man. The spirit of the church in each
city individually may enter heaven and stand before the
throne of God when they put off (their shoes) the
foreign teachings of mankind's fallen world so that their
presence there will not defile the dwelling place of God.
The word of God alone is what Christ recommends for
linking up the different bodies of the Christian fellowship.

The church, so history now unmistakably confirms,
chose a different course from that which Jesus Christ and
John advised. This may possibly explain the reason it is
so divided now against itself. It has always seemed a
contradiction to my mind that different churches send
out missionaries to the Jews in order to "convert" them
to "the Christian faith". The Jewish people have the word
of God with them. John, in this vision shows the
Christian church, the importance of the word of God for
uniting Christians first, before attempting any
"missionary" work. For you cannot unify the world with
your disunity. When that moment of full unity arrives,
trumpets will be given to each church community on
earth to summon all of Israel and warn the world about
the coming of the son of man. Yet even here, John tells
us that the angels of the churches must "prepare
themselves" for sounding them. The trumpets given to
the churches are not to be presumptuously blown.

***

John continues the chapter we are presently
examining in this way:

Immediately after that, the priestly spirit (standing
by the golden altar) took the incense pan, and filling it
with the power of God's pure word ("fire") from off the
altar, he hurled it directly at (mankind's destructive
system existing on) the earth. Instantly there followed

peals of thunder, rumblings and flashes of fire and earthquakes (public disturbances and social upheaval).

Then the seven messengers (of the churches) who had the seven trumpet warnings *prepared themselves* for sounding them. (In a parallel passage in Matthew's gospel, we are told they rose and trimmed their lamps.)

After the first (church) messenger of God had sounded his trumpet warning, hail and fire mixed with blood fell heavily upon the earth, and one third of all trees and all grass were burned up.

When the second messenger of God sounded the golden trumpet warning to the world, something like an enormous mountain (or world kingdom) all in flames (embroiled in violent public disturbances and warfare) was thrown into the sea (of turbulent mankind) so that one third of the sea was turned to blood. Consequently one third of all living creatures in it died, and one third of all ocean-going ships (institutions of world trade and commerce) were destroyed. (That is to say the spirit of Babylon the Great was present among the great world populace, destroying lives and people's means of livelihood.)

Following another great prophetic trumpet warning given by God's third messenger, a massive star like a flaming torch (illustrating the fallen spirit of mankind which had once been glorious) fell from the sky upon a third of all the rivers and springs of water (those predominant world philosophies expounded by the cultural and entertainment world through which the people generally refresh themselves).

The name of the star is "Vindictiveness" (literally "Wormwood"). (Because of it) a third of all (life-giving) waters turned poisonous and many people died from the waters that had gone bad. (The cultural waters of society as well as the waters of God's word would be made perverse and spiritually poisonous, and Satan, the spirit of mankind's opposition to God, won't miss a chance for poisoning them).

When the fourth messenger of God sounded his trumpet warning, a third of the sun (the monarch or chief of state) was struck, a third of the moon (whatever temple — secular or religious order which bolsters national philosophy) and a third of the stars (illustrious figures who have captured the imagination of the populace) so that a third of them turned dark, leaving a third of the day without light, as well as a third of the night.

While I watched, I saw an eagle (the swiftest and most far-sighted of God's messengers, which stand closest to his throne) whom I heard crying with a loud voice: "Woe, Woe, Woe (tremendously painful suffering and affliction) will fall upon all those living on the earth following the sound of the trumpets that the other three angels are about to blow."

***

When we see the High Priest of heaven (in response to all the prayers of those "whose blood is crying from the ground") take the altar fire into the incense pan and hurl it at the earth, we must surely think of those words Jesus is reported to have said: "I have come to cast fire upon the earth, and how I wish that it were already kindled." (Luke 12: 49) These words help us to understand that the fire which the High Priest took and threw upon the earth was symbolic of Jesus Christ's whole ministry. It was a ministry defined in a message Jesus sent to John the Baptist when he told John's disciples: "Go back and tell John everything that you have seen and heard: The blind receive their sight, the lame are made to walk, leprosy is cured, the deaf are made to hear, the dead are raised, and the poor have the good news preached to them. And everyone is blessed who does not turn away from me." (Matthew 11: 4-6)

Paul (Christ's missionary to the Gentiles) also itemized the elements of that sacred fire. In a letter that he sent to Roman Christians, he told them: "Do not repay evil for evil. Be careful to do what is right in the eyes of everybody. If it is possible, as far as it depends on you, live at peace with everyone. Do not take revenge, my friends, but leave room for God's wrath, for it is written: 'It is my place to avenge. I will repay,' Jehovah says. So rather than taking vengeance, if your enemy is hungry, feed him; if he is thirsty, give him something to drink. In doing this you will be pouring burning coals upon his head. (That is to say, you will be spiritually destroying all the values he has come to live by and to trust.) Do not be overcome by evil, but overcome evil with good." (Romans 12: 17-21)

The word of God is spiritually and physically revealed in speech and works. And fire from God's altar is spiritually symbolic of the power of God's pure, unadulterated word spiritually and physically revealed. Many Bible texts underline that point for us. For instance, when the Jewish prophet Isaiah tells us of his spiritual experience in Jehovah's temple at Jerusalem in the year that King Uzziah died, he symbolically describes what he has experienced in visual terms, telling us: "Then one of the seraphim flew toward me having a live coal in his hand, which he had taken with tongs from the (golden) altar. Placing this upon my mouth, he said, 'Now that this has touched your lips and taken away the uncleanness (of your words) it removes the sin (of their untruthfulness)." (Isaiah 6: 6-7)

Being given God's pure word to speak, Isaiah was thoroughly prepared for the work that God commissioned him to do. So now, when John shows us heaven's High Priest standing beside the golden altar (on which the blood of innocence was laid) and hurling fire upon the rebellious system of the world, we understand that this fire is effectually the fire of Jesus's whole ministry, a ministry which still, through the power of his spirit, continues in the world. The peals of thunder, rumblings, flashes of fire and earthquakes (which follow in the wake of that pure truth) are phenomena we find frequently revealed in many Bible texts. They were clearly present throughout Jesus's whole ministry.

There are many excellent examples of them in the book of *Acts*. Luke, the church's first historian, gave a brief description of the upheaval following Stephen's trial speech. Stephen, the first appointed deacon of the church, fearlessly addressed the judicial body at Jerusalem and drew a very violent response from those who heard him speak.

Luke, in his report, describes the incident in these words: "Now upon hearing the things (which Stephen had to say) his listeners were cut to the heart and infuriated, and they ground their teeth against him....They raised a great shout against him and put their hands over their ears and rushed together upon him." (Acts 4: 54-57)

Again, when Paul preached against idolatry at Ephesus, the local silversmiths and tradesmen there stirred up a storm of violence among the citizens. Luke, in his account tells us that "When (all the business people of the city) heard of (how Paul by his effective preaching was ruining the profits of their trade) they were furious and began (appealing to national and religious sentiments by) shouting "Great is Diana of the Ephesians!" And soon the whole city was in an uproar. The people having seized Gaius and Aristarchus, Paul's companions from Macedonia, rushed as one man with them into the theatre....The whole assembly was filled with confusion, some shouting one thing, and some another. Yet everyone was so confused that most of them didn't even know the reason they were gathered there." (Acts 19: 28-32)

When God's undiluted word is spoken or performed, we must expect violent reactions of some kind from those supposedly upholding the morality and values of Satan's stubbornly pragmatic world. Those passages which I have cited here surely testify to that. The ministry (of fire) which Jesus Christ himself poured directly on the earth (in speech and works) serve to illustrate the nature of the work his followers are called upon to do.

After being told that the High Priest threw fire upon the earth, we understand that the angels of the churches (in every city of the world) are called on to observe what he has done by carefully reviewing Jesus Christ's whole ministry so as to prepare themselves in the work that he requires from them—confidently sounding the trumpets he has given them. This deliberate action of the High Priest clearly serves the churches as a strong command to continue in the work that he began. His ministry would serve them as a guide in what they were to do. For this reason the whole ministry of Jesus Christ must be carefully reviewed by all the congregations every-where throughout the world — not as something done and finished with, but as a work that is still continuing.

So in John's vision, we are shown Christ's spirit commissioning each city's body of believers in God's work to sound the voice of God's own wisdom to the world. The trumpets they are given are representative of this. Like the talents in the story that I told you earlier, both symbols represent the wisdom of God's word. In each case the purpose is to bring salvation to the world, and rescue them from death row in Satan's prison house. In order to do this, the angels of the churches (so we are told) must of necessity prepare themselves. Otherwise the trumpet's voice will be of no effect.

It is the duty then of every church to systematically review not only everything that they have done in preparation for the tasks assigned to them, but they must carefully review as well the scheme of Jesus Christ's whole ministry, and see how it applies in every case, to each of all the warnings that they are called upon to give.

The first four warnings deal with (1) **leadership**, a topic Jesus spoke on frequently. Amongst the many things he said regarding it was "Do not be called Master for one is your master and you are all brothers. And don't call anyone on earth your father, for you have but one father and he is in heaven;" (2) **the world system**, of which Paul warned us saying: "Do not be conformed in any way to this world." (3) **the poisoning of cultural waters**, of which Jesus said: "By your traditions you have made the word of God of no effect." (4) **the darkness of world rulers**, of which Jesus said: "If the blind lead the blind, both shall fall into the grave." I touch but superficially on all these topics, for I leave it to the reader to do his own research on this, I merely try to show that Jesus clearly has defined the way for all of us.

It also is the church's great responsibility to see that every step in the whole plan Jesus Christ has given them has been thoroughly attended to. For the course of action from this point forward is a totally aggressive one. There is no turning back from it. The members of Christ's body must be thoroughly committed and totally involved in — spiritual, not carnal — war. And as Jesus told his followers centuries ago: "Notice that I am sending you as sheep into the midst of wolves. You must therefore be as cautious and shrewd as serpents, yet remain as harmless as doves."   (Matthew 10: 16)

That leaves no room for rifles, bombs or terrorist attacks of any kind. Such a mission requires much preparation, not maudlin sentiment.

Yet as the people of Israel well knew, the word of God can bless or curse the listener. God's word is "torah" or "instruction". If it is heeded and obeyed, men are blessed by it. Yet when it is disobeyed, the listeners are cursed. When God's word blesses mankind, it is spoken of as "dew" or "rain". When it comes upon them as a curse, it is spoken of as "fire" or "hail". So in reality, if we are fair to God, God doesn't really curse the world. It is mankind who brings down curses on himself. As it is written in the Psalms: "Declare them guilty (in your courts) O God! Let them be brought down by their own deceits for they have rebelled against you." (Psalm 5: 10) Or as Isaiah once observing said: "Wickedness burns like a fire. It therefore shall devour the briars and thorns and set ablaze the thickets of the forests, mounting upward like a great column of smoke. Thus shall Jehovah's anger burn up all the people, for no man will spare even his own brother."   (Isaiah 9: 18-19)

Warfare is certainly the warning mentioned here. The seven trumpet warnings lying underneath the seventh seal call to mind the *Feast of Trumpets* which were celebrated by the sons of Israel. *The Feast of Trumpets*, now called *Rosh Hashana* in the Jewish faith, was a solemn festival for those who celebrated it, and each solemn sounding of the ram's horn trumpet was part of a progressive plan of warning for an approaching

day of reckoning. We only need await the proper time
and be prepared for it.

Just who then will decide the proper time for us?
The truth is that the time has always been appropriate.
As Jesus said to his disciples long ago: "Do not say, that
there remains four months before the harvest comes. For
look and see: I tell you today, 'If you will only lift your
eyes, you cannot help but notice that the fields are ripe
already with their grain and waiting to be harvested.' So
anyone who reaps them will have wages and gather in the
fruit of everlasting life. When that is done, the sower
and the reaper will rejoice together."   (John 4: 35-36)

Yet though the time has always been appropriate,
neither the Christian nor the Jewish world have been
adequately prepared for waging spiritual warfare against
those invisible forces poised against them. "My people
are destroyed for lack of knowledge," Jehovah said. (Hosea
4: 6) You may recall that when Moses first brought the
tribes of Israel to the borders of the Promised Land,
they did not enter it. Even though the time was ripe for
entering, Israel had not spiritually prepared itself. They
grumbled, murmured, craved dainty foods the pagan
world supplied, and they were easily discouraged.

John has underlined for us in many ways the great
necessity of careful preparation for the battles we find
listed in the latter part of Chapter Eight. He starts by
telling us the awesome silence following the breaking
open of the seventh seal. For what the churches have
been called upon to do will totally expose the nature of
the world and the nature of the end toward which they
move. It also offers them the opportunity for choosing an
alternative.

But the sounding of the trumpets, we are told, brings curses on the world – which is to say on the world that walks in Satan's ways. So we should realise that Blessings and Curses are no more than the consequences reaped from what is done. Those who suffer from the law's misfortunes bring disaster on themselves. God is the sole avenger – not mankind. There is no place amongst the sons of God for righteous retribution – men who lie in wait with guns outside of abortion clinics, or who shoot Prime Ministers and Heads of State, or who store up arms in caves. The reactions of men like Simeon and Levi were to be abhorred. As Jacob said of such behaviour: "You have made my name to stink in all the land." Even Michael (God's archangel) when rebuking Satan, merely said: "May Jehovah rebuke you!" (Jude 9)

Curses fell on Adam and his wife, not because of God's ungenerosity toward them, but because of Adam's willfulness. Adam hid himself from God. He did not want to do God's will at all. In *Deuteronomy*, as well, Moses made it plain, the word of God which blesses, also curses them. Here Jehovah warns his people, that if they do not follow and respect the laws that govern all creation, curses will fall heavily on them:

"Cursed shalt thou be in the city, and cursed shalt thou be in the field. Cursed shall be thy basket and thy store. Cursed shall be the fruit of thy body, and the fruit of thy land, the increase of thy kine, and the flocks of thy sheep. Cursed shalt thou be when thou comest in, and cursed shalt thou be when thou goest out. Jehovah will send upon thee cursing, vexation and rebuke..."

(Deuteronomy 28: 16-20)

So it is that *anyone* who does the will of God is blessed, and *anyone* who willfully opposes it is cursed.

Still in all the passages that you will read, when curses fall upon the earth, you must realise that a triple interpretation is not only possible but entirely necessary for the full appreciation of the text. These interpretations are spiritual, political and physical. For instance, when we are told that the waters of the world are turned to Wormwood, and many people die as a result of drinking them, John is referring to the spiritual waters of communication, such as those philosophies expounded by the media, through which the people of the world generally refresh themselves, and even the waters of God's word polluted with superstition and false doctrines read into it by the ignorant.

Yet it also refers to the turbulent waters of mankind, which are polluted with evil practices so that, yes, the physical waters of the world themselves become polluted too — reflecting mankind's own polluted state. All three are poisonous, and undrinkable, so that many people die because of them. There is broad scope in all of these allusions, and we should be aware of it. But it is the spiritual base of all these woes we must consider first in every case.

However, when we read these curses, we should remember Jesus's own words: "God never sent his son into the world to bring destruction down on it. Rather he was sent into the world to save it." (John 3: 17)

For centuries the Christian world has said that angels of God would sound the trumpets heralding the last days. John, however, in the letter he has written us, has told us who those angels are. Since John has said that this plan was not his own but rather that of Jesus Christ, we should be able to determine from it whether Jesus was the true messiah or a charlatan. For his whole claim to be the Christ depends upon the working or the failure of this strategy.

After God told Moses, "I am who I prove myself to be," Moses used a plan by which he led the sons of Israel out of their captivity. Because the strategy he used was so successful in delivering the people from their Egyptian slavery and later bringing them — under Joshua — into the promised land, God's power was proved, and Joshua and Moses were revered as leaders who had heard the voice of God.

The final proof of any plan can only be determined by the ultimate success it has: Can it really work in setting people free? Is it sound enough to bring deliverance from slavery? and, in completion, does it lead the people to a place where they can live in peace and harmony with nature, their creator and their fellow man?

Now whereas Moses led one nation out of servitude, Jesus later had presumed to lead the whole world out of its enslaved addiction to a social order whose very way of life brought about destruction to all nature and humanity, and whose culture sowed the seeds of crime and violence and war. Jesus, by his plan, was to lead all those who followed him away from life-destroying practices which cursed the world, and bring them to a paradise on earth — where humankind and nature lived in perfect harmony with God. In other words, towards a unified and balanced universe. What is to follow then is a plan which can supposedly accomplish this. Upon this plan, and on this plan alone, the whole claim of Jesus's messiahship depends.

***

Now there are seven trumpet warnings which the church has been commissioned by their master to sound before the world. The fact that there are seven, illustrates the absolute perfection of the work God's servants have been called upon to do. These warnings have been significantly divided into four and three. The number four denotes the universality of the calamities the world has been alerted to, while three denotes the great intensity of suffering which will inevitably follow as a consequence of mankind's total disregard of them and of the creation God placed under him, the very glory of God's majesty and power.

No doubt you have noticed, though, the similarity which exists between the cleansing of the churches in Chapters Two and Three and the warnings given to a world divorced from God. The first of all these warnings has to do with leadership. When Jesus sat upon the hill (with his disciples) just outside Jerusalem, he warned them of the many false messiahs that would come and lead them to a fiery grave in war. He compared this fiery death in war to a massive garbage dump where criminals were burned. That garbage dump just outside the city gates was called Gehenna. Since the bodies thrown on it were already dead, it came to symbolize the second death in which the soul (or hope of resurrection) perished after the body was dead.

As I mentioned in the Prologue of this work, there are many Bible idioms of speech which (when we read them literally) impedes our understanding of the texts. One such idiom is the idea of fire and hail mingled with blood falling from heaven, another is fire from the altar of God being thrown from heaven upon the earth. Yet we find such idioms of speech not only in the *Book of Revelation* but in other Bible books as well.

For instance, we find in *Exodus* a passage which says that Jehovah told Moses: "I will rain down manna from heaven for you." What the passage means is that God will provide manna in abundance for the children of Israel. It does not mean that it will tumble from the sky. Yet it is surprising the number of Christians who insist on reading it that way.

Manna is a natural product of the wilderness. In his book *The Bible as History*, Dr Werner Keller speaks about it in these words: "Anyone who is interested in manna will find it on the list of exports from the Sinai peninsula. Further, its supplier is registered in every botanical index of the Middle East; it is the *Tamarix Mannifera, Ehr*.

"The general public has always regarded this Biblical bread from heaven as a miracle beyond explanation. Indeed, the question of manna is a perfect example of how difficult it is to eradicate prejudices and misconceptions that have gone on for generations and how hard it is for the truth to penetrate some people's minds. It seems that no one wants to believe that there really was such a thing as this 'bread of Heaven.'

"...In every valley throughout the whole region of Mt. Sinai there can still be found Bread of Heaven, which the monks and the Arabs gather, preserve and sell to pilgrims and strangers who pass that way."
                              (*The Bible as History* pages 115 - 117)

The "miracle" that God performed is in the abundance with which he supplied manna for all of Israel, like as when we read in Matthew's gospel of the feeding of the multitudes: "They all ate and were satisfied and the disciples picked up twelve baskets full of broken pieces that were left over." (Matthew 14: 20) The account which Moses gave was not to confound the reader with superstitious wonder, but merely to show him that God (the creator of all things) could supply their every human need.

So when John tells us here that after the first trumpet sounded, fire and hail mingled with blood poured from heaven, we should read these symbols in harmony with other Bible texts. And the calamities which follow false messiahs, John already has explained. They are warfare (fire), famine (hail — which devastates the crops), and death (or blood) which follows in the wake of these.

Here in this portion of John's vision, leaders and their followers are depicted as trees and grass to emphasize their innate mortality. "All flesh is grass," so Isaiah has declared to us, "and their glory is as the flower of the field. The grass withers, and the flowers vanish...." (Isaiah 40: 6) This first trumpet warning is not a warning solely aimed at false idealistic leaders whom men and women follow to their deaths, but it is aimed at every leader walking in the way of Adam's world and at the people who exalt them.

Let's start by looking at the kings of Israel. King Saul himself was actually a "people's prince". The people, in their stormy push to have a king, selected Saul to be a leader who would lead them into war. Oh yes, I know. You will tell me God selected him, and so he did. But the people didn't know he had, and God selected him to show that he already knew the sort of leader they would choose to govern them. Saul was the people's choice — a democratically elected king. And there was much to be admired in him. He was humble, self-effacing and conscientious — basically an honest and well-meaning man who did the best that he knew how for Israel. Yet in the end, he failed the nation, the people and the God who had anointed him. The great responsibility that was entrusted to him merely magnified his innate weaknesses and made them more conspicuous than they might otherwise have been.

He smarted from the gross ingratitude the people showed toward him. After all the victories that he had won for Israel, the people now preferred another man. The praises they once sang for him had dimmed. Another "people's prince" was hailed and praised more loudly than himself. Saul, therefore, took to brooding over this, a trait he had revealed before he was anointed king. Remember when he hid himself from those who sought for him? even though he really wanted to be found. We notice now that he was envious, covetous and jealous of his power and murderously assertive of his will. His kingship showed his weaknesses.

Even good King David ("a man after God's own heart") had weaknesses. Faithful, brave and wise in many ways, he was not wise where women were concerned. His relationship with his wife Michal is a good example in this regard. This loving wife who put her life in jeopardy to save her husband's life was scandalously treated afterwards.

In First Samuel, Chapter Eighteen, we read: "Saul's daughter Michal loved David." Yet later on Samuel tells us: "Michal despised David in her heart." (2 Samuel 6: 16) The story of what happened in between is more revealing than you might suppose, but the Bible does not try to be a scandal magazine. Whatever David wanted, he would take regardless of the feelings other people had.

In regard to Michal, after years of absence (when he himself had taken other wives) he ordered Abner (the captain of the guard) "Do not come into my presence unless you bring Michal, Saul's daughter back with you when you return." This was a hard command for Michal, Saul's daughter. For like David himself, she had taken another mate.

Michal had not heard from David now in many years, and we are told that "she was taken (forcefully) away from her husband Paltiel, Laish's son" who "followed behind her weeping all the way to Bahurim." (2 Samuel 3: 13-16) Yet David went on taking women as he chose. He even turned to murder and deceit in order to conceal his indiscretions from the world. It's a very sad story, all of this, but — as far as human leaders go — David ruled fairly and was a good king. What saved him really was a willingness to recognize his faults and change.

One only has to read *Psalm* 51 just to see how deeply David did repent of all his sins. In part he says: "Have mercy upon me, O God, according to your great unfailing love, and according to your great compassion, blot out all my sin. For I know how great my transgressions have been, and I have my sin constantly before me."

(Psalm 51: 1-3)

Even so, another "people's prince" rose up to challenge him. David's own son Absalom championed "the people's cause". In *Second Samuel* we read that Absalom "would get up early and stand at the side of the road leading to the city gate. Whenever anyone came with a complaint to be placed before the king for a decision, Absalom would call out to him, 'What town are you from?' He would answer, 'Your servant is from one of the tribes of Israel.' Then Absalom would say to him, 'Look, your claims are valid and proper, but there is no representative of the king to hear you!' Then Absalom would add, 'If only I were appointed judge in the land! then everyone who has a just complaint or cause could come to me and I would see that he gets justice.'"   (2 Samuel 15: 2-4)

This rebel son of David did win support and almost tore the land of Israel apart. Yet on the surface, everything he said seemed to be inspired by noble sentiments. However, all of it was motivated by a vengeful spirit of reprisal against a father who had recognized rebellion in his son and had tried to keep his son's hot-headedness in check.

The men who did tear Israel apart were King Rehoboam and his rival for power, Jeroboam of the tribe of Ephraim. Rehoboam was foolish and rejected the counsel of the wise. Jeroboam was stubborn and headstrong and introduced idolatry into Israel to keep them from going to Jerusalem to worship.

All these men who served as kings of ancient Israel, like the leaders of other nations, did lead their people to war and death. Following the reign of these last two leaders, prophets rose in both Israel and Judah to offer leadership directly from the mouth of God and promise them a coming messianic king who would bring peace into the world.

Yet many false messiahs were to come. Jesus even warned his followers of them (as had Moses centuries before). They included the idealistic leaders of Jesus's own day. Amongst them were the zealous patriots who led the great rebellion in the generation following Christ's crucifixion in Jerusalem. Their leadership, however noble its intent, only led the people to a fiery death and all the great calamities that Jesus spoke to his disciples about, upon the hill: false hopes, warfare, famine and devastation of Jerusalem itself. "Not one stone shall be left standing on another," he had warned. The devastation would be complete.

This warning of idealistic leaders and those who follow them is consistent with what John showed us earlier — a false leader seated nobly on a white horse holding a bow (the means of launching long-range missiles) in his hand. Violence — even in a just cause — was not taught by Jesus Christ. When his own disciples chose to take up arms in his defence, he told them candidly, "Whoever takes the sword (symbolic of all violence, armed rebellion and warfare) will perish by the sword." These words were consistent with his response when certain Jewish militants tried to make him king by force (of arms). He withdrew himself from them, and when they later followed him into Capernaum, he angrily and deliberately denounced them, for he wanted nothing to do with war.

What should be noticed most in all these leaders I have named is the manner in which the characters of all of them revealed the nature of the people that they served. As Arnold Toynbee said, people generally get the kind of government that they deserve.

It therefore must be evident that any church which has falsified the character of Jesus Christ (to make it fit the image of a "people's prince") must "return to its first love" or be unable to do the work that Jesus Christ assigned to them. There must be no confusion about leadership in this campaign, and the manner of the spirit that every Christian has been called on to imbibe. Churches (and individual Christians) which do not settle for themselves the matter of leadership, as it was stressed in the special message given to the church at Ephesus, will be among those following false leaders to their death.

After the first trumpet warning has been sounded, God's curse will follow shortly after it. It is the harvest reaped by those who put their "trust in princes" rather than in God. That is to say all leaders who rely on force of arms. The fire, hail and blood which falls upon the earth represent the fire of war, the devastation of harvests and domestic animals, and the death toll from the dread diseases following.

I know that there are those who seek a brighter side to this, by saying that the death predicted in these "prophecies" refers to those who shall "die, through baptism, to this world's way of life and be raised to new life in God's world." While I personally have no quarrel with their sentiment, John's emphasis in all these trumpet warnings is laid upon the unrepentant hearts and the consequence of disobedience to the way of the creator.

So when the Bible tells us that "one third of all trees and all grass were burned up," we are automatically reminded of what Jesus said regarding those unrepentant souls who had survived the wrath of Pilate after certain Galileans were put to death for rioting in Jerusalem at the time of Temple sacrifices there. Jesus said regarding this: "Do you actually believe that these Galileans were worse offenders than all other Galileans because they suffered in this way? I tell you they were not! So unless you change the focus of your lives, I tell you, you will suffer their same fate." (Luke 13: 2-3) His emphasis, like that in Chapter Eight of *Revelation* was the consequence of not repenting.

As Jeremiah said of such resistance to God's word: "This people lie about Jehovah, saying, 'He can never cause us harm! We will not see war or famine in our time. The words of his prophets are but wind....' For this reason my word shall become fire in your mouths and the people will be wood that it consumes." (Jeremiah 5: 12-15) Then Jeremiah further said to such unrepentant souls: "I have told you today but you still have not obeyed Jehovah your God in all that he sent me to tell you. So now be sure of this: You will die by the sword, famine and plague in the very place where you imagined you would peacefully reside." (Jeremiah 42: 21-27)

If you are really looking for a bright side though, it is this: that those who truly are of Israel will recognize the hand of God in what is taking place and come out of Babylonian captivity and chaos. As such they will proudly stand before the world as members of those tribes assembling upon the hill to let their light shine before the world.

According to the scriptures, the source of world confusion and disunity began in Nimrod's kingdom, Babylon (or Babel) directly following the great flood. In *Genesis* we are told that "from Babylon Jehovah confused the language of the whole world." So when Luke, much later, tells us that when the Christian fellowship "by agreement all came together in one place," and that "all began to speak in tongues as the spirit gave them utterance," we are being shown the power of God to unify all men when they submit themselves to the healing power of the creator. When "every man does what is right in his own eyes" there is confusion, divisiveness and war. When men and women willingly submit themselves to their creator, there is healing, unity and peace.

The second trumpet warning has to do with Babylon – the city of confusion and violence. John, by showing us a mountain all in flames, has identified the subject of this warning as that concerning Babylon the Great. This image is clearly a reference to the words of Jeremiah, who tells us that Jehovah said: "I am against you, O destroying mountain, you who destroy the whole earth...I will stretch out my hand against you, roll you off the cliffs, and make you a burned out mountain."

(Jeremiah 51: 25)

Many may assume that because the nation Babylon supposedly perished centuries ago that anything which might be said about it is irrelevant. But Jesus's apostle John was well aware that when a nation vanishes or falls, it leaves behind a spiritual residue that is inherited. For this reason, John shows us Babylon cast into the turbulent sea of mankind, which absorbs its character. If you have any doubt of this at all, you should take another look at our societies, and then at Babylon which mothered them. Babylon was a city full of merchants who had worked out many clever ways for accumulating wealth and property. The scriptures say they hated the sabbath day because it took away another opportunity from them to build up wealth.

Babylon was full of astrologers, fortune-tellers, mystics, and mediums, and they liked horoscopes as well. They sold hot cross buns — Ishtar cakes — during Ishtar festivals (the cross being the symbol for the sun) and they celebrated their god Tammuz's resurrection from the dead each year at sunrise on the first day of the week, upon their happy Ishtar holy day when eggs and hares were used as symbols of fertility, to celebrate a very joyous time.

They loved parades and grand processionals — with big floats carrying their gods. And every spring they celebrated the first day of the year with revelry and

sportiveness. In keeping with their manner, they would
have a spring fool festival at which they crowned a king.
The man they chose was someone that they had taken
from the prison house and was condemned to die.
Pretending that they served him, they would do him
mock obeisance, saying "yes your majesty," but when the
day was through, they hanged him from the city wall, as
their chief idea of humour was degradation of the fool
and mocking those who were despised. So it isn't difficult
to see why some historians believe that ancient Babylon,
more than any of the classical cultures of the past, was
actually the mother of the modern world.

However, it is mostly that this mountain represents
the confusion of wild hysteria, carnality and divided
loyalties that we are shown it hurled (in flames) into the
restless sea of mankind. The trumpet warning is to alert
the people to the consequence of foolishly surrendering
themselves to spiritual Babylonian captivity: Drugs,
occult practices, derring-do, intoxicated sensual hysteria,
and the wild abandonment to all things sensual will
indeed cause death and crime, and many businesses and
industries will flounder in the restless sea of the
Babylonish world (like the ocean-going vessels of trade
and commerce that they are).

Then literally as well, actual ships that sail upon the
oceans of the world, will (because of human greed,
carelessness and pride) in fact be responsible for killing
substantial amounts of life in the sea, and a substantial
number of ocean-going ships, say like oil vessels, will be
wrecked as well and cause death to all kinds of oceanic
life. Yet warfare is the ultimate calamity that Babylon
will bring upon mankind. The Bible does not look upon
warfare as an accidental aberration of society which on
occasion interrupts its peaceful flow. It sees war as a
chronic trait of Adam's world. For this reason we were

shown the red horse of warfare underneath the second seal as a constantly recurring plague upon the world. It is warfare that will fill the sea with blood – the sea of turbulent humanity and the seas which warships sail upon as well.

The reason then the Christian church at Smyrna was told to make a clear distinction between the teachings of the church and the customs of the world was so that they would not be part of that confusion they would be called upon to give warning. Yet as things now stand the Christian church is not exempt from any of the warnings they have been called on by their messiah to sound before the world. The description that Isaiah gave concerning the unhealthy state of Israel aptly fits the Christian state of health: "I have fed and brought up children, but they have turned against me. Though every ox knows its master and every ass its feeding place, Israel doesn't know or even consider it....Your whole head is injured and you suffer inner agony? From the bottom of your foot to the top of your head there is no healthy spot anywhere in you. You are covered with wounds, welts and open sores, and they haven't been cleaned, bandaged or soothed with healing ointments."

(Isaiah 1: 2-6)

Christianity, as well, has had many leaders who have split the Christian church into many isolated parts – each one supposedly "worshipping God in its own way," while at the same time feigning greater righteousness than all the other branches of the faith. Many too persist in saying, "We alone have the truth" (or "Lo, here is Christ.") "We are the people Jesus chose." They even glorify these leaders that have torn the church apart, preaching and worshipping in their name and even singing hymns of praise to them. In doing this they are

like the nations of the world, who all proclaim their own
superiority in culture, politics, philosophy and way of life
and, in addition, sometimes claim that they are radically
superior in race as well. Over such things they will even
go to war. In other words (as it now stands) the divided
Christian family is part of that same disease of
Particularism which they were sent to heal.

If they do not obey the wisdom of the scriptures,
including this prophetic letter sent by Jesus Christ, God's
word will prove to be a curse to them, coming down
upon them (not as dew and rain and sunlight but) as hail
and fire and bloodshed — their own blood and the blood
of many innocents. As was revealed beneath the second
seal, warfare with other leaders of the nations in the
world will be the consequence. For "there is a way which
seems right to a man, but in the end it leads to death."
(Proverbs 16: 25)

"If your eye is single, your whole body will be full of
light," Jesus once instructed his disciples, "but if you let
your eye be misdirected your whole body will be filled
with darkness. And as the darkness in you grows, who
possibly can tell you just how great that darkness is. You
just can't serve two masters, for you will either hate the
one and love the other, or you will loyally support the
one in preference to the other. You cannot serve God
and (any nation of) the world at one and the same
time." (Matthew 6: 22-24) You cannot let yourselves
become divided by being joined to any group or cause
that separates you from the rest of God's spiritual family.
"You shall have no other gods (great powers) before me"
is the command "written by the finger of God" to cover
that. God's people as a body must be of one spirit in
order to fulfill the calling of their lord.

This was a matter so serious that Jesus's own brother recommended dire measures for overcoming double loyalties. "Come near to God," he told the brotherhood of Jews throughout the world, "and God will come near to you. Wash your hands, you sinners, and purify your hearts you double-minded. Grieve, mourn and wail. Change your laughter to mourning and your joy to gloom. Humble yourselves before Jehovah and he will lift you up." (James 4: 8-10)

The most glorious of all governments on earth, of course, was the first government which God established when he told mankind (male and female) they were to "rule over all the earth and over every living creature that moves upon the earth." Male and female together as one species made in the image of God was (as God's right hand) to display the qualities of compassion, understanding, and mercy toward all creatures upon earth.
(Genesis 1: 26-27)

Adam was to be the brightest star to ever shine in the entire canopy of government that ruled the earth. But when Adam sinned, he "fell like a blazing torch from the firmament of God." In doing this, he poisoned all the channels of communication so that "many people died from the waters of the world which had turned bitter." We read in Genesis of just how great the devastation was that fell upon the earth because of Adam's sin.

In the beginning, Moses spoke of it like this: "The whole earth shall be cursed because of you; and only by the pain of heavy labour will you get to eat of its fruits. Even then, it will yield you mostly thorns and thistles all your days. (Life will even be so difficult and aggravating for you that) the herbs of the field (the bare necessities of life) is all that you will ever get to eat. And only by the sweat of your brow will you earn your food, until you return to the ground from which you were taken. For dust is all you are, and to the dust you will return." (Genesis 3: 17-19)

Nowhere is this fall of man so beautifully detailed for us as it is in the Lament of the prophet Ezekiel regarding the King of Tyre — mankind's representative.

> "Because of your overbearing pride
> you have told yourself, 'I am like God himself,
> sitting in the midst of all mankind (literally: "the seas")
> upon the throne.' But you are just a man,
> and not a god at all, even though you think
> yourself to be as wise as God.
> Even so, you once were full of wisdom
> and perfect in your beauty. For you were
> in Eden in the Garden of God,
> and adorned with every precious stone
> (for you possessed the noble qualities of God).
> All their mountings and their settings
> were of gold (godly wisdom). On the day
> you were created these were placed on you.
> (For in the image of God, I created you.)
> ...From the very day you were created
> you were blameless in all your ways,
> till wickedness was found in you.
> So I cast you from my holy mountain
> in disgrace...because your heart grew proud
> and you corrupted all the wisdom I had
> given you. So I threw you down to the earth..."
> (Ezekiel 28: 2-17)

That is the picture John described for us. The star that falls then is the proud, rebellious and stubborn heart of corrupted man — or rather the spirit (the drunken spirit you might say) that governs spiritual Babylon in opposition to the God of life. It is this wicked spirit known as Satan which contaminates "the waters of the world" (cultural activities, entertainment and recreational pastimes — with philosophies and imagery which lead to death). Such a spirit even poisons God's own word — so that there is a famine of life-giving truth.

The poisoning of the life-giving waters of communication is a retaliation against the creation of God. Therefore the name of the star is "Wormwood" or "Vindictiveness." Even Christianity's divided churches of today make almost any teaching possible, and the gospel of Jesus Christ has been distorted in many different ways. Not everyone who preaches teaches the same principles that Jesus taught. And many are so bound by sectarian loyalties they cannot be admonished by God's word. The waters of Christianity have been poisoned. Some even preach hatred and make vengeful reprisals on those who are opposed to them. And the irreverent waters of the modern sectarian world frequently teach violence or careless moral conduct or vain ambition to exalt oneself.

Since angels of the church communities are also spoken of as stars, we can't ignore the possibility that certain Christian bodies of prestigious stature in the world might choose to make alliances with Satan's world (as Balaam did) and distort the word of God, to satisfy the wishes of the powerful men who rule. Balaam, you recall, possessed great knowledge of Jehovah, but chose to serve a double loyalty and sold his services to Balac for a price.

Even so, it is the poisonous philosophies that guide the world which cause the people of the world to die. This is the message that the unified church was called to make. Corrupt teachings of any kind cause death.

"When the fourth messenger of God sounded his warning, a third of the sun was struck, a third of the moon, and a third of the stars, so that a third of them turned dark, leaving a third of the day without light, as well as a third of the night."

Poisonous philosophies which guide the nations cause the light of leadership to fail. The sun and moon and stars of heaven all grow pale because they represent the guiding powers that govern human life in Adam's world. Without the power of God's light in the leadership which rules the nations of the world, perversions grow and so does crime. Disease and death, you will remember, lay under the fourth seal broken open by the lamb. John here daringly predicts that those who govern and teach the world will progressively become more and more corrupt, so that the light of those who lead the nations will cease to wisely guide the populace.

As the psalmist accurately said of all of these: "Anyone who tells himself 'I don't need God,' is a fool. Such people are completely without morals, and all their dealings are detestable. They are incapable of doing anything good. Jehovah, out of heaven, has examined them and seen that none of Adam's offspring is sensible or wise enough to look for God. All of them have turned away from him and are corrupt. There is not even one amongst them all who lives righteously. Not one.

"Shall I not show these ignorant children of iniquity what they have done? They gobble up my people like bread (robbing them and killing them). Nor do they ever turn to me in thanks for anything they have. I shall therefore bring great terror down on them and fill their hearts with dread, for Jehovah dwells among the righteous. Although the wicked scorn and shamefully abuse the plans and counsels of the poor, Jehovah, their

protector, is their guardian. Out of Zion he will bring
forth great salvation for God's people, Israel. When
Jehovah brings his people from captivity let Jacob rejoice
and let Israel be glad." (Psalm 14: 1 - 7)

The "three woes" announced by God's messenger
affirms that human suffering will assuredly reach a
dreadful peak. The number three, like the word "Amen"
confirms that certainty. Men by their stubborn deter-
mination not to heed the warnings given, will definitely
bring human suffering to a tremendous height. As Jesus
said of this same period: "Unless the days of such
suffering were cut short, no life at all could possibly
survive, but for the sake of those who are obedient, those
days shall be shortened." (Matthew 24: 22)

But some, I know, will still continue asking, "When
will these things be? How will God's people know the
proper time to sound the warnings?" Jesus answered
them at one time in these words: "When evening comes,
you say, 'It will be fair weather, for the sky is red,' and in
the morning, 'Today it will be stormy, for the sky is red
and overcast.' You know how to interpret the appearance
of the sky, but you cannot interpret the signs of the
times. A wicked and adulterous generation looks for a
miraculous sign." (Matthew 16: 2-4)

The government of elders tried in the furnaces of
life, and the people of Israel who wear God's character,
will surely recognize the natural and appropriate times
for giving warning, and heed such sensible, strong advice
as has been given in Jesus's own words. They do not
watch for mystic miracles, but wisely use the means that
God has put into their hands.

CHAPTER NINE

The Gathering Storm

When the fifth spirit (of church community) sounded its warning, I saw a star (representing the law of God) fall down to the earth from the sky. The spirit (of God's law which can both curse and bless) was given the key to the bottomless pit (the collective carnal heart of man, where many spirits — legion in number — are restrained but stand ready to give birth to social movements of all kinds. Like the wilderness in many Bible texts, the bottomless pit is the womb from which those nations not yet born emerge.)

When the pit was opened by the spirit (of God's law), thick smoke (of oppression) — like that from a great furnace (of rigorous affliction) poured out of it so that the sun (or sovereign power of government) and all the sky (the source of spiritual guidance) were darkened by the smoke that came from it. (Without the guiding power of God's law in the governmental canopy ruling over us, we stumble blindly in the dark and curses rather than blessings come upon the earth.)

Then a massive human army, much like locusts, came out from the smoke on to the earth, and they were given power to sting like scorpions. (This curse is deliberately reminiscent of the plague of locusts Moses, by the power of God, brought down on Pharaoh's land. For these are the people exploited, overburdened and abused by the social order of the world. In this new instant, Satan is the spiritual Pharaoh who oppresses and afflicts life's underlings. This trumpet warning challenges the authority he wields for he destroys the glory of creation God called on humankind to watchfully attend.) This mighty army, which were like locusts, were given power to torment all God's enemies (and cause them dreadful pain.)

Those in this army were all told they could not indiscriminately harm the grass (the common people), the trees (illustrious citizens) or any other plant (all other classes in society), but only those who did not have the mark of God upon their foreheads (which is to say all those who had no place for God in any of their thoughts). This massive army was not allowed to kill. They only were allowed to torment those who did not have the mark of God on them. For five months (indicating this was only half the suffering this army eventually would cause) their victims would be made to suffer painful agony as from a scorpion's sting.

During all this time, people would yearn for death and not find it; they would want to die, but death would flee from them! (Macbeth's words in this case are most appropriate: "My mind is full of scorpions." This is the kind of torment God's enemies would suffer. King Solomon himself confirmed this view as we shall later see. People will despair because life will hardly seem worth while due to all the human misery encountered in the world.)

The long hair of the soldiers in this army was like women's hair (showing they were disadvantaged in society and their cases rarely came before the courts of law) and their teeth were (fierce) like lions' teeth (indicating that their words were frightening). Their breastplates (by which the rightness of their cause was known) were (impregnable) like breastplates made of iron (showing that the case supporting all their deeds and arguments was strong). Also the noise of their wings was like the thundering of many horses and chariots rushing into battle. (These words indicate the speed at which this movement was to grow and spread throughout the world. They also help us to appreciate how well organized and militant these movements were and how determined they would be to win).

They had tails which (is to say prophetic orators who, like the rear guard of an army) could sting like scorpions, and in those tails was the power to gall their victims with agonizing pain for five months. (As five is half of ten, this number indicates completion of the suffering this army was to bring. This army had fulfilled the purposes for which they had been called into the world. The great pain that this army first inflicted on the world was caused by their initial move into the social scene. It was inflicted by their very presence, their misery and the protests that they made. No argument on earth could talk away the justice of their cause.)

(Their presence in the world would sting their overlords and inflict great pain and inconvenience upon society. Their movement would gain ground, becoming strong, and many orators would speak on their behalf — causing even greater pain to the oppressors who ignored their obligations to humanity. So if remedy cannot be found for all the miseries which mankind brings into the world by their defiance of God's word, greater miseries will surely follow afterwards. Society therefore is called on to "repent", that is change its ways.)

These locusts had over them a king who was the angel of the bottomless pit (the spirit of God's law sent to curse the world) whose name in Hebrew is Abaddon, but in Greek is Apollyon (in English, the Destroyer). (Since the angel of the pit is the influence of the law — able to open and able to close, the leader of this army is none other than that side of the law which condemns the guilty and torments them by confronting them with "other peoples problems", thereby denying them repose: "There is no rest for the wicked," said

Solomon. The law is the destroyer of those who do not follow it. Righteous retribution is what the locusts from the pit exact. This army may not even know that they serve God. They simply are those people that the world system has (through injustice, persecution and oppression) harmed. So their condition is a sermon preached before mankind.)

One terror is over, but there are two more yet to come. When the sixth angel sounded his alarm, I heard a voice that came from the four horns of the golden altar (of incense) standing before God. It prayerfuly entreated the sixth angel who was holding his trumpet: "Set free those four spirits which are kept in bonds beside the great river Euphrates." (That is to say, "by the waters of Babylon." This prayer comes as one voice from people everywhere on earth, who in one way or another are heavily oppressed. The four corners of the altar illustrate how universal this plea is. The four angels, or spirits loosed from bonds, symbolically suggest that the spirit of oppressed and enslaved humanity everywhere on earth will rebel against the overlords restricting them.)

Then the four angels who had long awaited that day and hour and month for their release were well prepared to slay one third of all mankind. (As the psalmist says: "Let us break their shackles and smash the chains of our enslavement to the nations holding us."   Psalm 2: 3)

The size of the army that these spirits raised was vast—far past numbering, for the number of its horsemen, which was spoken in my ear, was two hundred myriad (beyond imagining). (We might recall the words of Isaiah at this point: "Listen! Do you not hear the great noise in the mountains? It is the stirring of people on the move. Listen to it! It is the tumult of multitudes of nations gathering together. Jehovah of hosts is assembling these

armies. He has called them from the very ends of heaven
and has brought them from far-off lands to devastate the
whole land of the Babylonians."   — Isaiah 13: 4-5)

Now this was the appearance of the horses and their
riders in the vision that I saw: They were wearing
breastplates of fire, (symbolizing that their cause was
just and righteous in accordance with God's word),
jacinth (resolute) and sulfur (could not be subdued). The
heads of the horses looked like heads of lions (formidable
to all foes), and from their mouths came out fire, smoke
and sulfur (overpowering oratory which ignited war).
Because of the fire, smoke and sulfur coming from the
horses' mouths, one third (a substantial number) of all
mankind were slain. In the mouths of the horses was the
power to do harm, and the power to injure was also in
their tails. For their tails, which were like serpents with
heads, inflicted deadly wounds.

All the rest of mankind who had not been killed, by
means of this destructive weaponry, still didn't turn away
from worshipping the work of their own hands, but
continued following the evil spirits guiding them: demons,
and idols of gold, silver, bronze, stone and wood — idols
that can neither see nor hear (such as photographs of
movie stars or rock celebrities). And they refused to
turn away from murders, magic arts of the occult, loose
sexual relationships and thievery (in all its forms. For the
great illusion of sophisticated modern urban man is self-
sufficiency. He looks upon himself as self-sustaining; and
a benefactor if he gives any of his earnings to help
balance the unequal biases of an unjust economic
system. He lives primarily to satisfy his own personal
whims, and doesn't see this as idolatry, even though he is
manipulated by the luring and enticing spirits of the
advertising and the entertainment industries, not to
mention partisan politics.)

("The humble shall inherit the earth." is the principle at work in many of these prophecies.)

*

A star falling from heaven; A bottomless pit; Smoke from a furnace (of affliction); An army of locusts; Yearning for death; The Destroyer; Prayer from the four horns of the altar of incense; Four angels in bonds set at liberty; A vast army of two hundred myriad: Only the most idolatrous of minds could possibly imagine that any of these images were intended as literal depictions of the truth. They are idioms of speech, and must be read as such.

Even today, we still retain in speech a great variety of idioms and colloquial expressions which help facilitate the way that we communicate ideas. "Johnny is always away up in the clouds," a primary school teacher says about a pupil who daydreams all the time. "Youth must try its wings to see if it can fly," a counselor consolingly instructs a parent whose son has ventured into unknown areas of pursuit — "They must take that daring leap into the great void." In speaking of a bad business venture, an executive might say, "We must cut our losses while we can. We can't go on forever pouring all our money into a bottomless pit."

Some of the things we read in these descriptions John has given us, cannot be seen. Others can. But the concrete imagery John uses, to describe the unseen world existing in the carnal heart of man, helps us understand the great force that unseen things can often have upon the world that's visible. It is unlikely therefore (considering everything the Bible says of it) that John actually believed there was a pit from which evil spirits rose and came into the world to trouble those who broke the law of God. But nations came into existence, apparently from nowhere and spread their influence across the earth. Spirits binding men to common causes came into the world from no place that was visible and shaped it in a multitude of ways. The words which Jesus spoke to Nicodemus (a ruler of the Jews) in regard to God's spirit in the world, can also be applied to this: "The wind blows wherever it may blow, and you hear the sound of it even though you cannot tell where it is coming from or where it is going. That's the way it is with all those born of (the spirit of) God."

Like the wilderness, from which nations yet unborn emerged, the abyss (or the bottomless pit) was like a womb that gave birth to spirits of infinite variety. Like the grave itself, it was a prison house where spirits were confined or kept in chains. Conflicting spirits and conflicting loyalties could lead to madness even.

In one of Jesus's own miracles, we find a reference to the bottomless pit, when we are told of a man tormented by the many spirits warring in his soul. Jesus asked the man whose soul was being torn by them, "What is your name?" and he replied, "Legion," because he was under the thrall of many spirits from the world, which troubled him. These spirits asked repeatedly that Jesus would not send them back again into the great abyss. (Luke 8: 30-31)

Moses, though, several millenia before, put the matter on a more prosaic base, when he told the nation in the wilderness: "Notice that I offer you today life and prosperity or death and destruction. For the command I give you today is to love Jehovah your God, to walk in his ways, and obey his commands, decrees and laws: then you will live and increase and Jehovah your God will bless you in the land that you are entering to possess. (Notice that the power, or star, set over them to guide them was God's law.)

"However, if you turn away from him and do not obey him but let yourself be drawn away by other spiritual powers (Elohim or 'gods') and become obedient to thcm, I tell you today that you will surely be destroyed." (In other words 'The Destroyer' will open the bottomless pit.)   (Deuteronomy 30: 11-18)

Or as Jehovah said through Jeremiah: "If any nation does not listen to my voice, I will completely uproot it and destroy it."   (Jeremiah 12: 17)

Other scriptures though identify the source of all evil spirits entering the world as being the human heart. For as Jesus said: "Out of the heart comes evil thoughts, murder, adultery, sexual immorality, theft, false witness, and slander." (Matthew 15: 19) And Moses, at the very beginning told us: "Jehovah saw the enormity of man's wickedness upon the earth and that the imagination of his heart was continually evil all the time." (Genesis 6: 5)

The collective carnal heart of man then is the bottomless pit from which all evil comes into the world, and it is the breaking of God's law which opens that great cess pool of contagion to defile mankind. We should note, however, that the army John describes did not emerge from the bottomless pit. Oppression did. The army served a righteous cause in rebelling against it.

There is a mean-spirited disposition in all those who defy God's law and live according to their own physical desires — making these their god instead. "I am the master of my fate. I am the captain of my soul" just isn't true. We are mutually dependent, all of us, on what others do. When people have no compassion for the needs of others and grow into themselves, the guiding star of God's law falls to the earth and opens up the prospects for a deadly world. We are our brother's keeper, as the scriptures say.

Those who walk according to the great creator's plan are called on to be generous and share their substances, and set up social measures to protect their fellow citizens against all unforeseen calamities. When industries and individuals live only for themselves — workers are thrown into the streets, the sick and the helpless are not cared for, and people, thinking themselves practical, will cut provisions for the needy any way they can. They are not building, therefore, a healthy social atmosphere, but are creating clouds of gloom throughout the world. Is such a world worth living in?

Who wants to see the city streets so full of misery? John, in this long letter, says: "During this time people will yearn for death and will not find it," which recalls its parallel echo centuries earlier when King Solomon of Israel expressed this sentiment: "It was then that I began considering the oppressions and injustices that were practiced in the world. For I saw the tears of the oppressed, and I realised that there was no comforter; for no one tried to help, as power was in the hands of the oppressors. So it seemed to me far better to be long dead than to live among such suffering. In fact it seemed to me even better to have never lived at all than to have lived and seen such injustices and suffering."

(Ecclesiastes 4: 1-3)

That God condemns such selfishness is evident. We read these words against the practices of greed in Isaiah's prophecy: "Jehovah has risen to present his case and to state the charges he has brought against his people. Jehovah's first charges are against the elder statesmen and leaders of the nation's industries: 'You have completely stripped your vineyards, taking all of (their fruits for yourself) what rightfully belongs to the poor into your houses. What do you mean by ruthlessly exploiting my people, and then grinding their faces into the dust?' Jehovah, the God of hosts demands of you."

(Isaiah 3: 13-15)

Later on he says: "Disaster will befall those who make unjust laws, and to those who oppress the needy, depriving the poor of their rights and denying justice to those in need, taking the property of widows and robbing the fatherless. What will you do when God requires a reckoning and brings destruction on you from a distant land?"

(Isaiah 10: 1-3)

The army of locusts, John describes for us in his account, were told they could not indiscriminately harm the grass, the trees or any other plant, but only those who did not have the mark of God upon their foreheads. The very wording of the second part of this command (referring as it does to people) clearly illustrates that John was not speaking about plants at all. He was talking about the common man (grass), illustrious citizens (trees) and those of every other class (any other kind of plant). So from the very start God makes it clear, his warfare is not based on class distinctions of some kind.

There was no mindless pitting of one group against another in God's plan. For man judges by the outward appearance but God looks upon the heart. God is no respecter of persons, so we are told, and in the words of John we are reminded of that fact. This plan is aimed at those who, regardless of their class, abuse the glory of God (which is creation) and who like Cain selfishly ignore their brother's need and everything that God requires of them.

In telling us that the hair of "the soldiers is like women's hair", John shows us he was well aware that women had for centuries been underprivileged in society, and would in time demand their voice be heard. The voice of women (in many prophets' minds) became the voice of justice crying to be heard. For this reason Solomon depicted Wisdom as a woman with a universal message to mankind. He said: "Does not Wisdom cry out to be heard? Does not Understanding raise her voice? On hilltops all along the road where pathways meet, and at the city gates, she cries out to be heard: 'Listen to me, everyone,' she says. 'I call upon all people in the world to hear my voice...With my mouth I speak for justice, for I detest all things crooked and perverse....'" (Proverbs 8: 1-8)

What John alludes to, in these symbols then, is all those people that the world deprives of justice in the courts of law, and abuses in the workplace and the social stream of daily life, because of prejudice or greed. Such a force as this lays great demands upon all levels of society, and the purposes that it pursues, according to the symbols John describes, are righteous, strong and resolute. All levels of society are held responsible, and John deliberately reminds us of the hardened heart of Pharaoh and the curses that this brought upon his world. Society is therefore called on to "repent" for this mighty army lays demands on all who are responsible for having laid such heavy burdens upon them.

This army of the underfed, the homeless, the persecuted, those wrongly tried in courts of law, and the socially abused will challenge and sting like scorpions, the consciences of all who callously ignore the magnitude of their responsibility to their communities and to people everywhere throughout the world. "Am I my brother's keeper?" we might ask again. God's word answers, "Yes," and the misery we cause condemns us by these scenes, for they are warnings God has given us.

Moses's voice is therefore heard in all of this: "How long will you refuse to humble yourself before me? Let my people go, that they may serve me. For if you refuse to let my people go, behold, tomorrow I will bring locusts into your country, and they shall cover the land, so that no one can see the ground; and they shall eat the remainder of what escaped and is left to you from the hail, and they shall eat every tree of yours that grows in the field; The locusts shall fill your house and those of all your servants and of all the Egyptians; as neither your fathers nor your fathers' fathers have seen from their birth until this day."   (Exodus 10: 3-6)

*

Now when Israel was in bondage to Pharaoh long ago, Jehovah told Moses: "I have seen the misery of my people in Egypt. I have heard their cries of suffering because of their oppressors. And I am much concerned with this. So I shall rescue them from the hand of the Egyptians and bring them out of that land." (Exodus 3: 7) So in John's vision, just as soon as the sixth angel sounded his alarm, we are told that a prayer went up from everywhere on earth, on behalf of all who were oppressed and heavy laden – all who suffered from injustice, persecution and drudgery.

In the symbols used by John, the voice came from the four corners (all areas upon earth) of the golden altar (where the prayers of suffering humanity are heard) beseeching the angel with the sixth trumpet: "Set free those four spirits which are kept in bonds beside the great river Euphrates."

We cannot possibly ignore the scriptural implication of these words. They bring vividly to mind the psalmist's plaint which says: "By the waters of Babylon, there we (captives) sat down and wept when we remembered Zion (the free city of God). There upon the willow trees we hung up our harps. For those who were our captors commanded us to sing songs, and they mirthfully asked us 'Sing us one of the songs of Zion.' How could we sing Jehovah's song (of freedom) in a hostile land?...O daughter of Babylon, you devastating one, let the one be praised who brings you down, and dashes all your little ones against a stone!" (Psalm 137)

That there are four such angels directly tells us that a universal spirit demanding freedom (like a great earthquake) would break out all around the world. All those suffering oppression would demand to be set at liberty, and a great army from everywhere on earth would rise. This army John describes for us is formidable in appearance and awe inspiring in its size. Nonetheless it is symbolically drawn so that the reader can appreciate certain qualities in it which otherwise could not be seen.

There are three attributes which John uses to describe the army God has raised: fire, jacinth and sulfur (which were the colour of the breastplates that they wore). And these three qualities are identical to those sharp words spoken by the lions' heads upon the horses that the army rides: fire, smoke and sulfur. Jacinth is a smoky blue stone, in case you're wondering. The significance of this is found in Jesus's own words: "Out of the abundance of the heart, the mouth speaks."
(Matthew 12: 34)

The spiritual significance of these words is that fire is the word of God, smoke the sacrificial offering, and sulfur tells us that the fire cannot be extinguished. Yet these are the same three elements used to describe war. It is vitally important, therefore, that we realise that while spiritual forces are at work in the world, and bring this army into being, the army itself is physical, and all who set themselves against it will be slain.

The breastplates of this army (which define the rightness of their cause) helps us understand that this army serves the purposes of God, is determined in its aims, and the vision leading it cannot be subdued. The horse which each man rides illustrates the militant spirit carrying each man into battle with the world. It is that driving spirit that enables each of them to speak as leader or as prophet of the cause, according as the situation may demand. For every man is led by the spirit (or angel) of liberty. The heads of the horses (illustrating each man's role as leader) are formidable, and their teeth which are like lions' teeth show us that they speak fierce words. The words they speak are belligerent and lead to revolutionary war — which slays one third of all mankind. Their tails (their prophetic voices) inflict deadly wounds on all who are opposed to them.

So it is only natural, I suppose, that many readers of these words see in them a direct allusion to the words written by the prophet Joel, who said: "A fire devours before them, and behind them a flame burns; the land is as the garden of Eden before them, and behind them a desolate wilderness; yes, and none has escaped the ravages of those devouring hordes. Their appearance is like the appearance of horses and as war horses and horsemen do they run."   (Joel 2: 3 - 4)

Many even go so far as to interpret these words as a reference to a modern war tank with a flame thrower in front and a gun in the rear. Yet the purpose of John's words is not so much to awe us with his skill for predicting modern weaponry as it is to illustrate the latent power residing in the countless men and women everywhere throughout the world, who, when the spirit of liberation calls them, will throw off the social bonds restraining them. For God does not condone oppression, drudgery, persecution or slavery of any kind — not even that which wears the euphemism "separate but equal," as a pretext for holding people in servitude. In fact, the words of Jesus at the outset of his mission were: "The Spirit of Jehovah is upon me, because he has anointed me to preach the gospel to the poor. He has sent me to proclaim the release of captives, and the recovery of sight to the blind, to set free those who are downtrodden, to proclaim the favourable year of Jehovah." (Luke 4: 18)

It is a powerful army in any way we measure it. Its size is past imagining, and frightening beyond words. For the actual number of its forces is not known. Although translators confidently give the number as two hundred million, the actual number whispered in John's ear was two hundred myriad. That is not the same thing at all. "Myriad" is a Greek word, which tells us that the number is uncountable and overwhelming in size. One myriad alone would be enough to frighten anyone, but two hundred myriad must have been a terrifying thing to contemplate. It staggered the imagination and was frightening beyond belief. Ezekiel would have used these words for describing the reaction of all those who would look on such a force: "Every heart will melt and every hand go limp; every spirit will become faint and every knee become as weak as water." (Ezekiel 21: 7)

It should be noted once again that this terrifying army had been called from every section of the earth. In spite of this, I have heard this passage used (during the Cold War waged between the "western nations of the world" and "the Communist bloc") as a direct reference to the Chinese nation. This was done to isolate the Chinese people from the so-called Christian nations of the world. Such reasoning was not only scripturally unsound, it was an ignorant attempt to divide the world into righteous and unrighteous camps, easily determined and defined by national and racial differences, and by the social system under which different peoples lived. Such thinking is frighteningly dangerous and irresponsible, as it overlooks the fact that (in John's vision) God was on the side of those who were oppressed. Since the army John describes was composed of these, to apply the number to the army of the Chinese people (who were communists at that time) would only mean that God was championing the communists.

World leaders and their followers have been counselled by this vision not to ignore the nature of their great responsibility, in just the same way Cain had been. For if they fail in this, there will be a consequence.

In some measure, Paul's words to the Corinthians are appropriate for he shows the latent strength residing in all those the world's powerful men despise. In his first letter to that church, he says: "Brothers, think of what you were when you were called. Not many of you were wise by the standards of this world; not many of you had any influence (in matters which pertain to this world's civic life); not many of you were privileged through birth. Yet God chose those lacking worldly wisdom to shame the wise; God chose those who were weak in the world to shame the strong. He chose the lowly and those who were despised. Then by revealing (to you) those things which have no existence in reality, he showed you it was possible to bring to nothing everything that has existence now. No one, therefore, has any cause to boast before him." (1 Corinthians 1: 26-31)

At this point in the *Book of Revelation*, spiritual deliverance had not yet arrived. Physical deliverance was what brought the armies out from the heavy smoke of rigorous oppression which John described. The Bible text leaves little doubt that God was on their side. It cannot be denied that physical deliverance (or Salvation) is desirable. But in the scenes that we are shown, Man with his unchanged nature was still in charge of finding his own way.

Isaiah said of those opposing such deliverance: "Wail (you Babylonians) for the day of Jehovah is at hand. Like a great destruction from the Almighty, that day will come, and it will make all hands limp with fear and will cause the heart in every man to melt. All will be terrified and overcome with anguish. Their pain will be like that of a woman in labour as they gape at one another in fear and their faces burn with astonishment. Take heed, for the day of Jehovah is coming — a cruel day of wrath and destructive fury — to devastate the land and to destroy the sinners who dwell in it."   (Isaiah 13: 4 - 9)

The devastation that he warns the Babylonians to fear is not torment in a fiery hell as some apparently believe. It is the fire of warfare in the coming overturn of nations. War is the most cruel of all torments in the world, and war against oppressors was a devastation the oppressors were bringing on themselves.

The King of Babylon became (for all God's people) the symbol of the great oppressor for centuries to come, and Isaiah's famous taunt of him, was seen (by many Christians) as a powerful prototype for a personified Satan, that evil force which governs social atmospheres, and makes humanity its slaves. There is much value then in studying the pattern of the evil spirit governing this man, and here is what Isaiah says of him:

"When at last Jehovah has relieved you from your pain and suffering and the harsh service to which you were enslaved, you shall revile the king of Babylon and say: 'This is the end the oppressor has reaped. This is the fruit and reward of his fury.' Jehovah has broken the strength of the wicked, and the rule of the tyrant has ceased, who ruthlessly oppressed the peoples with unrelenting cruelty, who, unhindered, aggressively went on unrelentingly subduing nations.

"Now all the lands enjoy peace and are at rest, and they break into joyous shouts and songs. Even the cypress trees and cedars of Lebanon are glad, rejoicing over you, and saying, 'Now that you have been overthrown, no one comes to cut us down.' The grave itself is anxious to receive you when you come; the shades of all its tenants welcome you, even those who once were great men on the earth, along with kings from all the nations whom death has taken from their thrones, respond and say: 'Have you become as weak as we are now? Are you now like all of us?' Your pomp and the music of your harps are gone, while in the grave you lie upon a bed of maggots and cover yourself with a quilt of worms.

"O Lucifer (herald of the day)! son of the morning, you have fallen (like light) out of the sky. You, who once did humble the nations, have been cast down to the earth, even though you told yourself, within your heart, 'I will climb (like the sun) to the very height of heaven (at noonday) to place my throne above the very stars of God (the sons of Israel, and humble them). I will sit upon (Jehovah's) throne (in the holiest of holies) on the mount of the assembly, upon mount (Zion) in the uttermost parts of the north. Climbing to a height far above the clouds (the hosts of common men), I myself will be (in all men's eyes) like the Most High.' Instead, you have been brought down to the grave and dumped into a pit.

"All those who see you, will look at you disdainfully and wonder: 'Can this be the man who made the whole earth shake and kingdoms tremble? who turned the world into a wilderness, destroyed its cities and wouldn't let his prisoners go free?'

"Though the kings of other nations are honoured in their burial, and lie each in his own sepulchre, you shall be cast out like the discarded branch (or criminal) you are, covered by the bodies of all who perish by the sword and are cast down into the stones of the pit to be trampled under foot. You shall not be honoured like other kings in burial, because you have destroyed your country and have slain your people. Nor shall any of your kind (that seed of evil doers) ever be honoured.

"Prepare a place for slaughtering the offspring of this evil generation, for the iniquity we have witnessed in their fathers, must never be allowed to rise again and take possession of the earth and fill the face of the whole world with cities (of their character). 'When I indeed shall rise against Babylon to utterly destroy it,' declares Jehovah of armies, 'I shall wipe out her name and leave no trace of survivors, offspring or descendants. I will sweep everything away with a broom of destruction and turn her into a place full of swamps inhabited by hedgehogs and porcupines.'" (Isaiah 14: 4-21)

So when we read Isaiah's words we may think of the second psalm which says: "Let us tear their fetters apart, and cast away their cords from us!" The resemblance of the sentiment expressed here to the great cry of the communist movement in the nineteenth century: "Workers of the world unite, you have nothing to lose but your chains," might surprise a few, but no honest reader of them can ignore the fact their basic sentiment is identical — to set at liberty those who were oppressed by ruthless exploitation of the powerless by those who take unfair advantage of the powers they have.

*

Of all the world's great analysts and philosophers, only Jesus Christ unlocked for us the great historic pattern of society in such a manner as to show its ills and all the dangers that would rise from them. Certainly if we could set aside, for just a moment, all our biases, our preconceived ideas, and all idolatrous objects of religious veneration, we would discover for ourselves, I'm sure, the logic of the things that Jesus said.

What he clearly placed before the people of the world was this: (1) Leaders leading all mankind to self destruction. (2) An unjust social system in which no one cares for his fellow man. (3) Violent and perverse philosophies (drunk like natural water from all avenues of communication upon earth) to shape imaginations and divide humanity into self-absorbed, exclusive cliques. (4) A darkened source of guidance from the powers that light our world. (5) Multitudes of people in our midst, who suffer from oppression and injustice. (6) The dread prospect of social upheavals throughout the world, because we do not listen to the peoples' voices in their pleas for justice, when the onus falls on us to right whatever wrongs become apparent in whatever land we live.

Through studying the pattern illustrated in God's chosen specimen, the nation Israel, we get some understanding of the warnings that these symbolic trumpets give. For we see in Israel the different stages of development that led eventually to its downfall.

(1) A rebellious nation (in opposition to the will of God) chose a leader who would lead them into battle with the world— King Saul. Yet God had warned them, from the start, about the consequences that would follow this (like the first trumpet warning that we heard). And God described, in great detail, for Israel, the great oppression that would start to build, and all who consequently would be made to suffer as it grew. Yet all the people (in opposition to God) chose Saul, and Saul (opposing God) led his people finally into battle and to death. Throughout history, we have encountered many leaders much like Saul. For Saul was not an evil man primarily. He was a leader forced to take responsibility for everything his people wanted him to do. As such the nation's flaws were all revealed in him—and the people didn't always like what they were shown. As in most men, personal ambition overrode the first priority of obedience to God.

Scotland's Macbeth sometimes comes to mind when I reflect upon Saul. Like King Saul, Macbeth was jealous of his power. Though he was highly praised at first, in time the praises for him waned, and nothing he could do could possibly restore him to the high esteem he once enjoyed. Like Saul as well, he turned to witches for advice, and along with those who fought for him, he lost his life in battle.

There is much in Wilhelmenian Germany, as well, to be observed. Like King Saul and like Macbeth, Kaiser Wilhelm II of Germany was actually a warm and generous man. His failing was the failing of many people in the world. He was unpredictably emotional, which was unfortunate, as his judgment frequently was rational and sound.

It was the pull of different factions in his land, and in Europe too, which pulled him gradually toward a tragic end, for they laid on him the great responsibility of building German confidence. The whole of Germany and her leaders were infected by the understandable desire of making Germany the equal of all other nations in the world. The vision (or shall I say the demon) of Weltpolitik dazzled many minds. The Kaiser, like the German people as a whole, was caught up in that dream, which his advisers (such as Admiral Alfred von Turpitz) had with such convincing confidence proclaimed. Yet that vision led to war. But Germany was not the only cause of it. The larger pattern of the world as well fits easily into the picture of this frame.

There are many leaders I could name as well, but now that you have seen the parallel, I imagine you can do that just as well as I.

(2) When King David first began his reign, he unified a spiritually divided land. Spiritually it might be said that Babylon was in the midst of them. However, David (being a man after God's own heart) was able to a great degree to overcome those differences and reconcile the land to God — even bringing those of Saul's own house into his court. He reconciled the hostile elements that had been tearing Israel apart for he had never set himself above King Saul, while Saul was still the ruling power of Israel, even though he knew the throne of Israel would in time be his. Yet as a man, King David did have flaws, and there were those who stood ready to humiliate him in the eyes of all the world.

(3) King David's own son Absolom — and the group he rallied round himself — began poisoning the channels of communication to bring his father down. This poisoning of those waters which sustained the life of Israel eventually led the nation to violence and the

weakening of King David's throne. Many lives were lost because of this.

Nor can we say the motives prompting Absolom were noble ones. He was completely motivated by vengeance, vindictiveness and hatred for a father who refused him audience. Strangely, though, many people now take up the cause of Absolom, David's peevish son. For example C. I. Scofield says: "Legalists have thought Absolom's wilfulness to have been due to over-indulgence on the part of David. There is no such intimation in Scripture. Rather it would seem that had David at this time taken Absolom into intimacy, the rebellion might have been averted."

What is overlooked in all these arguments is that Absolom was a self-confessed murderer whose case was still untried before King David's courts of law. To grant him audience would have meant that time could now be found for examining his case—and death would be the only sentence possible under Jewish law. Yet granting him acquittal or even executing judgment in this case would have alienated large sections of the populace. It was a far wiser thing to let his presence in Israel be ignored. For David loved his son, and he loved the nation that he tried to unify according to the will of God.

(4) Under King Solomon (the son of King David and Bathsheba) Israel became the light of all the world. His wisdom became legendary in his time. But the many political marriages he felt obliged to make, in order to increase his power and influence, brought idolatry into the land. It must be understood that, in ancient times, such marriages were seen as contracts of a kind for sealing trade agreements or finalizing military alliances with foreign powers. They were meant to illustrate the close relationship by which the nations entering these pacts were bound. They were also meant to illustrate

that the nature of their dealings with each other was familial. Yet due to these contracts the light of Israel was dimmed, and the burden that the people had to bear because of them became intolerable. One should always be aware that trade and military agreements which nations make with one another do affect the character and culture of their lands.

(5) When King Rehoboam (King Solomon's forty-nine year old son) first began to reign in 931 BC, the spirit of oppression grew in Israel, and the many burdens of the people were increased. Out of this oppression came the labourers of Israel to state their case before the king. The king and his advisers were upset by this and smarted from the protests that were made; so that ill-advised, Rehoboam threatened them with these words: "My father scourged you with whips; I will scourge you with scorpions (whips tipped with metal barbs)."

(1 Kings 12: 14)

These harsh words were what would tear the land of Israel apart. For the people justly told the king: "Since there is no share for us in any of the blessings David's House can give, we will have nothing at all to do with (King David) Jesse's son. Come on Israel, lets go home! (We'll look after our affairs); Let David's house take care of theirs!"

(1 Kings 12: 16)

Still King Rehoboam had been warned. God spoke to him. Rehoboam simply did not recognize God's voice in what the elder statesmen said. Their words had been: "If you will make yourself today like a servant to this people and serve them well, giving them a just and favourable reply, they will be your servants forever."

(1 Kings 12: 7)

But like Pharaoh he stubbornly refused to hear the voice of God which spoke to him.

(6) Then there rose a champion to lead the people. His name was Jeroboam. We are told that things suddenly turned violent in Israel. When Rehoboam would not hear the people's voice, the people stoned the King's minister of labour to death. After that they made Jeroboam their king—and consequently Israel was divided into two much smaller nations. Those ten tribes which followed Jeroboam (who took the birthright Jacob gave to Ephraim with them) were known as Israel. And those who stayed with David's house, were called Judea afterwards. So from that moment on, the glory which once had been the nation Israel was gone. Without the unity which once had strengthened them, they became the pawn and eventually the slave of other nations in the world.

*

However, in the plan that John is unfolding for us, there are seven trumpet warnings to be given. So far we have only been told of six of these. The seventh still is yet to come. Yet looking at the pattern of Israel's history to help us understand the sequence of these trumpet warnings, we discover that in between the sixth and the seventh steps we have been shown, there is a lengthy interval. Even so the seventh step, at last, did come and ushered in "the latter days" for Israel. Yet long before it came, the Jewish prophets told us what we could expect from it. It didn't come in unannounced. One such prophet, Daniel, writing in the sixth century BC (while the Jewish people were still captives in Babylon) had this to say of what still lay in store for them:

"Even while I spoke to Jehovah my God in prayer, confessing my sin and the sin of my people Israel, I pleaded with God to restore his kingdom upon earth (literally referred to as 'his holy hill'). (This matter still remained the great concern of many Jews in Jesus's own day, as is reflected in the question Jesus's disciples would ask him later on: 'Do you intend restoring the kingdom of Israel at this time?') While I was still in prayer, Gabriel, the man who had spoken to me earlier in this vision, approached me with great haste around the time the evening sacrifice was being made (upon the golden altar in God's sanctuary. So Daniel's prayer placed him spiritually in heaven, just outside the sanctuary there.)

"As he had special things to tell me, Gabriel carefully instructed me that I might know exactly what they were, saying, 'Daniel, I was sent with orders to instruct you on the meaning of God's plan so that you might understand the answer (which God sends to you). From the very moment you began to pray, I received an answer (to the words which still remained unspoken, in your heart). Now I have come to tell you what that answer is, for you are very greatly loved and held in high esteem. Pay close attention, therefore, to my words, as I interpret what that vision means.

"'Seventy times seven have been set aside for you and your people (1) to finish with transgression, (2) to put an end to sin, (3) to forgive one another of iniquity, (4) to permanently bring in fair, merciful and honest social practices, (5) to seal up (that is to fulfill) all visions and prophecy, (Notice that it was the burden of God's people to consciously fulfill God's word), (6) and to rededicate the sanctuary (where God resides) under a new covenant. (In other words, if we walk like citizens of Jerusalem today, we will spiritually be in the midst of it.)

"'So pay very close attention to my words and try to understand (what they require from you and all those serving me). From that moment when an order shall be given to restore and rebuild Jerusalem until the Anointed

One, the ruler God shall choose, appears (as messenger of
the covenant), there will be seven sevens and sixty-two
sevens. Although Jerusalem will be rebuilt with streets
and a trench (filled with water all around the city), these
things shall be done during difficult times. After the
sixty-two sevens (when God allows the Gentile nations to
reach the great peak of their maturity and power), the
Anointed One (the messiah) will be abruptly cut off and
nothing whatsoever will be left to him. (For he shall be
no more, and the kingdom that he sought to build will
not be realised.) Then the people that the ruler sends,
will come and destroy the city and the sanctuary. ("Not
one stone will be left standing on another," the prophet
Jesus of Nazareth said—no doubt thinking of the
prophecy that Daniel made regarding this.)

"'Finally war, like a great flood, will come, and will
continue right until the end, when desolations are
decreed. Then the ruler will confirm a covenant with
many for one seven (indicating seven steps in God's great
plan of salvation, corresponding to the seven days leading
to a new creation of the world). In the middle of the
seven (festivals) he will put an end to sacrifice and
offering. (For Israel will not be brought, at that time,
into the holy land.) Then someone who will desecrate
the holy place (i.e. Satan) will bring pagan practices into
the residence of God, and there they will remain until
the end when God pours out his wrath upon the world.'"
(Daniel 3: 13-15)

I quote this passage just to show the final step
involved in rounding out the great campaign as it applied,
in ancient times, to Israel. I must do this so that the
reader can appreciate the meaning of the warnings that
the seven trumpets give. There is very much in Daniel's
words which does require interpreting, but I have tried to
leave this mostly in the hands of churches and the

synagogues, as my sole purpose here is simply to reveal the way that Daniel's words apply to what John says and to show the fullness of the plan which Jesus was commissioned to reveal.

I should, however, clarify one minor detail that this scripture apparently presents to readers of our time. It concerns the line "the people that the ruler sends." Most translators are convinced these words refer directly to a leader of a foreign land. And in a sense they do. Not entirely though. For in the minds of those who wrote the scriptures, God is always in control. We read in Isaiah's prophecy, for instance, of the armies that the King of Assyria sent in to humble Israel. He said: "The Assyrian is the rod (the power and expression) of my anger, and in his hand I have placed the staff (the armies) of my wrath! I send him to humble a pretentious people whose hypocrisy has angered me, and I have inspired him to loot, rob, enslave and trample over them like mud in the streets."   (Isaiah 10: 5-6)

So we are dealing here with Bible idioms again. When Israel refuses (through ignorance or through lack of wisdom) the messiah that God send, they must take the consequence of what the world metes out to them. It is just as though God sent those armies in. That is the reason God is called "the Lord of hosts". All armies in the world are under his control. But God saves those who turn to him. So in Daniel's vision, the ruler sending in the armies in "the latter days" is God's messiah still, and it is God's messiah too who makes a covenant with many sons of Israel and puts an end to sacrifice.

Daniel tells us that God's messiah shall be suddenly "cut off and left with nothing." So rather than impose any special meaning on this text, I will simply quote the words Isaiah used regarding Daniel's usage of the term, "cutting off":

> "He was oppressed and afflicted,
> Yet he did not open his mouth;
> he was led like a lamb to the slaughter,
> and as a sheep before the shearers is silent,
> so he did not open his mouth.
> By oppression and judgment, he was taken away.
> And who can speak of his descendants?
> For he was cut off from the land of the living;
> for the transgression of my people he was stricken.
> He was assigned a grave with the wicked,
> and with the rich in his death,
> though he had done no violence,
> nor was any deceit in his mouth." (Isaiah 53: 7-9)

The words "He was cut off from the land of the living" unequivocally reveal that the messiah God would choose for Israel would die and nothing whatsoever would be left to him. For his countrymen would look upon him as having been "stricken by God". He would be despised because he would not satisfy the values that we look for in our world. He would be far too different in his ways from what most of us expect in leadership, and would lack that belligerence that most of us regard as necessary in a leader. The man of steel (or the iron lady) is the sort of person we most often choose to deal with foreign powers. "Peace through strength," we like to say, by which we mean strong arsenals of weaponry.

Daniel speaks of seventy sevens which, surprisingly, is taken very literally by many groups of Christians. I say surprisingly because they should be quite aware that Jesus himself used this same term when answering a certain question put to him. In *Matthew* 18 we read: "Then Peter came to Jesus and asked, 'Lord, how many times shall I forgive my brother when he sins against me? Up to seven times?'

"Jesus answered, 'I tell you, not seven times, but until seventy times seven times.'"   (Matthew 18: 21-22)

In both cases this number is used in regard to sin. The number is symbolic, and most Christians realise that when they cite the passage as Jesus used it here. Jesus did not mean we should keep a careful record of all our brothers' sins, but rather that we should (like God) go on forgiving our brother until perfect repentance is found in him, and perfect forgiveness is revealed in us.

Seventy times seven is the number of complete and perfect reconciliation with God and with man. It is seven taken to the nth degree or seven ad infinitum. That is 7 + 7 + 7 + 7 + 7 et al...or however many sevens it requires to reach the fullness of perfection God desires. Multiplying seven sevens by ten indicates that God's plan is not a narrow one, but includes all peoples of the Gentile world as well. The total number therefore represents an ideal restoration of mankind to the image of God. So the number of times that you forgive your brother (or your sister) indicates to God just how far you are willing to go to complete that perfect reconciliation with God and man, which Jehovah has called upon his servants to achieve.

However, I do realise that certain Christians are quite literal even about Jesus's own words.

"We don't have to go on forgiving people who offend us over and over again," one Christian woman told me with conviction. "Our church takes the word of Jesus literally," she said. By her emphasis upon "our church" and the exclusive attitude her manner seemed to indicate, I realised at once that I was not a member of that church

to which she had alluded. She had excluded me from her
magic circle. "We believe that once a person sins against
you four hundred and ninety-one times that he has
committed the unpardonable sin."

"Even if he is a brother in your church?" I asked.

"Most especially him," she said. "An outsider hasn't
been converted yet."

There was a motion picture cinema I passed one time,
which advertised its current feature as "The four hundred
and ninety-first sin." I knew immediately what the movie
was alluding to, although I never went to see it.

Therefore when Daniel uses this same number in
reference to time, we should pause before continuing, and
think about the many foolish "prophecies" certain
churches in the past have made on the basis of that
number Daniel gave. I say "foolishly" because even Jesus
Christ, who also was familiar with that text, declined to
set a time when his own disciples asked him: "Lord, is it
your intention at this time to re-establish the kingdom of
Israel?"

Jesus only told them: "Things like this are not for
you to know. Deciding upon dates and times is in the
hands of God alone. It is the Father who determines
these. The Holy Spirit you receive from me is given to
commission you for continuing my work as witnesses in
Jerusalem, Judea, Samaria, and in the farthest reaches of
the earth."   (Acts 1: 6-8)

Paul very aptly, at this point, tells us what that
mission was to be: "[God] reconciled us to himself
through Christ and gave us the ministry of reconciliation: for God was reconciling the world to himself in

Christ, not counting men's sins against them. And he has committed us to the message of reconciliation. We are therefore Christ's ambassadors, as though God were making his appeal through us. We therefore implore you on Christ's behalf: Be reconciled to God."

(2 Corinthians 5: 18-21)

God is the reconciler of mankind, reconciling all humanity. In Daniel's prophecy God, by using the number seventy times seven, shows the reader of this text just how far the great creator of the world will go to unify and reconcile the world. God will go beyond the extra mile required of him. Yet eventually there must be a reckoning. If men continue to refuse God's will, they will be destroyed by their own treachery.

*

(7) The seventh step in Israel's history took place in what is called "the latter days" of Israel. This time period roughly took in all that era from the latter part of the reign of Herod the Great in 6 BC (when the direct rule of Rome began in Palestine and King Herod was gangrenous with physical disease which mentally affected him) until the fall of Masadah in 70 AD.

They were difficult years, and Israel was torn by many factions. It seemed a land impossible to govern peacefully. Many spirits were at work in it, and the sea of mankind in it raged. Those who tried to rule the land had problems in all areas. Bethlehem especially was not a quiet place. It was a hotbed for revolt. Messiahs of all kinds arose, many of them were put down by fierce and bloody violence.

From the standpoint of the Roman authorities, anyone who claimed an hereditary right to rule (but was not chosen by the Roman emperor) was looked upon as dangerous. It was assumed that all such men were guilty of treason against Rome, and were put to death for it. The people living in the Roman province of Palestine were given the freedom to "worship" the way they chose, provided that they did not trouble Rome or challenge its authority to govern Palestine politically. The priesthood and authorities of Jewish temple life did not approve of Roman rule but, at the same time, they were concerned with the safety of the Jewish populace. The man whom we call Jesus Christ today—Joshua of Nazareth—was but one of many men which the common people, living in the land of Palestine, imagined might have been the great messiah they were told would come to re-unite God's people under him and re-establish Israel.

The latter days of Israel are now recorded history. Yet God did promise (through the prophets) that he would send a leader at that time, whose final rule would be more glorious than even Solomon's had been. Moses, who had nursed the embryo of Israel in the wilderness, told us just from where this leader was to come. He told us God would "raise a prophet much like (Moses) from among the brothers of Israel, and I will put my words in his mouth, and he will tell you everything that I command him." (Deuteronomy 18: 18). Since Israel, like the virgin bride of God she was, was destined to give birth to him, we must assume that he was in the midst of Israel just before her fall. History, however, reveals that Menahem and Eleazar, the two dagger men (or Ish Cariots whom the people did choose to lead them in their final push to gain freedom from the power of Rome) were false messiahs. For they led the people to their deaths and left the world no lasting heritage.

In the *Cyclopaedia Judaica* we read: "It is almost certain (Menahem) was considered a Messiah." Yet

whether he was given that official name or not, the people
followed him zealously to death. Menahem armed the
people with the weapons that had been stored at Masadah. Then returning like a king to Jerusalem he led a
revolution which brought warfare, famine and plague into
Jerusalem, and the complete destruction of the city and
the temple. Yet Daniel has told us that there was a leader
who could have "saved them" from that dreadful end.

So if we take our cue from this, we know in essence
what the seventh trumpet warning is to be. The only
question now which still remains for us, is whether
anyone will recognize that great messiah when he comes
to save the world? or will most of us just stand in awe of
all the world's strong men? then go through that same
cycle once again? What took place in Europe, following
the First World War, led step by step up to a second one.
For a false messiah (Adolf Hitler) rose in Germany, and
large portions of the world went after him. Because that
fearsome figure on the German scene dreaded anyone
who possibly might challenge him, (like King Herod, two
millenia before) he slaughtered all the "innocents of
Bethlehem" so that Israel's messiah could not challenge
him. (Of course I speak symbolically.)

Babylon was thrown into the midst of Germany, and
all the waters of communication were made poisonous.
Then great oppression rose in all those lands in which
their leader grew to be supreme, so that the blood of
innocence was shed and cried out from the ground to
God, till forces came from far off lands with mighty
armies that would humble him. That is the pattern after
all. The one great question we must answer now is how
to deal with it when it recurs. It is impossible to think
that God's voice was nowhere to be found in Germany
prior to the time that Hitler came to power. It simply
was ignored – in just the same way it has been ignored in

many lands before and afterwards. History teaches lessons we should study carefully and heed.

In Israel during Rehoboam's rule, when oppressed labourers confronted him, Rehoboam failed to recognize the voice of God. During the glory years of France (when monarchs ruled and France was looked on as the glory of the world that all nations tried to emulate) the voice of the oppressed went unheeded. This was the case in Tsarist Russia too. And what followed in each case were social upheavals that shook the world. In "the latter days" of every nation, messiahs did arise. In France, it was Napoleon, in Russia Vladamir Lenin. During "the latter days" of the Weimar Republic in Germany, it was Adolf Hitler.

Even Jeroboam, noble as his cause had been, led his nation to idolatry and ruin. Following his time, in other lands, many wars of liberation were consequently doomed and led to catastrophic ends — as may have been the case with the former Soviet Union, which put its faith solely in economic ownership, forgetting that "Man does not live by bread alone." The heart, the mind and the spirit must be freed and fed. Yet the Bible leaves no doubt, that physical liberation from oppression is something very much to be desired, but its success depends upon the spiritual rebirth and liberation of the heart and mind as well.

God, quite apart from words, therefore, speaks directly to us daily from reality in just the same way that he always has for the sake of all who are not blind and have the power for reading it. The Bible was designed to help us see the world and overcome the biases which keep us blind. God speaks to all mankind through his reality. That is how he spoke to Moses and challenged Pharaoh centuries ago. He challenges the ruler of this world today, where Satan has his throne. That spiritual tyrant who is said to rule the world, is far more dangerous than Pharaoh ever was, because we cannot see him visually. But we are influenced and manipulated by his power, if we are deaf to what God says.

Sin (according to the scriptures) is a social disease. There is no such thing as "private health" (spiritually or physically) in Israel. As was the case of Aachan, his "sin-sickness" put all Israel in jeopardy and contaminated them. Sin affects the whole of our society and every individual who winks at it. For social carelessness (or sin) like all diseases is malignant and becomes increasingly more deadly as it grows.

There is a common thread in all these warnings that the angels give, and it is this: A spirit of rebelliousness against the power which made all things exists in our society and, by the strength of its pervasiveness, rules all the world. The Bible calls that spirit Satan, for it opposes God and leads mankind and all the rulers governing on man's behalf, to their destruction by four great plagues which devastate humanity. It fills the world with chaos and destructive practices so that crime, perversions and civic violence abound. He poisons all the avenues by which mankind communicates and dims the light of all the powers which act as guides in civic life. The spirit of oppression he creates must eventually give rise to public protests and disturbances and fill the streets with misery. Because of this, rebellion will eventually arise. That is the cycle which afflicts man's world.

In the last three stages of its growth, the abyss, that spiritual grave, or hidden realm of misery is opened (like Pandora's box) by our disrespect for one another and for the marvellous creation of God, which the scriptures frequently refer to as "God's glory". When people, out of fear or prejudice, refuse to hear the voice of wisdom, calling out for justice, mercy and reconciliation with their fellow man through obedience to God, the spirit of the law (which can both curse and bless) is given the key to the bottomless pit. And if we close our ears to what the trumpet warnings call attention to, we are the slaves of Satan's world.

What follows at the end of all these warnings is formidable: devastation of the world we know if we should fail to recognize God's voice. Since "the Kingdom of God is in (our) midst," God's voice must surely speak to us. Those who serve him call upon humanity to recognize that voice, and make the necessary changes in their lives. For what follows all the warnings we are shown are curses, of which we (by our own nature) are the cause.

*

Although what follows this long line of ominous development has not yet been identified by John, our knowledge of those final days the scriptures have identified for us, unlocks the many secrets Christ reveals for bringing in a new world spirit, which can make our world a better place to live. "It was the best of times. It was the worst of times," so Charles Dickens said. And certainly in the best of times, we do lose hold of what is good; and in the worst of times the possibility of making our world a better place is imminent, provided that God's "angels" are obedient to him, and show mankind there is a choice.

As I said earlier, there are many levels on which these trumpet warnings can be read. Mainly though, their purpose is to alert God's armies, herald the coming of Messiah to the world, and call upon humanity to repent.

Nor is the reader left to any abstract notion as to what repentance means. The writer clearly indicates exactly what it is that God requires. No one is harassed or pushed into a corner and asked, "Are you saved?" – a question which, by its very repetition, has grown meaningless. God has shown the churches and mankind that there is something they are called upon to do. In concrete images that define his purposes, he has shown them what he wishes them to do.

Of course, by now, most of us are very much aware that there are those who look upon these "prophecies" as no more than a series of rigidly foretold events to be magically or supernaturally fulfilled in history, events that cannot possibly be changed. In every case this fatalistic method works against itself. For such a method blinds us to the part that Christ required his followers to play.

Many pious individuals, as well, believe that acting on these words will only force God's hand. It is their belief that we are only called upon "to watch and wait" then be caught up to heaven afterwards. Yet Jesus tells us otherwise. And he ends this whole communiqué to us with these words: "Blessed is everyone who does what is commanded in this prophecy." And elsewhere he asks openly all those professing firm belief in him: "Why do you call me Lord, Lord, and then not do what I command?"

To do God's will does not force God's hand. Indeed it was God's hand from which Jesus (God's messiah – the lamb of God) took the scroll which contained the plan. Then he gave it to every church community throughout the world. And Jesus (after carefully instructing his conscientious workmen in the plan) tells them that everyone who obeys it will be blessed. It is a plan therefore which must be acted on. For what God's messiah has proposed is a systematic strategy for overcoming all the ills which lead the whole world (governed by mankind) to death. Repentance consequently is the basic theme. Yet Jesus Christ, through John, lays out these basic principles like an organized well-orchestrated military campaign. Jewish history, as well, carefully defines for us the spiritual forces we are battling, and plays the role of second witness to Christ's words.

When considering the seven different rulers I have named, it is possible to lose a great deal of the meaning if we concentrate exclusively upon each individual as someone purely self-directed that we must either love or hate. The carnal heart of man is moved by different spirits in the world, many of them inimical to nature, to mankind and to whatever person who surrenders to their urge and makes himself the carrier of them.

All of Israel's rulers whom I have named, as corresponding to the seven warnings given to the world, serve as physical revelations of those spirits which we cannot see:

(1) *In King Saul* we have the spirit of personal ambition taking precedence over obedience to God.

(2) *In King David* we are shown the unifying spirit of personal humility and reconciliation (hindered by personal shortcomings). Nonetheless it was able to unite divided factions in the land.

(3) *In Absolom* we find the vengeful spirit of vindictiveness, which poisons public life and weakens those who rule.

(4) *In King Solomon* we watch the shining spirit of God's wisdom wane and pale through compromising alliances.

(5) *In King Rehoboam* we encounter the spirit of stern cold-heartedness which will not hear the voice of those who are downtrodden in the world (and justifies excuses for not hearing them).

(6) *The spirit of righteous indignation and rebellion* against tyranny (unguided by the wisdom and mercy of God) is typified in Jeroboam's rule. As such it leaves no room for liberation of the spirit. Although seeking liberty, it enslaves itself.

These, therefore, are the gods we often choose to heed: Personal ambitions, Failings of the flesh, Vindictiveness, Easy compromise, and Indifference to the needs of others. In every case, we put other gods before Jehovah — the God of Life.

(7) *The Great Messiah* (whoever he may be) must be in perfect unity with the spirit of God himself. He must have conquered personal ambition, carnal appetites, vindictiveness, the willingness to compromise God's word, hard-heartedness, and trust in strength of arms. He must exemplify God's spirit. To properly serve God, we must adopt the character of God's man of heaven (as he was shown to Daniel and Isaiah). This man of heaven, Christians say, was typified in flesh by Jesus Christ. You cannot be the followers of someone whom you cannot recognize within yourself, for who you are determines how you carry out commands.

When Jesus told us we must learn to read the signs of the times, he did not leave us without guidance as to what he meant. There was no mystic mumbling in anything he said. He carefully described the nature of the times that were to come and meticulously mapped out the sequence of events that would lead to world salvation or destruction, in accordance with the choices that we would make during "the last days". He has shown us all the different spirits with which we must contend and asks that we should recognize the voice that speaks for him. "My sheep shall know my voice," he says.

*

The flow of Jewish history helps us see that in between the sixth and seventh phase of this great plan there was an interval. During this interval, Israel and Judea allied themselves with other nations (much more powerful than themselves) to war against each other. In doing this they played the game that every other nation played in struggling for power. They ignored the voice of Elijah (and all the other prophets in their midst who succeeded him) and consequently they were brought into captivity. Israel was "lost" but the land of Judah was restored.

With Ezra and Nehemiah's help (who together acted as the voice of Moses in the midst of Judah) the temple and Jerusalem were both rebuilt and the city walls restored and the law of God was reaffirmed by them. Yet the temple that they built was not as glorious as Solomon's had been—indicating something yet was needed and desired if all the prophecies (God had used his prophets to proclaim) were to be fulfilled. Then since the nations of the world infringed upon their sovereignty, the Jewish people continued watching for a sign of that messiah God would send to liberate them from the great oppression that these hated nations laid on them. Like any people that have been restrained, the Jewish people sought liberation from the nation ruling over them. Those tyrants who desired "to set their thrones above the clouds of heaven" were still triumphant over them. So this whole period explains the gap that John has left between the sixth and seventh trumpets of this prophecy.

We cannot move on, however, without first briefly examining those similarities we find in the trumpet warnings given in Chapters Eight and Nine, and in the cleansing of the church in Chapters Two and Three. In each case a series of appeals is made for repentance. The first series of appeals is made to the churches of God in the various communities; while the second group of appeals is to the world communities themselves. What distinguishes them primarily is the response.

Most of us assume that the churches will repent voluntarily, while the individual communities (which are under the control of Satan) will resist and face the consequence. Yet what is most important in these similarities is that they indicate, to any reader, that unless the churches carry out the plan proposed for them, they cannot warn the world of those calamities that God will send. If they have any loyalties at all apart from Christ (who is at one with God) they cannot be a part of that great heaven that is being built to guide the world.

(1)   The message to the church of Ephesus was that they would lose their light if they did not return to a true vision of Jesus Christ and what he came to do.
    The first angel to the nations warned them they would lose their lives if they did not return to God.

(2)   The message to the church at Smyrna praised the congregation for its unity and steadfastness in holding to the truth of God.
    The second angel to the nations showed that great disorder and confusion had been thrown into the world to divide the nations into hostile warring camps.

(3)   The message to the church at Pergamos was to rid itself of all corrupting influences that were destroying them.

The third angel to the nations warned the people that the waters of their cultures and their national religions were corrupt and poisonous and would lead to death.

(4)   The message to the angel of the church at Thyatira was that if they overcame false teachings and idolatry they would rule with Christ (as stars in the firmament of God).

The fourth angel warned the nations that the firmament which ruled their world was dark and left them without guidance.

(5)   The message to Sardis warned that liveliness without the rule of God was dead.

The fifth angel to the nations warned them that without the light of God's law guiding them the spirit of oppression that would rise because of this would bring into the world an active army of protesters to harass and torment all those who do not have the mark of God on them.

(6)   The message to the church at Philadelphia was that the spiritual freedom that they had would make them in the image of their God. The door of heaven was open to them.

The sixth angel to the nations revealed great armies of men (such as Jeroboam led) overthrowing their oppressors in order to find physical freedom. But all these armies (like Israel itself) were spiritually still in the image of the natural man, as they would still lack spiritual communion with God.

(7)   Since the theme of the message to the final church was to seek the sabbath (or rest) of God, in the deliverance that his liberating message brings, we can predict that the final trumpet will bring both spiritual and physical deliverance (or Salvation) from Babylon and the enslaving nations of the world. Daniel shows us that this will be the time that God's messiah will appear.

Paul, the Christian apostle to the Gentiles, said this regarding the final trumpet to be blown: "Listen to me and I will tell you a hidden truth: Not everyone will die, but every one of us will be changed. Quite suddenly, in the blinking of an eye, when the last trumpet sounds, the dead shall be raised indestructible. All of us will be fashioned to endure."   (1 Corinthians 15: 51-52)

What is at work in the instructions to the churches and the warnings to the nations of the world is God's creative power. Whether by obedience and blessings, or by warnings and curses, God will bring about his plan. Of this you can be certain, for God is resolute.

Now you have met the cast: God, World rulers, Satan, Christ, the spirit of Babylonian violence and confusion, the congregations of God, the enslaving nations of the world, the nation of God (144,000 of restored Israel), and the armies of men desiring to be free. The drama following is based on what all of these performers do.

For those who do what the creator says, there will be blessings. But to those who unrepentantly continue in their ways, Jehovah (through all the prophets) says: "I have told you today, but you still have not obeyed Jehovah your God in all that he sent me to tell you. So now be sure of this: You will die by war, famine, and the plague in the very place where you imagined you would settle down in peace."   (Jeremiah 42: 21-22)

Those who are of God have their weaponry defined for them: "Stand firm therefore, having girded your loins with truth, and having put on the breastplate of righteousness, and having shod your feet with the preparation of the gospel of peace; in addition to all, taking up the shield of faith with which you are able to extinguish all the flaming missiles of the evil one. And take the helmet of salvation and the sword of the spirit, which is the word of God." (Ephesians 6: 14-17)

CHAPTER TEN

Commissioning God's Workman

Shortly after this, I saw another messenger of God descend from heaven. This majestic giant spirit, which was clothed in a cloud, had a rainbow around his head. His whole face shone like the sun, and his legs were like pillars of fire. In his hand he was holding an open scroll, and his right foot was planted on the sea and his left foot on the land. When he shouted his voice was like the loud roar of a lion, and after he had shouted, seven mighty thunders answered him.

Immediately I was on the verge of writing down what I had heard the seven thunders say, but another voice from heaven intervening said: "No! Keep secret everything that you have heard, and don't set down those things the seven thunders said." Only on that day when the seventh angel (of the church) prepares to sound his trumpet, shall this mystery from God be made apparent (in much the same way that the secrets of the prophets were revealed prior to their being brought about).

Then the voice from heaven spoke to me again and said: "Go now and take the scroll lying open in the hand of that messenger who stands upon the sea and on the land."

Not hesitating then, I approached this spirit messenger and I asked him for the little scroll he held. Immediately he responded with these words: "Here you are. Take the scroll, and be sure you eat it all. Even though it will be just as sweet as honey in your mouth, you will find that in your stomach it will turn extremely sour."

Obediently I took the scroll that the angel messenger was holding in his hand, and I ate it all. (Then, as he told me) I found that it was just as sweet as honey in my mouth. Yet when I'd eaten it, in my stomach it became extremely sour. (For the word of God is very pleasant to hear and read. But understanding it often requires actions that are extremely difficult to perform.)

So after I had eaten (God's word), I heard the spirit say: "Now it is your responsibility to go and prophesy before the many nations, before the tribes who speak in many languages and even before kings." (I should perhaps remind the reader at this point, that prophesying is not fortune telling. "To prophesy" means "to reveal the will of God". John was sent to reveal God's will to the world.)

*

God's will is in his word, and those who read his word and understand it, come to realise that (since they are no longer ignorant of God's will) their knowledge instantly obliges them to do those things his word requires: For "Jehovah, the God of the holy prophets has sent his messenger to show his workmen all those things which they must do immediately." (Revelation 22: 6). In this vision, John has been commissioned for a special work (by digesting a scroll which he was given to study carefully). And John, like Moses and all wise men who delegate responsibility, has commissioned everyone who reads this document to share the work which he describes for them. You may recall that in a manner similar to this, Jeremiah at an earlier time had been commissioned to do God's work through what he read. Jeremiah described his calling in this way: "When your words came, I ate them; they were my joy and my heart's delight, for I bear your name, O Jehovah, God of armies." (Jeremiah 15: 16.)

This instance, and that which John describes, resemble words once spoken by Ezekiel, another Hebrew prophet, who affirmed: "Then I looked and I saw a hand stretched out to me. In it was a scroll, which was instantly unrolled for me. On both sides of it, there was written woeful words of lament and mourning.

"Afterwards he said to me: 'Son of man, eat what is before you, eat this scroll; then go and speak to the house of Israel.' So I opened my mouth and he gave me the scroll to eat. Then he told me, 'Son of man, go now to the house of Israel and speak my words to them. You are not being sent to a people with a difficult language which is unknown to you, but rather to the house of Israel — not to many peoples whose language is obscure and whose words are difficult for you to understand.'"

(Ezekiel 2: 9 - 3: 6.)

What John reveals to us then, in this concisely drawn symbolic scene, is the basic method often used in scriptures to illustrate the manner in which an individual is selected and commissioned (by a spirit from God) to carry out a special work assigned to him. When correctly understood this dramatic scene becomes a firm command to "every faithful workman" serving Jesus Christ.

Fittingly the servants of God, in the interval between the sounding of the sixth and seventh trumpets, have been commissioned with specific duties to perform, which shall later be outlined in all the chapters which come after this. But this commissioning of an individual is always dependant on that person's knowledge of God's word, and his ability to read "dark sayings" and (through this knowledge of the scriptures) solve the riddles in the visions he is shown. By doing this, he establishes conclusively that he is able to undertake the task which God assigns to him. He does so with the full authority of God, because he has the power to read and speak the word of God with perfect understanding. As Jesus said: "Behold, I stand at the door, and knock: If anyone hears my voice and opens the door, I will come in to him, and will sup with him, and he with me."   (Revelation 3: 20)

There is no place in God's work for blind obedience. A follower of Jesus Christ cannot trust emotions, sentiments or biases to reveal the path of God to him. Quite simply (as a workman God has sent) he must know the blueprint he is following and carefully apply it to the structure of the work he has to do. To take any other course from what was given to the Church by John has no relevance at all. At this point (in the battle with the world) between the sounding of the sixth and seventh trumpets, the reader has been called upon to test his weaponry by answering the simple riddle he is shown. That prerequisite cannot be set aside. Because the interpretation of this vision orients the worker to the work he has been called upon to do.

Riddles (or dark sayings) are regularly given in the scriptures to challenge every reader of the sacred texts (and test him for his readiness to serve). In very early times, it was regarded as a sign of wisdom and learning to be able to unravel every kind of riddle that was posed. King Solomon of Israel (the wisest king of all, so we are told) could boast that he could solve every kind of riddle that was put to him.

Because such riddles were regarded as a means to test a person's skill and readiness to do the will of God, God's servants (in this strategy we are studying) are asked from their knowledge of the scriptures: (1) to identify the messenger whom they are shown and (2) to read the contents written in the scroll he holds, and study them. This cannot be done by those who are not properly prepared for it. If you do not accurately identify the messenger, you cannot possibly receive the scroll from him or know how it relates both to the messenger and to the plan which John stands ready to unfold.

1.
The Messenger

Because this commissioning of a servant of God is so important to the work Christ's workers have been called upon to do, of necessity we must take the time we need to carefully consider everything that John has told us of the messenger. He clearly tells us:

"This majestic giant spirit, which was clothed in a cloud, had a rainbow around his head. His whole face shone like the sun, and his legs were like pillars of fire....His right foot was planted on the sea and his left foot on the land. When he shouted his voice was like the loud roar of a lion."

Oh yes! Like you, I realise that there are many different groups and individuals within the Christian church who adamantly put forward varied views of who the angel "is", "might have been" or "seems to be". I have no wish to quarrel with anyone at all. But in the name of Christian unity I think it would be wise for us to first discuss a few of these conflicting views before continuing. In general they appear to fall into three specific categories:

There are those who say (1) that the angel messenger is symbolic of a latterday prophet (or an arch angel from God's throne) who has brought a fuller understanding of the gospel message in his hand — or similarly that the angel represents a foreview of some latterday church or church philosophy, or (2) that the messenger is none other than "the spiritual manifestation of our saviour Jesus Christ". (3) Others, prefer to take a more scholarly approach and speculatively weigh the pros and cons of who the angel possibly might be. They waffle on continually about the different choices we could make but come to no conclusion afterwards. It is almost as if they thought it really didn't matter who the angel was as long as the passage was thoroughly debated.

Sadly, all three of these approaches miss the mark. The first one (which says that the angel is a latterday prophet of some kind, some new church or some new church philosophy) is actually affirming that Jesus Christ had failed to do the work which he set out to do, and that the plan he gave his followers was totally inadequate — because it needed filling out by that new church or prophet who was predestined in the plan of God to follow him. Such a creed completely seems to justify the doubts which John the baptist had regarding Jesus Christ. When (sending messengers to Jesus) John asked the question: "Are you really he that was to come? or shall we look for someone after you?" (Matthew 11: 3)

Worse than this, however, is that such churches call upon their membership to put their "faith" entirely in those prophets and those leaders having no credentials other than their leaders' own assertion that they speak "the truth" and what they tell you is divine. Their only proof is that "they did not learn these truths from any man."

Challenge such a visionary with the scriptures, and he will tell you instantly: that what you quote to him has now been done away, or that copyists have altered Bible texts so much their meaning has become distorted, and their meanings far past finding out. Scriptures therefore have little relevance for him, because they have been "superceded by a new and better revelation from the throne of God". This makes it very difficult to share a common ground, because the scriptures once regarded as "the golden measuring stick of God" no longer measure anything. Not even the Bereans (that group of Jews so highly praised by Paul because they searched the scriptures regularly to measure the truth or falsity of his words) could possibly have qualified as challengers of them.

I do not wish to be abusive of such individuals or their doctrines. They must stand or fall on their own merits. Yet when they do presume to quote the scriptures and interpret them, they pass to me the right to challenge them. No longer can the veil of their prophetic infallibility be raised to hide them from admonishment. For as Paul once said to Timothy: "All scripture...is profitable for teaching, for reproof, for correction and for training in righteousness." (2 Timothy 3: 16). It was the duty of all Christians to admonish one another.

So it troubles me that those who are the members of such groups (are rendered instantly inferior to the person of the prophet leading them) and helplessly become dependent on his word. Believing that their leader's message is divine, he cannot be admonished or impugned by any equal brother in the church. To challenge what he says is akin to challenging God and calling God a liar. He may not claim to be divine, but he is worshipped all the same. Songs of praise are even sung to him. He is completely without peers. No one has the right to question him. To do so is instantly a breach of faith in God. As one devoted follower once told me: "There are some things we just don't question when it comes to God. We have to trust our leaders and have faith in them."

The only compensation that this prophet possibly can give to his followers is the feeling that they "worship" God upon a higher plane than other Christians do. Those who look to Jesus Christ alone as the sole High Priest and only mediator between God and man are seen by them as pathetically inferior. Yet neither Paul nor Peter nor Apollos, the foremost leaders of the early church presumed to be superior to any of the brethren.

In one letter that Paul wrote to the Corinthians, he unequivocally put to rest this question when he said: "What is Apollos after all? and who on earth is Paul? We are nothing more than servants who have helped you to believe....I simply planted the seed, and Apollos watered it. It was God who made it grow. Neither he who plants the seed nor he who waters it is anything at all. God alone who makes it grow should be revered."

(1 Corinthians 3: 5-7)

Furthermore, to say that the gospel message Jesus gave to Christians needed filling out is actually a breach in the contract that was made with him. Paul in speaking on this very point once wrote: "Just as no one is allowed to set aside or add to any human covenant once it is enacted and agreed upon, so it is in this case too."   (Galatians 3: 15)

So what makes Jesus Christ so different from the rest? I'm glad you asked. Wasn't he a man of flesh and blood? Of course he was. That was the quality that made him so distinctive. He used his humanity to transcribe the scriptures and reveal them written on the human character. He even took the Jewish holy days and used them (in the same way Moses did) as a well-laid plan for establishing a kingdom upon earth which was not inimical to nature and the world which God had made. Jesus made his own life a human revelation of God's word so that he became a living vision that all men could see. He therefore was "that prophet" Moses prophesied. And it was said of him, that he fulfilled the scriptures and did not alter them in any way. As God had said: "Let us make man in our image, after our likeness."

Paul defined his purpose in these words: "It was God's intention, from the start, that those whom he first chose (i.e. the Jews) would eventually become the image of his son (the man from heaven he designed). Jesus was the firstborn of the many brothers who would follow him. Moreover, God had planned when he first chose them (as his people) to make them in the image of his son, so that those he chose could be made right with him, and thereby glorified."   (Romans 8: 29-30)

This does not demand blind faith, but attentiveness and careful observation and inspiration from the man we see. That is the greatness of all true visions — that we learn from them. Jesus was an open vision that all the world could see. And there are many visions in the world today for those who have the eyes for reading them. God speaks through his reality.

The last of those three groups, who offer differing opinions on the angel messenger's identity, merely try to balance views and show their tolerance and open-mindedness. They are extremely clever in adroitly handling the various opinions which different scholars have advanced. Yet even so their scholarly activity in managing these points of view, while hiding any show of their real preference, thoroughly negates the plan which Jesus ordered all his followers "to quickly put into effect". The first six clarions have sounded the alarm, and Christian armies now are in the battlefield. The soldiers have advanced to take strategic points. And even now while danger threatens them, they stand ready to receive the next command.

So by giving Christians no definite interpretation of these words, such scholars leave God's troops without direction prior to the the final trumpet signal to advance. The trouble with the first interpretation that we have is that it only tells us that a bridgehead has been reached and everything which needed to be done is done now through the special message that their prophet has. All we have to do according to this first philosophy is join a special church, sing praises to a prophet who has given us "the truth" and wait for Jesus Christ to come and do the rest, or idly wait for death so that when we die, we may "go to heaven" where we will be acknowledged as having been believers in "the truth" and safely brought to God "in heaven" as members of "the true and only church". Even so the last of these is little better than the first alternative for it leaves Christ's armies in the field without a map, a plan or general.

The middle group assures us that the messenger we meet is Jesus Christ. Beyond all doubt, this interpretation puts us in good hands. All who hold this view cannot go far wrong with it, as they have good grounds for assuming this, since every angel we encounter in this book we have, is sent by Jesus Christ himself. Jesus Christ, the commander-in-chief of all God's troops, is master of the plan which he has taken from the hand of God. He alone can open and has opened all the seals upon the scroll for us, and what we now encounter is part of what he showed us underneath the seventh seal. So those who take this view have done the wise thing in turning to their ultimate superior. For God himself has placed us in his hands.

One must be very careful though not to force the text so as to make it fit some preconceived opinion that we have. We must consider thoughtfully how it fits into the context of the plan which John unfolds for us and how it helps God's workmen to fulfill their tasks. The angel messenger is not the person Jesus Christ at all, nor is he any latterday authority. He is that hope-inspiring vision of mankind united under heaven's government, to be "the new earth" God proposed to build. He is, in other words, the direct antithesis of that body of mankind so memorably described for us in Chapter Two of *Daniel*.

This is how the prophet Daniel, as he stood before the royal throne, interpreted a dream the King of Babylon had dreamed about the body of mankind as it existed under Babylon: "Before you, stood a large statue — an enormous, dazzling statue, awesome in appearance. The head of the statue was made of pure gold, its chest and arms of silver, its belly and thighs of bronze, its legs of iron, its feet partly of iron and partly of baked clay.

"...You, O king are the king of kings. The God of heaven has given you dominion and power and might and glory; in your hands he has placed mankind, the beasts of the field and the birds of the air. Regardless of where any of these might live on earth, God has made you the supreme ruler over all of them. You are the head of gold."   (Daniel 2: 33 - 38)

Now whereas this statue Daniel spoke of was made of different metals to represent the different nations of the world, John's spirit messenger is a carnate man of flesh and blood ("a son of man"). Clothed in a garment of clouds (of many witnesses), this man from heaven is mankind fashioned in the image of God — mankind as he will one day be. The head is Jehovah (and his government, made up of those whom he will choose). The rainbow that surrounds his head is that grace and truth (or forgiveness and peace) which God has granted to the world. And all the body parts are the people from the nations in the world — as Daniel said.

This man from heaven represents mankind on the new earth God will build. That new world (as the rainbow indicates) requires that we forgive and make peace with our enemies. It was the violence of warfare in the time of Noah that brought the great flood of heaven on the world — and it is the violence of warfare by which the man of Babylon sustains himself. It is the curse of war that threatens to destroy the world and which God's kingdom seeks to overcome. The man of heaven therefore is a man of peace sent (as Daniel said) to reconcile the world to God.

The man of Babylon, composed of different metals, is divided sharply by its many differences. It is lifeless, like an idol made by human hands, and it represents the best that man can do without the help of God. Unlike him though, the man of heaven is living spirit. Yet he stands upon the sea and land with legs of fire — showing that he rules all things by God's authority. The man of Babylon (while he still reigns) retains the same authority that God gave Adam at the beginning of all things. The man that God has chosen, after his own heart (who does God's will rather than his own) patiently awaits the time of the seventh trumpet to assume his rule.

Like other images that we were shown through John, the angel that John shows us here symbolically defines the aim that all the servants of God are called on to achieve. That aim is to replace the warlike metallic world of Babylon with a new enlightened world of peace. For this reason we are shown a shining angel, representing the new spirit of mankind, asserting his authority over land and sea, and in the heavens above the earth. He is a man governed by the wisdom which made all things – the creator of the universe.

The Jewish prophet Daniel also drew the picture of a man very much like him that John has drawn. It is, therefore, possible to visually appreciate the nature of the world which God designed, and which Israel was destined to become. In the visions Daniel draws, we are shown the nations of the world in the form of fearsomely aggressive beasts, suggestive of the way in which the nations actually perceived themselves. The new world God promised Daniel he would build, by contrast is presented as a man who wears God's crown of wisdom on his head. He describes that spiritual man of heaven in these words:

"In my night-time vision (or my dream) I looked, and saw before me someone like a man of flesh and blood (a son of man) approaching on the clouds of heaven. (Armies raised clouds of dust as they approached. So the armies that advanced with this new nation being sent into the world were all the saints who would one day bring their nation into power). This man (of spirit) drew near to the Ancient of Days (Jehovah, the father of all life on earth who installs all rulers and establishes all nations upon earth. John symbolizes him by the head of the man itself, surrounded by the rainbow of his grace).

"This spirit man was led into God's presence. There, God endowed him with authority, glory and sovereign power. (In John's vision, this is symbolized by legs of fire which stand upon the sea and land.) All peoples, nations, and men of every language worshipped him. (i.e. obeyed and honoured him). The extent of his authority (over all things upon earth) would be everlasting and never pass away. And his kingdom would be one which would never be destroyed."   (Daniel 7: 13-14)

This nation (of perfected Israel, which Daniel describes in his vision) was the seed and embryo for what was yet to come. Neither the Israel he saw, nor the new world which would one day grow from it, existed in the world. They were visions (or instructions) of what God desired from those who truly worshipped him. Daniel saw the nation God desired to build as one which would instruct the world. The followers of Jesus of Nazareth regarded their messiah as the seed from which perfected Israel and the new world was to come. Israel was called to lay the firm foundation for that world, and the messiah Daniel said would come was to be the corner stone. Israel was called to lead mankind into that now forgotten land of Eden, where God had been man's close adviser and companion, and had shown mankind the way to rule.

It was Israel which Daniel said was called on to perfect itself according to the method he was shown: through forgiveness and reconciliation. Then with the image of God's new man in front of them, they would be commissioned to rebuild the world. Thereby they would build a greater temple in the world than Solomon. For mankind in God's image is the temple he desires to build.

While considering this vision John describes, though, one cannot help but call to mind the great archangel who appeared to Joshua as "the commander of Jehovah's hosts". Joshua encountered him at the entrance to "the holy land" just before the great decisive battle had been fought. This is Joshua's account of him: "When Joshua was near to Jericho, he looked up and saw a man standing in front of him with a drawn sword in his hand. Joshua went up to him and asked, 'Are you for us or for our enemies?'

"'Neither,' he replied, 'but as commander of the army of Jehovah I have now come.' (God did not take sides

with any nation in the world—not even ancient Israel.
But in the scales of justice, Israel was the voice of the
oppressed—whose prayers the God of life had heard.)
Then Joshua fell face downward to the ground in reverence, and I asked him, 'What message does my lord have
for his servant?' The commander of Jehovah's army
replied, 'Take off your sandals (i.e. "put away the influence
of all worldly customs"), for the place where you are
standing is holy.' And Joshua did so."   (Joshua 5: 13-15)

Talking to this angel was like talking face to face
with God.

Both Daniel and Jude refer to this great prince by
name, calling him "the archangel" and "the prince who
protects his people." That John wanted those who
understood his words to see a close connection between
the spirit vision he has given us of united mankind in
the image of God and the great archangel Michael: "who
is like God" cannot be doubted in the least. This holy
spirit is able to inspire and strengthen all those he leads
by giving them a vision of the world to be. There is no
blind obedience to him for, by his very presence, he
identifies the goal toward which they move. He
represents mankind in the image of God.

In every facet of the strategy which John reveals,
there has been a steady stream of growing unity to be
observed amongst the people serving God, through
obedience to the plan which Jesus Christ has given them:
(1) the individual conforming to the character of Christ,
(2) each urban church community putting all corruption
from its midst, (3) the unifying power of prayer, (4) and
the high priest of heaven standing by "the golden altar"
giving golden trumpets to the seven church communities
(to offer well-considered warnings to the world to save
them from catastrophe).

In every case, it was the purpose of the task Christ called upon the churches to achieve which gave them unity. But neither God nor Christ forgot the people God first called. There is a larger goal to bring about than that which mere "religion" (as we think of it) could possibly achieve. That is why God sent his unifying spirit to commission those who honoured God, for the task of tearing down and building up again. Yet this vision we are shown is actually mankind and nature brought into perfect harmony with God.

Because a greater unity is needed amongst all people serving God, we are reminded of the angel that Jehovah sent to Joshua. Since this leader is a spirit Jews and Christians both can recognize, it makes it possible for them to easily resolve their differences and join together in a call to spiritual arms so as to free the world from prejudice, suspicion, crime, fruitless strife and oppression of all kinds. Churches in all cities of the world, who were formerly united by the spirit of their church community, will now find greater harmony and common cause with all the saints of God under Michael, the archangel who will lead God's hosts in battle with the world of Babylon. For he will bind together all of Israel, giving them the unity they need.

The scene which follows in the chronicle of Joshua which we just read is certainly appropriate for the battle being waged in this prophetic document, for it describes the trumpet calls and shout that led to final victory against that powerful city which had blocked the way to entering the holy land: "Now Jericho was tightly shut up. Because of the Israelites, no one went out and no one came in.

"Then Jehovah said to Joshua, 'See I have delivered Jericho into your hands, along with its king and fighting men. March around the city once with all armed men. Do this for six days. Have seven priests carry trumpets with ram's horns in front of the ark. On the seventh day, march around the city seven times, with the priests blowing the trumpets. When you hear them sound a long blast on the trumpets, have all the people give a loud shout; then the wall of the city will collapse and the people will go up, every man straight in.'" (Joshua 16: 1-5)

That we should meet the unifier of God's armies at this time does much in helping us explain the building of the temple afterwards and the two courageous witnesses who will prophesy before the wicked cities of the world.

This angel's face shone like the sun as Moses's face once shone after having been with God upon the mount. Clothed in a cloud, he showed himself in much the manner that Messiah was to come, and the rainbow around his head revealed like silent speech the grace and mercy of Jehovah the Creator, reminding this impressive army — before a major battle with the world — that the one they served was merciful and just. This angel spirit by his very presence awesomely revealed the multi-jewelled character of God.

Such a revelation tells us that if true world peace ever is to come, there must be mercy and forgiveness among men, regardless of the anguish and the pain endured. Seventy times seven must be the measure that we use to see how far that we should go in reconciling others to the way of God. Those serving God were not to be offended by petty slights, insults and rebuffs, for Jesus said: "You have heard it said, 'an eye for an eye and a tooth for a tooth,' But I tell you, 'Do not take offence at the petty evil others do to you.' If some one (pettily offends you) with a cuff across the cheek, turn the other cheek to him as well. And if someone wants to take

your tunic from you, let him have your cloak." (Matthew
5: 38 - 41) Do not keep grudges then.

Yet to what extent should we forgive the evil done to
us? Since Jesus was a living prophecy, his whole life
served as a way of teaching us. Forgiveness was a word
he often used, and the whole gospel of reconciliation was
based on it. That is the gospel we were told would save
the world. Even at the time when nails were being
hammered in his hands and feet, he said: "Father forgive
them, for they don't know what they do." (Luke 23: 34)
We can't afford to hold a grudge then. For our salvation
and the salvation of the world depends on it. And one
day upon Yom Kippur, all our sins must be confessed and
carried off into the wilderness upon the head of that
vengeful and malignant social spirit represented in the
Azazel goat (known as Satan). That wicked spirit must
be put away from us and sent into the wilderness. For it
is that compelling influence, under which all of us have
lived, which is the cause of all mankind's abusive and
destructive tendencies.

Yet the new-born spirit of community this great
vision has revealed must either come upon everyone who
has been liberated from the shackles of physical
oppression, or else their new-found liberty will be short-
lived. If people cannot overcome the power of that
demon spirit (sin) waiting for them just outside the door
of that enslavement which they hope to leave, they will
be devoured by it, as Cain once was. To be ready for
salvation from slavery, people must spiritually prepare
themselves.

As Malachi once prophesied: "Who shall be able to
live on the day of his coming (the day of Jehovah) and
who shall be able to stand when he appears."

(Malachi 3: 2)

2.
The Message

The messenger of God who stood with his right foot planted in the sea and his left foot on the land, held a small open scroll in his hand.

This short section of scripture visually refers to the first responsibility God placed upon mankind (male and female) when he gave them "dominion over the fish of the sea, the fowl of the air, over all domestic animals and over every living thing that moves upon the earth." (Genesis 1: 28-29). Yet Adam (or mankind) due to the curse he brought upon nature and himself, through his own deliberate abuse of nature, brought ruin on the work of God. So John now illustrates for us mankind's first calling so that those in the new community of God can see the role that they are called upon to fill. Perfected man was made to have control over all things God had made: "What is man," the psalmist asked, "that you are mindful of him? You have made him a little lower than God, and you have crowned him with glory and honour. You made him to have (responsibility and) control over the works of your hands. You have put all things under his feet: all sheep and oxen, fish of the sea, and whatever passes along the paths of the sea."
(Psalm 8: 5-8)

Such a man would not abuse creation or use it carelessly for trivial pursuits. So the vision John has shown us at this time is most appropriate, since all the armies of God's Kingdom have been struggling with the man of sin (the man of Babylon) for centuries and they need to see again the man of heaven in order to refresh themselves and reaffirm their purposes.

John defines all the aims of God throughout this vision in images that are strong and memorable. None of them are paltry, abstract words which lose their meaning over time. God lets us see the end he asks us to pursue, and it is the aim (and not the ingrown form of ceremonials) that unite the people God has trained to bring about his will. Since people are ruled more by their imaginations than by words we are given images that stick upon the mind and yet define the purposes of God. These images include:

(1) *The spiritual qualities* of the messiah depicted in visual form in Chapter One. These serve as (a) the model to be emulated by all those serving God, and as (b) the firm foundation on which all civic churches in the world are called upon to build.

(2) *A picture of heaven and the one who sits upon its throne* to define the structure of the government of God, its purposes and its responsibilities. While he who sits upon the throne defines the nature of the God they serve and represent.

(3) *The lamb with seven horns upon its head* to show the churches their sole source of unity and the equal status of the fellowship existing amongst all church communities throughout the world.

(4) *The scroll taken from the hand of God* illustrates the source of all commissioning. That the lamb of God alone can open it shows us that commissioning must come alone through him, and those he sends — not from any other prophet or messiah with a different plan.

(5) *Horsemen* memorably inscribe upon the mind the nature of those misfortunes that besiege the world and bring the curse of death upon mankind.

(6) *The Golden Altar* and the voices that come from below it tell us of the blood of innocence which calls to God to be relieved from all the misery that Adam's seed has brought upon the world.

(7) *The darkening of the sun and moon and stars* tells us that the governing powers (cultural and political) are spiritually dark. They lead the world therefore toward its destruction.

(8) *The seven angels by the golden altar with the angel acting as high priest* defines the nature of Christ's commission to the separate churches of the world — thus unifying them.

(9) Now *the man of heaven* is revealed to illustrate the nature of the aim God's people must achieve — a world where mankind ruled by God will rule responsibly: "A hewn rock uncut by human hands, struck the statue on his feet of iron and clay, pulverizing them. Then the iron, clay, bronze, silver and gold were broken into particles, which immediately became like chaff on a summer's threshing floor. Then the wind swept these away so that no trace at all was left of them. But the rock which struck the statue on the feet grew into a huge mountain filling the whole earth." (Daniel 2: 34-35)

It is not a question then of "to what church do you belong?" It is a question of "in what manner are you organized to carry out the plan which God assigned his workmen?" Surely it will help us if we understand the aims which we have set out to achieve. If these are always foremost in our thoughts our deeds will correspond to them, and God will find the means for helping us.

3.

The Greater Mission

"Then the messenger of God shouted with a loud roar like a lion, and when he spoke seven thunders answered him."

The great collective voice of all mankind united under God would be that mighty voice. For mankind was to be endowed with a kingly voice – someone who could speak like Jesus Christ, with authority, and "not as the scribes and Pharisees". For Jesus promised, God would grant requests to everyone who prayed in his name. That does not mean saying, "In the name of Jesus Christ our Lord we ask these things." Such lip service is meaningless. Praying in Jesus's name means asking for things which will bring glory to Jehovah and the world that he has made. Anything we ask of God is not for us to squander carelessly, but for the sake of God's community on earth, and so that we might relieve oppression, pain and misery. When we pray to further the work of God's kingdom, we are praying in Jesus's name, whether we utter his actual name or not. For the name of Jesus means "Jehovah saves" or liberates.

Man now speaking and acting with the authority of God will do all things in his name. But this is not a privilege that any man can individually assume. It only can be gained by imbibing the wisdom and nature of God, by studying and practicing his word, not from glibly quoting scriptures. John's vision, of the divine man of heaven, prepares us for understanding what will happen and what is about to take place. As Hosea said: "The people will follow Jehovah when he roars like a lion. For when Jehovah roars, his people, trembling, will come from the west. Trembling, they will hasten like

birds from Egypt (out of captivity) and like doves from
Assyria (out of bondage). 'For I will bring them home,
and let them settle there,' Jehovah says."

(Hosea 11: 10-11)

Jesus was to draw from this, his metaphor regarding
the birds of the air who would come and make their
homes in the kingdom he would build. In that parable
Jesus likened the man of heaven to a tree: "The
kingdom of heaven," he said, "is like a mustard seed
which a man took and planted in his field. Though it is
the smallest of all seeds, when it grows it becomes the
largest of all garden plants and becomes a tree, so that
the birds of the air come and perch in its branches."
(Matthew 13: 31-32) God, as we have seen, speaks
through his creatures, and the voice of man in unity
with God becomes the voice of God.

4.

The Seven Great Commands

"...when the messenger of God spoke, seven thunders
answered him (clearly telling what his purpose was).

"After the thunders had spoken, I was about to write
down what they had said, but I heard another voice from
heaven saying, 'Seal up (and make secret) what the seven
thunders told you now, and don't write any of it down.'"

This may seem like a very strange request, but let's
consider it. Daniel, much earlier, was given a similar
instruction: "Now, Daniel, close the book, and seal it fast
until the time of the end (of the age). For there will be
many who will strive frantically (even hysterically) to
disclose its meanings, wasting their time and energies in
their vain attempts."   (Daniel 12: 4)

Heaven didn't want the kingdom's enemies informed as to what all its planned strategies would be. Nor did they want their work reviled and trivialized.

That is not to say that God's own people wouldn't know about the kingdom's strategies and plans. For Jesus told his own disciples: "Now to you it is given to understand the mysteries and the secrets of the kingdom of God; but for others they are in parables (or symbols) so that looking they may look and not see, and hearing they may not comprehend." (Luke 8: 10) Or as Matthew worded it: "You have been chosen to know about the secrets of the Kingdom of heaven, but others are incapable of understanding them. Therefore, some will receive little, others more, according to their capability of handling them. But those who lack true understanding, will lose even what they do receive." (Matthew 13: 11-13)

The message then is still there for those "with eyes to see." And what the seven thunders said can be easily discovered in the context of the vision we are shown. It should be obvious to everyone that we are standing (in this vision) at the beginning of a new world. Surely any Jew can tell us from the Jewish Talmud that the seven thunders represent the seven great commands of God by which the heavens and the earth were made. The one most relevant to the context we are shown is, "Let us make mankind (male and female) in our image, after our likeness, so that they may rule responsibly over the fish of the sea and over the fowl of the air, and over the cattle and over all the earth, and over every moving thing that moves upon the earth."

5.
The End of Bondage

"Then the messenger of God whom I saw standing on the sea and on the land (indicating his authority over

them) raised his right hand to heaven and swearing in
the name of (Jehovah) who lives for ever and ever, and
who created the heavens and the earth, and all that is in
them, said, 'There shall be no more delay. (For the time
has come for us to act — and no more time shall be given
to all those who defy the will of God.)'"

One scripture that helps reveal the meaning of this
passage is found in *Deuteronomy*: "I lift my hand to
heaven and declare: As surely as I live for ever and ever,
when I sharpen my flashing sword, and my hand grasps
it in judgment, I will take vengeance on my adversaries
and repay those who hate me." (Deuteronomy 32: 40 - 41)

So the messenger (or angel) indicated that the time
had come to judge the world. It also meant deliverance
from oppression, as Daniel showed us with these words:
"Then the angel, raising his hand toward heaven swore
in the name of (God) who lives for ever and ever, saying,
'In another three and a half years, the bondage of God's
people will end, and all things (I have promised) will
come true.'"   (Daniel 12: 7)

Here then we should consider the word "salvation" and
what it means. Salvation means deliverance — complete
deliverance in mind, spirit and body from all enslaving
elements of the world: the physical tyrant, the over-
bearing task master, police harassment, from intellectual
ignorance and uncontrolled passions that shackle us to
the idolatry of this world (from dope, from alcohol, from
superstitions, and sexual enslavement, in fact from everything that hinders us from living happy and meaningful
lives in a healthy relationship with both God and Man).

The purpose of the Church was to sow those
spiritual seeds which would make it possible to handle

the great social upheavals when they do occur—lest we become enslaved when freedom opens up its door for us. For there is more to slavery than just being set free from oppressive rulers. We can be slaves to ignorance, and slaves to our own inhibiting desires. We can be slaves to our feelings of vindictiveness, reprisal and vengeance. We must be freed from them. Salvation must cover all of them, which tells us why so many revolutions failed.

The Hebrew Scriptures of the Bible tell us that both Israel and Judah fell to Assyria and Babylon because they did not properly imbibe the wisdom of God's word. Christianity, for the most part failed, because (as John and the other epistles tell us) the Church became polluted with false teachings and failed to cleanse themselves, loving the traditions of men more than the word of God. The monarchy of France reaped the blood harvest they had sown prior to the revolution, in their persecution of the Huguenots and other groups of Protestants. In the exact place where at the opening of the Reformation, the first stake for heretics was set up, the Revolution set up its first guillotine, "on the very spot where martyrs had been burned." As E. de Pressensé says, in his book *The Church and the French Revolution*: "The galleys and the prisons ran red with the blood of the priests. The galleys and the prisons, once crowded with Huguenots, were now filled with their persecutors."
(Book 3. Chapter 1)

So the Revolution didn't fair much better. Setting aside the Bible, they also set aside restraint of moral law. In world history France enjoys the rare distinction of being the first world state to legislate in their Legislative Assembly, that there was no God. After this was done, throughout all France, men and women everywhere (including the entire population of the capital) sang and danced in celebration of the news. Yet now there was no

moral law restraining them. The violence that followed
in its wake is now well known to history. What they
thought would free them from oppression, condemned
them to another kind of tyranny.

White America failed, through its narrow definition
of democracy. It did not include blacks and native
peoples of America in any of the benefits their world
might offer them. Thereby they themselves became
oppressors of the weak. By the way, it is also worth
mentioning that democracy did not find its way into the
modern world through ancient Greece. It was the
Christian Church which, in challenging the divine right
of kings, said that sovereignty lay in the people. This is
an historical fact too often overlooked.

The church was wrong of course and should have
known it was, for true sovereignty lay with God, who
gave power to the people in the first Chapter of *Genesis*.
That is if we are looking for a real Christian definition
of sovereignty. Democracy can fail to work, when people
aren't accustomed to its ways, and lack the moral stature
and knowledge for using it. In the revolutionary
democracies, very few work well because majority
opinion does not make right. Informed opinion (as
opposed to manipulated opinion) does. In the United
States a class system, and oppression, due to subtle and
not so subtle social barriers, does exist.

The overthrow of Communism in Yugoslavia, did not
create a happier world. Enslaved by ethnic differences,
the peoples there were unprepared politically to handle
the great changes that allowed them to decide their
destinies. Nor were they morally prepared, as their
loyalties were narrow and ungenerous, focused around
cultural differences. Therefore real liberation (or should
I say Salvation) eluded them. They were ruled by biases

and loyalties to what can only be described as idolatries that blinded them to their humanity.

However, when the seventh angel (or messenger of God) blows his trumpet, then God will reveal the secret plan (which the seven thunders uttered), of the great mystery that he announced and promised would one day be fulfilled.

6.

The Message

"Then I heard that voice from heaven once again, which spoke to me and said: 'Go now, and take the scroll from the hand of the angel who is standing on the sea and land, and open it.'

"So I approached the messenger and asked him to give me the small scroll, and he replied: 'Here, take it and eat it all. Though it be sour in your stomach (after you have eaten it), in your mouth it will be as sweet as honey.'"

As King Solomon is reputed to have said: "Honey from the honeycomb tastes sweet (in your mouth) in just the same way that wisdom does when you have found it. When you enjoy being wise, it will ensure you of a bright future."   (Proverbs 24: 13-14)

Therefore the scriptures tell us that it is God's wisdom that the scroll contains. The same is true of manna eaten in the wilderness. The manna eaten by the children of Israel in the wilderness was "as sweet as honey," symbolic of divine wisdom that would prepare the people for living in the new land they were approaching. For although physically liberated, Israel was not yet spiritually equipped to enter "the promised land", since they had not been spiritually set free.

In fact, this was to be their ultimate downfall — that Israel hadn't really eaten of the wisdom God had given them. Their insistence upon eating meat instead, indicated that they wished to live according to their fleshly appetites, rather than to live spiritually on the manna of wisdom which God was feeding them. Jesus, too, when he offered his own body to be eaten was not inviting anyone to cannibalism. He was offering the wisdom of God written on human life. They were to become like Christ and share in his ministry by continuing to do what he would do, saying those things he would say. They were to put on Christ. He was the word of God, written on flesh, rather than on scrolls or stones.

That he never wrote a book for posterity to read is itself a prophecy. His life was the scroll that he asked us to read. The laws of God once written upon stone and parchment were now inscribed on human life and sealed by God's own hand.

Those who "ate his flesh", were called upon to live, as he had lived, in accordance with the teachings and the works that he had taught them. Such living examples were the living testament of God. It was the eating of this wisdom and giving life to it which made it flesh. It was to be incorporated into the daily diet of living that John had in mind when he wrote in his gospel: "Though it was in the world, the world had no knowledge of it, and though it was given to God's own people, they did not receive it (into the flesh of their own lives)."

Neither John nor Ezekiel actually ate a book, they read and imbibed its wisdom thoroughly and lived according to its word, so that they would be ready for the divine mission to which they had been called. The book was sour in the stomach because of the great responsibility that the understanding of those words would place on them. It can be very pleasant just to sit in church and listen to the minister speak words that make you feel good afterwards. The question is, "What has God sent you to do?" John tells us what that is, and knowing what he says is troubling. In words and deeds, John's words must be acted on.

Those who hide these things are like the man in one of Jesus's own parables. In it the master said to him: "You wicked, lazy servant! So you knew that I harvest where I had not sown and gather where I have not scattered seed? So why didn't you put my money into use.... Take this servant's money from him...and cast him into outer darkness where there is weeping and gnashing of teeth (let him have the values that the world awards)."

(Matthew 25: 26 - 30)

7.
The Duty

"Then I was told, 'Now go and prophesy again concerning many peoples, nations, tribes and tongues.'"

John was commissioned in just the same way that Jeremiah was: "See, today, I have given you authority over the nations and the kingdoms to root out, pull down and to destroy."   (Jeremiah 5: 21)

Jeremiah's words deserve close scrutiny, for he makes it clear his words and deeds were not his own: "When your words came, I ate them; they were my joy and my heart's delight, for I bear your name, O Jehovah, God of armies."   (Jeremiah 15: 16)

Jeremiah had been sealed with God's authority to prophesy and teach. Now John has given a small book to all the Christian churches in the world. It contains the very wisdom Jesus Christ passed on to him from God and which he thoroughly imbibed. That wisdom which he was to prophesy through eating it, commissioned him to act on God's behalf, with the full authority, preaching in his name. So, now, to every church recipient of John's book of divine revelation is given, upon eating it (which is to say reading it again and again, thoroughly imbibing every word and thoroughly understanding what is said) a commission from God, with power to prophesy and speak on God's behalf. That power to prophesy depends upon one speaking only God's pure word.

Such a church or person now must show the nations of the world, God's will. So what we're called to witness now, is the creation of the world. "Let us make man in our image," God has said to us.

Isaiah spoke of this commissioning in these words: "Then one of the seraphim flew toward me with a burning coal in his hands that he had taken with tongs from the altar. When he had touched it to my mouth he said, 'See, I have touched this to your lips, and now your guilt is gone, and your sin is purged.' After that I heard Jehovah's voice as he said, 'Whom shall I send? and who will go on my behalf?' Then I replied, 'I am here. Send me.'"   (Isaiah 6: 6-8)

CHAPTER ELEVEN

God Is With Us — Jehovah Reigns

At this point, I was given a reed for measuring and told, "Go and measure the temple of God and the altar, and count the number of worshippers there. But do not measure the outer court, for it is under the control of the Gentiles (those nations of the world who are disobedient to God). They will trample on the holy city for forty-two months." During that time (which is twelve hundred and sixty days or 3 $^1/_2$ years, half the time required to carry out a major work), I will give my two witnesses the power to prophesy. (Those Jews and Christians who know the word of God and live by it) will dress themselves in sackcloth (to show that they foresee disaster for the Gentile world).

These two witnesses are like the two olive trees. Yet they stand like two lampstands before the Ruler of the whole earth. If anyone therefore should even try to injure them, (the) fire (of God's word) will come from their mouths and destroy their enemies. In this way, whoever tries to harm them will be slain. These prophets have the power to shut up heaven so that, during the three and a half years that they speak, no rain (symbolic of God's blessings) can fall upon the earth. These men also have the power to turn the waters into blood. (For the word of God, when resisted by those who hear it spoken, brings death and calamity of all kinds upon the earth.)

So when the witnesses will have finished presenting the evidence of the offences (against God, against man, and against nature committed by the nations of the world) the beast (of jingoistic nationalism) will rise from the bottomless pit and will attack them and, overpowering them, will kill them. Then their corpses will lie exposed in the great square of the city which is

spiritually called Sodom and Egypt. That is where the
one who governs us (Jesus Christ) was crucified. (Some
prefer the word "impaled".)

For three and a half days the people of every race,
language, culture and nation will gather round to gaze
upon the corpses of these men and refuse them burial.
Everywhere throughout the world, the people will be
glad and celebrate their triumph over them by sending
one another congratulatory gifts because of the great
relief they feel at being rid of them.

However, after three and a half days, the spirit of
life from God will come upon them and revive them so
that they will stand up, and great terror will come upon
all those watching them. Then a loud voice coming out
of heaven calling to the witnesses will say, "Come up
here!" and while their enemies look on, the two
witnesses will ascend in a cloud to heaven.

In that same hour, a terrible earthquake will level
one tenth of the city, and seven thousand people in it
will die. The terrified survivors will give praise to the
God of heaven who had delivered them. (i.e. They will
be saved.)

The second great calamity is past, but a third
calamity will follow speedily.

*

God's written word remains unchangeable. As
scriptures say: "The word of God endures forever." It is
because the scriptures are reliable, that John can be
instructed now to use them as a measure for
determining what is done in the temple. That is the
significance of the reed that John is given along with the

instruction to measure the temple, the altar and the services conducted there. For Jesus made it clear to all of his disciples that his congregation would be built upon the strong and solid rock of God's unchanging word.

Ezekiel goes on to clarify this truth for us when he says: "Mortal man, describe (or measure) the temple to the people of Israel, that they may be made ashamed of all their sins. Let them study carefully its plan, and if they truly are ashamed of all that they have done, then explain to them the details of the temple's whole design — its entrances and exits — the purpose of its regulations and laws. Write all these down for them, that they can see why everything has been arranged the way it has, and follow faithfully the plan and regulations I laid down for them."   (Ezekiel 43: 10-11)

Often when the temple or the city was measured, it signified that there was something wrong with it that needed to be changed. It needed to be torn down and rebuilt. Maybe you remember the physical enactment of a prophecy by Jesus, when he overturned proceedings in the outer temple court to signify its workings were corrupt and needed to be altered, saying afterwards: "Not one stone of it will be left standing on another."

In such a manner Jeremiah also prophesied: "Jehovah is determined to lay waste the city of the daughter of Zion. He has measured it off carefully on his rule, and is determined to set his hand now to destroying it."
                              (Lamentations 2: 8)

So Christians must take heed of what John says, for he lays heavy emphasis upon this matter, that something in the way we worship is extremely wrong. There is a work that must be done. And Jews and Christians have been called upon to measure up to it. Services are meaningless if they do not affect the way God's people live. Church doctrines weren't to be "deep mysteries". They were to be instructions on how to treat one's fellow man and how to care for the environment, which the Bible describes as "the glory of God." Spending one's life doing penance has little to do with repenting and changing the way we live. Penance may show us the great need for repentance, but of itself it does not accomplish it.

In the early stages of this plan the church was shown the urgent need to be united as one body in each of all the various communities. Heaven being opened to each community church, all church communities were then united through the power of prayer beside the golden altar of heaven, by the High Priest standing there. To accomplish even greater unity amongst those serving God a great uniting spirit comes to earth as the angel of God's people, the Holy Spirit. This is the leader of God's hosts. The uniting spirit, as John reveals him, is a vision of mankind united under God. He is reminiscent of the angel Michael who appeared to Joshua the leader of Israel before their onslaught of Jericho, which blocked their entrance to the Holy Land and the new nation which they hoped to build.

So now John (the Joshua of Christianity) recognizes the great need to break down walls which separate Christ's flock from their elder brothers — the Jews.

The worshippers in the temple also were to be counted, indicating that each individual was called upon to carefully examine what he was and what he did, to see whose cause he really served — God's or that of Satan's world. For counting the worshippers in the temple suggests numbering the people for service or the sword. "Stand up and be counted," is still a popular

expression used today, and means "Show whose side
you're on." Another expression once used was "Let's
separate the sheep from the goats on this matter."

We have here, then, a mustering of God's people,
called upon to be prepared. John's meeting with the angel
Michael in the last chapter gives us some indication of
what that change must be. Michael as the leader of
God's hosts was what strengthened and unified all those
who served Jehovah — the creator of the world. He
mustered, unified and strengthened the armies of God.
The meaning of the temple indicates that the narrow
loyalties dividing God's people must be revised in order
to embrace a greater loyalty. For even Christianity at its
best has something wrong with it. The temple of all
God's people must be torn down and then rebuilt so as to
better serve the purposes of God.

In the days before the Jerusalem of the first century
fell, there were many different kinds of Jews. Some
historians say the differences dividing them were great.
The number of sects and cults according to these
authorities were comparable to those of modern
Christendom. Although I have some reservations
regarding the extent which they suggest, I understand
the point they try to make. In Jesus's own day there
were Herodians, Nazoreans, Alexandrians, Sadducees,
Zealots, Essenes, Galileans, Pharisees, the sect of John
the Baptist and many other groups as well — some
adopting teachings of the pagan world. None of these
divisions were superficial ones. Yet all these looked upon
themselves as Jews. Samaritans were Jews as well, but
with a difference that greatly alienated them. Like many
modern Christians, they believed themselves to be the
only congregation of true worshippers. They therefore
wouldn't worship in Jerusalem.

Except for the Samaritans, all Jews were united by
the temple in Jerusalem. It was the common bond whose
yearly festivals healed and strengthened them and salved
their wounds making them one body with a common
hope. The temple in Jerusalem was the head and heart
of scattered and divided Israel. It was the spiritual home
of God. Even Jesus spoke of it as "my Father's House."
He never questioned that it served the purposes of God.
It didn't matter that it had been built by Herod the
Great. God's presence in it made the temple what it was.
The priesthood may have been corrupt but neither Jesus
nor Paul reviled the High Priest, nor questioned his
authority.

What made the temple in Jerusalem the House of
God was the people who gathered there. Regardless of
their differences they gathered in one place to be united
by one God. By alluding to this living temple, John has
emphasized the need for unity between God's people
(Christians and Jews alike). But he tells them not to
count the people "in the outer court" as having common
cause with them. The task they are to do requires
complete commitment. God's people weren't to let themselves become confused by mistaking what was done
outside their groups as having any common cause with
them. In John's view the whole city was the temple.

The Gentiles will trample on the city for forty-two
months, which signifies a time of testing, but even more
a time of grace. Now forty-two months is an interesting
number and is fraught with many meanings: (6x7
months = 42 months = 1260 days = 3 $\frac{1}{2}$ years) Six is
man's number of imperfection. Seven is God's number of
perfection. These people have been exposed to God's
word but have chosen to ignore it. Therefore, judgment
upon those in the outer court is imminent. Forty-two
suggests a time of extreme testing. Forty being the

number of testing, and two suggesting that the people were given extra time to repent. The Number three and a half says that the work is only half done. The other half will complete it. So we know these people have only come half way toward understanding God, and are a long way yet from what God expects of them.

Now John points out (as had the Pharisees themselves much earlier) that the Holy City could be any city anywhere on earth, if the spirit for worshipping God was right. For it is the spirit of the city that makes it holy or unholy. Cities filled with crime — crime that sometimes seems respectable as well as that which everyone can universally condemn — are cities that are trampled on: "Although your saints are for a little while now in possession of your sanctuary, your adversaries trample under foot your holy place." (Isaiah 63: 18) God sees the city as his temple, and the places set apart for worship and the study of his word as his sanctuary. So Jesus's cleansing of the temple's outer court of its gross commercialism, was a prelude to his cleansing of the city when he comes the second time.

In the meantime, the outer courtyard belongs to the Gentiles whose Babylonian businessmen say: "When will the New Moon be over that we may sell grain, and the Sabbath be ended that we may market wheat? — skimping the measure, boosting the price, and cheating with dishonest scales, buying the poor with silver and the needy for a pair of sandals, selling even the sweepings with the wheat." (Amos 8: 5-6) "O God, the nations have invaded your inheritance; they have defiled your holy temple, they have reduced Jerusalem to rubble. They have given the dead bodies of your servants as food to the birds of the air, the flesh of your saints to the beasts of the earth. They have poured out blood like water all around Jerusalem, and there is no one to bury the dead.

We are objects of reproach to our neighbours, of scorn
and derision to those around us." (Psalm 79: 1-4)

The Bible, throughout its texts, affirms that the way
of the unrighteous seems right to them, but that all their
practices lead eventually to acts of violence. Isaiah says
of them: "Their feet make haste continually to sin; they
are swift to shed the blood of innocents. Their thoughts
are thoughts which turn continually to wickedness.
Therefore ruin and destruction mark their paths."
(Isaiah 59: 1-3)

Still in their own eyes they see themselves as
virtuous. The Bible recognizes that and says: "There is a
way which always seems right to a man, but at the end
of it is death." (Proverbs 14: 12)

These then are the spiritual sons of Cain. And two
witnesses are called upon (on God's behalf) to plead with
them, just as God once came to plead with Cain. This is
the nature of what took place: "God, however, did not
respect the offering of Cain. And Cain let his anger get
out of control and he became sullen and downcast. And
Jehovah said to Cain, Why do you not control your rage?
and why are you sullen and downcast? If you do what is
right, will you not be accepted? but if you neglect doing
right, sin crouches (like a wild beast) at your door,
waiting to rule over you. Therefore you must learn to
master it." (Genesis 4: 5-7)

It is for this reason God advises us to measure
ourselves, the doctrines we believe and teach and the
practices of our sanctuaries — repenting of our errors and
correcting them. This is a repetition of the advice given
earlier to the messenger spirits of the churches. It is
repeated here in case we thought the messages did not

apply to us. And appropriately, it is given once again just prior to the final trumpet heralding the Christ's return.

We might remember now the parable of Jesus concerning the ten virgins: "Then Jesus likened the kingdom of heaven to ten virgins who took their lamps and went to meet the bridegroom. Five of them were foolish (and took no forethought of their needs); and five were wise (for they prepared themselves). Although the foolish brought their lamps, they brought no extra oil with them. But the wise ones brought a flask of oil along in addition to the oil their lamps contained. But the bridegroom lingered and was slow in coming, so all of them began to nod their heads and fell asleep. Then when midnight came, there was a shout. 'Look, the bridegroom comes! Go out at once and meet him!'

"Then all the virgins rose and trimmed the wicks of their lamps. Then the foolish said to the wise: 'Give us some of your oil, for look, our lamps are going out.' But the wise ones said to them: 'If we do that we won't have enough for ourselves. Hurry to the merchants, and buy some more oil from them.' But while they were gone off to buy more oil, the bridegroom came, and those who were prepared went in with him to the marriage feast; and then the door was closed.

"Later the other virgins also came, and said, 'Sir, Sir, open (the door) for us!' But he replied, 'I'm sorry but I do not know you.' Watch therefore, for you never know the day or hour that the son of Man will come."

(Matthew 25: 1-13)

Now ten is the number of Gentile completion, and virgins are representative of God's united congregations which are located in all cities of the pagan world. They carry the lamps which are to light the cities where they live. Trimming their lamps just before the bridegroom comes is the equivalent of measuring the temple in the city where they live so that their light may shine before the world. They were to discard false teachings and wrong practices which hindered them in making God's truth known. For outer darkness was the ignorance they were called on to expel. If their lamps did not expel that darkness they would be forced to be a part of it.

So if their lamps had no oil in them at all (no real knowledge of God to enlighten them) they would have to acquire it. "Buy it and sell it not." That is, don't let go of what you have just to satisfy another person's ignorance. Letting your lamp go out leaves you in the darkness you neglected to expel. Outside in the darkness (or ignorance) of the world, the door to the jubilant feast with Christ would be closed (in just the same way many doors have closed to us throughout our lives, when moments of true opportunity appeared for which we were inadequately prepared). Any door to opportunity is closed when moments for them pass which we cannot call back again. "My people perish for lack of knowledge," Jehovah said. There is logic to the scriptures if we look for it and patiently sit down to read them in a contemplative way. Yet they often appear foolish to those whose minds are giddy, frivolous or impatient.

We face now the mystery of the two witnesses, who are described as two olive trees and two lampstands. These are said to stand before the ruler of the whole earth. The imagery is an allusion to the fourth chapter of *Zechariah*, where it says: "There are two olive trees beside (the lampstand) one on the right side of the bowl and the other on the left, feeding it continuously with oil."   (Zechariah 4: 3)

"So I asked the angel who had been speaking with me, 'Sir, can you tell me what these (olive trees and lampstands) are?' Then the angel that I spoke to answered me and said, 'Do you mean to say, that you don't know what they are?' I answered, 'No, sir. I have no idea.' So he explained: 'These attachments to the bowl of the lampstands, which make it yield a continual supply of oil from both the olive trees is the word of Jehovah to Zerubabel saying, "Not by power, nor by might (not by size of armies or by weaponry of war) but by my spirit (of which the oil is a symbol)," says Jehovah of armies.'" (Zechariah 4: 5-6)

"So I asked the angel, 'What are these two olive trees on the right and on the left of the lampstand?' And then continuing I added, 'And also what are these two olive twigs that are beside the gold spout that empty out the golden oil?' Then he enquired, 'Don't you know what these are?' 'No, sir,' I replied. 'These are the two anointed ones who stand before the ruler of the whole earth (as his appointed representatives.)'" (Zechariah 4: 11-14)

In Zechariah's day these two anointed ones were Joshua the High Priest and Zerubabel the governor of Judah. Since we are dealing now with the larger spiritual temple rather than the carnal one, these two representatives are the Jewish people (representing Moses — the governor of Judah) and the Christian church (representing Jesus Christ, the High Priest who offered his own blood before the throne of heaven).

The two witnesses are representative of those perfected Jews and Christians who have taken time to measure themselves by God's standards and appear before their congregations and the world as spokesmen for God. Yes. The Jews. "For God did not forsake the people he first called." (Romans 11: 2)

It was the Jews themselves of whom Jesus spoke when he told the story of the Prodigal Father, prodigal in the sense that he had lavished all his love on both his sons. The faithful son who never left his father's home, was the Jewish people, and the wastrel son who squandered all that he had and was contaminated by his worldly practices, and therefore, indistinguishable from any other person living in the Gentile world, referred to those in the house of Israel who followed the idolatry of Jeroboam. Christians represent that portion of Israel called back into the house of God. To do this, a new covenant with God had to be made. For Israel had to be reinstated with God, for having strayed.

The Jews still spoke with the authority of Moses, as Jesus said: "The teachers of the law and of the Pharisees sit in Moses' seat. So you must obey them and do everything they tell you." (Matthew 23: 2) The Jews then spoke with the authority of Moses. And they still do. On the other hand, Christians spoke according to the promises of all the prophets from Elijah to Jeremiah to Malachi: "Consequently, you are no longer foreigners and aliens, but fellow citizens with God's people (the Jews) and members of God's household, built upon the foundation of the apostles and prophets, with Christ Jesus himself the chief cornerstone. In him the whole building is joined together and rises to become a holy Temple in Jehovah."   (Ephesians 2: 19-21)

The spirit of Moses then, was to be found in the Jews, and the spirit of the prophets was supposedly present in the Christian congregations. Like the two olive trees beside the lamps in God's temple, these two bodies were (by the spirit of God's word) called on to give light to the whole world.

This is what Jesus told a gathering of Jews who sat with him upon a mountain side, outside Jerusalem: "You are the light of the world. A city set upon a hill cannot be hid. Neither do men light a lamp then hide it under a bushel. Rather they set it upon a lampstand, where it can give light to all that are in the house. Therefore, let your light so shine before all men, that they may see your good works and emulate your father which is in heaven."   (Matthew 5: 14-16)

Some I know will be inclined to say, "But these were his disciples to whom these words were said." But Jesus's disciples were simply those Jews who, after having heard him speak to the crowd at large, returned to question him and learn the deeper meanings of his words. They were those "whom the spirit drew to him." These numbered in the hundreds and thousands if you count all those in the various communities who studied what he said. He was the sower who planted God's word in them, and "the common man heard him gladly." I do not stretch the point for Jesus clearly said, "Salvation is of the Jews." I merely speak to help some readers put aside a very hateful prejudice that still resides in some, and hinders Jesus's own plan from being used in just the way that he intended it, which was to gather and unite, not scatter Israel.

"I must ask you then, if you believe that God cast off his people?" Paul once asked an early branch of Christians living at that time in Rome. "In no way did he do this," he went on. "I am myself an Israelite who descended from Abraham and I am of the tribe of Benjamin. God in no way rejected those whom he first chose....When they stumbled did they fall beyond recovery? Not at all....Because I am talking to you Gentiles, I have made a great deal of my apostleship to you, hoping that my ministry to you might in some way stir *my own people* up with envy and ensure their own salvation too.

"If some of their own branches (Israel's lost tribes) have been broken off so that you, like a shoot from a wild olive tree, could be grafted in *among them* (the Jews) and *share* the nourishment of sap that comes out of their root, you have no right to boast or to exalt yourself above the natural branches. But keep this in mind, that you do not support the root! Rather *theirs is the root* supporting you.

"I realise that some of you will raise objections, saying, 'These branches (lost Israel) all were broken off (by God) so that we could be put in.' That of course is true. But they were broken off because of unbelief, and you by faith were grafted in. So don't be arrogant, but take care. For if God did not spare the natural branches (of the plant) why should you believe he will spare you. Try to understand the nature of God's generosity and sternness. He is stern toward those who fall, but will be generous to you as long as you remain and continue in the grace that he has shown toward you. Otherwise you as well shall be cut off by him." (Romans 11: 1-22)

A brief review again of history might help us some. Cain was the founder of cities in the world. Nimrod, following the flood, established nations and empires in the very early times. These men were cited as much to show the spirit from which these institutions grew as from any sense of historicity. Cain was a murderer and Nimrod was a hunter and a warrior. The sons of God were much slower in their development of society, for they were more attached to their affections for the world of nature which God made. Still they congregated regularly to share their knowledge of God. Abraham, isolated by idolators in a pagan civilization, dreamed of founding a holy nation to which all people of the world could turn to find communion with the creator of the world and learn his ways.

Moses attempted to make that dream a reality, by codifying all the lore and learning and the principles of wise and righteous dealing into a national law. Following a long captivity in Babylon, a certain segment of Israel was lost. This made a great impression upon Jewish minds including the early historian Josephus. Yet a certain group of Jews called Pharisees tried to give stability to a very unstable land by instituting a strict code of righteous conduct to prevent a further slipping of the Jewish people once again into the morass of immorality which would weaken them and lead them back into captivity again.

During the last days of that kingdom Moses built, an earnest Jew called Joshua (or Jesus) set out to gather those lost souls of the House of Israel by preaching God's word to them. For what divided Israel from Judah to begin with had been the creeping sickness of idolatry. Jesus therefore tried to gather scattered Israel, which is to say, those Jews who still remained outside the influence of the Pharisees. His hope had been to gather all of that Israel which remained, and make one house of them. Lost Israel to his mind were all those Jews who had flagged in righteous conduct and needed a shepherd who could bring them back. Jesus saw all these as being well within his reach.

He tried to plant God's word as seed in them so that solely by its power it would convert their lives. The parable of the prodigal son was told by him to illustrate this point, as was the story of the lost sheep. "All those in heaven" who rejoiced because of its recovery were those "sons of God" or rather "sons of Israel" who truly understood the way of God.

The dream of Jesus was to fulfill the prophecy of Ezekiel, who took two sticks in his hand and joined them. The story went like this: "Son of man," Jehovah told Ezekiel, "take a stick of wood and write on it, 'Belonging to Judah and the Israelites associated with him.' Then take another stick of wood, and write on it, 'Ephraim's stick, belonging to Joseph and all the house of Israel associated with him.' Join them together into one stick so that they will become one in your hand.

"When your countrymen ask you, 'Won't you tell us what you mean by this?' say to them, 'This is what the Sovereign Lord says: "I am going to take the stick of Joseph — which is in Ephraim's hand — and the Israelite tribes associated with him, and join it to Judah's stick, making them a single stick of wood, and they will become one in my hand."' (Making them the rod of God's authority.)

"Hold before their eyes the sticks you have written on and say to them, 'This is what the Sovereign Lord says: "I will take the Israelites out of the nations where they have gone. I will gather them from all around and bring them back into their own land. I will make them one nation in one land, on the mountains of Israel. There will be one king over all of them and they will never again be two nations or be divided into two kingdoms. They will no longer defile themselves with their idols and vile images or with any of their offences, for I will save them from all their sinful backsliding, and I will cleanse them. They will be my people and I will be their God.

"""My servant David will be king over them, and they will all have one shepherd. They will follow my laws and be careful to keep my decrees. They will live in the land I gave to my servant Jacob, the land where your fathers lived. They and their children and their children's children will live there forever, and David my servant will be their prince forever. I will make a covenant of peace with them; it will be an everlasting covenant. I will establish them and increase their numbers, and I will put my sanctuary among them forever. My dwelling place will be with them; I will be their God, and they will be my people. Then the nations will know that I Jehovah make Israel holy, when my sanctuary is among them forever."'"   (Ezekiel 37: 18-28)

Israel needed to be healed, and Jesus the great physician set out to heal them, and bring together both parts to make them one. Jesus was the planter of the seed of the living word of God. He did not build a church in any modern sense. He threw God's seed upon the scattered Jewish populace, even on the people of Samaria, because they too were Jews, although they did not worship in Jerusalem. The only church that Jesus ever spoke about was the church that God at last would choose out of all those who heard God's word and afterwards were influenced enough to do what was said in it.

Although Paul established "churches" in the various communities, building churches was not, by any means, his final goal. Churches merely were the means of giving mutual help to one another in establishing God's kingdom upon earth. By Paul's own admission, he himself was nothing more than a planter of God's word amongst those Gentiles who were able to receive it with intelligence. The so-called church that he established in each community was but a gathering of souls who shared a common dream and who shared their special gifts and the wisdom that the word of God had given them.

This congregation (or church) supplied the fellowship with a place to share their understanding and grow in the knowledge of God. The internal government of the church was no more than a mere convenience to give stability to them. Elders of the church were drawn from those experienced and mature enough to act as guides to those still young and immature in faith, while the overseer (or bishop) who wasn't any mighty potentate, acted as a focal point for organizing them and keeping order in their midst.

In the church of each community (for there was but one church in each of them) Christians tried to walk as citizens of that new world which God was building upon earth, whose values and customs differed from the ones they'd known. Because a different spirit guided Christians, they were not swayed by all the changing moods (or spirits) governing the world that Adam made. Even so, certain troubles entered these "communities of God" infecting them. The Bible clearly shows us what they were, and tells us how to deal with them.

One involved the splitting into groups — one saying "I am of Paul" another, "I am of Peter," and yet another saying, "I am of Apollos." Paul answered this by pointing out their only loyalty was to one leader, Jesus Christ — not to any other man who pulled the brotherhood apart by claiming special gifts or powers or even claiming to have spoken with angels. To divide the brotherhood was sin. It also was a sin to exalt one brother above another. John in one letter addressed this problem by showing the extremes that certain men would go to in order to exalt themselves.

Then there were those "wandering stars" who tried to make the congregation more like a place for indulging all their fleshly appetites. Jude in his short letter speaks of them. One other matter Paul addressed was the wilfulness of those outside the city church to exercise authority over them. They were allowed to listen to what those who came from other places said and perhaps learn from them. But they were not to surrender their autonomy and accountability to God through Jesus Christ alone.

More importantly the church in each community was asked to unify themselves through remembering "their first love" — the character of Jesus Christ and his ministry. "Hold fast to unity," Jesus earlier had said, "and be one, even as I and my Father are one." No man's will was ever to be exalted over that of God. "Not my will, but yours be done," was the prayer that Jesus gave. That is why the first step in his plan was to unify all segments of the church. Only then could the heaven of God be entered and observed. For only then could anyone appreciate the purpose of the plan which was "taken from the hand of God". In Chapter Eight, after the seventh seal is broken, the spirit that is Jesus Christ unifies all those in the world who are his people through the nature of the work that he assigns to them.

Following the messages these churches gave the world, John upon earth was confronted by a holy spirit from God (the angel of what mankind must be) having one foot on the sea and one foot on the land and wearing as a garment the rainbow arc of God's covenant with man. This angel vision then (of what mankind must be) had come, as a messenger from Christ under the authority of God, to bring greater unity to all the people serving God. To do this he commissioned John, by giving him a book to eat. What secrets were within that book we know from what John tells us afterwards: It was the unity that God desired from those who would capture and resanctify the Jerusalem of God.

There has been a lot of superstitious jargon surrounding the word "miracle". So let us clarify its meaning now. A miracle is any good work inspired by the spirit of God and performed in the name of God, or any mighty work done by which man or God's creation is benefited. Television is a miracle. So is the automobile and electricity, and so is a cold glass of water given to a thirsty man. Jesus told his followers that they would perform greater miracles than his own. And they have — if we have eyes for seeing them. They have built hospitals and schools. In fact Robert Raikes (a Christian) was primarily responsible for the public educational system that grew out of his simple act of taking street boys from the streets and teaching them the rudiments of reading and arithmetic.

Jesus's transfiguration, which gave three of his disciples a preview of his imminent return, revealed the witnesses of the end time as Moses and Elijah. (Matthew 17: 3) The miracles performed by both the witnesses in John's *Book of Revelation* identify the witnesses as those that Jesus earlier revealed. Moses established the first covenant with Israel, and Elijah was the initial prophet of the new covenant. Elijah also was a prophet to Israel and later to both Israel and Judah. So these two witnesses prepare the way for what is yet to come.

Two witnesses were called because, as God foresaw, one witness wouldn't be enough: "On the evidence presented by two witnesses, he who is worthy of death shall be put to death, he shall not be put to death on the evidence of one witness." (Deuteronomy 17: 6) And since the Christian congregation, in the eyes of their founder,

are one (Be ye one as I and my father are one) their
testimony forms only the basis of one witness, and John
clearly says that there are two: the two brothers — the
elder brother (the Jews) and the errant brother, the
straying son of Israel, (the redeemed Christian saved by
the good shepherd who went in search of him). You will
note too, that among all those who have the mark of
God upon their forehead, Judah's name is at the top of
the list.

Here then are Moses and Elijah, ready to give God's
message to the world. Do they have the power to close
up heaven or to open it? Of course they have. Jesus said
this of those Jews who were shutting out the masses of
the populace: "You shut up the kingdom in men's faces."
he told them. (Matthew 23: 13). Whatever animosity
there may have been in Jesus's words (if there was really
any animosity at all in them) was prompted by the
indignation which he may have felt from seeing so many
Jews amongst the poor excluded from the kingdom's
blessings. The elite, it seemed, had made themselves a
kind of social club. Jesus therefore gave his disciples the
keys to open God's kingdom to "the lost sheep of Israel".
"Behold," he told his disciples, "I give you the keys to the
kingdom of God. Therefore those things that you forbid
on earth shall be those things which God forbids, and
what you shall permit on earth shall be those things
which God permits." (Matthew 16: 19). "Thy will be done
on earth as it is in heaven," was to be the guiding
principle.

John says that the two witnesses he speaks of are
dressed in sackcloth, which signifies that their prophecy
concerns the downfall of nations. How then is it good
news? "Just as I watched over them to uproot and tear
down, and to overthrow, destroy and bring disaster, so I

will watch over them to build and to plant," Jehovah
says.   (Jeremiah 31: 28)

We arc told next that fire would come out of their
mouths and destroy their enemies. The picture painted
here is highly visual, but it means simply that no one
could stand against the power of their words. Also, the
words of God, which they were speaking, would no
doubt, too, reveal that the path which the nations had
chosen was the path of death, and so God's words would
bring judgment down on them. You will remember, I
said earlier this metaphor of fire was used by Jesus, in
reference to his own ministry on earth. Also, in
speaking to his prophet Jeremiah, Jehovah said: "My
words will be made fire in your mouth and this people
wood, and it shall devour them."   (Jeremiah 5: 14)

The symbolic time span of three and a half years
(affirming the work done here is not complete) also
serves to help the reader properly associate this passage
with the drought brought upon Israel by the ancient
prophet Elijah, since that was the length of time that he
had sealed up heaven.

It is written of these witnesses that they were men
who had the power to shut up heaven, turn water into
blood, and bring all manner of slaughter on the earth.

But the famine to be brought upon the world in the
final days was not to be one of literal interpretation
either — as the prophet Amos so clearly says: "Behold the
days come, says your God Jehovah, that I will send a
famine in the land, not a famine of bread, nor a thirst for
water, but a famine for hearing the words of Jehovah."
                                        (Amos 8: 11)

The message of the witnesses is defined by the
psalmist: "How beautiful on the mountains are the feet

of those who bring good news, who proclaim peace, who bring glad tidings, who proclaim salvation (deliverance from oppression), who say to Zion (the citizens of God's city) 'Your God reigns.'"   (Psalm 52: 7)

This is not the kind of news oppressors want to hear. Moses when he spoke these words was stubbornly opposed by Pharaoh, who responded: "Who is this Jehovah that I should obey him and let Israel go free?" (Exodus 5: 2) And what of the plagues (or catastrophes)? Peter says it for us: "Every soul who does not listen to and understand by hearing and obey that Prophet, shall be utterly exterminated from among the people." (Acts 3: 23) That is to say, he shall be cast out from the community and perish by his own immoral deeds and the diseases that they bring upon him. So in this sense the waters of God's word become blood in that they slay the hearer who adamantly sets himself against them.

In passing though we should take notice of the similarity between these witnesses and the two witnesses that entered Sodom prior to its destruction, to plead with the people of that city. Unfortunately, only Lot and his immediate family survived the great destruction that ensued. All other citizens in Sodom were destroyed because they would not listen to the messengers of God. For it is written in the book of *Amos*: "Surely the Sovereign Lord does nothing without revealing his plan to his servants the prophets." (Amos 3: 7) And the prophets, like trumpets, warn the people of the destruction they will bring upon themselves if they do not heed the warning given them: "If anyone hears the trumpet but does not take warning and the sword (of warfare) comes and takes his life, his blood will be upon his own head." (Ezekiel 33: 3) This was true in Sodom and, according to all Bible literature, it would remain that way until the very end.

Prior to its fall, two great prophets also preached in Jerusalem as well—John the Baptist and Jesus of Nazareth. Now, in the last days of the great enslaving system of the world, according to the apostle John the Revealer, two more prophets were to rise who would speak words which would bring destruction down on all who opposed them. Then when they had finished presenting the message of God in the clearest possible terms, the beast would rise from the bottomless pit and attack the witnesses, overpowering them by his might, perhaps exposing them in scandal magazines and then killing them (possibly through character assassination) and, of course, also literally (after sufficiently enflaming the populace with patriotic jingoism). The witnesses (the synagogues and churches) would continue to exist (in name) unburied, but the real life would have gone out of them.

"The beast" (or the "rapine warrior nation") which rises from "the bottomless pit" deserves our careful scrutiny. You see, *the bottomless pit* is more than just a symbol of the grave. It also represents the womb (or any place on earth or in the universe where new life is conceived). In Chapter One of *Genesis*, "the bottomless pit" is referred to as "the deep" (or "the abyss"). For everything which God made came from it. In the book of *Exodus*, "the wilderness" is "the deep" into which the children of Israel are placed to be reborn as a nation conceived by the spirit of the creator (so that God calls Israel his "firstborn son").

The book of *Revelation* (which we are studying now) tells us (in Chapter Nine) that the smoke of oppression rises from *the bottomless pit*. In this case, it is the human heart which is the source of it. Yet out of that smoke of oppression, a great army of oppressed men and women (depicted as locusts) emerge to sting and torment their oppressors. Now (like Israel) that army too has been reborn as a nation, but not as a nation serving God — rather as a nation which destroys God's witnesses. Just and righteous though their cause had been, this army lacked the insight to establish an enlightened nation upon earth.

History supplies us with many examples of the failed opportunities for establishing an ideal nation favourable to man and nature. Republican France threw off the oppression of its kings and the national religion supporting them, only to persecute and execute (not just their oppressors but) many who had championed their own cause. That same nation also passed a ludicrous law proclaiming that "there is no God." The revolution which gave birth to the Soviet Union likewise was prompted and inspired by righteous motives, but the revolutionaries set up mock trials against their own party members and made it a crime to worship God in any way at all. As is the case in many lands which rise out of the smoking furnace of oppressive tyranny, their leaders often lack the spiritual insight to bring about a more enlightened world.

So it is that a beast shall emerge from the bottomless pit and slay those two witnesses: the church and synagogue, whose teachings sting all guilty consciences. For there are assassins in the world — some have guns and some have bombs, and some have scandal magazines. Character assassination is just as fatal as a bullet is. But could the poisoned waters of the world (those fantasies and dazzling illusions the world itself promotes) not prove to be the most effective means of all for poisoning the institutions whose teachings are an irritation to their souls?

We saw the beast of course in Nazi Germany. For it exists in many forms. There we saw it murder many who belonged to God. Its treatment of the Jews was the most obvious sign of this. There is a beast in this world which shows itself spiritually in many unconsidered attitudes which citizens in many lands assume. For instance during the McCarthy era, good men and women in the United States of America and elsewhere were defamed in a poisonous atmosphere of words and recriminations. This beast is spiritual then and exists amongst many peoples of the world.

How then would the witnesses die? In the one isolated example I have given, of Nazi Germany, they died in death camps by the millions. Throughout the world they have often been imprisoned with no chance of parole. They could die by any means you can possibly imagine including character assassination. Yet there is another way that they could die as well. They could exist as bodies — as they do here in Chapter Eleven of *Revelation* — in name but not in spirit. There could be no life left in them. Like the church of Sardis mentioned in Chapter Three of *Revelation*, the churches and the synagogues of the world could become spiritually dead, by preaching doctrines contrary to the scriptures. So it is that those amongst the citizens who celebrated their success and triumph over these congregations, congratulated one another for their efficiency.

Sodom and Egypt are the names given to the place where the witnesses died, indicating two things: that there was an atmosphere or attitude that governed human minds and blinded them, and that the creation of God, including mankind, was in servitude. As the scriptures said of Sodom: "Now this is the sin of Sodom: she and her daughters (all other cities in the world which emulate her practices) were arrogant, overfed, and unconcerned; they did not help the poor and needy. For they were haughty and did despicable things before me."
(Ezekiel 16: 49-50)

Egypt of course is the land of sore captivity. Any nation throughout the world who subjugates people and binds them to unrewarded lives of oppression and servitude — spiritually is Egypt. In such a place, Jesus was crucified. Regardless of the geographical location — even if it is Jerusalem itself — the spiritual condition existing among citizens determines what it is. The poet John Milton, in *Paradise Lost*, and the playwright George Bernard Shaw, in *Don Juan in Hell*, both gave voice to such a view. But the Bible's words preceded them, as in the case when Isaiah called the citizens of Jerusalem, citizens of Sodom and citizens of Gomorrah. John here underlines these words with emphasis.

Yet, in what sense then did the two witnesses ascend to heaven, for after all, the reference here is not of two individual men but of communities of witnesses. Ezekiel again helps us out to some extent: "Then Jehovah said to me: Prophesy to the breath and spirit, mortal man, and say to the breath and spirit, 'This is what your God Jehovah says: "Come from the four winds, O breath and spirit and breathe upon these slain, that they may live."' So I prophesied as he commanded me, and the breath and spirit came into (the bones) and they lived and stood up upon their feet, an exceedingly great army. Then he said to me: 'Mortal man (literally Son of man) these are the bones of the whole house of Israel. They say, "Our bones are dried up and our hope is gone; we are cut off."'"   (Ezekiel 37: 9-11)

Having come alive again and played their role as witnesses, the forms of church and synagogue are taken from the earth, and in their place there stands (as one body) all the tribes of Israel — the sons and daughters of the patriarchs — armed with the word of God and equipped for every good work.

What John envisioned then, was a time when the churches and the synagogues would have fulfilled their role on earth, as perfect witnesses of God and the Kingdom that he was about to build. At first the nations of the world would seem to triumph over them. For the Churches and the Synagogues would remain on earth as lifeless bodies that really did not do the mighty works of God, or speak his word. Yet in time the spirit would return to them and they would rise again. Even so the part that they had been called upon by God to play would have been accomplished. So the form of church and synagogue would "go to heaven" or return to God, and in their place the members of the tribes of Israel would stand upon the earth.

Let us now go on to see what God will do. For the virgins all have trimmed their wicks and wait to see the bridegroom come:

* *

The Last Trumpet

When the time came, and the seventh angel messenger of God blew his trumpet, there were loud voices in heaven which cried, "The kingdoms of this world have become the kingdom of Jehovah and of his anointed delegate, and he shall rule over it for ever and ever!" ("For the kingdom is Jehovah's, and he has sovereignty over all nations." — Psalm 22: 28) Then the members of the (council of) twenty four elders seated before God on their seats (of authority) bowed their faces to the ground to acknowledge God as supreme (indicating that all God's people in the community of saints, speaking through their elders, had accepted God's sole rule in their lives. There can be no divided allegiance. When the united congregation of God in all cities does this, God will start to reign. The strength of his power will be felt throughout the earth.)

Then the councillors affirmed, "We praise and thank you, Jehovah, the Supreme High God, for asserting that authority and power which rightfully are yours, and beginning to reign. (For that malevolent spirit in man, called Satan, has been ruling until now.)* And the nations of the world (until this time) have displayed their anger and contempt for one another and for all creation. But now the day of your wrath has come! And it is time for you to judge the dead, and to reward your servants (the prophets and the saints who have revered your name) whether they are humble men or great — and to destroy all those who deliberately destroy the earth."

Then was the sanctuary (Greek: naos) of heaven opened, and there the Ark of the Covenant was revealed inside, and there followed   lightning (the understanding of God's word), voices (making God's word known), thunder (the power of God revealed in mighty works), earthquakes (the overthrow of governments and tyranny) and hail (God's judgment on the world).

*

The Ark of the Covenant was always the symbol of God's presence with his people. Yet when Judah went into captivity in Babylon, the Ark of God disappeared and those of the House of David never again ruled. But now Jehovah was to rule again, through a royal king of David's lineage. The significance of the Ark being

---

* The scriptures (speaking on this matter) tell us: "Then the devil said to Jesus, 'I will give all the power and authority of the nations of the world to you, and their glory, for I have power to give them all to anyone I choose.'" -- Luke 4: 6)

shown then, is to indicate that God's power now favoured those who had prepared themselves for him. "God is with us," is the message of the revelation here.

As God's heaven was opened to each church after it was cleansed from worldly practices, so the full strength of God's divine power returns to the united Israel of God. But this is an Israel that has no borders, as it is spread through all communities throughout the world.

CHAPTER TWELVE

The Virgin Bride of God

A glorious figure suddenly appeared in heaven: a dazzling woman clothed in the brilliance of the sun, having the moon under her feet and a tiara with twelve stars on her head. Pregnant and crying out in pain, she was ready to give birth. (Any careful reader of the scriptures should be able to tell you that this woman is the virgin bride of God — the community of righteous Israel. And the child she carries in her womb is the new world system — a Kingdom through which the offspring of Abraham were to bless the world.)

Afterwards another significant image was seen in heaven: an enormous venomous red dragon, having seven heads, ten horns, and wearing a crown on each one of its seven heads. (This is the ancient dragon of waste and ruin. It is frequently associated with death and darkness, ruinous floods, devastating drought, or war and slaughter and other world calamities. Here John uses it to reveal the spirit infecting world nations. Ancient Canaanites called this deadly beast Leviathan.) With its mighty tail (its powerful ruling figures of celebrity) this fearsome beast swept a whole third of the stars (those who are the representatives of God) right out of the sky and hurled them to the earth. Then the dragon stood before the woman who was about to give birth, hoping to devour her child the moment it was born.

When her time did come the woman gave birth to an infant boy, one who with an iron rod (which is to say by the strength and authority of Jehovah's word) was destined to subdue and rule all nations of the world. Yet for the moment he was caught away and carried to the throne of God, but his mother fled into the wilderness, where she found refuge in a place that had been prepared for her. There she remained for 1,260 days (which is three and a half years – being nourished by God's wisdom from the manna of his word).

Then war broke out in heaven. Michael and his followers fought against the dragon, so that the dragon and his followers fought back. But unable to prevail against (the superior weaponry used by) Michael's hosts, the dragon and his minions were completely driven out of heaven. That serpent called the devil or Satan, which from very ancient times has led the whole world astray, was thrown with all his angels out of heaven (the new world government).

Then I heard a loud voice cry from heaven: "Now God's power, salvation, His Kingdom and Christ's authority are firmly set in place, for the accuser of our brothers (and sisters) – who night and day never ceases to slander them before God – has been cast out. For they overcame him by (imbibing Christ's spirit) the blood of the lamb, and by the strength of their witness (the bread of deeds and words). Nor did they even cling to life so much as to be afraid of death. Be glad therefore you heavens and everyone who lives in them (as stars in God's new firmament). But let all those who live (by the standards of the corrupt system of things) on earth, and those in the sea (of fierce competition) be grieved, because the devil has come down to you filled with fury, for he knows his time is limited. (God's people – having put the devil from their midst – have infuriated the corrupting spirit governing the world because they are no longer easily deceived or manipulated by its sorcery.)

The dragon (seeing that his influence upon the children of heaven was gone) was cast down to the earth. Therefore he began ruthlessly persecuting (Israel) the woman who had given birth to the child. Two wings of a large eagle (the swift, far-seeing, holy spirit of God) were then given to the woman so that she might fly into the wilderness, out of the serpent's reach, where she would be cared for for a time, times and half a time (or three and a half years). (God's holy spirit would protect this body of believers and prepare them in a wilderness experience for the work to be accomplished in a complementary task for which they were to be prepared).

Then the serpent spewed out water—like a great flood—from its mouth to overtake the woman and carry her away. (For we must never underestimate the overwhelming power of a trivializing culture to wipe out and destroy all sense that many people have of their identity. The serpent has its own learning and philosophy prevalent in its entertainment, its educational system, its music, and its theatre—that is to say in its religious practices—which it spews out upon the kingdoms of the world, including God's community. Such is the weaponry of spiritual war). But the earth (the citizenry of Satan's own world system) helped the woman to escape the flood by opening its mouth and swallowing the water that the dragon had spewed out of its mouth. Furious, the dragon went away determined to wage war on the remainder of the woman's descendants—which is to say on all those who obey the commandments of God and preach the message Jesus taught.

*

Since we are dealing in this vision with a progressively developing theme in a logically planned strategy of action rather than with some crabbed and spotty piece of mystic mumbling, we must concede that the woman in this vision is the community of Israel—the virgin bride of God. She is a presence to be reckoned with in that heaven God is building for the world. The preceding chapters of this prophetic work have prepared our eyes for recognizing her.

John had been counselled and commissioned by the unifying spirit of perfected man. This was done (in Chapter 10) as a means of helping mankind recognize and acknowledge his responsibility as the overseer of God's creation — a creation mankind (at the beginning) was called upon to govern with integrity. The symbolism in that instance made this clear for the angel which John saw stood upon the sea and land designating his supreme authority over them.

King David, in one of his psalms, clearly defines the role of mankind in these words: "Oh Jehovah, our great governor, how magnificently displayed is the glory of your character throughout all the earth. The magnificence of your majesty overflows the heavens so that even infants and little children give you perfect praise. Nor do your enemies have any power to still the joyous praise that all creation gives to you. So I am moved to ask myself whenever I gaze upon the heavens, the work of your hands (at the moon and stars which you have created) what is man that you should be concerned with him? or the common man that you should even care for him?

"For you have made him just a little lower than the Elohim and have crowned him with all the glory and the honour of your name, giving him complete responsibility over all the works of your hands, and putting all things under his authority: all flocks and herds, wild animals, birds and fish and everything that inhabits the sea. Oh Jehovah, our great governor, how magnificently displayed is the glory of your character throughout all the earth."

(Psalm 8)

When earlier we heard the seven voices of creation speaking through the seven thunders "from heaven" we observed the progressive development in the nature of God's plan. For afterwards we saw the old temple reorganized, measured and refashioned to overcome disunity and thereby represent the perfect will of God. We were shown two witnesses (the Jewish synagogues and Christian churches) speaking to mankind before being carried off "to heaven". Now the next step obviously should be to show us a united Israel revitalized. And that is exactly what we have now been shown.

The whole description of the woman has been drawn from two essential scriptural references: Joseph's telling the members of his family of his dream, and Isaiah's reference to pregnant Israel's suffering. Joseph said: "I saw the sun and moon and eleven stars all bow down to me." Then his father in rebuking him replied: "Indeed! shall I and your mother and your brothers all actually bow down to you?" Joseph as the morning star of Israel was the twelfth star in Israel's crown and through the epic of his life, he heralded the work which Israel's messiah would bring about when he appeared to them.

Yet Isaiah in looking upon Israel as a pregnant mother said: "Have you ever known of a woman to give birth before she goes into labour? or heard of a male child being born before the birth pangs come? Does anyone who really knows about such things expect a land to be born in just a single day? or a nation to emerge (from God's people) in a moment? Though Israel is now beset with labour pains, she will very shortly give birth to children (who will honour God and the creation he has made.) "Do you imagine for one moment that I would ever bring upon this people pains of birth and then not cause them to bring forth?" Jehovah asks. "Can you actually believe that I would close the womb

after having brought the people to the point of·giving
birth?"   (Isaiah 66: 7-9)

So by these words, God reveals himself to be the
father of the child this woman is to bear. For he says
elsewhere: "Return to me O faithless Israel, for I am
your husband and I will choose you individually, one
from a city and two from a tribal family and bring you
back to Zion."   (Jeremiah 3: 14)

Yet many people may be confused when they are
told that the woman has appeared "in heaven", and that
the devil (or the great red dragon) persecuting her was
also present there. So we should realise that the heaven
we are speaking of in this instance is not "the heaven of
heavens", but rather the Council of the nations governing
the world, along with all the social and spiritual
influences which assisted it. This heaven, or government,
of ancient times (assisted by the social practices which
influenced imaginations) was one composed of deities
and influential men of state and public men of eminence
whose high positions of power and splendour dazzled
human eyes.

Such a heaven strengthened governments by giving
them control and influence over public attitudes. Only
through the adoration which the crowd bestowed upon
their gods and public figures could the imagination of
the public mind be captured and controlled. So grand
processions, public ceremonies, theatrical performances,
orations and victory parades and periodic holidays
helped to strengthen and command the public's loyalty.
All these together with the government itself made up
the heaven of the ancient pagan world. Because that
heaven was opposed to what John taught and preached,
the plan which he proposes in this strategy (that Jesus

Christ had given him) is that the heaven governing the world must first be changed to bring about sure victory.

Even today no government can rule effectively if it does not capture the imagination of the populace. Modern communists may go on saying if they wish that "religion is the opiate of the people," but a careful examination and evaluation of the former Soviet society reveals that even they themselves were not above creating their own myths and religion in an effort to sustain their nation's government. They had a heaven of their own. But the western nations of the world spewed out the water of a different philosophy and culture on them — and their heaven suddenly was changed. So was their government, and eventually their whole way of doing things was overcome and their former gods cast out.

No nation upon earth can possibly survive (even in this present world) without such influencing heavens guiding and instructing them, that is to say governing the mind. People in all nations are governed more by their imaginations than by any force or strength of law — civil, moral or any other kind. No world system can possibly survive for very long without that influential canopy of gods to stimulate imaginations and to set the tone of social life, and encourage aspirations and standards for the populace to reach. Yet so subtle, sophisticated and well organized has it become in modern nations of the world, few people are actually aware of any man-made heaven ruling over them.

We live today in a world that speaks frequently of stars. Television personalities, movie actors, popular musicians, athletes, and even emcees for game shows are all spoken of as stars. Yet we hardly seem to realise that the term is being used in exactly the same way the Bible uses it. The stars which God puts in his firmament (anyone excelling in the knowledge and the spirit of his word) are there as lights to guide the paths of those who look to them as shining examples to emulate (much like the "saints" of the Roman Catholic Church). So it is that this mundane world we live in also tries to glamourize its social life with its canopy of stars to set the ideal standards of fashion, dress, behaviour, speech, entertainment, music and moral conduct.

Ancient Babylon had its stars. So did Greece and Rome. The people of every age in history have had a heaven of some sort which they exalted high above themselves to be the powerful guiding force for ordinary citizens. And there have always been those individuals who fought ambitiously to be a part of it. Ancient peoples realised that law alone was not sufficient to supply the means for governing. There had to be a heaven over them with lights to guide the populace. The King of Babylon himself was known as Lucifer (the morning star). Yet these stars were no part of that heaven which God ruled. God's creation could be seen as reflecting his character, and that character was written on those humble individuals who had the spirit of their God with them. They were therefore part of God's true heaven. Ezekiel reveals that God said of them: "I shall put my sanctuary forever among them; I will be their God and they will be my people."   (Ezekiel 37: 27-28)

Nothing better illustrates the heavenly conception of that sanctuary in the midst of Israel than does the arrangement of the Israelite encampment during their wilderness experience. The whole camp's construction was designed to represent heaven itself. Like the life-giving sun in heaven's firmament, the sanctuary was placed directly in the centre of Israel's twelve tribes so that they all received its rays of wisdom directly. These same twelve tribes were also like the twelve heavenly constellations which moved in circles around the great polar star. In earlier times, the Sumerians had referred to this polar star as "the Good Shepherd of Heaven."*

Parents today who feel that they are being liberal and open-minded where religion is concerned, and fail to teach their children any kind of religion in their homes (lest they destroy an inborn natural aptitude which they believe their children have for discovering their own faith) don't seem to realise that society is itself its own religion. It is completely drawn, and its spirit permeates their children's world. Whatever spirit dominates the time will be the one that rears their children and teaches them the values of its creed. So far from freeing their children's minds as they believe they have, they will have made them slaves of a dominating world. Consequently their children will become whatever spirit that the world has made available to them—even idealistic Nazis.

Their hymns will be whatever songs are drummed continually into their minds, and the holy spirit guiding them will be whatever spirit happens to direct the times. Illusions, conditioning, appeals to phobias, angsts and lusts will all be used to lead them to whatever gods the spirit of the dominating world determines and provides.

Envy, hysteria, greed, imagined glamour, the strong desire to get ahead at any cost, to be famous, to make a name for oneself, to be popular, to have fun, to make lots of money, all help to serve the patterns of the mindless frenzy promoted by a world totally absorbed in their games of Chance and Destiny. These and the great game of "Beggar your Neighbour" moves the world

---

*Footnote: "Constellation", *Encyclopaedia Britannica*. VI, 311

progressively toward destruction of itself. Glorifying God or his creation is the least of its priorities and can find no place at all in the spirit of the world's concerns. Its gods (which do not seem like gods at all to them) go on poisoning the earth, piling it high in garbage and pollution so that the earth can scarcely breathe or yield as fruitfully as it could. These gods are poisoning our water and our soil and destroying the sky as well.

A healthy creator-based religion which makes creation its priority encourages knowledge and understanding of all life. It is a spiritual tree yielding healthy fruit that will help humanity survive. It does not outrightly condemn the sensual, as some apparently believe it does, but it gives discernment to behave responsibly and not destroy the earth or make oneself the centrepiece of life. The commandment, though, is not to abstain from satisfying the physical needs; it is to seek first the spiritual and make them the priority. The physical will be taken care of, if we get ourselves upon the right track first. Without the spiritual we will perish, for the earth will cease to yield its fruit, the skies will not answer prayers for rain. Before us the earth will be like a garden of Eden, and as we leave, it will be a barren waste. It isn't I who says these things. The Bible does.

According to the Bible, it was the imaginations in the hearts of men that brought the world of Noah to its end. The Bible frequently refers to this phenomenon as being the root cause of international strife, and of bringing down the curse of God upon the world. For instance we read these words in *Genesis*: "Jehovah clearly saw how great the wickedness of man had grown to be on earth, because his heart and mind continually were focused upon wickedness." (Genesis 6: 5) The mind is trained by what it hears and sees, and that heaven which we raise above ourselves is what in part instructs us in these ways.

Have you ever noticed how thoroughly "entertained" we are? Silent moments of repose are very difficult to find. Stores, doctor's offices, shopping malls, airplanes, even school halls are filled with "canned music" all the time. Car radios, tape decks, ads on street cars and on subway trains tell us what products we should buy, what shows to go to see, what television programs we should watch, what kind of music all of us should listen to, what kind of attitudes are chic, what moral standards are in vogue. Scandal magazines galore are used to titilate the evil tendencies in us and can be found in prominent places everywhere, even in the grocery stores and in subway terminals. Radios and television screens are rarely off. It's very difficult to find repose and think our own thoughts casually, commune with nature or have a life that's varied from the crowd. We are literally pressured and drowned in the great flood that Satan spews out on the world. That is to say that we are ruled by the artificial heaven reigning over us.

Those gods which nations raised above themselves in ancient times encouraged so much immorality amongst the populace, the psalmist was inspired to write: "Hide me from...the noisy crowd of evildoers, who sharpen their tongues like swords and aim their words like deadly arrows....They encourage one another in their evil plots...and they plan new crimes just to help them go on boasting how they have devised the perfect crime."
(Psalm 64: 2-6)

Isaiah spoke about this matter in another way. He said: "Their thoughts are thoughts of iniquity. Desolation and destruction are always in their paths. They do not know the way of peace, and there is no justice in anything they do. They have chosen crooked roads...and they grope and stumble like blind men even at the height of noon." (Isaiah 59: 7-10)

That is why John now, in this vision, daringly reveals a sight which challenges the kind of violence the imaginations men and women governed by the heavens of this world are taught to entertain. John dazzles them by letting them behold a woman splendidly arrayed entering the sphere of world celebrity. By telling us her countenance is like the sun, John shows us that her character reveals the glory of Almighty God. Her tiara of twelve stars is the glory of Israel's twelve tribes and the moon beneath her feet tells us that she rules the night and banishes this world's darkness with her countenance. The woman then is the Israel of God (which is to say "Holy Wisdom" carnally revealed in God's people). That she is pregnant means that she will soon give birth to a new world system and a new world government. The battle then which John describes as taking place "in heaven" is a battle to capture the imagination of the people.

Yet John is fully aware that "the woman" who appears in heaven will be opposed by the powerful ruling spirit governing the present world. When he tells us of the great red dragon waiting to devour her child at birth, his words awaken many overtones of past events. One of these recalls that time Balak (the King of the Moabites) saw Israel from afar approaching his domain. Just as the great red dragon in John's vision used its mighty tail against the stars of heaven, so Balak (the head of the dragon) called on his false prophet Balaam (the dragon's tail) to bring down the people of Israel with a curse.
(Numbers 22; 23; and 24.)

The striking thing about Balaam is that this false prophet really was a man who had an understanding of Jehovah, and could speak according to Jehovah's word. So it might seem strange to many that such a man, for the sake of material and monetary gain, would sell himself to the service of God's enemies. I'm sure there is a warning there for us. To some extent Balaam's words

reflect that quandary, for he said: "Curse Israel? How
can I possibly do that when God has not cursed them?
How can I bring down evil upon those whom God has
blessed? I stand here on this lofty height observing
them, and from this hill I have a perfect view. They are a
people quite distinctly set apart (from other peoples in
the world). Nor do they simply look upon themselves as
just another nation amongst nations of the world. Like
particles in clouds of rising dust, Israel is far past
numbering. Who possibly can count even the fourth
part of them?"   (Numbers 23: 8-10)

Then like a telling foreview of the vision John
presents to us of that Israel to come (when Jews and
Christians in obedience to God, will form one body
which will give birth to that nation God had called on
them to build). Balaam looked on them and said:
"Misfortune can be nowhere seen in Israel, nor is misery
to be found anywhere in her...Neither (the guile of)
sorcery nor (the deception of) divination can succeed in
overthrowing Israel. So it will be said of Jacob and of
Israel: 'Look and see what God has brought about!'
(There is no restraining her.) The people have been
stirred up (from their slumber) like a lioness. They
stand up like a lion which will not rest again until it has
(captured and) devoured its prey and drinks the blood of
all its enemies." (It will incorporate them into the new
world that it builds.)   (Numbers 23: 18-24)

John directly calls attention to the pregnancy of
Israel, reminding us again of Balaam's words: "God is not
a man that he should lie," Balaam said. "Does God make
a promise and then not bring it to fulfillment?"
(Numbers 23: 19) But the fulfillment of that promise
was a painful long drawn-out experience. But as we read
elsewhere: "A woman when she is in travail has sorrow,
because her hour is come; but as soon as she is delivered

of the child, she no longer remembers her pain, because of the joy she feels on bringing a living soul into the world." (John 16: 21)

Of this boy child that the woman was to bear, Balaam said: "Although I see him, I do not see him now. Although he is perceptible to me, he is nowhere near. Yet one day out of Jacob there will come a star and a (reigning monarch wielding the) septre (of God's word) shall indeed arise in Israel. He will utterly destroy the (Temples or) the heads of the Moabites, and smash the (capital cities or) craniums of all the sons of Seth. For Edom will indeed be conquered and Israel will grow strong." (Numbers 24: 17-18)

The woman in this vision, the virgin bride of God, is clearly drawn. She is clothed in the brilliance of God's character, stands upon the counsel of wise ministers (from the four areas of creation) and wears the twelve tribes of Israel as a crowning sparkling ornament. Because Jehovah is the husband of Israel, as Jeremiah said ("Return to me O faithless Israel, for I am your Husband and will choose you individually one from a city and two from a tribal family, and will bring you back to Zion." — Jeremiah 3: 14) the son that the woman in John's vision is to bear, actually will be the son of God—born from the wisdom of his word, which is the only seed God sowed in his community. His word, having the spirit of God in it, gives birth to a son.

It should not be surprising then that the Roman Catholic Church should say that the woman is the Virgin Mary and her child is Jesus Christ. John's words have many nuances, for the imagery is very rich and meaningful. We were meant to see that similarity. Jesus's whole life was drawn to be a prophecy of things to come. He was the spiritual founder and herald of that kingdom which was to follow him, when many sons of God would fill the earth. His kingdom was supposed to fill, and thereby rule, the world. God's very first commandment at the start was to "be fruitful and grow in number so that you might fill the earth and replenish it, governing even the fish of the sea and the birds of the air."

Then Jesus in speaking of God's kingdom said, "Blessed are the meek for they shall inherit the earth." "The meek", of course, are all those men and women upon earth who humbly submit themselves to the will of God, saying, "Not my will but yours be done."

So Jesus's own mother was indeed the herald and the symbol of suffering and rebellious Israel. Her very name was made suggestive of that fact. "Mary" or "Miriam" (so we are told) meant "rebelliousness". The name also suggested sorrow. Yet God foresaw in Israel (as he illustrates in Mary) a time when she would humbly submit herself to him and bring forth man in the character of God—the foundation stone on which the whole kingdom would be built. Her submission to God's will was meant to be illustrative of the attitude that the community of Israel herself must have toward God in order to bring forth the Kingdom he desired from her — the male child that she was to bear.

In contrast to this beautiful young woman called to be the bride of God, her nemesis is shown to be a fiery red dragon of enormous size. This dragon (tannûn) is a well-known symbol in the Bible and in all the literature of the ancient Near East. The seven-headed dragon symbolized all kinds of adversity which periodically afflicted mankind. This dragon was well known in ancient Sumer and was found depicted on a cylinder seal there from the third millennium B.C. From the cuneiform tablets found in Ugarit we learn this seven-headed

monster was called Leviathan.* The seven heads were
universally understood to be a graphic illustration variously used to depict seven days, seven weeks or seven
years of calamity. It even was symbolic of the seven gates
of death. The patriarch Joseph, who became a vizier to
Pharaoh in Egypt, you will remember had to deal with
seven years of drought. In other words, he fought
Leviathan and was victorious over its seven heads.

The sight of such a beast of "waste and ruin" should
remind the people of God of the seven great commands
used by the Creator to defeat the power of death when
he brought all life into being out of the "the deep" or
"great abyss" over which darkness had lain. This beast
of darkness and death which stalks the earth is shown
here as having its seven heads (or capital cities)
crowned. The seven heads and seven crowns indicates
that this enormous monster is familiar with the word of
God, but the ten horns show us that her rulers are
ruthlessly and adamantly opposed to it. The very image
then recalls for us that the churches are present in all
cities of the paganized world.

This dragon spirit governing the social system of
world nations moved by fear (as Balak the ruler of Moab
once had been) stands before the pregnant woman,
ready to devour her child the moment it is born. Such a
system cannot trust those "aliens" who practice customs
different from its own. It poses, in their minds, a threat
to their security. The striking similarity this vision bears
to other Bible texts is not an accident. We think for
instance about the birth of Moses, when the crowned
head of Egypt told the Hebrew midwives: "When you
help the Hebrew women in childbirth and observe them
on the delivery stool, if it is a boy child, kill him."
(Exodus 1: 16)

---

* Kramer, Samuel Noah. *Mythologies of the Ancient World.* p. 201

We also are reminded of the time when an angel in a dream warned Jesus's father Joseph: "Take the child and his mother and escape to Egypt. Stay there until I send you word, for Herod (the crowned head representing Roman rule in Israel) will search for the child to kill him." That warning came because "Herod gave orders to kill all boys in Bethlehem and its vicinity from two years old and under." For Herod knew the Hebrew scriptural promises, and he feared a King might rise in Bethlehem to challenge him.   (Matthew 3: 12-13)

Nor was this similarity contrived as certain scholars frequently have said. This similarity exists because it represents and illustrates a wide-spread social attitude which has been displayed throughout the course of history. For this reason John has called it "Satan" because it is opposed to the way of God. Need I tell you though, the dragon John describes is but a symbol of a social attitude we cannot see, so as to make it sensually visible and easily understood. However, it is an attitude that we continually encounter.

History is filled with many counterparts not the least of which is Anti-Semitism itself. We find the pattern woven into all of the accounts which deal with persecution of the Jews, the degradation of the Negroid race, the drowning or the burning of all witches in the 16th century and the slaying of so-called Christian heretics. We find it also in the armies sent against the virgin Republic of France to re-instate the royal family, in the armies sent, after the First World War against the young Soviet Union to serve no better cause than to vent their fear.

While Christian churches may sing, "It Came Upon A Midnight Clear" with cadences of hope, the world which watches every area of possible invasion with paranoid suspicion tells the ominously foreboding tale, "It Came From Outer Space." So we find this attitude reflected in the persecution of the intellectuals, writers and artists during the McCarthy years in the United States. The whole truth is there is never any place at all at any inn or lodging for sheltering the son of God – the true Christ entering the world. "Look!" John says to all of us, "even now he is coming on the clouds." Those same dust clouds that Balaam looked upon and said was far past numbering.

Don't mistake me, though. Movements initiated by those bodies seeking their own freedom, can indeed themselves become a part of that same dragon spirit of oppression that infects the world, and swallow up the child that holds out hope. France never did become the paragon of liberty, equality and fraternity. Nor did the Soviet Union fulfill its dream of offering the working man a workers' paradise. They did not produce, as they had once affirmed they would, that new being they had dubbed "the new man." Even Israel itself fell far short of the accomplishments which it set out for herself to build. Israel never lived up to any of the expectations God had set for them. Nor did Christendom which followed afterwards. They failed.

So God in calling on his people to unite and build a spiritual temple in the world, has set the stage for bringing God's true virgin bride into the full view of the crowd, by invading that religious heaven governing the satanic world. She appears there as a virgin ready to give birth to a son – God's son – the Kingdom of God to be born upon earth.

This then is the child which was prophesied by Isaiah when he said: "For a child is born unto us, a son is given unto us; and the government is upon his shoulder; and

his name is called Pele-joez-el-gibbor-Abi-ad-sar-shalom.
(Isaiah 9: 4-5) That is to say the kingdom of God (all
those who, as one body, honour God and his creation and
would establish responsible government over God's
dominion of the world). For God had said from the
beginning: "Let them (male and female) have dominion
over the fish of the sea, and over the foul of the air, and
over every living thing that moves upon the earth."

It was to the sons of Adam that this power was
given, provided they remained obedient to God's word.
Then the rulership of this dominion was again affirmed
in Psalm number eight. That rulership, however, was
dependent upon man governing in accordance to the way
of God, not merely for his own indulgence. Until the
moment comes when mankind acknowledges his true
responsibility, this condemnation lies upon the world:
"Your iniquities have separated you from God: your sins
have hidden his face from you, so that you will not hear.
For your hands are stained with blood, your fingers with
guilt. Your lips have spoken lies, and your tongue mutters
wicked things. No one calls for justice; no one pleads his
case with integrity. They rely on empty arguments and
speak lies; they conceive trouble and give birth to evil."
                                            (Isaiah 59: 2-4)

For this reason the speaker in this letter called
earlier on both the Jews and Christians to re-examine
their history and practices, and put away any animosities
they felt for one another, so that they might become like
two pillars (Jakin and Boaz) in the temple of God and
be ready for the bridegroom when he comes. Isaiah
speaking of this coming moment said: "Israel's enmity
(for Judah) must end, for all who harass Judah shall be
cut off. Ephraim (another name for the land of Israel)
must put away its envy of Judah, and Judah must put
away its hostility for Ephraim. (Only then), united they

will come down upon the Philistines on the west; united they will overpower the people of the east. Together they will possess Edom and Moab; and the people of Ammon will be subject to them." (Isaiah 11: 13-14)

To do this, God's community of Israel must put Satan from its midst. For just as those who keep a careful watch upon the heaven governing the pagan world, so God's people too must guard against the power of Satan entering their midst. We read for instance in the book of Job that when the sons of God came before God's throne, Satan was in their midst. And when Job was praised amongst the brethren by none other than by God himself, Satan just couldn't resist the opportunity to tear his reputation down.

There is something similar found in the *Genesis* account of Cain and Abel, when they offered up their sacrifices before God, and Cain was wroth because Abel's offering was seen as more acceptable than his own. We have to face the fact that the heaven we worship in is spoiled if we carry into it attitudes which have no place in it at all.

Job, during the period of all his misfortunes, went into the wilderness to sit alone and voice his pain and anguish before God. Yet even there the voice of pious Satan followed him and tormented him even more, in words of pseudo-comfort from his friends. For Satan cannot leave the godly man alone. He brings him down and makes him feel inferior to those "more holy than himself." The fellowship he brings with him is not one of mutual support but a moralistic and condemning one. For Satan loves to wear a godly face or mask of piousness.

Satan is the perfect picture of the hypocrite (or "play actor" if we actually translate the Greek) for he

loves to play the role of the untouchably perfect minister of God. God's people need to recognize the dragon
in themselves and in their midst and put it from their
lives, by speaking and by walking in the way of God.

God's brotherhood exists (not to show how good we
are but) for mutual strengthening and as a means for
helping one another in the process of godly growth. Paul
described the fellowship like this: "If there is any such
thing as one Christian encouraging another, or helping
one another out of love, if you actually have any
community Spirit at all in you, and you really have
compassion and affection toward all, then I sincerely
urge you to make my joy complete by being of like mind
in love, spirit and purpose — not doing anything out of
selfish ambition or from pretended superiority. Be
humble rather and look to one another's needs and
interests as being more important than your own. Do
not be so self-absorbed in your own affairs that you are
inconsiderate and ignorant of other people's thoughts
and pains and needs."   (Philippians 1: 1-4)

Yet the power of Satan has revealed itself in many
forms in God's community. When the children of Israel
were led by Moses out of Egypt, the voice of Pharaoh
followed them. When God fed his people manna in the
wilderness, the followers from Egypt wanted meat and
started all the people grumbling. They bewailed
everything that they had left behind in Egypt and
complained, saying: "Can't you even give us just a little
meat! We remember that in Egypt everyone ate fish at
no cost at all. There we also enjoyed cucumbers, melons,
leeks, onions, and garlic (and many kinds of dainty
food). But all that we have now is nothing in comparison
to it. All we ever see is manna all the time!"
(Numbers 11: 4-5)

It took Israel forty years to get the world of Satan out of them. Hence the wilderness experience for the New Israel in *Revelation* before the greater battle with the world. When Lot and his family came out of Sodom, the way of Sodom followed them. Lot's wife just could not stop herself from looking back, and ruing everything that they had left behind: the joy of all the merrymaking festivals, the friendships of the world, the happy marriage celebrations and the cosmopolitan trade which brought merchandise from every place around the world —for Sodom, we know now from cuneiform tablets found at Ebla, was on the main trade route of the ancient world. Lot's wife merely took a little time to pause and look back for a while wistfully remembering, until she couldn't move at all.

Lot, after losing his wife and sons-in-law was left with just his daughters. In order to relieve his misery, he drank heavily. His daughters versed in all the ways of Sodom did not hesitate to use them when they thought mankind's survival was at stake and dependent solely upon them. Satan was the chief guide in the heaven ruling over them. So that we read: "One day the older daughter said to the younger, 'Our father is old now, and there is no man anywhere on earth to come in to us and give us children as the custom always was on earth. So let's get our father drunk with wine and we will lie with him and thereby keep his seed alive.'

"So it was that the two daughters made their father drunk on wine that night. Then the older daughter (according to the plan that they devised) went in and lay down with him. And he didn't even know when it was that she came in or when she got up afterwards.

"Then the following day the older daughter told the younger one, 'Last night I slept with Father. (So it's your turn now.) Let's get him drunk on wine again tonight, so you can lie with him. In that way we will keep the family alive on the earth.' So they (put in operation what they said and) got their father drunk again that night by filling him with wine. Then the younger daughter went in as planned and lay with him. But as before he never once became aware of when it was that she came in or got up afterwards.

"And so it was that both Lot's daughters were made pregnant by their father." (Genesis 19: 31-36)

So now the New Israel is taken off into the wilderness to do battle with the persecuting monster who has invaded the heaven of their own community (thus darkening their sun). Just how much Isaiah's words concerning the spiritual pollution of the Israel of his time apply in this case to the newly gathered Israel, I leave up to the individual to judge. But Isaiah described Israel's condition in these words:

"They brazenly defy me to my face, by their perversity, doing things deliberately to anger me, like offering sacrifices in their gardens and burning incense upon bricks. Sitting among the graves and tombs (like witches who pretend communion with the spirits of the dead), they spend their whole night keeping secret vigils and eating swine's flesh as they drink from sacred vessels, soups concocted out of every unclean thing. Then these self-appointed ones will tell you, 'Keep away from us. Do not come too close. For we are holier than you.' Such disgusting words are sickening to me. Like suffocating smoke which rises from a fire that goes on burning ceaselessly, their dreadful works will not be tolerated long." (Isaiah 65: 3-5)

Before we simply wave our hand dismissing them, we should remember first that God often spoke symbolically, and visual religious acts were often used to illustrate the moral condition of the people's mind and heart. What filthy things do we imbibe continually which turns us into perverts and corrupts our soul. Israel must put these from its midst.

To rid themselves of every pagan influence, God's bride is taken briefly out of the community of Satan to do warfare for their heaven in the wilderness. John in one place says that she was given wings of the swift, far-sighted eagle to flee from the dragon which menaced her. One New Testament parallel of this is what took place following Jesus's baptism where Matthew clearly identifies those eagle wings for us: "Then was Jesus led of the spirit up into the wilderness to be tempted of the devil." So it was that Jesus did warfare for the heaven that would govern his own life, and it was the spirit of God that carried him away into the wilderness.

This warfare was recorded for our benefit so that we might gauge our own priorities in determining what powers in our heaven command us and rule over us. Should we live to satisfy our physical needs alone? Should we risk or waste our lives in trying to attract the awe, the wonder and admiration of the crowd? Should we do things contrary to the will of God just so we can get ahead in life? These three questions were asked and emphatically answered during the spiritual battle which Jesus waged with Satan in his wilderness experience. They were later raised in other gospel texts in order to help all those who choose to deal with Satan, to put him from their lives and make their heaven free. Christ's temptations are well worth our examining.

So turn off your televisions, radios and record players for forty days and forty nights, and live only upon the manna of God's word. Be certain, though, that you understand that forty days and forty nights of warfare is a symbolic period which stands for however long it takes to overcome the devil in your life. So there is spiritual warfare in the community of Israel itself for properly establishing God's heaven in their midst. For though God's people will undoubtedly have influenced the dragon's world, we must not overlook the great effect the dragon's world will have had on them. The dragon will be there unless a war is fought to drive him out of it.

New Israel consequently is commanded to take notice of the monster spirit lurking in their midst and put him from the heaven guiding them. They are not to be manipulated by the standards and the teachings of the world. They must be made immune to them. For this they need a wilderness experience. They must not be moved or influenced by flattery, triviality, resentments or superficial evidence, but must see through all deceptions which had deceived mankind throughout its history.

So in this chapter of God's strategy, the author shows us plainly at the start the field of influence on human lives over which the battle will be waged. God has set out to build "a new heaven and a new earth" for mankind and do away with those that Satan's world has built. Without a new heaven guiding it there cannot be a new earth. For this reason the last campaign begins its warfare in heaven. For this reason, we are shown (to begin with) the two great figures which affect all life on earth: the spirit governing God's Israel — his virgin bride; and the spirit governing the present world — a dragon fiery red with the blood guilt of sin. The struggle to gain control of heaven therefore is revealed as a struggle to establish the influencing power of God's ruling spirit in the social realm by first capturing the imagination governing men's hearts.

This Michael (embodying the divine vision of the world that is to be) is "the holy spirit" which inspires, strengthens and leads the messenger of God. The spirit of Satan offers those who follow him the egocentric dream of wealth, fame and power within the system of that jealously guarded and chaotic world that is. With the help of "the holy spirit" God gave his people, it took Israel forty years (in the wilderness) to overcome the influence of Egypt in their spiritual life and become strong. It took Jesus forty days and forty nights, and being then victorious because of Michael (the holy spirit of God that was with him) he could say: "Get away from me Satan. For it is written: 'You shall worship Jehovah your God and only serve him.'" Then the devil left him, and angels came and attended to him.

(Matthew 4: 10-11)

The dragon (the spirit governing world nations) is dangerous. Even those committed to the hope of Israel can be deceived and fall, as with his tail the dragon pulls them from the place of influence in the firmament of God. So here, to be part of the kingdom of God, this chapter reveals, those who claim belief in God must be led by the power of the Divine Vision (Michael leading them) to defeat the influence of Satan and his angels by throwing them out of the community of God. Yet this war is a spiritual war signifying that the spirit governing the present world and the spirit of the cities which are led by it must be driven out of God's communities. In being cast to the earth (i.e. excluded from its exalted place of influence), the devil is left solely to a corrupt and decaying world system, which is rapidly destroying itself.

With this "heavenly" defeat, God begins to reign and the charges that the devil makes against the brethren no longer influence those in the Kingdom of God. Even fear of death does not deter them now, for they see the complete victory of God's kingdom well within their reach. The sacrifice of Jesus and the power of speech this sacrifice has given to the descendants of Israel are the only apparent weapons that they use. This is occasion for rejoicing amongst the sons of Israel, but catastrophic for those who cling still to the traditions and practices of the old world, for Satan now has grown more fierce with the realisation that his remaining time is limited.

Yet the dragon spirit of the world, which deceives humanity with its own pretense of piety, will persecute Israel, the mother of the child. First it will try to overwhelm her with a flood of false teachings and philosophies. Christians now should be aware of all the lies that Satan tells. The serpent in the garden of Eden brought down Adam and Eve by convincing them they were immortal souls and could not die. Cain, deceived by envy for his brother, thought himself more righteous than his brother and was deaf to God. The Israelites, deceived by lust, chose meat to eat rather than the manna of God's wisdom. Balaam, with meat from pagan altars and with temple prostitutes, attempted to seduce the sons of Israel.

With things like this in mind, John warned the churches and the synagogues that Satan once again would flood the congregations of God with teachings and practices completely foreign to the way that Christ had shown. Then John assures his readers that the earth itself – Satan's own world system – would absorb these ways, so that the true Israel of God could still remain aloof from them. For God's people were no part of this world, as Jesus said.

Therefore, because God's kingdom would still be seen as a threat to the established nations of the world, the dragon (or spirit of the world) would continue to persecute the sons of Israel (who were the offspring of God's virgin bride). The next chapter will identify the nations that the dragon calls up from the sea and land to persecute the sons of God. Only God's true Israel can withstand the lures and violence the spirit of the world directs at them. That is to say all those who keep the commandments of God (his law), and who by their conduct bear witness to their messiah and to their God.

CHAPTER THIRTEEN

Brutish World Powers

Now the *Book of Revelation* is very rich in imagery. In it there is no imagery more rich than what we have found in Chapters Eleven and Twelve. It would be wise, therefore, for us to take the time to re examine it before continuing. For these chapters contain a wealth of knowledge worth considering. Here John was given a measuring rod to measure the temple of God, a final trumpet blown, two heavenly visions following—a woman giving birth to a child, and Prince Michael and his host fighting for possession of that heaven which will one day rule the entire earth.

We have encountered all of these in Bible texts if we have had the eyes for recognizing them. *The Measuring Rod*: Upon the entrance of Israel into the holy land, the law of God was carefully explained to them again, and all the tribes were numbered so as to meet the challenges that lay ahead of them. *The Final Trumpet*: All the pagan world had heard the news that Israel was rapidly approaching them, and "their hearts melted within them." *The Pregnant Woman*: From afar Balaam looked on Israel (the nation God had blessed) ready to give birth to a new kingdom in the world. *The Great Red Dragon*: Moab's King Balak spewed out water of his culture on the sons of Israel—temple prostitutes and meat from sacrifices to the pagan gods.

Before the Battle for the holy land, Joshua was met by the captain of God's hosts *Michael and his Angels*. He was the spirit that would strengthen them—the spirit that would continue strengthening everyone that did the will of God. This was the spirit Christians later would refer to as the Holy Ghost. But nowhere in the scriptures does the Bible speak of him as God, even though his name does mean "He who is like God." But this name only meant he reflected God's own character. Sometimes, then, the holy spirit is personified, and everyone who represents their God is filled with him. Those led by such a spirit (referred to as the captain of God's hosts) derive both strength and wisdom as he leads them in their spiritual battles for possession of that heaven governing the world.

It was Michael who led God's troops (the numbered sons of Israel) into the holy land and fought for them, and it is Michael once again who leads the sons of God in their battles for making the new heaven free from the influence of the former heaven which had ruled the world. I do not speak here superstitiously, but as I pointed out before, the world we live in has been ruled till now by spiritual influences of the gods that they themselves have made. In another battle with the world, the sons of God will take the holy land, which is the world itself. They will begin to rule under good King David's greater son, in New Jerusalem. The nations which they face will be a continuance of those that Israel once faced in Canaan long ago.

So it is well worth our attention now that Jesus's whole life was lived out as a prophecy, so that he could truly be the Messiah of the world. God's nation, Israel his virgin bride, gave birth to a son on the Feast of Trumpets, just following the final trumpet sound. Then it came to pass, the news went forth from Bethlehem, a saviour had been born, through whom the nations of the world would be blessed.

Eight days afterwards, upon the Day of Atonement, he was circumcised in accordance with God's law. But when Herod learned that a contender for the throne was born, he sent out a flood of massacre upon the innocents in Bethlehem. Yet Jesus and his family went to Alexandria for temporary residence, during the Feast of Tabernacles, returning on the last Great Day to bring judgment on the world. Still his message to them was: "I have not come to destroy the world, but to save it."

That's not biography, of course. That's prophetic utterance, and Christians would be well advised to learn the difference. For the second phase of Jesus's prophetic life began at Passover, when he was baptized and the Holy Spirit came on him. His life thereafter became the pattern of the strategy he gave his followers for battling those corrupting influences that made them any nation's slaves. It was the pattern for establishing God's kingdom on the earth. His prophetic life, as well as what he said, proclaimed the gospel he had come to preach: "God's kingdom had been born on earth." The warfare that he fought was spiritual, yet it had (for a long while) a great effect upon the world.

At his crucifixion, the third step of the revelation of his life began. He was crucified at Passover, after feeding what he was to those who followed him. Then his followers, in something like a wilderness experience — gained confidence during the perfecting days of Unleavened Bread. During them, their leader rose to be with them, before ascending to his God — like Moses who ascended the Mountain in the wilderness to speak with God. Then as Moses who, on Pentecost, returned to bring with him the laws to govern Israel and build the tabernacle in their midst so God could dwell with them, Jesus gave the character of God (in the holy spirit) to his followers bringing them into the temple God had built for them — His heaven and His world.

Those are the fundamental steps we go on following until we reach the final days. The covenant with God is sealed each year when we renew it in the evening meal that he commanded us to keep, and in the days that follow it. So we should now be ready for the final days, to meet the challenges of battle when they come. We have heard the trumpet sounds of warning. John, through Christ now, has alerted us. The holy spirit leads us into battle. But do we recognize the enemy.

The purpose of this chapter is to show the enemy to us:

As I stood upon the sandy shore, I saw a brutish beast (an oppressive world system of nations) rising from the (turbulent) sea (of mankind). The beast had ten horns (seats of government) and seven heads (all world capitals in which the word of God is known) and each horn wore ten diadems (meaning that their rulership of all the world which was complete at the same time was opposed to the will of God). Upon its forehead there were many names of blasphemy. (For its vile and evil thoughts brought about injustice and violence which are offensive to God).

This creature that I saw looked like a leopard; Its feet were like a bear's, and it had a lion's mouth. (For it stood for all the Gentile nations that had ever been before and were yet to be.) The dragon (whose spirit had supreme control of them) gave the beast all his power, his throne and great authority. (This reminds us at once of Satan's words to Jesus when he stood upon the mount: "All these nations will I give you and all their glory — the majesty, the pageantry, the throne, the absolute authority — if you will but bow down and worship me." — Matthew 4: 8-9)

(We might pause here too, just to remember the many world leaders and politicians throughout time who gained world power and prominence, many of them imagining the great things they would do once the reins of political authority was in their hands to use, only to find that national and world events and public moods conspired against their purposes.)

Then one of the heads of the beast was stricken with a deadly wound. But the death stroke soon was healed, and the whole world wondered and (filled with admiration for the beast) became his followers. (This is Babylon "which once was, and is no more but yet shall be". It is the spiritual head or capital city which throughout time has guided the actions of the beast of nations. Like spiritual Jerusalem, which rules God's people, Babylon is the city which the nations stand in awe of and obey.)

Then the people everywhere on earth worshipped the dragon because it was he that gave power to the beast. They worshipped him, asking one another, "Who (anywhere on earth) has power to match that of the beast?" and "Who possibly can be a match for him in any war?"

Then the dragon gave the beast the power to speak effectively and encouraged him to boast about himself and all his deeds. (In songs no doubt like this: "Where else but here, are you the master of your own little world? Where else but here do hearts beat faster when the flag is unfurled?") God allowed him full control of all the earth for forty-two months. (All of us have heard the boasts and songs of national superiority, the blasphemous call to arms, and the reviling of the poor and humbled classes of the world. For how we speak of other men and women is how we speak of God.) Opening its mouth, it slandered God, blaspheming his name, his temple (which is creation) and vilifying those who live in heaven (the community of God).

The dragon gave the beast the power to fight against God's people and to defeat them. This power extended (throughout the world) over people of all kinds in every nation, language and race. For people everywhere throughout the world will worship the beast, that is to say all those who, from the very beginning of the world, do not have their names written in the book of life belonging to the lamb that was killed.

If anyone has comprehension let him understand.

Some of you will be taken captive, others slaughtered by the sword. But (take heart and) do not be dismayed (for the ultimate victory is ours). However, it will require great patience and endurance on the part of all the saints (those who earnestly serve God).

It was then I saw another beast coming out of the earth (indicating it was the rise of the common man). Although it had two small horns like those of a lamb, it spoke like a dragon. (A beast rising from the common man with a dual government of apparent equal powers— seemingly peaceful and benign, but speaking with the voice of the warrior). This beast will exercise all the power of the first beast, as he acts on his behalf and makes the inhabitants of the whole world worship the first beast (Babylon) whose deadly wound was healed. (It is not really difficult to see where John found his ground plan for this beast. Gog of Magog as described in Chapters 38 and 39 of *Ezekiel* was the commander in chief of the two cities Mishech and Tubal, which were the two horns on the beast.)

Through his tremendous power to perform great deeds of amazing magnitude (literally miracles) on behalf of the first beast, such as making fire (a symbol of warfare) come down from the sky in the sight of everyone, he was able to deceive the people everywhere on earth. Then he ordered them to make an image resembling the first beast that was wounded by the sword (i.e. devastated in war) and lived.

Using the great power given him, the second beast gave life to the idol he had built of the first beast, so that the idol (seemingly alive) spoke, and all who would not worship it, the second beast put instantly to death. Then he compelled everyone, small and great, rich and poor, free and slave to have the mark of the beast placed on his right hand and on his forehead. (The mark of the beast as described by Peter is this: "Your conduct in the past was marked in doing what the Gentiles do: pursuing sensuality, lust, drunkenness, orgies, drinking bouts and the disgusting practices of idolatry. But now the Gentiles are surprised to find that you no longer dissipate yourself by running to the same extremes of wild excess and recklessness with them." — 1 Peter 4: 3-4)

For it was universally agreed that no one had the right to buy or sell unless he bore the mark, that is to say the beast's name, or else the number of its name. This calls for cautious wisdom. Therefore, let those with understanding carefully determine the number of the beast: because it is the number of Man. And that number is six hundred and sixty six. (Natural man in the extreme).

*

To read this chapter we have just read and to understand its meaning is to be thoroughly disturbed. Yet it is neither the strength nor the appearance of those beasts that John revealed to us which is unsettling. It is the recognition of that enemy as something we have seen and once thought beautiful. It is the terrifying feeling that up till now you and I have both been part of them. For what the enemy really is, is all of the established nations we were born in, raised in and have grown to love. They are the nations Jesus the Messiah saw when he was taken to the mountain top where Satan offered him the rulership of them. All he ever had to do was listen to the voice of Satan rather than the voice of God.

When Jesus looked upon them, he was shown the glory and the wonder they displayed. For there are many things we can admire in them. John, however, looking on them from afar, saw the ugly side of them. Those who live within these nations see themselves as pure and virtuous. It is only when we stand back from them that we begin to see the terrible effect that they have had upon the world which God had made. Then we recognize them as the wantonly destructive, ugly beasts they are.

I take no pleasure in pointing out these things to you – for they are frightening to me. I simply took it on myself to read John's document with care, interpreting the symbols and all the Bible passages to which John has deliberately referred. Yet having done this and uncovering the meaning that is there, I am reminded of what John said earlier after he had eaten up the scroll the angel gave to him: "It was as sweet as honey in my mouth, but after I had eaten it my stomach was extremely sour." For in understanding what he'd read he was obliged to "go and prophesy before many nations and tribes of many languages and even before kings." Like Jonah, he could not merely run away and hide. God had commissioned him.

My task, of course, is not as onerous as John's. However, I take care to point out here that what I say is not a mere interpretation I have forced upon John's words, but rather what the Bible (by its own power) clarifies. What gave John the power of vision to look beyond his own time in showing us these beasts was that he understood, or Jesus understood (or God who spoke to him understood) the nature of the world which would give birth to them. But having recognized in both these beasts the places we have all called "home", we can now empathize with Lot's wife and understand the way she felt when she looked back upon the city, its people and the customs she had grown to love.

John's depiction of the beast which rises from the sea deliberately alludes to all the various beasts vividly described in the *Book of Daniel*, and is meant to show us that these beasts are still alive in this much larger beast coming at a later time. For it is the spirit of a kingdom that makes it what it is, and the spirit ruling it is the true king of the land. Nations are nothing. They rise and they fall. It is the spirit giving birth to them that identifies them as the land of Babylon, just as the spirit of God's people can build at length the Holy Land. The waters that they rise from indicate the turbulent waters of mankind.

Still the idea of a nation rising from the waters of the sea appears to have been derived from the world's first federation of powers that rose under the conquering force of Nimrod, which came into being after the Great Flood, as a kind of defiant spirit rising out of the waters to oppose God:

"Cush was the Father of Nimrod who became a mighty man on earth. He was a powerful hunter who opposed Jehovah, so that the saying circulated 'Even like Nimrod the mighty hunter who challenged Jehovah in his might.' The beginning of his kingdom was Babel, Erech, Accad and Calneh, in the land of Shinar (Babylonia). From there he went into Assyria and built the cities of Nineveh, Rehoboth-Ir, Calah and Resen, between Nineveh and Calah; and incorporated them into one great city." (Genesis 10: 8-13)

This, because it was the beginning of the land of Babylon — the mother and spiritual capital city of all nations in the world — is the young beast that was the base or principle from which all other nations grew. From here then until modern times, this beast that rises from the waters of mankind takes on the form that John described for us, and is the same great beast of nations Satan offered to the young Prophet Jesus as a bribe to turn him from the purpose he pursued. We read about it in Luke's gospel, where he said: "Then the devil took Jesus to the top of a high mountain and showed him all kingdoms of the habitable world (across time) in a single moment, and told him I will give you all of these, the power to rule them and the glory they contain, for they are mine to give to anyone I choose. They shall be yours if you will only worship me." (Luke 4: 5-7)

This beast, then, is a beast that continues from generation to generation in different forms. To illustrate this, the writer describes the beast as having the appearance of a leopard, feet like a bear, and a lion's mouth, calling once again to mind the chain of nations Daniel described for us that rose individually from the Great Sea.

It is all the nations of the world throughout time. This is further clarified by the ten horns and the ten

royal diadems. The seven heads suggest that they are
familiar with the word of God, which is spoken in their
midst, and may even make pretense at representing it,
but the blasphemous titles on them—like the marks
upon men's foreheads—signifies the kind of thoughts
directing their activities. Isaiah clearly says of them:
"Their thoughts are thoughts of iniquity. Desolation and
destruction are in their paths. The way of peace they
know not, and there is no justice in their doings."
(Isaiah 59: 7-8)

Such things are a blasphemy of God's name. You do
not have to speak the name of God to blaspheme it. All
you need to do is deliberately perform acts that are
contrary to his character, which is the image in which he
fashioned all of us. For what we do, more than what we
say, either reveals or blasphemes God's name. The spoken
name is the communication of the lips that represents
the nature of God's character—holiness, truth, justice,
fair dealings, love, compassion, righteousness, wisdom,
creativeness, and whatever else the scriptures tell us
about God. The name of God is glorified in what we do,
what we think and what we say.

There is a reason why the Bible talks so much about
the character of God.

Blasphemy is how we treat our fellow creatures and
how we treat the world's environment that God made:
"For if anyone does not love his brother, whom he has
seen, he cannot possibly love God whom he has not
seen." (1 John 4: 20)

What does it matter what God is like? Why does the
Bible spend so much time describing and lauding God's
virtues? Is he an egotist? No. It is because the Bible is

addressing those who are called upon to carry out God's will. If God is merciful and compassionate, his children and all who serve him must reflect that character. The man who is proud and haughty and difficult to approach is not of God. The ungracious, arrogant man who has no compassion and no mercy is not of God.

Jehovah is gracious and full of compassion; slow to anger, and of great mercy. (Psalm 145: 8)

Jehovah is righteous (fair) in all his ways, and holy in all his doings. Jehovah is near to all those who sincerely call on him. (Psalm 145: 17-18)

God upholds the cause of the oppressed and gives food to the hungry. Jehovah sets the prisoners free, Jehovah gives sight to the blind, Jehovah loves the righteous. Jehovah watches over the alien and sustains the fatherless and widow, but frustrates the ways of the wicked. Jehovah reigns forever, your God, O Zion, for all generations. (Psalm 146: 7-10)

These six things does Jehovah hate: ...A proud look, a lying tongue, and hands that shed innocent blood, a heart that devises wicked imaginations, feet that are swift in running to mischief, a false witness that speaks lies, and he that sows discord among brethren.
(Proverbs 6: 16-19)

Evil deeds and thoughts are blasphemy. And evil thoughts are blasphemies that are written on the forehead.

This beast, however, has a name, as the later chapters of this book reveal. The name of it is the Hordes of Gog. That is to say it is the spiritual offspring of those nations Gog from the land of Magog (with the two horns) led to their destruction and will one day lead

again. Arnold Toynbee was not the first historian to
notice patterns governing the course of history. The
second beast will later be identified as Magog whose
leader Gog is one with him. I will talk, a little later, of
these names and what they mean.

John takes time to carefully call to our attention to
one head of the beast which was "killed by the sword".
This was understood to mean it had been totally destroyed in war. Yet it was revived and lived again. What
he is referring to Daniel has made plain. For Daniel had
depicted the nations of the world as a statue whose head
was made of gold. The feet of the statue were made of
iron mixed with clay. Since the iron mixed with clay are
the two beasts we are viewing now, then the head of
gold is that head on the beast which was destroyed.

The statue and the beast are one and the same. So
John alludes here to that illustrious and glorious capital
city of the world which was brought down by warfare
centuries ago. The whole world stood in awe of it. Yet
even though it was destroyed, the spirit which had
governed it was still present in the world, and had its
influence on human minds. Later on John will take a
closer look at it, for nothing in the book he gave us is
superficially passed over after being brought to our
attention so dramatically.

Later on, John will speak of it as a city "which once
was but is no more yet shall appear again." That city
which he speaks of here is Babylon, the spiritual capital
city governing the world. In contrast with it is the
heavenly Jerusalem which also is not seen, and is the city
governing the children of God.

Now the beast which earlier was pictured as
emerging from the bottomless pit and slaying the two

witnesses (the synagogue and church) is described now in this passage as coming out of the earth. This description brings us to the beginning of the world, for in *Genesis* we read: "Then Jehovah the creator, formed man from the dust of the ground and breathed into his nostrils the breath of life and man became a living person."   (Genesis 2: 7)

The word for 'man' in Hebrew is 'adam' and the word for ground is 'adamah', clearly showing the relationship. The number of the beast confirms this, by saying it was the symbol of his name. And the number is 666 — that is emphatically man in his natural state — primitive, violent and unschooled in God's word. Six is man's number — but six to the third degree is the ultimate degree. The number six is derived from the fact that Man was created on the sixth day. This is emphasized throughout the Bible texts.

"What is man that thou art mindful of him?" asks the psalmist of Jehovah in the King James translation of the Hebrew text, before he proceeds to answer the question himself. However, he has asked the question for the reader's benefit. Yet the answer to the question is deeper still than this one psalm alone reveals for us. For this reason, the matter is dealt with at greater length throughout the whole Hebrew and Greek Scriptures. In *Genesis* man is told: "For dust thou art, and unto dust shalt thou return."

This succinct definition of man, given in the third chapter of *Genesis* is apt, seeing that God made man from the earth. Yet, according to the *Genesis* text, man was created — male and female — on the sixth day of creation. The term Adam is not therefore to be taken as purely male — for male is not a species. Adam (the species made in the image of God) is male and female. No male is self perpetuating, nor is any female. Adam is a relationship—male and female being one flesh. No male exists apart from the female partner. And Man, made of earth, has the number six.

Genesis takes the attitude that mankind (adam) who is of the earth (adamah) at the beginning of his history, prior to the forming of cities, took the wrong turn. He began to look selfishly toward the creation only as a means to feed and satisfy his appetites, forgetting his first responsibility for the welfare of creation which God assigned to him. His number therefore was to remain six rather than the perfected seven—for seven stood for physical and spiritual completion, through obedience to God, by entering the sabbath that God made for him.

We waste our time in pointing out, as many people do, to different individuals in order to identify the beast. The beast, as is apparent from the description given here, is a world power or world alliance of powers, governed somehow by the common man, with a leader Gog— whose charisma wins the people's confidence. The two horns on the earth beast's head tell us that it has two ruling bodies of government. The horns being those of a lamb suggest that they appear benign and peaceable, but in speaking like a dragon, the beast shows by its words that it is warlike, calling men to arms, and inciting them to war. The message to the watchful is: "Do not be deceived by it." This nation or body of two nations (which Gog will lead) will be called to world leadership and act on behalf of Magog's hordes, the beast, or body of nations from the Sea.

I call attention here to Gog, Magog and Magog's hordes so as to identify them at this early stage. This will help us to follow the story line as it develops and unfolds in John's epistle.

But Magog, the beast from the earth, will be a nation of the people, and organize other nations of the world — making an image of them (an international forum of some kind) that appears to speak, but speaks with the words that Gog of Magog desires from them, slaying all who do not worship the image. Yet Magog, the people's nation(s) and its leader Gog can work miracles — calling fire (a symbol of warfare or violent destruction) from heaven. It is a miracle of such tremendous force and magnitude that all the world is awed.

Gog (which means mighty one, or doer of mighty works) was the symbolic leader of Meshech and Tubal whom Ezekiel said would join forces with the nations of the world against the land of Israel and be utterly destroyed in the ensuing battle that Gog led. The name Gog is a reference to the stormlike ability of this leader to bring a multinational assault against the children of Israel. His stormlike fierce attack was to come after Jehovah had gathered his scattered people out of the nations and restored them to the Mountain (or nation) of previously devastated Israel.

However, in the *Ezekiel* account Magog (which means the people of Gog) indicated the region or peoples from which he came. In the *Book of Revelation* account, the lands which Gog and Magog lead are referred to as "the Hordes of Gog". At one point, *Revelation* refers to Gog as the false prophet, no doubt because he is a charismatic individual who will lead the people's nation into war against God's Israel. The head (or spiritual Babylon) which instructs the larger body of nations is part of the first beast. The tail (or false prophet) which advises it, is in the nation from the earth.

Gog of Magog by leading this stormlike attack on Israel, incurs Jehovah's rage and brings destruction both on himself and the nations that he leads. Their bodies then will lie unburied on the battle plain and become food for the birds, and their bones will finally be buried in the the valley called The Valley of the Hordes which followed Gog, that is Hammon Gog.

Because the people of Israel dwell in, what appears to Gog, a land with no visible signs of protection, enjoying abundant prosperity, Gog is drawn into waging an all-out vicious attack upon them. He congregates a vast army from many nations for this purpose. But his assault sets off Jehovah's rage and brings terrible defeat and destruction upon Gog and his entire crowd. Their carcasses then become food for the birds and beasts and their bones are then buried in the valley called "The Valley of the Hordes of Gog" ("Hammon Gog").

It is doubtful that Gog ever was the actual name for any human ruler, but was chosen by the prophet John rather to signify the false prophet's great power and his ability to perform mighty works. The man Gog is symbolic of whatever charismatic individual rises to power on the confidence he is able to inspire in the people (whom he leads to their destruction). It may be of some small interest, though, to note that Magog, Meshech and Tubal were all names that were given to the sons of Japheth.

Gog was the commander-in-chief of Meshech and Tubal, (the two symbolic horns on the beast from the earth). He unified the nations of the world and led a multinational attack upon the Mountain of the restored nation of Israel after Jehovah had regathered them from all the nations of the world. We have, therefore, met the villains in the drama which will shortly begin. So we might logically expect to see next God's people, with a leader to deliver them.

The number of the beast (which is six, six, six) couldn't be more apt. It is the number of man to the ultimate degree. And yes it does mean "of the people, by the people and for the people." But John was not specifically referring to any nation in the modern world, only to the spirit which the number and the name suggests. John was writing of a phenomena he saw would have to be. He was therefore pointing to a type. You see the ideal nation should have been 777 — a government of God, by the sons of God, for the creation of God. For such was the charge first given at the beginning: "Then God said: 'Let us make man in our image, after our likeness, and let them have responsibility over the fish of the sea and over the birds of the air, and over the livestock, and over all the earth and over every living thing that lives upon the earth.' So God created man in his own image, in the image of God he created him — male and female."

Yet a better number still is chosen for the nation of God, the number mentioned earlier 144,000.

The warnings given here by John are words of warning to the world existing in all times. Being watchful isn't looking at the sky and saying: "Tomorrow he may come. Let's watch and see." Watchful is examining ourselves to see that we are taking care to do all the things that are required of us, so that the saviour when he comes might be proud of us and say, "Well done."

CHAPTER FOURTEEN

Harvesting the Earth

Now when I looked again to see, the lamb (the anointed Priest-King of Israel) was standing on Mount Zion, and with him were one hundred and forty-four thousand who had his name and the name of his Father written on their foreheads. And from that height came what sounded like a roar of mighty waters and the rumbling of loud thunder: the unified voice of a great choir singing to the accompaniment of harps.

For (the people standing on the mountain) were singing a new song before the throne of God, the four living creatures and the elders. Nor could anyone besides the one hundred and forty-four thousand who had been ransomed from their slavery on earth learn to sing that song. (For it was a song that celebrated freedom from captivity in Babylon—the spiritual Babylon which still enslaves most people in the world.)

These are the ones who haven't been defiled by women (the communities of an immoral world), for they have kept themselves unsoiled (literally 'virgins'). (By promptings of the spirit) they follow the lamb wherever he goes. Redeemed from slavery to the world they are the first fruits offered to God and the lamb. (For they are but the first of those released from slavery. God's hope is to save all men. Yes, saved means that a ransom price has been paid to take them from their bondage to an enemy—the enemy being those nations described in Chapter Thirteen, whose "thoughts are thoughts of iniquity, violence and destruction".)

No falsehood was in their mouths; and they were blameless before God. Another messenger of Jehovah appeared in heaven, hurrying with the good news (of everlasting freedom for the world.) (The picture here is

much like that of the charioteer who brings a message to
the city tower where the watchman passes on his word.
See Isaiah 21: 6-10. This good news is then passed on by
other couriers to every race, tribe, language and nation in
the city of captivity.)

Then he cried out with a mighty voice, "Honour God
and glorify him (with your works. Matthew 5: 16) for
the time of his judgment has arrived. Worship him (by
doing those things that he requires from you)...for he
made heaven and earth, the sea and springs of water."
Then another messenger of God followed in the vision,
prophesying, "Fallen. Babylon the Great has fallen, she
who made all the nations drunk with the wine of
immorality and violence."

Afterwards, another messenger of God crying in a
loud voice said, "If anyone worships the beast (that rises
from the sea) and his image (the symbols of nationalism
and its creeds — Daniel 3: 1-23)...and has the beast's
mark stamped upon his head and on his hand, will be
made to drink of the wine of God's wrath mixed at full
strength in the cup of his anger." (The wine of God's
wrath is war. Anyone mentally and spiritually enslaved to
the idolatry of national creeds will heed such an obscene
call to arms whenever it is given.) "Yes, and such a person
will be tormented with the fire and brimstone (of
warfare) in the presence of God's messengers (those
saints who tried to warn him and who stand on Mount
Zion) in the presence of the lamb."

And the smoke from their torment will continue
going up from generation to generation (for warfare shall
continue in every age and will never cease unless
mankind heeds God's warning and turns away from war).
For they who worship the beast and his image (the
symbols of nationalism) and receive the mark of his

name will never be at rest either night or day. Let God's people then be patient and steadfast in keeping the commandments of God and following the path that Jesus set for them. It was then I heard a voice from heaven saying, "Write this down: 'From this time on, all the dead who died in serving Jehovah will be blessed.'" "They certainly shall," the Spirit says, "for although they rest from their labour for a while (in death) their great rewards remain in store for them (See Matthew 5: 11-12)." (For we shall all be changed in a moment, in the twinkling of an eye at the last trumpet...and the dead shall be raised incorruptible.   — 1 Corinthians 15: 51-52.)

When I looked next, I saw someone resembling the son of man seated upon a white cloud. On his head he wore a gold crown and held a sharp sickle in his hand. (This son of man is the symbol of God's nation as described in *Daniel* as a contrast to the beasts of other lands. For as it says in *Daniel*: "I saw in the night visions, and behold, there came with the clouds of heaven one like unto the son of man, and he came even with the Ancient of Days, and he was brought near before him. And there was given him dominion, and glory, and a kingdom which shall never be destroyed." — Daniel 7: 13-14)

It was then another messenger (the Holy Spirit) of God left the temple sanctuary (the tutored heart of those who know the grace and love of God). This spirit called out in a mighty voice to (the congregation of God's people) the one who was sitting on the cloud, "Put in your sickle now and reap for the time has come to gather in the harvest from the earth for all the crop is ripe." So the messenger of God sitting on the cloud swung his sickle over the whole earth and it was harvested. Another messenger coming from the sanctuary (the human heart of those who put their trust in "holy war") also had a sharp sickle. After the messenger of God who was in charge of the fire (of warfare which nations would become embroiled in) came from the altar (of burnt sacrifices) and called in a loud voice to the one with the sharp sickle, "Take your sickle now and harvest the clusters of grapes from the earth's vine, because all the grapes are now ripe." (Nations would effectually destroy themselves with their feelings of self-righteousness.)

Then the messenger (warfare rising from the stubborn heart of Man), swinging his sickle on the earth, gathered the grapes and threw them into the winepress of God's wrath (the patriotic call to take up arms and go to war). Then the grapes were trampled in the winepress (of battles fought) outside the city, and blood spilled out of the press, rising as high as the bridles of the horses for a distance of 1,600 stadia (meaning over the entire earth).

*

Anyone who has taken time to read the Bible through, with even moderate comprehension of the texts, can't fail to recognize the strong resemblance which exists between these last two chapters in Revelation and the imagery found in the Second Psalm, which says:

"Why do the nations of the world (the beast from the sea) become so furious? and the great majority of people (the beast from the earth) consider such a vain (and stupid) thing (as war)? World governments take up arms, and their leaders sit in conferences together laying plans contrary to the way of Jehovah and his appointed earthly governor (the Anointed One). Let us therefore break their chains, and cast away the captive bonds which keep us bound to them. For he who sits on heaven's throne shall laugh at them and view them with contempt. From now on, he will only speak to them in anger, and cause them sore distress.

"But look, my governor is placed on Zion's hill. And this is what Jehovah told me that he said to him: 'You are my son. From this day on I shall establish you (as ruler of the earth). If you but ask me, I will give you all the nations of the world as your inheritance, and the farthest reaches of the earth for your possession. Then you shall break them with a rod of iron (the authority of God's word); you shall dash them in pieces like a potter's clay vessel.

"Pay heed then all you heads of government; be wise; take warning and correction and receive instruction, all you rulers of the earth. Learn to serve Jehovah with devoted reverence and joy; honour his son, or else Jehovah's anger will be roused, and you will perish (in battle) for having turned out of the way (of righteousness). Everyone who puts their confidence in Jehovah will be happy and enjoy the full protection that Jehovah gives." 						(Psalm 2)

I have no doubt that some may tell me I have changed the speaker of the words: "Let us break their chains and cast away their bonds from us." But I say look at the Hebrew text. It is not I who changed the speaker here. The words "they say" (which change the speaker of the phrase) was inserted by translators. God doesn't hold mankind in bondage; nations do. The Hebrew text clearly puts these words in the mouth of Jehovah's followers because they are a declaration of their freedom from any hostile and destructive practices which dishonour God and his creation. John underlines this truth for us by calling our attention to the new song being sung in heaven: "what sounded like a roar of mighty waters and the rumbling of loud thunder: the unified voice of a great choir singing to the accompaniment of harps". Harps were the instruments which celebrated freedom.

The purpose of the new song is to celebrate the newfound liberty which those who stand upon Zion's mountain now enjoy. Having cast away the bonds of nations, God's people have declared themselves to be a part of that new nation serving only God. The mention of their playing harps is not an accidental one. The children of God when they were in captivity (you may remember) had hung their harps upon the willow trees. They could not sing the glad songs of freedom as long as nations held them in captivity.

This complex picture John has drawn also calls another most important scene to mind. Surely you must think of Matthew's gospel when you read John's description of the multitude gathered with the lamb upon the mountain. You know the text I mean of course, where it is written, "And when he saw the multitudes, Jesus went up into a mountain. Then after he had seated himself, his disciples came to him, and he began to teach them, saying:

> "Blessed are the humble in spirit....
> Blessed are they who mourn....
> Blessed are the meek (the unbelligerent)....
> Blessed are they who hunger and thirst
>   after righteousness
> Blessed are the merciful....
> Blessed are the pure in heart....
> Blessed are the peacemakers....
> Blessed are those who are persecuted
>   because of righteousness...."

These are the ones (so Jesus told his followers) who shall be called the children of God and will sit as judges in God's government, for it is they who shall inherit the earth. To all those Jews who followed him into the mountain, Jesus said: "You are the light of the world. No city that is placed upon a hill can be hidden, nor does anyone light a lamp to hide it under a cover. Rather it is placed upon a lampstand so that it may give light to everyone in the house. In such a manner then as this, you also must let your light shine before mankind so that they may see your good works and glorify your father in heaven." (Matthew 5: 1-16)

One important purpose of this vision then is to quietly remind all those who claim to be the offspring of Abraham that their calling is to bless all peoples upon earth with many benefits and to comfort all who mourn. The reason that we earlier were shown a great crowd moving toward this mountain for comfort and for healing (and for refuge from a war-torn world) was so that we could see the means by which this nation was to grow and be established upon earth. No one possibly can find it drawn on any map depicting nations in the world. Nor will it ever be located in any isolated portion of the earth. It is a nation quite impossible to chart because it is a growing nation being built invisibly by God throughout the world. It is a scattered human family of different races spiritually united by a common dream, which they imagine they can turn into reality.

Regarding this, Jesus told a Jewish Pharisee he loved: "The wind blows anywhere it wanders and you hear the sound of it but you cannot tell where it came from or where it is going. That is the way it is with everyone who is born of God's spirit." (John 3: 8). How can we speak then of "a holy land" when it is written that God's people will inherit the earth? The psalmist even says "The earth is Jehovah's and the fullness thereof." (Psalm 24: 1). So the "holy land" is any place on earth where men and women have discovered God. The mountain (or the nation) of God, as Ezekiel and King David pointed out is the people of God themselves who carry the tabernacle of their God with them everywhere they go. This mountain (or nation) is a nation that will one day be located everywhere throughout the earth, and the tabernacle which it carries is the unified collective spirit that they share which emanates from that new heart God has given them.

In this chapter, John emphasizes for the second time that the number of those standing on the hill is 144,000 to reassure the reader that those whom God has chosen have been called out of every nation upon earth. From this number 144,000, which is (12x12)x(10x10x10), we also learn that the nation of Israel is complete. The presence of the lamb is interpreted by Christians generally to mean that Jesus Christ now stands among his loyal followers. But the lamb itself has deeper meanings too. The covenant Jehovah made with Israel, in Egypt, was sealed with the blood of the Passover lamb, which delivered all the firstborn sons of Israel from death. In the Christian covenant, the covenant was sealed in blood on the day of Passover. It was this sacrifice and covenant which ensured complete deliverance not just from bondage to the world, but from death itself.

Yet this same scene calls to mind that famous stone in Nebuchadnezzar's fearsome dream, mentioned in the Book of Daniel. It is that stone which Daniel said would strike the statue's feet of clay and iron (the beast from the sea united with the beast from the earth) and bring it crashing to the ground. Daniel's story ends like this: "Even while you watched, you saw a great stone that without (the help of) hands broke loose (from a crag) and struck the statue upon its clay and iron feet, smashing them in pieces. Then immediately the iron, the clay, the brass, the silver and the gold (of the statue) all crumbled and fell together, and became like chaff upon the summer's threshing floor. Whereupon the wind, blowing, carried them away and left no trace of them. But as for the stone which struck the statue, it grew into a great mountain and filled the whole earth." (Daniel 2: 34-35)

That stone was destined to become the mountain which would one day fill the earth. For the stone is the lamb and 144,000 sons of Israel who are standing with him upon Zion's mountain. And that mountain is the same mountain celebrated in the second psalm. For Zion is a mountain built of people who will one day fill the world. It is not a kingdom built in any one specific place that you can point to on a map. Nor will it ever be a literal mountain after it has grown. One only needs to think of all the different ways in which the Kingdom of God has been described to realise that fact. In one parable Jesus compared it to the seed of God's word scattered randomly upon the earth. It is a Kingdom then of people who share a common dream and live in hope of seeing it revealed in human attitudes toward nature and mankind.

We are so used to seeing nations being born from wars and bloody revolutions and carefully recorded afterwards upon charts and maps and globes and in atlases that a nation being planned and growing quietly from spiritual roots I'm sure will seem more than just a little strange. It doesn't even have an army to protect itself. At least not one that uses life-destroying weaponry. Jesus once explained it in this way: "The wind blows wherever it may go, and you only hear the sound of it, but you cannot tell from where it came or where it went. That is the way it is with all of those who are born of the Spirit, (or should we say, all who are citizens in the Kingdom of God.)" Remember now, he wasn't speaking superstitiously. "For the kingdom of God is not mere talk, but a real power," Paul said.

(1 Corinthians 4: 20)

It's not important that we know the number of the citizens. The Bible doesn't give us any population count. The kingdom, Daniel said, would one day fill the world, cannot be numbered. We only recognize it from the fruits of love and caring, exhibited by those who honour God. But unlike the warring nations of the world "they shall neither injure nor destroy in all this holy mountain." The only requirement for entering it remains turning our lives around and letting our natures be changed by God's Law and the way of Grace, reversing all the values we once learned. If we would change the world, we have to change ourselves, and let the new world come about by the way we think and speak and interact with others in the world. Doing for others what we would have them do for us, if we were in their circumstance.

Who makes up this government upon the hill of Zion then? this stone about to strike the statue's feet? They are the vocal minority who speak for God, and do his will. It was these that Jesus had in mind when he once said, "Straight is the gate and narrow is the way that leads to salvation, and few there be that find it." Like the small army led by Gideon, they shall be victorious against the Beast from the Sea and against the great majority of people in the world – the Beast out of the Earth. Even as Jehovah once declared, "Not by might nor by power, but by my Spirit," so this nation, after it has smashed the idol's feet and brought it down, will eventually become the mountain filling all the world. And as the waters cover all the seas, so will the nature of this kingdom be in the attitudes we breathe, after it has been established upon the earth.

Belonging to this very special group which stands with the lamb upon the mountain, according to the scriptures, is a most rewarding experience. Jesus compared it to a man finding a pearl of great price buried in a field, who sold everything he had, to buy that field. So there is every reason to rejoice, and those who stand upon the hill rejoice and sing a new song of celebration and of gratitude. Their new song is sung by them, and is heard as a united voice (like a choir). It sounds like many waters (for it has the power of God's authority in that it unites all cultures in the world), and it has the sound of thunder (for the strength of God is in its words) while the accompaniment of harps displays the joy of freedom from bondage (since they no longer hang upon the willow trees of Babylon). This joyful people sing in celebration of their freedom from enslavement to the world. Yet it is sung in heaven, in the sense that all who walk with God are standing there.

Yet no one besides the 144,000 standing on Mount Zion are able to learn the song, for only those who experience the joy of release from all enslaving bonds (and freedom of the soul and spirit) can understand the sentiment expressed in it. These were not defiled with women, but were virgins. How literal many preachers are with words like these! If taken literally we can easily see why the Kingdom of God could not possibly triumph over the enslaving nations of the world. Any nation that does not physically regenerate itself cannot possibly survive. In no place does the Bible advocate celibacy. The apostle Paul, who was himself a widower, defines the terms that we find written here: "For I am jealous for you with a godly jealousy; for I betrothed you to one husband, so that I may present you to Christ as a pure virgin."   (2 Corinthians 11: 2)

This congregation called from the world where they had wallowed in the vices and corruptions until then, now had been prepared as a pure virgin for Christ: "Do you not know that unrighteousness shall not inherit the kingdom of God," Paul formerly had said to them. "Do not be deceived, neither fornicators, nor idolators, nor adulterers, nor effeminate, nor homosexuals, nor thieves, nor covetous, nor drunkards, nor revilers, nor swindlers shall inherit the kingdom of God. Yet these are the things that some of you once were."

(1 Corinthians 6: 9-11)

Once they had been guilty of all these things, but now they had "washed themselves" and stood with other Jews and tribes of Israel on Zion's sacred hill.

The Bible frequently personifies the world's communities, as daughters, maidens or harlots, whose sons and daughters are the men and women who behave according to the spirit and the values that the various communities instill. Therefore, when John says that the chosen vessels for his work are virgins, he simply means they were not contaminated by the world's corrupt communities. The bride of Christ was depicted as a virgin community. For only a community that was entirely free from the crimes and vices inherent in their customs and their practices could possibly give birth to a better world and a new creation. For this reason, we are told as well that Jesus was of virgin birth.

Now John went on to say of those who stood upon the hill, that there was no falsehood found in them. But what are we to make of this? Surely you must realise how difficult it is to always tell the truth regardless of the circumstance. Abraham lied, Isaac lied, and so did King David. Yet none of these could be regarded as dishonest men. For falsehood wasn't found in them. They were true to God. Those who spied for Israel told lies frequently, and Rachab (the horé — or "holy woman" — in King David's royal line) lied as well, to protect the men who came to her. Having hid the spies of Israel upon the rooftop of her house, she sent the King of Jericho and his police upon a fruitless chase for them, outside the city walls. I don't believe that I have ever met a man or woman who has never told a lie, and I would be suspicious of anyone who thought he never had.

Can you imagine any soldier (or anyone for that matter) telling someone else "the truth" when human life would be endangered by his words? or a government official speaking candidly on any matter that would throw his nation into chaos internationally, yet at the same time realising that any reticence upon his part would be the same as publicly announcing it? I tend to be suspicious of all those people who are "plump and plain" and say everything they have upon their minds, regardless of the injuries they cause, because of some warped view they have of honesty. James (Jesus's own brother) tells us we should guard our tongues, and so we should.

However, the Bible makes it clear that in the normal course of life, guile and deceit are to be abhorred. Lies are demons from the dragon's mouth, and those in the government of God must keep themselves from speaking falsehood and know when not to speak. That is the principle, and those who are of Israel will practice it. They never give false witness in a court of law, although they may refuse to speak. That's their right, and that's what Jesus did.

What John primarily is referring to is the focus of these people's lives. To say no falsehood could be found in them, tells us their lives were honourable and that they did not blend the word of God (which was the foundation stone of their lives) with water from the dragon's mouth (those philosophies which were poisoning mankind). Instead they weighed whatever they were told upon the scales of God's unchanging word. They did not close their minds to truth, but always separated truth from dross. And because they knew the strategy which Christ had given them, they never lost sight of their aims.

Anyone who knows the word of God and is obedient to it stands upon Mount Zion with the lamb. (Matthew 7: 24). "For wherever the body (of Christ) is, there will the eagles (with their far-sightedness and the swiftness of their flight) be gathered." (Matthew 24: 28). For anyone who has wrestled with the beast and conquered it (Genesis 4: 7) will have the mark (of just and righteous thoughts) upon his forehead and the mark of (fair and honest dealings) upon his right hand which will identify him as a man of God, commissioned to bring God's Kingdom with all its benefits to mankind. The only question is, "Are we part of it?"

Those liberated from their slavery to the nations (from superstitions, illusions, idolatry and loyalty to anyone besides the great creator) can sing that song of freedom heaven teaches them. That freedom is the liberating gospel given to the world, and the spirit generated by the song God's people sing is the angel which proclaims it everywhere. I know that some denominations say that this angel is a special messenger of some kind sent by God to the leader of their church so that "the true gospel of Jesus Christ" can be restored. But John has shown us in this vision that any church which carries out the instructions that were given to them in Chapters Two and Three automatically has access to the throne of God. It isn't very likely then that all the offspring of Israel (Jews and Christians), who are standing as one body on the mountain of God, would look elsewhere for some new plan of action during a major battle with the world.

John tells us that this angel's message is: "Fear God and give glory to him...Worship him who made the heavens and the earth." At this point in the strategy of heaven, we are not speaking of Christianity or Judaism (or which denomination is the best). The angel which declares these things to all mankind is the spirit generated by the reunited tribes of Israel, who sing their song of freedom from the hill. And the joyous news they bring to all mankind is one that says:

"Let all the nations be gathered together, and let the people be assembled. Draw near you nations to hear, assemble yourselves and come, and harken you peoples. Cry aloud, lift up your voice like a trumpet. Let the earth hear, and the world: 'Let there be peace: Peace to him that is far off, and peace to him that is near.' Violence shall no more be heard in the land – wasting nor destruction within its borders. The land that was made desolate and the dry land shall be glad. The desert shall rejoice and blossom like a rose."

(A collage of texts from Isaiah)

Yet John (in this vision) tells us that there is another messenger from God, a messenger who warns mankind against worshipping the nations where they live, or any symbols representing them (referred to as the beast and its images). Early Christians (as history affirms) had no doubt of what that meant. In Rome, for instance, Christians who refused to reverently honour the Roman national emblems or gods of the empire incurred the wrath of Roman emperors. The Jews themselves similarly understood that national emblems were not to be served.

This was the case, in Jerusalem, when Pontius Pilate deliberately incited the anger of the Jews by bringing Roman ensigns into the city. It was the issue Jesus raised when he held a Roman coin up in the temple courtyard to enquire whose image was inscribed on it. Do you serve God or national emblems was the point at hand, and Caesar's face had no place at all (even on a coin) inside the temple of God. Of course, many Christians have conveniently misinterpreted these words.

It did not mean that you will divide your loyalties between God and Caesar. As Jesus said: "You cannot serve two masters." You serve God, not Caesar. However, you respect the nation where you live, doing whatever has been asked of you, if God approves of it, but saying no to anything that God does not permit. For the Christian is called upon to walk spiritually, at all times, in the kingdom of God on earth.

Those who chose to serve the beast of nationalism and the images that represented it, according to the texts we read, would be forced to drink from the cup of the wrath of God. For doing so they would suffer God's fury by burning in fire and brimstone. By this he meant war.

Malachi leaves no doubt of this, for he precisely says: "You shall tread down the wicked, for they shall be ashes under your feet on the day I am preparing." (Malachi 4: 3) The picture here is not of that fictitious realm we like to label "hell." It is of war with all its fiery violence. And the flames of war are never lit by God. They are ignited by men's uncontrolled passions, and these are the fruits of leading undisciplined and unruly lives — like Cain.

Those who wear the beast's mark (corrupt thoughts and perverse behaviour) John says, will drink the wine of the wrath of God. Daniel likewise warns us to beware of worshipping national emblems or images that personify the nations. As Jesus said: "You cannot serve two masters, for either you will love the one and hate the other, or else you will be loyal to the one and neglect your duties to the other. You cannot serve God and Mammon (the patriotic values and the narrow loyalties of this present world system)."

Now the wine of God's fury is warfare, ending in the destructive "fire and brimstone" of battle, or should we say today "napalm, gunpowder and the terrors of atomic weaponry." These would in time ignite the great gehenna (or lake of fire) to which the Bible texts refer. Yet how often have the Christian pulpits lauded war and called upon Christian men to serve their nations bravely, sending them to be a part of that gehenna — the great garbage dump outside Jerusalem where the bodies of all criminals were burned. This place served as a symbol for the fires of war where men would give their lives and spirits in the fiery heat of battle as they served the glory of some nation's pride. But its ultimate reward was death — eternal death.

From this gehenna, which men chose to serve, there could be no hope of resurrecting them. Completely dedicated to the way of death, they chose not to be warned, for the gods that governed them were far too dear. And so their smoke went up for ever and ever, reminding us that from age to age wars would erupt and bring destruction upon each succeeding generation. This is the end for those who place idolatry of nationalism above that of human lives and the great creation of God which they destroy.

In case we missed this point John says "There is no rest day or night for those who worship the beast and his image, or for anyone who receives the mark of his name." Valentine in Gounod's *Faust* certainly was in that crowd. Remember the Soldiers' Chorus there: "Glory and laud to the men of old. Their sons will copy their virtues bold. Conquer with trust in the sword at hand. We're ready to

fight and ready to die for Fatherland." And what are we
to make of that blasphemous hymn sung in many
Protestant churches today: "I vow to thee my country,
all earthly things above, whose love demands my loyalty,
my service and my love. The love that asks no questions,
the love that pays the price. That lays upon the altar the
final sacrifice." I wonder that it doesn't set the teeth of
every chorister on edge. How can they sing it with such
pious faces of serenity? For the final sacrifice in such a
cause is Eternal Death.

These things, says John, require patient steadfastness
on the part of all the saints who are dedicated in their
hearts to keeping God's commandments and remain
faithful to the teachings of Jesus. I wonder if the chief
commandments that he might have had in mind could
have been: "You shall have no other gods before me," and
"You shall not make unto yourself any graven images."

Next we are shown the son of man seated on a cloud
and wearing a gold crown, symbolizing mankind crowned
by Jehovah, the Ancient of Days, so that he might rule
the kingdom of God—which is not so much a nation, but
the entire world under the authority of God. The crown
that mankind wears is Jehovah's wisdom, which is more
precious than gold, and as Solomon said: "The wealth of
the wise is their crown, but the folly of fools yields folly."
(Proverbs 14: 24)

In the seventh chapter of *Daniel* in verses thirteen
and fourteen, we are shown the coronation of God's king.
Unlike the visions of the beasts preceding it (which are
archetypes of the nations of the world and the nature of
their king), Israel's king is presented as a man. That is to
say he is humane, compassionate and understanding. But
to be more accurate, the vision doesn't tell us that he is a
man. It says rather that he is "like a man," indicating he

is something more. He is the embodiment of the nation itself. He is given a diadem — the symbol of God's wisdom, so that we see he will rule the world with an understanding mind and a compassionate heart.

This is the spirit of wisdom which the children of Israel have been asked to put on. It is the same spirit which was typified for Christians in the person of Jesus Christ who served as a living example to those who studied him. Yet in John's vision, we are shown this spirit holding a sickle in his right hand, indicating that wisdom requires the followers of God to reap the harvest of the world. But the angel coming from the sanctuary of heaven cautions them that they are not to act without instruction first. As Jesus said: "The son of man will not do anything unless he sees his Father do it first. For only then will he be able to do it in the same way that the Father does." (John 5: 19)

As a son of Israel — natural or adopted — you too must follow this example of being led by Jehovah and the prophecies of those who have revealed his will. Then, the command is given to reap the harvest of the world. Would it surprise you now to learn that this command already has been heard? As Jesus said to his disciples: "Do not say, 'There are still four months before the harvest comes.' For look for yourselves and see. I tell you that the fields are already ripe and waiting to be harvested." (John 4: 35)

Ah, but there is a different kind of harvest too. Another spirit coming directly from God's sanctuary carries a sharp sickle and gives a second command to reap the earth. This is that spirit residing in the stubborn heart of those determined in their patriotic zeal to go to war. It gathers them as harvest for the sickle of battle to reap. This other angel swings his sickle over the earth and gathers harvest fruitage for the wrath of God — and blood flows for a distance of 1600 furlongs.

This number is significant, so I had better state its meaning now before we lose it in the maze of Bibles being printed with no regard at all for ancient languages. *The Living Bible* now, for instance, says for 200 miles. The *Good News Bible* does the same. And the meaning is completely gone. 1600 is the number that John gave which is the product of 4 squared by 10 squared — i.e. 4x4x10x10, meaning covering all nations in all areas of the earth. Four indicates all directions of the compass, and four squared indicates universality. And ten squared, as you know, indicates every nationality and race.

The Bible wasn't being literal in the numeral distance that it gave; it was speaking in the language of numbers. And the message it describes for us is this: All who serve the pride of nations and the vain idolatry they preach shall perish in the fiery flames of war. But all who do the will of God shall see God's whole creation flourish in its fullest splendour. This is the promised paradise.

As long as we regard the symbols in the chapters we are studying as merely pictures from a world beyond our own, we miss the urgency contained in them. That God is in our midst is the message we are asked to recognize. His sanctuary too is close at hand — not "up there" in the blue. And God's angels are continually addressing us. Where does God dwell then? is a question we must ask ourselves. Some place very close to us. His sanctuary is the human heart, and the voices from the heart which speak to us are the angels which lead us to salvation or destruction depending on the treasures stored up in the ark and the God who is enshrined upon its throne.

So from this sanctuary of the heart where our Elohim dwells emerge two angels, both requiring that the harvest which was sown in everyone be reaped. One angel represents a call to gather in all those in whom the word of God (sown by angels in Chapters Eight and Nine) took root, and now willingly respond and join the members of God's kingdom in the work of building God's new world. The second angel is the patriotic call to take up arms in a "just war" waged against an "evil empire" of some kind. These are led into the valley of decision for the glory of a nation they think worth killing for. The futility of such a war, however, is expressed by John in the words which say "and the smoke of their torment will go up for ever and ever." That is to say that warfare will continue in every age until the word of God (which speaks from God's creation) is obeyed.

I remember I once read that Xerxes (whom the Bible calls Ahasuerus) wept bitterly on one occasion, after he reviewed his troops and realised how short the glory of their lives would be, for in a few brief years not one of them would be alive. Reading that one passage made me meditate upon the transitoriness of every nation throughout history. I almost saw the faces of those men that Xerxes viewed as the individuals they once had been. They must have seemed like fine young specimens to him. But Xerxes wept to think how brief their stay on earth would be. How then can such inspiring scenes as these become unreal to us? Surely we must see the whole grand movement of the past parade like troops before our eyes. As all of us review the past and those inspiring worlds which once had been (Nineveh, Thebes, Troy, Carthage, Tyre, Athens, Rome, London, Paris, Washington) in all their pomp and splendour, are we not moved by what we see? Do you not feel inclined as Xerxes did to weep for them?

CHAPTER FIFTEEN

The Two Baptisms

I noticed then another extraordinary sign appear in heaven that was awesome and remarkable. I saw seven messengers of God, who had seven last catastrophes to bring upon the world—last in the sense that after them God's anger would be satisfied.

Shortly after seeing this, I noticed next what seemed to be a sea of glass mingled with fire. Standing beside it were all those who had proven to be victorious over the beast, his image, and the number of his name. (That is to say that they had been triumphant over the spellbinding power of the social environment, national idolatry and all social customs and illusions which enslave the human heart and mind). God gave them harps (so that they could celebrate their victory by joyously singing triumphant songs). Then they all began to sing the song of Moses (who had freed them physically) and the lamb (who had set their minds and spirits free):

"Astounding and magnificent are all your works, O Jehovah, Creator of all things. Generous and trustworthy are your ways, Supreme Ruler of the world. Why would anyone not want to turn to you respectfully and glorify your name, O Jehovah ("Who Causes to Be")? For you alone are reliable and cannot be corrupted. Surely every nation in the world should want to honour you and speak respectfully of your name, for the perfect rightness of your ways has been revealed."

After I had heard this song, I looked and saw that the sanctuary of the covenant had been opened. Then the seven messengers of God (the spirit of the seven earthly congregations) carrying seven great catastrophes came from God's sanctuary dressed in clean and dazzling linen (of God's righteousness). These spirits (of the congregations) wore golden sashes (of uncorrupted judgment) around their chests (revealing that their hearts had been refashioned by the power of God). Then one of the four living creatures handed each of the seven messengers a container filled with the wrath of the Creator who lives for ever and ever.

The sanctuary, then, was filled with the smoke (of awe-inspiring power) emanating from the great magnificence of the Creator's presence, so that no one could enter the sanctuary until the seven last catastrophes, which the seven messengers of God were carrying, were brought about on earth.

*

In Chapter Four of this book, when John entered heaven, it was to define the goals to be achieved on earth through looking on the organizational design of godly government. Here the purpose is to show God's workmen the means that they must use for accomplishing their ends. These seven messengers (or angels) represent the seven spirits governing the various communities of saints, located in all cities of the world. They are indeed the angels of the seven church communities whom we first met in Chapter Two of this book, but the congregation that they represent is the entire body of God's people — united Israel. The Christian church and Jewish synagogue have played their roles. Because God's greater glory is revealed in them, we are told that heaven's sanctuary was opened. In this sanctuary stood the Ark of God.

In Chapter Eleven, you remember, we were shown this symbol of God's presence with his people after the seventh angel sounded God's warning trumpet to the world. Now the open sanctuary in this present chapter is shown to indicate that God is with his people still. And because he is with them, they are unified. God is one, and his people are one. Jehovah unifies, and he unifies his people through the open sanctuary and the Ark of God. So it is essential that we take time to consider the reason it was built the way it was.

Being shown the Ark signified much more than a revelation of intent. God's people would have recognized it as a strong command from God requiring self-examination on their part, as the Ark of God had been designed to represent the human heart as God had fashioned it. The natural inclinations of the heart were to be overlaid with God's pure golden wisdom. Then inside it would be placed the perfect knowledge of God's law of liberty (the ten commandments), and the daily food of life (or manna) which Jesus told us was the doing of God's will on earth.

To anyone with such a heart, God gives the budding rod of spiritual authority. This ensures a perfect unity with Israel and bestows upon the individual possessing it the ability and the right to speak for God and act on his behalf. This is the power the ancient prophets had. The burning coal of God's pure word having touched their lips, God has commissioned them to do his will on earth —not their own.

It is with a heart like this that these messengers are sent by God to carry out his will on earth. The open sanctuary clearly indicates that God is present in the lives of all whose hearts have been molded by God and filled with the law and living wisdom of his word. Then united by the guiding spirit of God's congregation of believers, they are commissioned as one body to reveal the great catastrophes that human ignorance is bringing on the world.

No, there is no commissioning of terrorists. Yet God acknowledges the role he plays in all facets of real life. His message to the world (though urgent) remains unchanged: mercy to the meek who hear his voice and turn to him; and the burning fires of war awaiting those who stubbornly oppose his will. What has changed now is the tone these words take on. New conditions in the world require a different emphasis. Jesus had foreseen a time when his gospel having thoroughly been preached to all mankind would have divided them into two distinctive camps: those who followed him from those who still were rigorously opposed.

It is true, therefore, to say that the world—by this time—would have heard God's gospel preached. Also (if this strategy has been followed faithfully and used the way that Jesus ordered it) the nations of the world would have heard the trumpet prophecies which warned them and alerted them to the advancing "armies" of "the LORD", and they would know what the consequences which their disobedience would bring. They would have seen the evidence of their own destructiveness. So nothing remained for the sons of Israel but to condemn the nations for their willful crimes against creation. However, in condemning them, the hope remained that many still might turn from wanton disobedience to God and put an end to their destructiveness.

For this reason God's faithful workmen have been shown the method and the plan of action they are called upon to use in this final onslaught with the world. God's purpose is unchanged: it is to save the world. But these seven angel messengers (who represent the spirit of his seven earthly congregations) have been commissioned now to carry vessels which contain the seven last catastrophes about to fall upon the social orders of mankind. Those "with eyes to see" should realise what this revelation means. For it is not a call to violence. These containers which God's angels carry hold nothing other than the word of God itself. This is preached or "poured out on the world" as warnings, in order to reveal the great catastrophes which world governments are bringing on themselves and all who follow them. God's word remains the same. It is the way that it is spoken and applied which matters in this last stage of God's strategy.

There seems, however, at the present time to be a popularly held view amongst a few small groups of Christians that God calls upon his people to mindlessly condemn the world. Jesus Christ said otherwise. He said to Nicodemus: "God never sent his son into the world in order to condemn the world; he sent him rather that he might through his work preserve the world."
(John 3: 17)

The purpose therefore of this last campaign is to reveal a strategy which will effectively condemn the selfish and uncaring attitudes so prevalent amongst the nations of mankind and which are leading them toward an ultimate destruction of humanity and that creation which God made. God therefore shows a diagnostic remedy to turn the world away from following the dangerous course that it pursues and which is leading it toward a fiery death (in war). It is no mindless idle babbling that they are called upon to do. They are called on to intelligently persuade humanity to turn from all the selfish and self-destructive paths that it pursues.

God's people are said to be a priesthood dedicated to the preservation of the world, and they are called upon to play no favourites amongst the nations of the world. Their duty only is to God. They are in the wrong camp if they are promoting national ambitions or wars among the nations of the world. Their duty is to discourage these. The war they are engaged in is entirely spiritual. It is a war fought only with words and arguments in order to set the whole of God's creation free from those abusing it.

Since this campaign would be the very last campaign in the Messiah's strategy, it had to be well planned and carefully organized. Its course would have to be meticulously laid out, and in the chapters following we see just how thorough it would have to be. We shouldn't be surprised then to discover just how well defined it is in these decisive images preceding the initial actions of the chapter following.

God relies therefore upon a visual experience, serving as a blueprint for the work he asks his workmen to construct for him. He does this so that there will be no doubt amongst those serving him regarding all that he has called on them to do. It is for this reason they are shown a sea of glass mingled with fire. Those who stand beside it are those whom God will call out of the world. They are those who hear his voice and immediately respond to it.

John tells us these have overcome "the beast, his image and the number of his name". These are not mere words. Rather this symbolic imagery alludes to those powerful forces in the world which govern people spiritually. Although unseen, these forces nonetheless are real, and must be reckoned with. The purpose of these images (in the vision John creates) is to clarify these powers. Through giving us a visual experience of them, it had been hoped that his readers might better understand the nature of the war we wage against the unseen powers which rule the world. The "beast" refers to that great influence the social order wields in creating atmospheres affecting the thoughts of the populace both as masses and as individuals.

The "image of the beast" is apt because it was the practice of so many ancient peoples to make images of those tremendous powers which guided them. These powers, in ancient times, were seen as spirits of the nations that were served. Every nation's citizens openly did obeisance to them and worshipped them as gods, obeying all of their commands — with the priesthood and the government interpreting their will. In John's vision "the image of the beast" alludes to any image or symbols which helps a nation to depict the powers the people serve and to enforce the nation's right to make demands upon the consciences of men and command their loyalty. The image of the beast commanded service to the spirit of the nation. If rulers of the nations therefore called for any action not approved by the God who made the world, the prophets of the Bible made it clear that they were not to be obeyed. "My country right or wrong," is not an attitude which God commends in any of his followers.

The "number of his name" hits at the very heart of human frailty. By naming this as something to be overcome, God calls all individuals to personal account and reminds them of their own responsibility. They cannot simply point their fingers at their governments and say, "I was only following the orders that were given me." or "It would have been illegal for me to have disobeyed." Responsibility to God takes precedence.

The number of the beast indicates the unschooled nature of the individual himself, not educated in the way of God. The number six alludes to any individual who surrenders easily to human appetite and to the voice of social attitudes. "Judge for yourselves," Peter and John both told the powers of controlling human government, "whether it is right for us to obey you rather than God." (Acts 4: 19) You will recall how Esau (Jacob's twin brother) sold his birthright for a bowl of stew. He had no sense at all of value. His feelings governed him.

These are the things then that all those serving God must overcome: (1) the spiritual power of the social order, (2) patriotic idolatry and zeal, and (3) cravings of the human heart.

We are shown the scene of those who stand beside the sea of glass and fire to illustrate (as memorably as possible) the victories that shall be won by God in these campaigns. There will be those who turn to God. Repentance and baptism into new life will certainly reward the efforts that the sons of Israel shall make. Many shall be pulled out of the fire. Yet the final wrath remains for those who mindlessly pursue unrighteousness. That is why this picture makes allusion to the two baptisms prophesied before the first appearance Jesus made in the land of Israel.

Many scholars, in considering this image John has shown to us, are reminded of the priestly bath in Solomon's Temple found in 1 Kings 7: 23. But the idea of the coming wrath is more suggestive of John the Baptist in the spirit of Elijah standing in the greater Temple of God, beside the Jordan River, ready to baptize repentant sinners. For in this context, his words are most significant: "He that comes after me is mightier than I. He shall baptize you with the holy spirit and with fire."

The sea of glass illustrates the new life, without deception, guile or competitive frustration, into which God's people are baptized. The fire is for the disobedient. For there are two baptisms, defined by John the Baptist himself: "He will thoroughly purge his floor, and gather the wheat into the garner. But the chaff he will burn up with unquenchable fire." God's words give comfort to all who turn to him in trust. But the same words prove to be a fire for those who are opposed to them. For there are basic laws governing creation, which, if we do not obey, bring destruction down on us. Everybody has a choice as to the course he takes.

It is no accident that in the preceding chapter of this book, the writer John by allusion reminded us of Jesus's own words, that he could do nothing unless he saw the Father do it first. For such an allusion refreshes in the minds of all his followers, that they as well must take their lead from what the heaven ruling over them makes clear. Yet those instructions heaven gave its sons are carefully defined for them in the written word of God. "Thy will be done on earth as it is in heaven" was an essential part of that prayer pattern Jesus taught his followers. Then, when he gave them the keys to the Kingdom of God on earth, he instructed them to carefully observe this principle: "Whatever you shall see bound in heaven you shall bind on earth, and whatever you shall see loosed in heaven you shall loose on earth."

We know then, that as God's own messengers, we are asked to carry out the plan that John wrote out for us. Although the words were sealed, and made secret, they were not made secret to the followers of God. So heaven — in this vision — shows its own approval of the plan, and gives commands that must be followed when the time is ripe for them.

All who serve Jehovah upon earth will certainly rejoice at seeing anyone delivered from the strong enslaving powers of the social environment (which is the beast), from patriotic jingoism of all kinds — including national regalia (which is the image of the beast), and from all human frailties (which is the number of its name). The song of Moses is as valid now as it ever was at first. So is the song of Christ (the Passover Lamb).

I expect by now, you will have seen from studying this plan that it is based entirely upon God's power to unify. First the individual finds unity with God by imbibing the character of the man designed in heaven. Next the church community is unified by measuring itself beside the perfect word of God. After this the various communities are linked, and finally the whole community of saints — Jew and Christian. The plan also makes it clear that the Jews are not "converted" to "Christianity". Like the Christian, they are simply brought into harmony with God. It is God alone who gives them unity.

In contrast to the way of God, Adam's world displays a tendency to separate and be continually at odds. This disease is best described as "every man doing what seems right in his own eyes". "If it feels good, do it," is a saying many speciously promote. When we tell them anything is wrong, the question always is, "In whose opinion?" If you tell them God who made all things decided it, they will simply say, "There is no God," or "Who made God our judge?" "Everything is relative," they claim. The world therefore is radically divided between nations, races, provinces, cities, cultures, religions, schools, families, sexes, and individuals. And all of these are constantly at war.

Love perishes. People only love themselves. What is needed is a source of unity — "a marriage feast." The God of Israel, so Jews and Christians both believe, can heal that separationist desire which, like a great disease or plague gone wild, afflicts humanity. Whereas the world of Satan preaches competition and independence, God's world teaches co-operation and responsibility to God, to creation and to mankind. No man is an island unto himself," as the English poet John Donne said.

Time, therefore, is required in order to appraise the tasks which Christ has called on all his followers to carry out for him. To illustrate the need of this appraisal, the gospel writer Luke once wrote: "Consider this, when someone is about to build a tower, does he not first sit down and estimate the cost, to determine if he has the wherewithal for building it. Otherwise, when he has put the first foundation down, and then discovers that he cannot finish the tower, he will be ridiculed by everyone observing him who'll say: 'This fellow set out upon a task to build something too impossible for him, and could not finish what he said he'd do.'"   (Luke 14: 28-30)

So before endeavouring upon the work which Christ so carefully laid out, everyone must take the necessary time to see if he can do what God has called on him to do. Then, and only then, when that follower can honestly respond, in singing what is written in the song that heaven sings, can he possibly continue with the strategy laid out for him. For this is that moment which the gospel message has described, when Jesus warned his followers about the consequences of being his disciples.

"Anyone who wants to be my follower," he said, "must be committed totally and ready to abandon (everything he has including) his own life, and face the possibility of execution by the state. Those who (turn aside from this to) save their lives shall actually have lost them, but whoever willingly shall lose his life on my behalf shall truly find his life."   (Matthew 16: 24-25)

Heaven's song can only be appreciated by those who have experienced the liberating power that total obedience to God's word gives. It is a song of joyful, heartfelt exuberance of being totally set free. It rises from the realisation of the truth contained in it. To sing it superficially is not to know the song. Only those who have struggled with the three great spiritual powers that rule the world and overcome the beast that lives in them can truly know the meaning of that song. Only those whose minds and hearts have been set free can sing creation's song. Those who sing it know true liberty.

John tells us that they sang: "Amazing and astounding are your deeds, Jehovah, Creator of all things. All your ways are fair and reliable...." Such singing only can have meaning when those who join in singing such a song sing it from a genuine conviction born of real experience. So everyone must ask himself if he believes the plan which John presents is workable, logical and just? Only then will the song of heaven well up in his soul, and only then can he pursue the plan as someone who has properly prepared himself.

Heaven's vision unmistakably reveals that those standing upon earth beside the sea of glass are citizens of heaven, for they walk in all the ways of God. As such, they are given harps to symbolize the joyful celebration of their liberty, for harps were never played by people in captivity. In captivity, they hung their harps upon the branches of the willow trees. Taking down these harps symbolizes then, that they have been set free and so rejoice by singing the song of Moses in celebration of the freedom that the law of liberty had given them. Through that law and by "the Divine Vision" of the holy spirit of God, they overcome the spiritual Pharaoh of this world and his armies – the demon Satan and his minions whose influence is felt throughout the earth.

They also sang the song of the lamb, for the prophet greater than Moses made the Gentiles part of that same liberty which Israel enjoyed. They as well will share in all the promises which God once made to Abraham. What Israel has done, the Gentiles of the world can do as well. God gives liberty to all who follow him.

Isaiah told us how the nations would one day go to Israel to learn the law from them: "This is what Isaiah the son of Amoz saw in store for Judah and Jerusalem. In the end this is what will happen: The mountain (or Kingdom) of Jehovah's house (those people in his family) will become the most prominent (and esteemed) mountain (or Kingdom) in the world and will tower over all the hills (the prominent nations of the world), for all the nations will one day turn to it. And many people anxious to visit it will say, 'Come, and let us go to Jehovah's mountain (Israel) to the house (or people, who form the spiritual temple) of the God of Jacob; and he (God who speaks through his holy people) will teach us his ways, and we will walk in his paths.' For instruction (torah) shall come from Zion and the word of God from Jerusalem." (Isaiah 2: 1-3)

Yes, he said torah, the law, which wasn't done away. This was a vision of the final days before the nations fell. Zechariah speaking plainly revealed the words of Jehovah himself who said: "In those days ten men of all languages (symbolic of all languages on earth) will take firm hold of a Jew (Yes, he said a Jew) by the edges of his robe and say, 'Let us go with you, because we have heard that God is with you.'" (Zechariah 8: 33)

Then John saw that the Temple sanctuary had been opened. That is to say the full glory of God was opened to the world. And out of the sanctuary came seven angels with seven last catastrophes (or curses for mankind). What! you say, God's words curse? The answer is, Of course! They curse all those who curse themselves. As

Moses revealed: "Today I set before you blessing and cursing — blessing if you obey the commands of Jehovah your creator that I am giving you this day; and cursing if you disobey the commands of Jehovah your Creator and turn away from following what I have commanded you, to follow inclinations of your own imagining." (Deuteronomy 11: 26-28) What could be more fair, or plain. "Caution," says the sign upon the fence, "Dangerous voltage within." So you ignore the warning and go in anyway.

Great attention has been paid to the way the messengers of God have been dressed (as priests in dazzling white linen robes tied with a golden sash) for this is to show us they are dressed in the righteousness of God and girded with sound judgment or trustworthiness, which immediately recalls Jesus's command to his followers: "Be dressed and ready for service and keep your lamps burning, like men waiting for their master to return from a wedding banquet, so that when he comes and knocks, they immediately open the door for him. It will be good for those servants whose master finds them watching when he comes. I tell you the truth he will dress himself to serve, will have them recline at the table and will come and wait on them. It will be good for those servants whose master finds them ready, even if he comes in the second or third watch of the night."
(Luke 12: 35-38)

Beware of being literal with words like these, for Jesus showed his meaning in many other ways throughout his ministry. Yet he says that he will wait upon his followers, playing the servant to them. That immediately recalls for us, the memory of Jesus dressed in a towel as he washed his own disciples' feet. Spiritually, however, he was dressed in linen, and tied about the waist with a golden sash. How then can we exalt ourselves above our brethren.

This attention to the way we dress is stressed in the law where it says: "Then Moses brought Aaron and his sons forward and washed them with water. He put the tunic on Aaron, tied the sash around him, clothed him with the robe and put the ephod on him. He also tied the ephod to him by its skillfully woven waistband; so it was fastened on...."   (Leviticus 8: 6-7)

This shows us, then, that we are not ready to begin the tasks which Jesus has assigned to us until we have taken care of the spiritual manner in which we are dressed. We have fought the devil in the wilderness and driven him completely from the heaven of our lives.

After one of the living creatures gave seven golden vessels filled with God's anger to the seven angels to pour upon the world, the sanctuary was filled with smoke so that no one could enter until the catastrophes were poured upon the world. This reminds us of the words of the psalmist: "Jehovah is in his holy temple; Jehovah is on his heavenly throne. He observes the sons of men; his eyes examine them. Jehovah examines the righteous, but the wicked and those who love violence his soul hates. On the wicked he will rain fiery coals and burning sulfur (i.e. warfare); a scorching wind (a social attitude of violence) will be their lot."   (Psalm 11: 4-6)

Yet what terrible catastrophes were in these vessels? Why the full strength of God's word. Have the Jews and Christians forgotten what their calling was? It was to pour God's word upon the world and bring men out of slavery. This would overturn the armies of Pharaoh (or Satan) who would pursue them even through the waters of baptism separating them. Yet real catastrophes would overtake all those opposed to the people of God.

The same word of God spoken by Moses — which brought blessings upon Israel — brought cursing upon all those men opposed to it. The waters (symbolic of God's word) brought Israel out of slavery, but utterly destroyed Pharaoh and his armies who came in hot pursuit of them. The godless world doesn't give up easily.

When the word of God is spoken and obeyed, blessings follow afterwards. Yet when the word of God is spoken and opposed, it brings down curses upon all of those who are adamant and stubborn in resisting it.

CHAPTER SIXTEEN

Rewarding the Wicked

I heard a loud voice from the sanctuary of God's temple then, issuing a strong command, "Go and take the seven vessels containing God's wrath and empty them upon the earth." (For God's anger is the word of God itself. Those words which bless the righteous, also curse the wicked.) Directly after that command, God's first messenger went out and poured the contents of his vessel on the land (symbolic of mankind who as individuals are held responsible before God for their traits of character), and painful sores erupted upon everyone who had the mark of the beast on him and who worshipped the beast and his image. (For the word of God revealed the spiritual uncleanness that befouled their characters.)

When that was done, the second messenger of God emptied all the contents of his container on the sea (the community of competitive and turbulent mankind) and it turned to blood like that of a dead man (as God's word revealed that it was spiritually filled with murderers), and every living thing in the sea died (since the whole world community was full of competition, ruthlessness, violence, crime, murder and war).

After the third messenger finished emptying his container on the rivers and springs of water (or those entertainments, philosophies and values to which the civilized world all turn, to look for guidance and refreshment). These waters turned to blood as well (indicating that the cultural activities which refresh the world are actually the cause of all their social ills. The community was poisoned by these waters for they ultimately led to social sicknesses and death. "For there is a way that seems right to a man but the end of it is death." Murder, warfare and social violence therefore are identified in John's vision as being the product of all those easy codes of wisdom depicted and promoted in the world's media).

Afterwards I heard the messenger in charge of all the waters say: "Oh Holy One of Israel, who is and was, your judgments are entirely just and fair, for you have recompensed them for their deeds. Having shed the blood of saints and prophets, now they are given blood to drink as they deserve." (The war, violence, mayhem and crime of society are all the result of what society — left to its own devices — brings upon itself.)

Next the fourth messenger poured the contents of his vessel (which held the word of God in it) upon the sun, (the mainspring of human government, which was Caesar in the time of John). The sun (Ré or Roi) was seen to scorch the people with its fire. (For worldly governments, which are the sun around which all the people move, are harsher than the rule of God: "For my yoke is easy and my burden is light.") But those men burned by its heat cursed the name of God who (they believed) had placed the curse on them. They (stopped their ears and) gnashed their teeth, refusing to repent of anything they'd done. (Yet their anguish was of their own making.)

Then God's fifth messenger poured the contents of his vessel on the throne of the beast. (Satan's throne, the power behind the king, is the unseen ruler of the world). His whole kingdom (which occupies the whole earth) was plunged into darkness. So men, in torment, gnawed their tongues in pain, and blamed God, cursing him, for all their suffering and the painful sores (from those diseases) that afflicted them. Even so, they still refused to change their evil ways.

Jehovah's sixth messenger, emptying his container on the great Euphrates River (the defense system of Babylon), caused its water to dry up, clearing the way for the invasion by the (armies of the) eastern Kings (who could offer physical deliverance to them). Then I noticed three loathsome spirits having the appearance of frogs (lying prophecies from unclean lips) leap from the mouths of the dragon, the beast and the false prophet. These deceiving demons (notice that lies and false reports as well as deceiving prophecies are spoken of as demons) were able to achieve impressive results (literally 'miracles'), and these lies brought leaders into conferences over the whole world, and gathered them for battle on the great day of Almighty God. (Prior to and during wars of every sort, propaganda departments in the nations of the world deliberately inflame the populace with distortions of the truth so that patriotic feelings are aroused. John depicts such lies as frogs emerging from the mouths of all the beasts involved.)

"Stay alert, therefore, and don't be caught off guard. For I (this judgment that I bring upon the world) will come upon you unexpectedly, like a thief. Be careful, then, and guard your clothes (your ability to judge wisely with right judgment) so that you will not be caught naked and disgrace yourselves." For the rulers of this world shall all be gathered to (Mount Megiddo) a place called Armageddon in the Hebrew tongue.

When the seventh messenger had emptied his container into the air (the social atmosphere we breathe and absorb, and which invisibly affects our reasoning, our thoughts and judgments) a mighty voice came out of the sanctuary of heaven from the very throne of God, saying: "It is finished (for all things now have been attended to)."

Following this, there were flashes of lightning, rumblings, peals of thunder and a devastating earthquake of unprecedented magnitude. There never had been one like it since man first came into the world. The great city (of Babylon) was split into three parts, and cities everywhere in all nations were destroyed. Nor did God forget (the sins of) Babylon the Great. He handed her a cup which he had filled up to the brim with the fury of his great consuming rage and put it in her hands to drink. Then all islands (or smaller nations of the world) vanished, and the mountains (greater nations) disappeared. Hailstones (hard judgment in accordance with God's word) of tremendous size (a talent each in weight, i.e. 23 pounds) fell upon the people from the sky, making them curse God for the tremendous suffering that this great disaster brought on them because it was so terrible.

*

"Whatever you shall see bound in heaven you shall bind on earth, and whatever you shall see loosed in heaven you shall loose on earth," were the instructions which Jesus gave to those who sought to do his will. So even though we are shown a highly complex vision reduced to simple terms, such simplifying is essential as this field plan Christ has given us contains implied commands to be obeyed by all those serving in the army God has built. While other scriptures may fill out the deeper meanings that this vision has, God's warriors must be made to understand the outline of the plan which God proposed for them.

This is the last campaign God's warriors will wage against the world. If we read this chapter then, and understand what has been said in it, we will have little difficulty with the greater details given of it in the later chapters we are shown. God does not confuse us with the greater details first.

The angels we are shown (or messengers) are the spirits governing the communities of God on earth. For each of God's communities, being one body now, must move and act responsibly in concert with itself. It must plan its moves against an enemy it has been trained to recognize. There are seven angels having seven plagues, or catastrophes, to pour out on the world. But God does not commission terrorists. We know this from what Jacob said of his two sons Simeon and Levi. Such actions as theirs were to be deplored.

What then do these angels do? Quite simply, they pour out — or spread — God's word throughout the world in such a way as to reveal the end that shall befall it because of disobedience. And everything these messengers will say shall be brought about, not by what the messengers of God themselves shall do, but because world nations, bent upon destruction, shall bring catastrophes upon themselves.

In rebuking Judah another Jewish prophet, Isaiah, told of how Jehovah singled out the different segments of society for special condemnation before he let God's final fury fall on them. Moses, even earlier, when he confronted Pharaoh, humbled Egypt through a series of ten stunning catastrophes brought down upon the different gods in which the people, communities and rulers had put their trust. John's account is similar to both of these, for he divides the social structure of the world into those chief powers ruling and supporting the society which Adam, through free choice, made for man. After this he shows the messengers of God pouring catastrophic judgments down on them.

These chief powers expressed in symbols are (1) the earth, (2) the sea, (3) the rivers and springs of water, (4) the sun, (5) the throne of the beast, (6) the

Euphrates River, and (7) the air. These highly meaningful symbols, as you by now must realise, represent: (1) the individual people upon earth, (2) the fierce and competitive practices of the communities, (3) the teachings of the world, as they are found in recreational and cultural pursuits, (4) mankind's executive and sovereign government, (5) whatever body of individuals possesses the power to spiritually manipulate the people and politically instruct the government in ways inimical to nature and mankind, (6) national defence and (7) the social atmosphere.

All these areas of human life fall under the attack of God, who through his messengers delivers what becomes a curse to those receiving it – which is to say the word of God, that makes known the consequence of disobedience. For God has delegated his authority to those who know his word and are willingly obedient to him. Because they see the need for it, they are responsible for serving notice on those sections of society which John has named. These angels are the citizens of Israel, who daily feed upon God's word and readily obey his voice. They are not professional clergy, and they are not paid a salary for the work they do. They are workmen working directly under God's direction, and their rewards are spiritual.

The spreading of God's word, in times like those that John describes for us, will not be easy, for men and women of the world will surely say to them, "We have our own 'religion' now ('a form of godliness')." So the messengers of God (as Jesus said) "will be handed over to the local councils. They shall be flogged in their congregations (perhaps verbally abused and ostracized). On my account they will stand before administrators and rulers to present my case to them. In one way or another the gospel must be made known and spread throughout all the nations of the world." (Mark 13: 9 -10)

For it is the so-called 'layman' whom God calls — the rank and file Christian, because he has made "anyone who hears my word" individually responsible to him. To these he says: "When I tell the wicked man, 'You will surely die,' and you do not speak out to warn him or to dissuade him from his evil course he takes, in order to preserve his life, that wicked man will die for his sin as I have said, but I will hold you responsible for his blood."
(Ezekiel 3: 18)

With profound economy of words, John is able to convey the nature of these attacks upon the various sections of society, because, through allusion, he is able to refer to a great body of scripture, that he assumes his readers know. Those who aren't aware of them haven't pondered on the word of God sufficiently, and still are in the camp of those to whom God sends his messengers.

There is a wonderful consistency in scripture. There is no other library of literature on earth (ancient or modern) which agrees so perfectly with itself in all respects. What makes this so especially remarkable is the great time lapses which separate the writing of so many of these documents. We are not just speaking of a few decades or centuries. We are talking of millenia. I am particularly amazed at how precisely and how perfectly all these writings harmonize with one another so as to clarify and enhance meanings in preceding and succeeding Bible books.

It is the tendency of literature in other cultures to reject and change its philosophies as time progresses, and to build new ones, even to follow different aims. The Bible by contrast builds upon and clarifies a consistent idea, which blossoms in a constructive plan that the reader is invited to take part in. The scriptures are living scriptures in the sense that the reader's life becomes a part of them.

Through a chain of references, echoes and allusions, we receive a perfect vision of that world which God desires to build on earth. The scriptures are unique in this regard. They also leave no doubt as to how that vision is to be achieved. The Bible places in our hands the means for working toward that world which prophecy reveals. At this point, we have reached the last campaign. This is illustrated here, by John, as seven fierce attacks God's people make upon the different segments of the social order making up a world which is aggressively opposed to its being built, and which will frustrate that purpose any way they can, even making it seem trivial.

The first of these attacks is directed at the individual. The word of God condemns the populace for their spiritual sicknesses. Spiritually they are covered with sores and diseases of all kinds. John's description of their state of health calls to mind Isaiah's words: "Your whole head is injured and you suffer inner agony? From the bottom of your foot to the top of your head there is no healthy spot anywhere in you. You are covered with wounds, welts and open sores, and they haven't been cleaned, bandaged or soothed with healing ointments."
(Isaiah 1: 5 - 6)

So the Jewish prophet offers this advice to those that he addresses, saying: "Wash and make yourselves clean, and put away the evil of your ways. Stop practicing evil, and learn to do right. Ensure justice, give help to the oppressed, defend the fatherless and speak on behalf of widows (women who are disadvantaged by the

world). 'Come and make matters right between us,'
Jehovah says. Even if the stain of your sins is like scarlet,
they can be made white as snow, and if they are as red as
dyed crimson cloth, they can be made like pure wool. If
you are ready to obey me, you will enjoy the produce of
your land: but if you refuse and defy me, you shall all
perish by the sword (that is be slaughtered in war). For
the mouth of Jehovah has spoken."   (Isaiah 1: 16-20)

In a letter that Paul, the apostle of the resurrected
Jesus, wrote to Timothy we find a great deal that is said
about spiritual uncleanness: "People will be lovers of
themselves, lovers of money, boastful, proud, abusive,
disobedient to parents, ungrateful, unholy, without love,
unforgiving, slanderous, without self-control, brutal, not
lovers of the good, treacherous, rash, conceited, lovers of
pleasure rather than lovers of God—having a form of
godliness but denying God's power."   (2 Timothy 3: 1-5)

Yet Moses, much earlier, made the connection
between moral uncleanness and physical diseases.
Although many diseases spring from social causes (as
Moses also said) many of them come from what individuals themselves do. According to Moses the Egyptians
suffered from the diseases they did because their way of
living was morally unsound. In *The Book of Exodus*
Chapter 15, for instance, we read: "If you listen carefully
to the voice of Jehovah your Creator and do what is right
in his eyes, if you obey his commandments and do
everything I ask of you, I will not bring upon you any of
the diseases I brought upon the Egyptians, for I am
Jehovah who heals you."   (Exodus 15: 26)

This makes Egyptian history worth examining, as
the Egyptian in ancient times enjoyed a high reputation
in medicine. Medical papyri from the Middle and New
Kingdoms reveal for us a large body of information

concerning their medical practices, including the surgical treatment of wounds and fractures and prescriptions for various ailments. Also from studying their mummies, we know a great deal about the sicknesses they suffered from as well.

Some of the diseases which afflicted them included leprosy, dysentry, gout, arthritis, diabetes, diseases of the teeth and jaws, elephantiasis, smallpox, conjunctivitis, afflictions of the stomach and liver, deafness and bubonic plague. The Egyptians worked hard at trying to combat all of them, and as a result the Egyptians had specialists in many different fields of medicine. The words of the Greek historian Herodotus are extremely helpful to us in this regard. For he says, "The country (Egypt) is full of physicians; one treats only the diseases of the eye; another those of the head, the teeth, the abdomen, or the internal organs."

Modern medicine, however, does consider the Egyptian remedies for these diseases quite elementary at best and in many cases superstitious quackery. Yet even though no one would seriously challenge the superiority of modern medicine over that of ancient times, one medical researcher, Mary Dobson, does raise an interesting question regarding our advances in the modern world: "What, then, can be learned from a study of diseases of past ages?" she asks, and then goes on to say, "The general conclusion from a survey of the evidence seems to be that the diseases and afflictions of the remote past do not differ remarkably from those of the present....Apparently all the skills and efforts of patient research have done little to eradicate disease."

(Diseases in Ancient Man)

It is also evident that the people of Israel must, due to their superior hygienic practices described in the

Mosaic Law, have certainly escaped from many such ailments as beset the Egyptians. Their recommended low-fat diets and physically active lifestyles would have kept them free from heart ailments, and their strict moral code would have freed them from venereal diseases too. Nor should we forget that the modern practice of quarantine was learned from them — even to its name which stood for 40 days of isolation.

Yet there is a basic weakness in all individuals who lean upon others for support. *The Book of Judges* refers to this in these words about ancient Israel: "Whenever Jehovah raised up a judge for them, he was with the judge who rescued the people from the hands of their enemies as long as the judge lived; for Jehovah had compassion on them as they groaned under those who oppressed them and afflicted them. But as soon as the judge died, the people immediately returned to ways that were even more corrupt than those of their ancestors, following other gods and serving and worshipping them. For they stubbornly refused to give up their evil practices and perverse ways." (Judges 2: 18-19)

The Book of Revelation has depicted the wrath of God and the spiritual afflictions, brought upon the world of Adam, in physical terms so that we might understand our spiritual follies concretely as something to be pictured visually, and to help us realise as well that there is a physical consequence for our spiritual shortcomings. It also helps us to remember the role that Moses played in delivering Israel from Pharaoh, and to draw a parallel to what Moses did centuries ago, with what Jesus Christ can do today through his commissioned officers — the common sons of Israel: "Take handfuls of soot from a furnace and have Moses toss it in to the air in the presence of Pharaoh. It will become dust over the whole land of Egypt, and festering boils will break out on men and animals throughout the land." (Exodus 9: 8-9)

Just so, the word of God when poured out on men and women of the world, will show their spiritual uncleanliness. This can lead to deliverance from death, while disobedience leads to a final reckoning. We always reap the fruit of what we sow.

It is the turbulent sea of collective mankind that we look at next. That is to say, it is society's way of living. God asks us to consider carefully what is sometimes called our way of life, or the way of the world. This is the congregation of the unrighteous. It is the frenzied, ruthless, social practices that makes mankind a turbulent sea that never is at rest. John, again, in one definitive sentence lays bare the whole condition of society. It is this that the word of God is poured upon.

This sea which we are told was turned to blood, John reveals as a world of violence, causing every living creature in the sea to die. Not only are the people in the sea spiritually dead, but the wicked practices of men and women inhabiting it are revealed as murderers — envying each other, and despising one another without cause. It is a world of fierce competition and rivalry. This killing way of doing things is of very ancient origin. Yet surprisingly, it still survives.

God's curse first fell on it when Man — or Adam — chose the spiritual path on which to build his world. This is the curse the Bible tells us fell on him: "Because you chose to listen to your wife (the community) and to eat from the tree (the social practices) that I instructed you not to eat from, the earth shall now be cursed (because of what you do) and you will now work very hard to earn your food, and you will have to struggle all your life just to make a livelihood. The whole land will only produce thorns now (injustices and injurious practices) and weeds (things that do not turn out the way you

planned), and you shall eat (but meagerly) the herb of
the field. Until your dying days, you will sweat to earn
your food, and at the last you will die and turn to dust.
Because you have been made out of the dust, you shall
return to dust once more." (Genesis 3: 17-19)

The kind of fruit that Adam chose to eat is illustrated
in this passage that we find in Isaiah: "Jehovah looked
for (the fruit of) justice, but they yielded only oppression
and bloodshed; and he looked for (the fruit of) righteousness but only found the cries of sorrow and distress
(from the poor and humble of the earth)." (Isaiah 5: 7)

And the role that the community played, in leading
Israel to eat of it, is illustrated in these words by the
same writer: "The city that was once my faithful bride
has become a whore! It was once full of just men, and
caring righteous people lived in it; but it is now inhabited
by murderers. Your money has become worthless, and
even your beer has been watered down. Your leaders are
perverse and like common thieves, they take bribes and
chase after rewards: They offer no protection to the
fatherless, and the widow's case is never brought before
them to be heard." (Isaiah 1: 21-23)

He goes on to condemn the greed that makes them
do such wicked things: "Misfortune will befall you who
buy up house after house and (gobble up the land) by
joining field to field (in large estates and leaving nothing
for the people of the land), so that you alone are
provided for. In my own ears Jehovah has declared, 'All
these houses shall be made waste and even your splendid
mansions shall be left without inhabitant.' A ten-acre
vineyard will produce only a gallon of juice, and ten
bushels of seed will produce only a one-bushel crop."
(Isaiah 5: 8-10)

Paul, the leading spirit in Gentile congregations, summed up the sentiment in these words that have been quoted and misquoted everywhere: "The love of money is the root of all kinds of evil." (1 Timothy 6: 10) Yet it is the profit motive principle that runs the modern world and shows itself opposed to God. Jesus challenged those who live by it and said: "What good is it to a man if he gains everything in the world but loses his own life doing it? for what can a man offer (from all of his possessions) to buy his own life back again?" (Matthew 16: 26)

Little has changed since the time of Adam. Though men are greedy, they suffer for their greed, and the plight of the majority of people is clearly expressed in these tragic words: "Give careful thought to your ways. Though you plan abundantly, you take in little. Although you eat, you are never satisfied, and when you drink you never have enough. Though you put on clothes, you are never warm. And the wages that you earn you put into a purse that is full of holes (for all your money rapidly is gone)." (Haggai 1: 7-11)

James, who was the chief motivating spirit in the Jerusalem congregation after the execution of Jesus, condemned the social inequalities that wealth and poverty inspired, and he warned the followers of God to have no part in it. He told them in his forthright way: "If a man enters your gatherings having gold rings on his fingers and wearing splendid clothes and a poor man wearing shabby clothes comes as well; but you show a special preference for the well-dressed man and say: 'Sit over here in this good seat I have for you,' but tell the poor man: 'Stand over there,' or 'Sit down on the floor beside my feet,' then you are guilty of creating class distinctions and making judgments based upon evil perceptions." (James 2: 2-4)

The world is full of such distinctions based on wealth, race, sex, national biases, and Christian writers went to great lengths in trying to combat such prejudice. That God abhors such things is frequently affirmed. Even Paul (who has been challenged for some of his remarks) did say: "God makes no distinction between Jew and Greek for the same Jehovah is the ruler over all and blesses everyone who turns to him." (Romans 10: 2) And elsewhere too, he did affirm the undeniable equality of women and men, and left no doubt at all as to what he meant by it.

The term "Greek" which Paul uses here did not refer to the Greek people or to those of any special race. Greek was the international language of his day, and was spoken by people of every race throughout the world. The contrast that he made, therefore, was between the Jew and the rest of the civilized world. His remark made no exceptions based on any so-called curses of the past. It included people from all races and all nations upon earth. This was the new covenant, and it did not require revisions of any kind nor visions from heaven to make adjustments in the document. It was complete in itself, and had been sealed with blood.

Jeremiah emphasized a few of the prestigious acquisitions that people everywhere felt most inclined to boast about, and gave this advice to the followers of God: "The wise man should not revel in his wisdom, nor should the mighty man take pride in his might (the powerful armies he can raise against an enemy). Neither should the rich man feel smug about his riches. But if anyone takes pride in anything, let him take pride in this: that he understands and knows me. For I am Jehovah who practices loving kindness, justice and fair dealings throughout all the earth. For these are the things that I delight in Jehovah says." (Jeremiah 9: 23-24)

Because the way of the world is foolish, Isaiah could foresee a time when it would reap the harvest of foolish leaders leading them. Children finally would rule them in all things. He did not necessarily mean literal children, but rather people who in their thinking would be no wiser than children. Nevertheless the other, too, was possible: "I will give them children for their leaders and infants shall become their rulers, and people shall terrorize and cheat each other in that day, not only each his fellow, but everyone his neighbour, and children will even be rude and insolent toward their elders, and ruffians will intimidate the law-abiding citizen."   (Isaiah 3: 4 - 5)

His words come very close to the truth of what the world has witnessed even in our times. In such a sea of confusion as this, there certainly is blood, and every kind of creature in the world does stand in danger of its life. I could make a great deal more of many of these prophecies, and I'm certain you can too, but I am only trying to explain John's words. And as I expect most of us know, John, in this attack upon the system of things, was merely drawing to a boil all that the scriptures had been calling for, from the beginning—a reversal of the practices these writings claimed were destroying the whole creation.

They had looked for a time when "every valley should be exalted and every mountain and hill made low," when "the last should be first and the first should be last," and "the whole world would be turned upside down." Yes, in popular jargon "when the revolution comes." For we cannot doubt that what is spoken of in terms like these is a revolution "when people turn their lives around" and there is "a new heaven and a new earth." Be careful, though, for a revolution is not a rebellion. But there is great cause for society to repent and change the way it operates. David Suzuki, a world environmentalist, has expressed that need in these terms: "We need profound changes in our economic systems, in governmental structures and priorities, in the organization of our communities and in the way we live.

"We need a fundamental acceptance of our own biological nature. We must before all else, protect the basic capital that sustains all life."

The third spirit carrying the container of God's word, pours its contents on the philosophies by which the world lives. The way societies rejuvinate themselves through recreation, education, entertainment, art and spiritual guidance are all, therefore, called into question. Yet we must not assume that the Bible irresponsibly attacks these things. Paul, the most prolific of the New Testament writers, for instance, said: "Whatever is true, whatever is noble, whatever is right, whatever is pure, whatever is lovely, whatever is admirable, if anything is excellent or praiseworthy, we weigh and consider these things carefully." (Philippians 4: 8)

Such words are not surprising from one of the world's most widely read and educated men. For Paul was more than just familiar with world literature. As I pointed out elsewhere, his own style of writing reveals that he admired the works of Greek dramatists. What is being called into judgment, in John's letter, are the philosophies expressed throughout society that blind the people of the world to their own follies. Elsewhere in the writings of Paul, he speaks of the matter of philosophies that he finds most troubling:

"Now it is written (in the scriptures): 'I will destroy the wisdom of the wise (regardless of how wise that wisdom might appear to be) and the scholarship of scholars, I will bring to nothing.' Show me then the wise man, the scholar, or the great debater of the age. Has God not shown their wisdom to be foolishness? For the world with all its wisdom has failed to learn the way of God, and the way of God which they call foolishness has shown the way of true salvation for anyone who will believe.

"But the Jews demand a supernatural sign from heaven, while the Greeks (the whole Gentile world) want something practical, so when we tell them of a messiah who was crucified (who can deliver them) that becomes a barrier to the Jews (who look upon anyone who hangs upon a tree as accursed), while the Greeks can see no sense in it at all. Yet to everyone that God has called from among the Jews and Greeks, Christ represents the very essence of God's strength and practicality.

"That is because God's (so-called) foolishness is wiser than all human wisdom, so that what appears to be God's weakness is stronger than all human strength. For, brothers, consider what you yourselves seemed to the world when you were called. Very few of you, by worldly standards, were considered educated men with practical abilities, for you didn't have the social standing, and you were not born to wealth.

"However, God chose men like you, whom the world considered unschooled to put to shame all those the world considered wise, and he chose all you who were weak, to put to shame the strong. All the lowly people whom the world despised, God has chosen. And with those things that don't as yet exist, God will bring to nothing all the things that do exist." (1 Corinthians 1: 18-28) "I have a dream," he might have said to them.

Society in its unshakeable belief in the strong man who liberates, leads the world down the wrong path. Its super heroes — Batman, the Lone Ranger, Rambo, and all the rest—amusing as they sometimes seem, are but mere extensions of those other supermen of history, to whom men and women blindly give their souls. Napoleon, Xerxes, Alexander, Adolf Hitler, Jim Jones and all the rest only lead their followers to death. Nimrod, the mighty hunter opposed to God, was the forerunner of them all. The man with the bow, or with the gun, or with the world's most powerful fists, along with the glorious mighty man of armies is not the hero that the scriptures advocate.

As in all other things, God has turned the values of the world upside down. He reverses them. The master of all is the slave, not the powerful man of arms. By this standard the greatest person in the entire Bible is the woman Mary of Bethany. Matthew tells of the incident regarding her in these words: "When Jesus was in Bethany, at the home of a man called Simon the Leper, a woman came in with an alabaster jar of very expensive perfume, and she poured it upon the head of Jesus as he sat reclining at the table.

"Observing this, Jesus's disciples became annoyed and angry, asking her indignantly: 'Why all this waste? We could have sold this perfume at a high price and given the money to the poor.'

"Jesus having overheard them said: 'Why are you causing this woman so much trouble? What she did for me was very beautiful. As for the poor, they will still be in your midst. But I shall no longer be with you. The perfume that she poured upon my body was in preparation for my burial. And be assured, that wherever this gospel shall be preached throughout the world, what this woman did for me shall also be told and never forgotten.'"   (Matthew 26: 6-13)

Jesus, who has been called "the greatest of all teachers", by making himself the servant of all, humbly showed himself not to be above the meanest of all tasks in washing his disciples' feet. Now Mary herself is shown to be a servant to the lowliest of men, performing a task even lowlier than he — preparing a body for burial — so that Jesus says that what she did for him shall be preached wherever this gospel is preached.

We find this spirit reflected sometimes in literature. Jeeves, the servant of Bertie Wooster, is really his superior in every way, just as Figaro is more capable and wise than his employer, Count Almavira. What makes *The Crucible* by Arthur Miller such a great play, is that the very weak hero who loses his life because he would not defile his name by appending it to a false document, although losing his life, is victor in that he maintains his own integrity. There are some things worth dying for.

"But wait a minute," some of you will say, "Aren't you supposed to be condemning the world's philosophies and art." The answer is no. The word of God is poured upon the waters, and what is false and evil will be shown. God's word judges. I merely show the reader that intelligence and discrimination are essential to right judgment. God doesn't call upon his followers to picket plays or theatres. Just don't be deceived by what you see and hear. Paul expressed the thought in these words: "Be certain that no one leads you from the way of God with vain philosophies that are able to deceive you with their intellectual appeal but are really built upon human presumptions and traditions of this world rather than upon the principles you learned from Christ."

(Colossians 1: 22)

In this regard there is no greater example of a man being led astray and destroyed by vain philosophies than the hero Willy Loman in Arthur Miller's play *Death of a Salesman*. I find it one of the most moving dramas of the stage. Here is a man thoroughly deceived by the values and the teachings of the world, and by the world system promoting them. The best word to describe the play is "prophetic", in the truest sense of that word, for it is a perfect illustration of the meaning of Paul's words as found in the first chapter of *Colossians*.

Paul did ask Christians to seek out good things and to think on them, and there are many good things to be found if we but look for them. They simply aren't the philosophies that the world at large promotes. For instance, I remember sitting in an almost empty movie theatre in Regina, Saskatchewan, to watch a first local showing of the Charlie Chaplin film *Monsieur Verdeaux*. It gave me much reason for thought, as bad press throughout North America and a prevailing social climate had condemned this anti-war philosophy before it was even considered publicly. One must be careful then not to let prevailing public moods distort our judgments of what is worthy of our praise.

What is popular isn't necessarily right. For people under the influence of different social climates and prevailing voices of the nations will try to hinder God's word being heard and even misinterpret it. Yet God's wisdom must be spoken universally throughout the world. Nor should those speaking it judge too hastily or superficially. In regard to this, Solomon declared: "The ponderings of a man's heart are like waters in a deep well, but a man with understanding draws them out."

(Proverbs 20: 5)

I'm sure these words will make you think of Jesus's own words to the woman that he met beside the well in Samaria. In private conversation with her, he affirmed:

"If you knew what God can give you and who it is that asks you for a drink, you would have asked him and he would have given you living water." In reply the woman said: "Sir, you have nothing to draw with and the well is deep. How can you possibly draw up living water?" (John 4: 10-11) But Jesus was speaking to her about the wisdom of God — a wisdom that satisfied the thirst and "became a spring of water welling up within to give eternal life."

That is why King Solomon could say: "The words of a wise man are like deep waters, that pour forth like a fountain of wisdom in a life-giving stream." (Proverbs 18: 4) But there are other waters too, which lead to death, and the reader of John's letter is expected to use good judgment in discerning them. For as John, in *Revelation*, testified "they turned to blood," indicating that, "There is a way that seems right to a man but in the end it only leads to death."   (Proverbs 14: 12)

This then is the warning given by Moses regarding the waters that we drink: "Behold, I set before you the way of life and development and the way of death and destruction. For I instruct you this day to love Jehovah your God and walk in his ways, and to keep his commandments, decrees and laws, then you will live and increase, and Jehovah your Creator will cause you to prosper in the land that you have entered to possess.

"However, if you let the land that you are living in turn away your heart so that you disobey my words, and you are drawn by them to worship other gods (following practices alien to those I gave) and are obedient to them, I warn you earnestly that you will certainly be destroyed by them."   (Deuteronomy 30: 15-18)

The philosophies promoted by the nations of the world are dangerous as John has tried to show us by the words that he has written in this book: "When the third messenger finished emptying his container on the rivers and springs of water they turned to blood."

Standing before Belshazzar, the King of Babylon, Daniel—having read the writing on the wall—told him, "You have been weighed in the balances and found wanting." Babylon was to be overthrown. So now when John, in this *Book of Revelation*, tells us that the fourth container was poured out upon the sun, he was referring to the chief power governing the nation—its king, or sovereign government. In ancient times it was the King, who acted in the name of him who made the firmament, and was, therefore, himself regarded as the chief light in his nation's firmament, in the same way that Jacob was regarded as the sun that ruled his family.

When Isaiah wrote about the overthrow of Babylon's king, he did so gloatingly with these reviling words: "This is the end the oppressor has reaped. This is the fruit and reward of his fury. Jehovah has broken the strength of the wicked and the rule of the tyrant has ceased, who ruthlessly oppressed the peoples with unrelenting cruelty." (Isaiah 14: 4-6)

Kings (even at their best) were not viewed favourably. When Israel desired a government (or king) like other nations in the world, Samuel, the great wise seer of Israel, gave them this sharp warning:

"If you insist on asking for a king (or sovereign human government) to govern you, here is what he will do: He will conscript your sons to serve as soldiers in his war chariots and his cavalry, while others (in the infantry) will run before his chariots. He will make some of them officers who command units of thousands and others who command fifties. Some will be forced to plow his lands (in boot camps) and to reap his harvests (not their own) or to make his weapons and the equipment for his chariots.

"Your daughters will be called upon to make perfumes for him or to work as his cooks and bakers. In addition he will take a tenth of your own grain and vintage (in taxes) to give to his officials and attendants. Then he will take your menservants and your maidservants for his own use (a kind of goods and services tax) and he will also take the very best of your cattle and donkeys if he fancies them. He will take, as well, a tenth of all your flocks, and you yourselves shall be like slaves.

"When that time comes you will complain to me because of the king (or government) which you yourselves have chosen, but I will pay no attention to you then. (For you will have what you desired to have, and would desire again if freed.)" (1 Samuel 8: 10-19). Yet the people refused to heed this warning.

A thoughtful observation made by some historians and political scientists is that people generally get the kind of governments that they deserve. There is a general tendency in people to lean upon celebrities and leaders for direction in their lives, regardless of the wisdom of their ways. Leaders and celebrities are suns and stars which serve as guiding lights and give direction in the heavens governing the ordinary citizens of our societies. And charismatic leaders often lead men to their doom.

That Samuel's warning to the people of Israel proved true is shown in the complaint the people of Israel made to Rehoboam, the son of Solomon, following the so-called golden age of Jewish history. They told him:

"Your father made our yoke heavy. Therefore lighten the hard service and the heavy yoke your father placed on us, and we will serve you."   (1 Kings 12: 4)

Three days afterwards Rehoboam gave the people his reply: "Forsaking the counsel that the older (more experienced and wiser) men had given him, he took the counsel of the younger (inexperienced) counsellors and said: 'My father made your yoke heavy, but I will make it even heavier: and where my father punished you with whips, I shall punish you with scorpions (whips having barbed metal tips)."   (1 Kings 12: 13-14)

I have no doubt that this is why the psalmist gave the people this advice: "Do not put your confidence in mortal rulers or in ambitious men who do not have the power to save (you from the evils that assail you in the world) for in the day they die, they turn to dust again and all their noble thoughts and plans die with them."
                (Psalm 146: 3-4)

For even Israel's own rulers weren't in any way superior to those of other lands. Jehovah had much praise for the kings of other lands who ruled extremely well, although he often saw a bitter end awaiting them. For instance, Ezekiel reports these special words of praise that Jehovah gave the king of Tyre: "You were a model of perfection, in the fullness of your wisdom and your perfect beauty (the loveliness of human character). You were in Eden (the ideal pinnacle of earthly government) the garden of God (the people in it being like fruitful trees bearing the fruit of wisdom) very precious stones adorned you: ruby, topaz and emerald, chrysolite, onyx and jasper, sapphire, turquoise and beryl (noble qualities of character in men that reflect the qualities of God.)
                (Ezekiel 28: 12-13)

There could have been no higher praise for any of the sons of Israel, nor of those kings who governed it. But like all rulers – even good King David or wise King Solomon – the King of Tyre became corrupt. As we are told: "Your heart became proud because of your brilliance and you corrupted your wisdom because of your fame...By the many crooked dealings of your dishonest trade you have brought dishonour upon the once good name of all your industries." (Ezekiel 28: 17-18)

Because men and the institutions that they operate are corruptible, the followers of God are warned not to put their trust in them, regardless of how noble they intend to be. They are to remember always that God is their true king, and it is he alone that they are asked to serve. However, Peter does remind us of the respect we owe to every man, including Kings: "Show respect for people everywhere, and treat them well. Honour the brotherhood of believers, reverence God, and respect the ruler governing the lands." (1 Peter 2: 17)

Yet while honour is due to the king, the followers of God should be aware of the workings and the failings of human individuals and governments. For Solomon has alerted everyone devoted to the wisdom of God with these words: "I have considered very carefully what takes place on earth and I have often noticed how that men will oppressively dominate each other." (Ecclesiastes 8: 9)

Oppressive kings and governments, however, are answerable to God, and Isaiah specifies the very things that shall call them to account. He says: "Misfortune will befall all those who make unjust laws, and those who oppress the needy, depriving the poor of their rights and denying justice to those in need, taking the property of widows and robbing the fatherless. What will you do when God requires a reckoning and brings destruction on you from a distant land? To whom will you turn for help? Where will your riches be safe? You will have no option but to hide yourselves among the captives or to fall (in battle) with the slain. Yet even this will not turn Jehovah's anger away from you. His hand will still be raised against you." (Isaiah 10: 1-4)

Neither the miracle discoveries of modern science nor the three millenia of social development that has taken place in history has put an end to this plague of exploitation of the poor nor to the neglect of social responsibilities by those in power. Do you imagine human ingenuity will bring us any closer in the next few years? "Why of course!" some of you will say, "as soon as we pay off the deficit." Strange, there never is a lack of funds for war or for international intrigue. There only is a shortage of resources when it comes to taking care of basic needs of those that we are called upon to serve. As Samuel said, the people "have become like slaves" to those who govern them.

Such terrible hypocrisy and indifference to those in need, apparent in the affluent, led the Jewish prophet Jeremiah in his book to turn to God with this appeal: "Jehovah, you are always fair when I bring a case before you. Yet I must ask you about justice: Why is it that the way of the wicked flourishes and enjoys success? Why do the faithless people live at ease? You have planted them (like a tree), and they have taken root; they grow and they bear fruit. Although they have your name constantly upon their lips, you are very far from their hearts....How long will you allow the land to be parched and the grass in every field to die? Because those who occupy the land are wicked, the animals and birds are all perishing. And even the people themselves continually say: 'God doesn't pay any heed to what is happening to us.'" (Jeremiah 12: 1-4)

God does not irresponsibly condemn, or make judgments on the world. And human governments at times are just. Yet, as many people have been more or less aware throughout history, the world's official governments do not fully govern in their lands. Many people sense that governments, are somehow run by powers outside themselves. People sometimes speak about secret cabals, hidden governments and hidden agendas. Others call their statesmen nothing but mere puppets on a public stage who do no more than the bidding of another group of men, that no one as yet has irrefutably identified. The hidden government, apparently, has been successfully concealed behind a veil of illusions, and sits upon a throne that is unseen. It is that hidden throne of government which really rules the world, and Jesus met the one whose throne it was:

The King James Bible describes the meeting in these words: "The devil, taking him up into an high mountain, shewed unto him all the kingdoms of the world in a moment of time. And the devil said unto him. All this power will I give thee, and the glory of them: for that is delivered to me; and to whomsoever I will give it. If thou therefore wilt worship me, all shall be thine."
(Luke 4: 5-7)

That assertion clarifies John's words in the thirteenth chapter of the *Book of Revelation* when he said: "The dragon gave the beast his power, and his seat, and great authority." (Revelation 13: 2) John also, in one letter, said unequivocally: "The whole world is under the control of the evil one." (1 John 5: 19)

So the Bible does support the view that there is another power behind world governments. And yes, there is a secret agenda: Complete destruction of the creation of God. If nothing else, this doctrine of an unseen government has existed from the earliest of times. For "the dragon, that old serpent, which is the Devil and Satan," is intent on bribing everyone, inside and outside official governments, for he "deceives the whole world."

Since it is the throne of Satan that deceives the world, Paul is able to define the nature of the warfare being waged against the world: "Our struggle is not against flesh and blood, but against the rulers, against the authorities, against the power of this dark world and against the spiritual forces of evil in the heavenly realms."   (Ephesians 6: 12)

Satan then, according to the Bible, is the spirit that directs the headstrong rebellion at work in the world, that will not listen to wise counselling. And as a result: "The land is full of adulterers (those who mingle God's word with pagan beliefs and practices)! Because of this the land is parched and the pastures in the desert are withered. These false teachers (literally 'prophets') pursue an evil course and use their powers in ways that are not right. The preacher and the priest alike are godless (in that the ways they teach are not mine), and their wickedness is found even in my place of worship. ....Turn away from these false teachers who fill you with false hopes. The visions that they speak of are but mere inventions of their own minds and they are not visions of Jehovah (as they claim)."   (Jeremiah 23: 10-11, 16)

Perhaps it is a shocking thing to learn that God's own church is overrun with those who bring a bad name upon God and everything he says, but the words that say this are not mine. They belong to John. Jesus's own brother Jude, as well, addressed this topic, when he spoke about unscrupulous men who enjoyed celebrity in certain Christian circles, just as many do today. Here is what he had to say of them: "Certain people (whose wickedness has been condemned from long ago) have worked their way into our midst. They are opposed to God, and they have changed the meaning of God's grace into a licence for committing every kind of immorality. They deny that Jesus Christ is our only ruling magistrate and master. These same people (like those who died at Sodom and Gomorrah) live according to their own notions (or dreams), They sin against their own bodies and reject any kind of governing authority, and they lie about the powers of heaven.

"...These same people scoff and ridicule whatever they don't understand, and what they seem to understand is governed solely by the instinct of their feelings, as though they were unthinking beasts. Living by their instincts has corrupted them, and through this they destroy themselves. Misfortune lies ahead of them because, like Cain, they are falling prey to their own passions. Such people will do anything for profit and they do rush swiftly into Balaam's way, but like Korah's disobedient rebels they shall be destroyed.

"These dangerous men are filthy spots that soil the love feasts of the brotherhood, for they carry on at them with no thought or consideration for others, carousing shamelessly and only thinking of themselves. They are like clouds (passing over dry land) that offer no rain, (but merely move across the land) swept along by winds. They are like fruit trees at autumn (harvest time) that bear no fruit, and so are pulled up by the roots (and burned) making them twice dead.

"They are like the wild waves of the sea, tossing up their shameful deeds like dirty foam along the beach. Like stars that wander from their course, the blackest darkness lies ahead of them...These men are discontented grumblers who constantly blame others (for their own shortcomings) who pursue their own desires (for they are ruled by passions) and they love to boast about themselves. When they do praise others, it is just to flatter them for the sake of gaining some advantages from them." (Jude 4-16)

It is interesting to note that the apostasy of the Christian Church began right at the start, two millenia ago. Today there are more than 25,000 denominations and sects who do not live in harmony. Their doctrines vary in extremes, and more than local customs are dividing them. So John has given us a strategy to unify the brethren, and to overcome the world.

For the "Church of God" is not the churches of the world. It is the people God will choose from them for having done the work that he set out for them to do. Not prestigious individuals, nor the hired clergy, just humble men and women from the so-called "laity" who hear the voice of God and who do his will. They are those who speak the word of wisdom aptly when occasion makes it evident there is a need, and live according to the wisdom that they speak. But when I tell you Satan plays a big part in the churches of the world, I only say what anyone who studies God's word knows.

Paul confronted Peter for his ignorance in doing Satan's will and so did Jesus Christ himself. So when we read that God's word is poured out upon the throne of the beast, the world's chief source of inspiration (a source which takes in television, theatres, the new medias, and even the Christian church itself) we understand that it is the world's real government that is under attack: the throne of Satan (that unseen influence which controls the world's psychological atmosphere and the nature of its competitive activities). I doubt that any one body of men today has absolute control of it. Yet it remains the main force behind the suppression of the people, suppressed primarily in the sense that their full powers, as human beings, are never realised, and the better qualities of their natures are never shown.

As a power it does control the zeitgeists of the world. Yet when God's word is poured upon that throne, it will reveal the darkness that it brings upon the world and all the pain and suffering that people must endure because of it. The irony, however, is that people will go on blaming God for all their misery.

Satan's world is thrown into darkness because it cannot see the truth that is revealed to them: "Even if our gospel is veiled, it is veiled to those who are perishing. The god of this age has blinded the minds of unbelievers, so that they cannot see the light of the gospel or the glory of Christ who is the image of God." (2 Corinthians 4: 3-4) But the main reason for the darkness over Satan's world is expressed in John's own words: "This is the verdict: Light has come into the world, but men loved darkness instead of light because their deeds are evil."
(John 3: 19)

Having said these things, I will now turn to that other factor in these last campaigns I have not mentioned up till now, the qualities of God's creation which are inherent in all seven of these last campaigns. God, who by his very nature is creative, has used the power of his creative word to bring destruction down on Satan's world.

There were seven days in creation; now there are seven last campaigns. Now before the first campaign, as before the first day of creation we are shown a world that has become "tohu and bohu" — without shape or direction — and darkness covers all the sky.

In the first campaign, God says, "Let there be light," as the people are in darkness. Only this time they do not repent, and they suffer as a consequence. Then in the second campaign, God calls for separation of the waters so that the serene waters of heaven might calm the troubled sea below the firmament. But the people, having loved darkness rather than light only fill the world with violence, crime and murder, with none to help control or govern them. And so the sea is filled with blood. For when men in high positions can be bribed with favours, there is no separation of the elements. All is crime.

Now on the third day, God called for stable land to come out of the sea, so in the third campaign God exposes the unstable philosophies that guide the world and only lead to death, not to an enduring world that can't be moved. We are told that on the fourth day, God established the lights that ruled in heaven. So in the fourth campaign, God's word is poured upon those governments that rule the world. Because God's wisdom is not found in them, and there is no light found in the people of the earth, the world has no lamp at all to guide their feet.

The throne controlling all the world's activities and determining the nature of the social atmosphere, which God's word exposes in the fifth campaign, corresponds to the fifth day of creation when God called upon the seas to bring forth life abundantly and called for birds to fill the air. But the damning hand of Satan won't release that life so that people bite their tongues in pain and face the darkness of the world, cursing God for all the misery and darkness that they suffer in, and bring upon themselves.

If there is any real damnation in the patterns we have found, when God has poured his word upon the

world, it is because he does not force his will. He does
not rape the people that he woos. Those who eventually
receive eternal life, do so because they choose the way
that leads to it. That's how simple it all is. We choose
our misery if we choose the world system that causes it.

In the sixth campaign, the messenger of God now
pours his vessel on the Euphrates River, causing the waters
to dry up and clear the way for the invasion of the eastern
kings. Most people will remember now the attack made
by the Medes and Persians on the city of Babylon. Cyrus's
army, having diverted the water of the Euphrates River
that had run through the city of Babylon, walked down
the riverbed which had flowed beneath the city walls,
they entered the city, and they captured it. This is what
is now referred to in these words: "its water dried up,
making the way clear for the invasion by the (armies of
the eastern Kings)." The Euphrates River had given
Babylon a feeling of security, for it was the prime source
of their defence. Yet the great Euphrates River had not
defended them as the Babylonians supposed it would.

This act of defiance against the great city, is of great
prophetic significance, for it alludes to these words in
the *Book of Isaiah*: "(I am Jehovah) who says of
Jerusalem, 'She shall be inhabited;' and to the cities of
Judah, 'They shall be built again, and I will raise them
from the ruins.'

("I am Jehovah) who says to Cyrus, 'He is my
shepherd, and he shall perform all my pleasure and fulfill
my purpose;' even saying to Jerusalem, 'She shall be built
again,' and of the temple, 'Your foundation shall again be
laid.'

"Thus says Jehovah to his anointed, Cyrus, whose
right hand I have held: He shall subdue the nations

before him, for I shall strip kings of their power, for I
shall open the city gates for him, and their doors shall
not be shut. I will go before you and will level the
mountains (the mighty kingdoms of the world)—to
make the crooked places straight; I will break in pieces
the doors of bronze and cut the doors' bars of iron
assunder.'"   (Isaiah 44: 27 — 45: 3)

This scriptural passage immediately sets up an echo
about the coming of Jehovah himself: "Give comfort to
my people, says your God. Speak tenderly to the heart
of Jerusalem, and cry to her that her time of service and
her warfare are ended, that her iniquity is pardoned: that
she has received punishment from Jehovah's hands double
for all her sins.

"A voice of one who cries, 'Prepare in the wilderness
the way of Jehovah; make a straight highway in the
desert for our God. Every valley shall be raised up and
every mountain and hill shall be made low; the rough
ground shall be leveled and the rugged places smoothed.
And Jehovah's glory shall be revealed so that all
mankind will see it together, for the mouth of Jehovah
has spoken it.'"   (Isaiah 40: 1-5)

Such words too echo another verse: "For as daylight
comes from the east and is seen even to the west, so
shall the coming of the son of man be." (Matthew 24: 27)

The sixth step of the campaign, resembling the
sixth day of creation establishes that Man in the image
of God will be seen. For God's creation, and man as God
created him, is the glory of God. We are told that, in the
beginning, God saw everything that he had made and it
was very good. Man will have the beauty of all jewels
on the breastplate of the priest, for he will have all the

qualities of God. This is the meaning of the word of God made flesh.

But this is just a promise that the whole world fears, and because of it the nations of the world prepare for war.

Now God made the seventh day for man so that his mind could be renewed each week in the course of doing the will of his creator. The seventh day renewed the social atmosphere. It was a time to appraise what had been done and to consider what could yet be done to glorify God's name. But in John's mind, the atmosphere of Satan now pervades the world. Therefore in the last step of the last campaign, God's messenger pours his vessel on the social atmosphere of a world that hasn't been redeemed, and they respond in the only way they seem to know – in a violent earth-shaking war. So while the seventh day brings the peace of heaven to those who serve their creator, for those who have rebelled against his way, it brings the hell of man's destructive violence.

That is why God warns: "You must not worship Jehovah your God in the same way that the nations of the world worship their gods, for they do all kinds of detestable things that Jehovah abhors." (Deuteronomy 12: 13)

"Scoffers will no doubt say to you: 'Where is this coming event that's promised? Things haven't changed since ancient times. They go on in just the same way now as they did then.' But they deliberately refuse to face the fact there was a beginning when God made the heavens and the earth from water, with water. And don't forget there was a time once when the whole world (system) was flooded and destroyed. As that took place by the power of God's word, so by the power of that same word of God, the present heavens (governmental systems) and earth (the system of things) are reserved for fire (destruction by warfare and violence)." (2 Peter 3: 4-7)

The nations have fallen into the pit that they have dug; their feet are caught in the net that they have hidden. Jehovah is known by his justice; the wicked are ensnared by the works of their own hands. (Psalm 9: 15-16)

So when I think of all the people who have perished in the wars that outline history, I am amazed that many people thought that they were dying in the service of their God. Jesus left no doubt that such wars did not serve his cause. Even when his own life was in danger, he did not take up arms, and he forbade his own apostles to take up arms defending him.

If Jesus's own life was not considered a strong enough motive for assembling an army (and there were many Jews living at that time who would have gone to war for him if he had said the word), then what other cause has since that time shown itself to be more honourable. Jesus rebuked his own disciples' readiness to fight on his behalf with these few words: "Put your sword back in its place, for everyone who takes the sword will perish by the sword." (Matthew 26: 52)

When he told Pilate of the armies he could raise, his boast was not an idle one. A mob already had attempted forcing him to lead them into war. John relates the matter in these words: "The people when they saw the powerful work which Jesus did, took it as a sign, and began to say of him: 'This surely is that prophet which (Moses said) must come into the world.' When he realised that they would make him king through raising an army (to support his cause), Jesus immediately withdrew himself into the hills....When the crowd finally realised that neither Jesus nor his disciples were

anywhere around, they crowded into boats and went
looking for him in Capernaum." (John 6: 14 -24)

The crowds which lined the streets and cheered for
him on his entry into Jerusalem terrified the temple
priests because they feared the repercussions that would
come from Rome. Their fear was not unfounded. Jesus
had allowed himself to be acknowledged publicly as the
Messiah of Israel. That was treason in the eyes of Rome
and the puppet governments which governed in Judea on
behalf of Rome. Even though there were no outward
signs of organized revolt, none of the authorities was
quite sure what he intended doing after that. If the
priests allowed such public displays of devotion to
anyone apart from those that Rome had placed in power,
they themselves could be accused of allowing treason to
take root among the populace.

Jesus clearly showed that he had power. "The
common people heard him gladly." Jesus was quite
conscious of the power he had when he told Pilate: "My
kingdom is no part of this world system. If it were I
could easily have told my servants to fight on my behalf
to prevent my being handed over to the Jewish (priests).
However, my kingdom is of a different sort from this."
(John 18: 36) Yet Jesus, after being raised from death,
began to fight his sort of battle with the world.

So following the final step of the last campaign an
earth-shaking war will come. This is the final judgment
that God will heap on Man. Yet God, in his own words,
has told us long ago why this final judgment would
befall the world. For in the *Book of Proverbs* it is
written: "Wisdom calls out in the streets, raising her
voice in the public squares. She calls to everyone in the
whole land (literally 'at the city gates' — where the entire
city heard the daily news as it arrived): 'Just how long

will you foolish people still continue in your foolish ways? How long will you delight in mockery? and scoff at the counselling I offer you?

"'If you accept my reproofs and come to me, then I will lavishly pour out the spirit of my wisdom upon you so that you will understand my words. But I have called to you, and you have not come. Instead you have ignored my warnings, and rejected my reproofs spurning the redeeming hand that I stretched out to you. Since you have refused my counselling and the advice I offered you, I shall make light of your calamities, and I will laugh when terrors overtake you like a storm, when disaster sweeps over you like a whirlwind, and distress and anguish come upon you.

"'Even when they call upon me in their desperation later on, I will not answer them. Regardless of how earnestly they search, I shall not be found by them, because they hated all the knowledge that I offered them and did not choose to give honour to Jehovah's name at all. Because, therefore they have hated all my counselling and rejected my reproofs, they shall be forced to eat the fruit of their own ways and fill themselves with the devastation they have brought about by their own contrivances.

"'For the foolishness of those who are wayward will ultimately slaughter them, and the contemptuous complacency of fools shall bring destruction down on them. But all who heed my words shall live in safety without any fear of harm.'" (Proverbs 1: 20 - 33)

So it is that John, in this presentation, shows us now how in this last campaign of Jesus Christ, judgment will be brought upon the world. In this picture, John presents the messengers of God as completely unified in their obedience to him. There is no hesitation as they carry

out the highly organized program of verbal attack upon
the various institutions of the established order, to shock
the nations out of their complacency. Define, divide and
conquer is the apparent policy in this campaign. And by
the power of God's own word alone, the messengers of
God reveal the judgment being served upon the human
institutions that are creation's enemy — the well-
established order that controls the world.

God's words condemn: (1) the moral sickness of the
people whose diseases can't be cured by any of the
world's institutions of healing. (2) The frenzy of social
and economic competition, which by its nature encourages
ruthlessness, all kinds of violence, crime, murder and war,
(3) the recreation, entertainment and predominant
philosophies of society, which represent the way we live
and plant the seeds that re-create the cycle of continuing
violence, immorality and destructiveness, (4) rulers of
the lands and world governments that oppress the people
they pretend to serve and entrench the very powers
destroying the people and the world environment, and
actually promote the crime they seemingly oppose, (5)
the spirit of illusions that blinds societies — enmeshing
them in webs of confusion that bind them in
entanglements, (that power called Satan's throne). (6)
the defence systems of the world, which give the nations
a false sense of security, (7) and finally that spiritual
milieux of communication that manufactures the ideas
that become so entrenched in human minds, they seem
like a consensus of the ideas of the populace.

Moses, long ago, when he confronted the Pharaoh of
Egypt, attacked that nation's gods — the powers that
were commonly believed to be the main support of
Egypt. In overthrowing them, and showing them to be
inferior to the powers of the creator of the world, Moses
effectively negated any claim that Egypt thought it had

for governing. Now Jesus, in his plan (for John has told us that it comes from him) divests the nations he confronts of any claim to heal the sick world either morally or physically. Nor can it rid it of the crime and violence assailing it, since by its very nature it promotes these things.

God's word is extremely powerful when it is not diluted by apologists. When poured upon the world, God's truth not only shows the world how spiritually unclean it is, but it makes it clear the world system does not actually govern itself. It creates its own crime, and its so-called independent ways lead eventually to war. The Bible does not speak of anything more terrible, except eternal death.

One important symbol of significance we shouldn't overlook, John expresses in these words: "Then I noticed three loathsome spirits having the appearance of frogs leap from the mouths of the dragon, the beast and the false prophet. These deceiving demons were able to achieve impressive results, and their lies gathered leaders from all over the world into conferences, and drew them into warfare on the great day of Almighty God." These words seem almost impossible to misinterpret. Their meanings fairly leap from the page. Yet enslavement to the imagery itself seems to set up barriers for comprehending them. To translate them, however, into "plain language" robs them of the powerful feelings of abhorrence that John's images convey.

Frogs are unclean animals. As a Jew, John would have been appalled by the very thought of eating them. Yet these unclean things actually emerge from the mouths of those who instruct the people and lead them in the paths that lead to war. Such words remind us of what Jesus said regarding this: "It's not what goes into a man's mouth that defiles him. It is what comes out of a man's mouth that defiles him." (Matthew 15: 11)

We learn several things from this. Evil spirits or demons are those malignant human attitudes which spring from evil imaginations and the human heart which does not have the law of God inscribed on it. Lies spoken by the spirit which is Satan in every individual, the nations of the world and the Balaam (or false prophet or idealist) lead the nations into war. We should recognize the picture that is drawn for us, as it is prominent prior to all wars. Lies flourish in the form of propaganda from the mouths of leaders of the nations, propaganda departments, newspapers, people in the entertainment industries and shall I also say the church. That hurts, but unfortunately it is true.

If anyone drinks poison he will die from it. That is the principle at work in everything that we are shown. One well-known English dramatist and poet, William Shakespeare, devoted one whole play to just that theme. In *Hamlet* he showed how an adulterous affair between King Claudius and Prince Hamlet's mother, Gertrude, poisoned the whole Kingdom of Denmark.

It is said that Claudius poured poison in his brother's ear. That one symbolic deed expresses everything that took place after that. Poisoned in mind by his mother's adulterous behaviour, Hamlet's affections for Ophelia died, and he even slew Polonius, her father, because of what a spirit said to him. All relationships went bad. The line, "There is something rotten in the state of Denmark," is significant.

At the end of Shakespeare's play, everyone is dying from the poison that Claudius has spread, even Gertrude, the woman whom Claudius had loved. Then finally

Claudius himself is forced to drink, from his own cup, the very poison he had spread. Shakespeare's play is brilliant, for Shakespeare understood the principle John speaks of in this book.

What John teaches is that everyone throughout the world is perishing from the poison all of them have drunken from the cup the harlot Babylon has given them. Sin is the poison being spread throughout the world, and it is poured in the ear of all the populace. The messengers of God are called upon to spread the word of God throughout the world as an antidote and to make it clear to everyone, exactly what is happening. Therefore there are seven last campaigns.

These campaigns are logically divided into seven parts. The first step centres upon individuals, the second on communities, the third upon the teachings of the world as they are found in recreation and world culture. The fourth step focuses upon the governments, the fifth upon the hidden government (a power behind the throne), the sixth is one regarding national defence, and the last step takes on the social atmosphere. The plan is thorough and complete.

Such lies as those the nations of the world promote do achieve impressive results even as John has told us that they will. But Jesus warned his followers not to be deceived. "Stay alert," he said, "and don't be caught off guard for (these) will come upon you unexpectedly as a thief. Be careful therefore...that you do not disgrace yourselves."

As in everything, Armageddon also is symbolically used. It is not the geographical place that John is speaking of. It is what it represents. This is the battleground of history. The attitudes that lead mankind to war are all resolved in it. The name of God may be on the lips of all the warriors in such catastrophic battles, but God is not in their hearts. After the spiritual warfare of God is waged in the manner which Jesus Christ laid out, final judgement will be passed upon the world and be resolved according to the only way the nations seem to know, following their own pattern as they march into "the valley of decision" also known as Armageddon.

This final war will be more terrible than any we have seen before. As John says, "There never had been one like it since man first came into the world....The smaller nations and the superpowers all vanished." Yet we can see, from what John says, that he is not giving us a literal description of the actual events. He is concerned more with the role God plays in all of it. "Hailstones, a talent each in weight fell from the skies," he says. Their being each a talent in weight is significant, for you will remember that the master of the house in one of Jesus's parables gave each servant a number of talents. These were representative of the precious wisdom of God. Here this wisdom which would otherwise have enriched those receiving it, instead becomes a fearsome curse. The destruction is what man has chosen, not what God desired.

Having sketched the course of the role God's forces play in all of this, John's next task is to define the whole spiritual order of the monster he has just outlined for us.

CHAPTER SEVENTEEN

The Poisoned Chalice

Just then one of God's seven messengers which had carried one of the seven vessels came and spoke to me.

"Come with me!" he said, "and I will show you the way in which that infamous harlot, (or wicked city) whose residence is built on many (springs of) waters, will be punished. All the rulers governing the world without exception have been guilty of fornication with her (in allowing her to corrupt the social atmospheres) so that all the world's inhabitants are intoxicated with the wine of her adulteries (traditions, customs and deeds contrary to the way of God)."

God's messenger then carried me away in spirit to the wilderness, where I saw a woman (symbolizing a community) seated on a brutish beast (symbolic of mankind ungoverned by the spirit of God's wisdom). Scarlet (with sin) the beast had every kind of blasphemy written all over it. (Like the wild beast from the sea and its image we encountered earlier) it had seven heads and ten horns.

The woman who was seated on the beast was (regally) attired in red and purple clothes, and she was adorned in (holy ornaments) gold and precious gems and pearls. In her hand she held a gold cup (representative of her philosophy and wisdom) filled with every kind of loathsome immorality and the filthiness of her adulteries (perversely mixed teachings and practices). Written on her forehead was a secret name (which only could be read by those who were spiritually perceptive enough to recognize her true character and who were not blinded by the spell of her majestic countenance):

MYSTERY
BABYLON THE GREAT
MOTHER
OF
ALL HARLOTS (wicked communities)
AND
ABOMINATIONS IN THE WORLD
(perverse practices and crimes)

It was obvious to me from this that the woman sitting on that animal was drunk with blood – the blood of all those servants of Jehovah (whom she had slain) and with the blood of all who testified for Jesus (Christ). When I saw her, I was utterly amazed.

"What surprises you?" God's messenger enquired of me. "If you wish I'll tell you all about the woman that you saw, and all about the beast on which she rides. That frightful animal with seven heads and ten horns which carries her really had existence at one time. Though it exists no more, it will very shortly rise out of the pit again, before it goes to its destruction afterwards.

"When that occurs, like all the world's inhabitants since the creation of the world, those whose names are not recorded in the *Book of Life* will be dazzled and stand in awe of it, because it doesn't have existence now, though it will come into existence once again.

"This then is something you must, with wisdom, ponder on: The seven heads of the beast are seven mountains (or mighty kingdoms) that the woman is established in. Five of them have come and gone, but one is ruling now, and there is still another one to come, whose rule will be extremely brief. The beast itself, however, which once had been, but now exists no more, will be the eighth great power, ruling with the seven super powers that ruled before. When it appears, it too will go to its destruction like all the others which preceded it.

"Now the ten horns that you saw are ten kings (or sovereign state governments), which have not taken power as yet, but when they do, they'll rule together for one hour with the beast. Unified in purpose (and by treaty) all ten ruling states will give the beast their strength and power, and together they will war against the lamb. But the lamb will overcome them all, for he is greater than all lords and stronger than all kings (or sovereign states), and all his loyal and faithful followers will stand with him." (Like Cyrus, he was to be victorious against this seemingly unbeatable spiritual world capital.)

After that, the messenger of God went on to say, "The waters, that you saw the woman seated on, are masses of people out of every language, race and nationality. Now the beast, with its ten horns, will turn at last with hatred on the harlot, and will ruin her, stripping her of everything she has and leave her naked. Then they will eat her flesh and burn her in the fire, for God has put it in the hearts of all these ruling powers to surrender all their strength and sovereignty to the beast, so that the words of God will be fulfilled."

*

In Chapter Sixteen, we were shown the seven steps of the final campaign that Jesus Christ was to carry to fulfillment through his messengers. That Jesus Christ is present in the world and performs his "miracles" through those he has appointed as his messengers, clearly is attested to in scripture. For example, the *Gospel of Luke* and the *Book of Acts* comprise two parts of the same work. The first part tells us "what Jesus Christ began to do and teach", while the second part tells us what Jesus continued to do and teach on earth through "the power of the Holy Spirit sent down."

We may remember then, just how the prophet Elijah continued his own work, through his spirit that he sent down to Elisha after his departure from the earth, and how later, through the work of John the Baptist, the same spirit of Elijah (which came again through him into the world) prepared the way for Jesus Christ. In the same way, Jesus, through a faithful body of followers (the body of Christ) continued with that work which God assigned to him, by sending his own spirit down to them at Pentecost. It is remarkable as well that the *Book of Acts* ends so abruptly, for it indicates quite clearly that the book itself was never finished. Some readers have assumed from this that Luke must certainly have died a violent death. Others have suggested that such an ending indicates that even to the present day, the work which Jesus Christ set out to do never was completed upon earth.

Once a Roman centurion came to see Jesus, and begged him to heal his ailing servant. But when Jesus prepared to go with him, the Roman officer said something that was significant enough for Jesus to remark upon. Matthew recounts the incident in this way:

"After Jesus had entered Capernaum, a Roman centurion came to him and asked for his help. 'Sir,' he said, 'my servant has been struck down with paralysis and lies at home suffering terrible pain.'

"So Jesus said to him, 'I will come and heal him.'

"But the centurion replied, 'Sir, I'm not worthy enough for you to even come under my roof, but if you will only say the word, my servant will be cured. For I understand such things. Being a man under authority, and having soldiers under me, I only need to say to someone, "Go," and he goes. Or I can order another one to come, and he comes. And if I tell my slave to do anything, he will do it.'"

Jesus was so impressed by what the centurion had said, he indicated to his disciples that this was the kind of faith that he would like to find in all his followers. So he underlined how important such faith was, by saying: "I have not found so much faith as this in anyone in all of Israel. So I truly believe that the time will come, when many people from the east and west will come and sup with Abraham and Isaac and Jacob in the kingdom of God, while those who complacently believe the kingdom is their sole property will be turned out of it, to live in utter darkness, where they will wail and gnash their teeth." (Matthew 8: 5-12)

So we should notice that when Jesus sent out men to do a special kind of work for him, he conferred upon them all the power that he himself possessed. This is what he did, for instance, when he sent his twelve apostles to the cities of Judea to act on his behalf: "He called these twelve disciples to him, and he gave them the authority to drive out evil spirits and to cure every kind of disease and sickness...with the following instructions: 'Do not go among the Gentiles or enter any town of the Samaritans. Go rather to the lost sheep of Israel. And wherever you go preach this message: "The kingdom of heaven is in your midst." Heal the sick, raise the dead, cleanse those who have leprosy, drive out demons.'" (Matthew 10: 1-8)

If you have been observing the wording of the scriptures carefully, right from the time when God first spoke to Cain, you will realise that demons concern such things as uncontrolled passions, moodiness, wrong attitudes, lying doctrines, false prophecies, and any habitual practice that does not harmonize with God. For all of these are spirits which enslave everyone who serves the present world's established powers. Demons (or impulses and attitudes which were in conflict with God) were seen as being closely linked with idolatry and with the immorality associated with its practices. These demons were believed to be the cause of criminal activity, many kinds of sicknesses, emotional traumas and even madness. Drugs as well sometimes were involved with them.

A Christian then, if he has thoroughly imbibed the word of God, and carries out those tasks his master has assigned, is, to all intents and purposes, Jesus Christ himself. Through obedience to Jesus's own will, he has done what Jesus Christ would do. And whoever speaks demeaningly of him or treats him in a rude and unbecoming way has done these things to Jesus Christ himself: "He that listens to you, listens to me;" he said "and he that rejects you, rejects me; and he that rejects me rejects him that sent me." (Luke 10: 16) These were Jesus's own words, and he further said, "I tell you truly, insomuch as you have done these things to the least of all my servants, you have done them even to me." It is in this spirit then that Jesus says: "My sheep shall know my voice."

In this same sense, Jesus represented God. For he was sent by him. Therefore, to insult God's servant is to insult God himself, and to slay that servant God has sent is, in the truest sense, to murder God.

So now I call to your attention what sometimes has been called a contradiction in the scriptures, but which serves to illustrate my point. In the *Luke* account of the Roman centurion, when we compare it to the one that we already read in the *Matthew* narrative, there is such a

distinct difference, it often is commented on. Luke's
gospel says: "(In Capernaum) a centurion's servant, whom
his master valued highly, was sick and about to die. The
centurion heard of Jesus and sent some elders of the Jews
to speak to him (notice Jesus's good relationship with
Jews) and to ask him to come and heal his servant. When
they came to Jesus they pleaded urgently with him to go.
'This man is worthy and deserves your help, because he
loves our nation and has built a synagogue for us.' So
Jesus went with them.

"He wasn't far from the house when the centurion
sent some friends to say: 'Sir, please don't trouble yourself,
for I am not worthy to have you come under my roof.
That is why I didn't even consider myself worthy to
come to you. But only speak the word and my servant
will be cured. For I (like you) am also a man under
authority, with soldiers under me. So when I tell one man
to go, he goes; and when I tell another one to come, he
comes. If I tell my slave, 'Do this,' he will do it."

(Luke 7: 1-8)

That we are being told the same story, in a slightly
different way, in both these gospels cannot possibly be
denied or doubted in the least. The so-called contradiction that many have remarked upon merely illustrates
the point I made: If a man sends out his faithful delegates
to do his work for him, it is as though he went himself. So
when Jesus's own servants upon earth obey any of those
commands which Jesus Christ laid out for them in the
plan he sent to John, the person acting on Jesus's behalf,
essentially is Jesus Christ himself.

On the other hand it is a vain act, to pray for
something that Jesus Christ did not command and then
say after it, "In Jesus' name we ask it, Lord." Not even
being sure to whom you pray. To do anything in Jesus's

name means doing it on Jesus's behalf because he gave commands for it. As Jesus, himself, said, "I myself can do nothing, unless I see the Father do it first." And in case you think you can't be sure what you have been called upon to do, Jesus delegated his authority to act on his behalf by saying: "I tell you the truth, *anyone* who has faith in me will do what I have been doing." (John 14: 12)

So it is plain that *anyone* obeying God's commands has God's authority — and *anyone* obeying Jesus's commands has Jesus's authority. If God has told *all* men to speak for the disinherited, to be a voice for those who are denied a voice, to comfort the sorrowful, and feed the hungry and clothe the naked and show hospitality to the alien — what other special calling is there in the world? If Jesus has worked out a strategy for *anyone* who will obey his voice, then all who are obedient have his authority. To ask for God's help in doing any of these things is praying in his name. To pray for anything besides, is praying for ourselves, in our own name. The phrase, then, "In Jesus' name we pray. Amen" is vanity. And we have used his name in vain.

In the sixteenth chapter of this book, John outlined the sequence of the last campaign for all of the messiah's followers. These then are direct commands from Jesus Christ, to all of those communities on earth which possess God's wisdom and can understand the message which Jesus Christ has sent to them. If, in faith, these things are done on Jesus's behalf, and if his words are faithfully obeyed, then Jesus Christ himself (acting in the name of God) actually is doing them. That is to say, Jesus's own followers on earth are called upon to do a special work for him — a work for which Jesus made the plan. Jesus is the architect; his workmen are the builders.

To do such a work in his name carries all of the authority that Jesus Christ himself received from God.

And the commissioning for doing this work is given to all fellowships of Israel who have "eaten" the book that John has given them, and have meticulously fulfilled all of the preliminary acts of preparation for the task. In symbolic terms that is to say they have properly clothed themselves (as priests of God) for leading the world into "the holy land". By "the holy land" we mean a new world system without crime, without war, without pollution, without disease, without sexual or racial biases and where all life and all nature is honoured and respected as being the glory of the creator. "For God said, 'Let *us* make man in *our* image after *our* likeness, and let them have jurisdiction over the fish of the sea, and over the foul of the air and over every moving thing that moves upon the earth.'"

In the last chapter of this prophecy that we read, John in the clearest of terms precisely defined the various stages of the last campaign God's servants were to wage against the whole world system. That campaign was divided into seven comprehensive parts. Now, so that God's people might better understand the nature of God's enemy, John boldly draws a concrete image of the spiritual condition of the world. This image has the benefit of helping all God's servants to appreciate the total picture of those related parts which make up Satan's world, and clearly illustrates the way they operate.

The picture that we see is not a pleasant one. It is shocking and disturbing to say the least. We are shown a monstrous scarlet beast carrying a drunken, regally-dressed harlot adorned with holy ornaments who from the gold cup of her wisdom and philosophies pours her immoralities upon the world. This is the spiritual world system the angels of God were told to pour the wrath of God upon. The scarlet colour of the beast reveals it to be blood guilty from the lives it has destroyed throughout history – from Abel to Zechariah, to Stephen, to the slaughter of the North American Indians, to the rape of Africa and millions of the black-skinned race, to the murder of millions of Jews throughout history and in the Nazi holocaust.

Yet many people are apparently confused by the number of beasts which they encounter in John's prophecy. I expect that this is largely due to the exaggerated emphasis which is placed upon predictive prophecy. Although predictive prophecy is present in the plan of Jesus Christ, the beasts primarily are used to give definition to important areas affecting human life. These areas even in John's time were recognizable to anyone who knew the scriptures well. It is important therefore that we realise the similarities and differences which we find in all these beasts.

The great red dragon which we met in Chapter Twelve is Satan. This social influence is not a creature having personal independence apart from man. It is a spirit dominating all areas of social life through the power it has upon the public atmosphere. This spirit, or public overmind, found its origin in the selfish inclinations of the human heart. Referred to in the scriptures variously as "the god of this (present) world," and "the prince of the power of the air," it is the pervasive force compelling all men and women to conform to worldly practices and to indiscriminately emulate whatever social model of behaviour and appearance the spirit of the world makes popular.

This social overmind is powerful and compelling, oftentimes perverse and stubbornly opposed to God, the creator of all things. From its influence, the world of Cain and Nimrod took their form. Because of its attachment to society itself, it has the power to give its voice a highly moral tone or to clothe itself in popular acclaim. But it leads the nations of the world to war, death, crime and destructive social practices. It first found voice in mankind's personal desire "to be like God — each individual deciding for himself what was good or evil as he chose." "If it feels good, do it," may have been the motto which the dragon used. Its whole idea of freedom was for every individual either to ignore or else deny the social consequences of his deeds and his accountability for them.

Jesus clearly showed the difference between listening to the voice of Satan or the voice of God when he praised Peter for astutely basing his opinions upon the scriptures rather than what others said. Jesus said regarding this: "Well done, Simon, son of Jonah, for flesh and blood did not reveal this thing to you, but my Father which is in heaven." Then just a few lines down the page of Matthew's gospel, Jesus found good reason for rebuking Peter with these words: "Get behind me Satan! You are a hindrance and a snare to me for you do not speak the words of God, but lean upon the practices and opinions of men."   (Matthew 16: 17 and 23)

Robbie Burns was therefore wrong when he observed:

"O would such power the giftie gie us
To see ourselves as others see us
'T would from many a trouble free us
And many foolish notions."

Sorry, Robert, you should have leaned a little more on the "giftie" than upon the observation powers of other men.

Even Paul, at Antioch, found occasion for rebuking Peter when the latter gauged his actions by the favour he could win from other men rather than from God.

Jeremiah diagnosed the problem when he said: "The
heart (of man) is deceitful and perverse above all things.
Who possibly can understand it?" (Jeremiah 17: 9) All
gospel writers later would concur with him on this and
lay special emphasis upon the point he made. For
instance in Mark's gospel, we find these words: "Out of
the hearts of men come evil thoughts, sexual immorality,
theft, murder, adultery, greed, malice, deceit, lewdness,
envy, slander, arrogance and folly." (Mark 7: 21). In
addition the power of Satan, which governs the social
atmosphere, elevates or glamourizes those whose patterns
of behaviour and appearance serves the world as guides
for the human heart to worship and to emulate. This
then is the dragon – the spiritual ruler of the world.

The beast from the sea (which is introduced to us in
Chapter Thirteen) is a physical manifestation of the
aggressiveness of Satan, apparent in all world nations that
have risen from the turmoil of societies fiercely
competing with one another for personal or for national
dominance. All those nations of the past from Babylon
to Rome and beyond would be a part of that same beast
which from generation to generation would renew itself
in every age. Daniel, the inspired writer of the Bible
book which bears his name, had more than five centuries
earlier, in his interpretation of Nebuchadnezzar's dream,
taken these same nations and represented them
prophetically as a gigantic statue that the Kingdom of
God would eventually destroy.

The beast out of the earth (with the number 666)
which will eventually ally itself with the beast out of the
sea represents a nation which (according to this book's
predictive prophecy) would one day rise to assert the will
of the common people upon earth. Their form of
government would seem benign (to the people who were
part of it) but its voice would be aggressive and assert

the dragon's will. Since such a nation could not rise above the imaginings of the human heart, schooled only in its own desires, Satan's voice would always be the voice that spoke for them and ruled their land.

In predicting this, John (or Jesus Christ) was remarkably astute, but what he said was well within the realm of being understood by anyone who had a thorough understanding of God's word. The human will was what brought sin into the world. The human will was what led Israel to grumble against Moses and demand meat to eat, instead of manna sent from God. The human will destroyed the hope of entering the Holy Land when Moses first sent spies into the nation it was told it should replace. What was in the human heart caused Israel to demand a king. It also was the people's voice and will that divided Israel into two nations and made them weak. In recent centuries, it was the people's will that broke the church up into many parts in opposition to the will of Christ and it is the people's will that keeps it in that state – making it the people's church rather than the church of Christ (which is one body).

Nor was the Gentile world any less susceptible to what the people thought and did. The first labour strike known to Gentile history was staged in ancient Egypt while the pyramids were being built. Ancient Rome experienced a series of Servile Wars that stretched from 134 to 71 BC. John simply noticed what seemed obvious to him: that the people would eventually demand and win a people's sovereign state. John's vision did not come from psychic mutterings, but from an incredible understanding of the minds and hearts of men. Since the nation he predicted had not yet emerged out of the womb, but was still in embryo, we could say it was still in the bottomless pit or in the wilderness. John doesn't do this though. He says that it will rise out of the earth. For human beings who eventually would form that nation, were very much in evidence. He read the signs of the times (as Jesus said he should) and accurately interpreted them.

So the beast out of the earth with the number 666 — the will of man to the ultimate degree — signified a nation which would aggressively assert the people's will. Yet the beast with the number 666 is even more than this. It is man in the image of the beast, rather than the image of God — the Anti-Christ, "The Naked Ape" if you will — man with all his animal instincts, passions and desires glorified and worshipped, and placed like a statue on a pedestal for all to emulate. The Naked Heart undisciplined. Although the people would see themselves and their government as benign, their voice would be the voice of Satan still, for it would speak like the dragon.

The scarlet beast full of blasphemous names is by far the most unsettling, and by far the most difficult to define. It exists but it doesn't exist. "It had existence at one time, but it exists no more." Yet it is continually ready to reveal itself.

This picture that John draws is so prodigiously unsettling because it wakens in our soul the tantalizing feeling it is something we should recognize. And so we should. In Chapter Eight, we took a little time to consider the significance of God's tabernacle, which the children of Israel transported through the wilderness with them. This tabernacle was the centre of their lives and unified them in one body — as a nation built upon the pattern of the man from heaven, crowned with the wisdom of God. What we are seeing here is its antithesis. All the symbols of God's holy nation are there still, but in reverse.

God dwelt among his people and was present with them at all times. To illustrate this truth, the tabernacle of God with the Ark of the Covenant in it was constructed in such a manner as would convey this spiritual truth to them in physical terms. The Ark itself was especially designed to illustrate the spiritual design of the human heart of Israel with the throne of God above it. This was the heart that he had planned for every man. Within it was the law designed to govern every individual (the ten commandments), the manna (or the daily bread of life) was there, and Aaron's budding rod assured the power of God's spiritual authority to anyone who understood and was obedient to his word.

God's heavenly chariot therefore was moved from place to place on earth where people, with the heart of God in them — keeping careful watch on God's creation, called upon his name. God's people were the temple God designed. They were a temple called upon to fill the earth. Even wise King Solomon had recognized the limitations of the magnificent building he had made for God when he declared: "Behold heaven and the heaven of heavens cannot contain thee; how much less the house that I have builded." (1 Kings 8: 27)

King David too (whose heart was fashioned after God's design) declared: "Where can I go from your spirit? Where can I flee from your presence? If I ascend to heaven, you are there. If I make my bed beneath the earth you are there. If I ride upon the wings of the morning (soaring into space) or travel to the farthermost reaches of the sea, your hand is always there to guide me and your right hand strengthens me." (Psalm 139: 7-10) For it was the heart as God designed it which assured God's presence with all the sons of Israel. Yuri Gagarin should have read this psalm.

Where God's throne is, depends upon the nature of the heart which worships him. Gustav Holtz was well aware of that when he composed his famous song "The Heart Worships." King David, therefore, when he realised he had strayed from following the way of God, earnestly entreated him with these words: "Create in me a pure heart, O God, and renew an upright spirit within me. Do not cast me from your presence or take your Holy Spirit from me. Restore to me the joy of your salvation and grant me a willing spirit to sustain me." (Psalm 51: 10-12)

For that same reason, King Solomon observed: "As a man thinks in his heart, so is he." (Proverbs 23: 7), and Jesus Christ (King David's greater son) spent much time in speaking of a heart made clean within. On one occasion he said this: "Make a tree good and its fruit will be good, or make a tree bad and its fruit will be bad, for a tree is recognized by its fruit....For out of the overflow of the heart the mouth speaks. The good man brings out good things from the good treasure of his heart, and the evil man brings out evil things from the evil stored up in his heart."   (Matthew 12: 33-35)

It is no accident therefore that the garments and the head plate or tzitz worn by Israel's High Priest are so much like those which the harlot wears. Moses writing of them said: "And with the blue and purple and scarlet cloth they made them fine garments for Aaron, as Jehovah had commanded Moses....Then with a strip of pure gold, they made a holy crown (or tzitz) and on it was inscribed these words (as if they were a holy seal): 'Sacred to Jehovah.'"   (Exodus 39: 1 and 30)

What John was doing, therefore, was making an important distinction between those serving God (who were sealed with God's seal) and those who served the world of Satan (who had the mark of the beast on them). The distinction that he made was between the Synagogue of Jehovah (in the image of the man of heaven) and the

Synagogue of Satan (in the image of the beast). He was not foolishly just looking on and irresponsibly pointing fingers at the Roman Catholic Church or God's chosen nation, Israel, as certain groups of Christians in their ignorance affirm. John was simply making a comparison between God's people and those who served Satan, whoever they might be. As Jesus said: "By their fruits you shall know them (not by any name that they might call themselves)." "For man looks upon the outward appearance but God looks upon the heart."

The city which the children of the beast carry about with them is spiritual Babylon — a harlot who has no husband but who serves whatever spirit happens to gain dominance within the world. Her political stance changes with the times, according to whatever alliances she might choose to make. The sacred jewelry she wears serves to indicate how much her conduct has profaned the name of God. She is contrasted with the holy city of spiritual Jerusalem, which is the virgin bride of God devoted to one husband. That is to say one God. Through the use of an implied antithetic parallel, a traditional device often used in Jewish poetry, John contrasts those people who serve the lusts and passions of the heart, with those who serve the great creator of the world — bridling their passions and controlling them.

So what John shows us is the moral condition of the entire world. Just as God's people are one body — as a community responsible for one another — and together guilty for any wrongdoing in their midst, so the people of Satan's world are all bloodguilty of the crimes that it perpetuates. The people, drunken and enslaved by their illusions and their passions, comprise the beast that the harlot sits upon. Yet John's description of the woman is deliberately intended to remind us of Ezekiel's description of Jerusalem where he said: "I bathed you with water and washed the blood from you and put ointments on you. I clothed you with an embroidered dress and put leather sandals on you. I dressed you in fine linen and covered you with costly garments. I adorned you with jewelry: I put bracelets on your arms and a necklace around your neck, and I put a ring in your nose, earrings in your ears and a beautiful crown on your head.

"So you were adorned with gold and silver; your clothes were of fine linen and costly fabric and embroidered cloth. Your food was fine flour, honey and olive oil. You became very beautiful and rose to be a queen. And your fame spread among the nations on account of your beauty, and because of the splendour I had given you, your beauty was made perfect. That is the way it was, declares Jehovah the Creator."   (Ezekiel 16: 9 -14)

Since Jehovah made man in the image of God, such a passage serves to show us the height from which mankind has fallen. Although Ezekiel's words are more elaborate than John's description of the harlot, these verses which describe the virgin bride of God, call attention to important differences and similarities exhibited by these two women. Yet the prostitute's apparel certainly resembles that worn by the priests of Israel. John also calls our attention to the words the harlot wears upon her forehead to indicate the nature of her thoughts. Upon the tzitz she wears, we find these words:

MYSTERY
BABYLON THE GREAT
MOTHER OF
ALL EVIL CITIES AND PERVERSE ACTIVITIES

Such words recall Isaiah's prophecy for us which says: "Their thoughts are thoughts of iniquity. Desolation and destruction lie in their paths. The way of peace they

do not know, and there is no justice in any of their
doings."   (Isaiah 59: 7)

Those perverse activities which John refers to,
include not only crimes but the whole direction of life,
business practices and the kind of recreational activities
that are pursued. What we sow is what shall grow. And
the fruit of what we grow is crime and war — that is to
say "thorns and thistles." In John's view, and in the view
of all the early Christians, those sent to prisons for their
crimes were not the only evil doers in the world.

Jesus spoke his mind on this when he asked the
citizens of Judea: "Do you imagine that those eighteen
who died when the tower of Siloam fell on them were
greater criminals than all the rest of those people living
in Jerusalem? Not at all. Everyone was just as guilty as
they were." The way of life, the philosophies of society,
its values, recreation and the way it entertains itself all
help to plant the seeds of evil in the world, making all
of us guilty of those crimes we so despise in others that
we read about in shocked dismay.

Being part of the same community, everyone is
either purified or contaminated by the cup from which
he chooses to drink. In this regard there is an important
reference in the book of *Joshua*, found in the Hebrew
scriptures of the Bible, which begs to be observed. We
know it was the custom of soldiers in very early times to
carry away the spoils of cities they destroyed. This was
not to be the case when Israel destroyed the city of
Jericho. Joshua told his armies, they were not to take
anything from the fallen city regardless of whatever
value it might seem to have.

In Chapter Seven of that book we read of a man
called Achan who clearly disobeyed that clear command,

and committed what in his eyes was a harmless crime.
He confiscated a few things from Jericho that he thought
valuable, which the Bible refers to as "accursed things". I
will not speculate on what they may have been, for what
is most important is the effect that one man's errors had
upon all Israel. When the armies of Israel tried to take a
smaller city, called Ai, that was less fortified, they
couldn't capture it. The final verdict that God gave for
this was "Israel has sinned."

There is no such thing as independent crime or sin.
Everything we do affects the whole community of which
we are a part. This was the lesson that the book of *Joshua*
hoped to teach: that independent lust or greed convicts
the whole community. Being part of one body, our actions
mutually affect each other. We are either drinking from
the cup infecting us with these transgressions of God's law,
or else we are examples others will observe and emulate.

The words of Joshua as well as those of John and
Jesus Christ serve as warnings to the children of God "to
keep your garments unstained by the world." That John
really meant to warn his readers of shallow surface
judgments in identifying Babylon and Israel — the harlot
and the virgin bride of God — is confirmed by the words
which follow in Ezekiel's prophecy. For after he described
the beauty of Jerusalem, Ezekiel, in continuing his words,
prophetically affirmed: "But trusting in your beauty, you
used your fame to make yourself a harlot, freely offering
your favours to anyone who passed by, and you
surrendered all your loveliness to anyone who asked (to
any group, or nation or celebrity which rose in public
favour and gained prominence). Then taking the beautiful
garments I had given you (the teachings of
righteousness) you adapted them to suit the shrines of
idols, and in these shrines you built you carried on your
harlotries — such things as should never have been done."
(Ezekiel 16: 15 -16)

Let us take the necessary time, therefore, to examine both these women carefully so that we might recognize them when we meet them in the world.

JERUSALEM (or ZION) is	BABYLON (or Confusion) is
The City of God Serving One God	The City of Satan Serving Many Gods (therefore has divided loyalties)
The Holy City	The Wicked City
City of Peace	City of Confusion, Crime and Violence
Depicted as a Virgin (devoted to one Lord)	Depicted as a Harlot (having many paramours and discarding each of them in turn as whim or fashion of the world dictates to her)
The Spiritual Capital of the Kingdom of God	The Spiritual Capital of the Nations
The Scriptures are its written constitution	Various Philosophies compete for dominance
Does not make a show of being overly righteous	Appearing outwardly righteous
Admires the humble and industrious	Stands in awe of famous individuals (who personify their gods)
Citizens modeled after the Man from heaven	Citizens which glorify the beast by celebrating their perversions and animal desires.

Its Defence System is the Character of its people	Puts its faith in strong men and an arsenal of weaponry for national security
At peace with nature	Hunters of animals and destroyers of forests and habitats for animals.
The citizens co-operate and share their resources	Its citizens compete for Wealth, Honour and Fame
Charity, Righteousness and Peace are the Fruit of its Activities	Crime, Perversion and Warfare are the Fruit of its Activities

Like God's people, who by the manner of their walk, transport their city everywhere, those who serve the harlot Babylon carry her with them (along with all her many paramour celebrities) to wherever they may go on earth. They carry all her crimes, her adulteries, her filthiness and her loose moral conduct, being just as transient in their affections as the harlot that they worship is. For Babylon is very much a living presence in their lives, and they are morally diseased by all her sicknesses. While the people who serve God are governed by the spiritual capital city of Jerusalem (which is equivalent to the tree of life), the people who serve Satan are governed by spiritual Babylon (which is equivalent to the tree whose fruit is death).

What becomes apparent from such revelations that John shows to us is that he did not hold the nations of the world in very high esteem. He couldn't see them ever rising above crime and war and social violence as long as they continued poisoning the masses with their idolatry of lust, personal desire, ambitions and fierce competition for pre-eminence. Every nation was so bogged down in personal vanity, envy, vengeance and greed — that Satan's voice would always govern them. Yet his picture clearly illustrates John's diagnosis of the great disease infecting all humanity.

He also shows the remedy. Wars, crimes and perversions are but the sores upon the skin. The terminal disease lies at the heart of the nation itself. And the prescription Jesus recommends for it is in the method of attack: (1) upon each individual separately, (2) upon the customs practiced in the communities, (3) upon the philosophies, entertainments and recreations that are poisonous in what they teach, (4) upon the leadership that gives no light, (5) upon all those who rule the media and encourage vice, (6) upon the paths and occupations men pursue, (7) upon the social atmosphere which sets the tone of life and invisibly instructs. All these must be restructured and instructed from the cup of Jesus Christ, who by his own example taught the world to love.

Jesus chose to build his Kingdom upon the solid Word of God, which defined the difference between right and wrong. From this he instructed every individual, and with the body language of his life, helped to build the human character upon a perfect vision of the character of God. He chose the individual as his starting point rather than the mighty actions of the mob, regardless of how well motivated it might be in its desires to "liberate" the world. He put into the hands of every individual the power to talk with God, and to throw off Babylon.

This restructuring of individuals started with the human heart and was called conversion. Conversion, even in Jesus's own eyes, never was a sudden thing. The man of God was called upon to master all his fiery passions and look beyond his personal desires and sufferings. "For if you do not master these, that demon known as sin crouches like a wild beast at your door, ready to take possession of you. Therefore you must learn to master it."

Society, according to all scriptures that we read, created its own ills, and the individual human heart, by nature, turned to those who teased its hidden lusts, awakening the beast that lay slumbering in it. The social atmosphere engendered by the power of "Satan's throne" was the chief cause stimulating social immorality. It became the fountainhead of every sort of crime and social violence as it set the moral tone and standard which the people tried to emulate.

In John's day, Satan's throne was easily identified. It was evident, not just at Pergamos but, in every city where pagan temples, festivals, and worship of the nations and the symbols representing them, encouraged war, lewdness, wild abandonment to passions and the ruthless pursuit of wealth. For while Satan's people worshipped fleshly appetites and cravings of the flesh (personified in gods and goddesses) with the abandon- ment of the Bacchantes, Jehovah's people worshipped the creator of the world and sought to honour God and his creation by walking soberly and thoughtfully in the way of peace. Neither hunting nor war was ever glorified by them. For creation was the robe of God, and his living creatures were the temple where he dwelt.

Later, in the second century, Theophilus, a Christian bishop from the community in Antioch, had this to say about idolatry: "Is not Saturn found to be a cannibal, destroying his own children? And even his son Jupiter... suckled by a goat...is hardly recommended by his deeds of incest, adultery and lust."

Yet Jesus Christ's apostle Paul, was even more explicit and definitive, in all his arguments against idolatry. He looked more deeply into what idolatry involved. What he objected to was not the act of merely bowing down to graven images. Paul condemned the very inspiration lying at its heart, and the flood of personal and social immoralities that flowed from it. He referred to these as demons, for they created and sustained a demoralizing social atmosphere. "Is a sacrifice to an idol anything at all?" he asked, "or an idol in itself anything significant? No, but the sacrifices pagans make to idols, in reality are offerings to demons (or the spirit of those social practices that we abhor)...and I do not want you to be participants (in spiritual idolatry). For you cannot drink from the cup of God's messiah and the cup of demons too; you cannot have a place at Christ's table and at the table of demons as well."   (1 Corinthians 10: 19 -21)

Paul's argument takes us right back to the principle expressed by Moses in the *Genesis* account, when Jehovah declared that "Man must not be allowed to reach out his hand and take also from the tree of life and eat, and live forever. For Jehovah the Creator banished Adam from the garden of Eden to work the ground from which he had been taken. Then after he had driven Man out of the garden, he placed Cherubim on the east side of it, with flaming swords flashing back and forth to guard the way to the tree of life."   (Genesis 3: 22 -24)

So strong was the relationship between idolatry and immorality in both Jewish and Christian minds, that the two words often were synonymous to them. This association is quite evident in many of Paul's words. In speaking to the Galatians, he said: "The traits of a sinful nature are quite plain: sexual immorality, impurity, and debauchery; idolatry and spiritism; hatred, discord, jealousy, fits of rage, selfish ambition, dissensions, factions and envy;

drunkenness and the like. So I warn you in the same way that I did before, that anyone who indulges in such vices will not inherit the Kingdom of God." (Galatians 5: 19 -21)

Then in the third chapter of *Colossians*, Paul in speaking of these traits, actually defines idolatry from them: "Slay that earthly nature in yourselves which gives rise to sexual immorality, impurity, lust, evil desires and greed, for these *are* idolatry." (Colossians 3: 5) Then he enlarges on his words by saying: "You must get rid of all these things: anger, rage, malice, slander, and filthy language from your lips." (Anything that sends an evil spirit forth) (Colossians 3: 8) Or as God said to Cain, "A demon crouches at the door (ready to devour you) and you must learn to master it." So Paul, in actually defining idolatry for us, clarifies what John meant when he told God's people they must cast off Babylon.

Throwing off Babylon means mastering all passions and being freed from the enslaving power of a manipulating world. The harlot city, therefore, has been thrown into the restless sea of Man. The way of the world is a religion in itself regardless of how well it has succeeded in masking what it is. What makes its spiritual idolatry appear so natural to everyone involved with it is the constant use and practice that is made of it in human lives. Even faulty speech seems natural to those who have not learned properly how to communicate. Perversions too seem natural to those who practice them — as do perversions such as war and domestic violence.

So what Christians, in those early times, were teaching appeared to all of those who were rehearsed in pagan rites, like radical, alien beliefs. When the first few waves of Christianity began to flow into the ancient world, they aroused deep feelings of resentment among certain citizens. Such revolutionary teachings were alarming. They struck the very root of many Roman practices, such as pagan holy days which were based upon carnality and celebration of the flesh. Great outcries therefore arose in many areas. The ax-sharp words these Christians spoke hit many tender sentiments as though upon an open nerve.

Since merchants and craftsmen often owed their livelihood to the sale of special merchandise for all these gala festivals, they had little tolerance for what these Christians said. Something was the matter with these Christians for they also spoke against such entertaining pastimes as gladiatorial games. They didn't seem to have much fun in them at all. They spoke of love but would not celebrate the Lupercalia or lay with slaves and sacred harlots as normal men would do.

In challenging the gods and goddesses of Rome, Christians, to the minds of many Roman citizens, were more than just a nuisance. They were an economic threat to them as well. Merchants, shopkeepers and highly skilled craftsmen alike were fearful that important sources of their revenue were being put in jeopardy, as many were dependent on the manufacture and the sale of sacred images of gods and goddesses to assure them of a healthy income and a little comfort in their lives. So it isn't any wonder that the early Christians were harassed and persecuted in these early times. Had they come on to the stage of history at a later time, they would more than likely have been tarred and feathered, lynched or ridden on a rail— or like Joseph Smith, "the Mormon heretic" been murdered in their jail cells as they awaited trial.

When Paul of Tarsus preached in Ephesus, a howling and indignant mob was raised to silence him. Maybe you recall the stridency of that tremendous riot which arose there. Those who made the idols of Diana were inflamed at Paul's having preached against idolatry, and were in a state of unreasoning violence. Such outlandish views as Paul espoused would have forced the merchants of Rome to look elsewhere for ways to bring in wealth.

Nor were the leaders of the nation neutral or indifferent to the doctrine that was being spread by Christians. They were fearful of the consequences that were lodged in a philosophy which taught that "the last should be first," and "the meek would inherit the earth." Everything in Christian teachings seemed to be a challenge to the Roman way of life and thought. Romans looked on Christianity as a threat. And actually it was. So it was inevitable that persecutions would soon fall heavily upon all those who were contaminating Rome with such outrageously subversive views.

You must consider, too, the rigid stance that bureaucrats assume in every age. They are notoriously ill equipped for dealing wisely with such matters as do not fit into the mold and patterns of the guidelines set by them, and which limit them to doing only what is nationally expedient. They therefore judge such matters superficially, appraising them from their exterior appearance or from rumour, and they often take a rigid stance on matters which involve the national security.

Pliny under orders from Trajan was therefore to interrogate Bithynians with the ominous question: "Are you now or have you ever been a Christian?" ("Interrogavi ipsos an essent Christiani. Confidentes iterum ac tertio iterrogavi supplicium minatus. Perseverantes duci iussi." — Pliny to Trajan, Letters Bk X, XCVI) Unseating the harlot (spirit of idolatry with her many gods and goddesses) was not to be a very easy task for Christians then. And yes, she proved herself blood guilty in those days.

By referring to the harlot on the beast as Babylon, John shows us there is something in the nature of that ancient city which he wants his readers to take notice of. So in this prophecy, he calls attention to the well-known fact that Babylon was built on many waters. That conjures instantly the sound of Jeremiah's words for them: "O (Babylon), you who dwell by many waters, rich in treasures, your end has come, and the time of your duration is cut short." (Jeremiah 51: 13) But these waters in John's vision are purely figurative, for he tells us that they represent "the masses of people out of every language, race and nationality." So John depends upon us knowing something of the history of Babylon.

If you are not at all familiar with its history, I shall briefly give a very short account of it for you. Babylon was the capital city of ancient Babylonia. Most histories and Bible dictionaries will tell you that its beginnings are unknown, but the Bible says that it was built by Nimrod approximately four millenia ago. It was the capital of the first world order, which was erected following "the Great Flood." In early Bible literature, it was known as Babel, and we are told that all political world orders came from it. And historians recognize the truth of this, as many world religions can be traced directly to her influence, including those of ancient Greece and Rome.

The history of Babylon was a most chaotic one, but there are several things that are worth mentioning. It became an independent city state somewhere around 1894 BC, when the Amorite Sumu Abum founded a dynasty there, which reached its height under King Hammurabi. Hammurabi (1792-1750 BC) — after studying the varied laws and customs of the peoples who inhabited the land of Babylonia, gave the world the famous Hammurabi code of law, which many scholars claim served Moses in his compilation of the laws of Israel.

Far more detailed than any code of law preceding it, the Hammurabi code was comprehensive, covering all such matters as business, criminal, family and agricultural activity. And it was founded on the principle that the strong must not oppress the weak. Certainly, it was justly famous and may have been an influence on Moses, but there are many remarkable differences well worth noticing. Unlike the Hammurabi law, the Mosaic law did not observe class differences. Equality before the law began with ancient Israel. Israel's law was also based upon the principle of "love": Love for the Creator (and his creation) and love for mankind. And the ten commandments defined for them exactly what was meant by love.

However, I expect that it was because of the law code which Hammurabi gave to ancient Babylonia that the King of Babylon was given the name of the morning star, "Lucifer". For the King of Babylon brought the light of heaven — through "the law he brought with him" — into the world. But it was the far more glorious Babylon of Nebuchadnezzar II (605 - 562 BC) who humbled the land of Judah (586 BC) and brought her people into captivity, that made Babylon the most glorious city upon earth. In modern terms, we would call it cosmopolitan, as people came there from every place on earth — to visit, trade and do business — and many different cultures mingled in this large metropolis. Like the great Titanic, it must have seemed completely indestructible and thoroughly impossible to overthrow.

It was the sort of city of which strong men boast. And Nebuchadnezzar boasted mightily of his accomplishment. To ancient eyes, it was one of the great wonders of the world. This sprawling metropolis was built straddling the Euphrates River. Its armies were formidable, and the city's double walls formed an important part of Babylon's seemingly impregnable defence system.

Yet the Persian king, Cyrus the Great (a Zoroastrian devotee) was able to break through their strong walls of defence. According to Herodotus, Cyrus "diverted the (course of the Euphrates) river, by means of a canal, into a lake which was previously a swamp, (and) he made the ancient channel fordable, by the sinking of the river and (having made the river bed dry, his armies)...entered Babylon by this passage." (*Herodotus* Book I. sec. 191.)

So it was that Cyrus, King of the Persians, and Hapargus, Chief of the Medes (the Kings from the east) took over Babylon. Xenephon, however, offers us a few more details. He tells of how Cyrus diverted the waters of the Euphrates into trenches and then, while the city was absorbed in festival celebrations, laid siege to the city by sending his forces up the riverbed and past the city wall. The palace guards were taken by surprise, so that the troops of Cyrus were able to enter unhindered, through the very gates of the palace itself.

(*Cyropaedia* VII 5: 7-34)

Chapter Five of *Daniel* sheds further light upon the drama of that night which changed the mood of history in the ancient world. A further prophecy regarding it is found in Isaiah's carefully worded account. In the Bible book which bears his name, Isaiah says: "This is the retribution that is about to fall upon the land of Babylon, that desert near the sea: Just like a windstorm from the south, disaster will come raging out of the wilderness from a fierce and terrifying land. In a harsh and grievous vision shown to me, I have watched these treacherous men continue in their treachery and this destructive nation (of Babylon) continually destroy. Therefore Persia will come (and fall upon them); and Media will lay siege (and conquer them) bringing to an end the agony and suffering that Babylonia has wrought upon the world. Yet, even so, my heart is smitten and my soul is horrified by what I see, so that I am overcome with agonizing pains, just like a woman suffering in giving birth.

"My whole head swims and reels, and the nightfall which I had looked forward to (for rest) only sets my soul to trembling. But (in the midst of all this danger) the Babylonians prepare tables, and then spreading out rugs and carefully arranging seats, they eat and drink (in careless revelry).

"'Come, you captains, rise and oil your shields,' (I admonish them to no avail "Be alert and stand in readiness.) For this is what Jehovah says to me: 'Go yourself at once and place a watchman in the tower to loudly call out the report of what he sees, reporting instantly the moment that he sights any horse-drawn chariots or cavalrymen sitting upon donkeys or camels. Tell him to remain alert and instantly announce the news of what he sees.'

"When at last the watchman like a roaring lion, did call out to me, he said: 'Sir, day by day I have kept a faithful watch, and I have never left my post at night. But look! Only now a man approaches in a chariot drawn by a team of horses.' The message, then relayed to me, was 'Babylon is fallen. She has fallen, and the graven images of all her gods are shattered on the ground.' O Israel, my crushed and broken people, trampled on the threshing floor! I have told you everything of what Jehovah of armies, the God of Israel, has made known to me."

(Isaiah 21: 1-10)

We find from the vision John reveals to us in later centuries, that to his mind, Babylon survived, for she was the MOTHER OF ALL HARLOT CITIES in the world. Pergamos (for instance) was one of these. Babylonian culture had had a strong effect upon the world. She was present still in all their ways of measuring, in social pastimes and in many of the ways they entertained themselves. What helped her to survive was the multitude of idolatrous religions and their deities. These encouraged and indulged the people in passions of the flesh. But John was wise enough to look beyond his time and see it as a long-lived city having spiritual existence in the world since ancient times and continuing into the future.

There it would appear in different forms, and finally assume an organized existence which would deliberately and cynically enslave the populace in spirit. For spiritual enslavement always comes before physical enslavement. So in this way, the beast would assume a physical existence in this consciously manipulated plan for which the spiritual history of the people had conditioned them, as was the case in Nazi Germany or in North America during the Cold War years.

By identifying the harlot on the beast as Babylon, John also calls attention to the weaknesses existing in her seemingly impregnable defences. That weak point lies in the emotionally manipulated people themselves. The many waters of Babylon, so John has carefully instructed us, are "masses of people out of every language, race and nationality." Jesus Christ would build these up by revealing to them their own vulnerability. Then he would "heal their sicknesses" by rebuilding them on stronger principles which he would teach them from the word of God. Through this he would reconstruct their character and redirect their paths. This would make them strong because the word of God is sure and does not vary to appease the world. In this way he would divert the waters that protected Babylon.

So like Cyrus, Jesus Christ would begin his own campaign with an attack upon the many waters guarding spiritual Babylon. By focusing the first attack upon the individual citizen (previously described as grass and trees) the way into the city would be opened for a full attack upon the customs and the values by which people live. In such a manner he would alter the community itself. Like Cyrus, Christ's armies would have to take advantage of their lead and win the total victory so that Babylon would be both spiritually and physically overthrown. They could not rest alone upon the first step of the plan. Total salvation (spiritual and physical) was to be the object they pursued for every man. As was so often sung in that once famous Negro spiritual, "Didn't my Lord deliver Daniel? Then why not every man?"

Eventually these troops would have to concentrate upon weakening the strength of Babylon and then unseating her. They must completely overthrow the harlot city spiritually governing the God-defying world. All steps were separately aimed at doing this. From drying up its waters, to altering the social atmosphere in just the same way Cyrus once had done, they would establish justice, righteousness and mercy in the land. Yet their ultimate purpose is clarified in these words spoken by Isaiah long ago: "They will neither harm nor destroy on all my holy mountain (in the entire Kingdom of God, which will be spread throughout the earth) for the earth will be full of the knowledge of Jehovah as the waters cover the sea (indicating that the social atmosphere would be made whole and clean and mankind would be at peace with man and end his war with nature and with God)."

There is predictive prophecy as well, however, in John's words, but like all prophecy it fits into the whole great scheme which is laid out for us. For neither John nor any prophet saw the world as being in a static state. The beast which we contend with, changes constantly before our eyes, and has the power to hide or to reveal itself at any time. This is the reason we are told by John that it will very shortly rise out of the pit again, before it goes to its destruction afterwards.

"When that occurs," he says, "like all the world's inhabitants since the creation of the world, those whose names are not recorded in the *Book of Life* will be dazzled and stand in awe of it, because it doesn't have existence now, though it will come into existence once again."

This is not superstitious nonsense. It is real. So this matter calls for careful reasoning and not religious biases. What John asks us to apply is "The wisdom one receives from (the written word of God, given from) above (which) is pure, peace loving, reasonable, ready to obey, merciful, yielding good fruits, free from prejudice and is unfeigned.

(James 3: 17)

That means that we are not to make decisions based on superficial evidence. We must rely on scriptures, our knowledge of world history and use our observation powers to see what forces actually are governing our time. John told us that in considering the beast, "This is something you must, with wisdom, ponder on: The seven heads of the beast are seven mountains (or mighty kingdoms) that the woman is established in. Five of them have come and gone, but one is ruling now, and there is still another one to come, whose rule will be extremely brief. The beast itself, however, which once had been, but now exists no more, will be the eighth great power, ruling with the seven super powers that ruled before. When it appears, it too will go to its destruction like all the others which preceded it.

"Now the ten horns that you saw are ten kings (or sovereign state governments) which have not taken power as yet, but when they do, they'll rule together for one hour with the beast. Unified in purpose (and by treaty) all ten ruling states will give the beast their strength and power, and together they will war against the lamb. But the lamb will overcome all these, for he is greater than all lords and stronger than all kings (or sovereign states), and all his loyal and faithful followers will stand with him."

John here openly interprets his own imagery. He tells us that the seven heads are seven sovereign states. The first five which have come and gone can only be the five great powers that the Bible has already named for us: Egypt, Assyria, Babylonia, Medo-Persia, and Greece. These were the only great world nations that had come and gone. Rome was the one that still was ruling in John's time. All (if we believe John's words) were governed by the same confusion as Babylon, which at the time of Babel's tower, had spread confusion everywhere throughout the earth. The brutish scarlet beast then is the way of the idolatrous people and their idolatrous governments, in the final culmination of their wickedness.

Jeremiah said of these: "Babylon was a gold cup in Jehovah's hand, and she made the whole world drunk (with her idolatry). The peoples drank her wine, and because of it, they lost all sense of reason. (literally "were driven mad." — Jeremiah 50: 38). Because the people had gone mad, the people would destroy themselves — and that is what perversion is. "Babylon's waters will all dry up because her people have gone completely mad with her idolatry." (Jeremiah 51: 7)

World poets though mislead us in their views of Satan's throne. Dante Alighieri and John Milton both imagined that this throne was underneath the earth where a gigantic evil creature known as the Devil invisibly resided. Jesus's apostle John, however, tells a different tale. He shows us that this throne is very much in evidence, observable and a fundamental part of the material world where we reside. For it is that body of glorified men and women who exalt the passions of the flesh and make idolatry (enslavement to our passions) a "normal" part of life. So the passions of the flesh become our gods—so that any thought of God himself becomes superfluous. This is the beast that stands in the place of God—which the gospel writer Mark refers to as "the abomination which causes desolation." John in this prophecy informs us that it will one day (when it assumes the concrete form it had in ancient Babylon) rule together with all nations of the world uniting them.

To see what forms the harlot and the beast will take in future times, we must look at past and future history, past and future in the sense that we are standing spiritually with John in 98 A.D. John did not look at the future in the same way that we do today, for we look back on what he saw. What he foresaw though were the possibilities, and he sought to warn Christ's followers of them. He also was aware that in his own time many followers of Christ were flirting with the world and that the gravest dangers seemed to be in store for them and needed to be avoided at all costs. For the penalty was to be a part of Babylon. John was not alone in fearing this. All Christian writers warn us of the anti-Christ, that spirit in the Church itself that still retains Christ's name but whose deeds and words are not at all like his.

John, though, dares to make the prediction that Rome, which seemed so solid then, would fall and that another ruling power would rise to take its place, and that finally the beast itself would rule. We should therefore take a little time to stand with John and trace the course of "future" history as we can view it now in the light of real events.

The transition from ancient to modern history began somewhere around the year 300 AD, when the most terrible of all Christian persecutors, Diocletian, ruled. Diocletian was a genius. There is no doubt of it. Within twenty years he reorganized the whole administration of the Roman empire. We cannot doubt it would have fallen all apart if Diocletian, at that time, had not taken hold of it. To make his empire firm, he founded it upon the principle of his own divine authority. That is to say, he made himself a god.

Many people today, who seem to feel they do not worship any gods at all, might wonder what religion has to do with government. The truth is religion plays a major part in every social order of the world. Religion gives societies stability. It is the glue which holds them together and keeps them from falling apart. There has to be a common bond of sorts to define relationships in such a way that people see the sense of doing whatever social tasks they do. No social order can possibly be built solely upon abstract social principles. For these are cold and meaningless.

Every nation, therefore, has its shrines — even in the so-called atheistic nations of the world. France which by an act of parliament declared there was no God, still served Mother Liberty. The United States holds services in which its citizens solemnly pledge allegiance to the flag, sing hymns of praise to their nation's righteousness and sing the national anthem to open every sports event, while the Alamo and other places serve as shrines of reverence. It's history has become sacred mythology that warps the truth at times to satisfy the nation's image of itself. The Soviet Union had Lenin's tomb, and Volgograd with Mother Russia dominating it. Just in case you missed the strong religious connotation in the American pledge of allegiance to the flag, maybe you will see the similarity in this recitation that Stalin introduced as a responsive pledge of faith and loyalty to the Communist Party in the Soviet Union:

In departing from us, Comrade Lenin enjoined on us to hold high and keep pure the great calling of Member of the Party.

— WE VOW TO THEE, COMRADE LENIN, THAT WE WILL HONOURABLY FULFIL THIS THY COMMANDMENT.

In departing from us, Comrade Lenin enjoined on us to guard the unity of the Party....

— WE VOW TO THEE, COMRADE LENIN, THAT WE WILL HONOURABLY FULFIL THIS THY COMMANDMENT.

In departing from us, Comrade Lenin enjoined on us to guard and strengthen the dictatorship of the Proletariat....

— WE VOW TO THEE, COMRADE LENIN, THAT WE WILL HONOURABLY FULFIL THIS THY COMMANDMENT....
(Payne. *The Life and Death of Lenin.* pp 609-610)

Then what are we to make of such national personalities as John Bull, Johnny Canuck and Uncle Sam? Are they not gods? "Oh no!" you will say definitely. "They are merely symbols which represent the spirit of the nation that we serve." That's it, isn't it? You may not think you pray to them, but they represent an overriding spirit of the nation that can command and demand your loyalty. Those who can't join in with what the nations worship become, in most people's eyes, criminals, cultists or radicals. Is it any wonder, then, that Christians were despised in challenging such gods?

Diocletian made himself the nation's God, not because he was an egotist but because he had the knowledge of how to run the state and make it work. He began by delegating power, and dividing up the Roman empire into provinces which he called diocese. Then he appointed administrators that he called vicars, who wore long robes like those of modern priests. In addition to these Diocletian made more emperors, and he called them Little Caesars. To these he delegated his authority so they could, in the name of Rome and in the name of Diocletian, do whatever was required of them. The empire and the civil service under him had a very moral structure too. In them he was able to instill the strong belief that they were working for the honour of the empire and for the good of all, since both the empire and the emperor were looked upon by them as thoroughly divine—much like the attitude Americans at one time had toward their presidents.

Diocletian's persecution of Christians was inevitable. Because Christians served a God demanding total loyalty, they were regarded as a threat not just to Diocletian, but to the very fabric of the world which he had made. By questioning the Emperor's divinity which acted as the glue of Rome, they were threatening the whole supporting structure which Diocletian painstakingly had built around himself. As any patriotic man could see this couldn't be allowed. The persecution of Christians under Diocletian grew so severe, that eastern churches were to date their calendars from the time of this great persecution rather than from the date of Christ's own birth.

Was it any wonder then that all the Christian population in Rome was overwhelmed when on October 28 of the year 312, a great and sudden change took place? It was something that would soon reverberate throughout the world. Constantine the Great led his armies through the streets of Rome to stand before the house of Miltiades the local bishop of the Christian Church. Seeing them with drawn swords in their hands, Miltiades had every reason to feel ill at ease. But what took place was soon to change the world.

At that time, a Roman bishop didn't differ in his power from any other bishop in the world. A church bishop, in very early days, acted simply as a focal point for Christians in each of the various communities throughout the world. He along with various elder members of the community church, who were mature enough in faith to accept responsibilities, were able to assure order and stability amongst the various groups meeting often separately throughout the city and sometimes as a whole. It was the voice of fellowship, however, that was heard at the meetings of the church, and the bishop and the elders were charged to keep them orderly.

This did not always prove to be an easy thing. For the sake of keeping order in the congregation, Paul, on one occasion, advised a church community to have matters of contention and concern previously raised in church meetings discussed privately at home between husbands and wives. By finding unity at home, husbands would be able then to act as spokesmen for their family's concerns in congregational disputes. By doing this, Paul hoped to reduce the lengthiness and confusion found in open meetings of the church, where congregational differences were aired.

He did not mean it as a way of silencing the voice of women in the church. It had nothing at all to do with who "preached sermons" and who didn't. It had to do with settling a large body of community disagreements, and if families could not agree among themselves how could a church community? Paul called attention to the fact that the home was an important part of the church where family differences could be resolved. In settling community differences a family had to speak with one voice.

Although some history books may disagree in their accounts of what actually took place in this wedding feast between the Church and the Roman state in the time of Constantine, we know that Christians were exalted by the emperor to a very special place in Roman life. And that Constantine's decision marked the time when steady progress began toward the birth of National Christianity, which became complete in 394 A.D. when the Roman Emperor Theodocius outlawed all the ancient gods of Rome and made conversion to Christianity compulsory. However, we should realise that compulsory belief in Jesus's teachings had never been a thing which Jesus himself advocated or condoned, for he had said: "No man possibly can come to me unless the spirit leads him."

To say that Christians were confused by what was happening, after Constantine began reorganizing Christianity, is to understate their case. They were in every way completely unprepared for what occurred. Even the *Apocalypse* of John, as far as any one could see, offered very little guidance on what they were supposed to do in such a circumstance. Scripture even didn't seem to offer them a guide for understanding what was going on. Christians could only blindly feel their way and wonder what was happening. They didn't understand the circumstances, and they openly admitted it. It was as though the voice of God had stilled the waters of the world, and brought all persecution to an end.

Even so, I must correct a false impression many people seem to have about this early history. Christianity was not made the official state religion of Rome by Constantine. Rome's state religion was and still remained pagan sun worship. Sol Invictus was the god of state and his chief emblem was the cross. Its weekly holy day was the first day of the week. The birthday of the sun — Sol Invictus — was December 25th which coincided with the celebrations of Saturnalia, a season of good will, banqueting, visiting friends and relatives, wassailing (caroling) and the exchanging of gifts. Merchants did extensive business on such holidays as this. Other holy days included the great love feast of Lupercalia in February, honouring the Baalantine (pronounced Valentine) hunter of the wolf (whose symbol was the love god with his hunter's bow); and the resurrection celebrations of the Tammuz cult each spring.

Constantine's whole reign as emperor was hailed as a "sun emperorship," and he served as the High Priest of Sol Invictus during it. His banners and his coinage, as before, continued to display the cross (a symbol of the sun) as the sign of divine guidance. It should be mentioned, as well, that the Christian symbol up till that time had been the sign of the fish, and not that of the cross as some apparently believe.

Yet in the scattered empire that he tried to unify, Constantine did much more than merely tolerate Christianity. He adopted it. For he understood that Christianity alone, of all the sects, was represented everywhere throughout all the lands he ruled, and even those beyond his realm. Since he saw very little difference between the cult of Sol Invictus and the God

of Christendom who ruled the earth and sky, he took
God (the Father) as the special patron guiding him and
strengthening his reign. Constantine (as far as he had
been concerned) found nothing to conflict with what he
ever knew of God.

Jesus was the only problem that Constantine really
encountered in Christianity, but he decided he could
overcome that problem, for the moment, simply by
ignoring it. In his own eyes, Constantine looked on
himself as the anointed one of God. The role he played
in Roman life confirmed his view of this. Like Israel's
King David and King Solomon, Constantine brought
unity to the lands he ruled. And like those kings he had
consolidated his empire, oversaw and governed it under
the divine sanction of the God of ancient Israel. Jesus, in
his eyes, had tried to do these very things as well, but
failed, whereas he had taken up and done what Jesus
could not do.

One might wonder then, why he didn't choose the
Jewish faith instead of Christianity. The answer's not a
simple one, but Christianity had had a greater impact on
the world, and its influence was more widely spread. His
rule then heralded a kind of early democracy. For
Christianity, being the most widely spread belief in the
Roman world was, with a little mingling (for a time) of
other faiths, made one of the spiritual guiding forces —
the heaven if you like — governing the Roman world.
Rome, however, was not ruled exclusively by it.

The cult of Sol Invictus had been introduced into
Rome a century before the time of Constantine. Syrian
in origin, it had exhibited many elements of Baal and
Astarte worship. Still, like Christianity, it was
monotheistic. Since it conceived the sun god as
containing all the attributes of all other gods, it made it

possible to rid the Roman world of some of them without causing any friction as it peacefully accommodated all or most of them.

However, in the year 325 AD, Constantine inaugerated the idea of Church Councils by compelling the Christian bishops throughout all the Empire to meet at Nicea. As we might easily suppose, in a church so widely scattered in the world, there were many differences. So there was much confusion and disagreements found in them. But Constantine gave orders to resolve their differences, which might lead us to conclude, that the plan which John proposed for them, in *Revelation*, had not been understood or put into use at all.

Some began to wonder if the new Christian Empire possibly could be the long awaited Kingdom of God. There was much soul searching amongst all those gathered for the conference, and the re-evaluation of Christian principles ensued with many hot discussions and hot arguments. Some expressed the view that the church could only be corrupted by entangling itself in the Roman world's affairs. Others said that the Roman world with all its gods was still the Church's enemy. But the great majority of Christians disagreed with them and thought that it was wise to grasp the opportunity to spread Christianity throughout the empire and beyond.

From this safe distance when we read that Constantine as Pontifex Maximus of the Roman Empire offered bishops of the Christian Church powerful positions of prominence and wealth as officers of the Roman state, we cannot help but hear a multitude of echoes from the Bible. In Matthew's gospel we read the words of the tempter to Christ: "All these things I will give you if you will only fall down and worship me." or Balak's words to Balaam: "I thought to promote you to great honour, but you let Jehovah keep you back from it."

The Catholic Encylopedia itself is not ignorant of this for it says: "Some bishops, blinded by the splendour of the court, even went so far as to laud the emperor as an angel of God, as a sacred being, and to prophesy that he would, like the Son of God, reign in heaven." These words of course echo those of Paul who said: "Even Satan himself is made to appear like an angel of light."

At the council of Nicea, Constantine was able to resolve his one major problem with Christianity, Jesus Christ himself. He got the council to agree that Jesus Christ was God, and he wielded great influence upon the Church, sometimes making definite decisions for them when they failed to reach agreement on their own. Then throughout his reign, he blurred distinctions between Christianity, Mithraism and Sol Invictus, choosing to ignore whatever differences had separated them. So throughout his reign, Constantine could still continue erecting statues of Cybele and of Sol Invictus. On the latter of these, Constantine's own face appeared.

Christians now enjoyed a greater prestige in the world of Rome. Once hated everywhere, they now were loved. For in the mind of Roman citizens, they'd come to symbolize the spirit of the Roman world. So when Miltiades died in January 314 AD, Silvester was named pope and was crowned – dressed in richly royal robes – like any other earthly prince. Then he was housed in the beautiful Lateran Palace. Constantine, went on to fill many principal government positions with Christians and took an active part in building Christian churches throughout the Roman world.

No one possibly can doubt the absolute sincerity of those Christians who had suffered so long for their faith. How could anyone imagine that they merely stood aside and let the emperor of Rome have a free hand in reorganizing them? Yet there is an irony that we must recognize, and something greatly out of joint in what took place. For the church gave recognition to the very power that had executed Jesus Christ—an authority which continued to use crucifixion against all rebels of the state, and would continue persecuting Christians—renamed "heretics"—who weren't aligned with it. Even Jesus Christ—if he had come into this world to reassert his claim to be the heir of the throne of Israel—would certainly have met the same death he had met before.

Ironic too is the fact that the Christian Church would itself adopt the very dress, names and offices that Diocletian, the greatest of all Christian persecutors had introduced to Rome. It was the British historian, H. G. Wells who pointed out that Constantine brought politics and autocracy into a Christendom which was suffering from deep divisions in itself. In his *Outline of History*, he says: "not only was the Council of Nicea assembled by Constantine the Great, but all the great councils, the two at Constantinople (381 and 553), Ephesus (431), and Chalcedon (451) were all called together by the imperial power." What seems so puzzling about this whole affair is that not only were there no Church Councils prior to the time of Constantine, but an unbaptized Roman Emperor was allowed to settle many of the disagreements that they had.

Yet Constantine really needed something extremely vital in what Christianity could offer him. For what he needed most was an empire that was unified in politics, religion and in territory. Christianity, which was the most widespread religion in his realm, had to have complete agreement with itself. Christians, themselves must have seen much sense in this. So under his fatherly hand (and most Christians must have thought of it as that) Constantine led the churches to agreement with themselves.

In doing so, he made Christianity the new cement of Rome. Then throughout his reign, he skillfully blended the qualities of Mithraism, Sol Invictus and Christianity. However, H. G. Wells saw it in a harsher light than this and said: "The idea of stamping out all controversy and division, stamping out all thought, by imposing one dogmatic creed upon all believers...is the idea of the single-handed man who feels that to work at all he must be free from opposition and criticism. The history of the Church under (Constantine's) influence becomes now therefore a history of the violent struggles that were bound to follow upon his sudden and rough summons to unanimity. From him the Church acquired the disposition to be authoritative and unquestioned, to develop a centralized organization and run parallel to the empire." Gone was that special fellowship we mentioned earlier, where each considered the other as able to admonish when he spoke with the authority of God's word and to be admonished by all other brethren if he erred.

"Heretic" became the catchall word aimed at any Christian who would dare to challenge any of the dogmas and the canons of the church (church laws) promulgated by the Councils called by the Roman emperor, even if that Christian could substantiate his words with Scriptural evidence that refuted them. The search for heretics, as history reveals, became a ruthless thing. So what is anyone to make of it?

History, however, even at its best, leaves much to be desired. For regardless of how carefully historians might try to grasp the truth, nothing can recall the atmosphere that influenced decisions and events that were experienced by those who were its witnesses. Constantine could not have been a cynic as some historians maintain. Though I have no doubt that he was working primarily for the good of Rome, he must have had a strong

religious streak in him and a powerfully persuasive
manner that could gain the confidence of people who
would gladly have given up their own lives rather than
deny their faith. Amiable and soldierly, with something
of the priest in him, Constantine was able to establish an
atmosphere which Christians never had experienced
before. Upon command he was able to assemble
Christians from all places in the Roman world. It must
have been a terribly impressive thing. There never had
been any other time in the experience of Christians that
could compare with it.

Also history has a tendency to focus only upon the
larger movements in the world and ignore the smaller
ones completely. So it should be stated here, as well, that
although most Christians went along with those decisions
that Rome made on their behalf concerning the alliance
of the state and church, there were many Christians still
who were not persuaded and who did not go along with
it. These, in order to avoid the charge of heresy,
disappeared, some no doubt into the hidden shadowland
within the "church" itself, and others into the mountains
and the valleys of Europe and Asia Minor, and history
lost sight of them, since "they were no part of this world"
or its history.

Like slash editors who boldly eliminate the fine print
of additional material and anything that they regard as
trivial, historians concerned themselves almost
exclusively with what was happening in National
Christianity, because it was the larger group. Historians,
like journalists and people of all kinds, tend to look upon
the smaller movements more as rebels against established
practices. In reality, however, many Christians were
simply standing firm, and holding on to what they had
always believed. Seen, therefore, by historians, as too

inconsequential to observe, history glossed over them. What history preserved, therefore, was what appeared self evident from a surface scrutiny: that there was now ONE EMPIRE, ONE CHURCH, and ONE GOD.

This view of history, however, has frequently been challenged. For there never was a time when only one church body existed in the world. While it is true that there was only one "established church" given legal recognition by the Roman world, throughout history there were always many scattered groups of Christians who were treated like outlaws because they weren't aligned with it—Paulicians, Arians, Donatists, Albergensians, Waldensians, etc. So widespread were many of these groups, it would have been impossible for any one of them simply to have sprung out of one man's willful heresy. It is suggested therefore that these outlawed Christian groups should properly be spoken of as "Christians in hiding" for they blossomed periodically inside and outside of the legally established institution of the Church.

These were not allied with any kingdom of the world. It was said, for instance, of the Waldensians that they memorized whole books of the Bible, and that these sincere and courageous individuals often filtered down like mountain streams from mountain areas or outlying rural districts into other regions close to them where they spoke the written word of God. Some historians maintain that their clothes were so made they could conceal whole books of the Bible in their folded seams. As traveling tradesmen or workmen they would reside in different private homes before moving on to other places. Able to speak many parts of the Bible from memory they would discreetly engage others in conversation, speaking much of the Bible from memory to them whenever it appeared appropriate.

Because they were so transient, appearing and disappearing afterwards, some imagined, we are told, that they believed, after speaking to Waldensians, that they had spoken to angels. Perhaps they had, for their influence was spread almost supernaturally and was felt both inside and outside the established orders of the church. So-called heresies could not possibly have spread quite as quickly as they did without such independent groups of men. So that indeed we might question the historic outlook which credits individuals inside the church as originating and perpetrating heresies. Long before the time of Luther, there were other Christian outlooks besides those which official Christianity allowed, and Luther himself might possibly have been influenced by some of them.

Yet when Luther came on to the scene, he did not create an independent Church. He leaned heavily upon a worldly prince for his protection from the power of Rome. And it is remarkable that as world Protestantism gained momentum, just how many different groups of Christians came spilling from the fount of hidden Christendom. Unfortunately the Protestant movement was not a purely Christian one any more than Rome's had been. In many cases many Christian movements still remained political in origin — since the most powerful and influential of these groups were all allied with rulers and with nations of the world. In other words they served two masters. So it is remarkable that the Christian church, which had been charged by Jesus Christ with bringing peace to the world and bringing wars to an end, were now more than elbow deep in all the blood of actually promoting them, each allied with some other nation's cause.

So today there are more than 25,000 divisions and denominations that make up Christendom. Those which are vocally or tacitly supportive of their nations' governments are looked on as respectable. Others are spoken of derisively as cults. So where is Babylon? Was the Kingdom of God ever really established upon earth? Or was it deemed unnecessary after Constantine? Or did Christians lose the last campaign? It seems more likely it was never fought at all. Perhaps the time was never really ripe for it. Yet in making Christianity centrally controlled by an earthly city, rather than by the heavenly one, the focus of the strategy was changed from that which John laid out for them.

In John's campaign, each city depended directly only upon heaven and the word of God, and were only to be locally concerned with gaining unity amongst themselves. As local units, they were called upon to systematically conquer the city where they were, by drying up its waters, through conversions to their cause and through the changing of the social atmosphere. By this means they would re-establish the city of Jerusalem in every city of the world.

History, if it teaches anything at all, shows us where we failed. Yes, notice I say "we", for humanity (and nature too) fell victim to the subtle snares of Babylon. Notice that I don't say Christianity. The whole world was the victim of the atmospheres that Babylon could spin. So there continues to be crime and war, and blood spilled in the name of national morality and its many gods. I have no doubt, good Christians still existed in the world, both within and outside the mainstream movements that encompassed it. The one great folly, though, that shackled them remained the atmosphere that Babylon could spin.

It is too easy just to lay all burdens on the Christian church or on the Roman Catholic world, and say that these are Babylon. I have no doubt that Babylon is part of Christendom. But why should we ignore important facts? If we allow ourselves to be complacent, we are prone to overlook the other institutions of the world. We also blind ourselves to many benefits derived from Christendom. Unwholesome and corrupt in many ways it may have been. But history confirms that many wholesome principles flowed from it as well. Yet trying to find Babylon seems sometimes like looking for the wind, because it is so difficult to see. Let's examine, then, the question of Where is Babylon today?

Is there actually a strong community devoted to the creation and control of public opinion, social moods and attitudes? What is the prevailing social atmosphere that helps to shape our thoughts, our attitudes and our feelings about everything? and what has been the cause of it? Do social atmospheres just happen? "growing from the grass-roots up" as many people like to say? Or do newspapers? radio? and television? taken singly or in unison play any major role in shaping them? Is there any common group that governs them? In other words, is there actually a present physical manifestation of the power of Babylon? that spiritual force which rules the world, referred to in the scriptures as the power of the air?

If there is, then we have found the throne of Satan, which governs people's thoughts and human governments. For John (writing to us in the name of Jesus Christ) is very clear in his enigmatic riddling: "It doesn't have existence now, but it will come into existence once again. This is a matter that with wisdom you must ponder on."

This power, which can corrupt all human governments and infect the minds of all the world's inhabitants and turn them into willing slaves, believing they are governed by themselves, does periodically find physical realisation in the world. All of us, from time to time have witnessed or experienced how a mob incensed by common prejudice

will act in harmony with itself, doing things that no one
in it individually would have done all on his own. It is as
though another spirit governed each of them.

Some may feel that I have not gone far enough in
pointing an accusing finger in identifying the Babylon
that rules our time. But my concern is not to point
condemning fingers here and there. We can only ask
ourselves from the existing evidence if we ourselves are
moved by any social voice outside ourselves. What
power—if not God—rules over us. For the only choice
that we can make is between God and idolatry. And if
we have rejected God, that other voice which speaks to
us and governs us invisibly is Babylon. Different groups
in different lands have vied for men's devotion and their
loyalties. Whatever voice can gather men to slay their
fellow man is where we have to look for Satan's throne.

John saw the social atmosphere as the chief cause of
immorality, leading to all kinds of crime and violence.
Society, by the kind of social atmosphere that permeated
it, supplied itself with its own criminals. As Theophilus
maintained, the thieving, murderous, adulterous, rebellious, scheming, and incestuous gods themselves (notice
there are many named) had set the standard for society.
If these were qualities that formed the character of those
they worshipped, you couldn't much expect a different
attitude from those who worshipped them.

Let's take a moment then to consider briefly the
work of the Nazi Party, and how they subtly took control
of Germany, turning mere democracy into dictatorship.
If there is really any actual illustration of the riddle John
has given us, we might find it to some measure here. If
you have ever read such books as Trevor Ravenscroft's
The Spear of Destiny or Rusty Sklar's *The Nazis and the
Occult*, then no one needs to tell you of the role that

pagan rituals, horoscopes, psychic phenomena, the occult and worship of the ancient deities themselves all played in helping shape the thinking of a nation which sophisticated people everywhere believed to be humane and civilized.

Such books remind us with substantial evidence that Nazi Germany did not come from nowhere. It rose and grew out of ancient pagan practices and values, blooming in the modern world with all its ancient animosities. Nor did destruction of the beast ensure its end. It was still present in the world and waited for a time when it could be revived.

In the 1920s, when the Ku Klux Klan emerged in Canada, it was a mighty growth that gathered many followers. Its members held high offices in civic, provincial and federal government. It was composed of men of high ecclesiastical standing in the Protestant Church and in industries as well as politics. Even though the Ku Klux Klan in Canada lost prestige and its respectable veneer, and in effect vanished from the Canadian scene as an identifiable body, it would be completely wrong to suppose it was because the cultured individuals who once supported it had undergone a change of heart.

There was a beast in their community waiting for revival under other names to make it socially acceptable again. In such a way as this, the beast of Babylon still roves the world ready to acknowledge as its citizens, people everywhere throughout the modern world. Those always ready to adjust their principles to suit the social moods of the world's idolatry when convenience, respectability and lust all coincide. We only need define the city's qualities to find it in our modern world. Till then, it seems invisible and broods beneath the surface of society, ready to define itself concretely in any nation whose spiritual predominance and influence serve as the new spiritual world-leading capital.

In the 1950s, when Julius and Ethel Rosenberg were put to death in the United States, the public mood was such that people knowing almost nothing of their case, in their patriotic zeal clamoured for their death. Not even Albert Einstein the world's most celebrated scientist, speaking out on their behalf could pacify the public's cry for blood. The glib cliché so often used then, "It is far better that these two should die than a whole nation perish," still haunts my mind. Even at the time it reminded me of what was said by Caiaphas, the High Priest in Jerusalem when Jesus Christ was brought to him, "It is expedient that one man should die for the nation."

I wonder now and sometimes wondered even then, what these same people would have done and said if Jesus Christ had been brought to trial in front of them. So when the question does come up, "Who crucified Jesus Christ?" I say it was the beast that carries Babylon. The only other question we should ask is this: "Am I or you or we a part of it?" Yet even as I write these words I hear the singing of that once familiar Negro Spiritual: "Were you there when they crucified my lord?"

One thing every actor is aware of is stage atmospheres. A scene and the spirit of a scene dictates the way an actor must behave in it. For it is the creation of moods with which the actor is concerned. That is why every actor — if he is serious at all about his craft — studies the way real people behave in different settings and environments. Perhaps we too should be aware of this. Have you not noticed how a quiet cathedral, when you enter it, inspires a sense of hushed respect and an almost instant mood of reverence? Or how a bustling shopping street filled with traffic, falling snow, coloured lights, shop window displays that enhance the spirit of the season and enhance the merchandise with figurines, jingling bells and street music with the sound of shoppers milling everywhere, does create an atmosphere of expectancy, excitement, and a liberal buying mood?

Think about the different scenes we have encountered in society, the function that we serve in them, and the way that we behave because of it: waiting in a dentist's office, shopping in a grocery store, standing in a schoolyard (as a student, as a teacher, as a parent visiting the scene), the way that we behave in church (as a parishioner, as a priest, as a minister, as a choir member, as a pious worshipper, as a choir soloist, as a skeptic); in an office building (as an employee, as a person looking for a job, as an executive, as the cleaning man). In every case it is the scene and the way we think and feel about ourselves that dictates the mood. These in turn dictate the way that we behave in all of them.

In the theatre, as well, scenes dictate the different moods, and moods can alter many times to satisfy the action of the scene. So it is as well that in the very cities that we live, the mood can change each season of the year, or with the spirit of the times in which we live. Who sets the stage then in these important pageants of society? How does our behaviour change in every scene? and who dictates the part we play in them? and how we feel about ourselves?

Picture for a moment now, that while walking in the hills, you have come upon a scene that has deeply moved you with its spectacle. It seems to you a place where no one for a long, long time has been. The day is very misty, and a grey haze lies upon the hills, and high, high up on one of them there are the shell-like ruins of an old cathedral from a long, long time ago that causes you to wonder about its origins and history. Its very presence seems to cast a spell on you, and you are awed by what you see. We would say then that it has an atmosphere. The solitary sight of it in the grey light of the misty day, has a definite effect on you. That is what we mean by atmosphere.

Now, as you stand there rapt in thought and pondering the scene, you hear the sound of raucous laughter and of human voices drawing near. Then picnickers, dressed gaudily in ultra-modern clothes and revelling, appear. They seem unmoved by everything the scene reveals, and blind to anything ethereal. They drink from bottles which they smash upon the stones that once had seemed so beautiful to you. They change the mood. Their very presence alters all the values of the scene. It has become a different place. They change the nature of mood, and create a different atmosphere.

Atmospheres are not made merely by the setting of a scene but by the nature of the people that inhabit it. George Bernard Shaw in his play *Don Juan in Hell* made this very plain to us. It was the nature of the people that made hell or heaven what it is. Even Satan in John Milton's *Paradise Lost*, written something like three centuries earlier, expresses that same sentiment when he says:

> "Infernal world! and thou proudest Hell,
> Receive thy new possessor — one who brings
> A mind not to be changed by place or time.
> The mind is its own place, and in itself
> Can make a Heaven of Hell, a Hell of Heaven."

Although Milton, like most Christians even now, endorses a pictorial concept of hell that writers of the Bible wouldn't recognize, the sentiment which he expresses in these particular lines is one we can appreciate. God gave us the earth as paradise, filled with plants and animals and life of every kind, and we have spent our time destroying it. We have in our own hands the means of spending all our lives in paradise, but we have chosen to compete for whatever things that we can grab and for the prestige and positions that elevate us socially. With our love of money, wars and selfishness, we have indeed made a Hell of Heaven. Christ has challenged us to reverse this trend and, through faith, transform the Hell that Adam brought into the world, and make it Heaven once again.

CHAPTER EIGHTEEN

Throwing Off Babylon

One major theme John stresses in the *Book of Revelation* is that all of Babylon's social, business and religious practices survived the ravages of war and conquest so that Babylon itself remained the most essential element in every super nation which succeeded it as leader and as ruler of the world. Like a serpent which periodically will shed its skin, Babylon appeared to have eternal life. So when other nations one by one arose upon the stage of human history to take the place of Babylon, in all essential ways the spirit which was Babylon remained and continued its unbroken rule.

It well may be that we have now forgotten just how magnificent a city and an empire Babylon in early times had been. She was the wonder and the envy of the world for it was Babylon which gave the civilized world its social order, and vitalized the social atmosphere which captivated the imagination of all mankind. Yet John maintained that her smug self-confidence would one day bring her down.

Nor was John alone in saying such a thing. Much earlier a Jewish prince named Daniel, who served as the prime minister of Babylon in the royal court of King Nebuchadnezzar II, gave a most definitive account of what the destiny of Babylon would be. Called on by the King to interpret a dream which he had had, Daniel proved quite eloquent in giving us one of the finest specimens of political analysis ever to be made. You can read his brilliant thesis for yourself now in the second chapter of the *Book of Daniel*. For the King had dreamed a most disturbing dream about a fearsomely gigantic idol whose various body parts were made from different metals: Gold, Silver, Brass, Iron, and Iron mixed with clay.

Daniel carefully interpreted the dream, and identified both Babylon and the King who ruled it as the idol's golden head. Then he told the King that all the different metals making up the idol's body parts were actually those nations which in succession (one by one) eventually would take the place of Babylon as ruler of the world. What is so remarkable about this vision...revelation... prophecy?...(whatever you might choose to call it) is not so much that it was made prior to the fall of Babylon, but that it so aptly and so wonderfully describes the great dependency of one nation on another (throughout time) and incorporates them all into one body. He shows the nations to be mutually dependent on each other for their very existence. And the implication Daniel clearly shows is that the nations of the world together formed a giant idol all mankind would one day worship and adore, and look upon with awe and reverence.

In his analysis, therefore, Daniel has interpreted the worship of nations as nothing other than a shameless form of blind idolatry. He sees these nations as being one collective body — an image made with human hands. For this reason Babylon would have to fall and be replaced by something God would raise up without hands. For the Kingdom of God is spiritual in the sense that it is dependent on the attitudes of man toward God's creation: the earth and all its creatures (as well as all the sons of men). According to this prophecy (based upon a dream a pagan King had dreamed) the giant image (made up of powerful nations) would be smashed and become like chaff the wind would drive away or (as other prophets later on would say) like dust or like ashes that the sons of men would trample on. It could not last because it had been built upon wrong priciples: principles detrimental not only to mankind but to nature and the world's environment.

The Bible tells us that in "one great day of wrath" (which is to say in a terrible war) because of its accumulated sins, the great body of nations would one day have to answer for the magnitude of all the crimes it had committed throughout the centuries and great millennia it ruled. The present chapter of the book that we are presently studying affirms this when it says: "(Babylon's) sins are piled up to heaven and God has remembered all her crimes." (Revelation 18: 5). We might therefore wonder what these great sins possibly could be that we ourselves should be so judged as though we had committed them.

To find our answer, we must look to the great hymn of creation found in the first chapter of *Genesis*. There Moses has defined the role of human government when he tells us that God said, "Let us make mankind in our own image and after our own likeness so that he may rule (as God would rule: righteously and fairly) over the fish of the sea, the birds of the air, all domestic animals, the earth itself, and over every living creature which moves upon the face of the earth. Then fashioning mankind (from Adamah: the dust of the earth) in the character of God, he created them male and female."

(Genesis 1: 26 -28)

Using this criteria as our measuring stick, we might ask ourselves: How clean is our environment? the water that we drink? or the air we breathe? How free from all contamination is our earth? How well have all the species put into our care survived? Does it not seem as if we have divorced ourselves from those responsibilities which God commissioned us to do?

All mankind (of which we are a part) apparently decided on a different path from that which God assigned to him. That mankind chose to make the satisfying of

his sensual desires and carnal appetites his chief and sole
priority is indicated in the story that is told of Eve in
Chapter Three of *Genesis*: "The woman (i.e 'the community') looked....saw...it was a delight to the eyes...it was to
be desired...she took and she ate...." Deciding (only from
animal desires) on what was right or wrong, the community of mankind (the woman Eve) set the tone for governing the whole earth and structuring its social world. That
is why the wisdom of the scriptures say, "There is a way
which seems right to a man, but the end of it is death."
There is a consequence for everything we do.

The Bible tells us, as a kind of parable, that mankind
made a choice between two trees planted in the garden
of God. One of those trees was called "the tree of life",
and the other one was called "the tree of knowledge of
good and evil." Constant references to "the tree of life"
throughout the Holy Scriptures illustrates for us that
"the tree of life" and "the tree of knowledge of good and
evil" were but symbols which the Bible used to indicate
the means by which mankind communicated with the
God or Gods he served. Psalm Number One and the
legend of Jesus cursing the (sycamore) fig tree in
Chapter Twenty-one of *Matthew*, are but two of these.

One has only to reflect upon the words which say,
"The trees said to the fig tree, 'Come and be our King,'"
(Judges 9: 10) to realise that there were very strong
political implications in the the Garden of Eden story,
which decided the nature of the world and the type of
society early mankind (Adam) was about to build. The
fact that Babylon (at a later time) under Nimrod would
establish its own tower of worship (where the warrior
god Marduk was made Chief deity) contrasts sharply
with Abraham's centre of worship at Ur Salem (the City
of Peace). Here the one God El il or El Elyon was the

only deity and the great Melchizedek (known otherwise
as King Malki Sadeg) served as its priest and King.

That Kings of all these ancient nations were
regarded by their people as "the tree of life" in the midst
of their community is indicated by Ezekiel when he tells
the King of Tyre, "You were the model of perfection and
perfect beauty. You were in Eden the garden of God;
every precious stone adorned you..." (Ezekiel 28: 1) Yet
in an earlier chapter of this same book we are shown the
means by which the King of Babylon ("the tree of life" or
in this case "the tree of knowledge of good and evil")
communicated with his gods to learn their will: "The
King of Babylon will stop at the fork of the road, at the
juncture where the two roads separate. There he will
seek an omen (from the gods): He will cast lots with
arrows, he will consult with his idols, and he will examine
the liver..."   (Ezekiel 28: 1)

In the eyes of the people of Babylon, it was the King
who was looked on as the physical manifestation of the
tree of life because it was the King who communicated
with the different gods of health and healing. It was the
King who was the mediator between the gods and the
people. To the people, the King's voice was the voice of
the gods, but to the gods his voice was the voice of the
people. In the same vein Moses was the tree of life in
the midst of the garden of Israel during the Sinai
Wilderness experience. It was he who gave the people
water to drink, manna to eat, interpreted the word of
God for them, and healed them with God's word.
Likewise Jesus, whom Christians call "the Christ"
because he is anointed with God's Spirit, was the tree of
life in the midst of those who were his followers. He
gave them bread and water of the Spirit, healed the sick,
comforted the sorrowing, and offered all who followed

him eternal life. By doing this he showed himself to be the King of Israel ("the tree of life") within their midst.

I say these things to help you see that the great decision made by Adam "at the fork in the roads" was in reality a very complex one made between the King, his people and their God. And yes, it did take place about the year 4004 B.C. as James Ussher once said. Yet that decision mankind made (just prior to the civilizing of the world) would affect the nature of civilization and the kingdoms that would rise for great millennia to come. "Behold," God might have said to Adam at the time, "I set before you the way of life and the way of death. Therefore choose life."

However complicated and complex the actual events themselves may possibly have been, the writers of the Bible wisely chose to reduce the story to its elements and make it simple, meaningful and memorable. "Mankind chose the wrong course" was the whole point in the story which the Bible writers tried to stress before emphasizing the dire and fatal results which followed because he did. Then as the custom was in very early times, the destiny awaiting man was given. Mankind's actions had determined it:

Adam was told (by the God who ruled creation) that because of the choice he made, he would have to labour slavishly and painfully all the days of his life to earn his livelihood and the rewards that he would glean for all his labour would be largely thorns and thistles. Life would be extremely hard for him because he had enslaved himself to all his passions and his appetites. He would therefore only eat by the sweat of his brow until his dying day when he would finally return to the dust from which he had been made. Also all the nations he would build upon those principles he chose to follow would doom the nations that he built to "eat dust all their days", rising and falling one after another, and be constantly at war with nature and themselves, because the spirit guiding man refused to rule responsibly.

The seducing spirit of lusts and passions would constantly feel "enmity toward the real community of God (the woman) and toward her offspring (the unborn Kingdom that she carried in her womb). God at once dramatically illustrates for us the spirit of this enmity in the symbolic figures of two brothers, Cain and Abel. Notice that I do not say that the story isn't real. However, it is included in the scriptures, and has been greatly simplified, so that we might understand the basic truth which it reveals.

That all these early stories were intended to be read according to symbolic principles was emphasized by Paul when he interpreted the story of Abraham's two sons and the two women who had given birth to them. Regarding this Paul said, "These stories are symbolic and these two women represent two covenants.... (The woman) Hagar... represents the present city (of physical) Jerusalem whose children are enslaved. The second (woman, Sarah) represents the heavenly city of Jerusalem which is given from above. She is the mother of the free." (Galatians 4: 24-26)

It likewise is apparent from the words God spoke to Eve and to the serpent that both of them are figurative as well. If they weren't, then God's words to the serpent (the spirit on which man built his world), "I will put enmity between you and the woman and between your offspring and hers," would be quite meaningless. But when we read the passage symbolically, we understand world nations would resent God's Kingdom in their midst. In *Genesis*, this is drawn to our attention by contrasting the sons of Adam (born only of the flesh) with the sons of God (born of God's spirit and his bride) who walk according to God's word. For the community of God (from the very beginning) was destined eventually to give birth to a new and better world.

Eve's two sons Cain and Abel are used symbolically to represent the two roads taken by mankind: the way of the flesh and the way of the spirit. Cain's children were entirely physical by birth, driven only by their carnal lusts and willfulness. Although Abel had no physical children at all, he gave birth to children who were spiritual. They were born of the spirit he displayed, as they were those who having witnessed his example and the courage of his death, were governed by the spirit which had governed him (the spirit of the God which ruled over him) and they followed in his steps. They were those who looked to God for guidance in their lives. Therefore there were two lines of humanity spoken of in *Genesis*: the sons of Adam (born of Cain's line) and the sons of God (born of the spirit from above).

Some, I know, will wish to argue that there were only two people (besides Adam and Eve) living in the world at that time – Cain and Abel. If that were so, then that very silly question, "Where did Cain get his wife?" could not be looked upon as spurious.

I know what difficulties this presents to us. Yet these important symbols, which we find in *Genesis* and other portions of the Bible, have been planted there (as Paul once told his readers) to instruct them and give guidance to their lives. The spiritual was always present in the covenants which God made with man. Right from the beginning and throughout the whole course of his unfolding plan, the truths he had to teach were always evident and many lived by them. Yet mankind (as a whole) generally would warp these covenants to suit his own convenience. God's first covenant was not made with Moses. God made covenants with Adam, Noah, Abraham, Moses, David and, later on, with those who chose to be obedient to Jesus Christ. These covenants were all seen, even "The New Covenant" as measures to be used for restoring mankind to his first Edenic state with God — so that the earth (mankind) and nature would be ruled responsibly by those who acted in the name of God.

The line Paul drew to make a clear distinction between physical and spiritual Jerusalem was not a new idea at all. Many Jewish prophets (notably Isaiah) did the same. John, however, saw the need to be more forceful in his imagery, and so he chose two world capitals (Jerusalem and Babylon) to emphasize the difference between the two distinctive ways of living: the carnal and the spiritual. Moses also in the symbolism that he used laid emphasis upon the separating line which differentiated the spiritual from the carnal when he spoke about "the waters above the firmament...divided from the waters below the firmament." But John through the two distinctive cities (spiritual Jerusalem and carnal Babylon) can show the similarities and differences he saw in each of them. Both were carried (like tabernacles) in the hearts of those who honoured them. They were every man's internal government. We therefore only knew a person's citizenship by the way that he conducted his affairs and by his dealings with other people in the world in which he lived.

The prophecies of both Daniel and John, which visually depict the whole religious life of Babylon as something that has been passed on as a spiritual inheritance to all the nations of the world which followed it, is the same view that we find expressed in other Hebrew Scriptures. In *Genesis*, for instance, it is *consistently* made apparent in the separating line which has been drawn

between two sons throughout its texts: between Cain and Abel, between Ishmael and Isaac, between Esau and Jacob, between the sons of Leah and Rachel's sons, between Pharez and Zarah and so on. That line is also drawn between Israel's two kings, Saul and David. This is done so that we might understand the fine distinctions which God makes between even those who to all appearances are serving him. "For man looks upon the outward appearance, but Jehovah looks upon the heart."
(1 Samuel 16: 7)

God has done this in the scriptures so as to teach us that we, as those who choose the way of life, must learn to differentiate between the obvious physical exterior and the not so obvious spiritual interior. "You mean to say you are a teacher in Israel," Jesus said to Nicodemus, "and you do not understand such things?...If I have spoken to you only of physical things till now and you do not believe, how can you believe me if I tell you about spiritual things?" (John 3: 10 -12)

These words from the scriptures help the reader to appreciate the nature of the struggle which is taking place between those "born of the flesh" and those "born by the spirit" of God's word. John (an apostle of Jesus Christ), in the first chapter of his gospel, gave the following definition of spiritual birth: "The children of God are not born through any bloodline of human descent, nor by any act of the will. (You cannot merely will yourself to be a child of God). Neither can you force another man to be born spiritually. Spiritual birth can only come from God." (John 1: 13). Even Jesus said, regarding this matter: "No man can possibly come to me except the spirit draws him." (John 6: 44). You cannot force another human being to accept the things that Jesus taught. Forced conversion is a very ugly thing, and it can only be compared with rape.

Yet God's only purpose is to save mankind through the examples of his chosen vessels. For this reason God chose Israel so that we might see the struggle going on between the descendants of the flesh (Cain, Esau or Saul), and those of the spirit (Abel, Jacob or David). When the two lads Pharez (Shining Forth) and Zarah (Breaking Forth) were born, a great prophetic riddle (spoken by the midwife who attended Tamar) is memorably related for our benefit. "As (Tamar) was giving birth," so Moses wrote of this event, "one child put out his hand. Then the midwife took a scarlet thread and bound it to his wrist, saying, 'This child came out first.' But the child drew back his hand, so that his brother came out instead. Then the midwife said, 'How is it you have made this breach and come out first!' He was therefore called Pharez. Afterwards his brother who had the scarlet thread tied to his wrist, came out and was given the name of Zarah."   (Genesis 38: 28-30)

All these stories have been told to emphasize distinctions made by God and to illustrate for us that the first son (the man of flesh) always is the first man (or the eldest son) while the second son (the man of spirit), the one whom God designed in the beginning, is the second son. There are two births being illustrated here. All of us are born as those who serve the flesh. Only by imbibing God's word does the second child appear, "shining forth" as those who do God's will. The first birth is easier than the second for the mother bearing them. Rachel's suffering is indicative of this. Therefore the birth of God's spiritual kingdom on earth is very painful for God's community (His bride). And that is the significance of the words: "I will greatly increase the pain endured by you in giving birth so that you suffer painfully in bearing children."

Babylon (the first of two influential cities to be "born" on earth) bore children of the flesh. Jerusalem (the younger twin) on which God placed his name, bore children of the spirit. Therefore Babylon's religious life consisted of superstition and idolatry and all the fruits of it. Both Jews and Christians said that pagan gods encouraged every kind of immorality and they ultimately led to crime and violence and war. Babylon, Egypt, Medo-Persia, Greece and Rome, are indicated in John's letter as those heads upon the fiery beast which served as carnal governments that ruled the earth. Still they were not absolute in power; they were subtly controlled by something other than themselves — the throne of Satan ruling over them.

This throne consisted of a body of priests and priestesses steeped in all the mysteries of many kinds of gods and goddesses that through their conduct in the legends that were told of them, stimulated passions of the flesh, and enslaved the people by the superstitious attitudes that it brought out in them. Those spirits that the idols represented, Paul identified as human passions causing sexual immorality, impurity, and debauchery; idolatry and spiritism; hatred, discord, jealousy, fits of rage, selfish ambition, dissensions, factions and envy; drunkenness and the like. Enlarging on this same theme, he also (at another time) named such things as anger, rage, malice, slander, and filthy language from your lips.

He called these spirits, that the world imbibed, demons, for he perceived how they had poisoned all the social atmosphere of human life. The people and their governments indulged in all the vices named, and the gods they served gave sanction to their deeds, so that the beast that they became, was scarlet with the murderous nature of sin and the obscenities of their deeds were written everywhere on them.

Of course, we know, and I expect the writers of the Bible knew as well, that all the vices that Paul named were part of what was natural in man. No gods or demons (in the way that we have come to use this word) were inventors of these things. We find, for instance, envy and brooding anger in Adam's first son, Cain. The point is, that the gods the people served encouraged people not to bridle them. Anger is natural, but it must be curbed and mastered, as must even human sexuality.

"Hey!" some will answer now, "what's so wrong with sex. Sex is good." Of course it is! So good in fact that God's first command to the people he created was to multiply in number and spread out on the earth so as to care for it. In fact sex was considered a very sacred thing in early times. Abraham asked his servant, Eleazar, to place a hand under his thigh to swear an oath. This was a euphemism for putting a hand on Abraham's sexual organ to swear by his posterity. The blessing pronounced by Israel upon Judah, concerned all those who came from between his feet. Sex was looked upon as good.

But sex is certainly abused. Rape, murder, theft have followed in the wake of sexual passions. Sexual harassment is not at all unusual. Some are so preoccupied with sex they are enslaved, and seem incapable of thinking of anything besides. Yet unschooled passions when personified became the gods that governed human lives.

So when the people themselves would eventually become the final government, John said, they would rule in just the same way all the other governments had ruled, so that—in spirit—all those former governments would rule along with them. They would also join ranks with all the imperial rulers ruling on the earth, and together they would rule in just the same way that the former governments before them ruled. They could not rule in any other way, because they would still be drinking from the same cup of personified, exaggerated, uncurbed human passions that governed all humanity before. Yet John foresaw a time when the scarlet beast would free itself from the idolatry of Babylon — overthrowing all the media and the spirit feeding it with selfish ambition, slander, envy, lies, malice, jealousy, filthy language, and other such things poisoning their world.

I wonder if we know how many superstitions and traditions we employ in daily life: reading horoscopes "just for the fun of it", or tea leaves "from divining cups", consulting mediums or using palmistry to learn about the future, eating pork at Easter, kissing under the mistletoe, planning June weddings for a special blessing from Juno (the goddess of marriage), wishing with the wishbone from a bird, holding watchnight services to feel the holy awe of mystery inspired by them, making buildings with no thirteenth floor, carrying a rabbit's foot or other lucky piece, throwing salt over your left shoulder if you spill it from the shaker, throwing coins into a fountain, or wishing on a star, or on the first spring robin that you see each year, sensing something ominous if you break a mirror, using Abra-Ka-Dabra as a magic charm which means "Our Father which art in heaven", or saying hockus-pokus (originally Hoc es corpus) meaning "This is my body" used in the sacrament to change the bread into the flesh of Christ, etc. etc.

The whole so-called secular world is overrun with trappings from religions of all kinds. This is the product of religious Babylon. The main purpose of the unified community of Zion is to replace the heavens governing the Babylonish spiritual world capital.

Then, of course, there are the scandal magazines which make their livelihood from their malicious slanders, smears and general nastiness. These are the spirits of idolatry that plague the world. Interspersed with such malicious gossip are the words of psychic mediums and their so-called prophetic mutterings. Certainly the ancient gods continue to infect our world. But John says that the people will eventually turn on that parthenon of deities and bring it down. The eighteenth chapter we are reading now takes a closer look at how this will be done. Jesus Christ, through his helper John, tells us how another spirit will descend upon the world and lighten it. We read the details of it here:

*

Following these things, I saw another spirit from God descending from the sky (the spirit of the word of God made evident in human lives). This was a powerful spirit that lit up the whole world with the revealed glory (of God's word made flesh in humanity). Then with a mighty voice he cried: "She has fallen. The powerful (city of) Babylon has fallen! And now she has become a dwelling place for demons, and every filthy bird and unclean beast." (She has lost her subtle beauty and allure). Once all the nations had been drunken with the strong wine of her immorality, and all the rulers of the earth were guilty of adultery with her (for every kind of social sin was found in them), and the merchants of the world grew wealthy because of her excessive wantonness.

Then I heard (Jehovah's) voice from heaven say: "Come out of her, all who are my people, so that you take no part in all her sins and be forced to share the punishments I bring on her." For her sins are piled right up to heaven, and God is ready now to judge her for her crimes. Treat her in the same way that she treated you, and give her double payment, when you repay her for her crimes. Let her drink from her own cup, the same wine that she gave to you, at twice the strength of it. Let her drink the same amount of suffering and sadness that she allowed herself to have of luxury and pleasure.

For she loves to boast, "I sit like a queen upon my throne, and as I am no widow, I shall never mourn."

That is why, in one day, disaster will fall suddenly on her: death, sorrow and famine. She will be utterly consumed with fire, for Jehovah, the Creator who judges her, is formidable in power. When all the rulers of the earth who shared in her idolatries see the smoke of her destruction rise, they will weep and mourn for her.

Terrified by what they see, they will stand a long way off and cry: "O how terrible! How terrible it is! To think that in one hour this great and powerful city has been utterly destroyed."

The merchants of the earth, as well, will all be sad and grieve for her because no one any longer buys their merchandise — their merchandise of gold, silver, precious stones, and pearls; fine linen, scented wood and great varieties of articles made from ivory, costly wood, bronze, iron and marble; merchandise of cinnamon and spice, of incense, myrrh and frankincense, of wine and olive oil, of fine flour and wheat, cattle and sheep; horses and carriages and (slaves, which is to say) the bodies and souls of men. (They traffic in human lives.)

Now these merchants say (to Babylon), "All the delicacies you once craved have disappeared, and all your glamour and your wealth are gone as well, never to return!"

Those who once did business in her midst and heaped up fortunes for themselves now stand a long way off, terrified by all her suffering. As they bewail her end, they cry out mournfully: "What a terrible thing it is that this great city who used to be adorned with linen, purple and scarlet and ornamented with fine gold, precious stones and pearls, in one short moment should be brought to this!"

Standing a long way off, captains of ships, passengers, crews (commercial business executives, their staffs and workmen) and all who make their living from the sea (the restless savagely competing world), watch in terror as the smoke from the flames consuming her causes them to cry out in despair: "What city anywhere could possibly compare to her!" Then throwing dust upon their heads they weep and grieve, saying: "How terrible it is that this great city should be destroyed so suddenly."

Yet, let all those that heaven rules rejoice. Be glad all you people of God, apostles and prophets! for God has judged her for the way she treated you.

Then another mighty spirit from God, picking up an enormous rock the size of a large millstone, hurled it into the sea and said: "This is how the great city of Babylon shall violently be cast off, never to rise again." No more shall the music of harpists, flute players, trumpeters or any other musicians be heard in you again. Nor will any workman ever work in you again. Nor will the sound of the millstone grinding grain be heard in you again. No light from any lamp will ever shine in you again. The voices of the bridegroom and the bride will nevermore be heard in you.

Even though your merchants were regarded as the world's great men, you led the world astray with your illusions and deceptive practices. This is she who is guilty of having shed the blood of all the prophets of

God and the saints and everyone who ever had been killed on earth.

*

The pouring out of God's word upon the air (or social atmosphere) brings a different spirit into the world. We are told that another messenger — or angel — commissioned by God brightened the whole earth with the splendour of his presence. We cannot read this passage without hearing echoes from both the Hebrew and Greek Scriptures. Isaiah said, "The people that walked in darkness have seen a great light: they that dwell in the land of the shadow of death, upon them hath the light shined." (Isaiah 9: 2). Then Jesus Christ himself said prophetically, "As the daylight comes out of the east and fills the sky all the way from east to west, so also shall the coming of the Son of Man be." (Matthew 24: 27)

This light will be revealed in all those living by the word of God, and walking in that generosity of spirit which Jesus taught his followers. The angel is the spirit of Jehovah's people (in all four quarters of the world) who respond to that command which Jesus gave: "Let your light so shine before men, that they may see your good works and glorify your father in heaven."

(Matthew 5: 16)

That spirit lighting (or lightening) the whole world, also is an unmistakable fulfillment of what Jesus said: "Now if anyone should tell you, 'Look here is Christ' or 'Over there is where he is!' do not believe him. For there will be many false Christs and false prophets in the world who will show you evidence of their authority and perform impressive works so great in magnitude they could deceive even the elect if that were possible. So I warn you now ahead of time, so that you should not be unprepared.

"If anyone should tell you, therefore, 'Look, he is in the desert,' don't even go with them to see. Or if they say to you, 'Come and I will show you where he is. I know his secret hiding place' or 'He is hidden in the inner rooms,' do not let yourself be swayed or credit anything they say. For I tell you this with confidence (that you might be assured) that as surely as the light of day is seen from east to west, so the coming of the son of man will be." (Matthew 24: 23 -27)

Jesus couldn't have been more plain. And yet many sincere people have been swayed to follow charlatans who have led them to a death that served no cause. Jesus even made it plain just how that brightness was to come when he proclaimed: "Then shall the righteous shine like the sun in the kingdom of their father." (Matthew 13: 43). When that occurs it may be said: "The people who walked in darkness have seen a great light, and they who lived in the land of the shadow of death, upon them has God's light shone." (Isaiah 9: 2)

This messenger, then, is a spirit of hope, bringing God's unpolluted and undiluted word with him. This spirit from God will fill the whole world with the revealed glory of God through those people who have chosen to obey his word. This is not something to be done through pulpits, hidden in the recesses of the church: "A city set upon a hill cannot be hid. Neither do men light a lamp and then conceal it underneath a cover of some sort. Rather it is set upon a lampstand where it may give light to everyone within the house." (Matthew 5: 14 -15)

This angel messenger has little to do with "going to church" and listening to "inspiring sermons" preached by professional ministers. It has to do with the personal struggle of every individual to recognize and put off the enslaving habits of a world completely devoted to physical sensationalism. It is turning to the way of God and recognizing the needs and virtues of those who are near to us, and responding to them in a humane and under-standing way. It is doing what we have seen the messiah do, without pretending any special virtue in ourselves. So let's not fiddle with the works of religious quackery and humbug, or smugly let ourselves be governed by feelings of self-righteousness. "Beware the leaven of the Pharisees." But guard against despising them.

That is the message of the angel rising to give light to all the world. With such a spirit present in the world, Babylon will lose its hold. And in the universal light it gives, Babylon's loathsome appearance will be seen. There is nothing at all attractive in what the light of God's word will reveal of her. So by comparison she simply is a place for loathsome birds and beasts. John relies here on the picture that Isaiah drew when he described her in this way: "Babylon the jewel of kingdoms...will be overthrown by God like Sodom and Gomorrah. She will never be inhabited through all generations; no Arab will pitch his tent there, no shepherd will rest his flocks there. But desert creatures will lie there, jackals will fill her houses; there owls will dwell, and wild goats will leap about...." (Isaiah 13: 19 -22)

The picture then is one of complete desolation, one so stark and barren no one could ever be enticed by it. The lures and enticements of superstition, passion and lust would all lose their hold on people everywhere, and the advertising world could not rely again on any of these things to sell their products any more, and any church relying solely on age-old traditions or worship formulas would lose its following.

Then John explains the reasons for her fall. She fell because her people never learned to curb their passions or their lusts. She fell because of the dependence of her people upon greed, envy and idolatry, and also on the power of the enticing spirit of the advertising world. God's word had given people an immunity to such triviality.

John tells us next that Jehovah's voice was heard, giving his people a direct command to abandon Babylon. His words recall those which Jehovah once spoke to the Jews in this prophecy we find in the book of *Isaiah*: "Come forth out of Babylon, flee from the Chaldeans! With a voice of singing, declare this message to the whole world: 'Jehovah has delivered his servant Jacob from captivity.'" (Isaiah 48: 20)

Yet Isaiah's words were spoken to the Jews alone. But John—though writing to the seven churches—was addressing all God's people, which is to say, anyone who heard him speak and were obedient to the word which God had given him. For Jehovah's people are only those who willingly respond to what he says. Therefore, although most Jews may be God's people, some are not. This is also true of Christians living now. The phrase "Once saved, always saved" just isn't true. Although some Christians do belong to God, many Christians and some Jews belong to Babylon. So, to those that lag Jehovah says: "Thus says Jehovah of armies: 'Drink, be drunk, vomit, and fall to rise no more, because of the warfare (symbolically "the sword") which I shall send among you.'" (Jeremiah 25: 27)

Jeremiah further warns: "Flee out of the midst of Babylon, let every man save his life! Let not destruction come upon you through (sharing in) her sin and punishment; for the time of Jehovah's vengeance has come. For he will let her bring destruction on herself." (Jeremiah 51: 6)

But Babylon is not some place far off, "over there". It is right here in our midst, and we are part of it. For

Babylon is the present system of the world. To overcome its strong intoxicating influence, we must walk and speak like citizens of New Jerusalem. The way we live and how we speak betrays what city we spiritually are walking in. If we belong to Christ, however, we will desert those Babylonish ways that make us all blood guilty of her crimes. "Come out of her," Jehovah says to us. He wouldn't say that if we hadn't slipped and forgotten in some measure who we are and that we have been called to walk at all times, spiritually as citizens living in the city God has built.

There is a scripture that says: "Your sins shall find you out," that many Christians seem to read as "Your sins will be found out." That isn't what it means. It means that we must face the consequences of our acts and pay for them. There always is a moment when our sins will grow to reach maturity. These words then are a warning that applies to individuals, but they serve to warn the nations of the world as well. Therefore we are told: "Our service and our loyalty belong alone to him who loves us, and who freed us from the power of sin (and death)."

When John reveals that Babylon's sins "are piled right up to heaven," he means that God is ready now to call them to account. "MENE MENE TEKEL UPHARSIM" were the prophetic words, written in the Aramaic tongue upon the wall, that Daniel read on that Great Day which marked the end of Babylon. For Babylon had been weighed in the balances and found wanting, and judgment was about to fall on her. "Her sins had found her out."

"The last days" is a constant theme in Bible literature, but it also is a phrase that has been enormously abused. It has been overworked by charismatic enchanters, charlatans and confused Christians to engender superstitious fears and to lend enchantment to their words so that we miss the point the scriptures have in using it. Consequently Christianity has become the focal point of many false

"prophetic" utterances which have given rise to doctrines
that no scripture possibly can justify at all. Yet some of
these malicious doctrines have become so rigidly installed
in many branches of the Christian faith that to speak of
them irreverently is akin to sin or heresy.

While it is true we should be constantly aware that
one day our nations' sinful practices will be called by our
creator into account, no Christian should be constantly
crying "Wolf!" The last days (when a nation's sins bring
it into judgment) aren't a superstitious thing. Although
they do apply to Babylon and all the nations that are
part of her, many nations throughout history (some in
Bible times) have experienced the phenomenon of "the
last days". In our own time, we have observed the
crumbling of modern nations and empires. We have
sometimes seen these turn into ruined heaps. And we
have read about such things in the chronicles of history
so that we know the nature of "the last days" and the
foolishness that leads to them.

The Bible merely tells us there are signs to watch for
in predicting them. Reading the signs of the times is not
the mystical imagining that we have seen the face of
Jesus on a fortune cookie, a painted wall or on a racing
form. It is watching for the signs that indicate a nation's
weakening. And watching for Jesus Christ's return is not
looking at the sky and saying, "He might come at any
time." It is being constantly aware of what Jesus Christ
requires from us so that we are not fooled and caught up
in the snare of joining in with Babylon and fighting for
some cause other than the cause of Jesus Christ, in a
carnal war that shows no love at all for man. The only
war which Christians have been called to fight is spiritual.

The Bible tells us that there is a cause for any
nation's ills and weaknesses and that there is a remedy

for healing them—in the same way Jonah healed the nation of Assyria. The last days and the day of reckoning is not a thing to pray for as some Christians seem to think. Repentance and healing are more to be desired. But if they don't repent and throw off the yoke of Babylon, those nations who insist on "fornicating" with the spirit of the harlot city ruling over them, will perish in the flames of war and violence.

For this reason, then, John sets up an echo of the words which Jeremiah long ago addressed to us: "We would have healed Babylon (had she allowed us to), but she refused to let herself be healed. Forsake her then, and let us, each of us, return to his own country, for the guilt of Babylon and the judgment against her reaches up to heaven, and is lifted even to the skies."

(Jeremiah 51: 9)

I can think of no better example of such fires of fury in our modern times than the senseless slaughter that has consumed the lives and world of former Yugoslavia. All the narrow loyalties to different gods (or causes) have lit the fires of animosity and violence, striking out at even those who once were friends. Good people? Certainly. But deceived by gods of passion and the spells they cast upon the atmosphere. To speak prophetically: If ten righteous men had only lived among them, the healing of their nations might have come, for they would have lived to glorify the handiwork of God, without religious prejudice of "I have my religion. You have yours." Had they been obedient to God, they would have cared for his creation and their fellow man enough to know they should not follow men of violence or try to serve two masters.

The record of Christianity, throughout history, has not been glorious. The fault has always been that Christians served two gods and were not obedient to the teachings Christ had given them. Ireland is often cited as an example of Christians fighting Christians. But the problem is not Christianity. The problem is political in every way. There are those who are loyal to the crown of England and those who want to pull away from it. The war is therefore between loyalists and separatists. Those wanting separation are mostly Roman Catholics, but not all separatists are Catholic. Those loyal to the crown are mostly Protestant, but not all loyalists are Protestants.

The arguments and antagonisms between loyalists and separatists has nothing to do with the nature of Jesus Christ and his commandments. The quarrel is one based on racial differences and national biases. It is a quarrel based on loyalties to leaders other than God. Jesus has told us we cannot serve two masters, and now John, in this document, tells us that our loyalty belongs alone "to him that loves us." Christians therefore have been commanded to have nothing to do with such national wars. The only war that Christians advocated was spiritual— and to be fought only with spiritual weaponry.

So when we hear that Babylon has been destroyed — that multitude of voices of the different gods men serve —the rulers of the earth will weep. Yet do not think their tears, are tears of those who have repented. They are the tears of those who rue the loss of her who had helped them to deceive the whole world with superstitions veiled by ignorance and misplaced reverence. For as Ezekiel, the prophet says: "They take up lamentation over you and say to you, 'How you are destroyed and vanished, you that were won from the seas and inhabited by seafaring men, the renowned city, that was mighty on the sea, she and her inhabitants, which caused their terror to fall on all who dwell there!' Now the isles and coastlands tremble in the day of your fall; yes the isles that are in the sea are troubled and dismayed at your departure."   (Ezekiel 26: 17-18)

Such sorrow over this fall reminds us of Paul's words "Godly sorrow brings repentance that leads to salvation and leaves no regret, but worldly sorrow brings death."

(2 Corinthians 7: 10)

Sorrowing along with all the rulers are all the merchants and the export-import industries. In the full description that John gives, you can't ignore the direct reference to the corrupted business practices of the city, and how Babylon affects the way that we still buy and sell our merchandise today. Neither do the scriptures overlook the fact that no city can be judged solely by the name it bears. Not even historical Jerusalem can escape the judgment of God. The scriptures make that clear for us when they link historical Jerusalem (known universally as the City of God) to the cities of Sodom and Gomorrah whose citizens did not follow any of God's ways.

Isaiah, in a direct address to her, called her leaders and her citizens "you rulers of Sodom" and "you people of Gomorrah." Then Jesus in a desperate appeal, named her openly and said "O Jerusalem, Jerusalem, who kills the prophets and stones all those I send to her. How often have I tried to gather you together, in the same way that a hen will gather chicks protectively underneath her wings, but you refused (to let me gather you). But now, you see, your house will be left desolate." (Matthew 23: 37)

Be careful how you read now, for John has warned us against biases. Yet in these verses is the secret of real Babylon. The Bible takes the holiest of places upon earth, God's own city of Jerusalem, and finds in all the prophets condemnation for the rulers and the populace. Jesus says of those religious figures of his day: "Beware of the scribes, who like to walk around in long robes, and love respectful greetings in the market places, and the chief seats in the synagogues, and places of honour at banquets, who devour widows' houses, and for appearances sake offer long prayers; these will receive the greater condemnation."   (Luke 20: 46 - 47)

The careless tendency of many readers is to see in this passage, an attack made on the Jews or solely on the people Jesus named. They fail to realise that the gospels themselves are part of prophetic literature and took into account the larger picture of the world. Jesus spoke to the religious leaders of his day, those who enjoyed the prestige of their time. Jesus's warning was not to have his listeners shun the people named, but to avoid the practices he named, which were nothing more than sham and hypocrisy. For Jesus saw this danger in his own disciples. Had the danger not been there, he never would have spoken of these things.

For in *Matthew*, Jesus further says: "You know that the rulers of the Gentiles lord it over them, and their great men exercise authority over them. But this is not the way that it should be with you. The one you shall esteem the greatest in your midst should be the one who serves the rest of you. Therefore, anyone who wishes to be first among you, should work among you as your slave, in the same way that the Son of man did not look to be served but came among you to serve and to give up even his own life, for the benefit of everyone."
                    (Matthew 20: 25 -28)

He couldn't have been more explicit than he was. This is what he had against the Pharisees and scribes. And this would be his chief complaint against the hierarchy of modern Christendom.

None of us has any right to point the finger here and there and speak derisively of those who do not share the values that we have. That is not the point of any scripture that I know. The scriptures simply try to help us look into a mirror and correct ourselves. Are we idolators? loving the trappings of this world? Do we worship offices? prestige? honour? and celebrity? Do we idolize the famous entertainer and ignore the people close to us who do not emulate their ways? Do we exalt ourselves, and forget what Christ has called on us to do? Is the leader that we serve upon the throne of Babylon? or in spiritual Jerusalem?

Quite likely, in one way or another, we are all a part of Babylon the Great and share in her blood guilt. That is why we need a vision of the Kingdom God has called upon his people to build. That does not give anyone the right to exhibit feelings of self-righteousness. It was Jesus Christ who told his followers, "Beware the leaven of the Pharisees," and illustrated what he meant by telling them the parable of the Publican and Pharisee. He did not mean to tell them they should hate the Pharisees. Yet, sadly, that is what some Christians seem to think he meant. What Jesus was affirming was that self-righteousness had no place at all amongst the sons of God. No one should forget that many people who supported Jesus were the Pharisees themselves. To name a few, there was Joseph of Aramathea, Nicodemus and even the apostle Paul. There were many others too who go unnamed in scriptures but are alluded to in different Bible texts.

To appreciate the virtues of the Pharisees we must look back to their origins. When Simon, the Hasmonean prince was treacherously assassinated, his son John Hyrcanus became the head of the New state of Judea. After creating a mercenary army, he went forth zealously to carve out an empire. He subjugated the Samaritans and destroyed their temple. Then he gave Israel's ancient enemies, the Edomites, the alternative of exile from their land or conversion to Judaism. Nothing better reveals the perverseness of human nature than this sorry method that Hyrcanus used in spreading his faith, in the same manner that later Christianity would use, by the powerful use of military strength and violence.

His son Aristobulus continued and improved upon his example. He pushed his conquests up through Galilee and ultimately crowned himself king. He reintroduced the dreadful Oriental custom of destroying members of his family who could become a threat to the security of his throne.

It was at that time that a formidable party developed. This party rigorously opposed the policy of rulers who were abandoning the idealism of their faith. This party was the Pharisees. History reveals them to have been genuine liberals whose chief aim was to interpret the law which was their inheritance and make it fit the new conditions which they had to face. These Pharisees were sunny individuals whose energetic spirit renewed their nation's rapidly diminishing vitality. They became interpreters of the law, and they tried to make it flexible, while still retaining all its fundamental principles. It was their wish to make it workable, and retain it as the fundamental part of Jewish life. It was the courage of the Pharisees which helped their nation to retain the law and make it merciful. In doing this they stood up to the ruthlessness of kings whose policies were ruining the faith of centuries.

The chief opponents to the Pharisees was a group known as the Sadducees. Unlike the former group, the Sadducees were strong supporters of the royal policy of imperialism. Their outlook was a rigid one. It was unbending, and they saw it as their duty to destroy the roots of paganism any way they could — a practice matching that of later Christians in their ruthless battles against heresy. Their opposition to the Pharisees reached violent proportions at one time. Be careful, therefore, in the manner that you speak about these people called the Pharisees. The Pharisees lived in dreadful times, yet they saw themselves as keepers of the law, which others in their nation, through ruthlessness and violence, had set out to destroy. Remember these things, and keep them all in mind, whenever Pharisees are named.

Spiritual war is not a war expressing enmity against the Jews or Pharisees. And I confess I am amazed that anyone would ever think it was. The enemy is Babylon the Great whose spiritual atmosphere beclouds the minds of Christians, Jews and Muslims alike. Nor does the Bible invite anyone to be a terrorist. The only war the Christian has been called upon to fight is that war against the life-destroying forces Babylon the Great employs. This spiritual war is waged only with the power of words and deeds which can reveal the follies and illusions which deceive the mind and makes men slaves to them. It is a war against all forms of violence, fought only with kind deeds and wise words learned from God, spoken in the manner that this letter to the Churches has described. Pride, self-righteousness and prejudice are demons to avoid from which we must protect ourselves. For we are called upon to throw off Babylon in all our practices.

When we are shown the powerful spirit of a messenger of God throwing off a heavy stone which has encumbered it, it is to help us visualize our spiritual responsibility to throw off all those worldly practices of Babylon that we ourselves have thoroughly imbibed, and the tremendous effort we are called on to expend in doing it. For Babylon has blinded us with its illusions and enslaved us in soul-destroying ways. This enslaving power much like a grinding stone must be cast off. The powerful spirit in this vision teaches us that the spirit of God's word will strengthen us and help us overthrow the power of Babylon within ourselves. This is something all of us must do if we would free ourselves from all the cumulative sins that Babylon the Great has made us guilty of.

Her entertainment world, and all the industries supporting Babylon would all be stilled: "No music of harps, singers, flutes and trumpets will be heard in you again." Music and world culture would cease to be controlled by Babylon. Controlling these takes away the power of Babylon and helps to unify the world. No longer would world culture be a product of the market place — dividing men. So unable to sell music to the masses now, "no harps or singers, flutes or trumpets would be heard in her again." Music would become an honestly spontaneous joyous celebration of free Jerusalem. The wheeler-dealers of Babylon and her advertising men who mislead the people by deliberate deception and nasty business practices, no longer would be able to deceive.

One might easily question the deceptions (or the sorceries) used today in modern business practices — false lotteries, announcements of big wins to people desperate to survive, the many ways of wheedling money out of those who have difficulty even "making both ends meet" and "live from hand to mouth" each day. This in a world that spends more than $1,000,000,000,000 each year on arms and implements of war, but can't afford to keep up hospitals or find enough funds to educate its young. John couldn't possibly have guessed the structure of the modern world or the social institutions of today, but he knew what principles were governing the world: greed, deception, lust, heartlessness and social unconcern. Even Isaiah had spoken out against all these.

Surely this is Babylon, and surely we are part of it. Come out of her my people," is Jehovah's own command.

Who will willingly obey? Deceiving others in ads and business practices gets to seem like lots of fun. I mean look at how much fun it is to buy a lottery ticket and wonder anxiously if you will win, while you watch your money drift away. The whole trick is to get the money out of you and make you feel you don't mind spending it. Your own lust to win has actually made you a slave to those who pull manipulating strings.

The percentage of poor people in the world today is just as great as it was centuries ago — in spite of all our modern industries, inventions and mass production. Babylon impoverishes the world. How can it be otherwise when the basis of the world really hasn't changed. The guiding principle is to gain more power, more prestige and more goods than your neighbour and then lord it over him, perhaps as the celebrity with flashing strobes and screaming crowds. Such hysteria. And isn't it a lot of fun! Such are the gods that set the goals of Babylon.

It surely must be clear from what John says, that the Roman Catholic Church was not the target of John's words, as certain groups of Protestants have said. According to the words of John, the spirit which is Babylon is in the very fabric of the world in which we live: Religion, business practices, the superficial glitz and glamour of the advertising and the entertainment worlds, the wiliness of governments are all a part of it. It can be found throughout the whole breadth of society. The Roman Catholic Church, no more than any group amongst the Protestants can be accused of having traces of the world of Babylon in it. There are more than 25,000 different Christian denominations and sects in Christendom today, and by no means are they at peace amongst themselves. So where is Babylon? John has called on everyone to throw it off.

The record of Christianity throughout history has not been something we can call commendable. Protestants, as well as Catholics, have shed blood and have urged their people off to war with fiery sermons on both sides of world conflicts. It's time to stop pointing the finger and just look at ourselves and where we stand so that we can obey Jehovah's voice and come out of Babylon. Running here and there to some new church or new religious cult will never take us out of Babylon. John recommends that we conduct our lives so as to give God's light to the world, not stockpile weapons in a secret cave. There is no point in perpetuating modern Babylon with other kinds of violence, and bringing defamation on the name of God. That is the way of Babylon.

Now the angel in this vision is a mighty spirit, and the angel's act of hurling the boulder into the sea is shown to serve as a command to God's people everywhere to throw off Babylon in all its practices. When this is done on such a large and mighty scale it will certainly reflect a mighty spirit emerging in the world and doing it.

Too many people, reading this text, take the unfortunate position of "Jesus did everything for us at Calvary. There's nothing else for us to do. We have a free sleigh ride all the way." But that is not what the scriptures say. Jesus said, "Why do you call me Lord, Lord, and then not do the things which I command." Something commanded is a law, and in Jesus's own words, Moses's law and Jesus's law were both the same – because the principle on which they both were built was the law of God – the law which governs life.

John says this message is from Jesus. So this is one of his commands: "Throw off Babylon." This is one step in the series of commands in Jesus's strategy for establishing the new world. It's true that on the cross,

Jesus did speak the words: "It is finished." But many people tend to read into these words the idea that he did it all. He didn't. He did half of it. The other half is up to you. Daniel in his prophecy makes that clear when he says that in 3 ½ weeks the son of man (or the messiah) would be cut off and that another 3½ weeks would pass before the kingdom would be established on the earth.

Even Luke — as I said earlier — recorded in his gospel all that Jesus "began to do and preach." Then in the uncompleted book of *Acts* he told us what Jesus continued to do and preach through "the power of his holy spirit sent down." That is to say, he did his work through everyone that was obedient to his commands. That does not include all Christians — or all Jews — only those who take the time to understand what is required of them — responding to God's word with wisdom and intelligence.

Many people have actually misread the meanings of all the Bible measurements, and actually have counted days and months and years. One such man who counted time like this was the American evangelist William Miller, a very thoughtful and knowledgeable individual who lived a very moral life. In 1833 he foretold the second coming of Christ as being close at hand, and an almost miraculous confirmation of his words soon followed when a great meteoric display filled the heavens on November 13, 1833. It was said to be the most remarkable display of "falling stars" ever seen in recorded history.

Such an impressive visual "fulfillment" of prophetic utterings encouraged other ministers to do the same and look for verifiable fulfillments of God's promises in world events. To many ministers it seemed as if there were no nobler destiny for man than to watch the skies and wonder in what manner Jesus Christ would come from them. Joseph Litch, an American Christian, predicted the fall of the Ottoman Empire. According to his calculations, their power was to be overthrown "in AD 1840, some time in the month of August." Then at the very time he specified, Turkey actually did accept the protection of the allied power of Europe, and placed herself under the control of the so-called Christian nations of the world.

Such literal "fulfillments of prophecy" continued to impress many people. So others tried to gain attention from the sky-dazed multitudes by showing their own prophetic skill in fashions such as this. Literally hundreds of views (differing in time and manner) on how the second coming would take place emerged. The three most popular were the "Post-millennial Coming," the "Secret Rapture," and the "Spiritual Coming."

Of these the "Secret Rapture" gained most ground due largely to the efforts of an English clergyman called C. I. Scofield, who made this doctrine part of the *Scofield Reference Bible.* According to this belief, Jesus will return to this earth in two phases. First, He will return secretly to whisk away all true Christians to heaven to protect them from the time of "great tribulation", which Jesus foretold. It is therefore assumed by those who hold this view that the Church's promised place of safety is not upon earth, but up in heaven. The second phase is believed to be his "public" coming at which time all will be able to see and hear him.

But the rapture theory is a very recent one — even more recent than the post-millennial theory. The early New Testament Church never heard of the "rapture." Nor indeed had anyone else until about 1830. The first few advocates of the rapture theory fervently believed that they were living in the last three and one half years of earth's history. When that length of time was exceeded and Christ had still not "caught them away," they were forced to alter their doctrine to a general expectancy that Christ might return — unannounced — at any moment! Thus from those few people the doctrine of the "Secret Rapture" has spread to most of Protestantism today.

The Church of Jesus Christ of Latter-Day Saints, better known as the Mormon Church was founded in New England in 1830. Joseph Smith took the jump on other adventists of his time in that he gave the world another history and other scriptures that he claimed to be as authoritative as the Bible itself. The agreement that he reached with other adventists was that the world was living in the last days and Jesus would soon appear to establish the New Jerusalem in the United States of America.

William Miller, whom I mentioned earlier, was one of the founders of the Seventh Day Adventist Church. After careful research in Biblical mathematics, he determined that 1833 would be the year for the return of Jesus Christ to the earth. When 1833 survived his prediction he changed the date to 1834, then to 1843, and finally to 1844.

Charles Taze Russell, to whom our present day Jehovah's Witnesses owe their beginning, determined through his studies of scripture that Jesus Christ had come secretly into the world in 1874 and that in the year 1914 (in a period of forty years — or one generation) Armageddon, the last great battle between God and the devil would take place.

All this was the result of counting Bible numbers on the basis of literal interpretation, and not reading images and numbers symbolically. The number $3\frac{1}{2}$ being half of the perfected seven merely indicates whatever time it takes to accomplish what has been required.

When perfection has been reached, then the number seven heralds the accomplishment.

What is most disturbing though is that when Jesus Christ did not appear on any of the dates set by the adventists, none of these groups was willing to admit the errors it had made. Understandably, Jehovah's Witnesses took the outbreak of First World War as a vindication of their claim that the Battle of Armageddon had actually begun in 1914 as they had prophesied. But following the Great War, when the Kingdom of God was not ushered in, they re-interpreted the meaning of their prophecy.

The year 1914 now became the time that Jesus came invisibly into the world. Armageddon still remained a battle yet to come within the lifespan of the generation that was living then. The Seventh Day Adventists, when Jesus didn't come as they had said, merely re-evaluated their position — and instead maintained that Jesus Christ had cleansed the temple sanctuary in heaven. This was a phenomenon that no one possibly could verify except through "faith", but no one could disprove. The rapturists, however, even now continue saying, "He may come any time." And the Mormons who hadn't really set a date at all, went on doubling their efforts.

Do not mistake me. I am not ridiculing or mocking any of these people. Everyone makes errors all the time. We have to be prepared for that. But we must be prepared as well to recognize the errors that we make, such as allying Christian churches with various world governments, instead of being dedicated to maintaining peace in a brotherhood united under heaven. Errors such as making various world capitals the head office of denominations, or treating Christianity as if it were no more than a brotherhood of spectators called upon to watch a kind of supernatural picture show unfold, while ignoring all of the commands that Jesus gave. I have never understood why most churches have been built like lecture halls in universities instead of in the round where plans and views arc shared within a fellowship of equal brethren.

Instead of carefully adjusting old traditions and ideas, John's letter shows us we are called on to review the scriptures carefully and try to learn from them how we managed to misread them as we have. As the scriptures say: "Let God be true, but every man a liar." We make errors just because we try in superstitious or ambitious ways to cast our magic spells and pose as prophets of enlightenment. It is the kind of struggle for pre eminence which Jesus told us that we should avoid.

Why do we have to feel ourselves superior to other groups of Christians? Why do we have to act as if we thought that we are always right? Is there any harm in saying we are wrong? It seems to me that there is everything to gain from it. God may be right, but we have frequently been wrong, especially when we attempt to place ourselves "above the clouds of heaven". That is to say above the sons of Israel, who were to be past numbering — like particles of dust — the clouds which armies raise while they are marching toward an enemy.

How can we presume to set a date from reading the very texts which Jesus knew so thoroughly? and yet declined to set a date from them himself? It defies all reasoning. Jesus made a plan for us to follow. Such a plan was meant to be obeyed, not treated like a Ouiji Board. He showed us that we should not judge things superficially. Then he revealed the aims our mission had and told us everything we were to do in order to prepare ourselves for accomplishing that task. Being neglectful of our role as servants of God will not ingratiate us to him when he comes. And he will come. He has promised it.

CHAPTER NINETEEN

The Marriage Feast

Shortly after this, I heard what sounded like the great roar of many voices from heaven, which jubilantly cried, "Praise Jehovah for his marvelous deliverance. Honour and authority belong to God alone, for all his sound and righteous judgments. In his condemnation of the notorious harlot who had poisoned all the earth with her idolatry, he has let her bring down judgment on herself, so that she would pay the penalty for the blood of all his servants." (For Moses said: "Whoever sheds man's blood, by man his own blood shall be shed." Jesus, in complete agreement, extended this idea to war itself and said: "Whoever takes the sword will perish by the sword," condemning thereby man's aggressiveness.)

Again this multitude cried lustily, "Praise Jehovah, for the smoke from (the ruins of) the harlot city will continually go up from her forever." (This visually effective imagery serves to underline this truth: that rebuilding Babylon is a dangerous undertaking, and can only lead to more scenes of waste and ruin such as this. Babylon must never be rebuilt.) Upon these words the twenty-four elders and the four beasts around the throne instantly bowed before the throne and worshipped God, saying: "Yes, certainly, Let Jehovah's name be praised."

Then the voice (of him who stood) before the throne (namely Jesus Christ) proclaimed: "Let everyone who serves Jehovah praise him now and honour him (who has delivered you) both small and great!" Then I heard what sounded like a mighty crowd, like rushing waters and like a mighty peal of thunder roaring, as the people said, "Praise Jehovah, all you people, because Jehovah our Creator now rules." (What! What's this? You mean Jehovah didn't rule before? Of course he did. He rules those who are obedient to him. But don't we sing in hymns: "He rules the world." The hymns are wrong. Satan rules the world—and not with truth and grace. Only with Babylon destroyed, and only then, will God begin to rule the earth. That's why we say: "May your kingdom come. May your will be done on earth as it is in heaven." When men obey the will of God—taking care of all creatures, one another and the environment—then God will rule the earth with truth and grace, through the obedience of his servants and the social atmosphere that they engender in the world. For the care of the whole earth was delegated to them.)

Let us gladly celebrate then with exuberant shouts of joy and give him praise, for the time has come at last to take part in the marriage feast of the lamb, for the bride has now prepared herself for him, and she has been allowed to put on fine white linen that is bright and clean, which is the righteousness of those who serve their God.

The angel at that moment told me, "Write down these words: 'Everyone invited to the marriage supper of the lamb is especially privileged.'" Then he added afterwards: "These are God's own words." When I fell prostrate at his feet to worship him, he stopped me and he said, "No! Don't do that. I am no more than a servant like yourself and all the brothers. Do as Jesus taught and Worship only Jehovah, and follow every truth that Jesus has revealed."

Then heaven opened, and I saw a white horse, whose rider's name was Honest and Trustworthy, for with unerring judgment he will render his decisions and wage war. His eyes are burning flames of fire (piercing and astute. Thoroughly comprehending the mind of God he never judges superficially nor lets himself be swayed by superficial evidence), and on his head he wears many diadems (which indicate that his great wisdom makes him the King who governs all kings and the Lord who governs all lords). On his forehead (meaning "in his thoughts"), there is a name that no one knows besides himself. Arrayed in a garment dipped in blood, he wears upon his thigh the name "The Word of God". (Most Christians say that this is Jesus Christ.)

Behind this warrior all the armies of heaven riding on white horses, dressed in clean white linen of the finest quality, follow him. (See Luke 9: 26) From his mouth there came a keen swift sword (the word of God), and he will use it to defeat the nations and to conquer them. Then he will rule them with an iron rod (the authority of God's word) crushing out the wine in the winepress of God's wrath. On his robe and on his thigh were written: King of Kings and Lord of Lords.

Then an angel standing in the sunlight cried out in a loud voice to all birds flying in the air: "Come, all of you, and gather to the great supper of God! where you may feast upon the flesh of kings, generals and captains; the flesh of influential men; the flesh of horses and those who sit on them; and the flesh of all humanity, free and slave, great and small."

It was at that moment that I saw the beast (from the sea better known as Magog's Hordes and representative of the united nations of the world) and all the rulers of the earth and their armies who had assembled to fight against the one who sat upon the white horse and those who followed him. But the brutish beast was taken and so was the false prophet (the leader from the two-horned beast that had come out of the earth – Gog from Magog, the people's nation that misled the world) the one who had performed impressive works before the beast of Magog's Hordes and had succeeded in deceiving everyone who had the beast's mark on their head and worshipped the beast's image (the symbol of nationalism).

Then the beast (the nations of the world, which had come out of the sea — and known as Magog's Hordes) and the false prophet (the ideological — or religious — leader from the land of Magog, or the tail of the beast out of the earth) were hurled into the lake of fire (that fire which they had set ablaze with warfare) burning with brimstone in intensity. All the rest were killed with the sharp sword (of God's judgment) coming from the horseman's mouth, and all the birds devoured their bodies greedily.

*

Chapter Nineteen is a close-up view of those events depicted at the end of Chapter Sixteen, when turmoil followed after God's word was poured upon the seven branches of society. It is the climactic chapter of the whole Bible. It is the moment all have been expecting (But who could possibly survive this dreadful time?). The people of God have withdrawn themselves from Babylon and with a mighty spirit have thrown her back into the sea (which is to say the turbulent sea of mankind that had preserved the nature of her spirit through the centuries).

The appearance of the mighty angel picking up a huge rock is indicative of what God expects of man. Those wishing to stand with all the sons of God must put off Babylon. They must throw her back into the world and have no part of her. The mighty angel represents a mighty spirit that is widespread, so that in the unified act of doing this, worldly Babylon itself cannot survive the overthrow. This is not something that can be done with force of arms for Babylon will only rise again and again until united individuals will have no part of her.

No merchants now can make their livelihood from her. Religious charlatans no more can lead the people anywhere. Widespread immunity to the gimmickry and wizardry of Madison Avenue advertising men or strobe lights and hysteria of the entertainment world will mean that people are no longer slaves to her. Nor will the mysteries of cults and secret clubs have any hold on them. This is good reason to rejoice, and all the people of heaven (those on earth obedient to God) will cry exultantly "Let us Praise Jehovah. Yes, certainly, let us praise his name."

What greater time is there for celebration than the moment we discover, we are free from all enticements that the silly, mind-warping world of glitz and salesmanship can dangle in our faces. There is no need to make a great religious trek or pilgrimage. For God is glorified (as Jesus and the Pharisees both said) not so much in prayer books and religious rituals but by loving acts of real compassion for our fellow man.

Paul the apostle to the Gentiles put it in these words: "If I speak in the languages of men and of angels, but have not love, I am no better than a sounding brass gong or a tinkling cymbal. Even if I have the special gift of prophecy so that I can figure out and understand all mysteries and possess all knowledge, and if I have a faith that can move mountains (mighty world nations) but have not love, I am nothing. And even if I should give everything I have to the poor and surrender my body to the flames, if I am lacking love, I gain nothing from any of these things. For love is patient and kind. It doesn't envy others, and it doesn't boast its own accomplishments, nor is it proud. It is neither rude nor self-seeking. It doesn't anger easily and it keeps no record of any of the wrongs that others do to them. Love does not take delight in any evil practices but it rejoices in the truth.

Love bears up under pressure, and it is ready to trust, to hope and to persevere. Love never fails."

(1 Corinthians 13: 1-8)

The voice of Jesus Christ calls on everyone who serves Jehovah to praise him for the great deliverance he has given them from the harlot and her ways. The great response to what he says is thunderous. All those serving God would have every reason to rejoice: a spirit having great power has given light throughout the entire earth, and another mighty spirit has cast off Babylon. There is every reason to rejoice and to praise God. But how is God praised. James, the brother of Jesus, said: "This is pure and undefiled religion in the sight of God (our Father): to visit orphans and widows in their distress and to keep oneself unstained by the world." (James 1: 27)

The prophet Isaiah, too, in anticipation of this day, affirmed: "Is this not the fast which I have chosen: To loosen the bonds of wickedness, to undo the bonds of the yoke, and to let the oppressed go free, and break every yoke? Is it not to share your bread with the hungry, and bring the homeless poor into your house, when you see the naked to cover him; and not to hide yourself from your own flesh? Then your light will break out like the dawn, and your recovery will speedily bring forth, and your righteousness (i.e. your right dealings) will go before you; then will the glory of Jehovah protect you from behind. And when you call upon Jehovah he will answer you. When you cry to him then he will say: 'Here I am.' But you must first remove the yoke (of burdensome Babylon) from your midst, the pointing finger (of accusation) and if you give yourself to the hungry, and satisfy the desire of the afflicted then your light will rise in darkness, and the darkness all around you will become as bright as the noon day."

(Isaiah 58: 6-10)

This is the rejoicing John is speaking of. If we are doing God's will we are shouting his praise and affirming it in all our deeds. This is the rule of God. God's kingdom will have come to earth. I write these words while governments around the world are making drastic cuts and casting off the poor, even while they justify their need to build strong armies and speak piously of "just wars".

It seems that even three millenia were not enough to humble them. For this is what Jehovah said to those who live according to the "good sense" of the Babylonish world: "Jehovah has risen to present his case and state the charges he has brought against his people. Jehovah's first charges are against the elder statesmen and the princes of the people: 'You have completely stripped your vineyards taking all (their fruits for yourself) what rightfully belongs to the poor into your houses. What do you mean by ruthlessly exploiting my people, and then grinding their faces into the dust?' Jehovah, the God of hosts demands of you." (Isaiah 3: 13 -15)

"The kingdom," Matthew, in his gospel, said, "may be compared to a king who gave a wedding feast for his son. And he sent out slaves to call those who had been invited to the wedding feast (the Christian churches and the Jewish synagogues) and they were unwilling to come (as they had settled in the world and felt they had their own religion now). So that he sent out other slaves, saying: 'Tell all those who have been invited, "Behold I have prepared my dinner; my oxen and my fatted livestock are all butchered and everything is ready; come to the wedding feast."'

"But they paid no attention and went their way, one to his own farm and another to his business. ('I don't have time for any of this now. I have my work and my career to think about'), but some were irritated and they seized the slaves and mistreated them and killed them. (Isn't that the practice still with some: Tar and feathers, lynching, riding on the rail. We might recall what happened when 'Christian' men broke into the prison cell of Joseph Smith to murder him. Jehovah's Witnesses have been lynched, and tarred and feathered. Even Martin Luther King Jr. was cut down by a sniper's bullet. We know the attitude of those who will not hear what others have to say.)

"So the king was angered and sent his armies and destroyed the murderers and set their city on fire. (God is the God of all armies in the world and puts it in men's hearts, in spite of their intents, to carry out his will.) Then he said to his slaves, 'The wedding is now ready, but those who were invited are not worthy. Therefore go to the main highways and invite as many as will come with you to the wedding feast.'

"Then those slaves went out into the streets and gathered together all that they could find, both disreputable and good; and the wedding hall was filled with dinner guests.

"But when the king came in to see the guests, he noticed that one man who was there, didn't have a wedding garment on. 'Friend,' he asked him, 'can you tell me how it is you got in here without wearing any wedding garment?' But the man did not reply.

"So the king instructed the attendants, 'Take hold of him, and tie him hand and foot and throw him out of here into the outer darkness, where there will be wailing and gnashing of teeth.'

"For though many are invited, very few are chosen."
(Matthew 22: 1-14)

This is the wedding feast we find in *Revelation* now. The same feast that we spoke of earlier when I mentioned the virgins and the lamps. Yet these stories are not literal. It is the truth behind them we must understand. The individual is certainly a guest at this important ceremony. But this same dinner guest is also part of that community which becomes the bride. That is why the foolish now are left outside the feast—and the darkness they are left in is the darkness of the world—the world you know and see around you every day. The present darkness many people love so much and are contented in. Since they love the darkness of the present world, they are given no more than they have deserved—the trivial delights and ornaments, the superficial glitz and glamour and the final retribution afterwards.

This is not a vengeance that God craves. It is a retribution that they reap and bring upon themselves. The passion for crime as entertainment (murders, robberies and adulteries) and greedy business practices lead to civil violence and war. These grow from the very giddiness and foolishness they love. It is the same ferocious demon Cain was warned about that day when God advised him earnestly, "Your envy and your anger are like demon beasts crouching at the door, and they will soon devour you if you do not learn to master them." That is the principle at work which we find here.

God has said in terms that cannot be misconstrued: "I take no pleasure in the death of the wicked, for I would much prefer that he should turn from all of his destructive ways and live."   (Ezekiel 18: 23)

The demons to be cast out of us are those that we encounter everywhere: greed, envy, anger, lust, ignorance, pride, sloth, laziness...etc. They overtake our lives and smother us, and Babylon goes on tempting us and enchanting us with trifles, drugs or maudlin sentiments. That is why, when the Messiah comes, he will divide the sheep from the goats. As Matthew, the gospel writer, said: "When Messiah comes in his glory and all the angels with him (We have been witnessing those angels in these texts), then he will sit on his glorious throne. And all the nations will be gathered before him, and he will separate them one from another, as a shepherd separates the sheep from the goats; and he will put the sheep on his right and the goats on the left.

"The king will then say to those on his right, 'Come, you blessed of my Father, inherit the kingdom prepared for you from the foundation of the world. For I was hungry and you gave me something to eat, I was thirsty and you gave me drink, I was a stranger and you took me in, naked and you clothed me. I was sick and you visited me, I was in prison and you came to me.'

"Then the righteous will answer him, 'Sir, when did we see you hungry and feed you, or thirsty and give you something to drink? When did we see you sick or in prison and go to visit you?'

"Then the king will answer them, 'I tell you forthrightly, anything you did for the least of these my brothers, you did for me.'

"Then he will say to those on his left, 'Leave me, all you dreadful men, and take your place in the eternal fire prepared for the devil and his followers. For I was hungry and you gave me nothing to eat, I was thirsty and you gave me nothing to drink. I was a stranger and you did not take me in, I needed clothes and you did not clothe me, I was sick and in prison and you did nothing to take care of me.'

"Then they, as well, will answer, 'Sir, when did we ever see you hungry, or thirsty or a stranger or in need of clothes or food, or sick or in prison and did not try to help you?'

"Then he will say, 'To tell you frankly, when you refused to help even one of the least of my brothers, you refused to do these things for me.'

"Then they will go their way (doing what they always did) to their eternal destruction, but the righteous (by continuing in their way) will go to eternal life."

(Matthew 25: 31- 45)

Though that part which is the final judgment is yet to come, it emphasizes at this point, how we are expected to give praise to the name of Jehovah. Are we lightening the burden of our fellow man — or are we saying "Get rid of all the welfare bums", and then throw everyone into the street who has a job dependant upon "we the taxpayers" because we think it is an imposition now on our munificence.   Then for pious show, after we have pinched our coins, we make a small contribution to some charity, whose lottery might promise us a win.   A taxpayer, for your information, is an employer, and he should practice fair employment policies.

Rejoice in God, the scriptures say and cry Amen. That means worship him with exuberance and do so with great confidence. For the time of the wedding feast has come, and Matthew has described that vividly for us.

Now with the help of God's word, we must overcome the demons that inhibit us. Then we will be ready to start looking for a better world — a world that is described in all the Bible promises.

Having put on wedding garments, mentioned in the parable — that is to say 'repentance' and 'baptism' in the water of God's word — we are ready to begin the wedding feast. The marriage supper, which is the feast of Atonement, has overtones in it of the eating of the Passover lamb: "Then while they were eating, Jesus took some bread (unleavened bread, for that was the only kind of bread permissible for such a feast) and after giving thanks for it, he said, 'Here, eat this. It is my body.' (For it is written in the scriptures in any marriage, they shall be one flesh and Jesus emphasized the need of finding Union in the word of God, since it was on that rock that he had built his church.)

"Afterwards he took the cup, and when he'd given thanks, he told them as he passed it around to them, 'Let everybody drink from it, for it represents my blood in the new covenant that will be made with Israel — my blood which shall be shed (as dowry payment for the bride of God) to take away all condemnation of their sins.'"
(Matthew 26: 26 -28)

"Be ye one," he told his disciples, "as I and my father are one."

Another wedding, though, is well worth mentioning. The one at Cana where Jesus turned the water into wine. You remember that there were <u>six</u> stone waterpots (a symbol of the natural man) which were set out in accordance with the Jewish custom of purification, and they contained two or three firkins apiece (twenty or thirty gallons by modern reckoning, but the two or three in Bible terminology is far more meaningful as it affirmed the great significance of this first miracle. Two and three affirmed the perfect witness).

Jesus told the servants, "Fill the water pots with water." So they filled them to the brim. (There could be no half-heartedness in what we learned of God. There was a banquet here to be supplied and water was the symbol of God's word.) Then Jesus told the servants, "Now draw some out and take it to the banquet's Maitre d.'" Obediently the servants drew it out and brought it to the man in charge of the proceedings. Then when the Maitre d' had tasted the water which had turned to wine, although he didn't even know where it had come from (but the servants who had drawn it knew), he called the groom, and said to him, "It is the custom with most men to serve the good wine first, and then when everyone has freely drunk of it, then to serve the poorer wine, but you have kept the good wine until now."   (John 2: 6-10)

The message is, of course, that God's word turns to life blood in our veins, and gives life to those who have imbibed it.

Now consider the first words in John's gospel: "In the beginning was the Word, and the Word was with God and the Word was God." No. Not 'a god' or 'god' with a small g. The message is, there's no discrepancy at all between God and his word — and the living vessels filled with it have the life of God in them. Or as Moses said: "So God created man in his own image. In the image of God created he them: male and female."

Perhaps now we can understand the words: "And the word became flesh and dwelt among us." "For as many as received the word, God gave to them the power to become the sons (and daughters) of God." (John 1: 12) Or as Paul expressed the idea: "All those who are led by the Spirit (of God) are indeed the sons (and daughters) of God."
(Romans 8: 16)

This is what the whole new covenant is all about. "Behold the days come," Jehovah says, "that I will make a new covenant with the house of Israel and with the house of Judah, not like the covenant that I made with their fathers in the day when I had to take them by the hand to bring them out of the land of Egypt. My covenant, which they broke, even though I was a husband to them," says Jehovah. "But this shall be the covenant that I will make with the house of Israel," Jehovah says, "I will put my law on their inward parts, for I will write it on their hearts, and I will be their God, and they shall be my people. A man will no longer instruct his neighbour nor any man his brother, saying, 'Know Jehovah,' because they will all know me, from the one who is lowest on the social scale to the one who has most power," Jehovah has declared. "For I will forgive their wrong doings, and no longer will I remember their sins." (Jeremiah 31: 31-34)

The scriptures on this matter all agree, if you read them without prejudice. The wedding feast is a feasting on the word of God and the marriage is the marriage to God's word – God's word made flesh in us. In such a manner then, the son of man will come upon an impressive cloud of witnesses. And the linen in which God's bride is dressed represents all the righteous deeds inspired in the people of God (his saints) who do not boast their righteousness.

To give emphasis to something many might forget, John tells us how he fell down at the angel's feet to worship him but was restrained, and the words of Jesus Christ were emphasized: "Worship only God," the angel said, "according to the way that Jesus taught you to." What way is that? you ask. In the sixth Chapter of *Matthew*, Jesus taught his followers to pray to Jehovah, saying, "When you pray, you should pray like this: 'Our Father which art in heaven....'" Yet this was not a prayer to be mechanically recited, but was intended as a ground plan for those things we should pray about: Giving glory to the name of God and to help us by our deeds and words to hallow it, praying for the coming of God's kingdom and any matter concerning it, so that it might be brought to earth, praying for the food we need each day to nourish us, and to be forgiven for whatever sins we have been guilty of."

But nowhere in the prayer are we required to pray directly to Jesus or to angels of any kind. For even the angel closest to God's throne forbade it when John began to worship him. The only angel ever asking to be worshipped was Satan—in the wilderness, and Jesus there affirmed as he did many times: "You shall worship Jehovah only, and him only shall you serve."   (Matthew 4: 10)

You cannot ask Jesus to be more explicit than that. How then can we pray, "Blessed Lord Jesus." It makes no sense at all. Jesus is the king Jehovah chose to lead his people in their battle with the world of Babylon. He is God's only sovereign upon earth, and Jesus taught us we should pray only to Jehovah, who installed him "on the hill of Zion." (This symbolic phrase signified that Jesus was the King of Israel and represented the people before God. He therefore was "the tree of life" planted on "God's holy hill", that place where all God's people gathered as one body, in his temple, to hear the word of God.)

The marriage feast has taken place. The bride of Christ is now one flesh with him. "I am the vine," he said, "and you are the branches."

Now the great battle of God begins. It is the final battle led by a warrior on a white horse *whose name is known only to himself*. Following the great marriage feast, when all God's people are one flesh, it would be presumptuous for us to write a name where God has not. We are told that he wears many diadems indicating the great scope of his authority. (He is the King of all Kings and the Lord of all Lords) What gives him this authority is the many diadems he wears, which represent the full exent of that great wisdom God has given him to rule: He fully understands and incorporates within himself the the wisdom of God's word. Such a man is one who has conquered that man of flesh and walks according to the spirit God's word gives to him. He is someone who will not let himself be overcome by "the beast which crouches at the door."

The garment that he wears is stained with blood, and on his vestment is written in large letters, 'The Word of God'. For the sins of men result in shedding blood, and the Word of God requires "that whosoever sheds man's blood, by man shall his own blood be shed". And the blood of innocence must be avenged. For it is written "Your sin will find you out." Notice that it doesn't say, "Your sin will be found out." So what avenges the innocent is the folly of a man's own ways. He brings down vengeance on himself. Those following the Word of God are dressed in clean white linen, indicating righteousness. The leader and his followers are all mounted on white horses, and from the leader's mouth there goes a swift sharp sword – the only weapon that he uses to defeat his enemies. This sharp sword is the spoken word of God. And it condemns all those who take up arms and go to war.

This must certainly remind us of Paul's instructions to the Christian warriors: "Put on the full armour of God so that you can stand against the devil's schemes. For our struggle is not with flesh and blood, but against rulers, and the forces of evil in the heavenly realms. Therefore put on the full armour of God, after you have done everything to stand. Stand firm then, with the belt of truth buckled around your waist, with the breastplate of righteousness in place, and your feet fitted with the readiness that comes from the gospel of peace. In addition to all of this, take up the shield of faith, with which you can extinguish all the flaming arrows of the evil one. Take the helmet of salvation and *the sword* of the spirit, *which is the word of God."* (Ephesians 6: 11-17)

Where else would the sword of the spirit come from but the mouth. Truth and the power of words will overturn the enemy. This army (with its unnamed leader) will battle against warfare and its idolatry with the power of words.

Yet have we missed the writer's clever allusion, in this imagery, to the army led by Jehu against the idolatry of Israel. Like the leader in the army John describes, Jehu and his army in fulfilling God's prophecy were indeed the "word of God made flesh". And their purpose was to utterly wipe out all the vices of idolatry.

"The driving is like that of Jehu the son of Nimshi, for he drives like a madman," the watchman said when he saw Jehu approaching in his chariot. (2 Kings 9: 20) "When Jehu came to Samaria, he killed all that were there of Ahab's family, and destroyed them all according to *the word of the Lord* spoken to Elijah." (2 Kings 10: 12)

But who will be that King we see here in John's report? It's far too easy just to say — it will be Jesus Christ. If it had been that easy, John would not have told us, "His name was known only to himself." nor would anyone have followed the leader on the white horse we encountered earlier in Chapter Six, and Jesus never would have had to warn his followers: "Beware of false prophets, for many will come in my name saying, 'I'm Christ.'" Such will deceive many. How will you know. Easily. If you are married to the word of God, and have thoroughly ingested it at the marriage feast, you will know at once who is speaking it and who it is that speaks deceitfully.

Let me show you what I mean:

God's Voice Says **Satan's Voice Instructs**

The soul that sins shall die. God surely didn't mean to
(Ezekiel 18: 4) say that you will die.
(Genesis 3: 4)

Advice from the World

"Now I'm not forcing my ideas on you or anything like that, but I think, and I'm pretty sure you'll find most churches pretty much agree with me on this, God didn't actually mean that we would cease to exist. After all, we're immortal beings. What God actually said was we will be separated from him. And in Bible language separation from God means death." (Words of a clergyman)

Raise a child in the way he They have chosen their own
should go and when he is ways, and their soul delights
old he will not depart from in their abominations.
it. (Proverbs 22: 6) (Isaiah 16: 15)

"You've got to accept the fact that the world has changed a lot in the last few years, and you've got to give your child room to develop his own natural tendencies. You can't force your standards on him. You've got to let him find his own way." (Advice given to a parent at a High School home and school)

It's not that I encourage anyone to quote the Bible constantly, so as to hinder or inhibit you. But I do say,

Get to know its wisdom by digesting it and be able to weigh the wisdom of the world against God's word. Don't lean upon the learning and the strength of others to give you confidence, and never be impressed by titles or celebrity. For in God's kingdom popes and kings and potentates and entertainment super-stars along with honoured citizens will wait in line for audience before the judgment seat of single mothers thrown off welfare by the government and by the people who abetted them.

Now another spirit standing in the sunlight calls out to the birds to come and feast upon the flesh of fallen armies in the field. This passage doesn't tell us how they died. Yet we know they died somehow from ignorance. As Jehovah said: "My people are destroyed for lack of knowledge. Because you have rejected knowledge, I also will reject you." (Hosea 4: 6) The imagery, too, tells us that they died in war, because they lacked the knowledge of God. And had they known God, there would have been no violence. For as God's wisdom says: "When a man's ways please Jehovah, he makes even his enemies to be at peace with him."   (Proverbs 16: 7)

Warfare then is the final ruination of the world and is something that the nations bring upon themselves. It is in the Lake of Fire, which is lit by the nations themselves, that the false prophet and the Hordes of Magog shall perish. The psalmist has told us: "Let them fall by their own counsels; cast them out in the multitude of their transgressions; for they have rebelled against you." (Psalm 5: 10) And Isaiah has affirmed: "Wickedness burns like a fire: it shall devour the briars and thorns (those people who cause harm to others), and shall kindle the thickets of the forest (those who lean too heavily on others and have no knowledge in themselves), and they shall mount up like the lifting up of smoke."
                    (Isaiah 9: 18)

The false prophet is a type. We often have encountered such a man who is able to excite the populace (who feel the smart from some offence which has been done to them or suffer from the fear of xenophobia), so that all the people follow him because they "feel" he is their champion. Depicted as a beast out of the earth having two horns (a people's nation having two distinctive bodies of government) will follow such a prophet to their doom. These nations and their prophet will deceive the world with clever propaganda based upon distorted truths and lofty-sounding principles. Many such messiahs throughout history have deceived their nations and the world.

This will be the kind of folly which ignites the final war. But those who are of God (stable, calm and wise) will not be led astray by madness such as this nor put their lives deliberately in jeopardy to prove their bravery. As Jesus said: "It is written, you shall not test Jehovah your God (to prove that he is with you)." War, then, is the final consequence of human ignorance, and birds (or homeless wanderers as scriptures call them too) will come like vultures and other birds of prey and loot and steal amongst the ruined cities and the battle fields. Real birds too may also pick the bones of those who lie unburied on the plains.

This battle differs from all other battles fought throughout history, in that after it is fought, different values will begin to rule the earth, and humble men (not necessarily those who fill the churches now) will start rebuilding the world on different principles. We might regard this in the light of what the prophet Amos said: "They will rebuild the ruined cities and live in them. They will also plant vineyards and drink their wine, and make gardens and eat their fruit. I will also plant them on their land, and they will not be rooted out."

(Amos 9: 14 -15)

No one will doubt that God has come to earth and dwells among his people, for God is a spirit and his spirit will fill all the earth as water does the sea. It will be part of the atmosphere we breathe and will replace the atmosphere of giddy foolishness that leads to violence.

Yet Gog and Magog will survive — and later we will meet the slaves still serving them: slaves who had the brand of slavery upon their head and arms. But we should not deceive ourselves by being literal, or by any of the nonsense of tatoos on the head and arms or by the science fiction tales some branches of the Christian faith have given credit to, some translators even writing them into some modern versions of the Bible, as if it were the text itself that John had written down and wanted to communicate. Nothing could be farther from the truth. The mark of the beast is this: "They have corrupted themselves, and wear the spot of their corruption in their degenerate and crooked ways." (Deuteronomy 32: 5)

CHAPTER TWENTY

The First and Second Resurrection

After these things I saw a messenger of God, who had a great chain in his hand. (This messenger represented a new world spirit which would replace the old rebellious one). Coming down from heaven with the key to the bottomless pit, this spirit, immediately lay hold of that (rebellious spirit of the world depicted as a) dragon known as the Devil and Satan, and put him in bondage for a thousand years. The angel (or new world spirit) from God accomplished this tremendous feat by throwing the devil into the bottomless pit and locking it over him so that this evil spirit could not deceive the nations any more until a thousand years were done.

(The number one thousand can only be read symbolically. Ten symbolizes completion when applied to the Gentile nations of the world. In its present context, therefore, the number "ten" multiplied to the third power — 10^3 or $10 \times 10 \times 10$ — emphatically lays stress upon the fact that ample time will be given to mankind to understand the way that God requires him to live so that he might escape the wiliness of that rebellious spirit whose deceitfulness can only lead to death. To merely read the number literally is to lose its meaning and to miss the most essential warning in the words. As Jesus at the opening of this letter said, "There are many secret meanings in my words...." John's letter tells us then that following an indefinitely long period of time, Satan would again be freed for a short while, to see if it could still deceive the world.

(Such a visual depiction, as is given here, helps the reader to appreciate the powerful nature of that new spirit which will enter the world following the terrible war at Armageddon. With Babylon overthrown and the beast of national vanity destroyed, the rebellious world spirit of opposition to God — known as Satan — will no longer have the influence that it once had. The memory of the great destruction which it wrought upon the world will be too fresh in people's minds for it to exercise the same compelling power that it once had. You no doubt will remember that Isaiah centuries before John's time had said that all who one day would look upon this spectacle of death and devastation would be appalled and horrified by what they saw. — Isaiah 66: 23. Real events, like a great chain, will bind the former spirit of the world, and changed circumstances will be the key which locks Satan in. The key and the chain, like other symbols mentioned in this book, should not be looked upon as literal.)

During this time frame (of a thousand years or so) I noticed seats of judgment being set up (on the earth), and people being delegated special powers (to govern and) to judge sitting down on them. Then I observed amongst those judges certain living people who at one time had been put to death for following the faith of Jesus Christ, obeying the commandments of God, and for not worshipping the beast (of nationalistic zeal) or its image (patriotic regalia and national images of any kind) and who didn't have its mark upon their foreheads or their hands. (Since all their thoughts and deeds would be motivated only by their loyalty to God and his messiah, they would not be spiritually governed or influenced by nationalistic zeal or patriotic customs of the world). These were the ones who had been brought back to life and who were to rule with Christ a thousand years.

All other people who had died were not restored to life, and would not be revived until the thousand years were done. Those people resurrected (at this time to rule with Christ during this millenium) will constitute the first resurrection. These people are unique and especially endowed, since the second death will have no power over them. They will be priests of God and Christ, and shall rule with him during his thousand year reign.

However, when the thousand years are done, (that rebellious spirit against God and his creation known as) Satan will be released once more from that prison house (of social attitudes restraining it) which held it for a time in check. Then Satan briefly will possess the freedom and the power to regain control, so that people everywhere on earth (literally in all four corners of the earth) will be deceived and led astray. Using Gog and Magog (the people and their newly chosen leader) he will gather them for war. (Gog, like the title Caesar, which began apparently as a person's name, has in the text of John become the name of office for any leader of a peoples' movement which is at enmity with God. So the spirit of deceit will once more grow and firmly root itself in human hearts. And the whole world falling underneath its influence will be led astray.)

The troops that Gog from Magog gathered were immense and impossible to number — like grains of sand upon the shoreline of the sea. They swarmed en masse across the broad plain of the earth completely surrounding God's people and the city that he loves (Jerusalem, which may prove to be that place or any other place or places upon earth where men and women truly walk as citizens of heaven.) But fire came down from heaven and instantly consumed the armies (rebelliously opposing God).

(In these words we hear an echo from the *Second Book of Kings*: "The king sent to Elijah a captain of fifty with his fifty men. Then when the captain went up to him, he found Elijah sitting on the top of the hill. That was when the captain called to him and said, 'O man of

God, the king commands you to come down.' And so
Elijah, answering the captain of fifty said, 'If I am a man
of God, let fire come down from heaven and consume
your fifty.' At his words, the fire from heaven did come
down and instantly consumed the captain and his fifty
men." — 2 Kings 1: 9 -10)

Then the devil (that spirit of animosity toward God)
which deceived the people was thrown into the lake of
fire and sulfur (which the warring nations lit and) where
the beast (of national vanity) and the false prophet are.
(In this massive garbage dump, known elsewhere as
Gehenna, life and soul together perish — which is to say
the present life and all hope of future resurrection from
the dead). So now from age to age, both in bright
seasons and in dark this great torment (that rebellious
people have incurred by their own deeds) shall never be
erased from memory. (Certainly Isaiah's words again
occur to us: "All who look upon this spectacle of
devastation will be appalled by what they see.")

That was when I saw the great white throne (of
heaven) and (Jehovah) the one who sat on it. Before his
face the earth and heaven fled. (The world system and
the governments ruling "over it" would be wiped out. For
Jehovah, the creator, alone would now remain supreme.
Before him neither the old world system nor its rulers
possibly could stand. As it is written in the scriptures:
"But who may abide the day of his coming? and who
shall stand when he appears?"). These could find no place
to hide. ("For the arrogance of man will be brought down
and his pride will be humbled. Jehovah alone will be
exalted in that day, and idols will completely disappear.
Men will flee to caves and holes in the ground to hide
amongst the rocks, as the fear of Jehovah overwhelms
them with the brightness of his glory, which shakes the
earth *in social upheavals.*"   —Isaiah 2: 17-19)

I also saw the (resurrected) dead, the illustrious and the non illustrious, who stood before the throne as books were opened (to their understanding). That other book, called *The Book of Life*, was also opened then (so that the names of those now raised from death might also be put in if they fulfilled what God required of them. Such merciful provision makes it possible for the God of Grace to say: "Neither do I condemn you. Go your way and sin no more." — John 8: 11). Then the (resurrected) dead were judged (from that time on) according to the words that were written in the books (of scripture) which measured all their deeds.

First the sea (of turbulent mankind, whose resting places are unknown) gave up its dead (for judgment), then both death and the grave (where marked memorials designate the resting place of those who died more peacefully) gave up its dead as well, so that everyone was judged (from that time on, with absolute fairness) according to their deeds.

Now death and the grave were thrown into (Gehenna) the lake of fire (that symbolic garbage heap outside the ancient city where the bodies of criminals were burned). This lake of fire (or garbage dump of warfare) represents the second death. (Nothing there would ever rise again.) Anyone whose name was not now written in *The Book of Life* was thrown into the Lake of Fire (never to live again). (Death is death and life is life and those that die perish and all their thoughts die with them. There is no sadistic torture nor eternal suffering — only eternal life or eternal death. As God from very early times has said: "Behold, I set before you the way of life and the way of death. Therefore choose life.")

*

At this time a new social spirit enters the world, which in John's concrete imagery is depicted as "an angel from heaven". According to John, this new world spirit is a very powerful one and extremely durable. For the effects of it will be felt for a full millenium. The chain this angel (or new world spirit) brings with him and the key in his hand (as I indicated earlier) are symbolic images. The chain he carries is a chain of world events which have followed one another in succession so as to show, in no mistaken terms, Satan's unbecoming character to the world, and the key the angel carries with him is that new situation now existing in the world because of Satan's bloody reign of destructiveness.

Satan, the old world spirit which led a dazzled world made blind by its own passions and desires, is currently made helpless by a series of events that cannot be reversed. Securely locked away by the new set of social conditions, Satan can no longer move the populace. There will have been a strong psychological impact on the thinking of mankind. If we translate this imagery into real terms, we can imagine the tremendous effect that the overthrow of spiritual Babylon and the devastating war of nations led by Gog and Magog will have had upon the world and all its people.

It should also be apparent from these same texts that the thousand year reign of Jesus Christ and his specially chosen government (made up of those who, in past times and even present ones, were faithful to God's word and understood it, acting in accordance with his will regardless of the consequences which it may have had upon themselves) will not bring in what we might like to think of as "a golden age". Somehow or other it will have failed to satisfy the expectations many people have for such a rule. Many things will be difficult of course, as they were for Israel following its long captivity in Nebucadnezzar's ancient Babylon. The people will be called upon to build a world laid waste by Satan's power.

The opportunity, however, to learn God's law, his social practices, and to grow in ways respectful to creation will be there, as will be the hope and promise of building a new and better world. Not everyone, however, will be willing "to leave Sodom" behind. (Remember Lot's wife and her nostalgic backward glance into the past.) They will look back wistfully upon "the dainties of Egypt" (as the people Moses led into the wilderness once did) and will turn to Gog to help them re-instate the world which Adam chose to build.

So as the peoples of the world emerge into a new maturity, the memory of many things gone by will once more seem unreal to them — more like a dream than a reality. Many possibly might feel inclined to say, "Everything you speak of happened long ago, too long ago to really matter now. For those were times more brutal than our own, and people were barbaric then. We've grown since then and now we're civilized. We're living in a different age — a new millenium. We don't need God or any government inspired by him. All we need to do is what seems right in our own eyes. If it feels good, do it. That's my philosophy."

Jesus puts his finger on the problem when he says: "Now when the unclean spirit goes out of a man, it passes through the waterless places, seeking rest, and does not find it. Then it says, 'I will return to my house from which I came,' and when it comes, it finds it unoccupied and swept and put in order. Then it goes, and takes along with it seven other spirits more wicked than itself, and they go in and live there; and the last state of that man will become worse than the first." (Matthew 12: 43 - 45)

Unlike Paul (the advocate of Christianity) or Ezekiel (the Jewish prophet) John makes no attempt to describe the manner in which the first resurrection will take place. He merely tells us that it will occur. Yet not all Christians nor all Jews will be raised from death during this first resurrection from the dead. John simply states that he observed amongst the judges who were chosen to be co-rulers with Christ certain people who had died for their obedience to God, and for not bowing down to patriotic imagery. It is apparent from these words that only those who have had sufficient love and patience to search out and learn the will of God, and in real terms live by it, will be raised from death to rule with Christ during this most difficult time—a period of a thousand years.

The two major events which will mark this period shall be: (1) the coming of a new world spirit into human affairs to overthrow the old world spirit of hostility toward God, and (2) a resurrection from the dead of all those who have sufficient understanding of God's will to act as judges and rule with Jesus Christ on earth.

In effect the devil, like the Azazel goat on the Day of Atonement, which was turned out into the wilderness, will be thrown into the bottomless pit and locked away. That is to say that it will seem to be nowhere at all on earth. We should be aware though that the term "the bottomless pit" came from the Hebrew word abussos or abyss in the Greek, and often stood for the vast sandy tracts of the Arabian desert. In this context, it stands for the pit or the grave. But the combination of ideas is an interesting one because it does recall for us so well the idea of the Atonement Festival, when the High Priest of Israel, having brought the blood of the slain animal before the throne of God, returns to place his hands upon the "scapegoat" animal which in the Hebrew is "Azazel" (or demon animal) which is turned loose in the wilderness. The similarity in idioms used by both Moses and John is not an accidental one.

Every year, on the Day of Atonement, the High Priest of Israel would take two goats—very much alike in their appearance—to perform a rite of great significance to Israel. At the commencement of this ceremony, the High Priest through a sacred lottery known as the Urim and the Thummim determined which of the two goats would be used in the very special sacrifice. In ancient times a lottery was considered to be an extremely sacred means for determining the will of God. The Israelites performed it (according to some scholars) by means of two sticks (or perhaps two stones) representing a positive and a negative response—or more correctly stated, a blessing and a curse. These two sticks (or stones) were contained in a section of the ephod worn by the High Priest.

In Proverbs 16: 33 we read of them: "The lot is cast into the lap, but the decision is entirely from Jehovah." So even though decisions from them should seem accidental to all those looking on, according to the scriptures they were really brought about by God. To use the lottery then profanely was considered just as blasphemous as using God's name in such magic incantations such as "Allah Ka Zam," and "Abbra Ka Dabra". Yet magicians were notorious for stealing phrases from priests if they believed them to possess a magic power — such as the power to turn a sacramental wafer into human flesh — Hokus Pokus. The sacred lottery as well was taken over by magicians in order to determine human destinies, and later on it was adapted to such games of chance as could "magically" determine private gain.

Yet in the ceremony enacted on the Day of Atonement, the lottery was used to see which of the two (almost identical) goats would be selected as a sin

offering for Israel. Paul tells us that the goat sacrificed
in the real ceremony of atonement was Jesus Christ. The
Amplified Bible describes it in this way: "[Jesus] went
once for all into the [Holy of] Holies [of Heaven] not by
virtue of the blood of goats and calves [by which to make
reconciliation between God and man] but by his own
blood, having found and secured a complete redemption,
an everlasting release [for us].   (Hebrews 9: 12)

On the Day of Atonement Israel's guilt was purged
through the symbolic offering of an innocent life to God,
to impress upon the minds of all the citizens of Israel
the terrible consequence of sin, by showing them
symbolically at what cost Israel was restored to fellowship with him. The Israelites were to understand from
such a ceremony that it was but a part of a greater, more
far-reaching plan destined to bring salvation to the
people of God. The sacrificial animal was viewed by
them as a symbolic offering representing the perfected
life of a specially anointed High Priest of Israel who at a
crucial time in history would offer his own life to cover
the dowry price of Israel's past sins and by his blood
redeem Israel as the sinless (virgin) bride of God.

This explains why the confession of sins was so
important at this time. Man was to put himself in good
standing with God. As John said: "If we (freely) admit
that we have sinned and confess our sins, He is faithful
and just (true to his own nature and promises) and will
forgive our sins, and cleanse us from all unrighteousness."
(1 John 1: 9) The first goat then, so Paul has said, is representative of Christ. Christ was seen by him not only as
the life that was offered for atonement, but also as the
High Priest himself who carried his own blood into God's
sanctuary where he would offer it as a witness before
God that he had paid the full price for purchasing

(Israel) the virgin bride of God from the power of Satan's world.

In that ancient ceremony introduced by Moses long ago, the High Priest, after sacrificing the goat of innocence on Israel's behalf, would bring its blood into the tabernacle of God, before returning once again to place his hands upon the head of the Azazel goat, on which he would confess the iniquities of Israel. (See Leviticus 16: 15). This Azazel (or demon goat) was then turned out into the wilderness. By this means the responsibility for Israel's past sins was placed upon the head of the Azazel goat, that social spirit (or Satan) which had led mankind astray. This spirit then was put away from Israel and turned out into the abussos (which is to say the wilderness or bottmomless pit).

However, in John's vision, this ceremony of the Priest's return from the sanctuary to the congregation of God's people is depicted in a slightly different way. We are shown God's High Priest as a spirit messenger from God, entering the world with a chain and key so that Satan might be bound and locked away in the bottomless pit for a thousand years so he no longer can corrupt the world. This angel High Priest then can be none other than that quickening spirit generated by Jesus Christ himself who (anointed with God's spirit) had entered the world to drive the evil spirit of Satan from its midst. We are shown then in this manner how Satan—the instigator of all sin—will be put out of the world.

A similarity may be seen between John's words and those of Paul whose description of Christ's return in glory can be found in a letter written to the Thessalonians. There Paul says: "The Lord himself will come down from heaven with a loud command, with the voice of the arch-angel and with the trumpet call of God, and the dead in

Christ will rise first." (1 Thessalonians 4: 16) Although his letter was meant to be a source of encouragement to those Thessalonians who were losing hope of ever seeing God's Kingdom established upon earth, it has for the most part been a source of real confusion to many Christians living at a later time. Even though he makes no direct mention of any scapegoat in his words, Paul does speak of the first resurrection from the dead.

The term "scapegoat", however, is not entirely apt, for it implies the creature named has merely taken on itself the blame or guilt for what others do. Such a view has often led to grave errors and misinterpretations of this ceremony. The Azazel goat, as it should be called, indicates the evil nature of the spirit governing our present world. As has been affirmed by the Union of American Hebrew Congregations: "Azazel...was probably a demonic being....Appocryphal Jewish works, composed in the last few centuries before the Christian era, tell of angels who were lured...into rebellion against God. In these writings, Azazel is one of the two leaders of the rebellion. And posttalmudic documents tell a similar story about two rebel angels, Uzza and Azzael—both variations of the name Azazel. These mythological stories, which must have been widely known, seem to confirm the essentially demonic character of the old biblical Azazel."
(*The Torah—a Modern Commentary*, page 859)

So in John's vision of Jesus's own plan—we see this rite of the Atonement ceremony depicted as a marriage feast which is followed by the return of Jesus Christ to earth where he binds the devil for a thousand years, by placing him in "the bottomless pit". This bottomless pit or abyss is symbolic of the wilderness into which the Azazel goat was sent to put past sins and the enticements to sin out of the midst of the community.

All the Hebrew Festivals (which are better called the Feasts of Jehovah) were looked upon as foreviews of events to come. And Paul (the Pharisee apostle) whom almost everyone misreads, never said the Festivals of God were done away, although most translations of his writings force this questionable meaning on his words. Yet even he confessed the same sacred "Jewish" holidays (which early Christians still retained) as "shadows of the things to come."

To say otherwise would place Paul at odds with John. Even history records that Polycarp, John's disciple, in contending with Anticetus the bishop of Rome, asserted there was only one system of truth, and told Anticetus he would continue to observe the feasts of God as he had received them from the apostles. (*Ecclesiastical History* Book IV, Chapter 14, in the *Nicene and Post Nicaean Fathers* Volume 1). "Neither could Anticetus persuade Polycarp not to observe what he had always observed with John the disciple of our Lord, and the other apostles with whom he had associated."

Even Polycrates, Polycarp's disciple, at a later time contended with the Roman bishop Victor I over keeping of the Passover rather than Easter, saying, "We for our part keep the day (14th of Nisan Passover) scrupulously, without addition or subtraction." He also added with great emphasis: "Better people than I have said, 'We must obey God rather than men.'"

Paul (the apostle to the Gentiles), more than a century earlier, had been given a very rough time in Jerusalem for having abolished circumcision in the Gentile churches. If he had asked for anything besides this one request, you would certainly have learned of it in Luke's account of him. It took a massive assembly of Jesus's followers in Jerusalem to grant Paul that one request, because the matter was considered serious. To have changed the holy days as well would have created an even greater fuss than the one over circumcision did.

Even so circumcision still remained important in the church. But here it was interpreted spiritually. Circumcision was to be a cleansing of the heart, freeing oneself from the idolatry of passions. What was meant by cleansing of the heart was depicted in *Exodus* Chapter Four, when Moses (standing before Jehovah's angel) put his hand into his breast and found that it was leprous white. Then putting his hand a second time into his bosom, it came out clean—indicating God's power to cleanse the human heart. Paul expressed his view of circumcision in these words: "A man is not a Jew if he is only one outwardly, nor is circumcision merely outward and physical. A man is only a Jew if he is one inwardly; when circumcision is a matter of circumcising the heart, and done according to the Spirit, rather than the written code."   (Romans 2: 28-29)

There has been much speculation on the part of certain scholars in recent years as to what the significance of circumcision might have been. A surprisingly large number have speciously assumed it to have been a ritual to stress a man's maleness and thereby assert male dominance. Why they have made such an assumption in the light of existing evidence to the contrary is difficult to explain outside the boundary of a modern social trend to cut away male confidence or to use it in an arsenal of weapons in a spiritual war against male abuse. However necessary or justified such a war might be to gain female dignity, it should never be allowed to interfere with truth. And there is ample evidence to the real meaning of circumcision without inventing another meaning.

"Be ye holy for I am holy saith the Lord." This command given to Israel was to be the mark of God on them which would reveal his chosen people to the world. They were therefore told that every male child among them should be circumcised as a sign of their belonging to God. This association of symbol and command is what defines circumcision for us. But it does not tell the whole story. What is circumcision? and why was it practiced?

That there was a strong Egyptian connection in the practice of circumcision by the children of Israel is indicated by the circumstantial evidence surrounding Abraham's sojourn in that land. Circumcision had been an Egyptian practice for many years, and after Abraham's departure from Egypt, Abraham was promised that Sarah's child would become the heir to the Egyptian throne and inherit the entire Egyptian Empire. Those who know their history will realise that, when they read these words from *Genesis*: "Unto thy seed have I given this land, from the river of Egypt unto the great river, the river Euphrates...." (Genesis 15: 18) for what is described here is the entire Egyptian Empire as it existed at that time. This prediction was actually fulfilled when Joseph became in effect the ruler of "the two lands" (Upper and Lower Egypt) during the early part of what is now known in Egyptian history as "The Third Kingdom".

One must note, however, that circumcision as it was practiced by the children of Israel differed in one major way from Egyptian circumcision. In Israel circumcision was both internal and external. Circumcision (according to Moses) was to be of the heart. The external practice was a strong reminder of what must happen inwardly. Outward circumcision (painful as it was) was but a means of staying physically clean. It was well known, in ancient times, that impurities could be trapped under a man's foreskin, and therefore be, on occasions, the cause of certain physical diseases. Men's penises often became infected or sometimes swollen with physical impurities. Because men (through these physical impurities) passed diseases on to women, circumcision was seen as a form of cleanliness, and male circumcision ensured cleanliness in both women and men. The idea of a woman being circumcised, therefore, would have been ridiculous to them.

Like physical circumcision, internal circumcision also emphasized the need for cleanliness. It also was a painful operation because "circumcision was of the heart" and "the heart of man was evil from his youth." Many impurities in the social practices of the world became trapped in a man's heart, and Israel was called upon by his God to make his heart clean. To do this required cutting away willful, human presumption (and self-righteousness was itself one form of it). According to Paul, circumcision was a spiritual matter entirely. But since what we like to call "the Jerusalem church" did not respond easily to Paul's wish to do away with physical circumcision for Gentile converts, "the body of Christ" in Jerusalem had to be brought together to decide upon such a drastic change. We can only conclude then, that in the absence of discussion on any other topic by the church body, nothing else besides was altered in their view.

This suggests then that the army which we met earlier in Chapter Nineteen, led by "the word of God" — the spirit of their messiah, was made up of those whose hearts had been freed from the trappings and illusions of a vain world's idolatry. Pure in heart, and speaking from the treasures of God's word, their voice becomes the single voice of their messiah. That voice is depicted as the sword of justice issuing from their leader's mouth and used against all those who speak the words of Satan from their uncircumcised hearts — that subtle spirit governing the whole world.

Now the new spirit which has come into the world, lays hold on Satan and places him in the bottomless pit. The binding of Satan is the final act of the *Day of Atonement* (Yom Kippur). At this point we might be well advised to make a short review of the other days we have encountered in Christian and Jewish experience:

Passover: for Jews was a memorial meal of deliverance from Egyptian slavery. For Christians, it was also to become a memorial of Jesus's great sacrifice at Calvary to deliver his disciples from bondage to the slavish practices of a Babylonish world.

The Feast of Unleavened Bread: for Jews was a memorial of coming out of Egypt, passing through the Red Sea, and following Moses into the wilderness. For Christians, it was also a memorial for coming out of sin, being buried in baptism and raised to new life. Seven days stood for the complete act of disentangling themselves from sin as Jesus did when he faced Satan in the wilderness following his baptism.

Pentecost: for the Jews depicts the giving of the law to Israel at Mount Sinai. For Christians, it also represents the giving of the unifying Holy Spirit of the church community to all those born into God's family. It was this unifying act that took the church out of Babel's confusion.

We have these festivals reviewed for us in the *Book of Revelation*: *Passover* in the meeting of the resurrected deliverer in the temple on Jehovah's Day, in order to renew the covenant with God and to dedicate the churches to the work which God has planned. *The Feast of Unleavened Bread* in the ordered cleansing of the churches, and *Pentecost* in John's ascent into heaven to learn the final strategy of God where he witnesses the delivering of God's instructions to the Lamb of God who in turn opens the seven seals to the understanding of those who have obeyed the first commands. Contained beneath the seventh seal is the *Feast of Trumpets* heralding the warfare of Almighty God. This ends in the Battle of Jehovah at Armaggedon.

The Day of Atonement is marked by the wedding banquet, the return of Jesus Christ and the binding of Satan for a thousand years. *The Feast of Tabernacles* is the thousand year millenium (and it is a time of temporary dwelling upon earth under a government established by the messenger of the covenant). It will be a time of teaching the law of God's Kingdom to all people living upon earth. Following it will be *The Last Great Day*, where Jehovah only shall become supreme. John pictures this time as being the period when the final judgment takes place. Unlike the pagan teachings of vengeful retribution, John depicts this period as a time when all those raised from death shall learn the perfect will of God and be given opportunity to live by it. After that the city known as New Jerusalem (the perfect city of God) shall be established upon earth.

I mention these holy days at this point because they have a strong modifying effect upon John's words, and as you see, John had these days in mind when he wrote this letter to the Christian churches of his time. These days were celebrated by most Christians then. They were never "done away." As I have said, that is the reason Paul could speak of them as "shadows of the things to come." Perhaps we should take time to look at Paul's words once again. For I do not think we overstress the theme in re-examining those words which we find written in the second chapter of *Colossians*.

In the King James Bible, Paul's words are made to read: "Let no man therefore judge you in meat, or in drink, or in respect of an holy day, or of the new moon, or of the sabbath days, which are a shadow of things to come: but the body _is_ of Christ." Other "translations" garble the words even further adding "reality" instead of "body". These words, however, should read: "Let no one outside the body of Christ (which is to say "the Church") judge you in matters concerning what you eat or drink, or in relation to religious festivals, a New Moon celebration or a Sabbath day. For these are the shadow of things to come."

The Greek says "body" not "reality" and the needlessly inserted verb "is" in the King James Version cannot be found anywhere in the original Greek text. The modern renderings of this text therefore are forced, and translators know they are. The King James Version comes very close to the mark in its rendering of Paul's words but the translators got tied up in what appeared to be the awkward structure of the words and needlessly put in an extra word. Take out that one word "is" which they have added for the sake of balancing what seemed to be an uncompleted phrase, and we have the verse translated almost as it ought to be read. For elsewhere in the Bible "the body of Christ" means "church". We do not need to change this phrase to read, "the body 'is' of Christ."

Some might feel that "such a minor difference" doesn't really matter now since many things have changed in our "religion", and we are living in much different times from then. But still there are two far-reaching consequences worth examining if we continue to believe that Bible promises and prophecies mean anything at all or that those commands we find in scriptures actually were meant to be obeyed: The willful misreading of this verse sets up a needless artificial barrier between the spiritual brotherhood of Jews and Christians and presents them with a major hindrance to any final gathering of God's people. Secondly it destroys one of the keys we need for understanding the carefully planned strategy which Jesus Christ received from God and sent by his messenger to his faithful servant John. In addition it ignores an unmistakeable command which Jesus gave his followers.

Knowing that the Millennium is the *Festival of Booths* tells us something of what we can expect during this very special time. The festival is a time of celebration and growth. Leaving the old world, the people of God live in temporary dwellings as they begin afresh to build a new world upon better principles. We see from John's text that certain people will be raised from death to work with the messiah in building it. So we should realise that when the second harvest comes and is brought in on the *Last Great Day* of Jehovah, grain will be harvested in even greater abundance than it was during the first harvest.

No one will be raised from death just for the sake of condemning them and "throwing them into the lake of fire" so they can be destroyed again for all their wickedness. There would be no point in doing that. The truth is that the vast majority will be "gathered like wheat into the barns". On the last Great Day of God, many of those formerly deceived will be raised from death and tested individually by the scales of God. Books will be opened to their understanding by the people of God and the opportunity "to have their names written in *The Book of Life*" will be given them as they are judged thereafter by the way they live.

Now the Urim and the Thummim, which I mentioned earlier was more than just a lottery. It was representative of a fundamental principal in ancient Hebrew thought. As such it was a practice which required interpreting. And the priest who was wearing the sacred ephod and the jewelled character of God (which is to say the breastplate of Israel) alone was able to interpret what the outcome of the Urim and the Thummim was. Just as Samson drew strength (not from his hair but) from God's spirit, so the High Priest too required the spirit of God's word to speak on God's behalf.

The basic principal involved in the use of the Urim and the Thummim was the power of God's word to bless or curse all those who turn to it. To the true believer it is the spiritual water of baptism from which he can receive new life. But to anyone who treats it as a cloak to hide his vices, it is a devouring fire that will consume him like the dead branch that he is.

We find this principal at work throughout the scriptures. Between Mount Ebal and Mount Gerazim, Abraham received the blessings of God, for he was obedient to him. Later Joshua ordered that blessings and curses should be alternately called out from these very mountains to indelibly impress upon the tribes of Israel great rewards or great calamities to be harvested by either the obedient or disobedient sons of God. The two goats used at Yom Kippur alike reviewed this principal at work. It was determined by the curse or blessing of the Urim and the Thummim of the High Priest which goat would die and which should live.

This tells us something too about the last meal Jesus had with his disciples before being led away to death. Again the sacred principle of the Urim and the Thummim was at work. For in John's gospel it is said: "The one to whom I give this piece of bread when I have dipped it in the dish is the one (who shall betray me).

This action indicates that Jesus, as the High Priest, knew which of his disciples would betray him to the governing authorities.

God's word (on which the Urim and the Thummim had been based) does curse and bless. It therefore is depicted in a variety of ways—as dew from heaven or water of life to be contrasted with hail from heaven or consuming fire. The Urim and the Thummim therefore represent God's word, and those who truly understand its principles have the power to curse or bless. There are no magic objects possessing occult powers of determining. The word of God is a seed that grows in us and makes us wise, The paths we choose to follow determine whether by the lottery of God we are cursed or blessed.

Now when the thousand years were done and the spirit that was Satan once again appeared on earth, it did not come to men and women who had lived in ignorance. So John foresaw a time when men and women moved by the "lust of the eyes, the lust of the flesh, and the pride of life," would choose to live according to their own willfulness and rise rebelliously against God. But the curse that they would bring upon themselves would be fire from heaven, which is to say God's word which blesses the obedient or curses the disinherited. They would destroy themselves by the very devices they employed. God's word which warned them would be as fire to them and they would reap the fruits that they had sown. After that God alone would be supreme.

It should be evident to us as well from scripture that the one who sits upon the great white throne is the one God, Jehovah. We read for instance in *Isaiah*: "For Jehovah is our judge, Jehovah is our lawgiver, Jehovah is our king. He will deliver us." (Isaiah 33: 22) He does, however, delegate this work to all the people he has chosen as his representatives. And the 144,000 of God's perfected Israel who do not judge with superficial eyes will no doubt play a major part, by acting in accordance with what heaven has revealed. All of us each day are standing before God's throne, as will the whole world at the two fall harvests in God's year. The first harvest of the first fruits was regarded as a special gathering. It was looked on as a privilege to be part of it.

However, when the second harvest comes it will be satisfyingly more bountiful. So we are made to understand that though the wicked will be destroyed in the second harvest, the opening of the *Book of Life* indicates that new names will be written in. Many will profit from their past experience in discovering the unpolluted word of God. This is a picture that may not please a few who wish to see the direct consequences fall upon their enemies and all who wronged them in the course of life. So it might prove beneficial to recall the words God spoke to Jonah following the great repentance that his preaching brought about at Nineveh.

Jonah wanted to see great vengeance brought down upon the enemies of Israel. Greater vengeance than we find here in John's description of the final judgment. We have grown so accustomed to the pagan idea of eternal suffering for those whose lives we have despised, that many of us too might be displeased with what we read in John's account. In Jonah's document we read how Jonah reluctantly preached to the citizens of Nineveh, and how his preaching brought about repentance which saved them from destruction. Jonah was angry because of this for he felt betrayed, but when he saw a gourd plant wither because a worm destroyed the vine, his sympathy went out to it.

Then God spoke to him: "You have had compassion on a plant that you spent no labour on, and which you did not cause to grow, a plant that came up overnight and perished overnight. Why, then, should I not have compassion on Nineveh, the great city in which there are more than 120,000 persons who haven't known the difference between their right and left hand." (Jonah 4: 10-11) So Jehovah once again will have compassion on all those who consent to obey him and at last have understood his plan.

We should remember when we read John's words, that this is the final harvest in the year of God. Chaff and grist will certainly be burned (in flames ignited by the wicked, which is its own reward), but a harvest without grain is meaningless. The first resurrection, during the millenium (or feast of booths), was the first harvest. The judgment on the great day of God is the second harvest — and the second harvest always was more bountiful.

Many churches (because of human sentiment) have invented their own mystic rites and rituals in order to provide "salvation" for their dead relatives and friends who lived their lives out in ignorance of God. Baptism for the dead, for instance, or the buying of indulgences are nowhere to be found in scriptures. Sadly, many people are encouraged to waste their time and money on matters which belong to God alone when they could be much more profitably engaged in helping living people understand God's word or feeding, housing and clothing them. While it is not my personal intention to challenge the practices or doctrines of individual churches, I do feel obliged to make the meaning of the *Book of Revelation* clear. Therefore I cannot honestly sidestep this issue. When existing doctrines get in the way of understanding what John says and muddy up the waters of the stream that I am attempting to make clear, I feel obliged to take them out of it.

The churches have their own responsibility to weigh and measure carefully their practices and teachings with the word of God. This is what Chapters Two and Three instructed them to do. The reason this was commanded early in the strategy of salvation that John was expounding to the churches was so that false doctrines would not cloud or make confusing anything which he would later say. Jesus Christ demands thorough obedience, and pride in our own righteousness should not get in the way. It's no big deal to say we're wrong. It helps us find our way. False teachings and false practices separate us from the Messiah and from God.

In this scrutiny that Jesus asked from all his people, congregationally and personally, no church was set above another, nor was any made exempt from self examination. Those churches who failed to rigorously examine and thoroughly cleanse themselves—in God's eyes—would become a part of the religious Babylon whose practices confuse the world. The only point I wish to make is to show you from this chapter that God's own plan has made provision for the dead. The role of the church is to tend to the needs of the living—that is to say all corporal beings walking on the earth.

God will resurrect the dead and judge them wisely and with mercy. You will remember King David who put on sackcloth and ashes to appeal to God on behalf of his ailing dying son. However, once his son had died, David washed himself and put on his regular attire again, as he knew that nothing he could do now would be of any benefit to him. It is the living only with whom we are concerned. As Jesus said, "Let the dead take care of the dead. Follow me." (Matthew 8: 22). God alone will judge the dead. They couldn't be in better hands. Concerning the second resurrection, Jesus (during his

own personal ministry on earth) mentioned enough
people of other generations whom he said would have
repented if they had heard him preach (Matthew 11:
20-24) to indicate that there will be repentance and
salvation and a great harvest of redeemed men and
women when they hear him speak for the first time after
they are raised from death.

CHAPTER TWENTY ONE

The Nature of God's World

I saw then in my vision a new heaven (or new ruling bodies governing the whole world) and a new earth (for the world was filled with new relationships and social attitudes) as the first heaven and the first earth had vanished, and there was no more sea (no longer a disturbed and competitively turbulent populace struggling against itself). At that same time, I also saw the Holy City, New Jerusalem, whose appearance was like that of a bride adorned and beautifully attired for her husband, descending directly from God out of heaven. Then (as I watched and listened) I heard a loud voice from the (great white) throne affirm, "From this time on, God's peace shall be with men, and he shall live among his people. He shall be with them, and he shall be their God. And he will wipe away all tears from their eyes.

"No longer shall there be any death, nor sorrow, nor weeping, nor anguished pain, because the old order of the world (and the torments that it caused) will have completely passed away." Then he that sat upon the throne declared, "Write these words down: 'All the promises that I have made are definite and sure. They shall be carried out, for I am the A and the Z—the beginning and the end.'" (Of this you may be confident —that God who started a good work in you will carry it into completion.... Philippians 1: 6)

"To anyone who thirsts for it, I will give abundantly, without charge, water from the well-spring of life, that he may be satisfied. And whoever overcomes (this present world's delusions and his own lack of faith and courage) will inherit all these things (that I am showing you), and I will be his God and he shall be my son. However, all who are cowardly (from lack of faith), proudly skeptical, unbelieving, vile, murderous (using bombs or guns or any violent means for accomplishing these ends), immoral, practicers of spells and magic arts (using drugs, hypnotic suggestions and illusions to deceive or persuade others) and all liars (those who pervert God's word) will be thrown into the lake of fire and brimstone (war and violence of all kinds) which is the second death."

At that time one of the seven messengers from God who had held one of the seven vessels with the seven last catastrophes in them came and spoke to me. "Come with me and I will show you the bride, the wife of the lamb," he said. Then in spirit I was taken by this messenger to a large and lofty mountain where he showed me the Holy City, New Jerusalem, coming down out of heaven from God, and resplendent with God's glory, shining like a brilliant precious jewel that was as crystal clear as jasper (holiness beyond the power of language to describe).

Its broadly massive walls were very high and there were twelve gates by which twelve angels stood. On the twelve gates, the twelve names of the tribes of Israel were inscribed. There were three gates on each side—three on the east, three on the north, three on the south and three on the west. (4x3 is emphatically universal. This numerical description then, tells us something about Israel. Israel is a universal kingdom, drawn from every portion of mankind—every race, and every tribe—whose character and loyalties alone distinguish them from the nations of the world. So it will indeed be "a time when a man is judged not by the colour of his skin, but by the content of his character.")

Upon the twelve foundation stones (qualities of godly character) on which the city walls were built, there were inscribed the names of the twelve apostles of the lamb. The one who spoke to me had a gold measuring rod (the

wisdom of God) in his hand so that he might measure
the city, its gates and its wall. For the city was laid out
like a square, being just as long as it was wide. (It was in
fact a cube) for when he measured it, he found that it
was 12,000 stadia in length and it was just as high and
wide as it was long. (12x10x10x10 — men in the image
of God called out of every nation in the world). Then
after he had measured the thickness of the walls, he
found it was 144 cubits thick. (12x12 — signifying that
perfected Israel itself was the human wall protecting it).

(For the children of Israel, having thoroughly
measured themselves by the wisdom of God's word, will
have put off all extraneous superstitions which obscure
the word of God, and they are therefore the protecting
wall which guards against all uncleanness which might
enter the city from the polluting world. What we come
to realise from reading this is that the city John
describes for us is not one of buildings, but of citizens. It
is the character of the citizens and how they live which
makes the city of Jerusalem a holy place.)

The wall was made of jasper (holiness), and the city
of pure gold (divine wisdom), as pure as glass (without
guile or hypocrisy of any kind), the foundation stones
(the twelve apostles) of the city were decorated with all
kinds of precious stones (the traits which characterize
the nature of God). The first foundation was of jasper
(holiness), the second sapphire (purity Ex 1: 1, 26-28, 10:
1-4), the third is chalcedony (powerful works of faith),
the fourth is emerald (divine mercy), the fifth is onyx
(forgiveness), the sixth sardius (divine justice), the seventh
chrysolite (the power to teach and reveal), the eighth
beryl (the power to comfort others), the ninth topaz
(reliability), the tenth chrysophrase (generosity of
spirit), the eleventh jacinth (courageousness), and the
twelfth, amethyst (provider of needs).

The city's twelve gates were twelve pearls (a treasure of great price for which a man would sell all that he has to purchase it), each gate made of a single pearl, and the great plaza of the city was made of pure gold (wisdom so refined) that it was as clear as glass (unpolluted and without deception).

However, I didn't see a temple in the city anywhere, because Jehovah the almighty creator and the lamb (which dwell there) are the temple. There wasn't any need in the city for the sun (an imperial monarch) or moon (a holy congregation set apart) to shine on it, because God's glory (God's entire redeemed creation) gave it light, and the lamb (the word of God made flesh) was its lamp.

During the day, its gates will never be closed and there shall not be any night in it at all. ("For your gates will be open all the time, they shall not be closed either day or night so that men might bring you the wealth of the nations and their leaders would willingly submit to you as captives.) (Isaiah 60: 11). No evil thing will ever be permitted into it, nor anyone who is shameful or who lies, but only those whose names are written in the *Book of Life*. (Since the city is not the physical structure, but the citizens themselves and how they conduct their lives, it is impossible to enter that city if you are not obedient to God.)

*

We have reached now the denouement of God's work, which is actually a new beginning. The end is not the finish. It is the start. The Greek word used for new is "kainos" which unlike the word "neos" carries in it the meaning that it is a new world rising upon the ruins of the old. It is a revitalizing of the world. When Adam fell, it brought oppression not just on man but on all creation.

Paul had this in mind when he affirmed: "I consider the sufferings of the present time not even worthy of comparison to the glory eventually to be revealed to us. For all creation anxiously is waiting for the time when the sons of God will be revealed. For all creation has fallen victim to misuse, not from its own fault but from the fall of man to whom God had subjected it. Yet there is still hope, in that creation itself will be set free from this slavery to corruption into the freedom that the sons of God will bring with them. Until that time all creation groans and suffers from the pains of child birth until then."   (Romans 8: 18 -22)

So that is the reason then for all this fuss about another world. John tells us that it will be a world where God himself will dwell. That is to say that the glory of God will be seen at its most resplendent. Creation then will blossom as it never has been seen to bloom since Adam brazenly asserted his will over it. This dream which John and Paul reveal then is the same dream Moses had in mind when he told the children of Israel how God had said: "I will put my dwelling place among you, and I will not abhor you. I will walk among you even, and will be your God, and you shall be my people." (Leviticus 26: 11-12). Isaiah at a later time enlarged upon that sentiment in words that were akin to John's to tell how God would comfort his people: "God will abolish death forever," he affirmed, "and Jehovah the Creator will wipe away the tears from all faces."
(Isaiah 25: 8)

Yet to inherit such a world requires great faith. It won't come automatically. John stresses that important fact for us, in words affirming both a blessing and a curse: "Whoever overcomes (this present world's delusions and his own lack of faith and courage) will inherit all these things (that I am showing you), and I will be his God and he shall be my son. (That is to say that he will be "a tree of life" revealing the character of God in all the things he says and does.) However, all who are cowardly (from lack of faith), proudly skeptical, unbelieving, vile, murderous (using bombs or guns or any violent means for accomplishing their ends), immoral, practicers of spells and magic arts (using drugs, hypnotic suggestions and illusions to deceive or persuade others) and all liars (those who pervert God's word) will be thrown into the lake of fire and brimstone (warfare, brought about by their own violence)."

No choir without the necessary faith in its conductor can really sing. Disheartened people cannot do good work. Those who hope to see God's Kingdom must ask themselves what God requires from them. For Jesus told his followers: "I tell you honestly, that if you but had the faith and did not doubt you could say to this imposing mountain (of Babylon which burdens all humanity), 'Begone, and throw yourself into the sea,' and it would be accomplished." (Matthew 21: 21) "or you could tell this sycamore tree (symbolic of the tree of life or of God's Kingdom) be lifted up and planted in the midst of the sea, and it would obey you...." (Luke 17: 6)

True followers of the Messiah should ask themselves therefore what God requires of them, not merely fold their hands and blandly say, "Christ did it all. There's nothing more for us to do." For I do not know of any scripture that agrees with that. As King Solomon once said: "The sluggard buries his hand in the dish, but is too lazy to bring it to his mouth." (Proverbs 26: 15)

Jesus also indicated that there was very much to do: "Why do you call me Lord, Lord," he asked, "and then refuse to do the things that I require of you." (Luke 6: 46). "For I was hungry and you gave me nothing to eat, I

was thirsty and you gave me nothing to drink, I was a
stranger and you did not take me in, I was naked and
you didn't clothe me, I was sick and in prison and you
didn't even visit me." (Matthew 26: 42 - 43). And according
to Luke in the *Book of Acts*, Jesus continued his work
through the power of the Holy Spirit sent down to his
followers, which means he works through those who are
obedient to him. God will accomplish what he set out to
do, but the harvest is large and the workers are few.

"Have courage," Jesus told his disciples, "for I know
that in this world you will have great difficulty that will
test your endurance, yet I have overcome the world."
(John 16: 33)

If Babylon that city of confusion is not thrown off,
the entire world and all things in it will be destroyed.
That has been the message from the very beginning. It is
the message that we find now in John. Babylon is a Harlot
city. The Jerusalem of God is the Virgin City which allows
no corruption or defilement in its boundaries — nothing
that is evil and destroys — for that is what corruption is.
Comparing chapters seventeen and twenty-one of this
prophetic book makes an interesting study. Babylon (the
adulterous woman) is the capital city of this present
world system. New Jerusalem (the virgin bride of God)
will be the capital city of tomorrow's world. You cannot
necessarily identify them with your eyes or point them
out. It is the behaviour of their citizens and the
influence that they have upon the world which is the
mark identifying them.

It is said that Jerusalem is dressed as a bride for her
husband. Let's look first at how she is not dressed. Isaiah
in describing the women in the corrupted city of
geographical Jerusalem said this: "The daughters of Zion
are snobbish and haughty, and walk about with their

noses in the air yet with eyes that flirt and promise favours to the lusts of men as they walk about affectedly with mincing steps, their ankle bracelets jingling. For their trivial pretenses, Jehovah will ornament their heads with scabs, and Jehovah will cause them (as war captives) to be stripped naked, revealing their private parts.

"When that day comes, Jehovah will strip away the vanity of all the tinkling ornaments they wear about their ankles and their necks, the tiaras on their heads, their dangling ear ornaments, and bracelets and their veils, their scarves, their step-chains (attaching each foot to the other to ensure a measured step), their sashes, spice-perfume boxes and ear rings, their finger rings and nose rings, their negligees and party dresses, cloaks, stoles and ornamental combs, their mirrors, lingerie, and turbans with trailing scarves."   (Isaiah 3: 16 -23)

The beauty that he said Jehovah wished from them was: "But in that coming day, when the Branch of Jehovah becomes the beautiful and glorious ornament that people wear (what is spoken of here is the time when people put on the character of their messiah), the fruit of the land will be the pride and the glory of those who survive in Israel. For the time will come that everyone who is left in Zion and stays in Jerusalem will be spoken of as special — everyone listed among those living in Jerusalem.

"Jehovah will wash away the filth of the daughters of Zion, and shall purge all bloodshed from the midst of Jerusalem by the spirit of righteous judgment and by the spirit of fire (the spirit of judgment establishing the righteous, and the spirit of fire destroying all idolatry and wickedness as chaff). Then Jehovah will establish over all who dwell on Mount Zion, and over all of her assemblies, a cloud of smoke by day (reverence for God) and the brilliance of a blazing fire by night (the light of joyous faith and wisdom): and its glory will be a protecting canopy (for them). This shall be a shelter to give shade to them and protect them from the heat of the day (tyrannical oppression) and a protecting cover from the storm and rain (every kind of persecution)."

(Isaiah 4: 2-6)

And Peter, one of Jesus's apostles said: "Your beauty should not come from outward adornment such as braided hair and the wearing of gold jewelry and fine clothes. Instead it should be that of your inner self, the unfading beauty of a gentle and quiet spirit, which is of great worth in God's sight." (1 Peter 3: 3-4)

But John himself, in his imagery, says far more. If we interpret just a few of the qualities that John describes, we might read his description in this way: "The city shone with the glory of God and was like that of a very costly jewel for the radiance of its holiness was dazzling. She had great dignity and her faithfulness kept her unsoiled by the world. The illustrious deeds of Israel's twelve tribes adorned her entrances like pearls that were costly and beautiful, and the great missionary work of the apostles made her bearing elegant and adorned her with dazzling power of faith."

Does this city seem unreal to you? It shouldn't really. Throughout the ages, it was the universal dream of suffering humanity to build a city such as this: a city that did not oppress the poor or deal unjustly with the weak. John memorably describes this city in the vivid imagery of precious jewels and stones. Yet its foundations are actually the principles of holiness, justice, tolerance, fair business practices, equality of race and sexes in the social scheme of things, a readiness to forgive all personal insults, sensitivity to human needs and responsiveness to all created things (which the scriptures call "the glory of God"). For in all these things the character of God will be revealed.

It is unfortunate though that many modern Bibles now, in their attempt to literally convey the meaning of John's words, have taken the liberty of changing the numbers given in John's measurements to make them correspond with modern standards now in use. I say it is unfortunate because John was not concerned with literal modern standards in the least. When you change the numbers, you have changed the meaning John was trying to convey. John was not concerned with literal distances. It is only the deep symbolic meaning that these numbers have which tells us something of basic truth and magnitude his words imply.

This was a huge city, however, even by the measurements which modern scholars have imposed on it. In all directions—in hieght, width length—it covered the distance of 1,500 miles. That's impressive. It's certainly a tremendous size, and the vast areas it covers is extremely large, even for the sprawling cities that we build today. But John was not speaking of structural metropolis. The terms he used were spiritual. His measurements are symbolic of the universe, and he describes the qualities of citizens making up the universe of God. In speaking of a cube (not a pyramid as some maintain) he is alluding to the perfect balance of all things—in man, in nature and in heaven.

The angels standing at the gates recall for us the words recorded in the book of *Genesis*: "So Jehovah the creator banished Adam from the Garden of Eden to work the ground from which he had been taken. After he had driven him out, he placed on the east side of the Garden of Eden cherubim and a flaming sword flashing

back and forth to guard the way to the tree of life."
(Genesis 3: 23-24). The comparison of both the texts
clearly indicates that Eden was restored. This was the
paradise that God had returned to the earth.

It is no mere dream of pie in the sky, and it is
nothing like the myth of "going to heaven" after death,
which is the myth that grew from it. We can understand
it better if we think of Jewish history. Before the Jews
left Babylon to rebuild the city of Jerusalem, which had
been destroyed, Isaiah vividly described the ideal paradise
for them—a paradise they hoped to build on earth:

"This is what Isaiah the son of Amoz saw in store for
Judah and Jerusalem. In the end this is what will
happen: The kingdom of Jehovah's people will become
the most esteemed Kingdom in the world and will tower
over all the world's prominent nations, and the people
from all the nations will flow to it. And many people
anxious to visit it will say, 'Come, and let us go to Israel
to the people of the God of Jacob; and God who speaks
through his holy people will teach us his ways, and we
will walk in his paths.' For instruction (torah) shall
come from Zion and the word of God from Jerusalem.

"God (through his righteous nation) will render
judgment for the nations of the world and settle the
disputes of many people; and they shall beat their swords
into plowshares and their spears into pruning hooks:
nation shall not lift up sword against nation, neither
shall they learn war any more. O people of Israel, come
and (with this vision of the future) let us walk (today)
in the light of Jehovah's will."   (Isaiah 2: 1-5)

He elaborates upon this idea throughout his book.
Toward the end of it he says: "Behold, I will create new
heavens (new governing bodies) and a new earth (a new

set of relationships between all living things). The former things will not be remembered, nor will they come to mind. But be glad and rejoice forever in what I will create, for I will create Jerusalem to be a delight and its people a joy. I will rejoice over Jerusalem and take delight in my people; the sound of weeping and crying will be heard in it no more.

"Never again will there be in it an infant that lives but a few days, or an old man who does not live out his years; he who dies at a hundred will be thought of as a mere youth; and the death of anyone who fails to reach a hundred will be looked on as untimely. My people will build their houses and dwell in them; they will plant their vineyards and eat the fruit of them. No longer will they build their houses for others to live in them, or plant their food for others to eat. For the days of my people shall be as the days of a tree in their duration; my chosen ones will long enjoy the works of their hands.

"They will not toil in vain or bear children doomed to adversity; for they will be a people blessed by Jehovah, they and their descendants with them. Before they call on me, I will answer; and while they are still speaking I will hear. The wolf and the lamb will feed together, and the lion will eat straw like the ox, but dust will be the serpent's food. They will neither harm nor destroy in all my holy mountain."   (Isaiah 65: 17-25)

Then he asks: "Can a country be born in a day or a nation be brought forth in a moment? Do I bring to the moment of birth and then not give delivery? says Jehovah....I will extend peace to her like a river, and the wealth of nations like a flooding stream; you will be nursed and carried on her arm and dandled on her knees. As a mother comforts her child, so will I comfort you."
                                        (Isaiah 66: 8-13)

This was the Jewish dream to which Jesus Christ still subscribed — a land in balanced harmony with nature. Not just man with man but with all creation, which he was meant to rule. Man's fall meant that all creation suffered too. It was the Jewish dream to bring man and all creation back to God — that is to say ruled by vital principles that balance life and make it thrive, rather than upon those that tear the world apart and ultimately bring on death.

That was the world the Jews (whom the Bible calls the good figs) tried to build when they returned from Babylon. A mighty spirit had thrown off the yoke that held them in captivity, and the Jewish people — in the face of opposition from the Gentile world — set about the thankless task of trying to restore God's world. It wasn't just another nation that they tried to build. It was the Kingdom of God that would fill the world — a kingdom in which no one would injure or destroy the work of God — and God's glory (the creation that he had made) would fill the world and all the wastelands would flourish and rejoice because of them.

This was not religion in the narrow sense at all. Nor was it just a nation with another government. It was to be the government of God who made all things and set man over them to tend their needs and govern them with the wisdom of a balanced government that oversaw all things. Even so, contending with a world that lived in ignorance of God was difficult, and many Jews forgot the calling of the God they served. Not from insincerity, but from the influence of those nations of the world that dealt with them.

Protectionism soon set in and many little dams were made around their faith that broke it into many sects which caused divisiveness. The Pharisees were determined to retain the highest principles of what the Jews believed and began developing what today is called the Talmud, which is still retained and used by modern Jews. The Sadducees (the sons of Zadoc) were their chief opponents, denying any oral tradition, resurrection from the dead or any writing other than the written law. The Herodians were Jews as well, and saw no reason why the monarchy of Israel could not be of a different origin from either the Davidic or Hasmonean line, or why it could not harmonize its faith to blend with other nations in the world. The Essenes believed in keeping spotless from the world and watched for a messiah who would remove the yoke of this world's bondage from the holy city of Jerusalem.

The Zealots were fervent nationalists who wanted no polluting influence at all in Israel and advocated force of arms to overthrow whatever powers were tying them politically to nations other than their own. The Zealot dagger men (Ish Cariots) killed Jews or Romans or Samaritans or anyone who got in the way of installing an independent nation of Israel. There were other groups as well, too numerous to name. Many of these had adopted pagan practices and doctrines into their beliefs. It was a sadly mixed up and divided Israel.

Into such a world was Jesus born. Very little is known about this Jew's life who was born into the family that once had given Israel its line of kings. According to Eusebius (the first Christian historian apart from Luke) Jesus's father was the son of a Leviratic marriage, which meant that Joseph's mother had been married twice. That, of course, would mean that Joseph would have two lineages—his natural one and his Leviratic one. It had been a practice in Jewish families since very ancient times that when a woman's husband died, another family member would take her as his wife and raise up children to her in his brother's name.

In this way, early Jewish followers of Jesus understood that Jesus had the right to rule as Israel's king since the curse on Jeconiah's line had successfully been broken by the Leviratic marriage, for although Joseph was of Jeconiah's family line, it was "as though that king had had no son at all."

However, what is more important than a mere biography is what Jesus, in his ministry, had tried to do. Of that we have a record in Jesus's own words. In the synagogue he announced: "The spirit of Jehovah is upon me, because he has anointed me to preach the gospel to the poor. He has sent me to proclaim freedom for the prisoners and recovery of sight to the blind, to release the oppressed, and to proclaim the year of Jehovah's favour." And those words by and large do fit the picture that we see recorded of him in the gospels.

However, he attempted something even more impossible. He tried to unite divided Israel. We are told that he sat upon the hill and looked down on a Jerusalem he knew (that because of its disunity) was bound to fall. And he wept over it. For Jesus didn't want Jerusalem to suffer, and he said ruefully: "Jerusalem, Jerusalem, you who have slain the prophets that are sent to you. How often I have tried to gather you together, but you would not listen when I called to you."   (Matthew 23: 37)

Most people fail to understand that each of the four gospels in the Bible represents a great prophetic plan. We sentimentalize the meaning right out of all of them. The birth of Jesus as it is described in scripture, is a prophecy of Israel, the virgin bride of God. From Israel was to come the child who was destined to rule over the whole

world. That child would fill the world, for it was none
other than the kingdom of God. Throughout the
Hebrew scriptures prophecies quite often were acted out
by prophets. Jesus was the last great prophet of Israel,
so that in the gospels we can still observe the pattern of
a ministry which illustrates for us that the time had come
for the kingdom of God to be born and grow. The Jewish
people didn't have to bow their heads in slavish submission to the nations and go into captivity again. Jesus
told them, when he opened up the "secrets" of this new
covenant with them: "You are the light of the world."

The symbolism is there to be read, and to be
interpreted: born on the *Feast of Trumpets*, in 5 BC,
circumcised on the *Day of Atonement*, on the *Feast of
Tabernacles* he fled to Egypt (the symbol of death and
sin) and on the *Last Great Day* he returned to the land
of Israel to render judgment on the world. No. Not
literally, prophetically. There is a difference. But we
must learn to read the signs.

The cleansing of the temple was a warning to the
Jews that their temple and their city was to be
destroyed. In case they missed the point of it, Jesus told
his own disciples after they had left the precincts of the
temple, "Not one stone will be left standing on another."
Jerusalem would fall unless she repented, just as
Christendom would fall if it did not repent. But what
was Jerusalem to repent of? She was Jewish after all and
had all the promises of Abraham to make her people
confident. Just as the promises of the new covenant
made many Christians feel confidently certain they
couldn't err.

She was to repent of those divisive doctrines and
practices which were contrary to the spirit of God and
which caused disunity among them. As Jesus told them,

as today he might tell Christendom, "A divided house cannot stand." Jerusalem would fall. The temple would be broken down. That great temple which seemed imperishable.

Jerusalem would fall. But not forever. She would rise again, to be spiritually established on the earth so that she never could be broken down again. To illustrate this great impossibility, Jesus Christ (the prophetic image of the kingdom of God) rose from the grave, and spoke to his disciples of a spiritual conquest of the world. If we follow what took place historically with the Christian Church, we lose the thread. The church that slew heretics and witches and persecuted Jews was not the church of God.

Satan took Jesus to a hill and offered him the world if he would be subservient to him. Jesus refused saying, only Jehovah should be served. Jesus would not bow down to Satan (the spirit of the world). Serving Satan never had been part of that plan Jesus made.

John the evangelist, who wrote the *Book of Revelation* that we are reading now, took up the vision of his leader and in this book presented it to those with the ability to understand. The warfare of Jehovah would be spiritual. God's religion has no name. His followers are everywhere throughout the world and you cannot know them by their race, their language, their sex or by their nationality. God's people have put off Babylon and pursue the dream that Jesus gave to them—to build the Kingdom of God in every nation upon earth and to break down the walls dividing them.

Jesus spoke of it like this: "The wind blows where it will and you cannot tell from where it comes or where it goes. So it is with all those who are born of the spirit (of

God)." And in these last two chapters, John describes the city that will come. And the angel (or spirit existing among God's people) has a golden stick to measure it, signifying that it must be built and measured by the wisdom of God.

Shaped like a cube then—not pyramidal as some scholars say—it is fashioned on the principle of Solomon's Temple, but on a grander scale. The four sides and the grandiose dimensions show it will be established everywhere throughout the world. In case you missed it, it was the Pharisees who said, that God could be worshipped anywhere throughout the world, that he was not confined to just Jerusalem, as the Sadducees and other Jews maintained. Jesus, as the scriptures tell us, certainly concurred with them on this—as did Ezekiel.

So in this vision we are shown by John, the symbols that he uses to describe the city of God strongly indicate that New Jerusalem is a city which is to be established everywhere on earth. But it is a spiritual city which only can be recognized by the behaviour of the people who inhabit it. For New Jerusalem is a city founded on the jewels which constitute the character of God—jewels that once had been upon the breastplate of the High Priest of Israel. There will be no temple in the city because God is with his people, and his character is now written on the hearts and minds and deeds of every citizen who dwells in New Jerusalem.

When Babylon and all the citizens of Sodom are spiritually slain and raised again to new life by God's word; when the lure of Satan has no hold on anyone, then God himself will give the people his Jerusalem from above. New York City, Prague, Moscow, London, Berlin, Paris, Athens, everywhere the throne of God will be instantly in every place and God will walk among his citizens.

Now we can constantly go on saying, I'm a Jew, and I'm a Christian, or my sect or my political party has the true and only way. But God has called us from disunity to work toward a dream. When we forget the dream, we degenerate into little more than terrorists and fanatics. George Bernard Shaw once said it well, when he affirmed that a fanatic was a man who had lost sight of his goals and doubled his efforts.

****

CHAPTER TWENTY TWO

A City Worships God

The messenger from God then showed me the water of life (which is God's word) clear as crystal (for it was free from all pollution of false teachings). It was flowing from the throne of God (which is to say from Israel) and from the lamb (the humble servants of God who are one in Christ) down the middle of the city's street. All along each side of this refreshing river was an orchard filled with trees of life (people who had modeled their lives on the First Psalm) which bore twelve full crops of fruit (each year) yielding its fruit each month, (This Bible symbolism shows us men and women doing good works of the spirit and yielding solid benefits to be reaped from obedience to God). And the leaves of the tree (symbolizing prosperity) were for the healing of the nations. (We are our brother's keeper as all the scriptures indicate.) So there was no longer any curse.

The seat of God's government and that of the lamb will be in the city, and the servants of God who serve him will see his face and his name shall be written on their foreheads (for they shall have God's character) so that there will be no need for lamps (priests or elders) nor light from the sun (a national Priest-King) for Jehovah the creator will give them light, and they themselves shall be the priests that rule with him for ever. Then the angel told me: "You may depend upon these words for they are true. Jehovah, the creator who gave his spirit to the prophets has sent his messenger to you so that you can show his servants all of the things that are shortly to take place. For certainly, I am coming soon, and everyone who is obedient to my revealed commands in this prophetic book will reap the benefits."

Now I, John, who had seen and heard these wonders was so overcome by all that I had seen and heard that I

immediately fell down at the messenger's feet. Because I
was so moved by all the things I was shown by him, I
was actually ready to worship him. He quickly stopped
me though and said, "Please! Don't do that! I am no
more than a fellow servant like you and your brothers
the prophets and of everyone who is obedient to the
words you've written in this book. Worship only God!"
(That command then is essential to the fulfillment of
this plan and reminds us of Jesus's own words to Satan
when he was tempted by him in the wilderness.)

Then the messenger instructed me, "Do not keep the
words of this book secret. For the time for doing everything they say ('for fulfilling everthing') is very near."
(Not all those doing evil will repent). So you must be
aware that they will go on doing evil even more and
more. Those who are deliberately vile will make
themselves even viler than they ever were. (But do not
let their ways discourage you.)   All who do good things
must go on doing them. Therefore let anyone who is holy
continue to be holy still." (This text echoes words Isaiah
said to Israel: "O people of Israel, come and in faith, let
us walk today in the light of Jehovah's will (as though
his kingdom were already here.)"   (Isaiah 2: 5)

"Always stay alert, for I am coming soon! and I am
bringing with me that reward which I will give to
everyone according to the works which he has done.

"I am the A and the Z. the First and the Last, the
beginning and the end. (Jesus was the seed of the Kingdom and he would bring it to completion). All those who
wash their robes so that they may have the right to the
tree of life (the Kingdom God has planted upon earth)
and the right to enter through the gates of the city
(guarded by the cherubim) will be blessed. For outside
the city are only dogs (all those people whose natures are

perverted) — sorcerers, practicers of immorality, murderers, idolators and everyone who deals deceitfully and lies.

"Now it is I, Jesus, who have sent my messenger to you to tell all those in the churches of my purpose and my plan. For I am the root and the offspring of David, and I am the bright morning star (that ushers in a new day)." Both the Spirit and the bride (the Holy City) say, "Come." So let anyone that's thirsty, and let everyone who wishes to, come and take the water of life (the word of God) without charge.

I warn you, though, that everyone who hears the words of the prophecy that is written in this book: If anyone adds to them, God will add to him the disasters that are written here; and if anyone takes away from the words of the prophecy this book contains, God will take away his right to share in the benefits of the tree of life or the holy city which are described in this book; He who has said these things declares: "It's true. I am coming soon." So be certain then of this: Lord Jesus comes.

So let the generous and forgiving spirit of Our Lord, Jesus, most certainly be with all of you.

*

This last chapter of John's book rings with echoes from other Bible passages which readily interpret John's words even as they are read. When the messenger from Christ shows John "the water of life" we can't help picturing the scene of Jesus speaking to the woman of Samaria when he told her "Everyone who drinks the water that I offer him shall never thirst again, for the water that I give will become in him a flowing fountain of fresh water pouring out eternal life."   (John 4: 14)

We also are reminded of the first Psalm which tells us that whoever is delighted with "the instruction (torah) of God and meditates upon it day and night shall be like a tree planted by the flowing streams of water which brings forth good fruit in season. The leaves of such a one will never wither. For everything that person does shall prosper." (Psalm 1: 2-3)

This is true prosperity, not paltry money-grubbing gain. It is the satisfaction of knowing that what we do is meaningful. We can see then where John (or rather Jesus) had derived his imagery.

The water flowing from the throne of God reminds us of the words Isaiah said: "This is what Isaiah the son of Amoz saw in store for Judah and Jerusalem. And this is what eventually will come to be: The kingdom of Jehovah's people will grow to be the most prominent and esteemed Kingdom in the world and will one day be the most imposing power above all other nations upon earth, so that people everywhere will flow to it in crowds. And people everywhere will come eagerly to it and say, 'Come, and let us go up to Jehovah's Israel to the people of the God of Jacob; and God (who speaks through his holy people) will teach us his ways, and we will walk in his paths.' For instruction (or torah) shall come from Zion and the word of God from Jerusalem.

"God (through his righteous nation) will render judgment for the nations of the world and settle the disputes of many people; and they shall beat their swords into plowshares and their spears into pruning hooks: nation shall not lift up sword against nation, neither shall they learn war any more. O (Israel) house of Jacob! come, and (with this vision of the future) let us walk (today) in the light of Jehovah's will." (Isaiah 2: 1-5)

All these scriptures tell us that the trees of life which John speaks of here are the people of God — for God is enthroned in his people. "I am in the Father, and the Father is in me," so Jesus said. Zechariah also makes this point when he says: "It shall come to pass that...the inhabitants of one city shall go to another saying, 'Let us go speedily and seek advice from Jehovah....Indeed many people and even strong nations will look for Jehovah the Almighty in Jerusalem...taking hold of the garment of a Jew they will say, 'We will go with you for we have heard that God is with you.'" (Zechariah 8: 20-23)

This same truth was apparent too in the scripture which said: "Enoch walked with God." (Genesis 5: 21). Nor was he the only one to whom these words were so fittingly applied. But we are told that the government of God, which as trees bear life-giving leaves, is for the healing of the nations. This is true prosperity, and reminds us of the promise made to Abraham where he was told by God that in his seed all the nations of the world would be blessed. (Genesis 12: 3)

There is no denying that when the words of John are not obscured by human rhetoric they are crystal clear and unmistakable in meaning. John, as though anticipating much of what has happened in our world to pollute the meaning of the scriptures, tells us that a time is coming when God's pure word unmarred by men's traditions will course through every city street. The spiritual presence of God and Jesus's teachings will be so strongly felt and impressed upon the world that obedience to God's word will seem only natural to everyone. The citizens by their deeds, will bring about good things and fair dealings, and the offshoot of their deeds will heal the world with their bounty. The first Psalm helps to clarify this imagery as do the other scriptures I have named.

The destiny or curse which God awarded man "of thorns and thistles" resulted from a choice he made (in Eden) to live exclusively for his own benefit and ignore his duties to creation and his fellow man. "Am I my brother's keeper?" Cain would later ask. These "thorns and thistles" then were not so much the vengeance and retaliation of a wrathful God; they were the consequence of man's persistency in doing what was harmful to the world. The gross perversions of the mind and spirit are what causes nature to retaliate. And God speaks through his creatures and his handiwork.

In John's vision we are shown that it is obedience to the creator which heals the world so that creation once again can bloom and thrive in what scientists might call a balanced environment. Selfishness brought down the curse of God on man – polluting the air, the water, the land and the oceans of the world. Even the sky is melting over us. Mankind, through his stiff-necked stubbornness, has brought the curse of God upon himself and on his world (which is to say crime, violence, murder, warfare and human suffering). That's obvious isn't it? The warnings have always been apparent throughout history. But unfortunately even God's word has been polluted and trivialized and frequently abused by those espousing it.

With paradise restored and mankind in God's Garden once again, the curse which separated all creation from its God, would be gone and creation would begin to thrive again. Under the curse, the ground was (symbolically) to bring forth thorns and thistles, and so Jesus said: "You do not gather grapes from thorns or figs from thistles." Then in case you thought that he was speaking of plants and not of people, he said of all the false teachers that would come: "By their fruits you shall know them." Which tells us something of the Garden of Eden and of the world God wishes to restore.

Adam, in eating of the fruit of a corrupt tree, did many wicked and vile things because (even though they were harmful to creation) he found perverted selfish pleasure was derived from doing them. Knowledge of any kind in scriptures isn't just an intellectual understanding of some kind; it is the doing of something and the experience of it. What Adam did and continued doing brought harm upon the world. Now the New Adam (Jesus Christ) and his virgin bride (his holy congregation) would bring back blessing to the world and its sicknesses would all be healed.

A world obedient to God doesn't need priests or elders to instruct them, for they walk in the light of understanding. They don't even need a church or temple any more, for the city itself is the temple of God. God's name shall be written on the foreheads of all those serving him, which signifies that all their thoughts are godly since they bear the character of God. King David, in anticipation of this day, exclaimed: "As for me, I will behold thy face in righteousness: I shall be satisfied when I awake, with thy likeness."   (Psalm 17: 15)

This is understood to be the time when all mankind (male and female) in the image of God reflect the character (i.e. the glory) of their Creator. "Then shall the righteous shine forth as the sun in the kingdom of their Father," is another way that Jesus worded it. So when John is shown the city heaven has designed and is given the ground plans for building it, he understands these to be direct commands from Christ that he must now pass on to all the other followers.

The importance of obeying all of the instructions that John has written in this book is stressed by the angel spirit guiding him. Yet John (completely overcome with awesome wonder at everything that he had seen) was

ready to fall down and worship this powerful angel who
had shown these things to him. But the angel stopped him
doing this – saying he must worship only God.

Now there is nothing written in this book that John
has given us which is superfluous. There is a reason
everything is written as it is. We are told of John's
emotional response to show us that we must be careful
about reverencing any man or angel messenger God may
have sent to us. All messengers of God are equals in an
equal brotherhood. It is God alone who gave the
message —not the apostle, prophet, angel or charismatic
leader — we must reverence. And Moses tells us we must
study every message carefully – not merely take an
angel's word for it. We do not give our hearts or our
devotion to anyone besides God and the message sent
by him once it is understood. And the one essential
quality of any message sent from God is that it fits in
with the other scriptures that we have. In these there is
one theme: the Kingdom of God being built upon earth.
God's servant is to feed the hungry, strengthen the weak,
clothe the naked, comfort the sorrowful and lay the
foundations for a better world by preaching the good
news of that Kingdom which is being built.

It is ironic that an angel told John not to worship
him. For John, who'd deemed himself to be inferior to
the angel, is prayed to by some Christians, as are all of
the apostles. Yet the command the angel in the name of
Jesus gave to John is quite explicit: "Worship only God!"

In this letter Jesus tells us: "I am coming soon! and I
have with me the reward that I will give to everyone
according to the works that he has done." In saying this
we are reminded of a parable that he once told his
followers about a householder who went to a far off land:
"The kingdom of God will be like a man going on a trip

into a far off land. Having called his servants together he entrusted all his property to them, and he gave one servant five talents (115 pounds) of gold, and to another two talents (46 pounds) of gold, and to another one talent (23 pounds) of gold, according to each one's ability to handle what was given him. (Gold is the symbol of God's wisdom).

"Afterwards the householder left on his journey. Then the servant who had received the five talents instantly went out and invested the money that he had and gained five talents more. The servant who had the two talents also went out and gained another two talents. But the person with the one talent went off by himself and after digging a hole in the ground buried what he had.

"When a very long time had passed, the employer of those servants returned to settle his accounts with them. The man who had been given five talents presented his employer the five more talents he had earned. 'Sir,' he told him, 'You gave me five talents. Look, I have gained five more for you.'

"The servant's employer praised him saying: 'Well done, you good and worthy servant. Since you have been dependable in your handling of a few things, I will put you in charge of many things. Go at once and take charge of the rewarding duties I have assigned to you.'

"The servant who'd been given two talents also came to his employer and said, 'Sir, you entrusted me with two talents. Look! I have gained for you two more.'

"The servant's employer replied: 'Well done, you good and worthy servant! Since you have handled a few things well, I will put you in charge of many things. So now I will entrust you with much more.'

"When the man who had received but one talent came, he said: 'Sir, I know what a hard man you are to please, harvesting where you have not sown and gathering where you cast no seed. So I was afraid and I went and hid your talent in the ground. Here! This is what belongs to you.'

"Then his employer said to him, 'You wicked and lazy man! If you were so certain that I harvest where I haven't sown and gather where I've cast no seed, you should have put my money in the banks where I would at least have had the interest on the money that I gave you.'

"Here! Take the talent from this man and give it to the one with ten talents. For everyone who uses what is given him shall be given more and he shall have abundance then. But whoever fails to use the little that he has shall have even that taken from him. So throw this useless servant out into the outer darkness, where there will be wailing and gnashing of teeth.'" (Matthew 25: 14-28) In this parable, Jesus tells us something of the kind of government that he will build.

When John goes on to say that one is not to add or to take away from anything this letter says, he is doing far more than merely putting a copyright upon his written work. He is telling all Christ's followers, in no uncertain terms, that this is the only plan which Jesus ever gave his followers. It is the battle plan from the commander-in-chief of all God's hosts. To alter it would destroy the only hope God's people have for perfect unity. For Jesus came to gather not to scatter Israel or divide them into petty camps at war with one another. At Pentecost his followers received a spirit that was far

far different from the one which came from Babel's
tower. Christ's followers spoke a language all mankind
could recognize as theirs. To say that there is another
plan from the one which Jesus gave to John would scatter
Israel before its enemies. No prophet then — however
virtuous — can introduce another book which offers an
alternative to the only plan of battle Jesus gave.

By telling us that we cannot take away from it, John
means that no shortcuts can be taken in this plan. There
is a definite strategy to win the world for God and it
cannot be changed by visionary men. Every step of
action must be fully and carefully obeyed. That is why it
was so prudently mapped out for us.

Jesus tells us he is coming soon. Yet I wonder sometimes when I hear a minister leaning on the pulpit just in
front of him and speaking in a low and awe-commanding
voice, saying, "He may come at any time," why we
haven't followed the instructions Jesus gave. For the
scriptures have commanded all God's servants to make
the way straight for Jehovah and his messenger of the
covenant (the lamb of God who sealed the terms of his
new covenant with his blood).

EPILOGUE

What God Requires from Us

The Book of Revelation clearly shows that Jesus Christ mapped out a plan for establishiing a new world system. That is the reason Christians pray, "Let thy kingdom come; let thy will be done on earth even as it is in heaven," or sing that universal song: "We've a Story to Tell to the Nations." You see, it is the scriptures— not I — which say Jehovah will tear down and then rebuild. The scriptures also say that God will create a new world government ("a new heaven") and a new world system ("a new earth"). And it is the scriptures too which tell us that God's spirit will one day fill the world in the same way that the basins of the sea are filled with water. For it is the spirit of God revealed in men and women which will cause these things to be. That is the reason Jesus gave his "faithful workmen" a plan for building the kingdom of God upon earth, and instructed them to throw off Babylon.

The city that we walk in (whether it is Babylon the Great or New Jerusalem) is determined by whatever spirit we reveal in our thoughts, our words, our actions and our attitudes. Those who walk in the way of God's spirit are the citizens of the heavenly Jerusalem, and those who walk in the way of whatever Babylonian Zeitgheist dominates the world are citizens of Babylon. God has a plan to rebuild this world through the powerful spirit of his word revealed in those committed workmen who are dedicated to the way of God.

When God (through Moses) led the offspring of Israel out of Egypt and then (through Joshua) into the promised land, he used a strategy that he had carefully laid out and depicted vividly for them in festivals which served as steps or phases in his plan. There were seven strategic campaigns that were waged in God's plan of

Salvation. Three and a half of them brought Israel out of slavery, and another three and a half took them into the Holy Land.

When the last trumpet blew in the days of Joshua, the walls of Jericho fell down. Now in this plan which Jesus (another Joshua) gave to John, when the last trumpet sounds, all those serving Christ are asked to throw off Babylon. That this strategy which Jesus gave his faithful workmen is identical to the one which Moses used in ancient times is so apparent, there must surely be no doubt that Jesus is indeed that prophet very much like Moses, whom Moses said would come. Perhaps the reason why the churches in the different cities have never "immediately obeyed" the plan, as Jesus had instructed them to do, is because 1. the vast majority of Christians did not understand it because they did not really understand the parables which Jesus told. 2. Or maybe all the virgin churches in the different cities fell asleep while waiting for the messenger to call, "The bridegroom comes!" Yet it is written: "My sheep shall know my voice."

But Jesus in this strategy does far more than merely point out different steps to be obeyed. He actually identifies the enemies with which his followers must contend. These are 1. the difficulties that his people have to face and overcome: the false prophet, wars of all kinds, famine, epidemic diseases, persecution and social upheavals; 2. the nations of the world (depicted as a beast out of the sea) and their idolatries (the adoration of national emblems of all kinds); 3. the power of the people's governments and their elected representatives (depicted as a beast out of the earth); 4. the spirit animating all of the above (Satan — the great red dragon which persecutes Israel, the virgin mother of God's Kingdom upon earth). 5. Then finally the spiritual capital city of the world is identified as "Babylon the

Great" (depicted as a seductively beautiful woman riding on a scarlet beast and holding a gold cup in her hand filled with every kind of filthiness).

Jesus does this so that his followers will not be confused and make alliances with any of these foes when they arise. The whole world system though depends on Babylon the Great (whose media pours out corrupting social attitudes). Yet Jesus carefully identifies the weaknesses in her defences. By drying up the waters (of her culture) Jesus will be able to lead his armies into the city and conquer it in much the same way that Cyrus the Persian did when he brought liberty to all the captives in Nebucadnezzar's Babylon, and freed the people of God (the Jews) so that they might return and build the temple of their God. It was a liberal universal freedom that Cyrus brought with him. He let all captives go if they desired to leave.

Yet Jesus has carefully laid out his plan in symbols, which have the strange effect of partially, and sometimes totally — depending on who reads his words — concealing their intent. As he says: "Seal up these words and do not make them known until the time is ripe for them." Then by scriptural allusion he goes on to say: "For there will be many who will strive frantically (even hysterically) to disclose the meanings, wasting all their time and energies in their vain attempts." (Daniel 12: 10). Yet the meaning is still there to be found by those who have the eyes for reading it, which explains the words: "You may see this whole vision as nothing more than words sealed up in a scroll. For if you give the scroll to anyone who can read and tell him: 'Read this scroll for me,' he will reply, 'I cannot read it, for it is sealed.' Or if you go to someone else who cannot read and say: 'Please, read this scroll for me,' he will answer you, 'I don't know how to read.'"   (Isaiah 29: 11-12)

Now in all of these campaigns, Jesus gives his followers direct commands through allusions to specific Bible texts, or showing them what angels do, or sometimes by words spoken from the creatures around God's throne. Warning though is given the faithful labourers to avoid presumption: They are shown "one like unto a mortal man" who wears the crown of God's wisdom on his head and who sits upon a cloud with a sickle in his hand. For even he, a perfect son of God, must wait for his instructions from the sanctuary before he speaks to those who wait for his commands. Nothing simply is presumed — for whatever you shall do on earth shall be according to the word of God and what is done in heaven.

The ultimate end of this whole vision is to reinstate creation upon those principles which God laid down for Man (male and female) in the beginning. It was a new creation dependent upon God and those who acted in his name, rather than upon the way of Cain — whose self-righteous anger and outrage brought destruction on the world and filled the world's communities with every kind of crime. Learning and practicing the word of God is a fine art to be developed and used skillfully. Like a piano player, the one with the most freedom is the one with the greatest skill.

Now Joshua Ben Joseph was a Jewish prophet from Nazareth. We are told that the strategy he shows his readers came directly from the hand of God. And he illustrates this truth, not through any wild assertion but through Bible texts already spoken in the scriptures centuries before his time. He simply opens these to the understanding of the reader or the listener: "he who has ears to hear." This prophet saw the new creation as a city that would one day fill the world and all of its communities, if men and women (dedicated in their faith) would carry out the plan which he proposed, obeying all of those commands laid out in it. Only by this means could perfect victory be won.

Now if the plan which Joshua Ben Joseph gave his followers was understood, obeyed and proved successful, the whole world would be saved from the destructive hand of early Man, who had cursed it with human selfishness, destructive violence, and war. And if the followers of that now ancient prophet known as Joshua Ben Joseph, were faithfully to carry out the strategy which he had given them, and it should prove to be successful in delivering mankind and all of God's creation from the ruin brought upon the world by its first guardians (Adam and Eve) then Joshua Ben Joseph truly does deserve the title Jesus Christ which has been given him.

Yet how can we address him by that title if we refuse to give obedience to him and fail to carry out what was meant to be a highly organized campaign to save the world. If you say that you believe in Jesus Christ and yet reject his plan, you really don't believe in him at all. Faith is doing what he asks of you. Adam said there was a God, but by not obeying him he was an atheist. Therefore, he and all his offspring are condemned. As James, Jesus's own brother, so eloquently said: "So you believe there is a God. That's fine. The demons all believe that too and shudder." (James 2: 19) Throughout this book, I have mentioned more than once, that there are now more than 25,000 different ways of calling Jesus "Lord, Lord!"

So I fear these supplications may be all in vain, and Jesus Christ might say to all of us: "Why do you come trampling through my courts? Your hands are red with blood that you have shed. Your sins are piled as high as heaven, and you have not repented of your ways, and you do not give obedience to any of my words. Do you think

I care about your Christmas and your Easter Festivals? They are tedious and boring to me, and they do not lead you any closer to the throne of God or to Christian unity. Stop trying to appease the world. Disaster lies in store for it. Come out of Babylon and follow me!"

Finding unity, however, is a problem. Isn't it? Yet the Bible surprisingly has shown us how it's done. Everything begins with loyalty. And we are told that our loyalty belongs alone "to him who loves us," and to no other man on earth. And we are told that even praises sung are sung only "to him that sits upon the throne and to the lamb."

This prophecy of John (or rather Jesus Christ) has carefully defined the two world systems so that we can easily examine any similarities and differences they have. Jesus clearly shows us the character of that One God we claim to serve. He shows the method of creation, and has incorporated this into his plan. Nor does he call on anyone to blindly follow him. Rather he reveals the very end he calls upon his followers to reach. Then he systematically lays out for them all the different steps that they must take if they would reach that goal with certainty, knowing all their efforts are regarded as essential to a great, united, well-laid plan. This is the kind of faith that Jesus asks his followers to have. And it is what we should expect from any righteous man who is truly honourable. After all, he is not a charlatan. Jesus does not ask blind faith from anyone.

The only faith he asks from us at all is that we believe that the plan he gave us can be carried out. "If you say to this mountain (of Babylon) be lifted up and cast into the sea – if you have faith – you will accomplish it. Or if you say to this sycamore tree (the tree of life – the Kingdom of God to be established upon earth) be planted firmly in the midst of the sea (replacing Babylon) your faith will make it possible. For if your faith is no more than a grain of mustard seed, these things shall be done."

"I have a dream," said Martin Luther King Jr. and many people followed him to a freedom they had never known before. Jesus also offers those who follow him a new and greater freedom than they ever had. He shows them their goal and the path which leads to it. It is a world free from war, famine, disease, death and persecution, and a creation far more glorious than it was ever known to be. Knowing then the goal which is pursued is the first step towards perfect unity.

Another one is studying the festivals of God so as to learn what must be done to carry out the plan according to the method Jesus recommends. Yet these festivals must be read and studied with intelligence. For it is the meaning they convey, and not the ritual itself, which saves. The keeping of such festivals brings hope because they are rehearsals for that battle being fought outside the narrow world of sects and rituals. Yet they offer still, to those observing them, the hope and promise of a better world. That is why the chief apostle, Paul, referred to them as shadows of the things to come.

In order to fulfill this great dream dreamed by many men of God throughout the centuries, we must do what Jesus first set out to do: regather Israel and make them one in God: "Hear O Israel — Jehovah our God is One God." There were many congregations in Jesus's own day. It was a faith divided. There were Herodians, Nazoreans, Zealots, Alexandrians, Sadducees, Essenes, Galileans, Pharisees, the sect of John the Baptist (which still exists today) and many other groups as well. Nor were any of these various divisions superficial ones.

If only for this reason Jesus must have known Jerusalem would fall to all her enemies. "A house divided cannot stand," he boldly told his Jewish listeners. He would no doubt speak these same words today to Christianity. The fact is, however, that he has already said this to them. That is why the first step in his plan, after he reveals himself to them, is to call upon the body of the church in each community throughout the world to resolve their differences through the ancient festival of unleavened bread. With only heaven and the word of God to guide them, each city (independent of all other cities in the world) must thoroughly examine all their teachings and their practices.

While reading through this most important document which John gave to the churches, I was greatly impressed by how well organized it is. The greater steps that it involves, when we stand back from them, appear much like the great creative days. The seven days of creation which we read about in *Genesis* have the very elements in them that we find in the plan which Jesus sent to the churches of the world:

(1) On the first great day (the Feast of Passover) the imposing vision of the perfected man from heaven walking in the midst of all God's congregations throughout the world, is like a strong command to be obeyed: "Let there be light!" This is the spiritual man God calls upon his people to emulate (the man clothed in righteous garments bound with integrity, who never judges superficially, but with feet tried in the fires of adversity and crowned with godly wisdom, he speaks the word of God). Like the passover lamb, he is symbolic of the perfect servant of God whose flesh we eat. The light of the first day, which comes into the world, is a matter of putting on that character of God revealed in him. It

is the Passover meal which delivers us from death (the curse of darkness hanging on the world).

(2) On the second great day (the Festival of Unleavened Bread) God's congregations are called upon to cleanse themselves and make themselves spotless from the world. This is reminiscent of the second great command of the Creator: "Let there be a firmament in the midst of the waters to separate the waters under the firmament from the waters above the firmament." The people serving God must offer uncontaminated waters to the world. They must make a clear distinction between God's teachings and what the world at large might teach.

(3) On the third great day (the Feast of Pentecost) God's people are shown the troubled waters of the world, and they themselves are made like dry land called from it. They must not be a part of that troubled sea of false messiahs, wars, famine, disease, death and persecution. They must become a haven and a heaven for every kind of life that God establishes. So we receive spiritual guidance (torah) from God to accomplish this.

(4) On the fourth great day (the Feast of Trumpets or Rosh Hashana as it is now called) lights appear in heaven's firmament as new stars (or angels) governing the skies — godly spirits directing those who herald the new world. For on the fourth day God said, "Let there be lights in the firmamant of heaven." And stars or angels are but spirits men and women like yourselves reveal and reflect in all their daily words and deeds. So if the spirit guiding each of you reveals the perfect will of God, then heaven rules the earth through you and countless others like yourself. For men and women are those stars which shine as lamps within God's house.

(5) On the fifth great day (the Day of Atonement or Yom Kippur) God harmonizes into one camp all that is diverse amongst his people. He makes them one with him in what the Bible calls the marriage feast of God, and the power of Satan is put out of their midst. For there were creatures in the waters of the earth and creatures in the firmament of heaven.

(6) On the sixth great day (the Feast of Tabernacles or temporary dwellings) Man in the image of God is established upon earth. Yet there is an interval when some (like Adam) will rebel again but be instantly destroyed by the power of God's word. "In the moment that you eat of it (rebelliousness) you shall surely die." Man must bear God's image (having God in all their thoughts and all their deeds). That is the mark the scribe of God has placed on each of them.

(7) On the seventh day (the Last Great Day of God) which is the sabbath day, God rests from all his labour and resides now in the paradise that he has built, and all creation (by the glory of the way they live their lives) gives constant grateful praise to God. That is what true worship is.

It is a matter well worth noting that John (the messenger from Christ) deliberately took time to tell us that there is no church or temple in the holy city God has built. Yet God is glorified in every part of it, not by great pretentious affectations of a pious-seeming countenance or prayer-book attitudes but by the generous sharing of the many special gifts that God has given to its citizens. By drawing such a thing to our attention, John is telling us that church buildings are not really needed when the world is right with God. He would not bother saying this if churches were anything beyond a temporary means for drawing close to God. Such buildings only served to illustrate God's absence in the world outside of them. When man resumes his intimate relationship with the creator, the church and temple will no longer be regarded as essential in the city where he dwells.

In opening the scriptures to their understanding, John helps his readers recognize the tasks which God assigns to all "his faithful workmen". They understand therefore that God has called on them to be the builders of the new creation he designed. It therefore seems significant to me that throughout the revelation of this strategy, never once does John rely on any reckless claim of personal superiority to any other person in the Church. Nor does he ask his readers simply to believe the things he tells them solely on the basis that an angel spoke to him or that he saw a vision. Impressive though that vision is, John does not rely upon blind faith or anyone's credulity to verify his words. His strength lies in the soundness of the plan that he presents, and he lets the scriptures speak for him and interpret what he says. Those Scriptures which his imagery invokes are all the evidence he needs to show his message is from God.

In effect then, no one can reject John's words without rejecting everything that God has said. John's letter by allusion actually reviews the entire body of scriptures — from *Genesis* to the words of Jesus and the apostles. It is upon this rock that John establishes the authority of the vision he relates, and it is this word which singles out God's chosen ones, the good fish taken from the net. John would be offended if he knew that any Christian prayed to him for he did not exalt himself as someone others should bow down before. Neither was that angel which appeared to John, a messenger that any Muslim, Jew or Christian should adore.

Certainly no bishop or no angel in the churches called to read this letter to the fellowship could place himself above these words, nor could any member of the fellowship who heard it read, exalt himself. The letter also made it quite impossible for anyone to claim authority for adding to or subtracting from the plan which John had given them.

Bishops, though, were honoured in John's day, not because of any personal commission to act as intermediaries between God and any member of their flock, but because they were the voice of their community. The community had vested these men — by the laying on of hands — with the authority to speak in their name and act as their ambassadors between them and other church communities. They also acted as a focal point for periodically assembling the entire community of saints in their vicinity into one place. Bishops also served to link together all the various branches of the church within the same community where various elders represented different branches who met separately.

Such offices helped the Church maintain some degree of unity, even though communities were sometimes quite diverse. Meeting regularly as separate groups in private homes, they read God's word so as to learn their mission in the world. But the larger picture of the whole community and the spirit of the Church was never lost to them. For if the spirit of unity was ever lost, then they were like a branch cut off from the vine, and their light was said to have gone out. For the lampstand of communal unity was at the heart of Christian brotherhood. This unity (like the lampstand in the temple) was the only sign they were still united as one body in the temple of their God. "Hear O Israel, Jehovah your God is One Lord!" For as we read at Pentecost: "And they were all of one accord gathered in one place." "A kingdom divided against itself cannot stand."

John addresses that spirit of community. Speaking though, not to any bishop, John openly addresses the spirit of fellowship. Yet even so, it is not John who speaks. John identifies himself and then tells us of his vision of a man dressed all in righteousness, possessed with the pure wisdom of God and thoroughly reliable. This man, standing ready (by his own suffering and experience) to strengthen the weak, does not look at anything with superficial eyes, and every word he utters is the pure word of God. Though Christians everywhere assume this man is Jesus Christ, every Jew should recognize him as the man from heaven that Isaiah had described. He is the only man that God's people have been called upon to emulate for this is the man we read about in *Genesis*, whom God created in his own image.

The letter then that the King from God dictates to John is from Jehovah, Jesus Christ his messenger, and from the seven creative spirits of God which burn continually before him as lamps — that is from the spirit of God's ideal communities the churches have been called on to establish and perfect in every city of the world. This letter then communicates the idea of the character of God and the ideal spiritual government of the heaven which God designs to shine as stars upon the world.

We might wonder though why someone walking in the midst of all the Christian churches throughout the world would need to write a letter when he wanted to communicate with them. The answer is a simple one. These congregations all are out of touch with him and need a plan to follow which will make them part of that great body of mankind he hopes will rule the world. Even God, speaking through Isaiah, said: "Although I was always close to you, you did not hear me speak."

The churches were all so bound up in themselves and the impressive work that they were doing in the world, that they had completely lost sight of all their aims. So they are admonished in this letter for their failings — not by John or any member of a church hierarchy raised above the brethren, but by Jesus Christ who founded them. Yet even Jesus Christ does not speak like someone who exalts himself. It is God's word which rules, and for this reason the words which issue from his mouth are depicted as a sword because they are the power of God's pure speech.

In order to convey the whole idea of personal autonomy in each municipal church fellowship and to show them their responsibility to God alone, we are shown the image of the seven lampstands. No church in any other city was shown as being dominant. Each had a separate lampstand in their midst. No one church could dominate or rule over any of the others from far-away head offices. "By their own master they stood or fell". Each had the privilege of achieving direct access to God as the temple of God was in the midst of them and their only High Priest (Jesus Christ) was spiritually present in their midst. Although the apostles (those whom Jesus sent directly into the world) had been sent to plant the seed of God's word in various communities, after the seed took root their work was done. No bishop from another church community was ever called upon to interfere or meddle in what was done in any other city's church.

One community might ask another for advice, but no community had the right to usurp the role of Jesus Christ, the one high priest before the throne of God. The whole plan which is presented here presumes an independent growth and spirit in each church community, which constantly reviews its aims and keeps its work in line with them. That is why John's letter after he admonishes each church, calls on each of them in turn, to resolve whatever local problems they may have.

Each local bishop as the voice of his community could on behalf of his own fellowship admonish and advise another city's church with his knowledge of God's word, but he could never dominate, meddle or demand. As Paul once told the Roman Church: "Who are you to judge someone else's servant? To his own master he stands or falls. And he will stand, for Jehovah is able to make him stand." (Romans 14: 4) The seed of God was planted by the apostles. In doing this their work was done for they had planted it. Now the rain and dew from heaven (which is to say the word of God) would water it. They were never called upon to root out tares. Yet eventually the time would come, after all the grain had reached maturity, when God would send in harvesters. That is to say, the call to spiritual battle with the world, or the destructive patriotic call to arms and death.

Jesus showed the different churches how, through the Festival of Unleavened Bread, they were to regain fellowship with him, and through this process gain access to the mysteries of heaven. He assured the individual that he was always present at the door to counsel him, and he showed the church community itself how complete access to God's presence and heaven's glory could be gained when their fellowship put itself in perfect harmony with him. This was symbolized by heaven's open door. Before the time of Christ the heavens had become as brass. That is to say their doors and gates were closed.

To illustrate how heaven could be entered through this door, John goes in and shows the congregations everything that he had seen: God's ideal government — the supreme power of God (the guiding force of life) who was righteous, just and merciful, served by those who were the guardians and protectors of creation (the fish of the sea, the birds of the air, all wild life, domestic animals and even man himself). The turbulent sea has been made calm (having now been freed from guile and deceit) for night and day a royal government of twenty-four wise elders help to keep the world in harmony with God and his creation: a God who speaks through all his creatures to the elders who maintain a constant watch upon the world so as to satisfy its needs and free the social atmosphere from turbulence and violence through their wise counsel and advice. "Thy will be done on earth as it is in heaven" is the rule which guides the world.

To fulfill this aim and accomplish it according to God's will, God holds a scroll, containing the full outline of a plan, in his right hand. The only one who possibly can open it is the dedicated lamb of God (the humble servant who yields himself completely to God's will). This is the servant who says, "Not my will but thine be done." This is the servant who allows himself to be led "as a lamb to the slaughter." So the lamb in opening the scroll definitively shows us the nature of the turbulent sea of mankind in which the dry land of God must be established. "If you say to this sycamore tree, be uprooted and planted in the midst of the sea, it will be done — if you have faith."

Far from calling Christians "up to heaven" (where they will be safe from all harm) the man of heaven calls on all those emulating him to finish his work and bring heaven "down to earth." What could be more reasonable? "I did not come in order to destroy the world; I came to save it." These then are the aims that no Christian must forget. Those who dedicate themselves to it are called on to review the plan.

* * * * *

BIBLIOGRAPHY

BIBLIOGRAPHY

The Holy Bible: The King James Version; The Interlinear
    Greek New Testament; The Holy Scripturees of the
    Old Testament — Hebrew and English; The American
    Standard   Version;   The   Jerusalem   Bible;   The
    American   Standard   Version;   Revised   Standard
    Version; The Good News Bible; The Living Bible;
    New Century Version; The Anchor Bible; The Duay
    Version; C. I. Scofield Bible; The New International
    Version;   New   World   Translation   of   the   Holy
    Scriptures; La Sainte Bible. Paris; La Sacra Bibbia.
    Roma; Grosse Lutherbibel. Stuttgart; The Holy
    Scriptures: Jewish Publication Society. Philadelphia.

Baikie, James.   *The Amarna Age*.   A & C Black Limited,
    London: 1926.

Clayton, Peter A. *Chronicles of the Pharaohs*, Thames and
    Hudson,London: 1994.

"Constellation" *Encyclopaedia Britannica*. Volume 6, page
    311,   Chicago: 1960.

Danby, Herbert (trans)   *The Mishna*. Oxford University
    Press.   Oxford: 1933.

de Pressense, E.   *The Church and the French Revolution*

"Easter"   *Encyclopaedia Britannica*. Volume 7.   page 859
    Chicago: 1960.

Euripedes.   *Ion*

Frankfort, Henri. *Kingship and the Gods*, University of
    Chicago Press, Chicago: 1948.

Gunther, Paul W.,   *The Torah -- A Modern Commentary*,
    New York Union of American Hebrew Congre-
    gations, New York: 1974.

Herodotus,   *Book I* sec. 191

Jacobsen, Thorkild, *The Sumerian King List*, University of Chicago Press. Chicago: 1939.

Keller, Dr. Werner,   *The Bible As History*. (trans Dr. William Neil) William Morrow and Company, New York: 1956.

Kramer, S. N.   *Sumerian Mythology*.   University of Pennsylvania Press. Philadelphia: 1957.

The Lost Books of the Bible and the Forgotten Books of Eden. (introduction by Dr. Frank Crane), New American Library. New York: 1974.

Milton, John.   *Paradise Lost.*   The New American Library, New York: 1961.

Osman, Ahmed.   *Stranger in the Valley of the Kings.* Harper and Row, Publishers, San Francisco: 1987.

Payne, Robert,   *The Life and Death of Lenin.* Simon and Schuster, New York: 1964.

Perowne Stewart.   *Herod The Great.*   Arrow Books Limited. Toronto: 1960.

Redford, Donald B.   *Egypt, Canaan, and Israel in Ancient Times*, Princeton University Press, Princeton, New Jersey: 1992.

Sachar, Abram Leon.   *A History of the Jews.*   Alfred A. Knopf, New York: 1967.

Sklar, Dusty.   *The Nazis and the Occult.*   Dorset Press, New York: 1977.

Steinberg, Rabbi Shalom Dov. *The Mishkan and the Holy Garments.* (trans Rabbi Moshe Milton) Toras Chaim Institute, Jerusalem: 5752.

Stone, Nathan.   *Names of God.*   The Moody Bible Institute, Chicago: 1944.

Wells, H. G.   *An Outline of History,*   Cassell, London: 1920.

Xenophon,   *Cyropaidia,*   William Heinemann, London: 1914.